HIGHER
PERFORMANCE
SAILING

2006 World 29er Champions Silja Lehtinen and Scott Babbage sailing a 29erXX in a fresh breeze.

HIGHER PERFORMANCE SAILING

Frank Bethwaite

Adlard Coles Nautical

LONDON

TITLE PAGE Iker Martinez du Lizarduy and Xabier Fernandez Gaztanaga from Spain, Gold Medal winners at the Athens Olympics.

Published by Adlard Coles Nautical
an imprint of A & C Black Ltd
36 Soho Square, London W1D 3QY
www.adlardcoles.com

ISBN 978-1-4081-0126-1

A CIP catalogue record for this book is available from the British Library.

This book is produced using paper that is made from wood grown in managed, sustainable forests. It is natural, renewable and recyclable. The logging and manufacturing processes conform to the environmental regulations of the country of origin.

Designed by Susan McIntyre
Typeset in 10 on 12pt Minion
Printed and bound by C&C Offset Printing Company Ltd (Shanghai), China

Contents

PART ONE ▲ Perspective

PART TWO ▲ Wind

Chapter 10 ■ Hulls that Don't Baulk 146

Chapter 11 ■ More Power – Trapezes and Wings 163

Chapter 12 ■ Handicaps, Performance Equalisation, and Turns per Mile 169

Chapter 13 ■ Sail Forces in Steady Airflows   **176**

PART FOUR ▲ Performance Advances 1991 to 2008

PART SEVEN ▲ Handling

Chapter 28 ■ Sailing the Foil Moth BY ROHAN VEAL   399

PART EIGHT ▲ Racing at a High Level

Chapter 29 ■ Racing with Speed: 'Connecting the Dots'   407

LIST OF TABLES

Introduction

High Performance Sailing, published in 1992, describes how the wind works, how the waves work, how the conventional boat works, and how to shape and trim sail for best VMG (velocity made good) in different winds and waves.

Higher Performance Sailing, published in 2008, introduces the apparent wind sailboat and describes how its more complex dynamics meshes with new discoveries about the wind to tack downwind at three times the boat speed of its predecessors.

Apparent wind sailing

Ice yachts have been able to tack downwind at four or five times wind speed for 100 years, but there are so few of them, and so little about them appears in the media, that to the world's wet-water sailors they have always been mystery boats. How to sail them has been regarded as an irrelevant black art that was just that – a skill not relevant to 'real' sailors.

In the decades from 1970 to 1990, the Eighteen footer skiffs of Sydney adapted iceboat technology to wet-water sailing and tripled their downwind speeds. The new spectacle of these skiffs flying down the harbour at unprecedented speed attracted big harbourside and ferry spectator crowds, and within a few years this exciting new style had expanded into a sports television programme which achieved top prime-time ratings.

The phrase 'apparent wind sailing' was coined, and apparent wind sailing technique was promoted from 'irrelevant black art' to 'legitimate curiosity'.

In 1996 the unthinkable happened – the skiff-derived 49er was selected as the Olympic pinnacle class to bring spectacle to Olympic sailing, and in 1998 the 49er was followed by the 29er, a youth trainer that 'sails like a skiff to train for a skiff'. Within a year, the 29er was being built in six countries worldwide, and quickly became one of the two world youth trainers.

The designers of bigger boats are now adopting the technology developed by the skiffs to the point where a new genre of big swing keel apparent wind monohulls of America's Cup and Volvo size, and big multihulls, can also fly downwind at unprecedented speeds.

Quite suddenly, the apparent wind revolution has become global, and apparent wind sailing and handling technique has become very relevant indeed.

Higher Performance Sailing

In 1998, at the time of the second (of five to date) reprints of *High Performance Sailing* (HPS-1), I was requested by the publishers to revise it 'to cover the new science and technique of apparent wind sailing'.

As the work began to take shape, it became evident that the scope, extent and difference of the new material was more than could properly be accommodated within an internal revision. So what started as a revision has developed into this new work that extends and refers to, but does not repeat, *HPS-1*.

Higher Performance Sailing (HPS-2) introduces three new areas of sailing art to the sailor who wants to excel, and who wants to know what he would be letting himself in for if he made the change from blow-downwind to tack-downwind sailing.

Technology

The first part of this book introduces the apparent wind sailboat.

Chapters 1 to 22 explain the history and the evolution of high performance conventional sailing, and then of apparent wind sailing, to the sailor who wants to understand the technical background of this new way of sailing faster. It explains:

- How the wind works at three levels of its spectrum which have previously been little studied or discussed.
- How apparent wind boats work – the light strong materials from which they are made, the construction methods used, and the new dynamic principles involved in their design, rigging and handling; all of which work together to make the new performance levels possible.

Handling

The second part of *HPS-2* introduces the discovery that, at the subconscious level, two parallel handling techniques have coexisted for many decades. *Natural handling technique* is used, completely unconsciously, by the great majority of sailors. These are the sailors who always follow and never win. *Fast handling technique* is used, equally unconsciously, by the few champion sailors who always lead and share all the wins.

Consciousness of the importance of this as a separate subject area arose as a direct consequence of the much higher speeds at which the new boats sail.

The smaller apparent wind sailboats – the B-14, 29er and 59er (and no doubt others that I do not know) – are truly delightful, fast and exciting boats to sail, and are simple to handle in the same sense that it is simple to ride a bicycle or use a pair of skis once you have learned how to do it.

I have introduced large numbers of mature sailors who are still young at heart to these faster sailboats. The high point is to hoist the spinnaker and feel the boat accelerate and settle into its 'faster than the wind' tack-downwind mode of sailing. But both the sailors and I have been surprised to find that most of them experienced a totally unexpected difficulty. What was happening was that they had never previously handled any boat that could sail at sustained, really high speed, so had never learned either the balance techniques necessary to handle all fast sailboats, or the co-ordination necessary to handle *any* sailboat at real speed.

A few years later, much the same phenomenon arose with motivated sailors of conventional boats who improved their handling skills on the sailing simulator, but also experienced unexpected difficulty when they returned to the water with a new capability to sail at speed.

Access to the sailing simulator has been like having access to a microscope where previously the view has been through frosted glass. This has enabled me to look more closely at the handling component of sail training, and from there to look at the whole of 'sailing' itself. This has led to the seminal identification of the slower *natural* and the faster *fast* handling techniques, both of which coexist at the subconscious level and that we can now see have been responsible for so much woe in past years.

At root, natural handling technique is quick and easy to learn because no co-ordination is called for and its 'luff for everything' control of roll is consistent; this is why the great majority of sailors have learned natural handling and sail this way. But this simplicity comes at a cost:

- Because natural handling is intrinsically slower than fast handling, 'natural' sailors follow for all of their lives and never lead in, nor win, important races.
- Because fast handling technique as applied to both conventional and apparent wind sailboats necessarily involves the balance of the cyclist, the skater or the skier, and because the natural sailor has never learned this skill, this is why he or she characteristically has difficulty in controlling any boat either in strong winds or at real speed. This also explains the unexpected initial difficulties of motivated sailors in controlling the smaller, but still very fast, apparent wind sailboats.

Chapters 23 and 24 discuss this new way of thinking, and Chapters 25, 26 and 27 describe exactly what fast handling technique is and how to learn it – also, how and where it differs from natural handling technique, and why it is intrinsically faster. Access to the sailing simulator has enabled the way in which champion sailors handle their boats to be observed and described in more exact detail than has ever previously been possible. The material in these chapters has been developed over several years, and has reached the point where motivated 'natural' sailors, who want to excel, are now using it to learn the fast handling techniques used by the champion and in this way they are at last lifting their game, sailing at lead-group speed, and beginning to enjoy the occasional win.

Putting it together

Chapters 27, 28 and 29 describe in exact detail how today's champion sailors handle their blow-downwind and tack-downwind sailing, and fly both upwind and downwind to win world championships and Olympic medals.

As of 2008, Chapter 28 is unique. The technology of foil-borne sailboats has been a fringe activity for decades, but as *HPS-2* goes to press, it has recently and suddenly become practical. Moths equipped with foils are now consistently dominating their World Championships, and already on occasion are sailing faster than any other sailboats in the same winds. The potential is huge.

In Chapter 28, Rohan Veal, the helmsman primarily responsible for this revolution, describes how to sail these new craft.

Overview

In this book I record the history of the apparent wind revolution. It has been my good fortune over four decades to observe this whole process from within. Deep involvement with its developing technology, discovery and analysis of the new principles that have emerged, and association with the many gifted designers and sailors who have made it all possible, have been a year-by-year source of pleasure, excitement and deep satisfaction.

This book is dedicated to:

- Every young sailor who dreams of flying down the harbour twice as fast as his parents believed possible.
- Every mature sailor still young enough at heart to share the same dream.
- Every present follower who dreams of the fun and pleasure of sailing in the lead group, the deep satisfaction of the occasional win, and the enhanced self-esteem that will come from walking tall in his or her chosen recreation.
- Every reader who, for whatever reason, is not close enough to the water just now, but who dreams of taking the mainsheet and tiller and joining in the fun of this new way of sailing.

It is my privilege, and that of my many contributors, to share this new fun and pleasure with the reader.

Acknowledgments and thanks

While writing this book I invited a number of brilliant sailors to share their knowledge. They responded magnificently, and *HPS-2* has become a more useful, more authoritative and richer book as a result of their contributions:

Robin Elliott, of Auckland, New Zealand, a sailing historian, who has provided much of the early historical material and pictures in Chapter 1.

Ian Bruce, Montreal, of Laser fame, has provided the material and photos of the seminal Herrick Duggan years.

Harry C (Buddy) Melges has spent a lifetime among iceboats and lake scows. He is probably the fastest sailor in the world – on ice.

Lindsay Cunningham held the Little America's Cup for decades. He has held the open speed record for sailboats twice, and the speeds of his triscaphes are very close to those of the sailboards of Finian Maynard.

Finian Maynard was the world's fastest wet-water sailor, on sailboard at the time of writing.

George Chapman, assisted by his son Joddy, was for decades the voice of the aspiring foil sailor.

Ian Ward took the leap to sail his foil Moth, rather than just sit in it.

Rohan Veal has, by vastly refining and perfecting the new four-mode handling art, propelled the foil Moth from obscurity to centre stage.

Paul Cayard with his 'nature never reveals everything, and no sailor ever sees everything that nature reveals' states the essentials about scanning and planning.

Mark Bethwaite describes how a disciplined approach to scanning and planning, plus acute observation, can lead to eight World Championships.

Rob Douglass describes how calculated risk assessment and management can lead to a world championship by avoiding foreseeable disaster.

Scott Babbage describes how enlightened thinking about handling and performance detail, and focused practice to achieve flawless crew co-ordination to achieve full potential performance, is another way to a world championship.

Emmett Lazich describes how focused attention on crew co-ordination, with separation of strategy from handling, is yet another route to a Gold Medal.

Julian Bethwaite has originated far more than his share of the 'cut and try' developments – his three two-hander Eighteens, the asymmetric spinnaker, the flexible 'fibreglass' topmast, *Looney Tunes*' wishbone rig, the flat 'run-across' deck arrangement, the low-drag solid wings, the mainsail cuff to the deck – the list goes on.

As I have aged, my role has become to observe and measure, then later to analyse why some of the 'cut and try' changes work better than expected (for example, the cuff on the mainsail increases boat speed by enhancing the turbine blade effect over the lower jib). This follow-up analysis has often paved the way for the next intuitive try.

Between the author's often uneven draft 'proof-read' copy and the more polished, consistent, easier to read and well-reviewed copy supplied to the publishers lie the reviewers and proof-readers. I thank:

Professor Richard Spencer, University of British Columbia, Vancouver. Richard has assisted greatly with better and more accurate explanations of concepts, and particularly with replacement of words that carry a different meaning in North America from Australia.

Ted Hamilton is the most technically aware man that I know, and is ruthless with error, no matter how small.

Mark Bethwaite brings the champion sailor's 'no nonsense' overview to the task, and his comments have resulted in much re-writing to achieve clearer expression.

Nicola Bethwaite (Beijing would have been her fourth Olympics but shortly prior to the regatta she broke both arms in a mountain bike accident and could not compete) similarly brings the champion sailor's wider overview, but her corrections express it in finer detail.

Nel Bethwaite, my wife, deserves my particular thanks. For years she has put up with a husband who is so often 'somewhere else' as he searches for the better approach or word or phrase. Without her unfailing support there would be no book. She has provided the environment that has made it all possible.

Measurement systems

The world has not as yet agreed a uniform system of units. My professional background is aviation, associated with science and meteorology. The ICAO units used internationally by the aviation industry when I was flying were:

Distance:	nautical miles, tenths and feet.
Speed:	knots (nautical miles per hour).
Weight:	pounds.

These are the units I am accustomed to, and used in *HPS-1*, and will continue to use in general in this book. American readers will be comfortable with these Imperial units. But there is a steady global shift towards the metric system that affects all of us, and where use of the decimal system makes for simpler explanation, I now find myself using it naturally.

On balance, I believe that if I were to standardise on either all Imperial units, or all metric, the result would now appear to be forced. So *HPS-2* will be a creature of its time, and use whichever system best serves the subject under discussion.

Author's note

When notes in this format appear within the text, it is my note – not that of the contributor of the section concerned.

Frank Bethwaite

LIST OF ILLUSTRATIONS

PART ONE

Perspective

Chapter 1 • The Origins of High Performance

1.1 ■ Summary

Sailboat performance remained unchanged from its beginnings 4000 years ago until about 1800, and exceptions such as the Polynesian proas were rare.

The first speed increase, from 1800 to 1900, was to set bigger sails and use movable ballast to keep the boat upright.

The second speed increase, from 1895 until 1905 with a trickle-through effect until 1950, was to use lighter, flatter hulls to plane over the water faster than heavier, rounder boats could move through it.

The third change, from 1980 and continuing, is the apparent wind revolution in which downwind speeds faster than the wind have become routine.

A fourth change, in which foils lift the hull clear above the water, is just becoming practical (2007) in that Moth class dinghies now win regattas in all wind and sea-state conditions by using apparent wind technology on a foil rather than a displacement or planing support platform.

In a book about 'high performance', it is necessary to define what constitutes 'high performance' as opposed to 'everyday performance'. In recent years, accurate comparative measurements of speed by GPS (global positioning system) have become routine. In the years prior to accurate measurement, I have taken as my yardstick the behaviour of the interested onlooker – meaning that where people have reacted strongly with an 'If you can't beat them, ban them' response to a new performance level, we can be certain that the performance difference was real.

1.2 ■ The first 4000 years

Man has used small flotation – logs, coracles, dugout canoes – for tens of thousands of years. Use of substantial ships can be traced back to Crete at least 6000 years ago. The Phoenician traders of about 4000 years ago are reputed to have been the first to have used sails. From those beginnings, the craft of shipbuilding and the art of sailing and navigation spread worldwide.

All sailing vessels, wherever built, had two characteristics in common. They were heavily and strongly built for a long life in a severe mechanical and chemical environment. Their sail areas were modest so that they could survive the periodic unexpected sudden strong gust.

Because all sailboats were heavy and had modest sails, all boats of the same size would have sailed at about the same speed regardless of where or when they were built (see Fig 10.3). For this reason, until relatively recently, sailboat performance has remained almost unchanged since the development of the first sailboats.

1.3 ■ The century of bigger sails – 1800 to 1900

The first step towards higher performance in sailboats was taken almost simultaneously, 200 years ago, by two groups of boats on opposite sides of the world. Both the sandbaggers of New York and the skiffs of Sydney began to shift ballast to enable them to carry bigger sails.

1.4 ■ The sandbaggers of New York

The history of the sandbaggers goes back to the early 1800s. They were the fishing boats that serviced the fish markets of the growing city of New York. Oysters were a main food staple and were harvested in the Hudson river estuary by wide flat-bottomed boats that could skim over the oyster flats even when carrying a heavy cargo. The smallest were the lightest and flattest. Bigger, deeper sandbaggers fished the more open waters.

The estuary of the Hudson river was a natural area for both sailing and spectating, being a big area of water deep enough for sailing and protected from the ocean swells by a narrow entrance. The estuary also enjoyed a mild climate and in summer there was often a steady sea breeze. Inevitably, at some point, crews started racing each other. Onlookers began to gather on the vantage points of the shoreline to enjoy the spectacle and soon they started to gamble on the results. This led to a situation where the weekday workboats were re-rigged with longer, lighter spars and bigger sails for racing each weekend, but they remained rigged with mainsail and jib only.

To keep them upright under the press of the bigger sails and no cargo, they carried ballast in the form of bags of sand or gravel of a weight convenient to heft onto the windward deck on each tack. The length of the hull was the only rule for each class. Spars and sails grew progressively until they were enormous, and the bags of ballast became heavier and the task of shifting the bags on each tack became more demanding.

Initially the races were intermittent, but by the 1840s a regular match racing programme was underway. In a city that understood ships and the sea, this racing attracted increasingly large audiences and the interest grew.

It is interesting to make a comparison of the overall approach to sailing faster between the sandbagger technology and the open skiffs of Sydney of the same era (see Section 1.6).

The sandbaggers dealt with lighter winds and stronger winds by changing weight. They always sailed with mainsail and headsail only, plus sometimes a gaff topsail, and they never set or dropped extra sails such as spinnakers during a race. This approach allowed them to sail with a minimum crew of skilled sailors – probably a helmsman, a mainsheet trimmer and a headsail trimmer.

On light-wind days they would have sailed 'light': the boat, three skilled sailors, plus minimum sandbags and the fewest number of hefters possible.

On strong-wind days they would have sailed 'heavy': the same three sailors would not have set the topsail, and might have reefed mainsail and headsail pre-start, and would have carried more sandbags and enough hefters to handle the extra sandbags to give maximum efficiency and speed in the wind expected during the race.

Fig 1.1[1] shows the lines of *Una*, a small sandbagger-type dinghy which was built in 1852 by Cap'n Bob Fish and exported to, of all places, Cowes in England. Somebody obviously had a sense of humour because Cowes was then the spiritual home of keelboat yachting worldwide. In the Cowes environment of the day, conservative design was applauded, size won the social Brownie points, and a tiny unconventional 'foreign' sailboat had to be at the very bottom of the heap. But the import left its mark. With a centreboard and small single mainsail, she represented the extreme of simplicity and manoeuvrability compared with the local craft of her size and larger. Her speed and handiness in smooth water and moderate breezes made her popular, and that style of rig became known as and is still referred to in the UK as, a 'Una' rig.

Fig 1.2 shows the lines and Fig 1.3 the appearance when racing of a 27ft sandbagger of 1869. Fig 1.4 (the Sheridan Prize) shows the general rigging arrangement on the model. By the 1880s sandbagger racing had grown to the point where up to 40 boats were taking part in weekend regattas.

Sandbaggers and skiffs were the first racing yachts to employ movable ballast. In any breeze they were fast and impressive to watch, but when pushed beyond their limits they could come to grief in spectacular

---

[1] All of the original 'lines' drawings from which I have drawn Figs 1.1, 1.2, 1.9, 1.13, etc are in places faded or even obliterated by age or mildew to the point where I deemed them unsuitable for publication. In each case I have restored them by copying the original, 'whiting out' the blotches, copying the remainder very feint, and then hand-restoring the feint lines and gaps with the more even lines you see. The plan of *Mercia* (Fig 1.15) is the worst degraded, to the point where the area around the forward centrecase is uncertain. This and other small uncertain areas have been left blank in the restoration.

Similarly, the only pictures that now exist of breakthrough boats of a century ago are usually copier copies of faded newspaper or magazine pages. If the dots per inch are less than now deemed ideal, I take the view that this is a small price to pay. I thank Robin Elliott, Bruce Stannard and others for their welcome help in making these unique and invaluable pictures available.

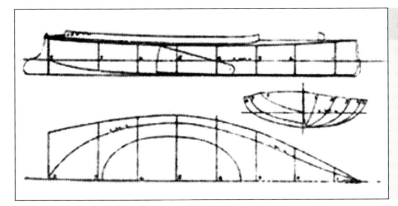

Fig 1.1 Lines of *Una*

A small sandbagger-type dinghy, built in 1952 by Cap'n Bob Fish, New York. Courtesy of Robin Elliott.

Fig 1.2 Lines of sandbagger *Bella* (faded lines restored)

LOA 27ft 3in, beam 11ft, draught 1ft 9in. Courtesy of Robin Elliott.

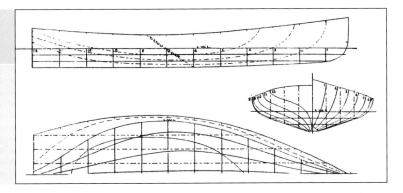

Fig 1.3 Sandbagger racing

Pluck and Luck LOA 23ft 7in, beam 10ft, draught 1ft 9in, built in 1875 by Jake Schmidt. Courtesy of Robin Elliott.

capsizes. These racing fleets attracted big audiences, and substantial gambling by both crews and spectators became a strong feature of the activity.

But success at this level begets envy, and the sandbaggers offended the 'establishment' sailors in three ways.

The New York establishment of the day followed English sailing culture, in which the ideal yacht was deemed to be a conservative craft as opposed to a dinghy-like craft with movable ballast. But these conservative craft simply could not match the speed of the wide, light, shallow 'skimming dish' sandbaggers that carried no fixed ballast, but in which strong hefters moved bags of sand or gravel onto the windward gunwale on each tack.

Their first sin was to sail so much faster than the 'gentlemen's' yachts. They did this because the 'power to weight' ratio of the best sandbaggers in racing trim (in this case the ratio of their sail-carrying power to their total weight) was much greater than that possible with a conventional design in which heavy ballast is carried either in the hull or fixed centrally on the keel.

The second sin, professionalism of the crew, was social. The sandbaggers were regarded as 'people's boats', often associated with, and usually crewed by, a team of longshoremen from a local waterfront bar. With prize money at stake, and the boat from the bar around the corner victorious last week, the strongest and best hefters of sandbags were paid to crew. In the eyes of amateur gentlemen sailors, this compounded the offence. Not only were the lighter, flatter 'skimming dish' sandbaggers much faster, length for length, than the amateur gentlemen's yachts, but the source of their speed was hard work performed by a paid crew.

The third sin, sponsorship of favoured boats, was the last straw. Wherever there are big gambling stakes, there has always been money available to help the favourites go a little faster, and sailboats are no exception. In the eyes of the amateur 'Corinthian' sailors, this combination of spectacular speed, based on the work of paid crews in sponsored boats, was unforgivable.

Nobody is suggesting that the two groups shared the same starting lines. The exclusive yacht clubs used high joining fees to exclude the sort of people who sailed sandbaggers, but there was no avoiding the fact that the slower yachts were publicly ignored, while the speed and spectacle of the racing sandbaggers commanded big public audiences. Magazines such as *Harpers Bazaar* featured sandbaggers racing on their covers. After a while, being ignored became too much to tolerate.

The reaction was double-edged. First, the sandbaggers were dubbed 'extreme and dangerous', and this accusation was pushed hard enough in the media to generate some public support against them. Second, around 1882 the Seawanhaka Yacht Club drew up its Seawanhaka Corinthian Racing Rules.

These rules banned entry from any yachts that shifted ballast, or were in any way crewed by professionals. This got rid of all three irritants: the boats that were fast because they moved ballast, the strong hefters who were paid to move the ballast, and the very skilled fishermen who sailed these extreme boats so well. As more and more clubs adopted this Corinthian philosophy, a divide – driven not by one but by *two* differences of approach – was created between this growing group of similarly minded clubs and the working-class sandbaggers. One difference was the Corinthian philosophy. The second, at root, was the 'respect for the rules' vs the 'respect for performance' conflict. The clubs introduced growing regulation – the requirement to furnish hull lines and rig plans, crew lists, and crew occupations – to enforce both their attitudes and stability. The sandbaggers had traditionally observed no rule other than the length of the boat and, when pushed, had simply set more sail or carried more ballast. Another factor was the encroachment of new piers which progressively deprived the viewing public of the close-up view of the spectacular sailing. As the years went by, the pressure on the sandbaggers increased, and political clout of the establishment sailors was sufficient to make the Corinthian rules prevail in the waters of New York. The sandbaggers were made unwelcome, and for this and other reasons organised sandbagger racing declined and vanished from the Hudson river estuary – for a while.

But they survived, and their first tactic was to roll with the punch and relocate further south. Some sandbaggers began to sail in and around Delaware Bay, where a few sail as 'vintage boats' to this day. Their numbers were small, their social impact was negligible, and they trod on nobody's toes, so they were left to sail in peace.

Their second survival ploy was to move west. They were purchased by mid-west sailors because they were the fastest boats of their time. We will look at the Inland Lake Yachting Association and their lake scows in more detail later, but the broad picture from the Inland Lakes Yachting Association's history is that recreational racing on the inland lakes near Chicago started in earnest in the late 1850s, and that many of the racing yachts from inception, until true scows were born about 1900, were the 'gravel wagons' imported from the east (see page 11).

The sandbaggers' third survival mechanism has been a modern reincarnation. A style of 'water-bagger' day racer and ocean racer has been developed through the 1990s that now loads and shifts water ballast from side to side exactly as the sandbaggers shifted sand or gravel ballast 150 years ago. Like the sandbaggers, they are wide, light, flat, and carry minimum ballast in light conditions and move maximum ballast to the windward side when sailing to windward in strong winds. The dynamic result is the same – the modern water-baggers enjoy superior sail-carrying power to total weight ratios and have abruptly begun to sail much faster than their lead-on-fixed-keels rivals.

The fourth reincarnation of the sandbagger is in the form of a vintage revival. Peter Kellogg has built two replicas of the biggest (30ft) craft; these sail at various venues. In about 1999, the venue was the Manhattan Yacht Club in New York; it ran a programme in which the two sandbaggers were called *Bull* and *Bear* and were joined by a chase-spectator-rescue powerboat, *Greyhound*. A club-sponsored programme encouraged those interested to first become club members, then spectators, then rescue crew, then sandbagger sailors, etc. This restored, for a year, not only the sandbaggers and sandbagger sailing to New York harbour, but also generated a growing support base which ranged from local enthusiastic spectators and crews to helmsmen. There were challenges by international teams, and in this way many contemporary sailors learned the art and techniques of racing these 'extreme and dangerous' sailboats.

It may be that some future archaeologist will assert that Egyptian skippers shifted slaves as ballast for speed as they raced flotillas of dhows up and down the Nile for the Tutankhamen Gold Cup in 2347 BC. Meantime, we believe that the sandbaggers of New York and the skiffs of Sydney were the world's first sailboats known to shift ballast to achieve dynamic ratios superior to conventional practice and so sail faster.

1.5 ■ The North American inland lakes

The Inland Lake Yachting Association's recently published *History of the Inland Lake Yachting Association*[2] notes that Wisconsin began to attract settlers in large numbers in about 1835. Many of the lakeshore settlements could be reached only by water, so substantial workboat building and sailing was an integral part of the growing economy. Into this environment, the 1851 triumph of the schooner *America* in England acted as a catalyst, and organised sailboat racing developed quickly.

I quote from the ILYA history: '*America*'s victory started a wave of interest in the sport which moved across the country. When it reached Lake Winnebago it changed Neenah's summer pastime into her major sport.'

This typifies the further dimension that sailing added to the leisure and social culture of many lake communities. Both the technical expertise of sailboat handling and racing, and the management and social expertise involved in organising sailboat racing at a consistently high level, became socially important. Fig 1.4 shows the ILYA's oldest major trophy, the Sheridan Prize (donated in about 1870). It is a hand-crafted sterling silver model of a sandbagger, large and beautifully accurate – the sort of trophy that has always been massively expensive. Nothing could better attest that by the 1870s sailboat racing had grown to the point where it was not only popular, but had become culturally important in these inland lake communities.

Fig 1.4 The Sheridan prize

Lake Geneva's coveted Sheridan Prize – a sterling silver model of the sandbagger *Nettie*. Courtesy of Lake Geneva Yacht Club.

Chapter 1 of the ILYA history is titled 'Before Scows'. In the late 1800s, the fastest sailboats known were the sandbaggers of New York. What we now see is that at exactly the time the sandbaggers were being pushed out of the Hudson river estuary by prejudice, a demand for them had grown in the inland lakes. They were eagerly purchased from the east coast and became known in the lakes as 'gravel wagons'. (The original bags of sand stayed wet and the fabric quickly rotted. Gravel dried more quickly and the bags lasted longer.) Their numbers were not large but their reputation for speed is attested by the Sheridan Prize.

Chapter 2 of the ILYA history, 'The Scow is Born', and subsequent chapters, chronicle the beginning (in about 1895) of the development of a local style of lighter, flatter scows more suited to the flatter waters and generally lighter winds of the inland lakes. These boats were designed to 'measure short (upright) and sail long (heeled)'. As their proportions were refined, the lighter finer-lined scows became consistent winners. They sailed 'on edge' in lighter winds and planed freely offwind when a stronger wind blew. They proved faster than the more powerful sandbaggers (or any other boat) in the generally lighter-wind inland lake

---

[2] The Inland Lake Yachting Association's history reports famous scow builder John O Johnson as saying that *Yankee*, built by Eugene Ramaley of White Bear Lake in 1898 for Lucius Ordway, was 'the first true scow he had ever seen'. It is said that the design of *Yankee* was influenced by Herreshoff's *Alfrida*, launched the previous year.

conditions, and superseded them to the point where the flat 'skimming dish' scow design-style soon became, and remains, the quintessential inland lake sailboat.

Buddy Melges adds these comments:

The very first A scow was an offshoot of Seawanhaka sloops and a cross with Canadian design of the first scows. As the competition grew for the Seawanhaka's Cup Challenge the Canadians built flatter and flatter sailboats soon to be known as scows. Interestingly, the first scows crossed Canada from the East arriving in Kenora, Canada, then filtering down to St Paul, Minnesota. The Ordway family of 3-M Corporation was the promoter and John O Johnson became the builder.

Buddy Melges again:

These very first scows had centreboards and when heeled to proper angles for reduced wetted surface they made too much leeway. Johnny Johnson then solved this dilemma with bilge boards (two angled centreboards), one in each bilge. Immediate performance gains became evident. These first scows were able to plane in winds as low as 12 knots.

The A scow is 38ft long, 8ft 6in beam and carries approximately 500sq ft of sail. They very well could have weighed 3000lb. The Class has survived because of [the simplicity of] *its so-called 'box' scantlings. Any boat which could fit into a box 38ft x 8ft 6in by a certain depth was an A scow. In fact in later years the E, C and M scows followed the same box scantlings which allowed all classes to keep current within the box. Certainly our present scows are very different and certainly much faster than those of 1890.*

Most of all the scow class, spinnaker or no spinnaker, sailed pretty much square to the true wind when running free before the wind. It was not until after World War II that so many performance advances were instituted.

Sail material improvement had much to do with boat speed. Stiffer materials that became more stable allowed for greater girths. Rigs were improved by flexing in order to shift gears as wind speed changed. Sail design had to be changed to compensate for bendy rigs and sail material became a very important part of the formula to new-found boat speed.

The scows being long, flat and minimum sheer height were well suited for the lakes of Minnesota, Wisconsin, Illinois, and any protected body of water. They were never popular on Lake Michigan because of its bigger waves, but in the smaller lakes in the state of Michigan the scows have thrived.

As a youngster aged 20 in 1950, and having a father who was very innovative, we began to copy our iceboat techniques for downwind sailing. We ventilated our sails by sailing close to true wind angles and therefore the increased boat speed moved the apparent wind forward. This new practice found our downwind track to first be high then almost matching the square runner because our speed was twice that of his, our sails sheeted more firmly and obviously brought the apparent wind forward of the beam. To say the least, we began to dominate the racing and even though we shared the information and coached it, it seemed like we always had the upper hand. Possibly it was because of the performance advance going into our production boats and sails and as designers we had a greater feel of what we were trying to accomplish in the fooling of Mother Nature.

1.6 ■ The skiffs of Sydney

Like the sandbaggers, the skiffs of Sydney come to notice about 1800 as the workboats that serviced the square riggers plying the growing port of Sydney. Before long, the skiffs also engaged in racing. They too re-rigged with lighter spars and progressively bigger sails for the weekends' competitions.

Few waterways in the world can showcase sailing as can Sydney Harbour. In most harbours the shores are flat, the view horizontal, and tactical subtleties cannot be seen by any distant viewer. Sydney is different. The warm summer climate is governed by the fact that the great dividing range is only 50 to 100 miles to the west, these hills are low enough for the prevailing westerly winds to blow over them and subside and warm, and become relatively cloudless as they flow down towards the sea. This gives rise to the characteristically clear skies and intense heating of the littoral, and this heating leads to the Australian east coast's prevailing strong regular summer afternoon sea breezes. Added to this is the topography of Sydney Harbour, which is a broken steep-sided fault aligned into the northeast through a 100m high plateau (see Fig 1.22). Down this valley the regular sea breeze funnels at an average 12 knots on summer afternoons. To cap it all, the steep high shores offer myriad

Fig 1.5 Skiff crew 'stacking'

This is *how* they sailed, stacked two or three deep on the gunwales. Photo from *Blue Water Bushmen*, courtesy of Bruce Stannard.

vantage points from which those who know sailing and the sea can look down on the racing skiffs and, because they are looking down, can follow the tactics as they tack and gybe in a way not possible where shores are flat.

Bruce Stannard's classic *Blue Water Bushmen* opens:

> *In the mythology of Australian sport, there are few legends more colourful or enduring than those which surround the great sail-carrying open boats. Throughout most of the nineteenth century, long before cricket and the turf became obsessions in the infant colony, vast crowds jammed every vantage point around Sydney harbour to gape at and to gamble on the incredible antics of the men who dared to race the big boats.*
>
> *In the 1850s Sydney is said to have had more amateur and professional sailors than any other city in the world.*
>
> *The twenty-four footers often carried up to twenty men – great chunks of 'live ballast' squashed triple-banked on the gunwales [see Fig 1.5].*
>
> *The boats were huge, powerful, beamy and very, very wet.*
>
> *They set colossal clouds of sail upwind and more before the breeze [see Figs 1.6 and 1.7].*
>
> *Long before spinnakers were invented they set their extras square-rigged on heavy spars like the great clipper ships.*
>
> *Judged by today's standards they were alarmingly, magnificently over-canvassed. Sometimes the boats simply buried their bows and drove themselves under.*

What was happening here was that while the skiffs and the sandbaggers both shifted ballast, the two groups employed different techniques. This was because the skiffs' big crews themselves constituted both more ballast – much quicker-moving ballast – and a huge skilled-sailor labour force to hoist and trim extra sail downwind. The sandbaggers had none of these advantages.

So in lighter winds:

- The sandbaggers sailed light by carrying minimum ballast and minimum crew, and set no more sail (always main and jib only, plus perhaps a gaff topsail).
- The skiffs reduced weight by carrying fewer crew, who set huge amounts of extra sail, particularly when sailing downwind.

Fig 1.6 Skiff with square extra

This is *what* they sailed; the year is 1889 – everything up. Photo from *Blue Water Bushmen*, courtesy of Bruce Stannard.

And in stronger winds:

- The sandbaggers reefed sail and carried more ballast and more hefters.
- The skiffs carried more crew for ballast and set a little less sail.

There was a difference too in the dynamics. While the skiffs and the sandbaggers used the same principle of shifting ballast, the method was different because the sandbaggers were decked. A small crew in the cockpit hefted inert bags of gravel from the leeward onto the windward decks which were shaped and strengthened to receive it.

There is a limit to how much weight even the strongest man can heft between tacks when short tacking, and this limit to how much ballast could be shifted became the 'natural' limit as to how much sail a sandbagger could carry.

Fig 1.7 A skiff with spinnaker

This is *what* they sailed; the year is 1890 with the then new triangular spinnaker. Photo from *Blue Water Bushmen*, courtesy of Bruce Stannard.

The skiffs had no decks and were completely open, so that large crews could move their own weight on their own feet very quickly from side to side and right onto the windward gunwale. The first there sat on the gunwale and those who followed sat on those already there – it was called 'stacking'. Sometimes skiff crews stacked three deep, and Fig 1.5 shows this way of sailing in action.

Sixteen normal adults weigh about a ton, and big men obviously weigh more. A crew of 20 on a 24-footer constitute $1\frac{1}{4}$–$1\frac{1}{2}$ tons of live ballast that can move very quickly, so the skiffs could – and did – shift more ballast quicker and further outboard, and so were able to carry far more sail than the sandbaggers. Further, the big crews were themselves a substantial labour force, so the big skiffs were also able to set and drop multiple extra sails on the long downwind legs.

To keep them from swamping when they heeled, 'lee-cloths' with props were attached to the gunwales. The leeward lee-cloth, propped upward and inward, acted as a leeward deck to keep water out of the hull when the boat heeled (Fig 1.5).

Fig 1.6 shows a 22- or 24-footer, in 1889, a period when some boats still used a square extra sail and some used the then-new triangular spinnaker. The jib, completely blanketed, is limp. To the right of the lower jib a water sail is set from the end of a square sail lower yard which is attached to the mast. Above the water sail is a huge square sail skewed out to windward. Above the square sail is another light square sail called a 'raffee', set from the top of the jackyard of the topsail. A topsail is set between the gaff and a jackyard which extends the mast upward. A huge 'ringtail' is set on light yards between the peak of the gaff and the end of the boom. This greatly increases the area of the mainsail. A second watersail is set along the full length of the boom under the mainsail. Zorba might comment: 'The full catastrophe'.

Fig 1.7, from 1890, shows what the then-new triangular spinnaker version of the rigs of that era looked like.

The skiffs, like the sandbaggers, sailed faster than any conventional boats, but in Sydney there were so many skiffs that the real problem was that there were too many boats and too little organisation. The skiffs ranged from the tiny 6ft class through the 8s, 10s, 12s, 14s, 16s and 18s to the big 22- and 24-footers. There were so many skiffs that the skiffs were the norm, but they were anarchic and, as a result, the whole sailing activity suffered serious and repeated organisational problems typical of early growth. The problem was that while the Sydney sailing scene of the 1850s to the 1890s was vital in the extreme, and concentrated, it was so diverse within itself that no single organisation could manage the competing interests of the different classes to everybody's satisfaction.

The yacht owners and their families valued social interests. The smaller 6, 8, 10 and 12 foot open boat classes were extremely numerous and needed local races, but their emphasis lay in 'local', and they needed sheltered waters.

The bigger 18, 22 and 24ft classes were very conscious of their image and public drawing power. They demanded regular well-organised races in the stronger wind and bigger wave 'showcase' area of the harbour.

Between the years 1856 and 1890, six clubs were formed, but all failed within a few years. It seems each of them tried to be all things to all sailors, but in practice their management policies pleased so few of their members that they failed to command authority and were unable to control their fleets effectively – hence the failure.

There was one exception, though. The Sydney Yacht Squadron (later the Royal Sydney Yacht Squadron) had been formed in 1862. It tried a different policy, by focusing exclusively on the needs of yacht owners, and never mind anyone else. This policy worked. The Squadron thrived – and thrives to this day; the lesson was not lost.

Because of the seminal importance of the Eighteen footer skiffs 100 years later, it is worth taking a moment to look at how and why they became so dominant.

A far-sighted businessman, Mark Foy, stabilised skiff organisation by employing the same policy of focusing on one class, and to this he added two brilliant promotion techniques. In 1891 he provided the financial support to form the Sydney Flying Squadron. It is now Sydney's oldest open boat club. The two new promotion techniques were:

- He encouraged the Flying Squadron's boats to carry big distinctive insignia on their mainsails so they could be instantly recognised at a distance by the onlookers ashore and the punters on the following ferries.
- He introduced what has locally been called ever since the 'Mark Foy start', in which handicaps are applied at the start, with the slowest boat starting first. The revolutionary change was that the first boat across the line became the winner.

These two innovations revolutionised the image of skiff sailing and turned it into an exciting mass spectator sport. The insignia enabled spectators and punters to identify and follow during the race the fortunes of any boat in which they had an interest. The Mark Foy start took all the mystery out of unknown handicaps applied after the finish. Sailboat races were suddenly transparent, vital, and exciting to watch. If crews sometimes pushed too hard and drove their boats under, that was just another part of the new vitality.

The Flying Squadron organised regular races in the most spectacular area of the harbour. Of critical importance, Mark Foy funded prize money of £20 each week – which was ten weeks' wages for a tradesman in the 1890s – and he kept this up until the club was self-sustaining. This incentive not only enabled the club to schedule regular races; the constant financial incentive lured the top open boat sailors away from other clubs and other classes, and soon established the Flying Squadron as the pre-eminent club for development, speed, spectacle – and gambling. Mark Foy had found and applied a management format that has endured for a century and become a part of the life of Sydney town.

That it was the Eighteen footer class and boats rather than the glamour 22- or 24-footers that were chosen turns out to have been almost accidental. In electing to try the same approach that was by then working with the Sydney Yacht Squadron, Mark Foy needed a vehicle to solve the previously intractable organisational problem.

What is not clear, even now, is how and why the Eighteen footers became blessed. In the 1890s, the 22- and 24-footers were the glamour skiffs, and Mark Foy himself owned more than one. It seems that he may have chosen the Eighteen footers precisely because the glamour 22- and 24-footer classes were more strongly 'organised' within themselves and were resistant to change, while the Eighteens of that period knew that they were 'orphans', and were amenable to being managed.

The history is that within a few years the dominance of the 22- and 24-footers withered, and the previously unremarkable Eighteen footer class, with their new insignia and Mark Foy starts, had become not only dominant but enormously innovative. They have remained so for a century. In this way, Mark Foy engineered the enshrinement of Eighteen footer skiff sailing as a part of the life of Sydney.

Fig 1.8 Spectator fleet

This is *why* they sailed; the skiffs and their crews enjoyed iconic status; spectators crowd the finish. Photo from *Blue Water Bushmen*, courtesy of Bruce Stannard.

Fig 1.8 attests that wherever spectacle is exciting, thousands will gather to watch. The Sydney skiffs were the world's first movable live-ballast sailboats. Their dynamic 'sail-carrying power to total weight' ratios were superior to conventional practice, they set more sail and sailed faster, and their greater speed and spectacle aroused great public interest. Fig 1.8 shows nine large ferries, three tugs and many smaller craft, all full of spectators, waiting at the finish line of an Eighteen footer Australian Championship race in 1924. Because of this mass level of support, they were encouraged to race regularly and publicly and, over time, achieved iconic status in Sydney.

Both the sandbaggers and the skiffs used movable ballast and bigger sails to sail faster. They were each the fastest sailboats of their size in the world, and the state-of-the-art message as the year 1900 approached was: 'To sail faster, move ballast and set more sail.'

THE PLANING EXPLOSION – 1895 TO 1905

1.7 ■ England – first stirrings and private planing

The first planing sailboats probably sailed alone, in private. In the late 1800s a type of fowling craft, the Norfolk punt, was used on the Norfolk Broads. They were flat bottomed with rounded ends to nose through the reeds; some of them were 'long, narrow and fleet, rigged with a small leg o' mutton sail and steered with an oar through a quarter rowlock'. What we are describing here is a primitive sailboard, and there is no way such a craft would not have planed fast with a good wind on the quarter. But their owners' objective was to shoot waterfowl and not to race other punts, so they probably planed alone.

Many years later wider punts specially designed for sailing round the buoys with centreboard and rudder and an efficient rig became an established class. Norfolk Punt class No 1, *Shrimp*, is in the UK Maritime Museum; and Mike Evans, who for many years was Executive Director of the IYRU, owns one of these boats. Concerning the planing performance of the earlier craft, Mike suggests that it was probably one of those things that was so commonplace that nobody ever thought to discuss it or record it.

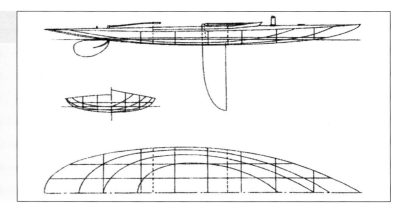

Fig 1.9 1 Rater *Sorceress*

Designed in 1894 by Linton Hope.
Courtesy of Robin Elliott.

Early records of planing-type hulls come from 1894. Creative designers – Linton Hope, closely followed by Arthur Burgoine, J M Soper and others – were designing unballasted 'A-raters' for use in restricted flat waters such as the Upper Thames (Fig 1.9). These boats were so perfectly adapted to their environment that they are still sailing, and I am advised that a mould has recently been taken from one hull so that cold-moulded FRP hulls will be available in the future.

Looking at their shape, it is self-evident that they must have planed freely and fast whenever they enjoyed a good wind on the quarter. The fact that the advent of planing in the UK tends to be associated with Uffa Fox's work 40 years later, rather than these early skimmers, suggests an absence of promotion rather than any absence of performance.

1.8 ■ New Zealand – Arch Logan, and the Patikis of Auckland

New Zealand offers a rich and complex history of early development of fast sailboats, and I am indebted to Robin Elliott for access to the extraordinary historical research conducted by Robin and Harold Kidd. What we now see is an explosion of creative design and sailing technology that started in Auckland about 1895 and developed lighter, flatter, faster planing sailboats so quickly that by 1900 they were being exported to South Africa, Australia and Honolulu. But at home they were beginning to be resented – they were first excluded from one club in 1900, and by 1905 the uproar was such that they were excluded from virtually all of the sailing clubs of Auckland in a repetition of the fate of the sandbaggers of New York 30 years earlier.

Until 1893 there is no record of any substantial sailing in New Zealand in unballasted sailboats, then one boatbuilding family that became dominant – the Logans – plus another equally good – the Baileys – changed history.

In the years 1893 to 1896 the Logans built a number of 'half-raters', some to the design of William Fife (UK) but more and more to the design of Arch Logan, who with four of his brothers traded as 'Logan Brothers'. All of these boats could, in theory, plane in ideal conditions.

In January 1897, the American barque *Sea King* sailed from Sydney for San Francisco with a load of coal. Mid-Tasman, she met extreme weather which damaged her to the extent that she put into Auckland, New Zealand, for survey and subsequent repair. In February 1897 the master's wide flat unballasted American sailing dinghy, also named *Sea King*, was purchased by an Auckland sailor and sailed on Lake Pupuke. Figs 1.10 and 1.11 show views of this boat from abeam and ahead. The origin of its design is unclear. It was certainly not based on any sandbagger philosophy, nor was it remotely like the ubiquitous New Jersey 'sneak box' style of workboat. She was unusually beamy with wide side decks and a very low profile. Whatever its origin, the lively performance of this unballasted sailboat triggered something latent in Arch Logan's mind.

By the end of 1897, the Logans had built three unballasted half-raters for a new division of the North Shore club, and the Baileys built another. In no way were these boats copies of *Sea King*. What they *did* do was extend the unusual features of light construction and a relatively flat aft bottom to a new level.

The following year, 1898, the newly formed Parnell Yacht Club asked Arch Logan to design and build some boats suitable for their youth division. Logan's response was to design an 18ft flat unballasted centreboard sailboat which he called a 'restricted half-rater'. The design was a smaller development of one of the three built the previous year. The *Auckland Star* newspaper, reporting on a club meeting of 30 July 1898, stated, 'on

Fig 1.10 *Sea King*

Sea King sailing in Auckland, New Zealand, 1897. Courtesy of Robin Elliott.

Fig 1.11 *Sea King* from ahead

Sea King viewed from ahead. Courtesy of Robin Elliott.

the suggestion of Mr T Ryan the proposed class has been given the appropriate name "Patiki", the Maori equivalent of "flatfish". ('Patiki' is pronounced Par-ti-ki, the 'a' in Maori being pronounced 'ar'.) Fig 1.12 shows one of these boats sailing in 1898, and Fig 1.13 shows the lines of a design by C J Collings, which was published in the American magazine *Rudder* in February 1905.

This exercise was innovative in five ways:

1 The first was that by this act the Parnell Yacht Club created New Zealand's first centreboard yacht class.
2 The second was the new flat, light, unballasted nature of the boats themselves.
3 The third was that this design approach gave this new youth trainer the ability to plane freely and thus offer a performance level far beyond the level normal to the adult conventional boats of that era.
4 The fourth was that, by consensus, 'restricted' rules were to apply to this class, rules that would require that all subsequent boats be very similar. Nowadays we would call these restrictions 'Class Rules', so this was a beginning of the 'Class' concept.
5 The fifth was to reinforce this idea of a class of similar boats with an appropriate name.

This design style was immediately successful. Six of the youth boats were built that winter, five by the Logans and one by the Baileys. In addition, two bigger, faster 22ft 1 rater and 1½ raters were built to the same design style. The genie was out of the bottle.

For the Intercolonial (Auckland/Sydney) championship of 1898–9 three 1 raters were built. Fig 1.14 shows a photo of Arch Logan's *Mercia* in Sydney a year later, and Fig 1.15 its lines. It did not win in Auckland, but was deemed the fastest boat. Along with the winner, it was sold to Sydney in 1899, where it dominated for a while. It was then sold to South Africa where it was re-named *Ibis*. Meanwhile, the Logans began to ship similar boats to Honolulu.

All heavy deep-bodied sailboats such as yachts with keels and the heavy sandbaggers, and the heavily crewed skiffs, sail through the water, and they suffer a very great increase in hull drag as soon as their speed exceeds that of a wave of their own length (see Fig 10.3). So in practice while those with bigger sails sailed faster than those with smaller sails, the speed differences were small and none of them ever sailed very fast on any point of sailing.

Fig 1.12 Patiki *Eka* by Logan Designed by Arch Logan in 1898. Courtesy of Robin Elliott.

Fig 1.13 Lines of *Maroro*

Lines of restricted Patiki *Maroro*, designed by C J Collings, published in *Rudder*, February 1905. Courtesy of Robin Elliott.

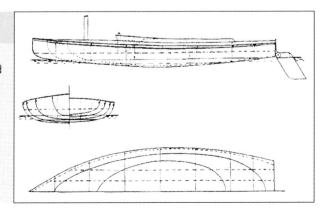

Fig 1.14 *Mercia*   A W Crane racing *Mercia* in Sydney, 1901. Courtesy of Robin Elliott.

Fig 1.15 Lines of Patiki *Mercia*

Mercia designed by Arch Logan in 1898 (faded lines restored). Courtesy of Robin Elliott.

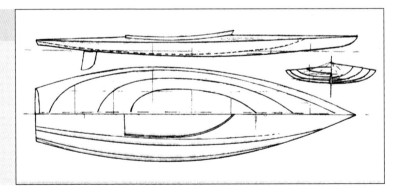

The performance of the new Patiki-style boats was beyond any previous experience. The new lighter Patiki-style designs with their flatter aft bottoms were able, for the first time in a sailboat, to avoid the crippling drag increase by lifting and skimming over the water instead of ploughing through it; so on broad reaches in a breeze, they were able to skim at speeds up to twice as fast as their conventional rivals. They were able to do this because of two innovations: the first was the shape of the aft bottom; the second was a construction innovation. The Logans and other Auckland boatbuilders began to use thinner (5mm) planking of lighter timber, together with lighter framing, and better engineering to make hulls that were much lighter than was customary, but still strong enough to offer a long racing life given care. Two men were able to lift one of these new 20ft or 22ft Patiki-style hulls when it was dry. They then went further and developed an

Fig 1.16 *Maroondah*

The Patiki *Maroondah*, at speed in Napier, New Zealand. Designed by Arch Logan in 1907. Courtesy of Robin Elliott.

even lighter and stronger structure with two even thinner skins, one diagonal, the outer one fore-and-aft, with oiled silk between, and all held together with myriad copper nails and roves. Fig 1.16 shows a 1907 Logan-designed Patiki, *Maroondah*, planing at speed.

In 1900 the offence of sailing too fast began to bite. Most of the members of the North Shore club were owners of 22ft mullet fishing boats known locally as 'mulleties', all of which carried some ballast for safety at sea. The ballasted 'mulleties' could not begin to match the reaching and broad reaching speeds of the new lightly built, finer-lined unballasted 'skimming dishes'. So, as in New York, the North Shore club voted to exclude future entries from unballasted Patiki-style boats from class starts for ballasted boats. While they remained in theory welcome to start in a separate race, the reality was that there were only ever one or two Patikis in any one of the five harbour clubs, so the practical effect was exclusion.

The name 'Patiki' suggested by Ryan for Logan's youth trainer was brilliant in that it encapsulated everything that was different about these new boats. So the appellation 'Patiki-style' quickly became attached to all new boats which 'had that look'. As a group, these Patiki-style boats had a problem – like the English International Fourteens of 30 years later, there were not many of them in total, there were never enough of them to form a class of their own in any one club, and it never seemed to have occurred to their owners to band together and form a club of their own or a separate class within a club.

For another five years, the Patiki-style was further improved, although not many were built. By 1904, a 24ft Patiki-style boat was conceding up to 96 (yes, ninety-six) minutes to conventional craft in club racing on the Manukau harbour west of Auckland.

Then came the coup de grâce and the riposte. The annual Auckland Anniversary Regatta was run by civic authorities so nobody could ever be excluded from proper entry to any of the classes. In 1905 in the 22ft division, three Patikis finished virtually together no less than 40 minutes ahead of the first conventional boat.

The uproar was huge! Their sin was to be so embarrassingly faster than all others in mixed fleets, and their fate was that henceforth entries from Patiki-style boats were not accepted from virtually all of the clubs around Auckland Harbour.

The decade from 1895 to 1905 saw explosive development in New Zealand from 'no record of planing' to the fully developed planing Patiki-style craft which was unbeatable in breeze and flat water. Arch Logan as designer was the giant who first saw the new opportunity and initiated dynamic change. The performance of his new designs in flat water and wind was so much faster than expected that they offended the Auckland establishment of the day to the extent that, like the sandbaggers of New York, they were excluded from club racing in Auckland Harbour.

1.9 ■ Canada – Herrick Duggan and the lake scows of Montreal

The Seawanhaka Yacht Club had sown the wind with its part in excluding the sandbaggers in 1882, and it was about to reap the whirlwind.

In 1895 the Seawanhaka Cup was presented by the club for competition in small boats, as an international match race series with challenge welcome from any club. In the same year, both the first challenger, from the UK, and the Seawanhaka defender had the relatively deep, narrow hulls typical of all coastal keelboats and the sandbaggers – that is, broadly similar to the underwater shape of Fig 1.2, or today's Yngling. These were the fastest, state-of-the-art boats of 1895. Seawanhaka defended successfully.

In the inland lakes, the deep heavy type of hull was beginning to be superseded by a lighter more lively type of boat. George Herrick Duggan, a civil engineer, had designed – and he and Fred P Shearwood had built and sailed together – a small yacht called *Gloria*, which dominated the racing on Lake St Louis, Montreal. Because of its long overhangs it was nicknamed 'the bug'. (Note Buddy Melges's earlier comment that scow-type design originated in Canada.)

In 1896 Royal St Lawrence Yacht Club tendered a challenge for the Seawanhaka Cup. Duggan had been Commodore from 1884 to 1890, and the notes that follow are drawn primarily from the club's beautifully presented history, *The Royal St Lawrence Yacht Club 1888–1988*. Chapter IV is titled 'Seawanhaka Cup: Days of Glory':

- The Seawanhaka defender, *El Hierie* (Fig 1.17), was designed by Crane to a 15ft waterline with 240sq ft of sail. The attitude within the club was that defence would be easy.
- Duggan elected to design a boat around a 12ft waterline and 300sq ft of sail. Fig 1.18 shows his challenger, *Glencairn*. It is already a lower, flatter, hull shape than either the 1895 challenger and defender, or *El Hierie*.
- The challenge awakened a ferment of innovation in the infant Canadian industrial machine. It became a matter of national pride that every part of the challenger should be 'Canadian made' – and in the end it was, even with the first challenger.

Fig 1.17 *El Hierie*

Seawanhaka Yacht Club defender, 1896. Courtesy of C E Bolles.

Fig 1.18 *Glencairn I*

Royal St Lawrence Yacht Club Challenger, 1896, designed and sailed by Herrick Duggan. Courtesy of Notman Photographic Archives, McGill University.

- Duggan was ably supported by Shearwood who, for the next nine years, acted as key helper in all things, built the boats and crewed with Duggan.
- *Glencairn* won the first race by 47 minutes. The record suggests that the defenders were so shocked that they did not regain their composure and sailed below standard in races two and three, which Duggan also won. The cup was now the Royal St Lawrence's to defend.
- Seawanhaka challenged in 1897, and put everything into the challenge. For Royal St Lawrence, Duggan defended with *Glencairn II* (Fig 1.19A), which appears to have been a detailed development of *Glencairn I*. The title of Fig 1.19B is confusing in that two different designs, or design studies, are shown. Both, though, are broadly similar and confirm the trend from the Vee bottom with deadrise of the sandbaggers and the Sydney skiffs, through the flat-bottomed scow, to the extreme of *Dominion* (see below).
- In *Glencairn II*, Duggan won again.
- Seawanhaka challenged again in 1898, and this time threw the challenge open to eliminations between challengers from any American club, so the Inland Lakes Yachting Association became involved. This was clearly starting to get serious. Some of the challengers were so flimsily constructed that they failed to survive the elimination series.

Fig 1.19A *Glencairn II*

Glencairn II. Courtesy of Notman Photographic Archives, McGill University.

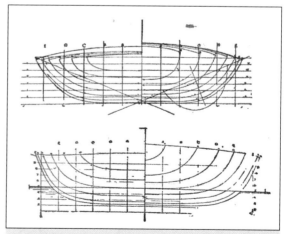

Fig 1.19B Sections of *Glencairn II*

These lines probably come from the magazine *Rudder*, 1897. Which one is *Glencairn II* is not stated, but both reflect the trend from the sandbagger shape through the scow shape to the *Dominion* shape. Courtesy of Robin Elliott.

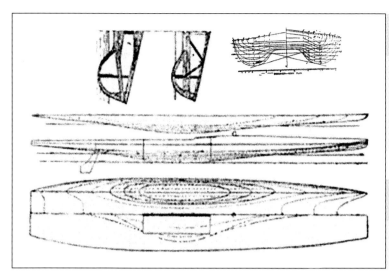

Fig 1.20A Lines of *Dominion*, 1898 (left)

Successful Royal St Lawrence Yacht Club defender. It was a brilliantly innovative boat. Designed and sailed by Herrick Duggan. Courtesy of Robin Elliott.

Fig 1.20B *Dominion* under sail (below)

Courtesy of Notman Photographic Archives, McGill University.

- For the Royal St Lawrence defence, Duggan created *Dominion*, a stunningly innovative design. Fig 1.20A shows the lines of this revolutionary boat, and Fig 1.20B shows *Dominion* under sail.
- Duggan won again.
- Following this challenge, the rules were 'adjusted' (read, 'if you can't beat them, ban them') to 'prevent the use of abnormal hulls such as *Dominion*, or flimsy designs such as *Seawanhaka* and *Challenger*'.
- Seawanhaka challenged again, and again employed the full national elimination process to secure the best possible challenger.
- For Royal St Lawrence, Duggan took the banning setback in his stride and built *Glencairn III* (Fig 1.21). Note how low and flat the hull shape has become, and that this boat is described by the magazine *Rudder* as a 'scow'. The transition from sandbagger to scow was complete. With it, Duggan won again.

And so it went on. Duggan designed, built, sailed and won the first challenge; he then designed, built, sailed and won the next five defences. He designed, and others sailed (and won), the sixth, seventh and eighth defences.

Fig 1.21 *Glencairn III*, 1899, under sail

Courtesy of Notman Photographic Archives, McGill University.

His craft were superbly proportioned and crafted for the light air, flat water, inland lakes sailing environment and his designs were tempered to the hilt as racing machines by the fire of nine successful international challenges.

This dynamic revolution in North America was taking place at exactly the same time as a broadly similar dynamic revolution was taking place in New Zealand, but from the point of view of the history of high performance sailing, the two thrusts were not the same.

In North America, Herrick Duggan was the giant who rewrote the book about what was fast in flat water, light air, inland lake sailing. He started from a near sandbagger displacement design in 1895 and finished with the modern lake scow. The scow is designed to 'measure short (upright) and sail long (on edge)'. When it is heeled and sailed on one bilge the wetted area is greatly reduced and the waterline length is greatly increased, so these boats enjoy lower drag up to higher hull speeds. This gives a higher ratio of sail area to wetted area, together with a lower drag than is possible with any 'upright' hull *of the same sailing length as the scow when heeled*. In the light airs and light to moderate winds and flat water that prevail in the Inland Lakes Yachting Association's area (generally the mid-west of the USA), this combination remains unbeatable. But for the reasons given in Section 9.9 (page 141) this approach is not efficient in either stronger winds or in waves, so Duggan's design solution, brilliant as it was for his area of the world, was not one that could be applied everywhere. Because of their shape, the scows planed freely offwind in the rare inland stronger winds, but in that area these are so rare that this was almost an accidental by-product. (The *Dominion* shape could not plane, but it did not matter.)

Arch Logan had sensed the planing potential of the *Sea King* shape and from that start point developed, over the next few years, a genre of fresh-wind planing sailboats that changed for ever the way sailors thought about sailboat speeds. But, like Duggan's approach, Logan's approach could not at first win everywhere.

At the stage both had reached in 1905, Duggan's lighter wind designs and Logan's stronger wind designs looked superficially similar, but their critical ratios were already very different. In Logan's case, in later years both he and others extended his initial work to create the vertical stemmed 'seagoing planer', and with this second development, the planing revolution was complete.

In 1895 the state of the art message had been 'To sail faster, move ballast and set more sail'. This message was true in both flat water and in waves. By 1905 it had become 'To sail faster yet in flat water, build light and flat. In lighter winds, heel. In stronger winds, plane'. This message was true only in flat water, and it was going to need another 30-odd years of further development before it would be true everywhere.

1.10 ■ The trickle-through decades – 1900 to 1950

In the years from 1905 to about 1955, the new planing designs were adopted with enthusiasm in New Zealand and South Africa and the Inland Lakes of North America, but not initially in either Australia or England, nor on the North American coasts.

It is easy to see why the British were cautious. Their climate is characterised by extreme variability. In special locations, flat-water boats like Linton Hope's I-Raters (Fig 1.9) were so good that they have satisfied their owners and their friends for more than a century. But a little further down the Thames, at Whitstable, conditions can be such as to capsize a big lifeboat end over end at a demonstration launch. It was going to need something more than I-Raters occasionally planing in their sheltered waterways to change the British mind.

The Australian situation was more complex. Most Australian innovation has come from Sydney, simply because far more sailing takes place there than anywhere else, and Sydney-siders have always been prepared to 'give a new idea a go'. But when you look at Sydney Harbour closely, it too has traps for the unwary. Fig 1.22 shows the shape of the 'showcase' area of Sydney Harbour. Of critical importance are the following factors:

- The prevailing summer afternoon sea breeze is a funnelling wind of 11 to 12 knots from the NNE.
- In this wind, Clark Island makes a natural leeward mark.
- The Sow and Pigs Reef, a little more than 2nm upwind near the heads, makes a natural windward mark.
- Shark Island makes a natural wing mark.

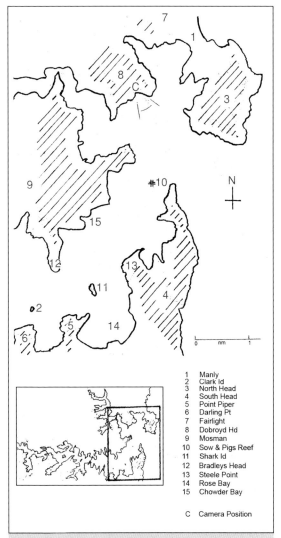

1	Manly
2	Clark Id
3	North Head
4	South Head
5	Point Piper
6	Darling Pt
7	Fairlight
8	Dobroyd Hd
9	Mosman
10	Sow & Pigs Reef
11	Shark Id
12	Bradleys Head
13	Steele Point
14	Rose Bay
15	Chowder Bay
C	Camera Position

Fig 1.22 Map of Sydney Harbour

This has been the Eighteen footer No 1 course since racing began; it is sailed far more often than any other course. When Mark Foy set up the Sydney Flying Squadron in 1891 its No 1 course became three laps from Clark Island to the Sow and Pigs reef 2nm to windward and back, with a dig around Shark Island on the first and third laps to make it more interesting. At first glance this looks like the familiar triangle, sausage, triangle course. But when you look at it closely, it is dominated by a number of unusual factors:

- The windward/leeward leg is more than 2nm long. This gives a lot of time to set and strike the multiple extras shown in Figs 1.6 and 1.7.
- Even in the nominally triangular laps, the intervening headlands and the wind shadow areas behind Steele Point and Shark Island make the downwind legs more of a run-reach-reach-run than two reaches. This is critical.
- So, between planing Patikis (such as the 1899 *Mercia*) and the 1899 non-planing skiffs, the Sydney situation was heavily skewed in favour of the non-planing skiff. Specifically:
  - On the few occasions when a course other than the No 1 course was sailed, the Patiki simply planed away from the non-planing skiff on the broad reaching legs, and sailed about as fast as the skiff on all the other legs, and won comfortably.
  - But when the usual No 1 course was sailed, there were no long reaching legs to plane on. Further, when wind is against tide up and down the harbour, the wave height increases to the point where the flat-water scow-shaped Patiki would be slowed to windward by its greater wave impact drag in rougher water, so it probably sailed to windward more slowly than the vertical-stemmed skiff, and no faster on the run, where the skiff carried so much more sail, and the reaches were too short to be decisive. In these circumstances, the skiff would have won.
- So the overall situation was that on a few occasions the Patiki would win by a large margin, but most times the skiffs kept on winning.

This was not enough to persuade Sydney. Sydney and Australia, like Britain, stayed with what they had and waited until something more convincing came along. Nearly 40 years later, in 1938, it came.[4]

1.11 ■ The South African interest

While the South Africans do not appear to have contributed creative design in the quest for high performance, their story shows how closely the 'high performance sailing' centres were linked 100 years ago. The principal drive was the annual 'Interport Challenge' between Cape Town, Port Elizabeth, Durban and Mozambique. All of these sailing waters favoured flat-water planing craft. It appears to have started with Logan's *Mercia*, which was designed and built in Auckland in 1898, sold to Sydney in 1899, and then sold to Durban in 1904 where it sailed for many years, renamed as *Ibis*. From this start, a regular traffic arose in designs, kits and complete boats between Auckland and South Africa, with constant enquiry and occasional purchase of lake scows from Wisconsin and Minnesota. What happened in practice was that whoever lost the Interport Challenge approached a designer somewhere to design a boat to beat last year's winner. Rules were vague, requests such as asking the New Zealander Logan for 'an American style boat to beat xxx' are revealing, and innovation was imaginative.

Fig 1.23 shows a 1909 Logan scow, *Shingana*, at speed on the Zwaartkops river. Note the 'American style' twin canted bilge centreboards. All New Zealand craft used a single central vertical centreboard.

Fig 1.24 shows the lines of *Merlin*, designed by Arch Logan in 1912 for Jack Grice of Durban. The horizontal bow has become broader.

These scows remained a feature of South African sailing for many decades. One of my South African contributors, Dave Cox, started as a bailer boy on 'the last of the scows' in Durban in 1932.

---

[4] A century later, in January 2002, six New Zealand 'M' class 'Improved Patiki 18 footers' (see Fig 1.27), which are still popular in New Zealand, visited Sydney and enjoyed a two-week revival festival with the (then six) Sydney 'Vintage Eighteens'. They raced the same courses. It was of interest to both me and Robin Elliott, who was one of the 'M' sailors (and my guest), to observe how exactly the scenario above repeated. We can be confident that the analysis above is reasonably correct.

Fig 1.23 *Shingana*

The Logan-designed scow *Shingana* on the Zwaartzkops river 1908. Courtesy of Robin Elliott.

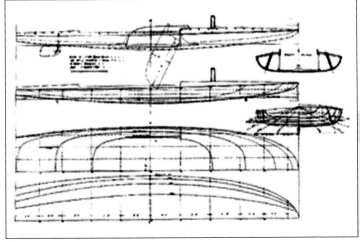

Fig 1.24 Lines of *Merlin*

Merlin, a 24ft 3in bilge board Patiki scow. Designed and built by Arch Logan in 1912 for Jack Grice of Durban. Courtesy of Robin Elliott.

Fig 1.25 Patikis in Napier, 1912

Courtesy of Robin Elliott.

1.12 ■ New Zealand after 1905

Like the sandbaggers, the Patikis survived – and magnificently – for a while. Odd boats had been sold all over New Zealand. In one particular location, Napier, recreational sailing took place on the 10sq mile Ahuriri lagoon which enjoyed reliable fresh sea breezes, was shallow enough to suppress big waves, and big enough for both good racing and picnic cruising. It was a natural home for the Patikis. Within a few years, a fleet of ten or more had concentrated there, were developed even further by local builders, and they raced spectacularly. Fig 1.25 shows some rigged pre-race in 1912. Because from 1910 to 1931 more Patikis were concentrated in Napier than anywhere else in New Zealand, the legend grew of 'the Napier Patikis'.

The end was savage when, in 1931, a huge earthquake devastated Napier. Part of the convulsion was that a great area of land, which included the Ahuriri lagoon, was lifted several feet. The lagoon drained, and it has subsequently become the city's airport. When sailing resumed decades later, the Patikis proved totally unsuitable for offshore sailing – they were slow to windward in ocean waves, and their construction was too light to be durable in rough water – and they never recovered.

Their legend lives on as 'the Napier Patikis'. Arch Logan's 'Restricted half-rater, Youth Trainer, to be called the "Patiki" class' had spawned the 'Patiki-style' boats, which were blindingly fast in strong winds and flat water. The seminal difference between the lake scows and the Patikis was that the lake scows shine in the inland light airs, and seldom see stronger wind. The Patikis were coastal craft which were both fast in light air and simply vanished when reaching in good coastal breezes (see Fig 1.16, *Maroondah*, and Fig 1.23, *Shingana*). By the time they regrouped in Napier, they had become simply the 'Napier Patikis'.

The legend now, 100 years on, is that the Patikis were unique to Napier. But they never were. In the legend, though, we honour one of the seminal design breakthroughs on the way to higher performance sailing.

The next step

Arch Logan had sensed the potential for speed that lay in *Sea King*, and created the lightly built Patiki which could plane fast in flat water. As soon as the design dynamics of the Patiki-style flat-water planer became understood, it became clear to both Logan and other New Zealand designers that the next logical step would be a seagoing craft which would combine both the advantage of the planing bottom with a topsides and deck design suitable for sailing in waves.

Both the New Zealand Patiki style, the North American lake scow style, and also Linton Hope's A-Raters all have low wide gunwales forward and low gunwales along the whole length of the boat. This is an efficient shape in flat water because, when heeled, the immersed bilge or chine presents to the water the longest,

Fig 1.26 New Zealand Z Class dinghies

Takapuna or Z class Youth Trainer, seagoing, planing design by R B Brown, 1921. Courtesy of Robin Elliott.

most slender shape with the least wetted area, hence the lowest flat-water drag. But in waves, this shape suddenly becomes grossly inefficient, because when sailing to windward the wide bottom between the widely spaced forward chines presents the maximum area to be hit and forced backwards by the crest of every advancing wave, and thus suffers added wave impact drag. Other considerations are practical. For sailing in waves, the gunwale height needs to be sufficient to keep the crew clear above the wave crests, otherwise the crests hit the crew and add even more drag. Further, the greater the speed, the greater the mass of flying water thrown over the boat with each wave, so the deck arrangements need to keep this water out, otherwise the boat will soon swamp (we are discussing here the days before suction bailers).

In the years following 1910 in New Zealand, a range of new 'seagoing' dinghy classes evolved, in which rough-water design features were progressively refined. Vertical stems with sharper bows progressively reduced wave impact drag, adequate gunwale height kept crews' buttocks above the wave crests, and large deck area with small cockpits kept the boats reasonably dry. Wellington boats added a fourth feature – adequate beam to handle Wellington's abnormally strong winds. This needs explaining.

The bulk of New Zealand innovation has traditionally come from Auckland with its gentler subtropical climate and more numerous boats, but Wellington has always been big enough to be important. No design that could not handle both harbours could ever become popular nationally, and the two climates are at opposite extremes.

Auckland is subtropical, its surroundings relatively flat, its average summer wind is about 9 to 10 knots and relatively steady, and the average wave height in the harbour is probably less than half a metre.

Wellington Harbour, further south, is temperate, and is in a deep valley amid high parallel north–south mountain ranges adjacent to one of the windiest straits in the world. Thirty-knot winds, unsteady in the extreme, and 3–4ft waves, are commonplace.

Following the interruption of the 1914–18 war, design development was brisk. In 1921 R B Brown designed the 'Z' or Takapuna class. (Takapuna is a northern beach suburb of Auckland.) These were 12ft 8in long, with a vertical stem, fine bow, flat aft bottom, and small cockpit. They were planing craft that could handle any waves, and were very fast downwind; Fig 1.26 shows two of them planing.

In 1922, following repeated calls for 'an improved Patiki class' from older yachtsmen who had raced the old restricted Patikis with the Parnell Sailing Club back in 1898 and who were now members of the Royal New Zealand Yacht Squadron, Arch Logan designed the 'M' class of Eighteen footer, which is basically a Patiki with higher gunwales and a vertical stem. It survived for 54 years within the RNZYS as its only centreboard class and thrives to this day. Fig 1.27 shows an 'M' class ('Emmy') planing very fast in a squall.

31

Fig 1.27 M class (improved Patiki) at speed

Courtesy of Robin Elliott.

Fig 1.28 New Zealand I class seagoing planing dinghy, designed in 1927

The photo shows the author, reefed down in *Merlin*, Wanganui river, *c* 1938. Courtesy of the Dave Nicholson collection.

Both the 'Z' and the 'M' classes originated in Auckland. Both have relatively modest beam.

Alf Harvey designed and built the first 'I', or Idle Along, class in 1927 (Fig 1.28). This was a wider-beamed boat for Wellington conditions, where strong winds are so common that club races are frequently started in winds of 30 knots with stronger gusts.[5]

As always, it was the class that encouraged development that showed the greatest advance. The New Zealand 'T' fourteen footer class had rules broadly similar to those of the International Fourteen foot class in the UK. In Auckland, Billy Rogers built the first of a series of brilliantly successful planing Fourteens – *Kismet* in 1923, *Shalimar* in 1928, *Treasure* in 1934, and *Vamp* in 1935. In all of these boats he dominated not only the 'T' class, but the whole fourteen footer presence in Auckland.

In Wellington, Harry Highet, a hydraulics engineer, designed a similar series of four outstanding fourteens: *Putorino*, *Indolence*, *Impudence* and *Innocence*. *Putorino* was not an extreme design, but in each of the following boats the bow was made sharper at the waterline and broader at the gunwale until the extreme 'aircraft carrier' shape of *Innocence* was reached. These boats could handle Wellington's worst winds and waves and still plane very fast when reaching or broad reaching. Harry's nephew Clive Highet sailed all four, and advised me that while *Innocence* was the fastest all-conditions boat, *Impudence* possessed the highest top speed in appropriate conditions.

These two streams of fourteen foot designs, both originating in the 1920s, were probably the world's state-of-the-art 'seagoing planing dinghies' of their era, and worthy successors to Logan's Patikis and Duggan's and Hope's flat-water planers of 20 to 30 years earlier.

---

[5] I built one of these as a youth in 1936, and enjoyed strong class racing on the river in Wanganui, which was another strong-wind area. I sailed periodic major regattas in and near Wellington (see Fig 1.28). When war broke out in 1939, I was New Zealand Junior I-Class Champion.

Fig 1.29 Billy Rogers's *Vamp*
(left)

Courtesy of Robin Elliott

Fig 1.30 Clive Highet's
Impudence (below)

Courtesy of Robin Elliott.

In 1938, *Vamp* from Auckland (Fig 1.29) and *Impudence* from Wellington (Fig 1.30) both entered the (Australian) Royal Hobart Regatta in Hobart, Tasmania.

Courses were laid in the wide estuary of the Derwent river, adjacent to Storm Bay. Unlike the narrow waters of Sydney Harbour where the No 1 course offered little reaching, these were normal triangular courses laid in wide waters with normal long broad-reaching legs. In Hobart's prevailing stronger winds the wide waters are rough, but the Wellington-bred New Zealand planing boats now thrived in big waves.

The performance advantage of the two light New Zealand seagoing planers over the non-planing heavy big-crew Australian fourteens was overwhelming. *Vamp*, sailed by Billy Rogers, won the 14ft Dinghy Championship of Australia, with *Impudence* – sailed by Clive Highet, Harry's nephew – coming second. *Impudence* won all three 14 footer races of the following Hobart Regatta.[6]

---

[6] Clive and I both became New Zealand Air Force pilots and friends. Clive was shot down over St Georges Channel in the Solomon Islands, late in 1943.

It was probably this seminal encounter in Hobart in 1938 that was primarily responsible for starting the shift in Australian thinking away from the heavy, big-crew, big-sailed skiffs. However, many other factors intervened. The 1939–45 war interrupted sailing for about a decade, and then there was a fierce split (the first of a number) in the previously monolithic Eighteen footer class. But the end result was that Australians at last changed their thinking. No more of the big-sail big-crew displacement skiffs were built, and Australia at last began to build and improve the design of lighter, faster, seagoing planing boats. As of 2007, these experiments and development show no sign of stopping.

Over the past few years, six 'vintage replicas' of the pre-war (1930s) 'Eighteen footer rag-carriers' have been built in Sydney. These sail regularly and gracefully.

1.13 ■ The English scene

The work of Uffa Fox, a famous English designer and dinghy builder in the 1930s, is well known. With respect to high performance, he did four things:
1 Altered the shape of the existing International Fourteen so it could plane.
2 Like the Logans, he developed a lighter hull construction technique.
3 Coined the word 'planing'.
4 Wrote, enthusiastically and well, about the planing dinghy.

These developments, taken together, caused English sailors also to change their minds and adopt the planing sailboat. In turn this resulted in the great growth in dinghy sailing led by England; this became worldwide in the 1950s, following the interruption of the 1939–45 war.

Shape

Fox's pattern of development of the International Fourteen was the reverse of that elsewhere. The Logans, Duggan and Linton Hope all started in the 1890s by developing craft that would plane in flat water. Logan then went further, and from this base developed the seagoing planer: the 'M' class. Fox started 30 years later with the International Fourteen class of open dinghy which had high sides and could already handle waves. He flattened the shape of the aft bottom so that this boat too could skim over the water and plane.

Construction

Like the Logans, Fox pushed the craft of building through-fastened timber boats to new levels of lightness. His approach was to use even thinner skins and to reduce the mass of the supporting structure by using a large number of close-spaced frames of extremely small sections plus myriad fastenings. This was labour-intensive in the extreme and his boats were priced accordingly – consequently, there were only a few of them. But they were light, and they did plane.

Planing

Many sailors worldwide believe that planing started in the UK in the 1930s and central to its development was the work of Uffa Fox. To an extent this is true because nothing prior to the 1930s seems to have been described as 'planing' whether it planed or not. It seems that Uffa coined the term 'planing'.

Uffa Fox's writing

Uffa wrote widely, enthusiastically and well, and was the messenger who brought to most of the world the news that sailboats could achieve, and sailors could enjoy, the higher speeds of planing. For the vast majority of sailors who knew nothing of the earlier work of the Logans in New Zealand, Duggan in Canada, Hope in the Upper Thames, and the South African Interport regatta planers, this was very exciting news indeed.

All the pictures and quotes in this chapter have come from newspapers local to each area, magazines from each area or nation, or books. The newspapers have reported the affairs of the sandbagger, scow or Patiki, and their triumphs and disasters, accurately and in detail. But precisely because they were local publications, nobody else in the world ever learned what was going on. What was so different about Uffa Fox was that the magazines he contributed to, and the books he wrote, were directed at a global market. Because most of the world learned about planing from Uffa, the legend grew that it was Uffa who invented the planing sailboat.

As we can now see, sailboats were in fact planing fast 30 years earlier so that is just another legend.

The planing sailboat developed between 1895 and 1905 at first performed well only in flat-water conditions, but by the early 1920s strong, light, fast seagoing planing sailboats were racing in numbers in New Zealand. By the 1930s, these had spread to England and Australia. By the 1940s, the whole world had accepted that the secret of higher speed was no longer bigger sails and moving ballast, and that lighter, flatter planing craft were now the fastest in all winds and in all sea-state conditions. No more heavy big-sail unballasted boats were built anywhere.

The best of the 'new' post-1939–45 war conventional dinghies, such as the Flying Dutchman and the 5o5 classes, were light planers, and they were very good indeed. On the water they proved to be about as fast as the 'new' lighter skiffs. It had needed the 50 years from 1900 to 1950 for this change to the planing sailboat to be adopted worldwide.

1.14 ■ The first half of the apparent wind revolution – 1970 to 1990

From 1950 until 1970 nothing very much happened worldwide. Boats such as the Flying Dutchmans and 5o5s, which could sometimes beat the bigger-sail Eighteen footer skiffs in 1960, could still sometimes beat them in 1970. But by 1980 it was silly even to try. The apparent wind downwind tacker was being developed, and the performance jump was enormous. The real question is, 'Why had it taken so long?'

There is nothing new about tacking downwind to win. In the 1880s and 1890s iceboats were tacking downwind hard and fast – they could sail downwind in no other way. As an example of how hard they sailed, the iceboat speed record in 1899 or 1900 was about 100mph, and this in a wind of 20–25mph.

Lake scows and iceboats are sailed in the same part of the world, so the scows had the iceboat example in front of them. Buddy Melges mentions that his father told him that some lake scow crews could win by tacking downwind in some boats in some winds, and this was before 1900.[7]

But the technique did not develop, despite this promising start. It lay dormant for 60 or 70 years, emerged tentatively for a while, then suddenly there was a great explosion of innovation in Sydney over about 15 years which rivalled that of Duggan in Montreal and Logan in Auckland nearly 100 years earlier. The end result was the same – a new and much faster breed of sailboat emerged.

An example of the tentative approach would be the Tornado catamaran. Designed in the late 1960s, it was initially sold with a whisker pole to goosewing the jib when running square. Before long it was found that a Tornado that tacked downwind with the apparent wind kept exactly on the beam usually arrived at the downwind mark a little before those that ran square. But an Eighteen footer that ran square with a big spinnaker would easily beat both of them. Some other light dinghies were similar, but most races were still won by crews who ran square.

Then a unique situation developed in Sydney where five separate factors were thrown together quite quickly one after another, and all in the same place. The Eighteen foot skiff class responded with its usual cut and try development in a changing situation, plus a measure of luck, and it was the interplay between these five factors that finally triggered a revolution in technology.

The way in which the narrower channel and bays of Sydney Harbour – as opposed to the wider waters of Auckland and Hobart – favoured the skiff over the Patiki in the early 1900s has been touched on in Section 1.10. Some 80 years later, different aspects of the same 'narrower waters' environment were again seminal in favouring one particular development thrust which then proved superior in all waters. This is so important that I make no apology for repeating here some elements of Section 1.10.

The first factor was the shape of Sydney Harbour. Fig 1.22 shows how the eastern part of the harbour is primarily a straight NNE–SSW valley aligned from the low sand spit of Manly (1) to and beyond Clark Island (2), and bounded by elevated plateaus 3, 4, 5 and 6 to the SE, and 7, 8 and 9 to the NW. Along this valley the prevailing summer sea breeze funnels at a mean 12 knots, sometimes up to 20 knots, always from the same direction. In this wind, Clark Island as the start, finish and leeward mark, the Sow and Pigs Reef (10) as the windward mark, and Shark Island (11) as a wing mark form a natural course.

---

[7] With the discovery of the critical ratios in about 2000 (see Chapter 20), we can now understand how and why some of these scows could win by tacking downwind in some winds and not in others. They were early 'marginals'.

Fig 1.31 Eighteens with parachute spinnakers

Courtesy of David Porter (helm in nearer boat).

The Sydney Flying Squadron's most-used No 1 course was three laps from Clark Island to the Sow and Pigs Reef and back, with a dig around Shark Island on the first and third laps to make it interesting. Fastest entry into, and exit from, Rose Bay calls for avoiding the light-wind areas that form behind Steele Point (13) and Shark Island. So the downwind legs with the dig around Shark Island called first for a square run, then a broad reach, then another broad reach, then a second short near-square run.

The second factor was that all the top Eighteens were equipped with not only three separate rigs for use in light, medium and strong winds; they also sailed with two spinnakers on board with each rig. One was a maximum-area parachute spinnaker (Fig 1.31). These were fast for runs that were square or near square, but were so big that they could not be held upright on even the broadest reach in any breeze. The other was a much smaller 'flattie' spinnaker that was set on those reaches that were too tight for the parachute (Fig 1.32).

So we start the 1970s with the established winning formula: 'On the downwind legs which include rounding Shark Island, set the parachute for the square-run from the reef to Steele Point. If the wind is fresh, change to the flattie for the two reaches into and out of Rose Bay around Shark Island, then set the parachute again for the second short run from Point Piper to Clark Island.'

The third factor was the emergence of the faster three-hander in the early 1970s. Not only were the boats faster, but the smaller three-man crews could afford only one man to make the spinnaker change so this sail-change took much longer. As between boats that changed spinnakers and those that did not, those that changed spent a much longer period sailing bare headed and slowly during the longer sail changes, and during this sail-change period they lost places to those boats that still had any spinnaker set – even if it was not the big parachute. So the winning formula changed to 'Do not change spinnakers on any downwind leg. Use the big parachute only on those near-square legs where you can carry it all the way. Set only a flattie and carry it all the way on any leg with a segment too tight for the parachute.'

Note that the fastest way to a leeward mark was still straight downwind with a big parachute spinnaker. Use of the flattie, which was slower on the run but faster on the broad reaches on the composite run-reach-

Fig 1.32 Eighteen foot skiff with 'flattie' spinnaker

Courtesy of Iain Murray (helm).

reach-run legs was for tactical, not dynamic, advantage. These were years of great uncertainty as crews made the right or the wrong choice of spinnaker in marginal conditions. The spectators and the punters loved it. The crews were blissfully unaware that they were laying the foundations of wet-water apparent wind sailing.

The fourth factor was the development of wings. These became progressively bigger until ultimately they reached the size shown in Fig 1.33. These hugely increased the sail-carrying power with almost no increase in weight. As they grew in size the winged Eighteens were able to carry progressively bigger sails and sail faster to windward and much faster on reaches and broad reaches with a flattie set. *But the wings made absolutely no difference to the speed on square runs.* At about the mid-stage of this process the magic point was reached where it became obvious that some winged boats in some winds were able to tack downwind with a flattie faster than any rival boat could run square with even the biggest parachute.

So it was wings that finally tipped the scales in favour of the downwind tackers. Nobody at this stage appreciated the full potential of this new development.

Any downwind speed advantage was still small. All thinking was tactical and biased towards the square run. Crews were uncertain and constantly experimenting to establish whether it was faster to broad reach 'deep' with the flattie set near square and dragging like a small parachute, or whether it was faster to sail higher and faster with the spinnaker pole near the forestay and the spinnaker lifting like a wing in the cross flow. There was expectation that further development of even bigger, squarer-shoulder parachutes might see square running become the faster option again.

After a year or two of this, the winning wisdom changed to 'Never run square. Never use a parachute spinnaker. Always tack downwind with a flattie.'

We can still place the time and the place and the quote that lead to the fifth factor. Late one afternoon in the Double Bay League bar after a race, it was Andrew Buckland (who sailed as sheet hand with Iain Murray on *Colour 7*) who commented 'They're never really fast until the pole is on the forestay.'

Fig 1.33 Eighteen footer with wings

Courtesy of Peter Sorensen (almost invisible in wing netting).

Over the winter, Julian Bethwaite's lateral-thinking response to this comment was to reverse his fundamental thinking about spinnakers. He threw away the gybing spinnaker pole, and substituted a fixed bowsprit to do the same job.

Much more importantly, he grasped the essential difference between blowing downwind running square and efficient tacking downwind. When running square with the apparent wind from behind, it is the spinnaker with the greatest possible drag (downwind force) that will be the fastest. But when tacking downwind with the apparent wind from on or forward of the beam, it will be the spinnaker with the greatest lift (crosswind force) and least drag (downwind force) that will be the fastest. Further, the faster the boat sails, the greater will be the change in the apparent wind direction, and the deeper the boat will sail (see Figs 26.8 and 26.9).

So Julian dreamed up a new sail, and worked with his sailmaker, Ian MacDiarmid, to develop a spinnaker with a luff deep enough for maximum power, and a clean flat leech which would develop the least drag in an apparent wind, which in future would always be from ahead. He reasoned that such a sail would be faster because it would be free of the drag of the hooked leech of every symmetrical spinnaker, no matter how flat.

And so it has proved. He had invented the low-drag full-luff flat-leech asymmetric spinnaker. With it, the braking effect of the earlier symmetrical high-drag hooked-leech sails was removed and the new apparent wind skiffs enjoyed a major reduction in drag (typically 40–50lb in an Eighteen in a breeze) and a corresponding significant increase in broad-reaching boat speed, and an even bigger jump in downwind VMG because the higher speed swung the apparent wind further forward and the boat sailed deeper as well as faster. Fig 1.34 shows *Prime II* of 1982, the second of Julian's two-hander Eighteens. This was the world's first fully developed wet-water, apparent wind sailboat.

Fig 1.34 Julian Bethwaite's *Prime II*, 1982

This was the true start of apparent wind sailing – the world's first asymmetric spinnaker (full luff and flat leech).

Over the following years this combination of light weight, great sail-carrying power and lowest-aero-dynamic-drag downwind sails (as opposed to conventional spinnakers which aim for highest-aerodynamic-drag) has been progressively refined. It has finally enabled sailboats to tack downwind at deep angles at VMG speeds substantially faster than the wind, speeds previously unimaginable except in iceboats.

When I wrote *HPS-1* in the 1980s, all of this ferment was taking place around me. However, I was too close to the action and it was all changing too fast for me to appreciate the broader picture.

This chapter has set the scene for *HPS-2*. It has been a broad sweep across the history of high performance sailboats, and gives a perspective about where we have come from, what forces have driven what changes, the changes that have made differences, and why, and who have been the creative people.

Fig 1.35 summarises the effect of the various changes on the downwind performance of the fastest notional 20ft boat of its period. It really does put into perspective the magnitude of the recent (and continuing) change to apparent wind sailing.

We need to note too that so far we have seen only the start of the apparent wind revolution. As *HPS-2* goes to press, tiny foil Moths are already

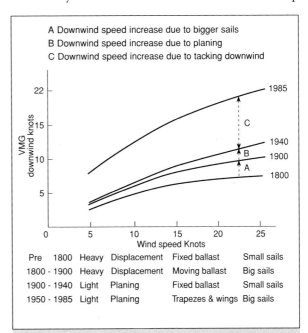

Fig 1.35 Increase of downwind VMG since 1800

matching the speeds of the bigger planing skiffs nearly twice their size. As soon as these more powerful boats develop appropriate foil technology, we can expect them to sail routinely at speeds somewhere between the present skiffs' speeds and the speeds of the iceboats.

In the chapters that follow I will try to explain the dynamics of this innovative and faster sailing, and how to handle these new boats in order to get the best out of them.

Author's note

Sources, referees and thanks

In writing this chapter, my principal sources have been:

1981	*Blue Water Bushmen*	Bruce Stannard (Sydney)
1988	*The Royal St Lawrence Yacht Club 1888–1988*	RStLYC (Montreal)
1989	*Traditions and Memories of American Yachting*	W P Stephens
1991	*Sydney's Flying Sailors*	Margaret Molloy (Sydney)
1994	*Emmy*	Robin W Elliott (Auckland)
1997	*Inland Lakes Yachting Association* (history)	Thomas A Hodgson (Wis)
1999	*Southern Breeze*	Kidd, Elliott and Pardon (NZ)
1999	*Fast Light Boats*	Grahame Anderson (NZ)
2001	*The Logans*	Robin Elliott and Harold Kidd (NZ)

Ian Bruce, of Laser fame, unearthed Figs 1.17 to 1.21 from the McGill University archives.

I wish to acknowledge and thank Robin Elliott for his co-operation in writing this chapter. Robin and his co-researcher Harold Kidd have researched and collated every word written about sailing in New Zealand newspapers and periodicals from 1860 to 1970, plus much else that influenced New Zealand – such as the US magazines *Rudder* and *Field and Stream*. From this enormous and accurate database, Robin has provided much that appears above.

I have furnished the draft manuscript of this chapter to all interested parties with invitation to comment. My thanks to all who have responded.

Chapter 2 • The State of the Extreme Arts

2.1 ■ Scope

This is a book about achieving higher performance from practical boats. By 'practical', I have in mind the sort of boats that have been described in Chapter 1. These have in common that they all float on water, can be handled by a self-contained crew without outside assistance, and can be sailed upwind, crosswind and downwind and back to the ramp, dock or moorings in all but extreme wind and wave conditions. Because it is easier and less costly to experiment with a small boat than a large one, the seminal advances have always been developed first in small boats. Some 20 to 30 years later the bigger boats get the message and copy the smaller ones. The current revolution in ocean racing speeds is based on the higher sail-carrying power to total weight ratios and the apparent wind downwind dynamics first developed by the skiffs of Sydney 25 years ago.

At the other extreme lie a tiny group of record breakers who pursue extreme speed for its own sake. Their definition of 'practical' is 'it's practical if it can break the present record'. The value of their contribution is huge. A record today by a craft deemed impractical by today's standards has a way of becoming tomorrow's commonplace for everybody's greater enjoyment. We all owe to these researchers and pioneers past and present both our thanks and an enormous debt for their making possible the performances we now enjoy.

In this chapter I have invited the five key present pioneers to comment on their passion, and on behalf of all readers I thank them for their contributions.

As at mid-2007, the list of recent world speed sailing record holders is:

Russell Long	*Longshot*	Trifoiler	43.55 knots	July 1982 at Tarifa
Simon McKeon	*Yellow Pages Endeavour*		44.65	February 1993 at Sandy Point, Victoria
Simon McKeon	*Yellow Pages Endeavour*		46.52	October 1993 at Sandy Point, Victoria
Finian Maynard		Sailboard	46.82	November 2004 at Saintes Maries
Finian Maynard		Sailboard	48.70	April 2005 at Saintes Maries
Antoine Albeau		Sailboard	49.09	2008 at Saintes Maries

Iceboat speed records seem not to be recognised.

2.2 ■ Fastest sailcraft: Iceboats   BY BUDDY MELGES

Author's note

Harry C (Buddy) Melges won Gold in FDs in 1964 and bronze in Solings in 1972. His name is synonymous with lake scows and iceboats. We all have to thank the iceboats for pioneering the dynamics of apparent wind sailing more than 100 years ago.

Most readers of *HPS-2* will be able to empathise with the wet-water exploits of Finian Maynard, Lindsay Cunningham, Ian Ward and George Chapman, so in their cases I have focused on the circumstances of the record sails.

Iceboats are different in that so little appears in the media about them that I have asked Buddy Melges to describe what iceboating *is* rather than to describe any one sail.

Iceboating is weather dependent to an extreme degree. The annual winter freeze turns lakes into ice strong enough to play on. For as long as good ice of adequate area offers itself, iceboating can be enjoyed, but only until the winter's first snow event turns the smooth ice into a snowfield. If the snow follows quickly after the freeze, there is no iceboating that year. For as long as they have good ice, iceboaters gather to enjoy their racing where and while they still can.

If you set an iceboat crosswind, get in and sheet on in a 10 knot wind, nothing will happen – partly because the runners are stuck to the ice, partly because there is not enough force from the tiny sail in a 10 knot apparent wind to get you moving. But if you push-run it up to 10 knots or more, jump in and pump hard, the stronger apparent wind and the free running runners enable you to accelerate. As apparent wind speed rises to 40 and 50 knots upwind and stronger downwind, the iceboat develops wings. On good ice and in a 10–12 knot wind Skeetas such as *Honey Bucket* can achieve about 30 to 40 knots upwind and 69 knots (measured 77mph by GPS) downwind. In stronger winds, maximum speed is limited by the roughness of the ice.

At the beginning of a race the iceboats are static with half facing each way. At the start signal each sailor push-runs his boat up to sailing speed and leaps in. Because of the speed of their craft, and the extreme wind chill factor, they typically sail multiple short races, each of which lasts no more than a few minutes.

Iceboating is an amazing case of performance advances! We still have stern-steering iceboats that are great big lumbering behemoths, but the real development came in the front-steering boats known as 'Skeetas'. The Skeeta is controlled by 75sq ft of sail area, 12in of roach and the pinhole in the headboard is 2½in aft of the bolt rope and 1in down from the top of the headboard. There are no restrictions on hull, runner plank, mast or boom and runners.

The first Skeeta was 16ft long, 12ft (transverse) runner plank, 16ft mast, 36in runners. My boat today (Fig 2.1) is 30ft long, 22ft runner plank, 28ft mast, 56in runners, with the same measured sail area as the 1930 Skeeta designed by Harry Melges Senior. The arms race in this class has affected its growth, with peaks and valleys over the years. The

Fig 2.1 *Honey Bucket,* **Buddy Melges' Skeeta**

Courtesy of Harry C (Buddy) Melges.

boats are now large enough to have outgrown and outspeeded many of our midwest lakes. I figure that we go upwind three to four times faster than the wind. As proven last year on near-perfect ice conditions using a GPS, the winner in 10–12 knots of wind had a maximum speed (downwind) of 77 miles per hour sailing a windward leeward course. It is conceivable that he could have gone faster by sailing a reaching course.

The things that soft water sailors do for speed, iceboaters do as well. Sail shaping is very important, but fitting the sail to the 13in wing mast is the most important starting point for winning iceboat races. The runner plank serves two purposes: as a shock absorber and platform stabiliser. The flexing of the sitka spruce plank is also very important to the ultimate boat speed.

The move towards a high aspect sail plan has dictated the size to be nearly two times larger than the first three years of the Skeeta iceboat. With all the new steels there are many options for runners; 440C stainless is very popular, and even titanium is used along with 62/50 steel. Iceboating is for the engineer. Because boat speed differential is so great between boats and because of the fact that one can sail a diamond course, accomplished soft water sailors do not always win! In fact, we have iceboat champions that have never sailed on soft water.

With carbon and Kevlar, the boats are lighter and therefore faster. Since 1990 the boats grew from 24ft 6in spars to 28ft 6in. Runner planks have gone from 18ft to 22ft, and overall hull length has grown by 4ft. The speed increase has been phenomenal; the new boats are a leg faster than the 1980s. There seems to be no ceiling in sight – the sky's the limit.

The solid wing masts that are showing up are not allowed to race with the Skeetas because of the soft cloth rule. It's pretty interesting to watch a wing mast back into the starting blocks. Iceboat racing starts from a standing start with half the fleet on port tack and half the fleet on starboard. A gun sounds, the flag drops, and you push-run to start your boat. This is a very important part of the race, and being fast off the line will have a big impact on your race results.

An iceboat well sailed in 10mph of wind will tack around 80° and sail downwind at 150° true wind angle. Interestingly enough, on the downwind leg of the course the windward boat has the right of way. This is for safety – to avoid capsizes that could be fatal.

Buddy Melges

2.3 ■ Fastest waterborne: Sailboard BY FINIAN MAYNARD

Author's note

Before a sailboard rider can break a world record, he or she needs:

- A very strong wind.
- A straight run of about 600m aligned at the optimum angle to the wind.
- No significant waves.
- Appropriate timing apparatus and staff to time a run of 500m.
- ISAF stewards to certify.

Because strong winds necessarily make big waves on open water, no open water venue can now be suitable for sailing at the speeds now required to break records.

As Project Founder, Finian Maynard invited a group of board riders interested in breaking world speed records to organise themselves into a Masters of Speed group; and they have built, near Saintes Maries, on a flat beach that is a part of the Rhône delta, a system of twin parallel retaining dykes 15m apart and about 1m high which enclose two straight canals or trenches, each about 550m long and 15m wide which meet at their mid point. High-volume pumps fill the trench to adequate depth when strong winds are forecast.

Finian describes in his contribution below the orientation of the canals to the directions of the prevailing strong winds. The organisational method developed is:

- A period during which favourable winds are likely is declared a record attempt period, during which all parties hold themselves ready to act at short notice.
- When during a declared period a suitable strong-wind forecast offers:
  - The trench manager floods the trench to adequate depth.
  - The timing group install their apparatus for the direction anticipated.
  - ISAF steward(s) attend to certify.
  - The interested sailboard riders sail as opportunity offers and as they see fit.

To date:

In November 2004 Finian Maynard claimed the world speed record with a sail at 46.82 knots. This beat *Yellow Pages Endeavour*'s 26 October 1993 world speed record of 46.52 knots. Fig 2.2 shows Finian sailing in the trench during this run.

In April 2005 Finian sailed faster yet to set a new world speed record of 48.70 knots.

As at May 2006, no less than seven world speed records have been set at 'the trench'.

Finian Maynard.

Equipment and 'feel' analysis

Holding onto a boom at 90km/h, and skipping along the water with such intensity that it is tough to even look at where one is going from the forces on the body, is quite something. It is a pleasure to have the opportunity to write this small piece, and I hope that my insight brings to life the essence of speed-sailing on a windsurfer.

The equipment in my sport has literally gone through a revolution since 1993 when symmetrical twist was introduced into the sails, the fins started to be both computer designed and computer-control milled to accurate shape, and the boards began to be built in lightweight and stiff carbon composite constructions. The torrid pace of development from a very competitive world cup racing circuit over the past decade has yielded the stable platform, and very fast speed capabilities of the modern set-ups. I liken this to the 'arms race' that fuels the rapid development to F1 car racing.

Currently I have eight world record boards, ranging in size from 33cm to 37.5cm wide and they are all in the range of 216–218cm long. All of my boards are made from a styrofoam core with a carbon/PVC sheet foam full-sandwich and all weigh under 4kg. I have several different rocker planforms and shape configurations to handle the different conditions that one can experience at the Canal with the fluctuations in wind direction and sea state. The 35cm board, with the lower rocker and straighter outline between the footstraps to handle the excessive power of the turbulent and aggressive Mistral wind, is the current record board.

My rigs for the past two records were only three sizes: being 5, 5.3 and 5.5sq m. After experiencing gut-piercing winds of 60–65 knots for two-hour periods in November 2004 and not being able to capitalise on the moment, I will be bringing a further three sails with the sizings of 4.2, 4.6 and 4.8 to further world record attempts. I have had a variety of sail foil/twist/luff curve sections in the past few years and the most effective combination so far has been a relatively fine entry with a locked draught at 30% and a flat exit on the foil for a quick release with a tight spot built into the luff curve to create a breaking point at the desired location of maximum rig deflection. The position of this critical point determines how the sail will digest the powerful gusts that are sometimes invisible when one is only 1m away from the bank.

The pre-preg carbon masts introduced to our industry in 2001 have brought into being a period when sail designers are able to create more skin tension through downhaul tension from the head to the tack. This, combined with refined and research and development – proven fast-shaping techniques with tensioned wide and stable luff sleeves has seen a new age – and the direction that windsurfing rigs will be able to go in the future.

Windsurfers generally use the dynamic flex of the rig and fin to absorb the relentless energy surges of world record calibre runs. I have passed 45 knots on 17 runs in the past 30 months, and every one of them felt quite close to the edge, but still manageable.

The fins are of a curved leading edge outline and 30% foil that has been well tested over a long period of time. They delay the onset of spinout longer than foil-borne boats or the fins of MI (Macquarie Innovations) because they simply are smaller, thinner and don't have as much lateral torque as the larger engined machines. The capability of the rider himself to make the subtle changes on the run directly into the rig and board right at the exact moment that the adjustment needs to be made creates an advantage, compared to more sophisticated but ultimately less sensitive ways of steering (the bigger machines). This quick reflex action enables the windsurfer to maintain control and post fast run after fast run.

In summary, the physical exhaustion that accompanies a hard and intense day is usually worth it because there is nothing quite like the feeling of looking down the run as the Canal lights up with a strong wind cycle coming through. The surge of speed once the little board gets up and going is phenomenal. We go from 0 to 44 knots in about 6 seconds and the boomerang sensation once the bow of the board is forced downwind onto the run is similar to being shot out of a cannon. Once powered, it is then time to line up the yellow start and finish markers and stay within 2m of the jagged edge while anticipating the onslaught of the gusts that could be coming just a little farther down the run. On the fast runs it is hard to see where I am going as my face wants to be pulled back perpendicular to the body. Trying to keep it all together is quite something – but the reward at the end is sweet and worth the risk.

The Canal

The 'French Trench' is possibly the most famous speed-sailing location in the world, with a total of seven out-right world records being set in the famous Rhône delta region of France.

The entire length of the run spans 1100m by a width of 15m and there are five different 500m courses accommodating the four wind directions of N, WNW, SE and SW, with the most common being N (Mistral) and SE (Le Marin). It has been noted from the past two winters that there is rarely a pattern with the weather systems, as world record wind can come at any time from September to May. Our favoured direction is definitely the Marin onshore wind, as it is warmer and more consistent in its behaviour. The wind itself is more laminar and the Canal stays very smooth as the wind is coming 'up' to the bank almost directly from the beach. The turbulent Mistral tends to come 'down' and hit the water from the upwind wall that sits behind the road, resulting in a much choppier sea state.

The biggest fallacy concerning the Canal is that it is artificial and therefore rock steady. The reality is that the location is very fragile when dealing with the onshore wind as we have had several banks break with the consequent flooding of the entire area – especially in the winter of 2003–4 when we experienced ten *vent est* storms of varying strength. The Canal needs constant attention to make sure that we have the perfect run at the perfect time to break records.

During the winter of 2004–5 we decided to push the envelope and raise the water levels 50cm in order to get the edge of the banks and the water levels at a more even height to reduce the turbulence created from

Fig 2.2 Sailboard in canal

Finian Maynard sailing in the trench for the world speed record. Courtesy of Finian Maynard.

the bank. The results were very good. The downwind bank tends to get 'eaten' away with winds over 40 knots, so we are constantly rebuilding the banks even after one or two windy days.

I find that the only possible way to achieve very high speeds is to be in a 'controlled' setting where you try to eliminate harrowing factors that will upset the nature and consequent stability of the run. It would be safe to say that even 20cm chop takes 1–2 knots off a run with the very narrow and sensitive boards and fins that we are currently using, so the relationship between the angle and consistency of the wind versus the exact timing of the run is critical. In short, it is difficult to read the wind cycles and it takes time to understand the behaviour of the two different winds in order to maximise the conditions that you are given.

Of course there are limitations with the run as it stands. We are forced to let the right wind angle come to us rather than us going to it. In a perfect world we would like to have several canals with slightly varying banks so as to maximise the strong wind more effectively. Reducing the variables is the big key to success in this game because it is hard to get all the 'ducks' to line up at once, so all sailors who chase the world speed record know that patience and perseverance are foremost if they expect to succeed. That is what makes success all that much sweeter.

Finian Maynard

2.4 ■ Recent fastest waterborne: Triscaphe   BY LINDSAY CUNNINGHAM

Author's note

Lindsay Cunningham has spent a lifetime designing and building very fast sailboats. He developed C class catamarans to the point where he dominated the Little America's Cup for several decades. More recently, he has extended his technical genius to achieve really high straight line speeds on wet water.

Background

In February 1993 *Yellow Pages Endeavour* (Fig 2.3) sailed at 44.65 knots, and on 26 October 1993 this craft became the world's fastest sailboat on water, achieving a speed of 46.52 knots in less than 20 knots of wind. The boat was crewed by Simon McKeon as helmsman with Tim Daddo on the mainsheet. The record was set at Sandy Point on Shallow Inlet about 40km northwest of Wilson's promontory in southeastern Victoria, Australia. The previous record of 45.34 knots was held by French sailboarder Thiery Bielak, who set the record in winds around 40 knots in a man-made channel in Saintes Maries in France.

Not only did *Yellow Pages Endeavour* establish both outright and 'C' class (235 to 300sq ft) world records, it also set new world records in 'B' class (150 to 235sq ft) of 44.65 knots, and 'D' class (over 300sq ft) of 41.66 knots – and also a woman's 'C' class world record.

The records were set over a 500m course, and the video cameras at each end of the course, used to record the start and finish times, also allowed the start and finish speeds to be estimated, with speeds of over 50 knots being recorded at the start and finish of some runs.

The syndicate behind these records already held the International Catamaran Challenge Trophy (then known as the Little America's Cup), and as no challenges were forthcoming for that trophy, the syndicate decided to move into the outright speed sailing arena.

There appeared to be room for improvement over the performance of the main contenders for the world record – the sailboards and trifoilers (which are craft that use hydrofoils to lift them clear of the surface and so reduce drag).

The sailboards carry a large penalty in the inherent air drag of the sailor, and so quite high wind speeds are needed to achieve the speeds they do reach. It is only the very precise levels of control that the sailor can bring to bear that enable such high speeds to be achieved. The trifoiler also hits a controllability limit, but at lower wind speeds than the sailboards. They have reached 43 knots in around 30 knots of wind speed.

Our target was to create a much more efficient craft that would need significantly lower wind speeds to break the records. Our initial estimates showed that a ratio of boat speed to wind speed of around 2.4 should be achievable, so long as we could get it planing. Hence a record would be possible in only 20 knot winds.

We were able to draw on our experience in 'C' class catamaran design where the craft operates primarily in an apparent wind regime, and where wing sails and all the latest lightweight construction techniques are used.

The first step was to examine the requirements for acceptance of a record claim, and then to look at the options available for each major element of the craft. The way in which each of the prime requirements were met in ice yachts, hydrofoils, sailboards and displacement craft were carefully analysed.

Location

Maximum speeds will be achievable in a location with as smooth a water surface as possible and very steady winds. The design of the craft has to be matched to the conditions available. We were very fortunate in having access to Shallow Inlet and Sandy Point, Victoria, where a curved low sandbank 1.5km long and about 1km wide separates the inlet from the open ocean.

The 500m course can be set at the appropriate point around the curve to get the true wind angle for maximum speed, with a range of nearly 50° of wind direction available. Even in conditions that appear very stable there is still significant turbulence in the air flow. Measurements of the variation of wind speed with height made to determine the amount of twist to build into the rig showed that the velocity at 4ft sometimes exceeded that at 35ft.

Sail

Carbon fibre sandwich and heat shrink surface materials make it possible to produce very light and strong aerofoils with the appropriate amount of twist off under load. As the craft is only required to travel in one direction, the foil is asymmetric. A record attempt is only started when the wind speed is in the range of 16–20 knots. As it takes only 20 seconds to travel the 500m, at a location where the wind is relatively steady, the range of automatic adjustment to rig geometry is relatively small. To minimise end losses, the foil is extended down as close to the water surface as possible, and is made in sections to allow the section below the beams to be let out fully when required.

Hulls

While theoretically a hydrofoil can give a much greater lift to drag ratio than a planing surface, it is seen that in practice planing hulls in power craft can reach much higher speeds than hydrofoil systems.

Hydrofoils hit a controllability limit first and then run into cavitation problems at around 50–55 knots. The difficulties in developing a low drag reliable control system that has to operate in the air-water interface have, to date, limited sailing hydrofoil speeds to the low 40 knots. The trifoiler *Longshot* currently holds the 'A' class hydrofoil record at 43.55 knots. Computer-controlled systems should have the potential to improve this figure, but it is not a trivial task, and malfunctions can be disastrous.

Foils

Efficient foils to resist the high side forces generated by the large righting moments are critical, and must be of sufficient area to allow the craft to reach planing speed. Hence at top speed, where the higher speed means that significantly smaller foil areas are adequate, the foil performance will be sub-optimal. It is believed that the complication of reducing foil area once planing is not justified. At speeds up to 45 knots, cavitation (where the water actually vaporises at points of low pressure on the foil) is not a problem.

However, even though the foils are located directly under the planing surfaces, air can still get to the top of the foils as the craft is sailing along the top of wavelets up to 50mm high. Hence fences have been fitted to the foils about 75mm from the top to prevent ventilation where air actually moves down the low pressure side of the foil and destroys the foil's grip on the water.

Three foils were placed across the stern of each hull in order to allow a more shallow draught, because of the shallow water at the southern end of the course, and also to reduce the twisting moments the foils apply to the structure.

Configuration

A crew of two was preferred, so that full attention could be given to the major controls – ie the steering to keep the boat off the sandbank, and the wing control to extract the maximum possible drive from the wing. The craft was then configured to the maximum size given the limitations of cost, size and

Fig 2.3 *Yellow Pages Endeavour* sailing at speed

Courtesy of Speedsail.

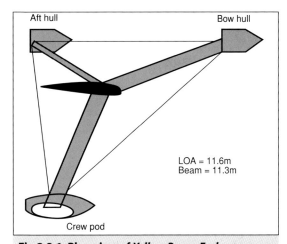

LOA = 11.6m
Beam = 11.3m

Fig 2.3.1 Plan view of *Yellow Pages Endeavour*

handling. The layout was decided primarily by the need to tie together the wing, the crew (in a streamlined capsule), the hulls and the foils, providing lateral resistance with a minimum weight low drag structure that had the stability required.

The layout is shown in Fig 2.3.1 – *Yellow Pages Endeavour*. There are two planing hulls in line to leeward, each 1.8m long and 1.3m beam about 10m apart to provide adequate fore-and-aft stability. The crew are housed in a planing hull or capsule positioned about 11m to windward to give the necessary righting moment. The hulls are joined together by streamlined carbon fibre/nomex beams joined at the mast step, with wire ties around the perimeter and solid carbon ties from each hull to the bottom of a strut extending down under the mast step. At speed the crew pod is lifted clear of the surface and held about 1m above the surface by adjustment of the mainsheet. The mast is positioned so that the forces on the wing are taken directly to the crew pod via the sidestay, and the line of action passes through a point midway between the two lee hulls so that the fore-and-aft foils share the side load equally. The foils on the front hull were used for steering as they were found to be more heavily loaded by the steering movements and, if they lost grip, the craft would turn away from the sandbank.

Performance predictions

The velocity made good (VMG) routines used for our 'C' class catamaran designs was adapted to fit the speed machine configuration. The lift and drag forces of all the elements of the craft were calculated as a function of the boat speed, apparent wind speed, weights, righting moments and incidence angles, using iterative loops in the VMG routines. The output produced gave the boat speeds achievable for each true wind angle.

The actual performance achieved in the world record runs was actually slightly better than calculated, but the closeness of the results to the predicted figures was gratifying. The measured boat speed was 46.52 knots when the wind speed at a point about 60m to windward of the course varied between 18 and 20 knots, a ratio of approximately 2.4:1. The total drag of the craft at 46.5 knots is estimated to be 1635 Newtons (370lb), representing a power output of 38kw or 50.4hp.

The concepts are relatively simple: minimise drag, configure the system so we get maximum forward force given the inherent stability and can get the thing started, and then hang on.

The execution, though, is not so easy. It took three years from concept to record, with four major repair jobs, as reality bit:

- The boat blew over on the beach and broke the wing when the wind shifted unexpectedly.
- The outboard motor on a tender malfunctioned, the wing swung around against a stay, and the boat capsized.
- Twice the craft slewed violently to leeward and was damaged when the bow hull bounced up and steerage was lost.

The systems were progressively refined until the record was broken in 1993.

A new boat, Extreme 50, was built in 1995 with a lower rig height that would give the optimal balance between greater forward force from the lower overturning moment and the greater induced drag from a lower aspect aerofoil.

The objective was to exceed 50 knots, but the required wind speeds from the right direction did not eventuate in the approved record attempt time period. Because cavitation effects begin to take effect at around 50 knots, design and testing of low cavitation foils was undertaken with Paul Brandner using the cavitation tunnel at Australian Maritime Engineering (now the Australian Maritime College), Launceston, Tasmania, prior to a further attempt to raise the record to above 50 knots.

By their nature, low cavitation foils have a centre of pressure in the trailing half of the foil because the leading half of the foil is symmetrical and points directly into the stream flow to minimise the low pressures that cause the fluid to vaporise or cavitate. All the lift or side force is generated by the shaping of the trailing sections.

Fig 2.4 *Macquarie Innovation*

Courtesy of Steb Fisher photography.

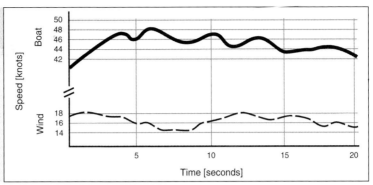

Fig 2.5 *Macquarie Innovation* achieved speed

20-second line trace showing boat speed and corresponding wind speed for *Macquarie Innovation* during a 500m record attempt run. Image courtesy of Speedsail.

These foils were manufactured and mounted on the boat, now named *Macquarie Innovation* (Fig 2.4) in honour of a new sponsor, and a further attempt to raise the record was made in 1998. The greater loads on the steering system resulting from the movement aft of the centre of pressure of the foils, together with excessive elasticity, and hence lag in the steering system, made the craft directionally unstable at speeds over 35 knots, and the attempt was aborted.

The steering system has now been modified with a worm/worm-wheel drive located right on the steering foils in the bow hull and carbon 'wires' used to reduce stretch under load.

Further attempts to raise the record are planned as opportunity offers.

Lindsay Cunningham

Author's note

Repeated attempts have been made in the years since, but the right combination of wind strength, direction, control and structural integrity has been elusive. Fig 2.5 is the speed trace of a run completed in early 2007, and leaves little doubt as to speed potential of this craft.

The Macquarie team's update reads: 'Fifty-six days on standby, 2 hours of available sailing conditions presented, best recorded run was 46.48 knots. Wind conditions from our 3 remote logging anemometers showed a max wind speed of 22 knots, a minimum wind speed of 9 knots and an average of 16.8 knots during the run. The max boat speed recorded was 49.55 knots' (Tim Daddo, Macquarie Speed Sailing Team).

2.5 ■ Fastest practical foilborne: The Flying Moths   BY DR IAN WARD

Author's note

In 1998 Dr Ian Ward of Sydney started experimenting with the bifoiler. This was a huge step towards efficiency, in that the bifoiler necessarily has only two-thirds of the foil form drag and skin friction drag of the trifoiler.

What Ian Ward did was reason that if he were prepared to develop the skill to balance and handle and sail a featherweight boat rather than just sit in it, he could potentially reduce foil drag by one-third, and this just might trigger foils into practicality.

He was right. It did, and he did it!

All subsequent bifoiler advances flow from Ian Ward's vision.

Introduction

To sail effortlessly just above the waves with exciting bursts of speed has long been an ideal for those who dream! The technical potential has always been there, but practical reality has been lacking. It seems to be such a simple concept to place a hydrofoil wing under the hull to lift it clear of the waves and go – and yet in practice it ends up being somehow far more complex than it seems.

The development of foiled sailing craft initially involved simple, passive surface piercing V-foils which were predominantly applied to highly stable, heavy multihull platforms. The more recent and most successful designs have instead used fully submerged lifting foils with active surface tracking and incidence control (see Fig 2.9).

By 2000, very little development of lifting foils had occurred in sailing dinghies, which is rather surprising since they have by far the most potential benefit from lifting the hull clear and skimming above the water. Initial attempts with dinghies generally involved trifoil arrangements of various configurations – with the most successful example being a flying International Moth, developed by Brett Burvill in Perth, Western Australia, in which he won two heats of the World Moth Championships in Perth in 2000. This design, however, was not without its problems – being difficult to sail downwind and rather impractical to rig and launch – but it exhibited impressive bursts of speed in flat water on reaches.

The International Moth is a development class, based on a singlehanded monohull dinghy with simple restrictions of length 3.35m, beam 2.24m and sail area 8.0sq m, but few limits on design, construction and weight. It is currently the only International dinghy class to allow lifting foils. This class provides an ideal forum for testing new developments against the fastest 'state-of-the-art' boats in all conditions around a race course. Therefore this was a very natural forum for foiling to develop.

Today, centreline foils on Moths look simple and very neat, but appear quite impossible to balance when sailing, which is perhaps why the concept was not considered previously. This method does, however, provide some unusual and significant advantages over previous arrangements. Unlike trifoilers, centreline foils or 'bifoilers' may be heeled well to windward, gaining significant righting moment from the weight of both skipper and the hull, as well as providing lateral resistance by aligning the lifting foil to the flow. There being only two deep foils and struts, the resistance is kept low and efficiency high. This arrangement is also very simple to rig and launch, unlike their more ungainly predecessors. It also requires some skill to balance these craft, thus retaining their dinghy-like handling characteristics. Hence the first 'dinghy foilers' were born.

Development history

The first successful attempt at sailing a dinghy foiler using the 'bifoiler' configuration was by Ian Ward in Sydney in 1999 in a Moth class dinghy. When Ward sailed a Hobie Trifoiler in 1996, the potential of a flying Moth became immediately obvious. He built a trifoiler Moth in 1997, but soon discovered limitations due to the high stability and difficulty in rigging and launching. He was further inspired by a 'unifoiler' sailboard developed by Rich Miller in California, which could achieve 30 knots on just a single foil, and reasoned that surely a Moth could do the same on two foils! He used a fully articulated lifting Tee foil on the centreboard with integral aft trailing wand and Tee foil rudder, which first sailed in 1999 and proved that the 'bifoiler' concept could work.

As early as 1987, Brett Burvill in Perth had dreamed of a foiling Moth and discussed this with John Ilett, but it was not until 1992, after seeing articles of Andy Paterson's attempts at a trifoiler Moth in the UK, that Burvill realised it was indeed possible. On his own initiative and with the help of Marc Pivac, he developed a trifoiler Moth in 1999 that had large wing-mounted surface piercing foils. He soon improved control with a larger fixed rudder Tee foil and used this configuration to win two heats of the World Moth Championships in Perth in 2000, proving for the first time that foiling Moths had huge potential.

Burvill then realised that adding a flap to the rudder would solve his control problems. He adapted a bicycle twist grip tiller extension to operate a flap on the rudder Tee foil, and this arrangement worked exceptionally well, even in low wind strengths, from its very first trial.

Frustrated at impending Moth class rule changes aimed at banning wing mounted foils, and being aware of Ward's bifoiler arrangement, Burvill decided to try dual fixed lifting foils, one attached to the bottom of the centreboard, and one to the bottom of the rudder. A control flap on the rudder foil was connected to the tiller extension for manual control of pitch attitude and height. While this arrangement only flew with heavy manual control, it showed excellent potential. The innovation with a bicycle twist grip control on the tiller to actuate the flap on the rudder foil made the entire craft controllable and was a significant breakthrough in the development of foiling Moths.

In 2001, Perth boatbuilder John Ilett also developed a foiling Moth utilising a surface-piercing foil mounted from the bow and a Tee foil rudder. While this design flew, it had many problems and proved to be too unreliable for practical sailing. Encouraged by the possibilities raised by Burvill's single centreline Tee foil (manually controlled via a rudder flap), he then developed a Tee foil Moth (ie a horizontal foil was attached to the bottom of the centreboard of his own boat) using the pre-preg moulded foils that he had already pioneered in

1999–2000. This foil section rapidly became the standard for the developments that followed, including one of the foils on Burvill's dual foil centreboard.

Ilett incorporated a trailing flap on his centreboard Tee foil; this was controlled by a bow-mounted trailing sensor wand. This system provided about an 80% automatic coarse-control of the boat and its foiling height. The remaining 20% fine-control was then achieved by a combination of the tiller extension twist-operated foil on the bottom of the rudder, together with positioning of body weight and adjustment of sail trim.

The development of the Ilett Tee foiler and its control systems took John Ilett several months and needed lots of assistance from his brother Garth, who was the 'test pilot'. The brothers worked through several modifications of the centreboard flap and fine-tuned the control systems. They also determined that it was necessary to move the rudder well aft on a gantry to provide the necessary longitudinal stability. While foiling on reaches then became rather easy, the boat had large deep foils that made it very difficult to hold upright when going upwind. The traditional Moth design did not have this problem as, unlike the foiler, the centreboard could be raised when sailing upwind. John therefore decided to make the foils much narrower, reducing the lateral area. This immediately resulted in the boats being easier to hold upright, making them capable of flying upwind as well as downwind – a significant breakthrough which then provided all-round performance. It was only then that Moths truly began to fly in all conditions and under control!

Ilett read widely about foil section shapes and has subsequently made contact with experts such as Tom Speer in the USA. He continues to gradually refine his foil shapes and size, as well as the control systems and location of the foils. However, the initial set-up has not changed significantly, and is a tribute to his foresight. Ilett's development can only be described as truly impressive and this breakthrough should be considered the first truly practical dinghy foiler or 'Flying Moth'. His unique robust construction technique in pre-preg carbon fibre, and production of a complete sailing craft as well as retrofit kits for existing boats, has singlehandedly made foiling available to many others in the Moth class throughout the world.

The development of the foiling Moth has not been without controversy both from individuals and associations. In 2002, the International Moth Class Association in Australia was concerned about the increased stability, legality and impact on the class of Burvill's original arrangement and decided to interpret the existing rules to outlaw the wing mounted foils, saying they constituted a multihull. This effectively banned Burvill's design. This ruling was not aimed at banning foilers altogether, but restricted their use to within the 'waterplane' of the hull. Since the breakthrough by Ilett, several local Australian designers such as Phil Stevenson, Chris Dey and Ian Ward in Sydney, as well as designers in the UK and Germany, have trialled many different foiling configurations. To date, though, none has been as successful as the now famous Ilett design.

Parallel development in 14s

Coincidentally, attempts were also being made to apply centreline lifting foils to International 14ft skiffs. David Lugg, also of Perth, followed his own path of development without knowledge of what was happening with Moths. In 1999, he responded to the challenge of the 14ft skiff authorities, who said foiling 14s 'could never work', and decided to trial centreline lifting foils which would at that time comply with the class rules. His first attempts simply lifted the boat uncontrollably out of the water.

Lugg continued his development with the assistance of Alan Smith in Adelaide, who proposed the use of a manually controlled flap on the rudder, via the tiller extension. In 2000, Lugg fitted a flap on the rudder controlled by twisting the tiller extension, and was able to satisfactorily 'fly' his 14. Lugg's foils were constructed by Bruce Proctor, and Brad Divine helped to develop the necessary sailing technique. Smith provided the dynamic stability analysis which determined the best foil size ratio to produce a stable, controllable 'man in the loop' bifoiler arrangement. This was the first ever two-man bifoiler, and the first to do this with crew on trapeze and with spinnaker.

Following Lugg's demonstration of speed and stability, the International Fourteen Association chose to ban 'flying'. While this arrangement provided the required level of control and showed significant promise, it has not had the same level of application to date as the Flying Moths with their 'automatic' wand control mechanism. Alan Smith suggested the reasons for this are that the wand system is easier to handle, has a lower work load, and permits a smaller rudder foil to be used. He also confidently predicts that it should be possible to significantly reduce the take-off speed, as well as to increase the top-end speed of the Flying Moths to around 35 knots!

The Ilett Flying Moth

The original arrangement developed by John Ilett utilises submerged Tee foils on both rudder and centreboard. Both foils have fixed Tee sections with a full-width 25% flap, and use a NACA 63412 section. The foils are 120mm x 800mm on the centreboard and 120mm x 530mm on the rudder. On the centreboard foil the flap is activated by an aft trailing sensor mounted on the bow. As the flap provides lift on the main foil, the angle of incidence of both foils increases and provides sufficient lift for take-off. The high-incidence angles enable take-off at quite low speeds of 7–8 knots and low wind strengths of around 6–7 knots. This is a significant advantage over previous sailing hydrofoil craft, which typically required 10–12 knots of wind for take-off. The flap on the rudder is used for manual trim, to promote extra incidence to get up early and to reduce height when going fast or downwind in waves (see Fig 2.7).

The International Moth hull and rig is already extremely well developed, being the fastest displacement sailing dinghy for its size. The existing features coincidentally provided an excellent platform on which to apply the foils. Their characteristics ideally suit dinghy foiling, as the hulls and rig are extremely light, with an all-up sailing weight of only 25kg. The fine easily driven hull has a very high speed in light winds, making it ideal for early take-off. The wings not only provide excellent righting moment, but the large dihedral angles used allow the boat to be heeled well to windward comfortably and without the skipper hitting the water – something not possible on many conventional dinghies. The fine, pintail stern also allows it to sink without excessive drag during take-off, and the deep, fine bow also allows recovery from major crashes as it spears into waves with little resistance and without submerging.

Performance

The performance of these small craft is nothing short of 'extremely impressive'. The Moth class began at Inverloch in Victoria, Australia, in 1930, and since then many significant developments have transformed the class – initially based on the original scow design with flexible rigs, pocket luff sails and walking stick masts in the 1960s. The ubiquitous 'wings' were also introduced in the late 1960s, and very narrow, minimum surface area, pintail hulls in the 1990s. Starting from a Portsmouth yardstick of around 130 in the early 1960s, these remarkable craft have continuously improved and now perform regularly to a yardstick of around 70, faster than almost all mono-hull dinghies and even most catamarans.

Nothing really prepares you for the incredible performance of the Flying Moths. Only the Olympic Tornado catamaran and 18ft skiffs are faster around a course today – an amazing feat for such a small dinghy! Even in the infamous Port Phillip Bay chop in Melbourne with big waves and strong winds, it is quite surreal to see the Flying Moths leaping bow up, strapped down and heeled far to windward, pointing high and flying well above the waves, travelling at 14–16 knots to windward and up to 25 knots downwind in 18–20 knots of breeze. Upwind, they seem to have it all sorted out; downwind, there is the occasional crash, but they recover quickly and easily. In lighter winds they are up to 50% faster than the conventional displacement designs, which are themselves not slow by any measure.

Rohan Veal saw the potential of Ilett's foils and bought a set in 2003. After a steep learning curve with much dedicated practice, he mastered the necessary techniques and applied these to come third in the 2003 World Moth Championships in France and to win the 2004 Australian Championships, and cap this by winning the 2005 World Championships in Melbourne very convincingly in difficult conditions. This is the first time in history that a foiled sailing craft has won an International Class World Championship. He won every heat and attributed his performance to a good technique, coming from lots of practice. Fig 2.6 shows Veal and the foiled Moth in action, and Fig 2.7 shows a typical foil array.

One new technique has evolved from Veal's observation that heeling the boat well to windward when sailing upwind gives extra lift from both rig and the foils as they resist leeway, providing exceptional performance and early take-off, especially in light airs. His tireless efforts in refining technique and also publicising the achievements of foiling Moths has led to enormous interest in the class and highlighted the development of the Flying Moths.

Veal's performance against 'A' class catamarans is also astounding, regularly winning by 1–2 minutes around the course. He is also significantly faster than 14ft skiffs and 49ers. While a modern Formula sailboard can at times pace a foiled Moth when the wind suits them, they need 11–12sq m of sail to get going, whereas the Moth achieves this with just 8sq m of sail. In flat water in Perth, the foiled Moths have clocked 19 knots in 10–12 knots of wind, nearly double the wind speed. This is far more efficient than most other sailing craft,

Fig 2.6 Foil Moth sailing

Rohan Veal sailing a foil Moth – note the typical windward heel. Courtesy of Rohan Veal.

Fig 2.7 Moth — main lifting foil

Courtesy of Rohan Veal.

especially when the small sail area is considered. Even the world speed record, which was established by a sailboard, achieved a relative speed of only 1.3 times the prevailing wind speed.

Handling

Author's note

Since Ian Ward wrote this section, Rohan Veal has contributed Chapter 28.

Further developments

Flying Moths are an incredible innovation and have certainly led to the possibility of a new breed of sailing dinghy. The centreline foil arrangement has broken new ground in terms of being able to sail upwind, even in light airs, and with a new level of efficiency not seen before in around the buoys sailing craft.

It is interesting to observe that parallel developments have occurred virtually simultaneously, that one set of ideas has spurred the next development, and that design rules have also significantly shaped the response of designers. This experience also confirms that it requires quite different sets of skills to conceive, construct and then successfully race a new concept such as this. One thing in common for all of those involved in these foiling developments is their enjoyment of every step of the innovation process, which has at various times been inspiring, frustrating, sometimes physically damaging, but well worthwhile for those priceless Eureka moments!

There is an obvious opportunity to apply the same dinghy foiler principle to many new dinghy designs in the years to come. In addition, there seems ample room for further development, and even better performance in the future. Certainly, unifoiler and bow rudder arrangements, retractable and freely pivoting foils for light airs, and variable foil area for higher speeds, are all possible sources of improvement. While the most successful foiling developments in Moths so far have initiated and continue in Australia, further development is now under way in Germany, Japan and the UK, and it will be truly fascinating to see what the future holds.

Dr Ian Ward

References

This section has relied on contributions from: John Ilett, Brett Burvill, David Lugg, Rohan Veal and Alan Smith.

2.6 ■ Fastest foilborne: The Trifoilers BY GEORGE C CHAPMAN

Author's note

Commander George Chapman RN, together with his son Dr Edward 'Joddy' Chapman, have spent many decades at the cutting edge of the development of foil-borne boats with three foils. George was both a researcher, designer and sailor of his own marques, and also served as chronicler of the genre.

It was my privilege to spend a day with George and Joddy at Plymouth. I enjoyed sailing *Calliope* – predecessor to *Ceres* – and observed how practical and effective the boat was, and the Chapmans' approach, and was mightily impressed with the scope and accuracy of their on-the-boat measuring equipment and the subsequent printout of the day's sailing.

Sadly, George passed away shortly before *HPS-2* went to press.

Lifting hydrofoils

Currently used lifting hydrofoils – 'lifters' – and their associated leeway resisting struts which 'fly' a boat's hulls clear above the water incur much less hydrodynamic drag than displacement or planing hull forms over useful ranges of speed. For example, if we compare two craft each carrying two people, a 49er and *Ceres* (see later), both of which are reaching at 17 knots in the same 11 knot wind, *Ceres*'s hydrodynamic drag is around 65% of the 49er's. But these are entirely different craft, and on other points of sailing – for example, sailing to windward – the 49er can sail very much faster while the heavier *Ceres* goes best to windward with hulls and foils sharing the loads: a mode called 'skimming'.

The very much lighter Moths have recently enjoyed a revolutionary development to the point where they are now flying at higher speeds on all points of sailing in all but light winds. The overall speed advantage is real and practical. Moths on foils which are sailed with great skill are now winning their world championships.

It was the potential for speed off the wind that spurred competitors to experiment. They met at the Weymouth (UK) Speed Weeks which started in 1972. Initially they used surface-piercing lifters, and their initial success led directly to the present state of the art, where the envelope of foiling performance has widened dramatically.

Finally, lifting hydrofoils – lifters – arrived in mainstream sailing via their adoption by the International Moth Class.

The following sections will look first at the foil systems available, and then at the background development of the heavier boats from which the Moths are now benefiting.

Basic hydrofoil principles

Just as the hull of a conventional sailing boat has to support the weight of the craft from sinking, enable it to resist heeling forces, roll and pitching, and allow it to be steered, so the overall foil system of a hydrofoil flyer must do all these and, additionally, fly the boat so that the hull(s) do not touch the wave tops.

Many experimenters have started with as many as four foil elements, one at each corner of the craft; some still do. However, quite early on, Baker (USA, 1950s), then Hook, and in 1971 Hansford (UK), realised that if two main supporting elements are placed close to the fore-and-aft centre of gravity, one on either side, the boat can be made to resist heel, and the combined leeway resistance is centred close below the centre of effort of the sails. Only a single element aft is needed, the rudder, to ensure yaw stability and provide a means of steering. A lifter at the tip of the rudder, making the element an inverted T, provides stability in pitch.

Thus we can see that the elements that provide vertical forces are similar in function to the wings and tailplane of a conventional aircraft – though the analogy is not dynamically exact.

The above remarks apply equally whether you adopt two main elements, one either side of the boat to form with the rudder a 'trifoiler', or a single main element – as has been adopted in the Moth Class – as a bifoiler.

Inclined surface-piercing foils

From the very beginning, all of the work on the heavier boats has been based on the trifoil configuration introduced above. Two main elements are widely spaced abeam and a smaller stabilising foil is attached to the bottom of the rudder. This configuration gives maximum stability.

In the early years, inclined surface-piercing foils were favoured, both on the grounds of simplicity and the fact that as speed increases and the boat rises, so less wetted area of foil is required. These foils combined the lifting and leeway resisting functions and therefore required less total area.

The principal disadvantages are that, despite the fences, ventilation remains prevalent, leading to loss of lift; also, the windward foil may easily develop negative leeway force, adding to total drag. In addition, because of the cross-coupling of lifting and leeway forces that can easily interact with rudder steering force, steady steering is necessary. With this arrangement it is easy for a helmsman to overcorrect with the rudder and put the boat into an oscillatory porpoising motion. What is remarkable is that people still occasionally build such craft.

At non-flying speed the whole of the foil structure is submerged and creates considerable drag. This was acceptable for a 500m record-attempt boat getting back to the start, but not for an all-rounder.

Inverted T lifters with surface sensors

Inverted T lifters were developed next. These have vertical struts (daggerboards and rudders) to resist leeway and steer, and horizontal lifters at the bottoms of the daggerboards and rudders to raise the boat's hull(s) clear of the water and, in the case of windward main lifters, to hold the windward side down when necessary. The rudder lifter can reverse its lift to stabilise in pitch and prevent pitchpoling.

Fig 2.9 shows various arrangements of inverted Ts. The starboard side shows the sensor system generally used in the UK, with a straight 'feeler' sensing the sea surface ahead or close to the strut, similar to that used on the Moths. To port is the system generally used in the USA, with a steeply inclined 'wand' sensing the surface close to or aft of the strut. Either control system could operate the full-span trailing edge flap as illustrated on the port foil, or move the whole foil about a horizontal axis as shown to starboard. This latter, balanced, lifter is comparable to a balanced rudder in that, correctly proportioned, it requires a minimum torque to control it; without that torque, it self-feathers to the stream.

To date, only the UK feeler has been found appropriate on a bifoiler, where there is a single lifter under the daggerboard and the sensor can be pivoted from the bow.

As a foiler rises on its lifters, so the sensor's tip falls relative to the boat, reducing the foil's angle of attack or the downward deflection of the flap. If effective angle of attack becomes zero, but the boat continues to rise, elastic shock cords ensure that negative angle is applied to keep the lifter in the water.

Although more complicated and costly, submerged inverted T foils have shown that they are the better choice, if only because they do not have the disadvantages of the surface piercers noted above. A practical advantage is that they give a smoother ride and are not prone to crashing or pitchpoling.

When unable to fly, such a foiler can adjust the demanded 'flying height' so that the lifters keep the hull(s) just touching the water. This is called 'skimming', and for heavier craft is appropriate – particularly when sailing to windward.

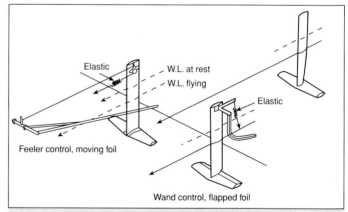

Fig 2.9 Submerged foil arrangements

With submerged foils the struts are usually carried like centreboards, in the outward hulls. Or in the case of a bifoiler, in the hull. Alternatively the strut/foil units may be mounted outboard like leeboards and pivot up to reduce draught. This sketch shows the UK sensor system – a 'feeler' on the starboard side and a US 'wand' on the port side.

Scat and *Ceres* – trifoiler multihulls

These two craft were the leading US and UK flying foilers in the early years of this century. They were derived from conventional trimarans and beach cats respectively. Both have been developed and designed with flying being their principal method of sailing quicker than non-flying siblings. They are the products of many years' work by their respective design teams.

Dimension	*Scat* (Fig 2.9)	*Ceres* (Fig 2.10)
Designer: Hull	Nigel Irens	Dr E J Chapman and
Foils	Dr W S Bradfield	Cmdr G C Chapman
Length overall	37ft	19ft
Beam	42ft	10ft 10in across hulls
Boat weight	7000lb*	440lb
No in crew	2 to 4	1 or 2 (occasionally 3)
Mainsail	711sq ft	149.5sq ft
Jib	392sq ft	38.7sq ft
Reacher	793sq ft	–
Total sail area	1896sq ft	188sq ft
Best speed	31.6 knots (briefly – GPS)	27 knots (briefly)
		22 knots over 500m, 2003

*7500–8000lb in ocean racing mode which requires four crew.

Scat – an ocean-going trimaran foiler

Scat was commissioned by Dr Bradfield of Hydrosail Inc, Florida, in 2002. The hull structure and rig were designed by Nigel Irens specifically as an aeroplane trifoiler, but with the ability to ride out rough weather. The two main beams converge just abaft the point where the amas carry the main struts, the after curved main beam encompassing the cockpit area. This provides a full-width cockpit, netting-decked outboard of the centre hull, with steering positions almost against the amas.

The wands are outboard of the amas, controlling flaps on the lifters that are fixed relative to the struts. Controls brought to the cockpit enable adjustment of the depths of strut and wand deployment and lifter incidence, as well as adjustments for the inverted T rudder. These allow fine tuning, analagous to fine tuning the sails.

In early 2004, readings of speed (by GPS) and masthead wind speed when sailing on the relatively flat water of the Intracoastal Waterway confirmed that in winds above 12 knots *Scat* can sail at up to 1.9 times wind speed, touching 31.6 knots in a wind varying between 15 and 25 knots, on a beam reach with main, jib and reacher set. *Scat* eases through the wake waves of larger boats with no difficulty.

On the 2004 Miami–Nassau, Bahamas, Race, Phil Steggall led a crew of several experienced RAVE sailors. With an easterly wind up to 40 knots, the first 125 miles were a beat, hull borne. The final 50 miles were close reaching, skimming and with some flying. Of the nine multihulls entered, only two finished – a catamaran called *Green Flash* won in 25½ hours and *Scat* was second, having taken an hour off the cat in the final 50 miles. Of 13 monohulls, only 6 finished, and their leader was 2 hours behind the multis. The return trip to Florida further demonstrated the ability of *Scat* to make a fast comfortable passage in a variety of winds and seas.

Fig 2.9 Scat flying

Courtesy of Dr Sam Bradfield.

Fig 2.10 *Ceres* flying

Courtesy of Georger Chapman.

In the 2005 Race, starting last on a broad reach, in half an hour and over 11 miles, *Scat* overtook the whole fleet, including a 40ft trimaran. She did not do so well on the wind, which dropped, and she finished third of the four multihulls.

Ceres – a daysailing catamaran trifoiler

Ceres first went afloat in 1998. Following earlier development work on the smaller *Calliope*, she has balanced lifter foils mounted at the bottoms of the main daggerboards. These are controlled by light tubular feelers mounted inboard of the hulls. These lifters are at all times set by the feelers to the appropriate incidence, so the boat does not need the added strut-and-fixed-lifter adjustment of *Scat*. Rudder-lifter incidence can be set afloat, but does not normally need adjusting.

The proportions of *Ceres* differ from those of most beach cats. There is less length of bow forward of the mast, and there is an additional beam right aft to support the single rudder. Bow burying is not a problem, and when sailing to windward skimming, with the lifters active, the boat remains upright and level in pitch and roll – and is very stable due to the damping of the lifters. Switching the feeler-controlled height between flying and skimming is done using a single cord across the boat, toggling the strut-top clutches. Nevertheless, because she is overweight the windward performance is not impressive. New much lighter hulls will further improve performance.

As with *Scat*, sailing through wake waves poses no problem. Sailing with swell or wind waves revealed that on the descending slope, the orbital motion of the water can seize the lifters and dump the hulls suddenly onto the water, but this can be avoided by sailing diagonally across the waves. Sailing into waves does increase the heave motions, but the lag between feeler 'command' and lifter response causes the boat to fly relative to the wave tops rather than the mean sea level. This is exhilarating! Provided the struts are long enough in relation to wave height, the lifters will not break surface; if they are not long, they will, and care will be required.

Pacing against comparable beach cats has not been possible, so for *Calliope* and *Ceres* we developed instruments to measure and record apparent wind speed and direction and boat speed. The data is then processed to give a polar diagram of performance for each outing, or portion thereof, showing boat speed for winds up to a chosen value. This has been a useful tool in development, and led in 1996 to the writing of a Velocity Prediction Program (VPP), which further aids design and improvements.

The Speedwatch boat speed meter, which displays speed and provides input to the recorder, has briefly indicated 27 knots. More realistically, 22 knots has been achieved and recorded at Weymouth over 500m.

Ceres has been, and will continue to be, a useful platform for development, and provides a delightful ride for one to three people in suitable conditions, with calm water, a steady breeze and sunshine. And she sails faster than most of the boats we come across!

George C Chapman

PART TWO

Wind

Author's note

I sense ambiguity in the understanding of the word 'veer'.

The Oxford dictionary definition is 'change direction, esp of wind, sunwise' – ie in the northern hemisphere a veer is a clockwise change of direction, but in the southern hemisphere it is an anticlockwise change of direction.

Macquarie gives the definition: 'change of direction (either way) – ex. the road veers left'. Alan Watts, a professional meteorologist, defines veer as 'a change of direction, clockwise'.

My observation is that many – probably most – authors and sailors agree with Alan Watts. But one of my sailing proof-readers picked me up on error if we define it according to the Oxford definition.

So, to avoid ambiguity, I will use the words 'clock' to mean change of direction, always clockwise, and 'back' to mean change of direction, always anticlockwise.

FOREWORD TO CHAPTERS 3–6

HPS-1 (1992) discussed some of the different winds we sail in, their driving mechanisms, and the typical gust and lull, and back and clock patterns that characterise each wind. These patterns were then analysed and grouped into those that are most likely to repeat with sufficient regularity to justify strategy based on prediction, and those in which repetition will more likely be random, and in which no prediction accurate enough to be useful is possible.

The later sections of *HPS-1* dealt with sailing in these winds, and in particular:

- Adjusting sail shape and sail trim and sailing technique in response to change of wind speed in gusts and lulls, which is a handling skill.
- Planning the fastest path through oscillating backs and clocks which are predictable, which is a particular strategy skill.

Recent developments

In the years since I wrote *HPS-1* there have been five major developments in our understanding of the sailor's wind. Of these, 1 and 2 below have been seminal:

1 Gust peaks

We have realised that within the gust pattern that repeats, on average, at about 30 seconds gust and 30 seconds lull, a pattern of substantial 'mini gusts' often occurs in which the wind speed changes significantly every few seconds. This rate of change of wind speed is much faster than any sailor can respond to with manual adjustment. The design response to this has been the development of the automatic rig. This calls for:

- A new look at the wind's unsteadiness. When does the wind blow most steadily, and when most unsteadily? How much does the wind speed change in these quicker gust peaks?

59

- Discussion of the modern automatic rig, and the new skills called for to handle the very different dynamics of these rigs.

2 Surges and fades

The second development is that apparent wind skiffs now sweep widely from side to side of the course as they sail downwind at three times the boat speed of conventional 'blow-downwind' boats. The result is that the big areas of stronger wind that previously were usually ignored – because, for blow-downwind boats, they were too far off-course, or too distant to access with advantage before they faded – can now be accessed quickly. This has led to a new situation in which sailing for more of the time in these wide, stronger-wind areas has become the key to winning the downwind legs.

This calls for a new look at the wind's wider spectrum, and at the properties of surges and fades.

The remaining three developments, while not seminal, are none the less important to our understanding:

3 The turbulent layer

With the addition of gust peaks, and surges and fades to the lexicon, we now have a continuous spectrum of four identifiable motions within the turbulent layer of the wind, all of which are of critical importance to the sailor. These are:

(i)   The *gust peaks* every few seconds.
(ii)   *Gusts and lulls* about every minute.
(iii) *Surges and fades* about every five minutes.
(iv)   *The backs and clocks of the roll* mechanism – usually about every ten minutes.

Three of these (i, ii and iv) are special in that they are all creatures of the 'turbulent layer' in the sense that if there is no turbulent layer, none of them can exist and, further, when a turbulent layer *does* exist, the properties of all three will, to a large extent, reflect the nature of the turbulent layer itself. This can vary from shallow and cool with regular oscillations, to deep, heated, energetic and unstable, and with irregular and unpredictable repetition of everything.

The third motion on the above list (iii) *surges and fades* is not yet well enough understood to know where it originates, but it will be surprising indeed if it turns out to be independent of the turbulent layer. The turbulent layer is discussed in Section 3.10.

4 The nexus between heat and unsteady wind direction

The fourth factor is that there is a fundamental difference between all cooled winds and all heated winds.

In cooled winds:

- Short-term direction is always true within a narrow range.
- Longer-term direction seldom changes unexpectedly.

In heated winds:

- Short-term direction is never true, and does not stay within a narrow range. It routinely changes direction quickly and irregularly by up to three times as much as in the cooled wind.
- Longer-term direction always changes widely and irregularly.

This difference between cooled and heated winds becomes a major factor in race planning.

5 Divergent flow within gusts

The fifth development is the realisation that the wind direction is divergent within each gust. This turns out to be a major factor in both optimising VMG to windward, and also as a second strategy option when approaching the windward mark.

Chapters 3–6 below discuss the wind and its patterns from these new perspectives. Chapters 27 and 28 discuss the strategy options that they open up.

Chapter 3 has become a review that blends this new thinking into the previously accepted wisdom:

- It looks at the flows of the laminar and turbulent boundary layers at the water's surface and at the deep turbulent layers above them. These are universal in that they are the norm everywhere from mid-ocean to over a lake in the middle of a desert.
- It then looks at the thermal winds which occur only near shores. These have the same surface boundary layers, but much shallower turbulent layers above them.
- It touches on the cold drainage winds that occur only where cold dry land is sloped. These are different again.

Later chapters develop the technical, the handling and the strategy logic that flow from this new thinking.

There is a further point. Sailing ceased to be black art and became respectable science with the 1925 publication of Manfred Curry's *The Aerodynamics of Sails* in which he stated, 'Sailboats follow Aerodynamic law', and described his work with the primitive wind tunnels at Gottingen University in the early 1920s.

Tony Marchaz had vastly more sophisticated wind tunnels and measuring apparatus to work with and his 1971 *Sailing Theory and Practice*, and his subsequent works, greatly reinforced the original work by Curry with precision.

Through the 1970s and 1980s, I took a wider route. As I travelled to attend the major boat shows and regattas each year, I observed and recorded winds over water worldwide, identified and studied the patterns within them, endeavoured to design and build faster rigs and foils and boats to sail in those winds, and studied the racing techniques of winning sailors.

This enabled *HPS-1* to cover a wider segment of the art of sailing, because I was able to describe how the various winds work, how the waves work, how the boat works, and how best to sail the boat in the different winds and waves. To the best of my ability, I researched sail and foil shapes in my own and the local university's wind tunnels, and confirmed the end results of this research and development with on-the-water testing.

It was only some years later that I realised that what I had written in *HPS-1* could not be applied 'across the board' because it had all been conducted in selected conditions.

The whole point of wind tunnels is to provide smooth steady airflows in which small differences in performance between different aerofoil sections and different sail shapes may be observed and measured and compared with confidence.

The whole point of our on-the-water testing had been to select the smoothest winds in which we might measure and compare small differences in performance with the most reliable repetition possible, and in this way confirm on the water what we had learned from the wind tunnels ashore. Chapter 13, Sail Forces in Steady Airflows, summarises this basic body of knowledge.

What I now realise is that we had selected only smooth conditions in which both to develop our rigs and to confirm their relative performances. The consequence is that everything written in *HPS-1* should be regarded as true and proven as best possible in smoother winds, but it may not remain true in rougher winds, because we never attempted either to measure performance nor compare equipment in rougher winds because it is never possible to measure and compare anything accurately in unsteady conditions.

This book describes the practical development and handling of the new apparent wind craft and the more automatic rigs we have developed. These are both easier to handle in the unsteady winds in which we usually sail, and they sail faster than the best manually adjustable rigs. Chapters 21 and 22 and the following chapters on handling and racing describe what we have learned to date about this new art.

Chapter 3 • Review of Wind Dynamics

3.1 ■ The wind's driving force

The Earth has sufficient gravity to hold an atmosphere about 20% oxygen, 80% nitrogen plus traces of other gases. The mean hydrostatic pressure at sea level is 14.7lb/sq in, 2117lb (nearly a ton) per sq ft, 1013.2 millibars or hectopascals (depending on where you live) which is 10.13 tonnes per sq m. From the point of view of the aircraft designer, the International Standard Atmosphere has a surface pressure of 1013.2 millibars, and a density of 0.001185, as compared to water with a density of about 1.0.

Note that one millibar is a substantial pressure – about 2.2lb/sq ft, or 10kg/sq m. To give a sense of scale, the rigs and righting moments of most dinghies and yachts are designed to balance when sailing to windward at a sail loading of about one pound per sq ft, or 5kg/sq m, ie half a millibar. More than that calls for eased sheets, or otherwise you capsize. The isobars on the weather map are usually drawn every four millibars, so the pressure difference between any two isobars is eight times what your sail can stand. No wonder the wind whistles when the isobars are close.

The thickness of the atmosphere is such that half its density lies below a height of about 17 500ft (5.3km) and three-quarters below about 35 000ft or 10km. Its upper limit tapers into space. The space station MIR orbited for 15 years at a height of 390km (244 miles). The fact that it ultimately slowed suggests that some atmospheric traces still create aerodynamic drag at that height. That it needed 15 years for this drag to take effect suggests that the resistance was almost negligible.

If there were no heating there would be no wind. What happens is that the sun's radiation passes through the atmosphere without heating it, and instead heats the Earth's land and water surfaces. It heats the top several metres of transparent water only a tiny amount each day, so ocean and lake temperatures change little and slowly. As an example, the east Australia current off Sydney usually peaks at 22°C in about March, and falls to about 17°C in September.

On the land surface, only the top few millimetres are heated each day, so diurnal increases vary from trivial in high latitudes (low sun) to 40–50°C and more in the tropics (sun overhead at noon).

This surface heat from solar radiation is the primary energy source that drives the wind. The Earth's surface is heated most at the Equator where the mean surface temperature is about 30°C, and least at the Poles where it averages about –20°C. Air in contact with the surface is heated or cooled by conduction. Heat is distributed upwards by convection and latent heat, and in this way the whole air mass soon reflects the temperature of any warmer surface over which it flows. Above the surface, the temperature falls by a surprisingly constant 6°C per km (2°C per 1000ft) to about –40°C at 9km above the Poles, and –75°C at 18km above the Equator – as in Fig 3.1. Above this surface (the tropopause) lies the stratosphere in which the atmosphere attenuates to nothing and the temperature remains almost constant.

The atmosphere below the tropopause is called the troposphere and all weather phenomena occur within it. Huge thunderheads may reach and penetrate the tropopause, but cannot rise much higher because they keep expanding and cooling as they rise; this means they quickly become colder and denser than the surrounding stratospheric air which no longer gets cooler with increasing height. This now cooler air subsides and spreads horizontally to form the characteristic 'anvil' tops of thunderheads. The horizontal tops mark the level of the tropopause.

The greater solar heating at the Equator causes a temperature difference between the Polar and the Equatorial troposphere. Via a two-stage process, this causes a higher surface pressure at the Poles and a lower surface pressure at the Equator, and this pressure difference drives the surface wind. The mechanism is interesting.

Consider the situation at the surface S–S in Figs 3.2A and 3.2B, at about 17 500ft or between 5km and 6km at the Poles – above which half the atmosphere lies. Pressure at this surface will necessarily be constant. Let us call this pressure p1.

If there were no sun, there would be no temperature difference anywhere and the pressure at each height would be the same everywhere and the air would be calm. The height above sea level of the surface with half the atmosphere above it would be the same at the Equator as at the Poles. This notional starting situation is shown as Fig 3.2A, in which the height of this surface at the Poles is called h1 and at the Equator h2, and h2 is the same as h1. Also, p1 at the Equator is at the same height as p1 at the Poles.

Now let the sun shine and warm the equatorial regions. The column of air between the surface and the height we are considering (about 17 500ft) will be warmed about 40°C (Fig 3.1) and expand about (40/273 × 17 500)ft = 2564ft, or about 800m. This will raise the height, at the Equator, of the surface with half the atmosphere above it by about 2500ft above its original 17 500ft – ie to about 20 000ft – to h2 in Fig 3.2B. It will not be raised at the Poles.

At the Equator, the pressure at 20 000ft will now be the same as at 17 500ft over the Poles. The pressure at 17 500ft (p2) will now be greater because above it there will be both half the atmosphere (pressure p1), plus now the hydrostatic pressure of the 2500ft (800m) of air (shaded in Fig 3.2B) between its original and its new height due to the expansion. At this height, pressure changes about 1mb every 60ft, so the pressure p2 at 17 500ft will now be p1, plus about 42mb. At the Poles it will still be p1. So thermal expansion at the Equator has caused a pressure difference at and above 17 500ft between the Equator and the Poles of about 42mb, or 90lb/sq ft, or 440kg per sq m (Fig 3.2B).

It is this pressure difference that drives the upper-level air from above the Equator towards the Poles. This high-level counterflow of real air with real mass (about half a million tonnes per cubic kilometre at that height) starts the process.

As soon as the upper-level air moves away from the Equator towards the Poles, the hydrostatic pressure at sea level at the Equator will become less because real upper-level air with real mass is flowing away, and the sea level pressure at the Poles will become greater where real upper-level air is now 'heaping up' above. So the second stage is that at low levels a pressure difference develops, with new higher surface pressure at the Poles and new lower surface pressure at the Equator. Low-level air will respond by flowing from the Poles towards the Equator. This is the low-level flow we call 'wind'.

Coriolis

If the Earth did not rotate, the flow would be a simple loop – air would flow from Pole to Equator at low level, be heated, and then expand and rise over the Equatorial regions. There would be a counterflow from Equator to Poles at high level, and subsidence would occur over the Polar regions, all driven by the pressure difference caused by Equatorial solar heating, as in Fig 3.3.

But the Earth rotates, and anything that is accelerated and then left to its own devices will try to follow a straight line in space (Newton). The consequence of the Earth's rotation is that anything that moves straight in space will trace a curve over the surface of the rotating Earth.

Try this in your imagination: walk all day towards a fixed point in space, such as the sun. At dawn you will start by walking east. If you live in the southern hemisphere, by noon your path on the Earth's surface will have curved left and you will be walking north. By sundown your path will have curved further left and you will be walking west. In the northern hemisphere your path will have curved to the right. What is happening is that you are indeed walking straight in space, and it is the Earth rotating beneath you that causes the trail of your footsteps to curve relative to the Earth's surface.

If in your imagination you start walking again towards the sun from the same starting point the next day, but this time walk along a straight road

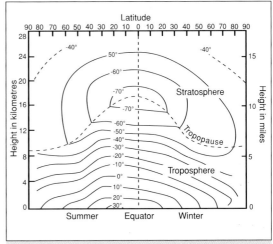

Fig 3.1 Change of temperature with height

Vertical section through the atmosphere showing the distribution of mean temperature in degrees centigrade. From *Meteorology for Aviators*, Sutcliffe.

that runs due east, the trail of your footsteps will diverge from yesterday's 'straight line in space' path, so this time your path along the Earth's straight road is *curved* in space, and some sideways force must be acting on you to curve your path.

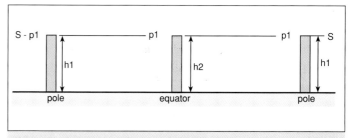

Fig 3.2A Situation without solar heat

You can sense this force if you imagine that you are walking along a meridian away from the North Pole, away from the Pole star. (A meridian is just one more straight line on the Earth's surface.) As you depart from the Pole you will incur an increase in circumferential speed due to the increase in radius from the Pole, and the only way to increase speed is to accelerate. In this case, the acceleration is sideways. This force is called the Coriolis acceleration (Coriolis for short) after the man who first worked it out.

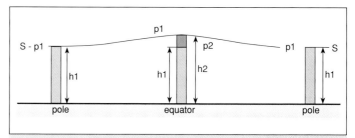

Fig 3.2B Effect of solar heat on upper level pressure

Water in your sink will curve similarly. When you pull a plug in the southern hemisphere, every water particle will curve left as it flows towards the plughole – this causes the familiar swirl, almost always clockwise in the southern hemisphere and counter-clockwise in the northern. Air behaves similarly.

The weather map

The consequence of Coriolis is that the flow of air is always subject to two different horizontal forces. The first is the local pressure difference that rotates with the Earth. The second is the momentum force that works relative to a fixed direction in space. It is the interaction of these two conflicting forces that causes the wind to blow around highs and lows, and not directly away from or into them. If you look at the forces from the standpoint of an observer in space, their interaction becomes simpler to follow.

Imagine the following: you are observing the Earth from above the North Pole, the Polar high is below you, there is a low pressure system over Stockholm in southern Sweden, somebody has painted a cubic kilometre of air over northern Norway red, and that you then watch that air for a while.

At the start at Stockholm at noon, you, above the Pole, the red air over northern Norway, and Stockholm, and the sun are all in line. The pressure difference between the higher pressure over the Pole and the lower pressure over Stockholm starts the air accelerating south towards Stockholm – that is, towards the sun.

The moving air now has momentum and will want to keep moving in a straight line towards the sun. The mass is surprising. Every cubic kilometre of low-level air will weigh about $(1000 \times 1000 \times 1000 \times 0.001185)$ = 1.2 million tonnes, and this sort of mass – once it starts moving – will have a mind of its own.

The Earth rotates anticlockwise at 15° per hour, so three hours later, at 3 pm, our red air, which started flowing south towards Stockholm, will have curved to the right with respect to the Earth's meridians and will be moving southwest towards France due to momentum (still directly towards the sun), while the low pressure area over Stockholm will have rotated with the Earth to the left and will now be pulling our red air to the left. Note that the air is now being swung right by Coriolis, and being pulled left by the pressure difference.

By 6 pm, Stockholm with its low pressure will have rotated 90° to the left. The pressure force between the high over the Pole and the low over Stockholm will now be at right angles from both its original 'towards the sun' direction and the original momentum direction, and will be strongly forcing our red air to curve left, not right.

By midnight, the world and Sweden will have rotated 180°, the pressure force will now be away from the sun, and will directly conflict with the original momentum which was towards the sun. But in the meantime, the anticlockwise rotating pressure force will have turned our red air 90° to the left.

The end result is a balance between the pressure forces that rotate with the Earth, and the momentum force that is slaved to space, which makes moving air reluctant to turn at all. The consequence of this balance is that air – both low-level air and high-level air, and also the water in your sink – will only initially flow directly away from the higher pressure and towards the lower pressure. After a little while – only a few seconds in the case of the water in your sink – it settles into a stable pattern with the flows around the low-pressure and high-pressure areas.

In an ideal, frictionless world, the rotating pressure force and the delaying momentum force would find a balance, with the air blowing exactly along the isobars – the lines on the weather map indicating constant surface pressure that circles the highs and lows.

In the real world, surface friction slows the surface wind a little so it mimics the water in your sink. Instead of blowing exactly along the isobars it skews inwards a little to spiral inwards around the lows and outward a little around the highs. The effect

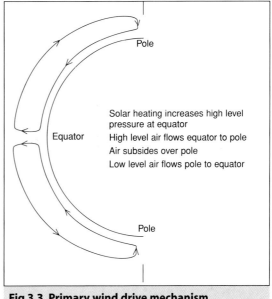

Solar heating increases high level pressure at equator
High level air flows equator to pole
Air subsides over pole
Low level air flows pole to equator

Fig 3.3 Primary wind drive mechanism

of this is that 'Highs' are areas of higher surface pressure within which the air subsides and diverges outwards, and 'Lows' are areas of lower surface pressure within which the air spirals inwards and converges and rises.

An important point for the sailor is that there is a difference in the 'spiralling' as between land and sea. Over the sea, the surface friction is low, so the wind direction settles at close to the isobar direction. Over the rougher land, the surface friction is greater. Every particle of air brought to rest by every obstruction will start to move again, not along the isobar, but directly towards low pressure. In practice it will be swept up in the turbulent flow, but the end result is that the surface wind diverges more towards low pressure over the land than over the sea.

The more closely the isobars are packed together – their gradient – the faster the air will flow. This is why we call it the 'gradient wind'.

The end result of this process is that the low-level flow from Pole to Equator actually takes the form of the complex series of lows and highs so familiar as the weather map. On these maps the lows, highs, ridges, troughs and fronts appear to be the dominant features. In this they mask what is really going on – which is that the low-level air, despite all the swirls and detours, is moving inexorably from Pole to Equator, where it rises in what sailors call the doldrums, land dwellers call the monsoon, and aviators call the inter-tropic front. It returns poleward as a high-level generally westerly counterflow which subsides in the Polar Highs to complete the loop shown in Fig 3.3.

This is the energy process that drives what we call the gradient wind.

THE WIND AT THE SURFACE

3.2 ■ Cooled and heated winds

Figs 3.4, 3.6, 3.8 and 3.10 are 15-minute traces showing the speeds and directions on a second-by-second basis of 3 knot light air and 6 knot, 10 knot and 20 knot winds respectively. All of these are 'cooled' in the sense that the water temperature is the same as, or cooler than, the air.

Figs 3.5, 3.7, 3.9 and 3.11 are similar traces of winds of about the same speeds, but which are heated. In each case the water temperature is warmer than the air.

These traces are from the meteorological tower that was moored 8nm offshore from Kingston, Ontario, by the Canadian Department of the Environment in 1975, the year immediately prior to the Montreal Olympic Games. The recording instrument is a U2-A anemograph, which operated each day of July from

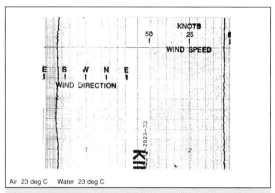

Fig 3.4 Light air, cooled

Air 23 deg C   Water 23 deg C

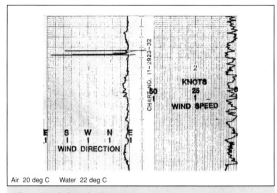

Fig 3.5 Light air, heated

Air 20 deg C   Water 22 deg C

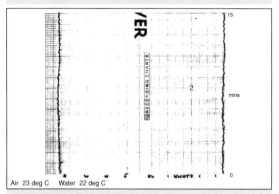

Fig 3.6 A 6 knot wind, cooled

Air 23 deg C   Water 22 deg C

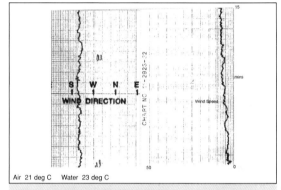

Fig 3.7 A 6 knot wind, heated

Air 21 deg C   Water 23 deg C

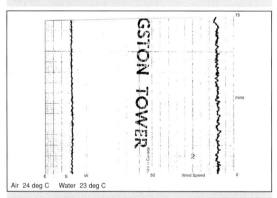

Fig 3.8 A 10 knot wind, cooled

Air 24 deg C   Water 23 deg C

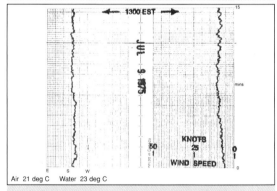

Fig 3.9 A 10 knot wind, heated

Air 21 deg C   Water 23 deg C

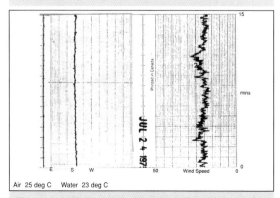

Fig 3.10 A 20 knot wind, cooled

Air 25 deg C   Water 23 deg C

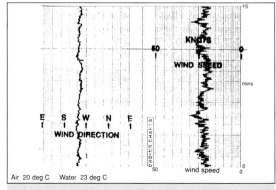

Fig 3.11 A 20 knot wind, heated

Air 20 deg C   Water 23 deg C

9 am to 4 pm and provided about 240 hours of traces of this detail. I thank the Department for their permission to use this data.

In *HPS-1* the gusts in wind speed and the oscillations in wind direction were discussed, but little reference was made to heat. In the years since writing *HPS-1*, I have come to understand that heat has a profound effect on both the speed and the direction flow patterns of winds of all speeds. The following sections and chapters will refer to the diagrams above.

3.3 ■ The boundary layer

When the air is calm, there is no boundary layer. When air flows over any surface, the molecules that touch the surface come to rest, so the wind speed right at the surface is always zero. (This remains true at even the highest speeds – eg space vehicles re-entering the atmosphere.)

Viscosity between the molecules of this surface 'at rest' air and the molecules of the adjacent moving air will slow the adjacent air. The slowing will become progressively less with increasing distance from the surface until it becomes negligible:

- The slowed air between the surface and the unslowed air is called the *boundary layer*.
- The unslowed air beyond the slowed boundary layer is called the *free stream*.

3.4 ■ Laminar and turbulent boundary layers at the small scale

When air flows over sails or water flows over hulls or centreboards, the nature of the flow at the surface always takes one of two very different forms.

Osborne Reynolds (1842–1912) was a pioneer who experimented with the flow of water through glass tubes. He observed that:

1 At low flow speeds a thin filament of dye introduced into the middle of the flow at the entry moved as a straight line through even the longest tube. This indicated steady laminar flow, in which each layer of fluid flowed smoothly over the slower layer closer to the surface, and did not mix (as in Figs 3.12A, 3.13A, 3.14 and 3.17).

2 With increasing speed, a condition was reached some distance down the tube where the dye stream first wavered and then suddenly broke up and became evenly diffused throughout the tube. The flow had become turbulent. The flow was now a mass of myriad eddies all circling around each other because each eddy was to some extent within the circulation fields of its neighbours, and so all the eddies were linked into one well-mixed flow (as in Figs 3.12B, 3.13B, 3.16 and 3.18).

3 The change from all-laminar to all-turbulent in the tube was near instantaneous.

4 As the flow speed was further increased, the point at which the flow became turbulent moved closer to the entry.

5 The slowest mass flow at which the flow would trip turbulent was found to be constant. This observation led to the concept of the critical Reynolds Number (RN).

Ira H Abbott was Director of Aeronautical and Space Research, NASA, and Albert E von Doenhoff was a NASA research engineer. Their *Theory of Wing Sections* is the authoritative industry aerodynamics text.

Fig 3.12A, taken from *Theory of Wing Sections*, shows the way that the flow speed changes across a tube when the flow is laminar. (The ribbons in Fig 3.14 mimic this flow.) Fig 3.12B shows the very different way it changes when the flow is turbulent. (The ribbons in Fig 3.15 mimic this flow.)

The way the speed changes within the boundary layer is called the *velocity gradient*. In the laminar flows of Figs 3.12A and 3.14 the flow speed starts at zero at the surface and increases steadily with increasing distance from the surface. This is called a linear velocity gradient. In the turbulent flows of Figs 3.12B and 3.16 there is rapid increase of speed very close to the surface and relatively little further increase at increasing distance away from the surface.

Fig 3.13 repeats Fig 19.4 of *HPS-1*. Dr Walker (Dept of Hydraulic Engineering, University of Tasmania) set an aerofoil section with a chord of about 6in (150mm) in a channel through which water flowed at about 5 knots (8ft per sec; 2.5mps) and drew a line of ink on the foil surface from a to b using a squeeze bottle with a fine nozzle.

He set the foil at a small angle, which develops a laminar flow boundary layer – that is at the dynamic condition that develops the low-drag laminar flow 'bucket' from –1° to +1° in Fig 13.15 – and drew his line of ink. A smooth and gentle shading formed and drifted slowly towards the trailing edge (Fig 3.13A). The slowness and evenness of the process was as arresting as its smoothness. Even after ten seconds, traces of ink still clung to the trailing edge.

Dr Walker reset the foil to a greater angle – dynamically equivalent to say +4° in Fig 13.15, at which angle the foil runs with a turbulent flow boundary layer and with about twice the drag. The flow speed was unchanged, and he drew another line of ink. A coarse harsh streakiness instantly developed (Fig 3.13B). The detail of the pattern changed rapidly and many times as the ink tracer was diluted, until after about half a second all the ink had been swept away. The harshness of the pattern, the rapidity with which it changed, and the speed with which all the ink was swept away were surprising.

What this demonstration showed was not only the profound difference in the nature of the boundary layer flow and the energy at the surface as between laminar and turbulent flow. It showed too the way the eddies of turbulent flow organise themselves into 'parcels'. The dark streaks were parcels of water within which the ink was diffused and that were momentarily attached to the surface and near stationary. The intervening clear areas were newly arrived parcels of water without ink.

That there must be greater shear stress under the turbulent flow is obvious. To quote Abbott and Doenhoff: 'For turbulent flow ... the shearing stresses near the walls are considerably higher.' The low-drag 'bucket' in the drag curve of the NASA laminar flow aerofoil in Fig 13.15 (page 188) shows how great this difference is. Over the water surface the drag of the surface that holds back a parcel of air which is turbulent with high speeds at the surface will be about double the drag when the flow is laminar with gentle flow at the surface.

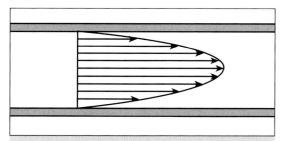

Fig 3.12A Velocity distribution across pipe

A When flow is laminar.

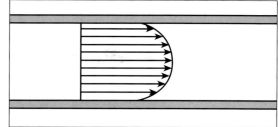

Fig 3.12B Velocity distribution across pipe

B When flow is turbulent.

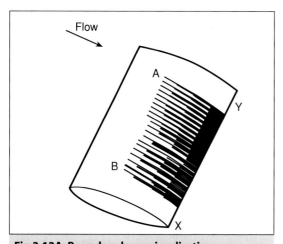

Fig 3.13A Boundary layer visualisation

A Appearance of ink in laminar flow.

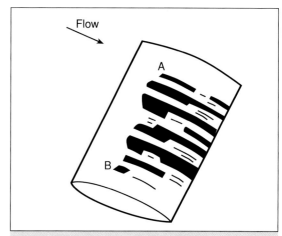

Fig 3.13B Boundary layer visualisation

B Appearance of ink in turbulent flow.

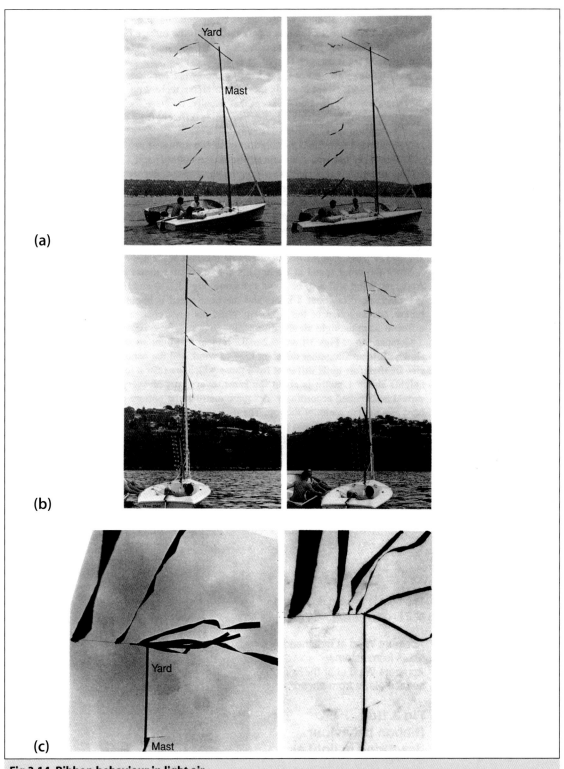

Fig 3.14 Ribbon behaviour in light air

(a) Ribbons show true wind of 4 knots at 6m; boat stationary.
(b) Broad reaching at 2 knots; view from astern.
(c) Broad reaching at 2 knots; view up ribbon halyard.

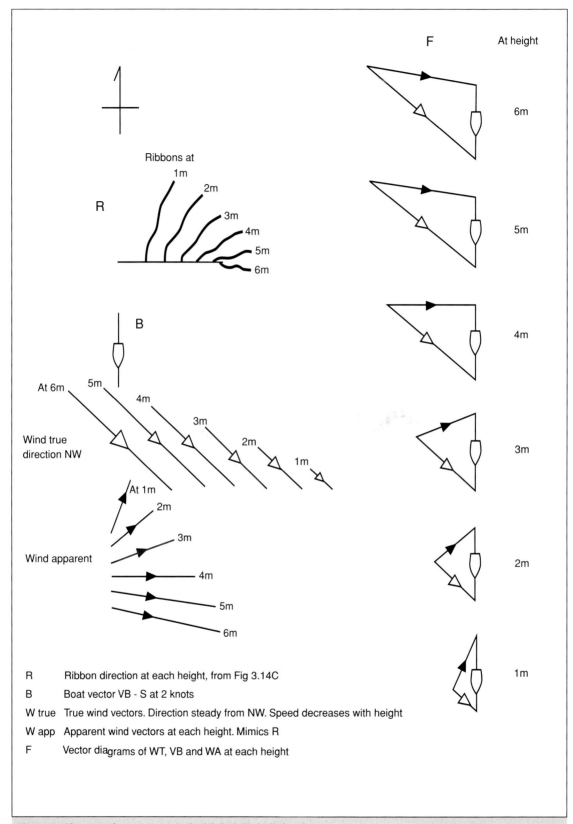

F At height

6m

Ribbons at
1m
2m
R 3m
4m
5m
6m

5m

B

4m

At 6m 5m
4m
Wind true 3m
direction NW 2m
1m

3m

At 1m
2m
3m
Wind apparent
4m
5m
6m

2m

1m

R Ribbon direction at each height, from Fig 3.14C
B Boat vector VB - S at 2 knots
W true True wind vectors. Direction steady from NW. Speed decreases with height
W app Apparent wind vectors at each height. Mimics R
F Vector diagrams of WT, VB and WA at each height

Fig 3.15 Change of apparent wind with height in light air

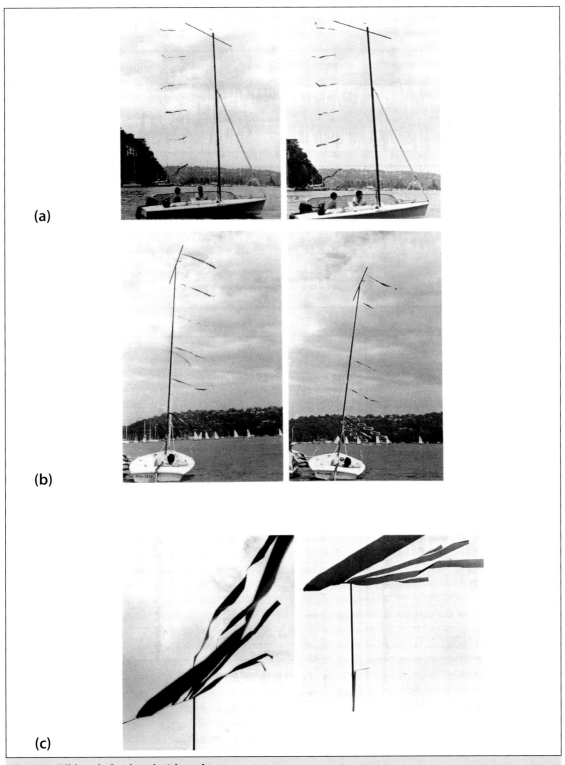

Fig 3.16 Ribbon behaviour in 8 knot breeze

(a) Ribbons show true wind; boat stationary.
(b) Ribbons show apparent wind in 4 knot broad reach; view from astern.
(c) Ribbons show apparent wind in 4 knot broad reach; view up halyard.

3.5 ■ Differences in scale between laboratory and nature

As between the glass tubes in Reynolds's laboratory, and the water surface of a bay or harbour, the three vast differences are depth and area, both of which are differences of scale, and the lack of any particular starting point, which is a difference of kind.

These turn out to be of critical importance to the racing sailor, because in a situation where there are patches of breeze and patches of light air there will be a very big difference in wind speed and drive force over the lower sails between sailing in the slow-moving lower layers of the thick laminar boundary layer of light air and sailing in the much faster-moving lower air above the thin boundary layer of the turbulent breeze a little distance away. The following sections explain why.

Depth

When the flow at the wall of one of Reynolds's relatively small tubes first trips turbulent, the turbulence only needs to thicken to the dimension of the tube radius before the whole of the flow becomes turbulent, so the transition from laminar to turbulent in a small tube is near instantaneous.

But over the harbour, the atmosphere is miles deep and the radius approaches infinity.

How far will the turbulence spread, and how long will it take to spread to its maximum depth?

Area

We have seen in Dr Walker's experiment (Fig 3.13 top) that the eddies of turbulent flow organise themselves into 'parcels'. Again, at the scale of the small tube, when the flow at some point on the tube wall first trips turbulent, there is not much option for the water adjacent to it to behave differently.

But even at the scale of the channel in which Dr Walker's model was immersed, we see that separate parcels can form and behave for a brief moment in a way different from the parcels adjacent.

The harbour, with a surface area millions of times that of the tube, offers each parcel and group of parcels a freedom to respond to the forces affecting them at that moment which is very different from the constriction of Reynolds's tubes.

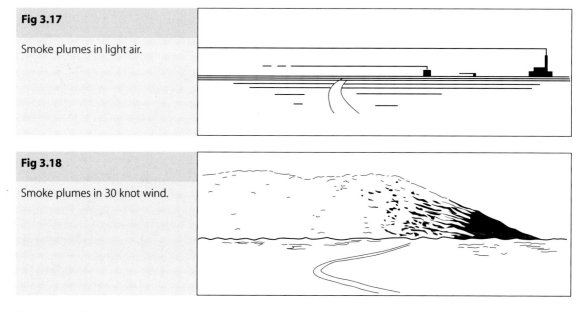

Fig 3.17

Smoke plumes in light air.

Fig 3.18

Smoke plumes in 30 knot wind.

Starting point

In Reynolds's tubes, there was always a starting point. At the entry of the tube the flow speed accelerated from zero in the holding tank to some finite speed in the tube. The boundary layer necessarily started at the entry of the tube, always thin, always laminar. As fluid passed along the tube, the boundary layer grew thicker. If the speed exceeded the critical flow rate, the flow tripped turbulent. These flows were always nascent, growing, changing. They are typical of the flows over the hull, the foils and the sails.

In nature, over the harbour, there is no single starting point nor starting time. Whether light air and laminar, or breeze and turbulent, the flow has everywhere started long ago and has grown and thickened and developed as fully as it is going to develop. Whether the wind speed is light air and the boundary layer laminar, or is faster breeze with a boundary layer fully turbulent, the flow everywhere has stopped growing and changing. Except at the critical speed at which a laminar flow will trip turbulent, or vice versa, it is everywhere mature and unchanging. It will carry on indefinitely as it is until the wind speed changes.

3.6 ■ The racing sailor's wind

How fast you can sail will depend partly on the wind speed, and partly on the way the wind speed changes between the water and your masthead. Between two sailors who sail the same sort of boat in the same 5 knot wind measured at a height of 50ft (the World Met Organisation standard), but with one sailing in a 5 knot wind with a velocity gradient such as Fig 3.19B (cooled), and the other in the velocity gradient shown in Fig 3.19A driven by a hot rough surface (reeds or waves), the second will sail about twice as fast as the first because he will get so much more drive from the stronger wind over his lower sails.

The velocity gradient

The way the wind speed changes with height above the surface is called the velocity gradient.

Most small high performance sailboats have masts 6–7m high, so the racing sailor is particularly interested in the wind from the surface up to about 6m. To understand what goes on in this layer, we need to look at several areas:

- Earlier work
- The light air (laminar flow) boundary layer at natural scale
- The velocity gradient in light air (laminar flow)
- The turbulent layer at natural scale
- The breeze (turbulent flow) boundary layer at natural scale
- The velocity gradient in breeze (turbulent flow)

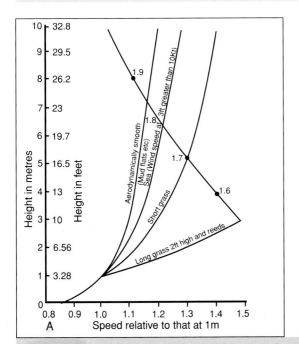
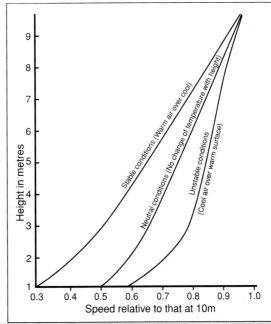

Fig 3.19 Change of speed at height with heat and roughness

Reproduced from *Wind and Sailing Boats*, by Alan Watts.

73

Earlier work

Alan Watts, in his 1965 *Wind and Sailing Boats*, presented the two diagrams that are repeated here as Fig 3.19A and B.

In Fig 3.19A he states that surface roughness such as adjacent reeds in a sheltered waterway, or waves in an open waterway, will not only promote turbulence, but can cause abnormally fast flow at a height of 2–3m. (It is interesting to note that Lindsay Cunningham (see Chapter 2) reports that the wind structure on the inland side of Sand Point sometimes reveals this characteristic.)

In Fig 3.19B Alan states that when conditions are unstable (ie when the water is warmer than the air) the thermal excitation will encourage the boundary layer to trip or remain turbulent. (This we can see as between the glassy water and ribbons showing laminar flow in Fig 3.14 and the rippled surface and socks showing turbulent flow in (a) in Fig 3.21. Both are in winds of about 4 knots.)

The light air (laminar flow) boundary layer at natural scale

In the 1980s, as part of my research into light air sailing, I needed to know more about the light air velocity gradient. The only published work at that time were the diagrams in Alan Watts's *Wind and Sailing Boats* (Fig 3.19). Alan states that the velocity gradient will vary with both change of surface roughness, Fig 3.19A, and will also change according to whether the air is being warmed or cooled by the water (Fig 3.19B). He says nothing about change of flow with change of wind speed.

Because of my understanding of aerodynamics and my practical experience with model aircraft, I believed that at low wind speeds the wind speed itself would probably have something to do with the velocity gradient, so in the late 1980s I set up the ribbon experiment shown in Figs 3.14 and 3.16, repeated from *HPS-1*, plus Fig 3.15.

This work was completed in the sheltered valleys of Upper Middle Harbour – the narrow waterways to the north of the main harbour shown in the inset in Fig 1.22. All the stability factors were towards the stable extreme. The scale of the waterway was small – about 2000m E–W and 400m N–S – the water was glassy smooth in calm or no more than rippled in breeze, and the warmer autumn air was being cooled by the cooler water. The ribbons of 'half ounce' spinnaker cloth weighed about 1g each.

From this ribbon experiment we observed that in those stable conditions the boundary layer and velocity gradient will take one of two forms – laminar or turbulent – and which form it takes will depend on the wind speed itself:

At free stream wind speeds from 0 up to about 5 knots, each layer of air up from the surface flows a little faster than the layer (lamina) below. The layers flow smoothly over each other and do not mix. This is like the filament of ink in Reynolds's tubes, or the smooth shading of the ink in Dr Walker's first demonstration (Fig 3.13A).

This laminar flow light air boundary layer is of particular interest to the small-boat sailor because it is so thick that he sails almost entirely within it. The wind in the free stream at height will blow at the speed governed by the gradient. When this speed is from zero to up to about 5 knots, the boundary layer in stable conditions takes the form revealed by the ribbons in Fig 3.14(a).

In Fig 3.14(a) the boat is stationary, so the ribbons of light spinnaker cloth at metre intervals are blown by, and reveal, the true wind. Because the air molecules that touch the surface come to rest, the wind speed at the surface is zero. This is indicated by the glassy appearance of the water surface; also, the near-vertical angle of the lowest ribbon. The other ribbons indicate progressively stronger true wind by streaming at progressively more horizontal angles with every extra metre of height up to about 5m. The angles of the ribbons at 5m and 6m are not much different. This shows that the boundary layer here is about 5m thick.

The rate of change of speed with height is called the velocity gradient. Fig 3.23B shows what the ribbons show: that the velocity gradient in light air is approximately linear; that is, if the speed at 5m is 5 knots, it will be about 4, 3, 2 and 1 knot at 4m, 3m, 2m and 1m above the surface. This mimics the near linear laminar velocity gradient in the tube (Fig 3.12A). There is never much wind speed nor drive force in the lower few metres of wind in light air.

Most small boats have rigs between 5m and 7m high, so what the ribbons show us is that in stable light air small boats sail almost entirely within this boundary layer. Only above 5m is there the free stream wind that is not slowed. This too remains laminar, as is shown by the smoke plumes in Fig 3.17, which were observed shortly after dawn near Narva in Estonia. The plumes remained pencil thin for distances of several miles.

This is called laminar flow. What is happening here is that the viscosity of the air is sufficient to suppress all turbulence. The sailor's principal visual clue that the boundary layer is laminar is the glassy surface of the water.

The effect of the lower wind speeds near the surface in light air on the direction of the apparent wind and the drive force from the sails is profound, in that it introduces huge and adverse twist in the apparent wind (the wind shown by the ribbons).

In Fig 3.14(a) the boat is stationary in a true wind of about 4 knots at the masthead, so the ribbons show the *true wind* at each height between the masthead and the surface.

In Fig 3.14(b) and (c) the true wind is the same at about 4 knots, but the boat is moving at 2 knots in a broad reaching direction, so the ribbons are blown by the *apparent wind*. Fig 3.14(b) is a view of the ribbons from behind, and Fig 3.14(c) is a view looking straight up the ribbon halyard.

Fig 3.15 is a series of vector diagrams that show in more detail what is going on in Fig 3.14(c). Vectors are arrows that show both the direction and also the speed – the longer the arrow, the faster the movement in the direction of the arrow.

'R' in Fig 3.15, 'ribbons at 1m, 2m' etc, shows the average direction of the two ribbons at 1m, 2m, etc (one from each picture) in the two photos in Fig 3.14(c).

'B' in Fig 3.15 is the boat vector. The boat is moving steadily south at 2 knots.

'W true' in Fig 3.15 gives the true wind vectors. The direction is steady from the NW, and the speed becomes progressively slower at lower heights. I have assumed that a gradient wind of 4 knots at and above 6m will blow at 3.8 knots at 5m, 3.2 knots at 4m, 2.4 knots at 3m, 1.6 knots at 2m, and 0.8 knots at 1m above the water surface.

'WA' gives the apparent wind vectors at each height. At 6m, the apparent wind is from a little north of W at 3.1 knots. As the true wind speed decreases and the boat speed stays the same, the apparent wind becomes lighter and swings forward until at 1m it blows from near ahead at 1.6 knots. The twist in the apparent wind between 6m and 1m is near 90°!

Column 'F' in Fig 3.15 gives the vector triangles from which the vectors in 'WA' are derived:

- The boat vector shows the boat to be moving steadily south at 2 knots.
- The True Wind vectors repeat the True Wind vectors of B.
- The Apparent Wind vectors, drawn bold and with the solid arrow heads, repeat the W apparent vectors, and show why the apparent wind goes light and swings so far forward at low level.

The WA vectors in 'W apparent' and 'F' closely mimic the ribbon speeds shown by the droops in Fig 3.14(b) and the ribbon directions shown in Fig 3.14(c). These are the two factors that result in so great a loss of 'power' from the lower sails when the surface goes glassy. They also point the way to recovering some of it – by twisting open the upper jib and mainsail leeches to extreme.

The velocity gradient in light air (laminar flow)

In light air the unchanging nature of the thick, viscous boundary layer defines the velocity gradient, as shown in Fig 3.23B. Every molecule is governed by viscosity. There is no other way it can flow. It has no energy to do otherwise.

The turbulent layer at natural scale

At some critical wind speed of about 6 knots in stable conditions, as low as 3 knots in unstable conditions (water warmer than air), and as high as 8 to 9 knots in extreme stable conditions (water much colder than air), the shear stress between the air momentarily touching and stuck to the surface and that moving freely above it becomes more than its viscosity can suppress, and the air then begins to roll and break up into tiny random eddies. What is happening is that the air is being rolled off the surface in a manner similar to the action of rolling your hand over a number of round pencils. All the eddies start by spinning in the same direction in a 'fine grain' flow. Every eddy is within the extended circulation of every other eddy, so in this way all the eddies are linked to and circle around each other in a well-mixed flow that sweeps along at a uniform average speed.

Close to where it starts, the turbulence is always 'fine grain' as in the smoke plumes in Fig 13.20, where the turbulence starts at the nozzle. This is typical of the flow over wings, sails, hulls and foils, where the turbulence starts where the boundary layer trips turbulent near the mast, bow or leading edge of the centreboard or rudder blade. Tufts on sails tremble in this 'fine grain' flow.

But the longer it lasts, the coarser the grain becomes, because any two adjacent eddies that spin in the same direction can merge and become one bigger eddy containing the energy of both. (You can see how this works if you make two eddies that spin in the same direction in your coffee cup – usually they will merge.) In this way, a tiny population of eddies, given time, can and do become very big. So in the case of the wind where the turbulence started many miles upwind, or many hours ago, the flow becomes a turbulent layer that is characterised by a

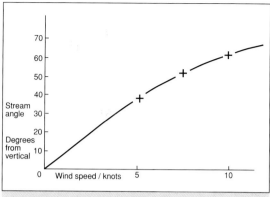

Fig 3.20 Windsock stream angle

coarseness of grain that at its extreme manifests itself in the universal gust-lull pattern of the wind.

In Fig 3.21(e) the displacement of some of the windsocks indicates the presence and effect of eddies of 2–3m in diameter. In Fig 5.2 the patterns indicate both the coarseness of the 'grain' and the presence of eddies of hundreds of metres in diameter.

In Fig 3.18 a brief intense grass fire released copious smoke into a 30 knot NW wind. The smoke viewed crosswind from 20 miles distance revealed the fully developed turbulent mixing process. The top of the turbulent layer was at about the 10 000ft level. The mixing, spinning eddies carried the smoke edge upwards at about 30° from its source – that is, at about half wind speed. This was observed looking SW near Goulburn in NSW.

| (a) | (b) | (c) | (d) | (e) | (f) |

Fig 3.21 Windsocks in katabatic and gradient winds

(a) and **(b)** 6 knot katabatic wind. **(c)** and **(d)** 7 knot gradient wind. **(e)** and **(f)** 9 knot gradient wind.

The breeze (turbulent flow) boundary layer at natural scale

Unlike laminar flow, each eddy is mobile and can move towards and away from the surface. Every eddy is to some extent within the extended circulation pattern of every other eddy. This results in intense mixing that carries all of the air along at about the same speed, except for a relatively thin layer about a metre thick just above the land or water surface.

In turbulent flow, eddies at free stream speed descend and scrub the surface and stick to it momentarily and are slowed by viscous shear, as we saw in Fig 3.13B. As soon as they are slowed, they are almost immediately undercut and replaced by newly arrived fast eddies. This 'scrubbing' action by high-speed parcels of air ripples the surface of the water. This rippled surface (as opposed to the glassy surface of light air) is the most visible indicator that the boundary layer has tripped turbulent. In Fig 3.16(a) the boat is stationary in a true wind of about 8 knots at the masthead, so, as in Fig 3.14(a), the ribbons show the *true wind* at each height. Only the lower ribbon droops steeply. The other ribbons all stream at about the same near-horizontal angle. What this shows with certainty is that only the lower metre of wind flows slowly, and that all wind at and above about 2m flows much faster. (But these ribbons are so light that once they stream near horizontally they cannot show us whether some may be in yet faster flow. This is a point I missed when analysing this experiment 20 years ago.)

Above the thin 1m thick boundary layer, the ribbons all stream at about the same angle, and this indicates a speed distribution that mimics the speed distribution of turbulent flow through the pipe in Fig 3.12B. Note the rippled water surface in this diagram.

In Fig 3.16(b) and (c) the true wind is the same at about 8 knots, but the boat is moving at 4 knots in a broad reaching direction, so the ribbons are blown by the *apparent wind*. Fig 3.16(b) is a view of the ribbons from behind the moving boat, and Fig 3.16(c) looks straight up the ribbon halyard. Because there is little change of speed with height in the true wind, there is little change in the direction of the apparent wind – that is, there is almost no twist.

The velocity gradient in breeze (turbulent flow)

Some years later I wanted to know more about the velocity gradient at 2m, 3m and 4m in winds of between 6 and 9 knots. When I looked more closely at Fig 3.16 I realised that a weakness of this experiment was that the very light weight of the 1g ribbons that made them so sensitive to changes in wind speed from 1 to 5 knots was so light that they were not sensitive to speed changes in stronger winds. This degree of lightness meant that they just streamed near horizontally in all winds stronger than about 5 knots.

So I ran another experiment, and this is the one shown in Fig 3.21. I made six tubular wind socks 485mm long and 75mm in diameter from 3.6oz sailcloth. Each weighs 25g – about 20 times the weight of the ribbons. We hung a sock from the end of a batten tied across the roof of a car, and measured the angles at which the sock streamed when moved at 5, 7.5 and 10 knots through calm air (Fig 3.20). As in Fig 3.14, the socks were then attached to a halyard at 1m intervals. A jetty with a boat-lift crane at its end is sited on the northeast corner of Lyne Park, which is the rectangular projection on the south shore of Rose Bay just south of the '14' in Fig 1.22. (It used to be Sydney's old flying boat base.) I used the crane and an 8m alloy tube to position the halyard 6m clear crosswind from the end of the jetty. A submerged half brick tied to the bottom of the halyard kept everything taut and steady.

On 12 September 2006, the usual early spring morning drainage westerly of about 12 knots under the bridge was as steady as wind can be. Water was at 18°C and the air flowing off the cold land at the water's edge was at the overnight minimum of 10°C. By the time it reached Rose Bay 3nm to the east, the air had been warmed to 16°C, was surging and fading

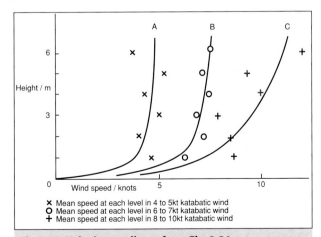

Fig 3.22 Velocity gradients from Fig. 3.21

from 7 to 4 knots – sometimes 3 knots – every few minutes, and slowly dying. Note the extreme instability of very cold air over warm water.

Figs 3.21(a) and (b) are two of ten images taken between 0930 and 1000; the view is northeast across the dying NW katabatic (drainage) wind.

The angle of every sock in every image was measured and a speed assigned from Fig 3.20 and the average speed calculated. Two images show the socks in a mean wind velocity of 7 knots, three in a mean wind of 5 knots, and five in a mean wind of 4 knots. In all ten, the socks were oscillating slightly in turbulence, but all streamed at consistent angles. Velocity gradient A in Fig 3.22 is the average of all ten of these pictures of the socks streaming in this shallow cold unstable drainage wind.

This is a classic turbulent flow boundary layer. As compared with the glassy water and steady laminar flow of Fig 3.14 in the enclosed valley waters of Upper Middle Harbour, the wind and water in this open fetch of the main harbour showed no trace of glassy surface nor laminar flow.

The conditions were different from those in Fig 3.14 in three respects:

1 The scale of the main harbour is ten times or more the scale of the narrow valley waterways. Further, there was stronger wind and a rougher water surface not far upwind.
2 The water surface was roughened by small waves instead of being glassy smooth.
3 The cold drainage air was being strongly heated as it flowed over the warmer water.

All three of these differences are unstable and encourage turbulent flow. From this experiment we see that the lower wind speed limit at which the boundary layer can trip turbulent may in some conditions be as low as 3 knots, possibly even as low as 2 knots.

The key clue of 'A glassy surface indicates laminar flow and the need to twist the sails' remains true.

As the day warmed, the cold drainage wind died to calm. By 1230 a gradient wind had started to blow from the east and over the next hour it filled in to a maximum of 9 to 10 knots, with peak gusts to 13 knots; air was 20°C over the water at 18°C. The prominent visible gust-lull pattern confirmed the presence of a deep turbulent layer. I identified approaching gusts or lulls, and when I judged the flow steadiest I measured the wind speed at 3.5m (eye level when standing on the jetty), picked up the camera, and took a picture. The field of view of Figs 3.21(c), (d), (e) and (f) is north-northeast across the east-southeast wind. Of 16 images, two have a mean velocity of 6 knots, four of 7 knots, three of 8 knots, five of 9 knots, and two of 10 knots. Velocity gradient B in Fig 3.22 is the mean of the 6 and 7 knot pictures, and C is the mean of those of 8, 9 and 10 knots. More samples would give smoother curves, but there are no surprises. These are all typical of turbulent flow boundary layers.

The most unexpected feature of this work was the way in which the behaviour of these extremely mobile and sensitive socks revealed the presence of vigorous eddies of 1, 2 and 3m diameter with a clarity that I have not previously seen.

About half the images show the socks streaming at about the angles expected. Fig 3.21(c) and (d) are two of these.

The surprise was that every few seconds a large and vigorous eddy would abruptly, momentarily and forcefully displace several socks. In Fig 3.21(e) the socks at 3m, 4m, 5m and 6m are being driven apart in an orderly manner by a large eddy; and in Fig 3.21(f) the 5m and 6m socks are being driven strongly apart by a smaller eddy. Note that some have been driven well above the horizontal. This contrasts strongly with the horizontal-only streaming in Fig 3.16.

The lessons from this day with the heavier socks, and in the much wider and more unstable arena of the main harbour, were:

• In the strongly unstable morning conditions (water much warmer than air) the boundary layer had tripped fully turbulent in winds as light as 3 knots at 3.5m.
• In the very normal later gradient wind the behaviour of the sensitive socks revealed that vigorous eddies of 2–3m diameter occur routinely in the 0–6m layer.

3.7 ▪ Summary of Section 3.6

Referring to Alan Watts's earlier work, plus the light ribbons experiment of Fig 3.14, and the heavier socks experiment of Fig 3.21 in different temperature stability regimes, we can summarise the findings.

The nature of the velocity gradient can change hour by hour according to three factors:

1 The wind speed.
2 The surface roughness – that is, whether or not there are waves.
3 The thermal stability – that is, whether the water is warmer or colder than the air.

Examples:

• At its most unstable – in large waters when the water has waves and is warmer than the air:

– In 0 to, say, 2 knots   The velocity gradient will be linear up to 5m to 6m.

– In more than 2 to 3 knots   The flow will trip turbulent with much stronger wind at the 1m to 4m levels than in stable conditions.

This type of velocity gradient is indicated in Fig 3.23A. On such days, the boat will sail fastest with little twist.

• At its most stable – in smaller waters when the water is smooth or rippled and is cooler than the air:

– In 0 to 5 knots   The velocity gradient will be linear up to 5m to 6m.

– In 5 to 10 knots   The velocity gradient will change more smoothly and with less wind speed between the 1m to 4m levels between 5 and 9 knots than in unstable conditions.

This pattern of velocity gradient is shown in Fig 3.23B. On such days, the boat will sail fastest with the upper leech wide open, twisted to extreme.

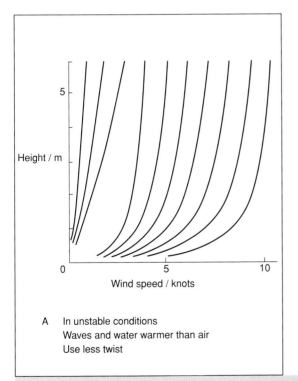

A   In unstable conditions
Waves and water warmer than air
Use less twist

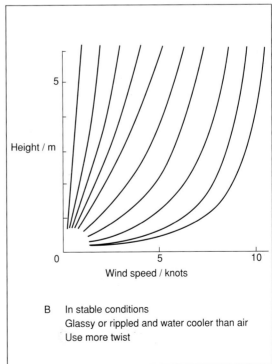

B   In stable conditions
Glassy or rippled and water cooler than air
Use more twist

Fig 3.23 Change of velocity gradient with wind speed, surface roughness and heat

3.8 ■ Consequences

The discovery that such big changes can occur in the wind's 'power' at the 2, 3 and 4m height in the same nominal low wind speeds, and that such big changes can occur as between relatively smooth flow and extremely rough and unsteady flow in the 6 to 10 knot wind speed range, go far towards explaining some 'mysteries'. For example:

- Why battened sails are faster than unbattened sails
  - The battens stiffen the sail and prevent it from distorting in the big eddies.
- Why some intolerant wing mast shapes behave poorly in unsteady winds
  - The momentary change in angle of attack can be very great, and outside the range of tolerance of that mast shape. Once flow is separated, these intolerant shapes are reluctant to reattach flow.
- Why automatic rigs behave so well in unsteady winds
  - Self-evident.
- Why some purported apparent wind 'skiffs' fail to deliver in some winds
  - That is, when the wind at 2, 3 and 4m is lighter than was expected.
- Why abnormal performance is sometimes observed
  - That is, when the winds above 2m are stronger than expected.

An example of abnormal performance

The object was to measure the on-the-water performance of the production 59er. It was a strange spring morning, with abnormally warm air at 30°C ahead of a weak front. The water was still at that year's winter low of 16°C, so the difference between the warm air temperature and the cold water temperature was huge.

For about 40 minutes the wind over the flat water in North Harbour (near Manly in Fig 1.22) alternated between glassy patches and rippled patches of about 100m to 200m diameter. From an adjacent motorboat I measured wind speeds of 5, 6 or 7 knots with a turbometer at eye level about 2m above the water. What was so strange was the performance of the 59er. Tacking downwind, it repeatedly sailed steadily at 12 knots and gybed through about 90°, even when passing through some of the glassy patches.

The 59er is quick – but it is not, and cannot be, *that* quick. I kept measuring these abnormally high speeds and waited for the wind to increase to get a range of measurements at higher wind speeds.

This did not occur. Clouds suddenly formed, erupted, the heavens opened and we retired in torrential rain, thunder and lightning.

It was only later that we realised that the abnormal performance of the boat in a wind measured at 6 knots at 2m was probably due to the abnormally great difference between air and water temperature that suppressed turbulence. The very cold water had stabilised the boundary layer to the point where it remained laminar at a wind speed at which it would normally have tripped turbulent. Had I been able to measure the wind at 3m, it would likely have been 8–9 knots, and more at higher levels, and this stronger wind at height would account for the higher-than-expected performance observed.

From my earlier ribbon experiment, I had assumed that any wind of 6 knots or stronger would trip turbulent. But in these chilled conditions, the wind stayed laminar. Therefore my measured 6 knots at 2m implied a wind of probably 8 to 9 knots at 3–4m, and the high boat speed was explained.

Summed up, these four sets of data from Alan Watts's book and my light ribbons and my heavier windsocks, and the abnormal boat performance in abnormally stable conditions, suggest that between, say, 2 knots and 8–9 knots there is no such thing as a 'normal' boundary layer, or a normal velocity gradient, or a normal intensity of turbulence.

We cannot see the wind; we understand that it is an unsteady flow. What we see from these indicators is that whether the boundary layer stays laminar or trips turbulent depends critically on both the wind speed, and on the temperature difference between air and water, and to a lesser extent on whether the water has small waves or is smooth. The lighter winds we sail in can vary widely in their flow speeds at different heights above the surface, in their unsteadiness, and in the 'grain size' of their turbulence. In some conditions, the unsteadiness can be much more unsteady than we might expect.

Through all of this the key indicator is whether the water surface is glassy or rippled. To sail fast when the surface is glassy, sail with maximum twist and ease to keep the *upper* leech ribbons alive. When the surface is rippled, trim with normal twist and trim to keep *all* the leech ribbons alive.

THE WIND ABOVE THE BOUNDARY LAYER

3.9 ■ Calm

Cooled air

Imagine a day with no gradient – for example, in the middle of a high.

If the water or land surface is at the same temperature as the air or colder, then the air at low levels will remain motionless. At a higher level it will become part of the generally westerly flows which always exist in the upper atmosphere.

Heated air

If the surface is a little warmer than the air, isolated thermals will form and rise. Often these take the form of intermittent bubbles that rise from the same warmer source. Between the isolated rising columns, air will subside gently over large areas. At the surface, a local, intermittent inflow pattern will establish towards the base of each thermal to complete the loop. In this situation, the surface wind speed will be greatest close to the base of the rising air, as shown in Fig 3.24.

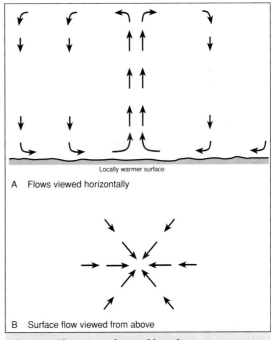

A Flows viewed horizontally

B Surface flow viewed from above

Fig 3.24 Flow near thermal in calm

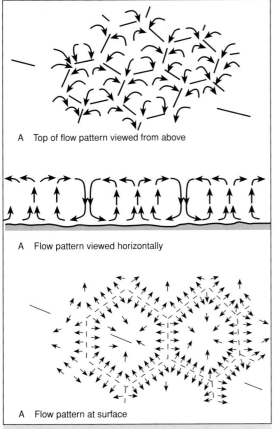

A Top of flow pattern viewed from above

A Flow pattern viewed horizontally

A Flow pattern at surface

Fig 3.25 Flow patterns within clustered cells

As the surface becomes progressively warmer than the air, the rising thermals will become more numerous, cluster more closely, and finally may assume a hexagonal cellular pattern, as in Fig 3.25. As they cluster more tightly the viscosity difference between warmer air ('thicker' viscosity) and cooler air ('thinner' viscosity) changes the dynamics at height and the nature of the surface flows. The rising cores are necessarily warmer. Between the cores it will be the coolest air that subsides, and because it flows more easily this cooler less viscous air will concentrate into thin relatively fast-moving 'curtains' of descending air that split at the surface and flow outwards in both directions. These become the highest speeds at the surface in this pattern.

Looking at Fig 3.25, it is clear that two boats only a few metres apart can experience completely different winds.

3.10 ■ Light air and its two layers

In light air the wind flows in two layers:
1   The first layer, from the surface to about 5m, will be the slowed laminar boundary layer as described in Section 3.5.
2   Above the boundary layer is the free stream.
   • It is not slowed.
   • It is not turbulent (Fig 3.17).
   • It flows horizontally (Fig 3.17).
   • There is no inherent limit to its depth.

Cooled air

When the surface is cooler than the air, or at the same temperature as it, both wind speed and wind direction will be relatively steady. Fig 3.4, 'Light air cooled', is a typical trace of light air over a cool surface. Fig 3.17 is a sketch of smoke plumes in Estonia over a cool surface in light air.

Heated air

When the surface is warmer than the air, the surface flow near any isolated thermal that is carried along within the light air will be a combination of the flow near the thermal in Fig 3.24 and the flow of the light air, and this will develop a local surface flow pattern such as that shown in Fig 3.26. A boat on starboard tack that sails from **a** to **e** would sail in, say, a 4 knot easterly at **a**, a 2 knot southeasterly at **b**, a 3 knot westerly at **c**, a 7 knot northeasterly at **d**, and be back in its 4 knot easterly at **e**.

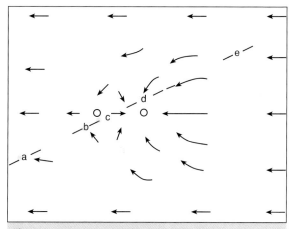

Fig 3.26 Pattern near thermal in light air

When more intense heating forms clustered cells that move with the light air, the speed and direction trace of Fig 3.5 represents the extreme of the unsteadiness that can develop. On this day, a 3 knot light air at 20°C was flowing over the water of Lake Ontario, which was at 23°C. The resultant intense clustered cell circulation generated inflow speeds of about 3 knots – that is, about the speed of the wind itself. So the speed trace shows a series of gusts of 3 plus 3 knots = 6 knots, and a series of lulls of 3 minus 3 knots = momentary calms.

The direction trace swings wildly and irregularly through plus and minus 20° as the crosswind inflows bias the direction. The backs and clocks are not correlated with the gusts and calms.

The size of the cells that drove these inflows can be calculated. There are 13 gust peaks in 15 minutes, so there was one every 70 seconds. The mean speed is 3 knots or 5ft per second, so these cells were spaced about 210ft or 65m apart.

Above the surface, thermal loops will be present in the lower levels of the free stream, but their influence on its flow will be trivial.

This two-layer organisation of the atmosphere contrasts profoundly with Sections 3.11 and 3.12 below.

3.11 ■ Breeze and its three layers

In breezes, the air flows in not two recognisably different layers, but in three:
1   At the surface there is the slowed turbulent boundary layer that is about 1m thick.
2   Above this is a turbulent layer, deep, which looks like a free stream, but isn't quite free:
   • It is uniformly turbulent throughout its depth.
   • It is slowed towards the surface because turbulent mixing links it to the boundary layer and its surface skin friction. A 10 knot surface wind will typically blow at 15 knots at 1000ft.

- Its depth is inherently limited.
- Its flow will be horizontal on average, but within it parcels of air move freely away from, and towards, the surface as indicated by the spread upwards of smoke from a grass fire (Fig 3.18).

3 Above this turbulent layer is the free stream; like the light air free stream, this:
- Is not turbulent.
- Is not slowed.
- Is not inherently limited in depth.
- Flows horizontally.

3.12 ■ The turbulent layer

The turbulent layer is of critical importance to the sailor because within it are born four of the patterns that are so important to him when racing. That is:
1 Quick gust peaks every few seconds.
2 Gusts and lulls about every minute.
3 Surges and fades every five minutes or so.
4 Roll motions, usually every ten to thirty minutes.

These creatures of the turbulent layer reflect its properties. On a day when the turbulent layer is low-energy and stable, all of its offshoots will be similar and at their most predictable, and vice versa.

Only the cold drainage wind mechanisms occur below, and relatively independently of, the turbulent layer. A good 'feel' for this turbulent layer is the starting point for anticipating the behaviour of the day's wind. The turbulent layer is one major meteorological entity that the sailor can rely upon *not* to change quickly, unless:

- A cold front changes the air mass.
- A local sea or lake breeze develops. This will create a new, local, more shallow turbulent layer within, and at the base of, the existing layer.

The three key properties that will influence the nature of the turbulent layer are:

- *Depth*. This will be influenced by wind speed, heat and the subsidence inversion.
- *Energy*. This will be controlled by wind speed and heat.
- *Stability*. This will be influenced most strongly by the presence of a strong subsidence inversion.

Depth

We can estimate the depth of the turbulent layer in several ways, but the primary indicator is wind speed. Published meteorological texts suggest that in cool conditions and when there is no added heat and no subsidence inversion:

- When the surface wind is 6 knots, the layer is about 500m thick (1600ft)
- When the surface wind is 10 knots, the layer is about 1000m thick (3000ft)
- When the surface wind is 20 knots, the layer is about 2000m thick (6000ft).

What happens is that the turbulence generated by surface friction spreads upwards until it is balanced by the natural stability of the atmosphere which resists the lifting, expansion and cooling due to turbulence. The smoke plume shown in Fig 3.18 gives a good mental picture of the process.

Fig 3.27 shows what happens. As surface air is lifted by the turbulence it expands and cools. The rate of change of its temperature as it rises is about 10°C per kilometre (3°C per 1000ft), and is shown by the slopes w–x and y–z. This is called the dry adiabatic lapse rate (adiabatic means that no heat is added or removed).

Over the whole of the Earth's surface the average lapse rate is about 2°C per 1000ft. You can understand why if you consider the heat budget of the lower-level air as it makes its tortuous way from Pole to Equator. At the Pole, it is heated by compression as it subsides in the polar highs, but it is then cooled by contact with the cold ice over vast areas. At the Poles there is not only little sun; heat is lost by radiation into space through the clear skies of the polar highs. From that cold start, as it moves towards the Equator, it is heated not by one heat source but by *two*. The obvious one is that it picks up heat at low level from the progressively warmer land and water surfaces over which it flows. The less obvious one is that about half the radiant energy received by the Earth from the sun is expended in evaporating the oceans' water into water vapour which is carried, dissolved in the air, for many thousands of miles, until it becomes part of a low, front or trough where air rises and expands, cools as it expands, and condenses into water droplets that form clouds which rain. As the water vapour condenses into liquid water, the vast amounts of latent heat that were used to evaporate it in the first place are released into the atmosphere, but this time not at the surface but *at cloud level*. This is why the upper levels of the lower atmosphere are warmer than one might expect.

Now back to our turbulent layer. Let us start in imagination in the middle of a high with no gradient, no wind, no turbulence, no turbulent layer. At any point and time the ambient lapse rate can differ widely from the average, but must always be less than the dry adiabat. Let us assume the global average 2°C per 1000ft shown in Fig 3.1; this is the wavy line A–B

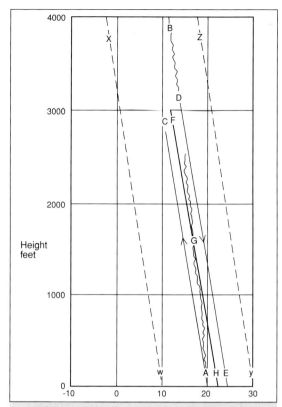

Fig 3.27 Mechanism of turbulent inversion

in Fig 3.27. The high moves, a gradient develops, the wind speed rises to 10 knots, and the boundary layer becomes turbulent. The turbulence spreads upward, and the rising eddies mix the air which then behaves more like a uniform mass, and so cools along the dry adiabat A–C (parallel with w–x). Air rising from the surface from A to C is replaced by air which subsides from D, compresses, and warms as it subsides along D–E (parallel to A–C). Air going up and cooling mixes with air coming down and warming, so the turbulent layer stabilises about the temperatures F–G–H.

Note that the cooled air at F is now colder than the adjacent air just above at D, so will sink to G unless kept at level F by the energy of the turbulence driving it upwards. This energy derives ultimately from the surface friction and is not limitless. The deeper the layer becomes, the greater will be the temperature difference between F and D, and the more energy will be required to keep the expanded colder upper level of the turbulent layer at its new height.

So the turbulence will spread upwards until a balance is reached between the energy generated by surface friction which becomes the turbulence which drives the air up, and the energy expended in keeping the top of the colder denser turbulent mixed layer higher than it wants to be.

This explains why, everything being equal, the depth of the turbulent layer will be thinnest in 6 knot winds and will become thicker as the wind speed becomes stronger.

Note particularly that because F must always be colder than D, every turbulent layer must be capped by a 'turbulence inversion'.

These depths will change when other things are *not* equal. The two primary factors are heat and the subsidence inversion.

Heat

Consider an onshore gradient wind of 6 knots or stronger which is blowing onto a flat tropical coast at about dawn. The temperature of the land surface will be about the same as the temperature of the sea. No heat will be added, so there will be no change in the thickness of the turbulent layer as between far out to sea, the coast, and a small lake at a distance inland from the coast.

As the day progresses and the dry land surface (but not the ocean's water) heats to its mid-afternoon maximum temperature, heat will be added, by conduction, to the air flowing over the land – but not over the water. So the thickness of the layer over the sea and coast will not change, but the thickness over the land will increase until the energy generated by both the unchanged surface friction, plus now the extra energy added by the hot land surface, balance the energy absorbed by 'keeping the top turbulent air up'.

Smooth green fields will heat the air least, and the bitumen, concrete and tiles of a built-up city will heat it most. At the extreme, tropical heat can double the thickness over inland desert areas and will greatly increase the instability.

So a group of sailors racing at the coast and another group racing on the inland lake can expect to sail in about the same wind speed because the gradient is the same, but in very different patterns of quick gust peaks, gusts and lulls, surges and fades, and oscillating winds because the depth, energy and unsteadiness of the turbulent layer over the inland lake will be greater than at the coast because of the intervening heated land surface with its heating of the lower air.

Subsidence inversion

The highs and lows of the weather map indicate not only where the pressures are higher and lower. They also indicate where the air is rising and subsiding.

Lows are areas of low pressure where the surface air spirals inwards, converges, rises, cools as it expands, and the cooling condenses water vapour into water droplets that form clouds and rain. As it condenses, the water vapour releases huge amounts of latent heat that warms the air which rises further and so tends to deepen the lows and tighten the gradients around them. This release of latent heat in low pressure areas is one of the factors that drives local winds. The extreme example is the hurricane.

Imagine that somebody has painted a piece of air blue so that we can watch it for a week or more. At a latitude of about 30° north or south the high–low repetition frequency averages about seven days, and the huge 'waves' with highs as the crests and lows as the troughs are at a wave-length of about 3000nm, so they can be thought of as waves that are flowing through the atmosphere west to east at about 20 knots. The air of the lower atmosphere will be flowing from Pole to Equator at an average speed of about 5 knots, but via a tortuous route. Let us start watching as a high approaches. On the first one or two days we might see our blue air moving some hundreds of miles towards the Equator in the leading edge of a high. At this point there will have been no time for the air to subside far, so there will be none or only a trivial subsidence inversion. As the middle of the high moves over the area, our blue air will spend several days going nowhere except down. During this period a subsidence inversion will form and grow more and more intense. Then, as the next trough or front approaches, there will be a day or two moving polewards, then another day being spun around and rising in a low; it will then do it all over again, but each time closer to the Equator.

Highs are areas where the air spirals outwards away from the higher pressure towards the lower pressure all around. The air that flows away can be replaced from only one source – higher-level air subsides to 'fill the gap'. In the middle of each high the whole mass of air sinks – well, *almost* all. As all the air in the high tries to sink, the air nearest the ground or water cannot sink because the ground or water surface is there, so what happens is that all the air above some lower layer sinks until its divergent spiralling allows it to escape outwards. The lowest layer stays put because it cannot do anything else. The air that subsides compresses and warms, and the longer the high lasts in that area the further it subsides and the more it compresses and warms.

In practice, the subsiding air treats the blocked air as if it were the surface, and separates from it by the mechanism of a subsidence inversion. Their typical height is 3000–4000ft. Subsidence inversions start small, but in latitudes where highs last several days they grow day by day until they become intense. Above this the air subsides and spirals outwards and diverges. Below it, the blocked air stays blocked.

Fig 3.28 shows what happens. The mechanism is the same as in Fig 3.27, but is reversed and is larger. Let us assume that a front has just passed, that the air at 20 000ft is at −20°C, and that the ambient lapse rate is the world average of 2°C per 1000 feet. This is the wavy line A–B in Fig 3.28. The dry adiabat of 3°C per 1000ft is shown by the dashed line A–C. As the days pass, the air at A subsides to level D, but as it subsides it compresses and warms (parallel with A–C) to finish at E. Air from D finishes at G, and air from F finishes at H and K. All air above K has warmed from DFJ to EGK, and is subsiding and spiralling outwards. But the air at J cannot subside, so does not compress and warm, and stays at its original temperature.

J–K is the subsidence inversion. It becomes more intense day by day.

When the subsidence inversion becomes strongly established it will combine with any turbulence inversion and push it lower, and in this way will limit the depth of the turbulent layer to something lower than might be expected due to the wind speed and temperature.

As with the much weaker turbulence inversion, the wind usually blows more strongly above the subsidence inversion. When clouds are present, the slope of the clouds reveals the gradient between the two winds. (Air in the centre of a non-raining cumulus cloud always rises.)

Whether or not a subsidence inversion exists has a profound effect on the steadiness of the wind below it. The flows of the turbulent layer under subsidence inversions are among the more stable of the atmosphere's motions:

- Fig 3.29B is repeated from *HPS-1*. It shows a plot of the wind direction traces hour by hour at Kingston airport on 'low dominant' days – that is, days when the isobars were curved as around a nearby low. On such days the air will be rising in a 'low dominant' synoptic situation so there can be no subsidence inversion. The dominant characteristic of these plots from the sailor's point of view is the unsteadiness and unpredictability of the wind direction.

- Fig 3.29A is a plot of the Kingston airport traces on 'high dominant' days on which a subsidence inversion would have been suppressing and capping the height of the turbulent layer. It shows that on such days the wind direction is very much more consistent.

- Roll motions that are regular are normal. When fair weather cumuli form, their flattened tops mark the presence of – and the height of – the subsidence inversion, and their arrangement in 'streets' reveals that the rolls are in ordered and regular arrangement. Fig 3.30, a photo of roll clouds taken from space (repeated from *HPS-1*), shows such order.

Note that the high overhead–low overhead repetition frequency grades from weeks in the great subtropical anticyclones with their regular trade winds, through progressively shorter periods at higher latitudes, until at the latitude

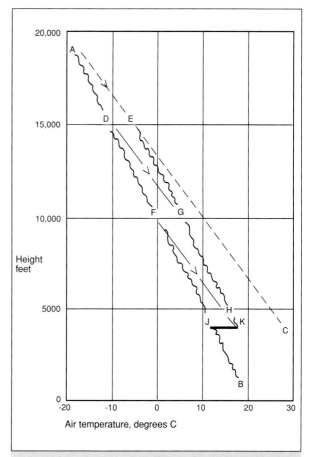

Fig 3.28 Mechanism of subsidence inversion

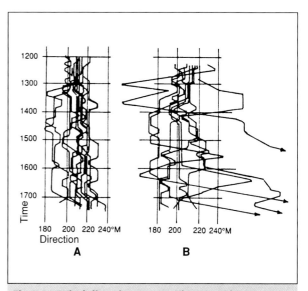

Fig 3.29 Wind direction traces, Kingston airport

A On high dominant days.
B On low dominant days.

Fig 3.30 Roll clouds from space

Cumulus cloud lines are spaced about one and a half miles apart near the centre of the photo. Courtesy of NASA.

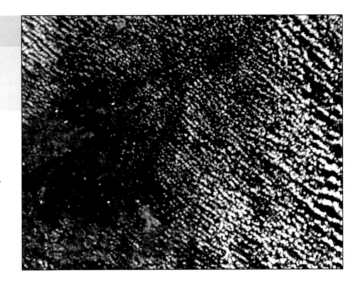

of Helsinki there may be one or more high–low cycles per day.

Because air takes time to subside, it follows that the stabilising influence of the subsidence inversion will be greater nearer the Equator, where a high can persist over an area for many days – and less nearer the Poles.

Summary

The concept of the turbulent layer as the matrix from which the gust peaks, the gusts and lulls, the surges and fades, and the backs and clocks of the roll motions all originate provides sailors with a powerful race planning tool:

- Depth can be estimated from the forecast or observed wind speed. When clouds are present, depth can be observed directly by their flattened tops.
  - The deeper the turbulent layer, the less predictable will be the wind patterns.
- Heat excitation can be estimated from latitude, season, time of day, cloud cover, albedo (heat absorption characteristics of the upwind surface – water will heat the air least, green fields not much more, the bitumen and tiles of a city the most).
  - The greater the heat input, the more coarse-grained, energetic and irregular will be the patterns.
- If the local isobars are curved as around a low (ie a low dominant situation), there can be no subsidence inversion.
  - In any low dominant situation, expect irregularity.
- The presence of a subsidence inversion can be inferred from a high on the weather map. If the local isobars are curved as around a high (ie a high dominant situation), there will be a subsidence inversion, and the longer the high has been locally dominant, the more intense will be the subsidence inversion.
  - In any high dominant situation, expect regularity. The longer the situation has persisted, the greater will be the regularity and stability.
- Any inversion can be observed directly if clouds are present.
  - Flattened cloud tops reveal its depth; an arrangement of roll clouds in streets reveals both the presence of rolls, and the fact that the rolls are regularly ordered.
  - Oscillating backs and clocks in the wind direction will be correlated with the cloud streets in the sense that the bias in the direction of the surface wind will be towards the base of the column/curtain of rising air, the top of which is indicated by the cloud street (sometimes there is displacement because the curtain may slope).
  - Observation of roll clouds approaching and passing overhead can be used for quite accurate anticipation of the next back or clock.

The following notes about the turbulent layer are included for interest:

- The even distribution of the all-pervading turbulence can be sensed from Fig 3.18. There is no change in the slope at which the smoke from the grass fire spreads upwards.
- The extraordinary range of the sizes of the eddies can be sensed from Fig 5.2 (Sherlock and Stout).
- Whenever you depart from or approach an airport, you can feel the aircraft move restlessly in the turbulent layer. In the free stream above the subsidence inversion, all is usually silky smooth.

- When even the smallest clouds form, they indicate the top of the turbulent layer clearly. Often, when there are no clouds, the turbulent layer contains dust and other particles that are swept up from the surface in volume sufficient to make the lower air more opaque. A pilot who looks through the clearer upper air along the upper surface of the more opaque lower air can see the upper surface clearly for a few seconds as he climbs or descends through the layer. I have seen this often, but I have never even *once* seen it without waves. Always it has looked like a low ocean swell with a wave-length of several miles. These waves indicate the presence of roll motions.

3.13 ■ Aspects of the turbulent layer

Quick gust peaks

Gusts form in the turbulent layer, and quick gust peaks form within the gusts. Chapter 5 (page 101) discusses these unexpectedly quick changes in wind speed.

Gusts and lulls

Gusts are creatures of the turbulent layer. A tiny proportion of eddies keep on combining with other eddies and continue growing until they become huge, and Fig 5.2 (Sherlock and Stout) reveals some of them. Of these, some will stay at their level and dissipate with time. Some will be overtaken by a slightly faster average wind and spiral upwards like an undercut tennis ball until they twist the edges of any clouds that may have formed at the top of the turbulent layer (*HPS-1*, page 38). These I call 'curlies'. Some will enter wind slightly slower and, still moving at their higher mid-turbulent-layer speed, will wind themselves down through the progressively slower lower air like a topspun tennis ball until they reach the surface where they will undercut the slower lull wind and spread themselves over the surface. These we call gusts.

Fig 3.31A shows how a rising plume of heated smoke is being twisted by a series of big eddies at a spacing that will pass over a fixed point at about 1 minute intervals. After about 2 minutes in moderate wind, 4 minutes in strong (20 to 25 knot) wind, surface friction will slow the gust to the surface wind speed appropriate to the gradient. This slowed flow we call 'lull'.

In the same way as big waves cannot form in shallow water, big eddies cannot form in thin turbulent

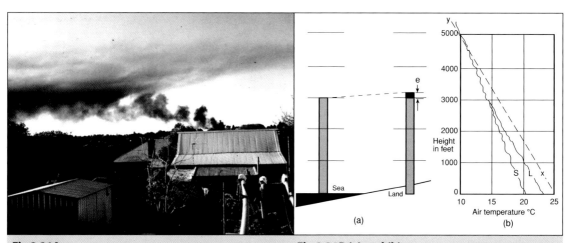

Fig 3.31A
A sea breeze mechanism revealed by a smoke tracer

Fig 3.31B (a) and (b)

The photo was taken at Naremburn, Sydney, Australia. The fire was caused by a burning fuel tanker 6km away at Forestville (approximately 20 000ft to the north). The coast is 10km to the east (to the right). The easterly sea breeze is about 12 knots (20fps); there is counterflow from WNW. Note smoke forming an inverted 'puddle' at the height of the inversion at the top of the sea breeze and base of the counterflow is at 2500ft. The spacing of the big eddies is about one every 1200ft. This is the gust mechanism made visible.

layers, so the smoothest breezes (turbulent winds) are the lighter breezes with the shallowest turbulent layers over cool surfaces, and particularly the abnormally shallow turbulent layers of the sea and lake breezes. (Fig 3.31A is a classic sea breeze situation.) The biggest and harshest gusts are the creatures of the deep turbulent layers of strong winds over hot surfaces.

Surges and fades

These are discussed in Chapter 6 on page 108. We do not yet know enough about surges and fades to be certain from where they come. But because they appear to exist only when the turbulent layer is present, it seems highly probable that they too are creatures of the turbulent layer.

The roll mechanism and oscillating winds

Rolls form in the turbulent layer, and they are often revealed by cloud streets, as in Fig 3.30. Rolls cause the wind's oscillating back and clock patterns which may repeat regularly or at random.

3.14 ■ The thin turbulent layers – the sea and lake breezes

The sea and lake breeze mechanism was covered in detail in *HPS-1* (Chapter 9). These notes summarise the mechanism and cover the new thinking between 1992 and 2008.

Wherever dry land, which can heat many degrees during daylight hours, meets water that barely heats on any one day, sea breezes are likely to be common. These are shallow, thermally driven loop flows that occur at the base of either the free stream in light air, or of the turbulent layer in wind. The mechanism is identical, but at a miniscule scale compared with that which drives the global gradient winds, and it is strongly influenced by the direction of the local gradient wind.

Consider a featureless coastline at dawn. The gradient wind is calm, and the sea and the land surface temperatures are the same – say, 20°C. The surface air temperatures will usually be very close to the surface land and water temperatures. Let us assume that the air temperatures and pressures at the surface and at every height both offshore and a little way inland are the same as column 'sea' in Fig 3.31B(a) and that the ambient lapse rate is the world norm of 2°C per 1000ft as S in Fig 3.31B(b).

As the day warms, let us assume a very modest surface air temperature increase of 3°C over the land. The air temperature plot will now look like L in Fig 3.31B(b). The warm bubbles rising from the surface will expand and cool at the dry adiabat of 3°C per 1000ft (x–y), and reach equilibrium with the local air at 3000ft. The atmosphere from surface to 3000ft will have become on average about 1.5°C warmer than over the sea. It will have expanded about 1.5/273 × 3000ft = 16.5ft ('e', shaded and not to scale at top of the 'land' column). At sea level, the change of pressure with height is about 1mb every 30ft. So what has happened is that the increase in land surface temperature has expanded the lower air over the land and caused a pressure increase of 0.55mb at and above 3000ft, but not at the surface. (The mechanism is identical with that in Fig 3.2.) Therefore no change has occurred anywhere over the sea. So at and above 3000ft an offshore flow of air starts, driven by the now higher pressure over the land towards the unchanged pressure at the same level over the sea. This offshore flow of air with mass reduces the hydrostatic surface pressure over the land and increases it over the sea. A surface flow then starts of air from the now higher surface pressure over the sea towards the now lower surface pressure over the land. We call this flow a 'sea' or 'lake' breeze. Note that there is now warmer air flowing offshore over cooler air flowing inshore (see Fig 3.31A). The air flowing inshore – the sea breeze we sail in – has itself become a turbulent layer capped by an inversion, but in this case its depth is so shallow that it can exist within whatever normal deep turbulent layer may exist at the time.

From the viewpoint of a pilot who is flying at 10 000ft across a coastline in an offshore gradient wind during the hour or two after dawn, he will see an uninterrupted offshore wind from far inland to far out to sea. But at mid-afternoon on days with a well-established sea breeze he will see the offshore surface wind die, say, 15 miles inland, and be replaced by the onshore sea breeze about 10 miles inland. The onshore sea breeze will typically extend across the coast and from 2 to 10 miles offshore, depending on whether the gradient wind is convergent or divergent at the coast. (Refer to the paragraph below.) Further out to sea the offshore gradient wind will re-establish. At the pilot's height of 10 000ft or above, the offshore tailwind will have blown steadily all the time, completely unaffected by the shallow goings-on below. From his vantage point he sees the sea breeze as a shallow surface flow local to the heated coast.

If somebody could paint the sea breeze flow blue, the pilot would further see that the onshore surface flow was part of a flattened loop. He would see a slower deeper offshore counterflow just above the shallow faster onshore surface flow, and observe that the offshore counterflow slows offshore, subsides to fill the void formed by the onshore surface flow, is cooled by contact with the cooler water, reverses direction, and becomes part of the shallow cool onshore sea breeze flow. As soon as it crosses the coast, this flow is strongly heated by the hotter land surface, expands, and rises. In expanding, it lifts the air above it which then starts to flow offshore (the counterflow). In rising, it becomes part of that offshore counterflow. Because it has been heated it is now warmer than the cool onshore flow, so there is a temperature inversion (hotter air above cooler) between the lower onshore flow and the counterflow above it – thus they do not mix.

The whole system is a closed loop. Fig 3.31A shows this mechanism in action over Sydney, as revealed by smoke as a tracer. Sydney's climate is one in which NE sea breezes are the prevailing winds in summer. Bankstown, the city's second airport, is 30km inland and records regular sea breezes from late morning until late afternoon in summer, so the sea breeze front routinely extends 40km or more inland. The photo in Fig 3.31A shows the behaviour of copious smoke and heat released into this sea breeze mechanism at a point 10km from the coast (to the right).

The heat causes the plume to rise, and the ENE sea breeze flow sweeps the plume to the left as it rises, and twists the plume with the sea breeze's own eddies. These are spaced at about 1200ft, which in a 12 knot or 20fps flow is one eddy per 60 seconds, so this is the gust–lull mechanism made visible. At about 2500ft the plume reaches the inversion, can rise no further, so forms an inverted 'puddle', from the top of which it is swept to the right, from the WNW, in the counterflow.

Every part of the loop must flow freely, or the fragile sea breeze will die. This is why what starts and is driven by local heating is so strongly influenced by other factors.

From a sailor's viewpoint, he may have sailed the morning races in an unsteady, unpredictable offshore gradient wind at the base of a turbulent layer many thousands of feet deep. The wind from 0900 to 1200 in Fig 3.32 is typical. With the day's heating, a sea breeze will set in, and this is what he will sail in for the afternoon races, as from 1200 until sundown in Fig 3.32. He sees it as a turbulent layer from an onshore direction and of different depth – one so shallow and so stabilised by a low inversion that its stability and predictability are legendary. Compare both the speed and the direction traces pre-noon and afternoon in Fig 3.32.

The strength of the sea breeze and depth of its turbulent layer will be profoundly influenced by the direction of the gradient wind, due to the quadrant effect. This was worked out by David Houghton, a British meteorologist and Olympic coach and author of many books on wind. It is discussed with respect as to whether or not a sea breeze will develop and its strength in *HPS-1* (Chapter 9). The notes below will add the further considerations of the depth of the turbulent layer and the consequent stability of the surface flow.

As an example, let us start by assuming a sunny, relatively cloudless day over the English Channel, that the gradient wind is calm, and that a southerly sea breeze has established from the Channel onto the English south coast and a northerly sea breeze from the Channel onto the French north coast – as in Fig 3.33.

Let us look at what happens to the sea breeze over the English coast when the gradient wind begins to blow from different directions:

Southerly gradient wind

Let us assume that a southerly gradient wind starts blowing. Far from augmenting the existing southerly sea breeze, this wind at height will oppose the offshore counterflow, and the sea breeze will fade or die. Unless the gradient wind is weak, the southerly gradient wind will replace the sea breeze. This may be the same strength and direction as was the sea breeze, so it may look like a sea breeze. But there will be a critical difference: the turbulent layer will be between two and five times as deep, and what was a steady oscillating sea breeze with trivial gusts will develop significant gusts and become irregular in both speed and direction. A further point is that a sea breeze will clock with Coriolis (unless local factors make it a funnelling wind). The gradient wind is already fully clocked, so will not clock further.

A sea or lake breeze cannot exist in a moderate or strong onshore gradient wind.

Easterly gradient wind

If the gradient wind blows from the east, this creates a convergent situation along the English south coast. The 'east' column in Fig 3.33 shows the mechanism. For there to be an east gradient, there has to be higher

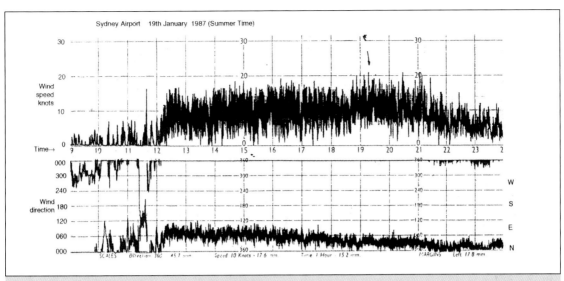

Fig 3.32 Dynes anemograph trace of a sea breeze

pressure to the north, over England, and lower pressure to the south, over France. Over the relatively smooth water of the Channel, the wind will flow almost along the isobars east to west. But over the rougher land surfaces, every parcel of air that is stopped by an obstruction will start again by flowing, not along the isobars, but towards the lower pressure over France – that is, from north to south. So the flow near the surface over the rougher land surface of England will be skewed towards the south and will converge with, and heap up against, the east–west flow over the smoother water in the Channel.

The offshore counterflow will be inhibited by this heaping-up converging mass just offshore, so it will become weaker. It will also be blocked from subsiding by the upward welling convergence. With the counterflow resisted in two ways by the convergence, the sea breeze will slow, thicken, become uncertain, less regular – or may die.

Convergence makes a sea or lake breeze thicker, weaker, and its patterns less regular.

Northerly gradient wind

If a light to moderate gradient wind starts blowing from the north, this will assist the counterflow, will not inhibit anything, and the sea breeze will become stronger.

If the northerly gradient wind becomes progressively stronger, at some point the scrubbing action of its turbulent layer and turbulent boundary layer must sweep the whole local thermal sea breeze loop away. The gradient wind speed at which this will occur will be a balance between the strength of the heating and the fragility or robustness of the sea breeze loop system, and the progressively increasing strength of the gradient wind.

An offshore wind makes a sea or lake breeze stronger, up to a point.

Westerly gradient wind

If the gradient wind blows from the west, this creates a divergent situation along the English south coast. The 'west' column in Fig 3.33 shows the mechanism. For a west gradient wind to blow there has to be lower pressure to the north, over England, and higher pressure to the south, over France, so in the gradient westerly wind the flow over the Channel will be more along the isobars, but over southern England the surface flow will be skewed away from the Channel coast towards the lower pressure, and the over-the-sea and the over-the-land low-level winds will diverge.

In this situation, the offshore counterflow will be accelerated towards, and can subside easily into, the 'gap' created by the divergence. Nothing is inhibited, so the sea breeze will become shallower and steadier and much stronger.

Divergent situations make a sea or lake breeze shallower, stronger, more regular.

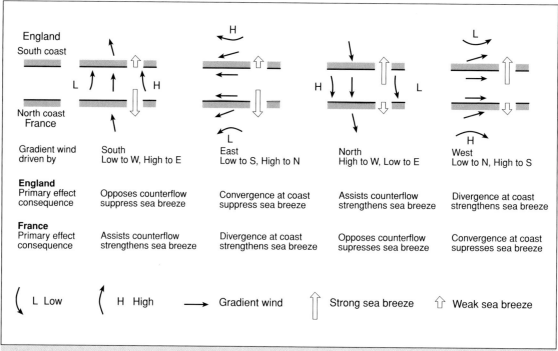

Fig 3.33 Effect of gradient wind direction on sea breeze

Over the north coast of France the situation will be the reverse of that described above, and the sea breeze will blow from the north:

- A southerly gradient wind will make it stronger, up to a point.
- A westerly gradient wind will cause convergence and make it thicker and weaker.
- A northerly gradient wind will oppose the counterflow and destroy the loop.
- An easterly gradient wind will cause divergence and make it shallower and stronger.

The notes above and the easy-to-follow examples of Fig 3.33 show how and why gradient winds from different directions affect the sea or lake breeze. To make a practical forecasting tool for the sailor, we can group them and write a simple 'quadrant effect' rule that will work in both hemispheres.

Grouping

In the northern hemisphere English example above:

- An onshore wind from the S made the sea or lake breeze weaker.
- A transverse wind from the E made it weaker in a different way.
- An offshore wind from the N made it stronger.
- A transverse wind from the W made it stronger in a different way.

If we group these by quadrant we get:

- A SE gradient wind will make it weakest. S and E are both minus.
- A NE gradient wind will have little effect. E is minus, N is plus.
- A NW gradient wind will make it strongest. Both are pluses.
- A SW gradient wind will have little effect. S is minus, W is plus.

If we make this general, we can apply it anywhere in the northern hemisphere:

'Stand with your back to the sea, facing the land. Call the quadrant left front 1, left rear 2, right rear 3, and right front 4.' With this approach, a gradient wind from each quadrant will have the effect:

From Q1	The sea breeze will be strongest and regular.	Offshore, Divergent.
From Q2	The sea breeze will be moderate and regular.	Onshore. Divergent.
From Q3	There is little chance of any sea breeze.	Onshore, Convergent.
From Q4	The sea breeze will be light and irregular.	Offshore, Convergent.'

Try this on the French coast in Fig 3.33. Everything is reversed properly and it works. It works equally well anywhere else in the northern hemisphere – in Florida, Vancouver and Japan.

To make it work south of the Equator in Sydney, Auckland, Perth or Cape Town, reverse the quadrant rotation:

'Stand with your back to the sea, facing the land. Call the quadrant right front 1, right rear 2, left rear 3, and left front 4.'

Practicalities

The east coast of Australia enjoys some of the most regular sea breezes anywhere in the world. At their strongest – when a northwest gradient wind and fierce heating combine to give a 'Sydney Harbour black nor'easter' – they can blow at 17 to 22 knots, be as shallow as 700ft, and the temperature drop as an approaching aircraft descends through the inversion at this level can be as much as 4°C.

The shallower the layer, the steadier will be the wind, and the smaller will be the gust factor. And yet it was in exactly one of these 20–22 knot winds that I watched the sails of the two Eighteen footers flash every few seconds (Section 14.12), and was in this way alerted to look more closely for evidence of quick gust peaks.

Wherever big temperature differences develop over relatively short distances a strong shallow 'thermal' loop flow will develop. Always there must be a deeper, slower upper level counterflow to complete what is essentially a local 'loop'. The strong winds through San Francisco's Golden Gate, the abnormally strong winds through the Columbia river gorge, the regular lake breezes into the source of the St Lawrence river near Kingston, Ontario, and the characteristically strong sea breezes over the coastlines of southeastern Australia are all examples of this.

Where coastlines are relatively featureless, flow will start directly onshore, develop mass and momentum, and then continue to flow towards some fixed point in space. As the world rotates under this moving air, to an observer on the ground the flow will clock in the northern hemisphere – for example, from east to southeast – and will back in the southern hemisphere – for example, from east to northeast. Fig 3.32 (repeated from *HPS-1*) is a trace from the Dynes anemograph at Sydney airport. It shows a fickle northerly morning gradient wind replaced by a 12 knot sea breeze, which starts from 060° at noon and backs to 020° by 10 pm.

A few miles to the north, in Sydney Harbour, the topography of the harbour valley with its steep shores and the high hot plateaux on either side of the waterway (Fig 1.22) constrain the flow to an 'along the valley' wind only. In this and similar locations, the sea breeze will start as a weak onshore flow from the east and back, but only until it flows along the valley. It then becomes a 'funnelling wind', in which the direction does not change further. Fig 3.34 shows a hand trace of a 15 knot Sydney Harbour 'funnelling wind' from 1300 to 1530 hrs.

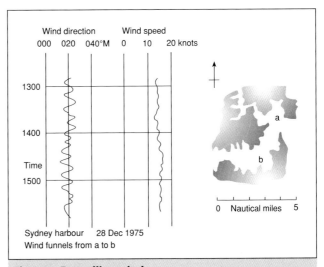

Fig 3.34 Funnelling wind

3.15 ■ The katabatic or drainage wind

Sloped land that cools at night generates katabatic or drainage winds. When these reach the sea they are called land breezes.

On clear nights the top few millimetres of the land surface radiate heat into space and the surface becomes cold. Air in contact is cooled by conduction and becomes denser, so stays on or near the surface and forms a thickening film of chilled and denser air. If the land slopes, this film drifts downwards, and concentrates into substantial flows down any valleys to become the regular early morning drainage or katabatic winds. These flows are abnormally steady and stable in that the fastest and coldest and densest air is closest to the surface, and speed decreases with height (apart from the 5m laminar or 1m turbulent boundary layer right at the surface) so that they are both thermally and dynamically stable. For all these reasons there can be no gusts. These are the smoothest of all winds.

In lake or coastal areas the water is necessarily at the lowest level, and early morning sailors can enjoy these steady winds where they flow onto the water.

Because any temperature change in the water occurs through metres rather than millimetres, the day–night change in water temperature is miniscule. So the water will usually be much warmer than the chilled dawn air, and will heat it strongly. For this reason, the coldest and strongest and steadiest flow will be at the water's edge. Offshore, the flow becomes progressively warmer and weaker and more unsteady as it becomes heated light air. Fig 3.21(a) and (b) show windsocks in such a flow.

At the scale of the mountain lakes in the great valleys in the southern slopes of the European Alps of northern Italy, the mass and momentum of the down-flowing air is so great that it regularly provides 12 to 15 knot winds all morning at the upwind lake shores.

At the scale of Sydney, which lies in the Cumberland basin, cooled air drains out of the four waterway valleys of Broken Bay, Sydney Harbour, Botany Bay and Bate Bay. The harbour drainage wind is strongest at the narrowest constriction which is where the bridge is. At dawn in winter, the speed at the surface is typically 6 knots, but the flags on top of the arch at 600ft are still limp. An hour later, the surface speed is 10 knots or more and the flags stream from the west. By 1100, the land has warmed and the katabatic wind has faded and vanished.

These shallow cold flows occur underneath, and completely isolated from, any overriding free stream or turbulent layer.

3.16 ■ Two unsteadying factors

The flow of the turbulent breeze is always unsteady to some degree. If either of two factors are present, the degree of unsteadiness will be significantly increased:

Heat

Heat always increases irregularity. Whenever there is strong heating, either because colder air has flowed over warmer water, or because close upwind land surface has been heated by sunlight, the wind will always become more unsteady, more irregular, and rougher.

This is because air that is heated by the warmer surface will rise; all air cannot rise simultaneously, so a pattern establishes in which some air rises and some descends, like the water at the bottom of a boiling kettle.

In calm and light air, rising 'bubbles' of warmer air rise from the warmest patches, and intervening cooler air descends. Viscosity of gas increases with heat, so the cooler air is 'thinner', and it tends to form 'curtains' of descending air which move faster because the air is thinner. The descending air splits as it reaches the surface into horizontal flows both ways away from the bases of the descending curtains and towards the rising cores of adjacent cells (Fig 3.25).

In calm and in light air – that is, where there is no turbulent mixing – the pattern of rising bubbles and descending curtains is at the scale of the isolated thermal or cell. In light air this pattern will be carried along in the wind as in Fig 3.5, where the cells are spaced about 70m apart.

In breezes, the intense mixing of the turbulence obliterates all small-scale-cell patterns, but the massive energy of heating will not be denied, and expresses itself as a similar mechanism at a larger scale.

Figs 3.6 to 3.11 are traces from the Kingston Meteorological Tower of broadly similar south to southwest winds. The fact that they are all from the 'prevailing sea breeze' direction during daylight hours implies an overriding thermal lake breeze component, and also that the turbulent layer in all cases was probably relatively shallow – that is, as in Fig 3.31A of a Sydney sea breeze. Half of these are traces of heated winds, and the effects of heating show as consistent differences between the heated and cooled samples.

Figs 3.6, 3.8 and 3.10 show cooled wind traces of 6, 10 and 20 knots respectively. In these, the direction traces all 'vibrate' as they respond to each passing eddy, but the band within which they vibrate is narrow, typically +/– 5°. In the short term, these traces are all smooth and steady; in the longer term, they are all consistent, without any abrupt change of direction as they back and clock smoothly in the roll pattern. These traces are typical of cooled winds.

Figs 3.7, 3.9 and 3.11 of 6, 10 and 20 knot heated winds are very different. The eddy by eddy 'vibration' sweeps a wider range, so the energy of each eddy is clearly greater. The short-term flow has become much less steady in direction, but the big difference is that the heat has added major abrupt inconsistent swings of direction at the next scale up. Fig 3.7 shows 10 or 11 of these changes in a 15-minute trace; Fig 3.9 shows 8 changes; Fig 3.11 shows 9 changes. They tend to occur at about 90 to 100 second intervals on average.

So we have two patterns, in which the practical observations are:

- The direction traces of cooled turbulent winds with shallow turbulent layers are smooth and consistent
  – They do not change direction quickly nor unexpectedly.
  – At a scale of, say, 100m they do not blow in different directions – in other words, two boats sailing 100m apart will both be in much the same wind.
- As compared with the consistent direction flow of cooled winds, *all* of the heated winds show substantial unsteady direction changes consistent with crosswind surface flows due to large random thermal cell activity
  – At any point, substantial change of direction is likely to occur at random at intervals of about 90–100 seconds on average.
  – The local direction at any point can be significantly different from the direction 100m distant.

The driving mechanism appears to be that heated winds develop thermal cells with surface inflows from all directions. Cell spacing appears to be about 250m at 6 knots, 500m at 10 knots, and 1000m at 20 knots.

This cell activity with its inflows will also increase the unsteadiness of the wind speed. About half the gusts will be a little stronger, and half the lulls will be a little lighter.

The fact that the cooled wind is reliable in direction, but the heated wind is not, is of the greatest tactical importance whenever match-racing is appropriate. In the final races of any closely contested regatta a situation will normally develop in which it becomes more important for a particular boat to finish ahead of a certain rival than to finish well in the fleet, and in these situations these two boats will often race each other and ignore the fleet.

When the water is cooler than the air, there are likely to be no surprises, and the match-racing will proceed according to its set piece rules that favour the windward defender. But when the water is warmer than the air, the situation becomes completely different. Two boats not far apart will often find themselves in quite different wind directions, and these random changes in direction can be used by a leeward attacker to steer a windward covering boat into headers, and then escape.

The deep unstable turbulent layer – low dominant situation

When the turbulent layer is deep and is itself unstable due to the convergence natural within a low dominant situation – nearby low or trough overhead – the whole turbulent layer becomes much unsteadier than usual. These are the days when passengers in low-flying aircraft have uncomfortable rides. The surface wind reflects this unsteadiness with harsh gusts and big unsteady changes of direction even when the surface is cooler than the air. When it is heated, the wind just gets rougher still.

Fig 21.4B (sea breeze), 21.4C (stable gradient wind), and 21.4D (unstable gradient wind) display in speed trace and direction trace form what to expect when sailing in these three winds.

3.17 ■ Surface flow patterns within gusts

In Section 29.4, Mark Bethwaite asserts:

A gust is simply a parcel of higher-altitude air penetrating the slower-moving lower-altitude air and impacting on the surface of the water. As it impacts, it will not only move downwind, it will also splay across wind in the same way as if a glass of water is thrown onto a table. Most of the water will continue in the direction it is thrown, but a significant element will splay to each side.

It is this splayed wind propagating from the centre of the gust that allows you to cut the corner by sailing the lifted tack on the outside of the gust – on starboard tack if you are on the port side of the gust looking upwind, and on port tack if you are on the starboard side of the gust looking upwind.

This is a powerful and simple tactical tool. Some sailors are aware of it and use it in gusting winds – others do not.

On a recent summer day with a gradient easterly wind of 11 knots with gusts to 16 knots, Mark and I conducted a series of measurements in Rose Bay to quantify his assertion. Mark, in one inflatable, identified each suitable approaching gust, moved quickly north or south to what he deemed to be the gust axis, signalled, continued 100m, stopped, and measured wind direction in the pre-gust lull then through the gust. I was adjacent in another inflatable, followed closely, reversed direction at the axis, and motored 100m the other way, stopped, and similarly measured both speed and direction in the pre-gust lull and then through the gust from a position about 200m distant and on the other side of the gust axis. We measured seven gusts.

The clock on the left-hand side was	Min 10°	Max 20°	Mean 15°
The back on the right-hand side	Min 0°	Max 15°	Mean 7.5°
The divergence in any gust was	Min 10°	Max 30°	Mean 22.5°

These measurements were conducted in a cooled gradient wind with a deep turbulent layer. It would be logical to expect more divergence in strongly heated winds, and less divergence in the smoother winds of cooled shallower turbulent layers with lower gust factors.

3.18 ■ Summary of Chapter 3

In this chapter we have reviewed the wind's basic drive forces; also, the factors that cause steadiness and regularity, and those that cause unsteadiness and irregularity. (See *HPS-1* Stability index.)

The thinner the turbulent layer and the more it is cooled by the surface, the steadier will be the wind and the more predictable will be its patterns.

The deeper the turbulent layer and the more it is heated by the surface, the rougher will be the wind and the less predictable will be its patterns. The table below summarises the key factors:

Table 3.1 Key wind speed factors

Wind speed

Light air	**(Laminar flow)**
Cooled	Will vary slowly and smoothly.
Heated	Will vary quickly, widely and irregularly.
Breeze	**(Turbulent flow)**
Cooled	Will always have gusts.
	Gust/lull factor will be about 35% to 40%.
	Gusts will repeat at random, but at about 30-second gust then 30-second lull on average.
	Quick gust peaks will be embedded within the 30-second gusts.
Heated	Will have harsh irregular gusts.
	The greater the heating, the more the gust/lull factor will exceed 40%.
	Gusts will repeat at random, but at about 30-second gusts then 30-second lull on average.

Table 3.2 Key wind direction factors

Wind direction	
Light air	**(Laminar flow)**
Cooled	Direction may be steady or wander smoothly.
Heated	Direction will vary widely and irregularly.
Breeze	**(Turbulent flow)**
Cooled	Direction will vibrate within about +/– 5°.
	Will be steady short term.
	Will back and clock smoothly in the longer term.
	Will be consistent over a wide area.
Heated	Direction will vibrate within about +/– 10° or more.
	Will vary irregularly short term.
	Will back and clock widely and irregularly longer term.
	Will be inconsistent between even close areas.
Direction within gusts	Refer to Section 3.17 above.

Notes

1 Direction 'Steady' includes normal oscillation.

2 In open water direction changes are not correlated with gusts. They do not occur at the same time as speed changes, nor at the same frequency.

3 Deep turbulent layer, low dominant situations can give big unsteady direction changes whether heated or not.

4 In situations where the gradient wind blows diagonally over a valley system, gusts will strike down from the direction of the gradient wind, while the lulls (gradient wind) will flow more along the valley. Such situations can give systematic gust/lull back or clock bias either way in either hemisphere.

Sydney's Upper Middle Harbour (Inset, Fig 1.22) is an example of this. In normal sea breeze conditions the flow above the plateaux is NE, and gusts generated in this NE flow reach the surface as NE gusts. Along the E–W valleys, the lull surface wind is more E along the valley, so gusts strike from the NE – that is, the gusts are backed with respect to the lulls.

But on the next leg of the course up the N–S valley the surface flow is again more along the valley, but this time more from the N. The gust direction does not change and strikes from the NE, so on this leg the gusts are clocked with respect to the lulls.

Chapter 4 • The Spectrum of the Wind

4.1 ■ The emergence of wind tactics

Prior to 1960 there was virtually nothing in sailing literature about what is now called 'wind tactics' – that is, local differences of wind at the scale of the round the buoys course. For example, descriptions of America's Cup races in the 1930s discussed tide and current in detail, but did not touch on possible differences in wind between the two boats as a relevant factor.

In the 1960s three seminal books, or series of books, were published. In *The Tactics of Small Boat Racing* and his subsequent books, Dr Stuart Walker asserted that winds either oscillated in direction or shifted persistently one way, and described the benefits of 'sailing the lifts' in oscillating winds and of sailing the headers in persistent shifts.

In *Wind and Sailing Boats*, Alan Watts, a sailor and forecaster, opened up the whole structure of wind motions at the scale of the racing helmsman, and introduced the concept of a spectrum of motions each about ten times bigger than the one below. He also observed that in some circumstances gusts favoured starboard tack in the northern hemisphere and asserted that this could be relied upon as normal. (In this he foreshadowed what has since become known as the Eckman spiral.)

David Houghton described in formidable detail the convergences, divergences and counterflows that drive the local wind speed differences on which race success so greatly depends.

It was primarily the work of these three authors that gave birth to the science of wind tactics. Sailing literature since 1970 has developed their pioneering studies, and has been focused primarily on wind patterns at the typically 10–30-minute time scale of roll motions (oscillations, etc) and the one-minute time scale of gust motions.

An example of this is that the wind section of my 1993 *HPS-1* was driven by both my own interest in wind tactics, and by my interest in Stuart's and Alan's work. I wondered how relevant their assertions might be in the southern hemisphere. In the late 1960s, I could find nothing about oscillating winds, nor persistent shifts, nor the bias of gusts, in the scientific or meteorological libraries. I therefore set about amassing a database of my own.

Starting in the late 1960s, wherever I was in the world and where I could see wind blowing over water, I drew at an open scale the way the estimated wind speed and the wind direction changed, at that place and in those conditions, as the minutes passed.

By 1972 it had become clear from this increasing data bank that, given enough time, all winds oscillate (except for synoptic change), so I concluded that oscillating winds were real, and that in oscillating winds 'sailing the lifts' was fastest *provided the mark ahead was not closer than one full cycle*.

Conversely, no wind shifted persistently in one direction for an indefinite period, so there was no identifiable feature called a persistent shift. I concluded that 'persistent shift' was a useful name to give to that situation within a race in an oscillating wind where the next rounding mark lies too close for the 'sail the lifts' mechanism to work with advantage – that is, closer than one full cycle. This clarification led to the development of the fastest three-quarter cycle, half cycle and quarter cycle techniques, and Gold medals (two at the Kiel Olympics) rewarded those who thought at this new level. (Chapters 10, 11 and 12 of *HPS-1* developed this thinking.)

Further, there was no evidence that either tack was systematically advantaged by gusts in either hemisphere, except in some very special conditions. Indeed, in some conditions the bias can go either way in either hemisphere – as in the example given at the end of Chapter 3.

A story from Kingston, Ontario, prior to the 1976 Montreal Olympics, is relevant. (Mr Justice) Livius Sherwood had been appointed Director of Sailing for the forthcoming Olympics. I had been Meteorological Coach to the Australian Olympic Yachting Team at the Munich Olympics in 1972 (sailing at Kiel), and was studying the winds at Kingston, Ontario. One evening in 1974 at the Kingston Yacht Club, Ian Bruce (of Laser fame) introduced me to Livius Sherwood. Livius advised us that an instrumented meteorological tower would be moored in the course area and that printouts of the wind averaged every 10 minutes through daylight hours in July 1975 would be made available to all competing countries during the year prior to the Olympics.

I happened to have spent that day on the water in the course area and had in my pocket my hand-drawn plots of the oscillations of that day's wind and the way they correlated with the streets of roll clouds moving overhead. I showed these to Livius, advised him that oscillations every 7 to 15 minutes were the norm worldwide, and that about 10 minutes (as I had observed on that day) was the most common frequency. I pointed out that on any day with oscillations close to 10 minutes any data averaged at 10-minute intervals would mask the oscillations.

He listened and thanked me, and a few months later I learned that an open scale U2-A anemograph had been added to the tower's instrumentation. The 240 hours of open-scale traces from this U2-A instrument in July 1975 certainly proved invaluable in understanding more about the oscillations (ie the roll motions) in that area in that season.

They continue to be uniquely useful. As an example, to design better flexible and automatic rigs we now need to know more about the short-term fluctuations – that is, the quick gust peaks. It is primarily these open-scale Kingston Tower U2-A traces that have provided me with the seminal database for the study of these fluctuations. (These are discussed in Chapter 5.)

4.2 ■ Explaining the spectrum of the wind

The atmosphere is in constant motion. Recognisable patterns occur and repeat at different sizes, frequencies and levels of energy, but these motions are never steady.

The World Meteorological Organisation uses a common language worldwide to describe the present and the forecast weather. With respect to areas of wind with similar speed, in ascending order they use the terms 'gusts', then 'squalls', then 'pressure lines', then 'fronts'. These descriptors take huge bites. A gust 100–200m in diameter may cover 20 000–30 000sq m of surface. A 20 knot squall that lasts for 30 minutes may be 5–10km in diameter and cover 25 000 000sq m, or 1000 times the area of the gust. Pressure lines hundreds of miles long, and fronts thousands of miles long, represent equally big jumps in scale. These jumps are too big to be relevant to the round-the-buoys racing helmsman.

In his 1965 *Wind and Sailing Boats*, Alan Watts describes 'The Spectrum of the Wind' in much smaller divisions. He saw the wind as what we would now regard as a fractal series of recognisable patterns, each about five to ten times bigger than the one below it. He defines the smallest of these as 'friction eddies' with repetition frequencies of about 10 seconds, then 'minor gusts' with lives of 1 minute, then 'medium gust cells' with lives of 10 minutes, then 'long gusts' with lives of 1 hour. He offers no further description of the properties of these other than references to the winds local to Hayling Island and Thorney Island, nor does he suggest any causes. But simply by stating this progression he alerted us to the spectrum of observable features in the real wind that are important to the small-boat racing helmsman.

My mainly temperate-latitude observations worldwide led me to refine Alan's spectrum in the following way:

Quick pulsations

These have a repetition frequency of about one second. They seem to exist only in some circumstances. Two indications of their presence are:

- Thistledown sometimes exhibits quickly erratic trajectory in light breezes.
- When sailing a light dinghy with a stayed rig in a strong wind, the rig is sometimes shaken quickly in strong gusts in the way a dog shakes a bone.

I have not seen them referred to previously in the literature, and they may not be important except in understanding the behaviour of automatic rigs on model yachts. My point in mentioning them here is that one of the considerations in the design of the automatic rig (see Chapter 21) is to understand what is the fastest rate of response called for. In this connection these quick pulsations need at least to be considered, so for completeness I have included them here.

Fluctuations or 'quick gust peaks'

In *HPS-1* I described these as fluctuations that increase or decrease the wind speed generally by about +/– 7% every 6 to 12 seconds with surprising regularity. At that time my focus was how to sail fastest with a manually adjustable rig which was assumed to be reset every minute or so to match the speed of the imminent gust or lull, and at that time I regarded these fluctuations as 'background noise'.

In the years since, the seminal importance of the more energetic fluctuations as 'gust peaks' in their own right has been recognised, and this has led to the development of the fast-response automatic rig. (Chapter 5 looks at what measured data we have and what we know of their properties.)

Gusts

These are areas of stronger wind, generally about 200m crosswind dimension and longer upwind and downwind in 10 to 12 knot winds, and about double that size in 20 knot winds. Their origin is that myriad small friction eddies, almost all of which spin around a horizontal axis in one direction (top goes downwind) and can and do accrete at about mid-height in the wind's turbulent layer into a small population of very big eddies.

Some of these big eddies rise and reveal themselves by twisting the edges of any clouds present at the turbulence inversion level. Some find themselves in slower air and wind themselves downward in the manner of a top-spun tennis ball. Those that descend to the surface become gusts. They tend to hit hard and taper off as they are slowed by surface friction. Their higher speed makes the ripples on the water surface steeper, and these steeper faces reflect less light so that gusts appear as darker areas on the water surface.

Large gusts in 10 to 12 knot winds can remain recognisable in this way as areas of stronger wind for about 2 minutes. The much fiercer and bigger gusts of 20 knot winds can remain visible for up to 4 minutes. At any time, the water surface area tends to be about 50% gust and 50% lull – the lull areas are simply recent gusts that have been slowed by surface friction to gradient wind speed and are waiting to be undercut by the next descending eddy of faster, more energetic air. Gust/lull cycles repeat at random intervals, but their average repetition interval is always close to 60 seconds, and this remains constant regardless of wind speed.

How rough the wind is – the gust factor, the gust speed/ lull speed ratio – is governed by two primary factors:
1 The first is the thickness of the turbulent layer.
2 The second is heat – thermal excitation. (See Chapter 3.)

Surges and fades

These are areas of stronger wind generally of about 500–1000m or more in diameter. These mark the water, but do not seem to be related to anything. In a practical sense they are generally referred to indirectly as 'There's more pressure over there' – but so often it vanishes before you can reach it. They are not gusts. They are not squalls. They are not rolls. As yet, they have no agreed descripton. I will refer to them as 'surges', and the lighter air areas between the surges as 'fades'. At present they represent a mystery area because we know neither what causes them, nor much about their properties. (Chapter 6 discusses what we know to date.)

Rolls

These are systematic wave trains in the turbulent layer which cause wide areas of wind to oscillate in direction or to freshen or die at an upwind–downwind scale generally about 5–10km. Their size is such that wind over the whole affected area backs or clocks, becomes fresher, or dies, generally with a cycle time between about 10 and 30 minutes in deep boundary layers, and less in the shallow sea and lake breeze flows.

When looked at from the 2008 standpoint of what we know about the wind's spectrum:
1 Stuart Walker's 1960s *Oscillating Winds and Persistent Shifts* was a discussion about roll motions.
2 Alan Watts's 1965 'Gusts favour starboard tack ... etc' was a discussion about gust motions, and in what conditions what is now called the Eckman spiral is significant.
3 David Houghton's descriptions of the drive mechanisms become more and more relevant as we learn more.
4 My 1993 *HPS-1* focused on gust and roll motions.
5 Today, in order to design better automatic rigs, we need to know more about the quick gust peaks.
6 Also, to race apparent wind sailboats downwind more intelligently, we need to know more about surges and fades.

Quick gust peaks, and surges and fades, are discussed in Chapters 5 and 6.

Chapter 5 • The Quick Gust Peaks

5.1 ■ The quick changes in wind speed

Central to the logic that a crew will sail faster if they adjust their rig manually to every significant change of wind speed and sea state are three assumptions:

1 The first is that in wind speeds from calm up to the design wind, the fastest way to sail to windward will be to set the sails at the shape that has been found best for that boat in those wind and sea conditions, and to change sail shape as appropriate only when either wind speed or sea state (or both) change significantly.
   - Up to the design wind, balance is controlled primarily by body movement (hiking), so systematic change of sail shape for each gust and lull is not necessary.
2 The second is that as the wind speed increases further and exceeds the design wind, the gust-lull sequence becomes dominant because
   - A boat with sails that are not flattened in the gusts will begin to stagger under the too-full sails and will sail more slowly through the gusts.
   - A boat with sails that are flattened manually to match the stronger wind in the gusts, and then restored to the fullness optimum for the lull, will sail faster through the gusts than a boat that is not adjusted, and will sail at the same speed through the lulls, so its mean speed will be faster than the speed of a boat that is not adjusted.
3 Central to this assumption is another assumption: that the wind will change its speed as it gusts and lulls at a rate that will give crews opportunity to adjust their sail shape manually to each significant change of wind speed.

At root, these reduce to a broader set of assumptions:

- That the only significant speed changes will be the changes from the stronger gusts to the lighter lulls, and vice versa.
- That gusts and lulls repeat on average with about a 1-minute cycle time, which is slow enough to admit manual adjustment, *and*
- That no further significant speed changes occur within the gusts or lulls themselves.

This chapter will suggest that this approach is not true.

The modern adjustable rig emerged in the late 1960s. Initially this took the form of a mast flexible enough to bend, plus adjustable outhaul, downhaul and vang controls to bend it. These rigs were quick to adjust and crews soon found that if in stronger winds they flattened their rigs both to keep the 'power' of the rig matched to the weight of the crew, and also to reduce the aerodynamic drag of the rig, the 'depowered' boats sailed faster than those that did not adjust.

Over the years, adjustment technology has been refined at the expense of greater complexity to the point where a skilled crew can now set exactly the shape they want, but it takes them time to do it. The sail then holds that shape regardless of wind speed until it is next adjusted. On the questionable basis that if two or three adjustment controls made a boat a little faster, then three times as many controls would make it three times faster, more and more controls were piled on. The mammoth Eighteen footers of the late 1980s had 13 separate adjustments and the job of the sheet hand was as much to be an adjustment engineer as a sailor. Today's 505s and similar boats have even more controls and rope ends to pull, so take even longer to get a different desired sail shape exactly right.

It is self-evident that the wind's roll motions cause it to freshen and die every 10–30 or so minutes. Crews can adjust every few minutes. Friction turbulence causes it to gust and lull every minute or so. Skilled and motivated crews can make simple adjustments every minute, but that seems to have been accepted, almost by mutual consent, as the limit. Nothing in past or present sailing literature discusses shorter-term unsteadiness.

In the late 1980s, three events occurred that broke this mould:

- A style of rigid-lower-mast, flexible-topmast 'flexi-tip' Eighteen footer rig was developed in response to emerging cost and mechanical problems with the conventional complex adjustable rigs.
- These simpler rigs on tiny 'budget' boats sailed faster than their highly developed and costly mammoth predecessors.
- On one particular late afternoon when the light from a low sun was parallel with the sails of adjacent budget and mammoth competitors racing in a strong-wind race, I was fortunate in being able to watch the upper mainsail of the budget boat 'shimmering' as it yielded to quickly alternating aerodynamic loads during a single gust, while the mainsail of the adjacent mammoth was more rigid – and such flex as occurred affected mainly the middle of the leech, and not the top. (This incident is described in Section 14.12.)

This observation threw up a new possibility – that the wind speed may also change significantly several times within a gust, at a rate much too fast for any crew to respond to with appropriate manual adjustment. If this were found to be true, the assumption that even the most skilled and motivated crew can adjust efficiently to each change of wind speed becomes a nonsense, and the whole logic of the complex adjustable rig collapses.

This chapter will look at what we now know about very quick changes of both wind speed and wind direction.

5.2 ■ The Dynes anemograph

The first appeal must be to the millions of hours of traces archived from the World Meteorological Organisation's standard Dynes anemographs. Fig 5.1 is a trace of the most common of all winds – a gradient wind of moderate speed. This trace is about as 'clean' as is available – it is a trace from the Sydney airport instrument of a southerly wind, which blows across the unobstructed 5 mile fetch of Botany Bay, so is free of all turbulence from upwind hills or buildings or hot surfaces.

It is obvious from inspection that even an ideal reading such as this cannot give useful information about wind speed changes at a time scale of less than a minute. The design of the Dynes instrument is such that each day's wind is traced on a chart 24in long, so the paper moves under the pen at 1in – 25mm – each hour. At this speed, the thickness of the ink line represents about a minute of time, so the detail of changes faster than this cannot be either recorded or read, and this is true for all the Dynes data worldwide.

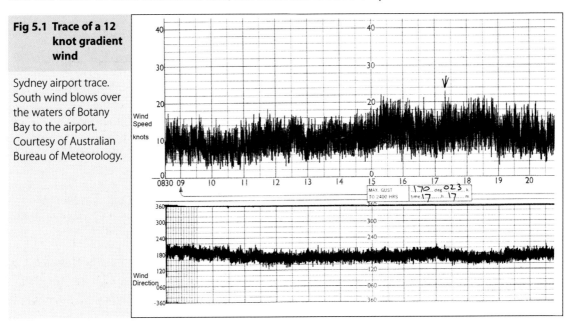

Fig 5.1 Trace of a 12 knot gradient wind

Sydney airport trace. South wind blows over the waters of Botany Bay to the airport. Courtesy of Australian Bureau of Meteorology.

5.3 Sherlock and Stout

At the other end of the scale is the work of Sherlock and Stout, who measured the detail of the wind's friction turbulence with an array of 12 quick-response recording anemometers. Eight were mounted in a horizontal N–S line, with every instrument 50ft above the ground and each 50ft from its neighbour. A further four were mounted on the vertical 250ft tower that carried instrument No 6 at 50ft, No 7 at 100ft etc, up to No 10 at 250ft. Each recording instrument measured and recorded the wind speed every half second.

Fig 5.2 shows 30 seconds of a run in a westerly wind of 40mph – about 35 knots. These measurements were taken over an open moorland surface; I do not know the temperatures, so have no idea to what extent thermal excitation may have been a factor. This instrument array measured in miles per hour and did not measure direction.

The top diagram in Fig 5.2 shows a plan – that is, horizontal presentation. Note that north is to the bottom of the page, so in the westerly wind the flow is from right to left. If 1–12 were a start line, the boats on it would experience the speed variations shown in the diagram during the following 30 seconds (provided nothing changed during that time, which would be unlikely).

The lower diagram is an elevation that shows that the change of speed with height is at least as unsteady as the change of speed with horizontal position.

The presentation of data in Fig 5.2 as lines of equal speed conveys a vivid appreciation of the intensity and complexity of the turbulence of this 40mph – 35 knot – wind. It is of interest to note that the width of the predominant gust is about 100m.

In Fig 5.3 I have drawn the changes of speed with time in the manner of the Dynes anemograph trace of Fig 5.1, except that the chart paper would notionally have been running at 300mm per minute, 18 000mm per hour, or 720 times faster than the Dynes' tape. The traces for six of the twelve instruments are given; the trace of instrument No 1 is shown as 5.3A, that of No 3 as 5.3C, etc.

This 30-second record is much shorter than the average life of a gust, so cannot show more than the occasional random gust onset or fade. The speed range is generally between lows of 30mph and highs of 50mph (one or two are much higher). I have assumed those periods of the traces when the recorded speed is wholly above 40mph to be gusts.

This analysis shows very clearly that:

- The wind speed changes frequently and significantly during each gust.
- The interval between the individual 'gust peaks' is only a few seconds.
- The speed difference between the 'gust peaks' and 'gust lulls' is significant.

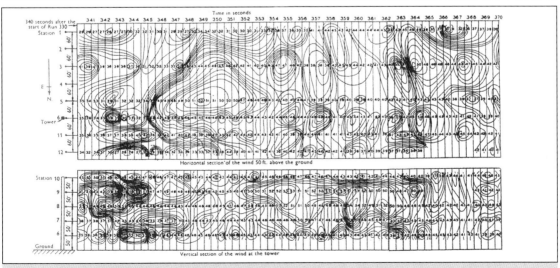

Fig 5.2 Sherlock and Stout

Flow detail of 40mph wind over moorland, as measured by Sherlock and Stout. Courtesy of British Weather Office.

In Fig 5.3C, the wind from 340 seconds to 348 seconds (from the start of the run) is less than 40mph so is not a gust, and therefore is ignored in this gust peak analysis. The following quick gust peaks of 48, 50, 50, 52 and 49mph average 49.2mph. The intervening quick gust lulls average 41mph; 20 seconds elapse between the first and last quick peak. So trace 5.3C reveals that:

- Mean gust peak speed was 49.2mph
- Mean gust lull speed was 41.0mph
- Mean gust speed was (49.2 + 41)/2 = 45.1mph
- Mean fluctuation was 49.2–41 = 8.2mph or 18% of 45.1
- Mean interval between peaks = 20/5 = 4 seconds

If we treat all six traces in this way and average them we get:

- Mean gust peak speed 46.9mph
- Mean gust lull speed 39.6mph
- Mean gust speed 43.25mph
- Mean fluctuation 7.3mph or 17% of 43.25
- Interval between peaks 25/125 = 5 seconds

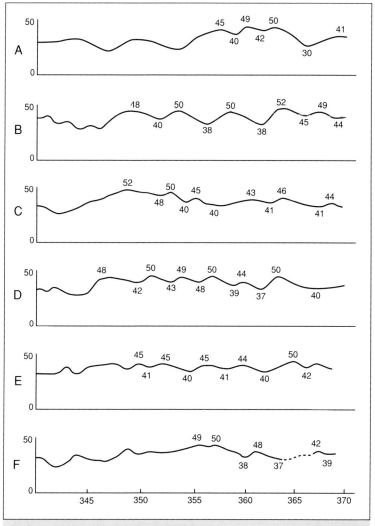

Fig 5.3 Quick gust peaks from Fig 5.2

Seconds after start of run.
Speed of quick gust peaks and lulls in miles per hour.
Fig 5.3A trace is from sensor No 1, trace 5.3B is from sensor No 3, etc.

A 17% average increase in wind speed implies a 37% increase in heeling force, and is clearly significant. The change in the apparent wind will be less, but the change between peak quick gusts and lulls (as opposed to average) will be much greater.

So the lesson from Sherlock and Stout is that the wind speed does change, and, change significantly, every few seconds within 'normal' gusts and lulls in strong winds.

5.4 ■ The Kingston Tower traces

It may be that these Sherlock and Stout measurements were of an abnormally rough wind. Fortunately, the U2-A records from the Kingston Tower enable us to get another look at gust peaks, and Fig 5.4 gives gust peak data from the recorded traces.

The July and early August 1975 traces from which Figs 3.4 to 3.11 were selected were made available by the Canadian Dept of the Environment to national teams prior to the 1976 Montreal Olympics. Their book takes the form of tables which give air and water temperature etc, every ten minutes plus 118 pages of traces

Page	Date	Hour	Air deg C	Water deg C	Dir deg T	Gust High (W/V kts)	Gust mean	Gust Low (W/V kts)	Lull High	Lull mean	Lull Low	Num hghs	Int Secs	Temp A-W	W/V kts mean	Ratio Gm/Lm	Ratio Gh/Ll
COOLED WINDS																	
82	24.7	1330	26	23	210	32	30	26	25	21	21	5	6	3	####	1.43	1.52
3	2 7	1440	24	22	225	18	17	16	16	14	13	4	8	2	15.5	1.31	1.38
3	2 7	1350	24	22	225	17	15	14	15	14	13	3	10	2	14.5	1.15	1.31
81	24.7	1105	25	23	205	22	20	18	18	17	16	8	8	2	18.5	1.25	1.38
2	2 7	1220	23	22	220	16	15	13	14	13	12	8	8	1	14.0	1.25	1.33
37	8 7	920	23	22	185	13	12	10	11	10	9	4	8	1	11.0	1.33	1.44
91	27.7	1305	23	22	180	18	16	14	14	13	12	9	6	1	14.5	1.33	1.50
94	28.7	1320	22	21	240	21	19	18	16	15	14	8	8	1	17.0	1.36	1.50
100	30.7	1315	23	22	220	15	14	13	12	11	10	6	10	1	12.5	1.40	1.50
38	8.7	1150	23	23	200	15	14	13	14	12	11	4	8	0	13.0	1.27	1.36
55	14.7	1030	22	22	200	16	15	13	13	11	12	6	8	0	13.0	1.25	1.33
56	14.7	1130	22	22	210	14	13	12	11	11	10	6	8	0	12.0	1.30	1.40
65	17.7	1120	23	23	1120	14	13	12	11	11	10	8	8	0	12.0	1.30	1.40
68	18.7	1155	23	23	210	14	13	12	12	11	10	4	8	0	12.0	1.30	1.40
69	18.7	1335	23	23	210	19	18	17	17	16	15	8	9	0	17.0	1.20	1.27
70	19.7	945	23	23	200	23	20	19	19	17	15	4	12	0	18.5	1.33	1.53
74	22.7	1045	23	23	220	14	14	12	12	12	12	5	12	0	13.0	1.17	1.17
78	23.7	1245	23	23	210	15	14	13	11	10	9	8	8	0	12.0	1.56	1.67
79	23.7	1330	23	23	230	15	14	12		11	10	7	9	0	12.5	1.40	1.50
93	28.7	1240	22	22	240	18	17	15	14	13	12	6	9	0	15.0	1.42	1.50
97	29.7	1430	22	22	230	18	17	16	14	13	12	9	7	0	15.0	1.42	1.50
99	30.7	1130	22	22	210	15	14	13	13	12	11	5	10	0	13.0	1.27	1.36
													188				
													8.5				
HEATED WINDS						Gh	Gm	Gl	Lh	Lm	Ll						
27	4 7	1415	22	23	215	15	14	12	13	12	11	6	10	-1	13.0	1.27	1.36
39	8.7	1415	22	23	200	15	14	12	13	12	11	7	6	-1	13.0	1.27	1.36
42	9.7	1340	22	23	220	16	15	14	14	12	11	7	6	-1	13.5	1.36	1.45
58	15.7	1020	21	22	210	17	16	15	13	12	11	4	8	-1	14.0	1.45	1.55
59	15.7	1205	21	22	215	18	17	15	11	13	13	8	8	-1	15.0	1.31	1.38
60	15.7	1350	21	22	210	15	15	14	14	12	11	5	8	-1	13.5	1.36	1.36
71	19.7	1225	22	23	180	28	25	22	22	20	18	9	7	-1	22.5	1.39	1.56
75	22.7	1250	22	23	215	22	21	20	18	16	15	7	9	-1	18.5	1.40	1.47
76	22.7	1345	22	23	215	22	21	19	18	16	14	9	7	-1	18.5	1.50	1.57
80	24.7	910	23	24	190	24	23	20	19	18	15	7	9	-1	20.5	1.53	1.60
90	27.7	1112	21	22	180	21	19	18	17	16	14	8	8	-1	17.5	1.36	1.50
47	11.7	1240	20	22	230	19	17	15	16	15	14	6	10	-2	16.0	1.21	1.36
48	11.7	1350	20	22	225	18	17	17	15	14	12	3	6	-2	15.5	1.42	1.50
89	27.7	930	20	22	205	15	14	13	12	11	10	7	9	-2	12.5	1.40	1.50
92	28.7	915	20	22	265	16	15	14	13	12	10	8	8	-2	13.5	1.50	1.60
46	11.7	920	19	22	260	19	17	15	17	15	12	5	8	-3	16.0	1.42	1.58
84	25.7	1245	20	23	240	29	25	23	23	21	17	5	6	-3	23.0	1.47	1.71
85	25.7	1310	20	23	245	29	26	23	25	22	20	7	9	-3	24.0	1.30	1.45
88	26.7	1412	20	23	225	22	21	19	19	18	16	5	6	-3	19.5	1.31	1.38
83	25.7	1040	19	23	250	28	24	21	20	18	15	6	6	-4	21.0	1.60	1.87
													154				
													7.8				

Fig 5.4 Quick gust data from Kingston Tower traces

	Cooled	Heated	Total
Gust high/Gust low	1.19	1.19	1.19
Gust mean/Lull mean	1.33	1.23	1.28
Gust high/Lull low	1.42	1.51	1.47
Interval between peaks, seconds	8.5	7.8	8.1

from the tower's U2-A anemograph. Each page shows two hours of the tape full size – that is, at 250mm per hour. The tape was run from 0900 until 1500 hours each day. Figs 3.4 to 3.11 show 15-minute runs from these tapes. I am grateful to the department for this data and their permission to use it.

The traces on 76 of the 118 pages show winds wholly less than 12 knots – that is, wind speed less than the design wind of the typical dinghy. Since adjustment is not relevant at these wind speeds, I have ignored these pages.

From the other 42 pages I have selected gusts and adjacent lulls, one from every page, each chosen as typical of the wind on that page.

The sample has been sorted into those in which the air was cooled – that is, the water was at the same temperature as or cooler than the air – and those in which the water was warmer than the air so the air was being heated. Some 22 were cooled; 20 were heated.

With a magnifying glass I then read:

Gh	Gust highest	Highest speed during gust
Gl	Gust lowest	Lowest speed during gust
Gm	Gust mean	Mean speed estimated from trace
Lh, Ll, Lm		Lull highest, lowest, mean
Number of highs		Number of peaks during that gust, *and*
Interval, seconds		Mean interval in seconds between the peaks

The means and ratios are:

Gust peak properties from Kingston Tower traces

	Cooled	Heated	Mean
Gust high/Gust low	1.19	1.19	1.19
Gust mean/Lull mean	1.33	1.23	1.28
Gust high/Lull low	1.42	1.51	1.47
Interval between peaks, seconds	8.5	7.8	8.1

It is relevant to point out that the Olympic courses were chosen within, and the Kingston Tower was deliberately sited within, the area normally covered by the Kingston lake breeze. As has been pointed out in Chapter 3, sea and lake breezes are among the world's smoothest winds. It follows that such roughness within gusts as shows in the Kingston Tower traces is likely to be less than would normally be expected in winds with deeper turbulent layers.

The purpose of this 'gust peak' study is to better understand the environment in which both adjustable and automatic rigs work.

5.5 ■ Conclusions regarding wind speed

1 *Speed change.* The wind speed does indeed fluctuate by close to 20% several times within the life period of every gust.

2 *'Gust high/Gust low'.* The 'Gust high/Gust low' ratio of 1.19 from the Kingston Tower data is directly comparable with, and almost identical with, the mean fluctuation of 17% – that is, 1.17 from the Sherlock and Stout data. This fluctuation appears to be independent of wind speed and thermal excitation.

3 *Interval.* Gust peaks appear to repeat at intervals of about 8 seconds in, say, 15 knot winds, reducing to 5 seconds in 35 knot winds.

4 *Handling consequence.* The assumption that a motivated crew can adjust efficiently to each change of wind speed is no longer realistic.

5 *Dynamic consequence.* The design object for an efficient rig has changed:
   • It is no longer that the rig should be manually adjustable for changes in wind speed.
   • It has become that at every change of wind speed above the design wind, the rig should begin to flex automatically and near instantaneously towards the shape that will give the highest ratio of drive force to drag at the acceptable heeling force at the new higher or lower wind speed.

A philosopher might observe that we have been overlooking the obvious and living a huge mistake for the last 30 years.[1]

5.6 ■ The quick changes in wind direction

From the sailor's point of view this is the oldest subject, but from a design standpoint it is completely new.

Prior to the 1960s, there was almost nothing at all in the sailing literature about adjustment. In recent decades it has become a subject in its own right, but the whole focus has been on what sail shape is fastest in each wind speed and how best to adjust to that shape as the wind *speed* changes.

That the wind *direction* changes too has always been accepted, but it has similarly been held that because the business of being a sailor is primarily the ability to steer a boat to the wind, it will be the helmsman's responsibility to hold the angle between the changing wind direction and the sail constant, and no further consideration by the designer is required. This assumption remains true for all slow changes of direction, but the new reality is that it cannot be true for changes of direction faster than the helmsman-plus-boat combination can respond to.

The conclusions 1–5 in Section 5.5 above are about quick changes in wind speed flow from data such as the Kingston Tower wind speed traces. Inspection of the associated wind direction traces reveals that the continual small quick changes in speed are always mirrored by near identical, although not synchronous, small quick changes in the wind direction. Figs 3.4 to 3.11 are typical. They reveal how constant the direction changes are, how their frequency tends to be always in the range of a change of direction every 6 seconds or so on average, that the factors that cause greater unsteadiness in wind speed similarly cause greater unsteadiness in wind direction, and that the larger of these quick changes are routinely of the order of 10°.

A point of interest is that if the vectors that give a 17% change in wind speed – for example, +/– 0.85 knots in a 10 knot wind – are applied in the crosswind sense, they give a direction change of +/– 5° – that is, 10°, which is what we observe. It seems probable that the driving mechanism is a system of close-spaced eddies with near-vertical axes.

5.7 ■ Conclusions regarding wind direction

The notes above suggest that, in the same manner as with the wind speed, quick and significant changes in wind direction occur about ten times a minute. (The consequences of this observation are developed in Chapter 21.)

What seems to have happened is that a simple flexi-tip rig developed for mechanical and cost reasons in fact delivered a much more efficient dynamic response to both quick gusts, and also to quick changes in wind direction. Further, the response time of the flexible rig was near instantaneous, so it responded to every change of wind speed, no matter how small these were or how quickly they repeated. The combination of the efficiency of the 'twist open from the top' shape now so characteristic of the flexible topmast, and the instantaneous flattening response of the springy rig to every quick gust and lift, tipped the balance and delivered performance superior to the best of the highly developed adjustable rigs. A new field of development lay ahead. To make progress, we needed to know more about the frequency and degree of the wind's short-term gust peaks.

These are in no way the end of this story. Many excellent 'Nature' TV programmes show great eagles and albatross in flight. Their tip feathers can be seen to be in constant motion as they flex to unsteadiness at half-second rather than 5-second intervals, driven by motions within the next level down of the wind's fractal spectrum. These wings have evolved over millions of years, so it is unlikely that the observed flexing is not efficient.

In Chapter 21 we will see that instantaneous initial flexing towards the best shape can already deliver drive to drag benefits of up to 40%. Our next task is to find how much further down the wind's fractal spectrum we can go with even greater advantage.

---

[1] In HPS-1, I drew attention in Chapter 5 to the constant presence of fluctuations in wind speed. At that time I thought them to be an ever-present background 'noise', but one which was so small that, for practical purposes, could be ignored.

In the years since we have learned that the factors that cause the wind to become rougher (see Chapter 3) also cause the fluctuations in speed to become more prominent, to the point where they are now a significant factor in the design of very fast rigs (see Chapter 21).

Chapter 6 • Surges and Fades

6.1 ■ A question of scale

My 1992 *HPS-1* was unusual in that much of the section on wind was based on my own observations, and encouraged sailors to think at a different level if they wanted to understand the wind better, and win. *HPS-2* repeats *HPS-1* in this respect.

The much higher downwind performance level of apparent wind skiffs calls for understanding a previously ignored level of the wind's fractal spectrum: the level between gusts and rolls.

Crews who win in apparent wind sailboats need to think in a new and different way. Upwind, their boats are faster, but not much faster, and the old ways of avoiding lighter-wind areas, working the shifts, and tacking on the headers in the short stuff still work. But downwind they sweep sideways at three times the boat speed of the conventional boat and approach the downwind mark more than twice as fast, so they can hunt for and access better wind from a search area about ten times as big as that available to the conventional sailboat. Their increased speed, and particularly their crosswind speed downwind, has made the relatively small areas of advantage in the 100–200m diameter individual gusts no longer relevant. These boats have jumped one level of scale and their crews now need to look for, and use, when sailing downwind the kilometre-size areas of stronger wind that have always been used when sailing upwind, but that were never until now readily accessible when sailing downwind. This new art calls for study of, and understanding of, the properties of surges and fades.

We have known about surges and fades for a long time, but have never really taken them seriously. Why?

At root, the dynamics of the conventional sailboat are such that there was little to be gained from studying them closely. But the advent of the apparent wind sailboat that tacks downwind has reversed this situation, and now there is everything to be gained.

In Section 29.4, Mark Bethwaite offers exact advice about the sailing that wins in Lasers:
- *When sailing upwind, scan at two distances*
  - *Scan at the limit of vision to see whether the wind on one side of the course is stronger than on the other side, ... and for backs and clocks.*
  - *Scan at closer range to track existing and forming gusts.*
- *When sailing downwind, scan for existing and forming gusts immediately behind the boat and a little to either side ...*

Between the lines, what Mark is saying is this:

- Stronger-wind areas (surges) and weaker-wind areas (fades) exist, and they can be identified at distance.
- When sailing to windward
  - The stronger-wind areas can be accessed by a boat that tacks from side to side across the course as it sails.
  - Because of the fast speed of closing when sailing to windward, they can be reached while they still exist. (The surges come to you as fast as you approach them, so the speed of closing is close to twice the wind speed.)
  - The sailor who sails to and in the stronger wind of a surge will beat the sailor who did not look and, as a result, often sails in the weaker wind elsewhere.
- When sailing downwind, these areas are not worth chasing, because
  - Surges and the boat both waft downwind at about half wind speed, so you have to sail to them.
  - The crosswind performance of the conventional 'blow-downwind' boat that luffs 15° is about one-eighth of the wind speed. At this low crosswind speed it takes too long to reach an identified surge. If you luff more than 15° you lose too much downwind VMG.
  - Practical experience is that most surges die while you sail slowly towards them.
  - So chasing nearby gusts is much more rewarding.

This advice wins in conventional boats, but the downwind tacker is utterly different, and there is now everything to be gained from knowing more about surges and fades.

This subject has never been studied, so there is nothing about it in the scientific literature. So, once again, I have started to amass a data bank of personal observations, and in this chapter I present what I have observed to date.

6.2 ■ The 'new kid on the block'

In the late 1980s when I was completing the manuscript of *HPS-1*, I was astonished by the performance of the Eighteen foot skiffs. They were in a league of their own, both upwind and downwind. And downwind, they seemed to have two gears. Sometimes they were fast – and sometimes they were *so much* faster that they passed with ease the competitors who were just sailing fast.

The other skiffs were unremarkable – the 16s of that era were heavy and uninspiring; we saw few 14s, and they were not fast; and the 12s were more concerned with keeping their huge rigs upright than with real speed to the finish.

All the conventional boats were just that – conventional – and sailed downwind at about half wind speed. There were no surprises there.

Now, 15 years later, and with a few seasons of hands-on experience in sailing the 59er under my belt, I think I have discovered what is the difference between ' fast' and 'so much faster'. Conventional blow-downwind boats tend to sail downwind at speeds close to the hull speed of the boat, and leaders who sail in gusts for more of the time than followers sail 3% or 4% faster. But apparent wind sailboats sail downwind at a speed that is proportional to the speed of the wind, so those which sail in large areas of wind that is probably 10%–15% stronger can sail up to 10–15% faster than followers who do not. This puts a much higher priority on finding and staying in the large areas of stronger wind when sailing downwind.

At the '100m diameter gust' level in the wind's fractal spectrum, the water surface at any time shows about 50% gust, 50% lull.

At the '5 to 10km roll' level of the wind's spectrum, the wind is clocked about 50% of the time, backed for the other 50%. This scale gives the oscillating winds.

At the '0.5 to 2km' diameter level between gusts and rolls, the surface wind is stronger over about 50% of the surface, lighter over the other 50%. This level of the wind's spectrum has become all-important to all of the new tack-downwind boats.

As yet, motions at this level do not have an agreed official name. I have discussed this with the Australian Bureau of Meteorology scientists. In this book I will refer to them as 'surges' and 'fades'.

6.3 ■ The new opportunity

To illustrate the difference between the approach that wins with conventional boats and what is needed to win in apparent wind boats, let us look at the way two skilled crews, both lead group sailors, one in a conventional boat and one in a contemporary boat, will handle their downwind legs.

There are two primary differences between racing a conventional sailboat and racing an apparent wind skiff.

The first difference is obvious. The conventional sailboat blows straight downwind at about half the wind speed. The apparent wind sailboat tacks downwind three times as fast through the water and approaches the downwind mark about twice as fast.

The second difference is not at all obvious at first. It is this – the area from which the apparent wind sailor can select better wind is huge as compared with that of the conventional sailor.

The apparent wind sailor hunts the best wind from a wide area, sails to it, and sails in it. The conventional sailor gathers what he can from a tiny area.

Figs 6.1, 6.2 and 6.3 show the mechanisms.

Fig 6.1A shows the performance diagram in true winds of 6, 9 and 12 knots of the popular (conventional) 5o5. The performance of the Flying Dutchman and the 470, both of which have been or are at this time Olympic, are similar.

Fig 6.1B shows the performance diagram of the Olympic 49er, a slightly smaller boat. The performance diagrams of the Grand Prix Eighteen foot skiffs of the early 1990s are a little faster than the 49er, and those of apparent wind boats such as the 29er, B-14 and 59er a little slower.

For those unfamiliar with polar diagrams, try looking at Fig 6.1A this way. Imagine that you are in a helicopter that is hovering, and that directly beneath you is a start boat with a number of 5o5s tied to it, all pointing away from the start boat. The wind speed is 9 knots. At the moment of start all the ties are released and the boats sail directly away from the start boat as fast as they can, each on a different heading. One sails close hauled; one close reaches; one beam reaches, etc. Before they vanish, you take a photo vertically downwards. Later you print the photo and draw a line through all the boats. You have just drawn the 'boat speed in 9 knot wind' 5o5 polar diagram in Fig 6.1A. The start boat is at 0. The speed at which each boat sailed away from the start boat on

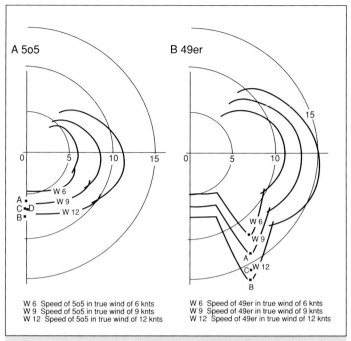

W 6 Speed of 5o5 in true wind of 6 knts
W 9 Speed of 5o5 in true wind of 9 knts
W 12 Speed of 5o5 in true wind of 12 knts

W 6 Speed of 49er in true wind of 6 knts
W 9 Speed of 49er in true wind of 9 knts
W 12 Speed of 49er in true wind of 12 knts

Fig 6.1 Performance diagrams 5o5 (A) and 49er (B)

each point of sailing in 9 knots of wind is given by the distance it sailed from '0' to the curve in the period between the start and when you took the photo; the faster it sailed, the greater the distance. Had the wind been 12 knots, the boats would have sailed faster and you would have drawn the 'boat speed in 12 knot wind' polar diagram.

Let us consider the options open to, and the decisions called for, first of the 5o5 crew and then of the 49er crew as they start a downwind leg in a true wind which averages 9 knots.

6.4 ■ Conventional downwind technique

A gust in a 10 knot wind will cover an area of about 200m crosswind and 200m upwind and downwind, and double that size in a 20 knot wind.

We make the following assumptions:
1 The 9 knot wind is 50% the 9 knot gradient wind lulls, interspersed 50% with gusts that average 12 knots.
2 The gusts typically extend 200m crosswind and 200m upwind and downwind.
3 The gusts blow at 12 knots for 2 minutes, then fade to 9 knots.
4 The gusts move at 12 knots.
5 The 5o5 sails at 6 knots in the 9 knot lulls, and at 7.33 knots in the 12 knot gusts (points A and B in Fig 6.1A).
6 A novice crew who do not hunt gusts will sail half the time in lull and half in gust at an average speed of 6.67 knots (point C).
7 The skilled crew are prepared to 'hunt' any gust they can reach within 60 seconds, on the expectation that they will enjoy the stronger wind within it for a further 60 seconds.
8 The skilled crew are prepared to sail up to 15° from the rhumb line and incur a distance penalty of 3% to access an observed gust.
9 The leg length is 1nm, 6080ft, 1.85km.

In Figs 6.2 and 6.3 the true wind is from the north – that is, from the top of the page.

Fig 6.2A shows the essentials: the vectors B0–B1, B0–B2, B0–B3 represent the boat speed; the vectors G0–B1, G2–B2, G3–B3 represent the true wind speed.

If the 5o5 is at B0 when a gust appears at G0, 300ft (100m) upwind and the crew hold their course, the gust will overtake the boat at B1, 60 seconds later, and 600ft (200m) further down the leg from G0. If a gust appears at G2, 100m upwind and 50m crosswind, and the crew clock 15°, the boat will meet the gust at B2, and a gust at G3 will meet the boat at B3.

As the boat approaches to round the windward mark, the instantaneous scan area is therefore the triangle B0–G2–G3, 100m upwind of the mark and 100m total crosswind. Any gust further upwind than G2–G3 will not reach the boat within 60 seconds. Any gust outside the lines G2B0 or G3B0 cannot be accessed with a turn of 15°.

Fig 6.3A shows what happens during every subsequent minute as the boat sails downwind at 6.67 knots from B0 to E:

- The instantaneous triangle is repeated as the starting scan area.
- Every minute the boat will sail at 6.67 knots – 3.4m per second, so 204m per minute downwind. B0–E is this distance, to scale.
- Every minute half the existing gusts will vanish. They will slow to lull speed and become a 9 knot lull wind.
- Every minute a similar number of new gusts will appear in random positions and begin their 2-minute (average) lives as gusts.
- So during every minute the crew can discover and access any gust that forms within the area BFEDC. Because they cannot reach anything beyond this area, nothing outside this area can affect them or their speed.

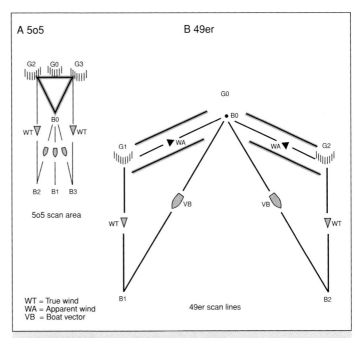

Fig 6.2 **Instantaneous scan areas or lines**

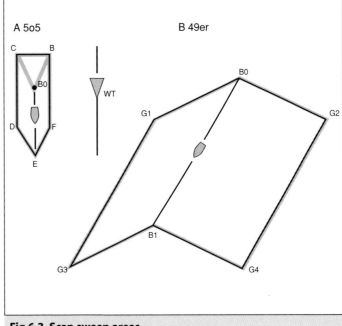

Fig 6.3 **Scan sweep areas**

This is the 'scan sweep area' per minute from which the skilled 5o5 crew can identify and access additional gusts. A reasonable assumption would be that with diligent scanning and hunting, they will sail in gusts for between five-eighths and three-quarters of the time rather than the expected half the time of the novice crew, and their average speed will become about 6.83 knots – point D in Fig 6.1A – or 2.5% faster than the novice crew who does not scan.

This is the reward to the skilled crew of a conventional boat for scanning and hunting gusts when sailing downwind. They scan the search sweep area outside the boat and access all the suitable gusts they can reach. In this way, they control the wind that they sail in to the extent that they can, and sail a little faster.

Note two points:

1 The crew of the blow-downwind boat can hunt and use gusts efficiently when sailing downwind because we have a solid understanding of the properties of gusts – their size, how strong the wind is within them, how fast they move, how long they last. With this knowledge, a crew can assess the potential cost and benefit of accessing each identified gust, ignore the marginal ones, and focus on those that will move them ahead of their rivals.

2 While surges and fades are of critical importance when sailing upwind – if you sail in fades you will lose to those who sail in surges – they do not rate when sailing downwind. They are usually too far away to be reached at the low crosswind speed available with a blow-downwind boat, and when you do try they tend to die before you get there. Put another way, this adds up to acknowledging that we know almost nothing about them, but what we do know, coupled with the glacial ability of the blow-downwind boat to hunt crosswind, is that they are not worth trying to use, so they have never been worth studying.

6.5 ■ Apparent wind downwind technique

Fig 6.2B shows the scan dynamics of the 49er, using the same logic and drawn to the same scale as Fig 6.2A. The boat is at B0, directly crosswind from B0 in Fig 6.2A. At this point we enter new sailing art.

In the 9 knot lull wind the 49er will sail at 14 knots, 7.1mps on a heading 35° from directly downwind (point A in Fig 6.1B). In the 12 knot gusts it sails at 17.25 knots, 8.8mps, at 25° from directly downwind (point B in Fig 6.1B). Its average speed and heading through 50% lull, 50% gust will be 15.6 knots, 8mps, at 30° from directly downwind (point C in Fig 6.1B). In Fig 6.2B the vector B0–B1 of 530m shows this starboard gybe boat speed and direction vector to scale, and B0–B2 gives the potential boat speed vector on port gybe.

G1–B1 and G2–B2 are the vectors of the true wind; they show how far a parcel of air will move during 60 seconds in a true wind of 10.5 knots. G1–B0 is the vector of the apparent wind; its speed is 9.7 knots in the direction G1–B0 when the boat is on starboard gybe, and from G2–B0 when the boat sails on port gybe. This vector triangle of 1 minute runs of the true wind, the apparent wind and the boat shows that if, when the boat is at B0, a gust appears at G1 300m to the ESE, it will meet the boat at B1 60 seconds later. If a gust appears at G2, the crew can gybe and meet it at B2. So the instantaneous 'search area' is no longer an area 100m wide upwind of the boat, but has become the 300m line B0-G1 crosswind and slightly downwind to the WSW from the boat. This is the wind you will pass through in the next 60 seconds if you do not gybe. Because you are tacking downwind you always have the option of sailing the other way, so if you see better wind on the other side you can gybe and access a gust at G2 300m to the ESE within 60 seconds. So your instantaneous scan is to look 'up the apparent wind' in *both* directions – that is, to search both the line B0–G1 *and* the line B0–G2. This is an instantaneous scan search width of 533m – that is, more than five times wider than G2–G3 in Fig 6.2A.

Fig 6.3B, to the same scale, shows what happens as the boat sails. During any minute in the 10.5 knot average wind WT, the 49er will sail the 530m from B0 to B1. So the scan sweep area per minute (the area any part of which you can access within the next 60 seconds if you want to) becomes B0–G1–G3–G4–G2. This is more than ten times the scan sweep area of the 5o5.

From the notes above we see that the seminal differences between handling the two types of boat are:

- The skiff's instantaneous search area is not upwind, but is crosswind both ways.
- The skiff's instantaneous search area is five times as wide as that of the blow-downwind boat.
- This wider width multiplied by the much higher downwind VMG means that the search sweep area per minute from which to discover and access gusts becomes nearly 11 times the search sweep area available to the blow-downwind 5o5 crew in the same time.
- This search sweep area is all downwind. Even if the best gust of the day forms 10ft behind you at G0, it will be useless because it will move downwind at 12 knots and you will be sailing downwind away from it at 15.6 knots.
- So the upside is that you have a huge area from which to pick the youngest and biggest gust each minute.

- But the downside is that the gusts are no longer of much use to you. You will pass through the 200m width of the typical gust in less than 30 seconds, and due to the sequential nature of the apparent wind gybe (see Chapter 26), you will necessarily lose 4 to 5 seconds every gybe; therefore, gybing back and forth in a 200m wide gust is not an efficient race-winning strategy (except sometimes in light air).

At this point it is helpful to look again at Mark Bethwaite's digest (Chapter 29) of the 'wind tactics wisdom' that has evolved for many decades in the high-level racing of conventional boats. In summary:

- When sailing upwind, look for and take advantage of the wider areas of stronger wind (surges) that are observed by crews who scan. These can be accessed relatively quickly by a boat that tacks upwind because the boat necessarily sweeps widely from side to side as it tacks, and the speed of closing between the boat sailing upwind and the surge drifting downwind is high.
- When sailing downwind, don't bother – because while surges remain of great potential advantage, their speed of closing with the boat seems near zero so they do not come to you, and you do not have the crosswind speed to sail to them; therefore, experience is that they usually die before you can reach them. Chase the smaller gusts that you can access with certainty.

6.6 ■ The new reality

What we see from the notes above is that the doubled downwind speed and hugely increased crosswind mobility of the apparent wind sailboat has reversed this hard-earned 'surges are not worth chasing downwind' conventional wisdom.

In its place is the new apparent wind wisdom that the way to win in future will be to 'forget the gusts; hunt and sail the surges downwind as well as upwind'. At the present time, this is easier said than done, because we do not yet know enough about surges and fades to be efficient in our hunting.

We can hunt gusts with confidence in a blow-downwind boat because we know:

1 How long they live, *and*
2 How fast they move, *and*
3 How much faster we will sail if we access them.

From 1 we can estimate how long it will take to close with them if we steer to intercept; from 1, 2 and 3 we can estimate what benefit we will enjoy, and from this decide either to access or discard. An important point is that if we make no decision, or decide to discard, we lose very little.

All we know about surges and fades at this moment (2007) is:

- They are visible, sometimes just visible, so their extra wind speed is likely nearer 10% to 20% than the gust's 30% to 40%.
- They have no defined edges – these are always graded and indefinite.
- They seem to drift downwind.
- They typically live long enough to access with the high speed of closing available when sailing upwind, but tend to die when accessed slowly. The best estimate would be 5 to 10 minutes, but it's extremely variable.

What this leads to in practice is great uncertainty. My experience from 59er racing in a mixed but relatively evenly matched fleet of 29ers (slower in lighter winds but faster in stronger winds due to trapeze) and B-14s (about the same in lighter winds, but faster in stronger winds due to wider wings) is typical. Club courses of about 1nm upwind–downwind were set either in Rose Bay or in the harbour near Shark Island (Fig 1.22). Typical times were 10 to 12 minutes upwind, 5 to 6 minutes downwind. Multiple two-lap races were sailed.

As we sailed upwind we would naturally elect the side on which stronger wind appeared, and try to fix both the time we first saw the stronger wind and how big it was. As we approached and rounded the windward mark, we knew:

- The view of the course, *and*
- How long the surge we were in had existed, *and*
- Whether it was 'big'.

We tried various approaches. Typical would be:

- Sail back into what you can see if it's young, *but*
- If a small surge has already existed 5 minutes, or a big one 7 or 8 minutes, expect it to die and that better wind will appear on the other side.

No system worked reliably, and the surges did not behave consistently.

There are further major differences unique to apparent wind sailing:

- With the apparent wind boat you cannot 'make no decision' and lose little by making no decision. You have no option but to go one way or the other.
- The downwind speed of the skiff is proportional to the wind speed (Fig 6.1B). So, as between two skiffs, if one sails downwind in stronger wind than the other, that boat will make huge gains. This is totally unlike the situation with conventional sailboats, in which gains or losses downwind are relatively small and making no decision loses little at worst.
- The speed with which you sail away from the windward mark in wind is often breathtaking. In good wind you can access anything you want to access, at any distance, and fast. But it had better be the right side, because when you choose the wrong side, sail a long way, and the wind then dies, you are a very long way from where you now see you should have gone, and in the lighter wind it takes a longer time to sail back.
- Despite this, a technique of gybing back and forth down the rhumb line seems to offer less overall success than any other.

My conclusion after a season of this racing was to realise that we simply do not know enough about surges and fades. To become proficient and confident in this new way of sailing downwind, new art needs to be used.

It turns out, though, that we need more than new art. We need new names. We also need new data and new analysis. In short, we need new research.

To this end, I decided to find out what I could about surges and fades.

6.7 ■ Steps towards a good experimental design

It needed about a year of indifferent but progressively more useful work before I arrived at what seems to be a good experimental design. The sequence was as follows:

Logic suggested that any crew who had well-based rules as to which side to go for would be able to make better decisions sooner about which surge to hunt, and win more races.

So my objective firmed – as with my wind observations of 30 years earlier, I would observe and amass records of the wind, but this time over the whole course area during a large number of downwind legs. I hoped that analysis of these observations would lead to simple rules that crews could apply to make better decisions about which side of the course would be faster downwind in the particular conditions of the day.

I considered undertaking more detailed study of the traces from the several recording anemographs that had been installed around the harbour prior to the 2000 Sydney Olympics.

This turned out to be not realistic. Synchronous traces from two instruments about 1000m apart cross-wind would have been ideal, but no such pair existed. And it was when I contemplated more intense analysis of the trace from any one instrument that I realised that observation from one point can never tell you anything about nearby stronger or lighter areas.

I considered mooring two recording anemographs, one on either side of the course, during races. The logistic problems, though, were more than I could reasonably handle.

At about this point I recognised that the only new information available to any crew during a race comes from eyeballing the water. Finally, the penny dropped. I realised that I too could get useful information if I eyeballed the water over the whole of the course area and recorded what I saw, and repeated this often enough to build a useful database.

It was at this point that my focus shifted from acquiring synchronous speed and direction traces from two adjacent recording anemographs, and I began to think about direct observation of the wind over the whole of the course area.

At first I considered the relevant areas to be the two sides of a course while boats were actually racing, and for a while I pestered friends who had harbour views which faced the prevailing sea breeze to let me observe the course areas during races. This proved unrealistic because the wind over the course area upwind of the closest observation point (Point Piper, 5 in Fig 1.22) is churned up by Shark Island directly to windward, and all other vantage points were either too low, with unacceptable foreshortening, or too distant and/or too oblique.

The next development was to use a camera and photos of areas of water were exposed using different films and shutter speeds. It turned out that very normal 100-ASA colour is as good as any to record the darker areas that mark stronger wind. Surprisingly, filament electric light seems to reveal contrast in the emulsion print better than natural daylight.

Short-course (1nm) racing in fast skiffs tends towards upwind legs of about 12 minutes and downwind legs of about 6 minutes. I reasoned that a useful record of observable changes in wind speed over such times would be given by a 12-minute set of 24 frames exposed at 30 second intervals. The expectation was that each set would then be analysed for best side of the course both upwind and downwind. Initially I believed that the ideal set would be taken with the camera looking upwind from a position just downwind of a notional leeward mark, and I started this photographic work in about May 2000.

The first few sets to this format proved to be both encouraging and disappointing. All were exposed from elevations so low that the foreshortening precluded reliable analysis of surges more than a few hundred metres upwind. But what I could see in those few hundred metres certainly revealed wind speed differences in the crosswind sense. The concept was valid and had potential, but the application needed improvement. A rethink was called for.

6.8 ■ Better observations

I found a vantage point on Dobroyd Head 93m above the water (on the scarp edge at C in Fig 1.22). This overlooks the harbour between North Head and Middle Head, and was the area of course D in the 2000 Sydney Olympics. I found that sets of photos exposed from this height showed surges up to 3km distant without unacceptable foreshortening, and two practical consequences flowed from this enhanced clarity:

- The first was that there was no longer any perceived need for the camera to face upwind. Given the clearer view of the whole larger area, the wind direction ceased to matter. A notional upwind–downwind course could be inserted anywhere in the field of vision and the flow of surges along both sides of it could be studied regardless of its direction with respect to that of the camera's field of vision.
- The second and more important consequence was a change in the object itself. I realised that with this new capability I could study the properties of the surges themselves rather than the effects of surges close to a notional course.

So rather than asking 'What will be the stronger-wind side of some course at some future time?' I changed the objective to answer the more fundamental questions:

- How often are surges visible?
- How do they start? (Do they just appear, or drift into view from upwind?)
- How long do they live?
- How fast do they move?
- How big do they grow?
- How do their lives end? (Do they just vanish, or drift out of view downwind?)

And, at a second level:

- Is there pattern to their behaviour? And, if so, is there pattern always, or just sometimes?

At this point I felt that the design of the experiment had been sufficiently developed to get on with it, and in May 2001 I started a second series of sets exposed from Dobroyd Head.

The tripod position is constant. The camera is zoomed to its widest (50°) and is centred towards South Head 2.6km distant at 155° true. The useful field of vision covers about 10sq km.

The following parameters are noted when each set is exposed and developed:

- Surface wind speed and direction.
- Air temperature.
- Water temperature.
- Turbulent layer type – whether gradient wind or sea breeze/funnelling wind.
- Synoptic situation – whether high dominant, low dominant or neutral.
  (These are the Stability Index factors from *HPS-1*, Chapter 10.)
- The photos are exposed at 1-minute intervals, and when developed are dated and numbered in sequence.

6.9 ■ Analysis

To answer the questions above, I needed to get the crowded and foreshortened surges in each photo onto a plan so that I could study the start, growth, size, movement and decay of each surge. This was a three-step process.

Step 1

I drew on clear plastic a foreshortened perspective graticule to the scale of the photos (Fig 6.4). This shows what the photos would look like if the water were painted in chequerboard rectangles 500m NS and 250m EW.

Each photo is studied to identify the visible surges. Those beyond about 3km are ignored. Sometimes the combination of the sun's position and the ripple direction degrades contrast on one side of the picture. In Fig 6.5, I have analysed what was clear ahead and to the right, and ignored what was less distinct on the left.

The transparent perspective film is placed over each photo and is registered on the horizon and on a physical feature on the horizon in the photo.

Each surge within 3km is outlined on the clear plastic with fine white-board marker.

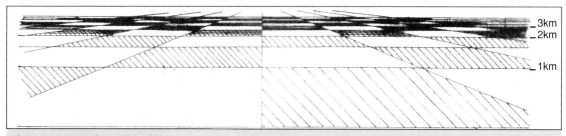

Fig 6.4 Perspective graticule

Step 2

I drew a regular plan-position 'chequerboard' graticule (Fig 6.5). This is what the camera would see if it photographed the painted water of Fig 6.4 vertically downwards from directly overhead.

Each outlined surge on the perspective graticule (Fig 6.4) is then drawn by hand on the plan-position graticule. The corresponding chequerboard patterns make the transfer task unambiguous and simple, if tedious. Each plan graticule is numbered to correspond with the photo.

At the end of this process I have a numbered sequence of 24 of the plan graticules, each about half covered with a near-random 'blob' pattern of the outlines of surges of varying size.

These are the key observations, but in this form they are still too jumbled and confusing to convey any clear message. Fig 6.5 shows a typical sequence.

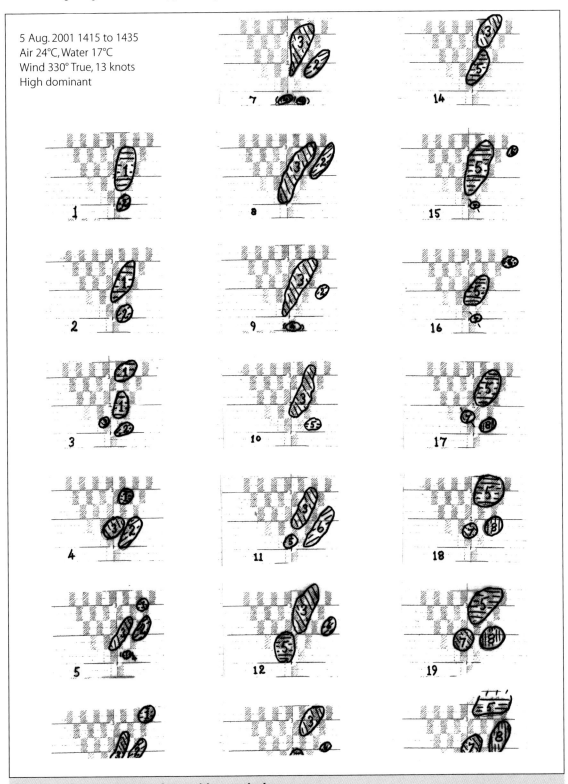

5 Aug. 2001 1415 to 1435
Air 24°C, Water 17°C
Wind 330° True, 13 knots
High dominant

Fig 6.5 Surge sequence on plan position graticule

Step 3

Use of colour reveals order and pattern. I colour the most obvious surge in plan-position graticule No 1, say, dark blue. I follow this surge from graticule 1 to 2 to 3, colouring dark blue as I go, until it vanishes or drifts out of the field of vision. I then colour every other surge similarly, but in a different shade. I now have an overall picture that is easy to comprehend, one that shows each of the surges over that area during those 24 minutes. In Fig 6.5 I have used numbers and different black and white hatching instead of colour to show how it works.

If the 24 pages of the set are assembled in order and riffed, the coloured surges appear to move. The properties of each surge can now be measured – where it starts, how it grows, its size, its speed, its end, and how long it lasted. At a second level, I can see how consistent any surge is with the others in that set.

This whole process is tedious and time-consuming. Each photo of the set needs much focused attention to get it to the stage of coloured blobs on the plan-position graticule.

6.10 ■ Data to date

It was my intention to expose and analyse at least 50, and preferably 100, sequences so as to be able to present statistically useful conclusions. By September 2002, I had exposed and analysed 25 sequences. I paused to look at what I had learned, and to reconsider what to do next.

The philosophical lessons to that point were:

1   I have yet to see a photo that does not reveal surges. Surges, like fluctuations, gusts and rolls, appear to be an always present natural feature in the wind's spectrum.
2   Surges occur on all days – that is, on days when the air is being cooled as well as on days when it is being heated, so their driving force is not heat and must be dynamic.
3   A necessary consequence of differences in surface wind speed in adjacent areas is that vertical motions at the scale of the surges must be involved.
4   Surges that occur on days when the water is warmer than the air will necessarily be driven by thermal excitation in addition to whatever the other dynamic forces may be.
5   Surges usually move downwind at about one-quarter the wind speed; this is about the same as the speed at which roll motions seem to move downwind. But sometimes they just appear and vanish and move little.
6   Very occasionally a stationary surge occurs within a field of moving surges, in the manner of a lee wave downwind of a mountain range. This is not surprising in this locality.
7   Surge size and surge life are very variable.
8   It was my intention to have a colleague moor a motorboat in the field of vision and measure the wind speed every minute during a sequence, but we did not proceed to this stage. My best guess would be that the typical difference between surge and fade would be about half the difference between gust and lull – that is, about 20%. If it were much less, they would not be so visually obvious.
9   It is relevant to note that I had raced in these waters with the Balmoral Tasar fleet for many years, and that everything that I observed from height was consistent with my memory of racing in those waters.

The practical conclusion was that the whole process of acquiring the observations and processing the photos as above, while accurate and the best I could do, was so time-consuming that it was absorbing all of my spare time and had, for the past two years, precluded all real progress on the book. So I had to decide whether this was to be a book about apparent wind sailing, or a book about surges and fades. I considered the use of high-quality digital photography with computer manipulation to enhance the contrast, then bleach the whole image until only the darker surges remained, plus writing a program to transform them from perspective to plan position. But while this would speed up the supply of images, it would take much time to establish, and would make no difference to the time needed to analyse each of a larger number of sequences.

So my decision, with regret, was to get on with the book, be satisfied with introducing surges and fades into the sailing lexicon, and to leave accumulation of adequate samples for more thorough statistical analysis to some future group of PhD students as their theses subjects.

Fig 6.6 tabulates data from the best 8 sequences.

Data from best seven sequences

Date	W/V	Air C	Water C	Turb Layer	Synop Sit'n	Surge No	Start	End	Life Mins	Size km	Dir (to)	V kts	
11 5 01	155/11	18	20	Gradient	H Dom	1	1	12	>12	1.5 x 1.5	0		
21 5 01	270/06	16	19	Gradient	H dom	1	1	12	>12	0.5 x 0.5	0		
						2	6	18	12	0.5 x 0.5	0		
26 5 01	160/15	15	19	Gradient		1	1	4	>4	1.5 x 1.5	N	8	
					Isobars	2	1	8	>8	2 x 3	N	4	
					straight	3	13	18	5	2 x 1.5	N	8	Mobile
						4	20	23	>3	1 x 2	N	3	patches
7 7 01	270/8	18	15	Gradient	H dom	1	1	2	>2	1 x 1	E	3	Big
						2	3	11	8	1.5 x 1.5	E	4	Surges
						3	20	24	>4	1 x 2	E	4	
22 7 01	330/8	17	16	Gradient	L dom	1	1	6	>6	2 x 2	0		
						2	2	8	6	1 x 2	0		
						3	7	11	4	1 x 1	0		
						4	9	12	3	1 x 1	0		
5 8 01	330/13	24	17	Gradient	H dom	1	1	6	>6	1 x 1	S	2?	
						2	1	7	>7	.5 x .3	SSW	5	
						3	3	13	10	2 x .5	SSW	5	
						4	7	9	3	.2 x .2			
						5	10	20	>10	1 x 1.5	SSW	5	
						6	15	16	2	.2 x .2			
						7	17	20	>3	.7 x .7	SSW	5	
						8	17	20	>4	1 x .6	SSW		
29 9 0`	045/13	23	19	Sea Breeze	H dom	1	3	9	6	.5 x 1	SW	10	Short
						2	2	5	4	.7 x .8	SW	10	lives
						3	6	16	11	.5 x 1.5	SW	5	
						4	9	22	13	1 x 1.5	SW	4	
						5	14	24	>10	.5 x .8	SW	5	
						6	17	20	4	.5 x .5	0		
						7	22	24	>3	.5 x .5	SW	6	
1 12 01	045/12	24	20	Sea Breeze	H dom	1	1	24	>24	1 x 1	SW	2	Slow
						2	1	7	>7	.5 x .5	SW	2	Slow
						3	12	16	4	.8 x .8	SW	7	Fast

Fig 6.6 Summary of surge observations

6.11 ■ Postscripts from left field

It never seems to occur to sailors to think of the wind as other than a horizontal flow – though not everybody agrees with this view.

From the perspective of the paraglider

The refinement of the original 'Rogallo kite' hang glider into paragliders with very reasonable performance has led to the ability to thermal soar these machines for duration and to dynamic soar them to fly cross-country. These machines depend on the pilot's legs when landing, so they are designed to touch down at not more than 14mph. The literature of this small-glider community is of interest to the sailor. Below are some quotes from paragliders:

'*Wind tends to destroy thermals by continually mixing the air ... turning what could have been a decent thermal into a ragged mess, especially close to the ground ...*'

'*It's important to understand that the lift and sink generally balance each other out, especially in relatively small areas. If your climb rate is 1000ft per minute (about 10 knots), expect at least 1000ft per minute sink when you leave the thermal. If the thermals are large, expect big areas of sink ...*'

'*I picture the vertical structure of thermals as a root system that touches the ground. At increasing height each thermal combines with its neighbour until a great "trunk": feeds into the base of the cloud above.*'

The scale of these observations would be consistent with smaller (0.5–1km) surges.

From the perspective of the sailplane pilot

The pilots of sailplanes – advanced sophisticated gliders with very high ratios of lift to drag and with no limitations on their approach and landing speeds – think at a different scale. Philip Giffard, an ex-dinghy sailor who now lives near the coast south of Brisbane, writes:

I was flying with a friend in his Stamm. This is a very high performance sailplane with at best about a fifty to one glide angle, but more importantly its full-span trailing edge flaps give it a tremendous speed range. When slightly down they enable it to near hover at very low speed with little sink, and when slightly up they enable it to shallow dive at more than 100 knots again with a surprisingly low sinking speed.

We were thermalling about 20 miles inland when suddenly a cold wind set in from the coast. Getting home became a problem. It was useless circling in lift because we simply drifted further inland. So we headed directly for the coast. In lift we flew as slowly as possible to spend as long as possible in the rising air. When we flew out of that area of lift we retrimmed the flaps and shallow dived at high speed to pass through the area of sinking air as quickly as possible until we came to the next area of lift. The long periods climbing at low speed in rising air and the headwind were enough on balance to keep us above the minimum safe altitude as we shallow-dived across the areas of sink, and in this way we made it back to the coast against the wind.

Note again that the air was assumed, and correctly, to be everywhere either rising or sinking. In this case the scale appears to be of areas some kilometres in extent.

These excerpts give us some clue as to what might drive the surges and fades. If, for whatever reason, the atmosphere is indeed everywhere either rising or subsiding to some extent, there have to be horizontal flows at the surface away from the bases of the subsiding areas and towards the bases of the rising areas.

It may be that these cross-flows are what we will in future call surges and fades.

PART THREE

The Boat

Chapter 7 • The Drive to Sail Faster

7.1 ■ Seminal performance advances

For 4000 years the relative performance level of sailboats everywhere changed almost not at all, but over the last 200 years we have witnessed three major performance advances and a string of minor ones. Why?

In chronological order the key advances have been:

- **1800 to 1900 – Moving ballast**
  Moving of ballast in sandbaggers and moving of bodies in skiffs enabled them to carry more sail. The advantage was faster sailing, principally by maintaining more speed through the lulls (see Chapter 1).

- **1895 to 1905 – Planing**
  Until the planing sailboat was developed, all sailboats had been limited by their hull speed and were relatively slow. Planing sailboats were not limited in this way, and could sail faster (see Chapter 1). The development of the planing sailboat altered all future expectations of performance.

- **1925 – Recognition re aerodynamic law**
  In 1925, Manfred Curry realised that sailboats follow aerodynamic law, and wrote a book about it called *Yacht Racing, the Aerodynamics of Sails, and Racing Tactics*. In doing this, he was the first to document the technical principles of sailing.

- **c 1935 – Trapezes**
  Trapezes were invented in different forms in both New Zealand and the UK in the late 1930s, but their advantages appear not to have been well exploited, and they were ignored. They were re-invented in Europe in the early 1950s.

- **1960s – Wind tactics**
  In the early 1960s Dr Stuart Walker published *The Tactics of Small Boat Racing* in which he categorises winds as either oscillating or persistent shifts. Also in this decade, Alan Watts published *Wind and Sailing Boats*, in which he asserted that gusts favour starboard tack in the northern hemisphere. David Houghton published a series of smaller books in which he described the driving mechanisms of the wind features useful to the racing sailor.

  These three authors together introduced the concept of 'wind tactics' – the art of taking advantage of short-term local changes in wind speed and direction to reach the next mark sooner.

- **1960s – 'Bendy' masts**
  In the early 1960s, when masts were meant to be stiff, Moth sailors wanted the lightest possible masts. Inevitably, some were made too light and bent a little, but it was observed that these sometimes sailed faster.

  Over about two years, perception of these slightly flexible masts changed from 'Not stiff enough. Defective. Undesirable' to 'Faster, Desirable'. This was the first of several cases in which unexpected performance increase was observed – and in this case the cause was manufacturing error.

- **1960s – Adjustment of sail shape**
  Outhaul, downhaul and vang or backstay controls were then developed that were powerful enough to hold a 'bendy' mast at any desired bend independent of wind speed and mainsheet tension. Sailors used these

controls to adjust their mainsails flatter for sailing upwind or in stronger winds, or fuller for sailing offwind or in lighter winds. A datum mark system was developed to enable any desired shape to be instantly and accurately repeated.

Crews who adjusted sail shape efficiently sailed faster than those who did not.

- **c 1975 – Wings**
  The principle of shifting ballast to the windward gunwale and then of shifting the crew further to windward by use of the trapeze was extended by the use of wings to increase effective gunwale beam with no change of hull shape and an insignificant increase in weight (see Chapter 11).

- **c 1975 – Tacking downwind**
  Between 1975 and 1990 the ability to tack downwind faster than running square, and then faster than the wind, was developed by the Eighteen footer skiff class of Sydney (see Chapter 1). Up to that time, all sailboats (but not iceboats) had sailed downwind with wind-from-behind technique at a boat speed and VMG always substantially slower than the wind speed.

  Since then, some boats can sail downwind with a wind-from-ahead technique at a boat speed faster than the wind, and some with VMG faster than the wind. This was a huge performance increase which fundamentally changed all future expectations of sailboat performance.

  The term 'apparent wind sailing' was coined to encapsulate this new technology.

- **1988 – Flexible topmast**
  In 1988 a new distribution of flexibility within the mast structure – an almost rigid lower mast and a much more flexible topmast – was developed to overcome mechanical and cost problems. Increased performance was observed – this was another case of unexpected performance increase from a structure created for a different reason.

- **1992 – The dynamically humpless hull**
  Tow-testing of some skiff hulls at full scale has revealed drag curves that do not show a 'hump' just above hull speed. This was an unexpected discovery that has not yet been adequately explained by present theory. A pragmatic approach has incorporated this feature within the design of some advanced sailboats (see Chapter 10).

- **1999 – The critical ratios**
  Many new 'skiff copy' products failed to deliver apparent wind performance at all wind speeds. Analysis has revealed that true apparent wind performance is possible if – and only if – three different ratios are all satisfied *and* the boat remains controllable in strong winds (see Chapter 20).

- **c 2000 – Towards automatic rigs**
  Four developments have flowed from the bendy mast and the more flexible topmast:
  - Observation of the behaviour of a flexible rig when sailing revealed that it yields not only to gusts that typically last about half a minute, but also to 'mini-gusts' that occur every few seconds (see Chapter 14). (This was yet another unexpected discovery.)
  - Study of the available records for evidence of 'gusts within gusts' – that is, at the 'fluctuations' level of the wind's spectrum – revealed that significant changes of wind speed can, and do, occur every few seconds. These repeat far too quickly for any crew to respond to with manual adjustment (see Chapter 5).
  - It follows that the advantage enjoyed by crews who adjust every minute or so is only a part of the potential advantage that could be enjoyed if a rig could self-adjust automatically and instantaneously to the quicker changes.
  - Development and optimisation of such automatic rigs is a current goal.

- **c 2000 – Further wind tactics**
  The much higher downwind boat speeds of the apparent wind skiffs has reduced the relative importance of the 100m diameter gusts and focused attention on the 1000m diameter surges and fades – the next level up in the wind's spectrum. This level appears not to have been systematically studied, so no detailed analysis of wind motions at this scale appears in the scientific literature. In order to sail the faster boats more intelligently, we need to know more about the properties and probabilities of surges and fades. An initial pilot study has now been completed (see Chapter 6).

After 4000 years of so little change in performance, all of the changes above have occurred within the past 200 years, and all of these except one within about the past 100 years.

Further, of all these changes three are of overwhelming importance because it has been first the bigger sails, then the planing sailboat, then the apparent wind sailboat that have contributed to the big jumps in performance that have altered all future expectations (see Fig 1.36). While each of the other changes has added something to the developing technology, the importance of each is trivial compared with these three.

What has driven this ferment? And what has made these advances possible?

7.2 ■ The cradles of individually driven change

Between 2000 BC and AD 1800 sailing was obviously of interest to sailors, but of little or no relevance to anybody else. Therefore the truly fundamental change appears to have been when sailing became 'public' in about 1800. Probably because of the growth of literacy, the media, and the spread of gambling, the outcome of sailboat races began to be of importance to a wider public than simply the sailors themselves. This stimulated imaginative sailors to think of possible ways of sailing faster.

Inventive individuals abound, and $E = mc^2$ is probably the ultimate expression of the lone innovator. All of the changes listed above, other than the three 'big' ones, are typical of the work of a single highly motivated innovator or inventor.

These need no further explanation.

7.3 ■ The cradles of group-driven change

With respect to the moving ballast sandbaggers and skiffs, the Duggan and Logan planing sailboats, and the development of apparent wind sailing, all these were the creatures of co-operative groups. In looking at the history of each of the groups, they all possessed four common factors and they all survived for only as long as these four common factors remained strong:

1   The first and most important one has been the character of the key people, with the essential need being that one man or woman should dare to think differently. No change is possible until it is first created in the imagination – that is, until somebody dares to think differently.
2   The second was that the key brain(s) should enjoy both a supportive working environment and the positive support of a group of like-minded men and/or women to work among. True creativity is a fragile flower; it takes little to crush it.
3   The third was that the ideas had to work – in other words, that boats built to these ideas should indeed sail faster.
4   The fourth was that the group itself should feel supported by a substantial public audience who would enjoy the new spectacle and be vocal in their approval.

7.4 ■ The bigger sails era

New York

The sandbaggers appear to have been the creatures of the New York waterfront taverns. The fishermen provided the boats and the sailing skills, and the longshoremen provided the brawn to heft the sandbags. The tavern clientele provided the fiercely loyal close support. The public who watched from the shorelines and wagered provided added depth to the support.

For some decades it all worked, but the balance was fragile. The loss of a supportive environment – a result of a decrease in the foreshore viewing area because of pier development, plus the focused opposition from sailors opposed to change – tipped the balance, and the sandbaggers withered and vanished from New York.

Sydney

The Sydney skiffs (*c* 1840–1938) expressed the 'jack's as good as his master', 'give it a go', and 'go for broke' character of Sydney after the decades of the gold rush. Contempt for restrictive laws led to the minimum possible rules – 'the length shall not exceed 16 (or whatever) feet, the race starts at half-past two, and the first boat across the finish line is the winner'. No restrictions, no excuses, no handicaps. In this environment large numbers of home-designed skiffs were built with high hopes and their crews crowded on more and more sail in their 'cut and try' search for more speed (Figs 1.6 and 1.7). The wider populace loved it; they crowded the steep foreshores to watch and wager. When Mark Foy organised the previously uncoordinated activity into regular weekly programmed spectacular races, the skiffs quickly achieved an iconic status in Sydney that survived for a century.

7.5 ■ The planing sailboat explosion

Montreal

The Herrick Duggan 'displacement sandbagger to planing Lake Scow' 1895 to 1905 era appears to have been the careful methodical expression of genius from one engineer's brain. The Royal St Lawrence Yacht Club's centenary history tells us that Duggan had been Commodore from 1885 to 1890; also, that in the years before the Seawanhaka challenges, starting in 1895, he dominated Lake St Louis racing in his small yacht *Gloria*. Buddy Melges tells us that 'lake scows' started near Montreal and first migrated west through Canada, then south into the USA through Minnesota, so it is now obvious that Duggan and Shearwood had an extensive and unexpected background of experience from which to draw. Having said all that, it remains obvious that Royal St Lawrence's successful challenge and eight consecutive successful Seawanhaka Cup defence matches were the expression of Duggan's creative genius and the smooth working of the Duggan–Shearwood team and their close supporters. The St Lawrence Yacht Club history also tells us that Duggan and Shearwood became Canadian sporting icons during and following those years, so the wider public was well aware, appreciative and vocal.

Duggan's legacy is a record of nine successive challenge matches prior to each of which he designed a new and different boat which was sufficiently faster than the one before to win again. This was not an immediate thrust towards planing. *Dominion* (Fig 1.20) expresses the ultimate in a displacement design which 'measures short (upright) and sails long (when heeled) with minimum wetted area'. Only when this approach was banned did Duggan move towards the planing hull, with its need to tread delicately within the complex of wetted area and sail area and total weight ratios. He sensed what was needed better than his opponents and kept on designing faster boats. But then the challenges ceased and the Duggan era came to an end.

He had started with sandbagger-like displacement yachts, and his final design was the model for the modern, faster, light-air flat-water planing lake scow. As a sustained creative exercise by one designer, this probably remains unique.

Auckland

Arch Logan's planing 'Patikis' seem to be another case where the dominant drive was one man's brain. While Arch was one of five brothers who traded as 'Logan Bros', all of whom were nominally as good as each other so their designs were all signed simply 'Logan Bros', it was Arch who focused on design rather than management, construction or property development. The explosive development of the planing Patiki started with Arch's sighting of *Sea King* and his leap in imagination as to what could be done with this new unballasted, lighter weight, flatter-lined approach if it were to be built to a different vision.

Arch's brothers provided the close support; enthusiasm for the progressively faster boats, both from their owners and the media, provided the wider support. But this environment, like that of the sandbaggers, proved fragile. Growing resentment of the faster boats by conservative sailors and clubs who resisted change diminished the appreciative public support. Then in 1910 the Auckland port authority took over the Logan Bros shipbuilding premises to make way for a new wharf, and the brothers never did re-establish permanently as a unified, focused group. With the removal of these two essential elements, the drive for explosive change evaporated.

The Arch Logan era had started with ballasted displacement craft. In a surge of unprecedented creativity he and those he led quickly established, and further developed, the blazingly fast-planing Patikis which revelled in strong winds and flat water.

In later and quieter years he continued to design superb craft like the seagoing 'M' class.

7.6 ■ The apparent wind revolution – Australia

A purely Sydney scene

The drives behind the relatively recent development of apparent wind sailing through the 1970s, 1980s and 1990s by the Sydney Eighteen footer skiffs were transparently simple:

- All conventional rules-bound sailboats worldwide were unconsciously locked into a 'no change, no greater speed, no spectacle' mindset which led ultimately to the 'no television interest in sailing' at the Atlanta Olympics and the International Olympic Committee's demand for spectacular sailing that would flow from that.

  The surviving 'no rules' Australian skiff classes are the 12s, 14s, 16s and 18s.
- The 12s still followed a nineteenth-century mindset that bigger sails were faster despite the obvious fact that beyond an optimum size in any wind, bigger sails are in fact slower. In reality, the 12s' relatively huge rigs are at about the limit of control, and for this reason the 12s are challenging to sail and spectacular to watch. This satisfies both the sailors and their supporters, despite the fact that their speeds – for example, in the Two of a Kind races – were quite slow.
- The 14s of those days were concerned with cost minimisation and suspicious of anything new if it cost a dollar more. So, like the 12s, the 14s were focused on things other than speed and also were sailing quite slowly.
- The 16s were potentially fast, but until very recently were locked into slow dynamics by the common strong local culture that supported each 16ft skiff club and its fleet. For many decades, the 16ft skiff clubs had developed within, and remained locked into, the pre-war social attitudes of their upper harbourside working-class suburbs, and their rules expressed a culture that demanded that their boats race with as many crew on board as possible so that the greatest number of families and friends would contribute to club patronage. These clubs all fiercely resisted any suggestion that the boats should be encouraged to sail faster by lightening up and carrying smaller crews. (This environment has recently changed quickly and dramatically, due partly to the gentrification of the inner suburbs, but primarily to the vacuum left by the withdrawal of the Eighteen footers from the development scene since 1996.)
- The Eighteens alone had managed to survive without crippling historical, technical or social mindsets. They were based in two clubs, both in relatively affluent suburbs. Most importantly, the two clubs co-ordinated their services to provide the most supportive environment possible. Membership of each club was recognised by the other, and the race programmes were co-ordinated. The Sydney Flying Squadron in Careening Cove on the North Shore managed the Saturday races, and the NSW League in Double Bay on the South Shore managed the Sunday races over near identical courses.

This was the Eighteen footer environment that evolved after the 1939–45 war. It grew as a warm, pleasant, friendly, and mutually supportive community. Within it was a core of vital, anarchic, creative, fiercely competitive sailors, all of whom were focused solely on speed. Ashore, they socialised and helped one another and carried each other's boats to and from the water. But from race start to finish, they were different personalities with knives in their teeth. Then, back ashore, co-operation reigned again. Design innovation and experiment was not only welcome; it was expected. Most Eighteen footer sailors and builders were traditionally pragmatic 'cut and try' advocates, but as the decades passed an increasing number began to calculate, predict and design by numbers.

The 1945 to 1975 phase

The era from 1945 to 1996 was divided into two parts: from 1945 until 1975, it was 'normal' in that funds were scarce and innovation limited; from 1976 until 1996, the situation reversed and research and development – whether by measurement and calculation or by cut and try – was strongly encouraged by generous funding.

From 1945 to 1954 I routinely flew flying boats from the flying boat base in Rose Bay (14 in Fig 1.22). I watched while the residue of the pre-war multi-crew, huge-sails displacement skiffs of the style that had been so thoroughly beaten in Hobart just before the war was replaced by a fleet of planing Eighteen footers with lighter hulls, a crew of four with three on trapeze, and the skipper steering from the gunwale, and separate rigs for light, moderate and strong winds. These new Eighteen footers were back on the harbour together with the shoreline crowds, the ferries and the punters. A young designer named Bruce Farr from Auckland had a good eye for line, and his boats began to dominate the race results. From 1945 to about 1970, this was the Sydney Harbour scene at weekends.

The economics had shaken down into a pattern in which the winning crews were sponsored at about \$A20 000 per season, with less for those not yet winning.

Innovation was limited. Starting in 1960, Bob Miller (later Ben Lexen) designed and sailed two three-handers which were sometimes very fast but were too inconsistent to be convincing. Despite winning one world championship, they did not change most sailors' way of thinking, and minor variations on the four-hander theme continued to be the norm.

From 1971 until 1975, David Porter tried three-handers again. He built and sailed five progressively faster, more consistent and more successful three-handers. Over those five years, these five boats changed everybody's way of thinking, and after he finally won the World Championship in Brisbane in 1975, nobody built another four-hander.

The 1876 to 1996 phase

For several years after 1976, Iain Murray was sponsored in *Colour 7* by the Channel Seven TV network which had just converted its TV signal to colour. This became the boat to beat and Iain won the World Championship several times (these years are described in Section 1.13). Fig 1.32 shows Iain's first *Colour 7*, broad reaching with a symmetrical flattie spinnaker. This boat had no wings; but year by year thereafter, wings appeared and grew wider, rigs grew bigger and broad reaching speeds increased.

In 1982 Julian Bethwaite invented the asymmetric spinnaker system and rigged it on his two-hander Eighteen footer *Prime II* (Fig 1.34). His system used a long fixed bowsprit in place of a free spinnaker pole, and an asymmetric spinnaker with a full powerful luff and a flat low-drag leech. The more powerful three-handers immediately adapted the asymmetric rig. Times to set and drop the spinnaker reduced from 30 seconds to 5, the crippling drag of the hooked leech was removed, and the boats suddenly started broad reaching routinely at previously unprecedented speeds. This was all good spectacular stuff, and the harbourside crowds exploded. The Seven network helicopter routinely swept the harbour on Saturday and Sunday afternoons on its way to and from news assignments; it filmed *Colour 7* and other skiffs, and Channel Seven showed these clips as part of its own station promotion. The viewing public loved it.

From the point of view of the sponsors, the increased speeds, excitement and exposure abruptly increased the promotional value of having a good skiff carry their logo on its spinnaker. In this atmosphere, the sailors were encouraged, and paid generously, to experiment with whatever they thought might make their boats sail faster. Once the *Grand Prix Sailing* programme was launched, this process simply accelerated. (Chapters 14, 15 and 16 describe how this promotion opportunity was perceived by Brian Keane and how Julian Bethwaite and his crew responded.) All the other top boats were trying equally hard and being paid similarly to try anything and everything, so it is hardly surprising that R and D, whether by cut and try or by measurement and calculation, reached an unprecedented level of both activity and effectiveness.

The public flocked to the harbour foreshores to watch – and wager. The newspapers devoted half-pages to sailing results with large photos, usually of skiffs at speed. This was the skiff environment that I came to know from the early 1970s when my younger son Julian became involved in the class, and the beginnings of my book *HPS-1*, written in the decade 1980 to 1991. The onshore environment was comfortable and supportive, and over those years this tiny crucible of perhaps 50 crews in total contributed an input into the global art of sailing faster that was altogether disproportionate to their numbers.

The environment felt stable and secure – but it wasn't.

The end of an era

In 1993 one of the two clubs, the League, abruptly reversed its policy of co-operation, withdrew mutual support, and withdrew the long-standing reciprocal invitation to Sydney Flying Squadron members to start in League races. It barred and bolted the gate by banning from League membership any sailor who started in Sydney Flying Squadron races. To emphasise the difference, they adopted a club class rule that called for shorter wings. Why?

At root, the League's traditional business was to provide race management on Sunday afternoons for an Eighteen foot skiff fleet in the 'showcase' part of Sydney Harbour. The spectator interest and media promotion generated by the fleet was exploited by providing either support for 'owner and sponsor' teams, or a 'whole provision and management of a boat and its crew' package for such sponsors as preferred to rely on club management of their sponsorship. The whole exercise attracted strong club membership and patronage. This was all local to Sydney and the harbour.

The League and the Sydney Flying Squadron (who managed the Saturday races over the same courses) had for decades co-operated in providing an environment in which crews were encouraged to engage in both R and D and also 'cut and try development' in this vital class – and, above all, in making all crews welcome on both start lines.

Over the decades 1945 to the 1970s, this policy of co-operation had encouraged crews to experiment with design, and in measured steps the heavy, big-crew rag-carriers had been replaced by the four-handers that in turn had given way to the three-handers. Over these years, the style of sailing did not change – all downwind sailing was wind-from-behind sailing – and the speed increases had been modest.

Abruptly, the three-handers began to broad reach progressively faster, and unconsciously they were developing a new technique of apparent wind sailing. The emerging excitement, spectacle and uncertainty (for the punters) of this faster sailing excited interest far beyond the harbour and Sydney. Both the League and the Squadron either failed to see the wider promotional opportunity, or thought about it and then elected not to become involved.

One sports TV programme producer, Bill McCartney, saw the opportunity, created the TV programme *Grand Prix Sailing*, and within a few years had generated audience demand such that the programme was broadcast free to air in prime time on main commercial TV channels in the capital cities. The audience for this Sydney icon had increased a hundredfold, and in the ensuing commercial rush to get a skiff into the Grand Prix programme, the League suddenly found itself bypassed and becoming irrelevant. It seems to have been this that triggered its action.

The League directors' response was to think small and salvage what they could of their traditional Sunday afternoon race influence by a process of 'cocooning'. The first move was to isolate 'their' local and modest fleet and exclude from it particularly the faster, more charismatic 'Grand Prix' sailing craft. Within a few years, they purchased a fleet of slower shorter-winged one-design Eighteens which are easier to sail, and they now manage this captive fleet by matching sponsors with crews. This has restored the League's influence over its traditional Sunday afternoon patch of the harbour, but at a price.

The first casualty was the thrust to take Eighteen foot skiffs to the world. Far-sighted skiff enthusiasts in Europe and the UK, with vision to grow the class globally, looked to the vital Sydney skiff fleet for leadership. They blinked, and when they looked again they saw only petty squabbling.

The second casualty was the skiffs themselves. The International Olympic Committee and the International Sailing Federation, both looking for a way to introduce spectacular skiff-style sailing into the Olympic Games, very reasonably concluded that a class that could not govern itself better than this at a local level could not be relied upon to behave responsibly globally, and began to think of a different approach. The 49er now stands where the Eighteens could have stood.

The third casualty was performance development itself. The active innovative crews transferred to the Sydney Flying Squadron, and for a few years the 'open' Eighteen R and D culture accelerated and continued very strongly (see Chapters 14 and 15). Its base was the Squadron. Its *raison d'être* was contesting the 'Grand Prix' regattas organised by the high-rating *Grand Prix Sailing* programme, as well as the traditional Squadron Saturday racing, and the Australian and World Championships.

But behind the scenes, the International Olympic Committee/International Sailing Federation thrust for an alternative approach to spectacular sailing was gathering momentum. The promulgation of the High Performance Olympic Dinghy (HPOD) Criteria in 1995 (see Chapter 17), the HPOD Evaluation event at Lake Garda in September 1996, and the selection of the skiff-derived 49er as Olympic, triggered the floating of two new sports TV programmes, both based on the 49er. Neither achieved critical mass, so neither proceeded. But the end result of this upheaval was that the previously successful 'Grand Prix' skiff TV programme based on the Eighteen footers was terminated.

Under these blows, the fire in the belly that had created these progressively faster Eighteen footers in the 1970 to 1996 era went cold. All effort now is directed towards improving racing technique (see Chapter 29), and there is no longer any drive to increase speed.

The one-design fleet of Eighteens still races, but the crowds and the media coverage are gone. Some open Eighteens still race from the Squadron, and in a few years they may find magic again. Meantime, the Sixteens have taken fire with development and are sailing faster, but with their existing 'no wings' and other rules they can only go so far.

At present, as we look for yet higher performance through the following pages, we will no longer find it among the Eighteen footer skiffs of Sydney.

My best guess is that somewhere in the world a new 'no rules' class of two-hander foiler will arise and it will be these new boats that will learn to race at speeds somewhere between the skiffs and the iceboats. These will provide the new focus of development and spectacle in the years ahead.

Chapter 8 • Hulls – The Materials Revolution

8.1 ■ Properties of shipbuilding materials

Typical properties of the materials used in shipbuilding – timbers, iron and steel, aluminium alloys, and 'plastics' – are given in Table 8.1.

Table 8.1 Materials specification

Material	Specific Gravity Water = 1	Density lb/cu ft Water 62.4	Tensile strength ton/sq in, typical	Deformation % stretch to fracture, typical
Mountain Ash	0.7	43	8	low
Silver Ash	0.72	45	8.3	low
Dense timbers used for hulls. European Oak, etc probably similar				
Coachwood	0.61	39	7.5	low
Huon Pine	0.54	34	6.5	low
Kahikatea (NZ White Pine)	0.45	28	4.8	low
Medium timbers used for superstructure, European Beeches probably similar				
Sitka Spruce (Europe)	0.44	28	5.1	low
Klinki Pine (N Guinea)	0.46	29	5.5	low
Lighter woods used for spars				
Balsa	0.1	6.25	low	low
Steel	7.8	486	27.5 to 125	25 to 0
Alum 6061-T6	2.7	168	22.5	12 to 0
Glass fibre	2.54	158.5	85	5.4
Kevlar fibre	1.45	90.5	80	2
Carbon fibre	1.76	110	93	1.2
Polyester resin	1.1 approx	68.5 approx	low	2
Epoxy resin	1.1 approx	68.5 approx	low	6

Timber

Until the Industrial Revolution introduced iron and steel as potential shipbuilding materials, all boats were built of wood. In England, the shipbuilding industry of the Cumberland coast, centred in Harrington, Workington and Maryport, was based on the hardwood rainforests of the Pennines. They built many of the ships on which Britain's reputation as a seafaring and exploring nation was founded, but at the cost of depleting the hardwood forests.

During the early Industrial Revolution, the only source of heat hot enough to smelt iron was hardwood charcoal, so the demand for charcoal timber was added to the shipbuilding demand. By the time smelting with coke made from coal replaced smelting with charcoal, and iron and steel became plentiful, the Pennines timber was worked out, and the Cumberland shipbuilding industry based on building wooden ships died. Among the skilled craftsmen who left the area for New Zealand or Australia in the early 1800s were my forebears.

Iron and steel

After this period, most of the big UK ships were built of iron on the Clyde and the Tyne. Iron and steel come in a huge range – from the softest iron to the strongest piano wire.

Small boats continued to be built exclusively in wood for almost another two centuries.

Aluminium

Aluminium and its alloys are creatures of the twentieth century. Like iron and steel, the range of properties is wide. It is used extensively for aircraft construction and for the hulls of the straighter-lined smaller powercraft, but has never been popular as a construction material for sailboats.

Plastics

Prior to about 1935, plastics were laboratory curiosities. But their potential was already recognised, they enjoyed accelerated development during the 1939–45 war, and became generally available to light industry in two waves.

The initial wave was in the late 1940s when the first two of five new products became available to boat-builders. These were:

- Fibres of glass that were either woven into cloth or presented as 'mats'.
- Polyester resin that could saturate the cloth or mat as a liquid and then cure into a long-chain-molecule solid to make 'Fibre Reinforced Plastic', or FRP, which the world came to know as 'fibreglass' or 'glass fibre'.

For the next 20 years the sailing world knew 'fibreglass' only in the form of hulls that were cold-moulded of glass fibre bonded with polyester resin into 'solid' laminates. The skins of dinghy hulls were usually between 2mm and 4mm thick. A 'solid' FRP laminate is four to five times as heavy as wood, so typical 14ft hulls built of solid FRP weighed about 20lb per foot.

In the late 1960s the range was suddenly and substantially extended:

- In addition to the established glass products, fibres of aramid and carbon became widely available at affordable prices.
- Resins based on the epoxies and vinyl esters were added to the staple polyester resin.
- The manufacturing process for waterproof closed-cell PVC (polyvinyl chloride) foam was developed, and this product too became available at affordable prices.

This made possible the foam sandwich revolution, in which laminates are laid up with a 'foam core', as opposed to a 'solid' laminate.

8.2 ■ Modes of failure

There is an important difference in the way one of the FRP structures fails as compared with all other materials.

All of the plastic fibres will stretch under load, then return to their original length, until the load increases to the point where they fail by snapping.

Many metals will at first behave in the same way – that is, they will stretch and then return to their original length, but only up to a point called their 'elastic limit'. Beyond this, there is a narrow range between their elastic limit and their ultimate tensile strength within which they will yield by stretching and deform permanently. Only when the ultimate load is applied will they snap. Generally, in the case of both steel and aluminium, the softer the product the more it will deform; and the more highly tempered it is, the more brittle it will be.

An FRP rod gives no such warning, except in the special case of glass/polyester discussed below.

Polyester resin is a 'thin' (low-viscosity) sticky liquid which, when catalysed with a peroxide, will gel and cure to become a solid block of long-chain-molecule material. The cured solid has tiny capillaries through it so is porous to water vapour. It shrinks a little as it cures. The tensile strength of the resin is low as compared with any of the fibres; its elasticity is such that it stretches about 2% before it snaps by local crazing.

Polyester gelcoat comes as a 'neutral' pale grey base liquor of polyester resin, into which very fine particles of pigment have been 'ground' rather than just mixed. The addition of these fine particles, plus the thoroughness of the ball-mill mixing process, almost completely eliminates the capillaries that occur in normal resin. For this reason, gelcoat is almost, but not totally, impervious to water and water vapour. Pigment of any colour can be added to achieve the final colour of choice.

Epoxy resin comes as a 'thick' (viscous) sticky resin component and a viscous hardener component which, when mixed in exact proportions, combine on a molecule-by-molecule basis to cure slowly into a block of long-chain-molecule solid. It does not shrink, and has no capillaries through it. It is totally impervious to water and water vapour. Its tensile strength is low compared with any of the fibres, and its elasticity is such that it stretches about 6% before it snaps.

The vinyl esters have properties between the polyesters and the epoxies.

The fibres

- *Glass* has a tensile strength of about 85 tons per sq inch. It stretches about 5.4% before it snaps. This 'springiness' explains, for example, the great flexibility of a glass fibre fishing rod.
- *Aramid* (Kevlar) has a tensile strength of about 70 tons per sq inch. It stretches about 2% before it snaps.
- *Carbon* has a tensile strength of about 93 tons per sq inch. It stretches about 1.2% before it snaps.

The fibres of glass, aramid and carbon are all produced as fine filaments. Fibres are available in three broad presentations:

1 Chopped Strand Mat (CSM)
This is the most common, most easily worked and most inexpensive presentation. It is a 'felt' of fibres each 40mm to 60mm long which lie at any angle (isotropic) and are lightly glued together, usually with a cornflour paste.

2 Cloth
This is the woven or knitted presentation, and is available as glass, aramid or carbon, and often as a mix of two. A very large range of weight, style and fibre orientations is available.

3 Uni-directional (UD)
This is available as glass, aramid or carbon. In this presentation, almost all (or all) of the fibres of a bolt of cloth or roll of tape run in the same direction, and are held in place by transverse beads of glue or minimal weft threads, often of a softer, thinner thread.

8.3 ■ The elastic limit

Let us consider what happens if we make a rod of each of the materials in Table 8.1, and then apply and release progressively increasing tensions until they fail.

Most metals have a property called an elastic limit. The steel rod will stretch and return to its original length, like a rubber band, until at a tension close to its ultimate limit it reaches its elastic limit. This is called elastic deformation. Above its elastic limit it will deform by stretching permanently and will no longer return to its original length. This is called inelastic, or plastic deformation, or yielding.

Progressively increasing load will stretch-deform softer steel by up to 25% of its original length before it snaps. In practical terms, if a metal fitting or wire is overloaded, it may give some warning by deforming before it fails. But not always. Special-purpose steels can be as strong as 110 tons per sq inch; these will snap with almost no yielding.

The aluminium rod will behave broadly as does the steel one – that is, it too has an elastic limit beyond which it yields. However, it does not stretch as far as steel before it breaks. Different alloys and tempers have strengths that can range from less than 10 tons to about 25 tons per sq inch. The stronger they are, the less they will stretch-deform before they fail.

Timber has no similar elastic limit. The wooden rods will stretch only so far, then snap. Because no two trees are identical, there will necessarily be some inconsistency, so while the broad limits of any timber can be predicted with confidence, the exact limit of any sample cannot be known.

With respect to Fibre Reinforced Plastics, or FRP, neither the resins alone – nor the fibres alone – are of much use for making things. The useful 'plastic' structural material is the FRP. The behaviour of the mixes under load is interesting. Put very simply, if you mix a stiff fibre with a stretchy resin, the results can be magic. But if you mix a stretchy fibre with a brittle resin, the result is surprising and can be disappointing.

Rods of just resin are weak in tension, so resin castings are of little use as structural materials by themselves. The resin's job is to be the glue that binds the fibres together.

As a group, FRP laminates have no elastic limit, but one mix behaves as if it had but for a different reason.

As an FRP carbon/epoxy rod takes the load and begins to stretch, the epoxy stretches with the carbon and nothing changes or lets go until at a tension of about 83 tons per sq inch (of the carbon; ignore the intervening resin) and an elongation of 1.2%, the rod will snap without warning. This is 20% stronger than tool steel and a quarter of the weight, so it is a very efficient structural material indeed.

A carbon/polyester rod will behave in exactly the same way.

And a glass/epoxy rod will behave similarly, except it will stretch 5.4%, become thinner as it stretches (like a rubber band), and will snap at about 76 tons per sq inch.

8.4 ■ Failure by softening

We might expect the glass/polyester rod also to stretch 5.4% and snap at 76 tons per sq inch. But it doesn't – it behaves quite differently. The problem is that with this mix the resin cannot stretch as far as the glass.

As it stretches under load, nothing happens until at about 28 tons per sq inch and 2% elongation, the resin reaches its elastic limit and begins to fail. The next bit is interesting. When any material is stretched it must necessarily become thinner – any rubber band is an example of this. As long as the glass and the resin stretch together, they both get *thinner together*, and no glue-line fails. At 28 tons per sq inch, the rod is 2% longer and the cross-section is 2% thinner. As soon as the stretched and thinned resin begins to fail, it relaxes locally and returns to its normal shorter length and larger cross-section. So the holes in the cracked resin that originally held the glass fibres firmly become locally about 1% bigger in diameter than the still-stretched glass fibres. This is the action that breaks the glue-line between the relaxed resin and the still-stretched and thinned fibre of glass, and the thinner glass fibres then start to pull out of the now-larger holes in the resin. The end result is that the glass/polyester mix will fail by progressive yielding at about one-third of its expected strength. It will fail progressively at about 28 tons psi, the tension at which the resin reaches its elastic (stretch) limit, and not snap at the 76 tons psi – which is the ultimate tensile strength of the glass.

I have explained this property in some detail because from the late 1940s until the 1970s most of the world knew 'plastics' only as the polyester resin and glass fibre FRP laminate called 'fibreglass'. General availability of the carbons and the epoxies and foam was still in the future. 'Fibreglass boats' were made of thin laminates of glass/polyester FRP. The failure mode of a thin laminate is exactly the same as that of the glass/polyester rod. When a lightly built boat is either stressed as a whole by sailing in strong winds and big waves, or stressed locally as in any bump severe enough to make the resin begin to fail, the laminate will begin to craze and slowly the boat will become softer, like a toughened windscreen hit by a stone. So the nature of lightly built FRP dinghies was to become softer and lose speed year by year.

Through the decades 1950 to the mid-1970s, sailing dinghies were built of plywood or FRP. The glass/polyester FRP hull was quicker to make so less expensive, but heavier (15–20lb/ft), and its nature was to become softer and lose speed year by year. When compared with a carefully built glued plywood hull, the end result was that the ply boat was more expensive to build but lighter (10lb/ft) and it remained stiff, retained its speed, and so was preferred by top-level sailors. The timber boatbuilding industry continued to thrive until about the mid-1970s.

8.5 ■ Foam sandwich

Into this milieu, the advent first of foam, then of the aramids (Kevlar) and the carbons, the epoxies, and the whole foam-sandwich technology, wrought a mighty revolution. Again, it was the aircraft industry that showed the way. Featherweight aircraft cabin partitions and doors of astonishing strength and stiffness were made by gluing paper-thin three-ply skins to both sides of a core of almost weightless balsa. In the aircraft environment these panels stayed dry and lasted for ever. But when boat hulls were made like this, the balsa saturated, became 'dozy', soft and heavy, and soon failed. Replacing the ply with thin strong glass skins was no better because water permeated through the porous polyester and the balsa again saturated. The vision for something as light and strong as balsa, but that would not saturate, drove the development that resulted in rigid PVC (polyvinyl chloride) closed cell foam. The moon project was largely responsible.

The NASA Apollo missions culminated in the late 1960s in men walking on the moon and returning to Earth. They flew in a carbon/epoxy foam-sandwich box called a space capsule. In the decades since, a progression of more efficient materials and methods based on the space technology have almost completely replaced both the earlier timber and 'solid' FRP as boatbuilding materials.

The structural facts of life of foam sandwich can be appreciated from two loaves of bread with crisp crusts. If you cut the side crusts off both, you now have two foam sandwiches. Both have the top crust, the intervening light fluffy cooked dough, and the bottom crust intact. Note how hard they are to bend in the plane that stretches the top crust and compresses the bottom one, or vice versa. Now cut the top and bottom crusts off one, put the crusts together, and note how easy it is to bend the doubled crusts when they are not held apart, and how very much stiffer is the uncut sample where all that the light fluffy cooked dough is doing is holding the top and bottom crusts apart. That is the primary function of the foam core in a foam-sandwich laminate. In engineering terms, it is the web between the two flanges of a girder.

The effects on the stiffness of a panel are enormous. Consider a panel of 'solid' glass fibre 2mm thick, and a sandwich of two 1mm thick skins on either side of an almost weightless foam panel that is 8mm thick. The total thickness of the sandwich will be 10mm, but its weight will be almost the same as the 2mm thick solid panel. The stiffness of a panel will vary with the cube of the distance between the fibres that carry the load, in this case, 2mm and 10mm for the extreme fibres, and something less than 2mm and 10mm for the other load-carrying fibres, so the foam panel will be at least $5 \times 5 \times 5 = 125$ times as stiff as the solid panel. A bump that will bend the solid panel 100mm will bend the foam less than 1mm!

In the case of the FRP foam sandwich, because the whole panel is so stiff the flexing under load is so small that nothing is overstressed and nothing fatigues unless, or until, very high forces approaching the ultimate strength of the FRP panels themselves are applied.

Minimum practical weights work out like this: a solid FRP skin 2.5mm thick weighs about 1.1lb/sq ft. This is about the typical skin thickness of the heavy dinghies which softened quickly. A foam sandwich with an outside skin of FRP 0.4mm thick, then 8mm of foam, then an inner skin 0.3mm thick, weighs about 0.5lb/sq ft – that is, less than half the weight – and it stays stiff and sails with undiminished speed for up to 30 years.

To sum up: there is less material cost, but more labour cost, in a foam-sandwich structure, so it costs more; however, it is worth it because it is much lighter, lasts much longer, and holds its speed.

To make the foam, four products are mixed simultaneously. Two are the resin and hardener that would normally combine to form a dense block of solid PVC. The other two are foaming agents that combine to release nitrogen gas. As it is formed, the gas creates a myriad of bubbles or cells that are uniformly distributed throughout the mass. Every bubble is unique and closed. The resultant foam is chemically stable and completely impervious to water and water vapour. The process can be controlled to produce 'buns' of foam of any density, which are then sliced into sheets of any desired thickness. In practice, foams of about 6lb/cu ft, or 75–80kg/cu m, substitute perfectly for the typically 6lb/cu ft balsa originally used in the aircraft industry.

Chapter 9 • Hulls – The Design Response

9.1 ■ The modern skiff

Skiffs look like no other sailboats. The general arrangement that evolved within the Eighteen footer class over the past few decades is characterised by a low, light, almost triangular, hull with long straight forward gunwales and bilges, and an unobstructed, slightly dished deck. Cantilevered wings of an optimum, not maximum, span extend from the gunwales. Taut netting is stretched between the forward and aft tubes and the gunwales and the outer tubes that form the wing tips. These trampoline-like surfaces, together with the unobstructed deck, form a single working surface across which crews can move fast by running on their feet, as opposed to sitting and swaying from the hips as is normal dinghy control practice. Big, fully battened sails are set on a flexible mast that is well raked aft and bent further aft at the top. The spinnaker is asymmetric and, like the wings, is of optimum, not maximum, area.

The light total weight, together with the extraordinary sail-carrying power generated by all crew trapezing from the tips of the wide wings, gives a power to weight ratio high enough for these boats not only to plane, but to plane fast on all points of sailing in all but light winds.

Why have they evolved into this particular shape? And why are high performance yachts worldwide now following their lead so closely?

9.2 ■ Structural evolution

As our starting point, we will take the structural design used for the first 'sailing dinghies'. The waterproof glues, marine plywood, glass fibre, foam core material, foam-sandwich construction and incredibly stiff and strong fibres – such as the aramids and carbon – were all in the future.

At that time, all small boats were built of wood. Fastenings were double-ended rivets, each made by driving a copper nail through the work, placing a conical copper washer called a 'rove' on the projecting point of the nail, tapping it down to the wood with a hollow punch, cutting off the excess length of rivet, and peening the stub to capture the rove. It was tedious, skilled and costly work. Most small boats were open, with no decks at all. Uffa Fox's small-sail two-crew International Fourteen footer featherweights were built of thin, light wood, while the planks and ribs of the big-sail big-crew Australian skiffs were thicker and made from stronger species of timber, but both were built in the same way because the design objectives were the same. These were:

- Underwater, the hull was shaped for minimum resistance at hull speed when carrying the design weight.
- The topsides needed to be high enough so that the undecked boat would not swamp when heeled and/or sailed through waves. Further, the forward topsides needed to cut through the wave crests when sailing to windward with as little wave impact drag as possible.

The 'classic' design

Fig 9.1 shows the classic starting point: an undecked rowing dinghy into which a mast with three stays has been fitted. Provided that the keel at the mast step was strong enough to hold the mast up against the tension of the shrouds and forestay that were pulling it down, this approach worked, and this was the classic 'sailing dinghy' starting point. The whole thing was flexible, rather like a shoebox without a lid, and twisted when the crew hiked strongly.

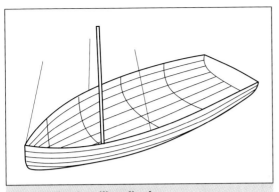

Fig 9.1 Classic sailing dinghy

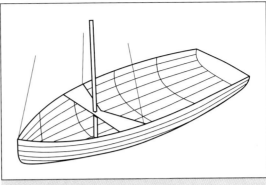

Fig 9.2 Classic dinghy with partner

The 'classic plus partner' design

As more sail was added, the gunwales at the chainplates needed to be made strong enough so that the chain-plates would not pull out, nor the gunwales at the chainplates buckle inwards under the increasing shroud tension. To stop the gunwales from buckling inwards, sailing dinghy and skiff builders everywhere started to use a gunwale to gunwale 'partner' to keep the gunwales spread apart, and to steady the lower mast, as is shown in Fig 9.2. This was a big improvement in mechanical design. At the extreme, this approach was good enough to support the huge rigs of boats such as those shown in Figs 1.6 and 1.7. The twisting problem was alleviated by the use of a running backstay or 'runner' to the aft gunwale which was set and released tack by tack. This both helped to keep the forestay taut, and carried much of the twisting load. (It can be seen in Fig 1.5.)

The floor needed to be a reasonably clear surface for the crew to walk on, and strong enough to support their weight. The gunwales had to be wide enough to sit on with reasonable comfort.

That was about it. In those days nobody thought much about crew movement, because all crews adopted a sitting stance when sailing, and never needed to move far. In the 1950s, the previously monolithic Eighteen footer class split in fierce dispute about the eligibility of new boats 7ft wide being in fleets of Eighteen footers which were customarily 8ft wide. Either way, it needed only one or two steps when moving from sitting on one gunwale to sitting on the other gunwale each tack or gybe. And the idea of designing the hull for less aerodynamic drag was still many years in the future.

The framed and decked design

Pictures show that a new sort of small-boat structural design appeared in the late 1920s and early 1930s, and this seems to have been a New Zealand initiative. Fig 1.26, and Figs 1.28 to 1.30 show a genre of hulls in which designers from New Zealand have created a lighter, stronger stiffer boat by 'putting a lid on the shoebox'. I myself made one of these.

As a child, I had made two nondescript sailing canoes. In 1936 I made an Idle Along (Fig 1.29), the internal structure of which is shown in Fig 9.3. A full frame of thin timber has been placed at each end of the cockpit. The hull was then fully decked except for the cockpit cut-out (indicated by the dashed lines). This design approach gave the whole structure the rigidity of a shoebox with its lid glued on, plus strong points to carry the mast socket and to

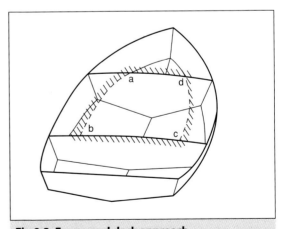

Fig 9.3 Frame and deck approach

which the stays could be attached. Because of the natural strength and rigidity of this framed and decked design, the timber used could be thinner than had been customary in the hull skins of the undecked designs, so the finished weight was surprisingly light. We were fortunate in that in those days a local 'New Zealand white pine' (kahikatea) was readily available. It was light, strong, did not split easily, was easily worked, and ideal for making small boats. I recall that the port and starboard topside panels were each a single piece of timber about 14ft long, 15in wide and five-sixteenths of an inch thick (4250mm × 375mm × 8mm). As was then customary, I finished the structure and, prior to painting, soaked the whole thing in linseed oil for some weeks, until it would absorb no more. This soon crystallised and thereafter stopped it from soaking up water with use, and it remained relatively light throughout its long life.

As a spin-off, this framed and decked approach provided fore-and-aft buoyancy, so these boats could be rolled upright and sailed on following a capsize. The penalty was a ton of water in the cockpit, so a capsize relegated you to the back of the fleet, but you could still sail under control, and hence did not need outside assistance. This feature provided a new measure of safety and independence from the rescue team.[1]

9.3 ■ Advanced wood design

Following the war, major changes in construction technique were made possible when the new 'plastics' industry made available the first three of a number of products that were about to change the face of small sailboat construction. The three initial products were long-life waterproof glues, and the marine plywoods that were made possible by these glues, as well as the Fibre Reinforced Plastic, FRP, which is near universally known by its original trade name of 'fibreglass'. The late 1940s, 1950s and early 1960s were the decades in which hulls made from heavy through-fastened timber were replaced either by craft of lighter timber and plywood that were fastened by glue, or by the early fibreglass hulls of heavy laminates of 'solid' FRP. Because solid fibreglass was both heavy and suffered progressive softening, this construction was never used in high-performance boats such as skiffs.

The aircraft industry had already developed the technology of using glued plywood to make strong but light airframes, and the boatbuilding industry quickly adapted this technology with marine ply and waterproof glue to make strong stiff sailboat hulls that were a fraction of the weight of the pre-war solid timber through-fastened craft. These lighter hulls planed sooner and faster than the earlier, heavier boats, and this performance increase was a major contributor towards the final adoption of the planing design – certainly in Australia, and probably worldwide. The new breed of Eighteen foot skiffs of the 1950s and early 1960s were all built of glued plywood.

The key difference between the Australian solid-timber pre-war skiff hulls and the post-war ply hulls was the adoption by the skiffs of framed hulls. The earlier solid-timber hulls had thick skins over close-spaced ribs; there were no transverse frames and no decks. These boats *could* twist and squeeze, but were made of material thick enough *not* to twist much nor squeeze, and were strong enough to hold their shape for many years of enthusiastic use. But they were heavy. Six vintage reconstructions of typical pre-war 'solid timber' big-sail Eighteen footer hulls typically weigh about 750lb 'dry', and more like 800–850lb when saturated during the season's sailing. This is about 40–44lb per foot of length. Uffa Fox's featherweight small-sail International Fourteens, built from thinner, lighter woods with a very large number of fine fastenings (and thus very costly to make), would have weighed about 15–20lb per foot. Less expensive boats, made from thicker wood with fewer fastenings, typically weighed 30–40lb per foot.

The new 1950s to 1960s skiffs used ply structures (see Fig 9.3) with thinner, lighter plywood skins. Small-sail Fourteen footers built in this manner weighed about 10lb per foot. The four-handers built like this were about one-third the weight of the earlier thick-skin boats and much stiffer. The typical four-hander hull weighed 240lb 'dry' and 270lb saturated – that is, between 15lb and 20lb per foot. Before important championship races it was common for top boats to be 'cooked' for a week in a shed with the temperature held at 30–40° to dry them out. This could reduce the weight by up to 30lb.

During this period it was customary for the top crews to build a new boat every year. This was partly because the lightly built boats began to yield and lose speed, but the main reason was the pace of design development. New designs were generally a little faster.

The two four-hander Eighteens shown in Fig 1.31 would have been early examples of plywood boats of this nature. They were big, flat, beamy boats with a vertical transom at the stern (which is in fact a frame),

---

[1] In 1939, immediately prior to joining the New Zealand Air Force, I won this class's NZ Junior Championship. During the years of the 1939–45 war, there was no recreational sailing for me.

and another frame at the mast. A thwart at the height of the aft end of the centrecase stabilised the centre-case and centreboard. The gunwales and deck at the chainplates were usually reinforced with doubled or trebled ply.

These additions prompted a key philosophical change in the approach to their racing of *all* of the skiffs. The Sydney Flying Squadron's shingle reads 'Australia's Oldest *Open* Boat Club' (the italics are mine). Open boats swamp when they capsize, and need rescue. If their steel centreboards were heavy enough, they sank, and the sailing annals are full of stories of a boat that capsized and sank on Saturday being located on the bottom and raised in time to race again on the Sunday. For 150 years, all skiffs of every size had prided themselves on a core racing ethic of 'Stay upright. If you capsize, you're out'.

The new mast frame and deck necessarily created a space that could be enclosed as flotation. There was, though, initial resistance. When Bob Miller, later Ben Lexen, took his three-hander *Taipan* to Auckland in 1960 he was forced to cut big holes in his decks so that his boat would indeed swamp should he capsize. But within a few years the common sense of self-rescue prevailed, and the frames then doubled as both structural members and as watertight bulkheads for forward flotation. Aft flotation was added so that, following a capsize, a boat could be righted and sailed on.

The early three-handers were built of ply, and became lighter still, for two reasons. The first was obvious – they were smaller boats. The second was that the approach of 'If it doesn't break, it's too heavy' was becoming the norm. (We saw this in some of the early Seawanhaka challengers in Chapter 1, so it was nothing new.) But the three-handers applied it so enthusiastically that it resulted in an inconsistent performance record and poor reputation, even by outstanding boats, and an understandable reluctance by more conventional sailors to adopt the dynamic advances they demonstrated. An extreme example of this was that Bob Miller built his two three-hander Eighteens, *Taipan* and *Venom*, in 1960 and 1961. They were blindingly fast when they finished – but unfortunately they did not finish often enough. *Venom* in fact won the World Championship in a light/moderate wind series in 1961, but from the point of view of other sailors in the class they were so inconsistent that they were ignored. For some years, another three-hander would appear here or there, and some were successful. The New Zealanders in particular kept plugging at three-handers, but four-handers continued to be the mainstream boat until David Porter tried again some years later. He built five 'KBs' in all from 1970 to 1975, each better designed, better built, more reliable and better sailed as he and his crew came to terms with this new style of sailing. The fifth year he won the World Championship. After that, nobody else ever again built another four-hander; his persistence and skill had changed the way people thought.

David's fifth *KB* in 1975 was still a glued timber and plywood boat; its rigged hull weighed about 180lb. These boats were still very lightly built and had a one-year life at peak performance. No two-year-old or older boat ever came near to winning the major events.

9.4 ■ The second structural revolution

The early 1970s became a time of developmental ferment, with three construction methods all competing to make light sailboat hulls.

Timber in the form of thin plywood had enjoyed a long and successful history in the aircraft industry, and the new marine glues were now reliable in water. But the lightest boat weights needed skilled handwork; because they could not be mass produced, they were becoming expensive.

'Solid' glass and polyester hulls laid up in moulds could be repeated relatively inexpensively by industrial process, but suffered from weight, flexing and softening. The basic problem was that the resin and glass FRP mix was about five times as heavy as timber, so had to be about one-fifth the thickness if it was not to be unacceptably heavy. Panel stiffness varies as the cube of the thickness; $5 \times 5 \times 5 = 125$, so a relatively expensive timber skin 5mm thick is about the same weight, but more than 100 times stiffer than a fibreglass skin 1mm thick.

The recent development of closed cell PVC (polyvinyl chloride) foam ushered in the age of foam-sandwich laminates; they promised enormous potential, but they were still very new and not as yet well understood.

Four examples will illustrate the strengths and problems of each approach from the 1970s viewpoint:

1 Comparing the same high performance boats made of different materials, the fastest boats, the Eighteen foot skiffs, continued to be made from plywood regardless of the expense. FRP was too heavy, and foam sandwich not yet reliable enough.

2 As between the same boats made of the same material but of different ages, the solid-skin FRP hulls suffered from flex, softening and loss of speed. As between a new hull and one some months old, the new one was so obviously faster that the policy of the national coaches of many European nations with Olympic aspirations was to give their top teams a new 470 hull at least twice each season.

3 As between the same boats, one made of solid FRP and one of foam sandwich, the new foam-sandwich technique was already beginning to show its dynamic advantage. The relatively flat topsides of a thin-FRP-skin Starboat flexed substantially in waves. As between a thin-FRP-skin Star and a 1971 Eurostar with foam-sandwich topsides, they were equal in speed in flat water, but the Eurostar was consistently faster to windward through waves. The added dynamic pressure of each wave crest momentarily flexed the topsides of the FRP Star inwards, the aft end of the temporary dent was necessarily at a blunter angle to both the wave and the centreline (ie temporarily giving the boat a blunter bow), and so the resultant of the dynamic impact force of each wave crest pushed the flexible FRP boat backwards a little more efficiently. I recall exactly this conversation with David Forbes, an Australian Star helm, then sailing well. His question was, 'In flat water I can match the Eurostars. In waves they get away. Is this my wave technique or is there a technical explanation?' We discussed the stiffness difference above and its consequence on performance. He thanked me for the explanation, chartered a foam-sandwich Eurostar, and won the Star Gold medal at Kiel in the 1972 Munich Olympics.

4 As between a new-technology boat and an old-technology one, whenever a new method supersedes an old one, unexpected problems will always occur. In *HPS-1* I described some of the experiments and developments that led to the Tasar. The Tasar, designed in 1975, was far ahead of its time. It was the first boat to have bottom, sides and deck all fully cored with the then-new rigid PVC foam. The inner carlins and cockpit side panels remained normal FRP. The good mechanical performance of the cored bottom, topsides and deck pleased us, but we were surprised to find that the joints between the stiff foam-core deck panels and the more flexible side bulkheads of the cockpit gave trouble, and ultimately needed to be made much stronger than initially expected. With the benefit of hindsight, it is all so obvious. If you clamp a wire in a vice and bend the free end back and forth, it will always fatigue and fail where it exits the vice. In the same way, flexible panels joined to foam panels will always fail at the edge of the foam, because that is where almost all of the flex will be concentrated. We soon learned to taper the strength from very strong at the join to normal flex at a distance, like a fishing rod. The failures stopped. It is called development, and learning. Once these initial problems were cured, the long-term performance of the lighter-foam panels in these early foam-sandwich boats has been superb.

When glass is glued to foam it cannot bend locally so it does not yield and soften. Well-maintained, low-stressed polyester/glass/foam sandwich Tasars, now 30 years old, have lost no speed at all and can still win championships. As higher mechanical performance is demanded, as in Eighteen foot skiff hulls with their very high rig tensions, practical experience is that for foam-core structures of equal weight a glass polyester hull will last a year, a Kevlar vinyl ester hull will last nearly two years, and a well-designed carbon/epoxy structure will last many years.

The comparison between the lighter FRP/glass/foam-sandwich hulls of the 1970s, which could give a 30-year life of undiminished stiffness and speed, and the earlier, heavier solid FRP hulls, which needed replacement twice each year because they softened and lost speed so quickly, is stark. This sort of advantage was irresistible. From the late 1970s, it has been foam sandwich all the way for the faster boats.

9.5 ■ The new dynamic design factors

As so often happens, advances in several fields all surge together, and the result is that the whole culture moves to a new paradigm. With respect to the skiffs of Sydney, the new glass/polyester, then aramid/vinyl ester, then carbon/epoxy foam-sandwich materials from the aerospace industry, were eagerly adapted by a sailboat class that was driven by total respect for performance and which deliberately structured its rules to encourage anything that would give more speed. The astonishing gains in skiff performance during the closing years of the twentieth century, as new materials combined with new design dynamics, has been fore-shadowed in Chapter 1. The detail within each field is the stuff of the chapters immediately ahead.

Hull shape and mechanical design changed profoundly in response to seven new drives. Five of these – the new compromise in underwater shape; the need for control at planing speeds; the new demands on topsides shape; the need to satisfy the new ergonomics; and the need to reduce aerodynamic drag – were dynamic. The sixth and seventh – the need to withstand extreme rig load with near zero yield; and the need to withstand torque (twist force) greater than anything previously demanded – were mechanical.

9.6 ■ Underwater shape

The underwater shape of any boat is a compromise. If you want minimum drag at relatively low speed, the well-proven best shape is the long, slender semicylindrical rowing shell – but these are hard to turn. So if you want both speed and the ability to turn, a shorter and wider hull is for you. The question of where to put the volume then becomes important. If the boat is to spend its life at modest speed, a distribution of bulk like a sine wave gives minimum drag. The Flying Dutchman has such a distribution. If a slightly higher working speed is expected, a distribution biased with a slightly longer bow and a correspondingly shorter stern seems to be preferred. Up to the 1970s, most of the world's good sailboats, including the Eighteen footers, fell within this range. From the mid-1970s onwards, the three-handers began to sail significantly faster – first because they were lighter and had better dynamic ratios, then wings appeared, then the asymmetric rigs were developed. These led to very great increases in both the expected and the achieved mean speeds of the Eighteen footers. Not surprisingly, designers experimented with both the distribution of bulk – a square barge would be one extreme and two cones joined base to base the other – and with the bias from symmetry of the curve: two equal cones base to base would be the symmetrical norm; and a longer nose cone, and a progressively shorter aft cone, would be an example of asymmetry. From time to time, some strange-looking boats have appeared. So far, nothing has been able to beat a very conservative approach to this dynamic – a sine wave biased a little to stretch the bow and shorten the stern.

9.7 ■ Control at planing speeds

The greater mean speed triggered a control problem. Any sailor or observer will be familiar with the way that any boat designed with rounded waterlines or buttock lines that 'close' the water aft will begin to 'death roll' uncontrollably if it is pushed too fast downwind. Conversely, any boat with straight lines aft will run true at speed. All planing motorboats demonstrate this feature. So the recent fast skiffs have converged on a design style with conservative distribution and position of buoyancy and long, smooth cone-like rounded bow sections that harden into near-straight keel line and straight, sharp chines aft.

9.8 ■ Topsides

When sailing to windward in flat water, only the bottom of the hull is wet. The topsides develop aerodynamic drag only. But when sailing in, say, 15 knots of wind and waves typically 2ft high from trough to crest, the situation becomes very different because the topsides have to go through the wave crests as well.

In any wave system, each particle of water describes a circular orbit. In the case of normal waves 2ft high, the water in each crest moves downwind at 1.7 knots – about 3ft per second – that on the back face falls, that in the troughs moves to windward, and the water in the advancing face rises, all at the same speed. (This subject is covered in detail in *HPS-1*, Chapter 13.)

Let us consider the dynamics of two imaginary 14ft boats with vertical stems when sailing to windward in 2ft waves at speeds of 5 knots and at 10 knots. Both boats, below the chines, have the bottom shape of the 29er. The flat-water drag curves of the 29er are given in Fig 10.10. Above the water, one boat has a bow like an Optimist, a flat square, say, 1sq foot in area. The other is like a surfboard with a deck at waterline level, but with a thin vertical fore-and-aft panel above its centreline.

In flat water, the drags of the two hulls will be identical, because both are of the same underwater shape. Both develop a drag of 18lb at boat speed (Vb) 5 knots, and 55lb at Vb 10 knots.

In waves, the performance difference between the two boats becomes profound. We will look first at the situation of the boat with the blunt bow at 5 knots.

The calculations are sobering. The speed of closing between the bow and the crest is the 8.5fps boat speed plus a component of, say, 2fps of the 3fps orbital speed of the wave crest – say 10–10.5fps. The coefficient of drag (Hoerner, *Fluid Dynamic Drag*) of the square pram bow is about 0.8. So the momentary peak drag with bow fully immersed is: Area = 1sq ft × Density = 1 × Coeff drag = 0.8 × Speed (fps) squared, say, 10 × 10 =100, which equals 80lb.

If we assume that only half the bow usually immerses, and that this immersion of the bow increases from nothing to a maximum and falls to nothing, and that the adverse orbital speed of the crest increases from nothing, rises to a maximum, and then decreases to nothing wave by wave, a correction of about × 0.14 looks reasonable. (Half immersion at maximum = 0.5, times rise then fall of immersed area = 0.7, times rise then fall of orbital component = 0.8, all multiply to a total correction, say, × 0.28. This applies only through the crests, and so for half the time.) Thus the mean drag increase in waves would be about (80 × 0.14) = 11.2lb. The mean total drag through waves rises by 11lb – that is, from 18lb to 29lb. We see here why waves affect boats with blunt bows so badly.

For the other boat, the drag increase is much smaller because the water particles glance along the fore-and-aft panel rather than splat directly against the square bow. The key point is that in this case the wave impact pressure acts across the boat and increases the side force; it does not push the boat backwards at all. Only the skin friction pushes the boat backwards. This would be a maximum of, say, Area = 10sq ft × Density = 1 × Coeff drag (turbulent flow skin friction (NASA) 0.003) × Speed squared, say, 100 = total approx 3lb, to which we apply the same corrections as above, so 3 × 0.14 = 0.425lb. Therefore the mean added drag is about 0.5lb – that is, from 18lb to, say, 18.5lb. We see here why the big record-breaking catamarans have knife-like bows and topsides as close to fore-and-aft panels as possible.

This is bad enough, but at 10 knots boat speed, it gets much worse. The calculations become: Optimist-type-bow; Area = 1 × Density = 1 × Coeff drag = 0.8 × Speed now 19fps squared, say, 361 all equals 289lb. Corrected as above becomes 289 × .28 = 81lb, and for half the time = say, 40lb. The waves have increased the total drag from 55lb to 95lb. We see here why the old Patikis and the present lake scows could not, and still cannot, match the vertical-stemmed fine-bowed boats to windward in waves.

For the fore-and-aft panel boat, the skin friction, corrected, rises to about 1.5lb.

Table 9.1 displays this in a table format.

Table 9.1 Relative wave impact drags (to windward)

Boat Speed Kts	Fine bow			Pram bow >		
	Drag lb in flat water	Drag lb in waves	Inc %	Drag lb in flat water	Drag lb in waves	Inc %
5	18	18.5	2.5	18	29	61
10	55	56.5	2.5	55	95	73

These drag increases are sobering. The effect of bluntness is horrifying, and the faster you sail, the worse it gets. Note very carefully that there is no advantage in waves for any boat that is fine at the waterline but blunt at the gunwales – which is the design style of about 99% of conventional boats. Only submarines and wind-surfers can escape wave impact drag. Every normal boat must necessarily have a topsides bow wedge angle that lies somewhere between the impractical zero of the fore-and-aft panel above, which gives about 2.5% skin friction drag increase and the 90° 'pram' bow which gives the 60–75% increase in wave impact drag.

The skiff response has been to rake the bow forward to reduce the gunwale wedge angle, and to approach a triangular topside shape with long straight gunwales and bilges from the bow to as far aft as is possible. This geometry gives the minimum wedge angle at both bilge and gunwales, the most knife-like topsides, the lowest wave impact drag at speed. The skiffs became triangular for this reason 25 years ago. The fact that every fast keelboat and catamaran now copies the skiff lead attests that this was indeed a major advance.

9.9 ■ Waves and scows

Waves disadvantage shapes such as the old Patikis and the present lake scows even more than vertical stemmed boats when sailing to windward. Let us assume an extreme scow shape – for example Fig 1.24 – with near parallel topsides, between which a flat bottom necessarily slopes upward from about mid-length to a bow that is a low horizontal knife edge. This shape will suffer substantially greater disadvantage in waves than will a vertical-stemmed pram hull, partly because of its greater area and partly because some of the favourable corrections above cannot apply.

The wide bottom is of much greater area than that of any reasonable topside. A greater width of boat hits each advancing wave; the same impact pressure is generated over a greater area, and so the total force and the total adverse component are greater.

The second disadvantage is that there can be no assumption of 'only half the area may be immersed'. The whole of every wave crest will necessarily impact on the whole of the advancing bottom area between the chines or bilges.

This is why the 1895–1905 early Patikis and lake scows that introduced flat-water planing to the world did not, and still do not, shine in waves. Arch Logan's 1921 'improved "M" class Patiki' was a re-design in which he was among the first to re-shape the forward half of his hull into a vertical stem. His genius not only shared the earlier 1900s introduction of the planing sailboat with Herrick Duggan; in later life he was at the forefront of the more wave-tolerant design that has since been systematically developed over the subsequent 80 years into the quintessential triangular shape first developed by the Sydney skiffs, and that is now becoming a universal design trend worldwide.

9.10 ■ Aerodynamic drag

If you put an open shoebox in a wind tunnel at an angle to represent an Optimist sailing to windward, and measure its drag, this is substantial. Not only does the wind hit the windward end and windward side of the box, it then hits the leeward inside and the downwind inside end of the box as well. There is also reduced pressure on the leeward faces of all the vertical surfaces. This example is typical of all open dinghies. In the days of running downwind slower than the wind, aerodynamic drag of the hull was a disadvantage when sailing to windward but assisted when sailing downwind, so sailors could rationalise that it was not too important. But with the development of apparent wind sailing, with the apparent wind now from ahead of the beam all the time, aerodynamic drag is also disadvantageous all the time, and the skiffs have led the development of lower-aerodynamic-drag design.

If you replace the open-top shoebox with a solid brick, the drag becomes much less. The wind now hits only the windward end and side of the brick, and gently tugs the leeward faces backwards. The effect of raising the deck to gunwale level (next section) improved not only the ergonomics, it substantially reduced the drag as well.

If you now round the top corners of the brick, the reduction of drag as the round-down approaches 10% suddenly becomes substantial. (A brick 10in high with a 1in radius rounding of its top edges is said to be 'rounded down 10%'.) In the dinghy case, whatever the gunwale height above the water may be, nothing much changes until the rounding approaches about 9%. But by 10% the flow smoothes and follows the curves, and the drag reduces to about half.

When wind flows away from a surface such as a vertical transom, the effect is like a filter pump; the core of dead air behind the transom is dragged downwind by the viscous drag of the surrounding moving air, the pressure decreases, and the pressure difference between the undiminished pressure on the windward face and the reduced pressure on the leeward face shows up as drag. But if the transom is sloped so that the air flows smoothly down to water level, no such pressure difference develops. The skiffs were the first to develop the triangular hull with a smooth deck at gunwale level, rounded-down gunwales and a sloped transom. The reduction in the aerodynamic drag of such hulls is substantial.

9.11 ■ Ergonomics

What we are talking about here is the new requirement that, to control the new wider, lighter boats, crews need to move further, so they have had to start moving faster, and on their feet.

Pre-war, the gunwale to gunwale beams of conventional boats were about 5ft for Uffa Fox's Fourteen footers, and up to 8ft for the widest of the displacement Eighteen footers. These boats were body-hiked from the gunwales. Every time such a boat tacked or gybed, the ship's company needed to stand up and walk one pace or two at most, then sit on the other gunwale. Toe straps were still in the future. The most efficient cockpit geometry for this movement was a flat floor to walk on and a gunwale about 18in above the floor to sit on, and that is exactly how the boats were proportioned.

The post-war New Zealand skiffs started to use trapezes again in the 1951–2 season – the same year that van Essen designed his Flying Dutchman with its side decks. Very soon it became normal practice for the helm to 'hike' with his feet hooked under the new toe straps and, in stronger wind, the forward hand trapezed with feet against the gunwale. The trapeze height was set so that the forward hand when coming off trapeze was at the height of sitting on the side deck. So for both helm and forward hand the tacking or gybing body movements remained the same as pre-war, except that the forward hand had added the going-out on trapeze or coming-in from trapeze to the central movement. For this movement, the same shape – a flat floor to walk on and a deck 18in higher to sit on – remained efficient.

The late 1970s and early 1980s saw the introduction of wings. At first these were simple stubs that increased the width of the gunwales outwards a little, but soon wingspans began to grow and a substantial gap developed between the gunwale and the tube that formed the outer rail of the wing. This posed completely new ergonomic demands on trapezing crew – which in the case of the new three-hander Eighteens now included the helmsman. Every tack or gybe now required that each crew member move, still on trapeze, from the wing outer rail across the gap to the gunwale, then step down to the floor while he/she unhooked, then walk across the cockpit floor to the other side, hook up, climb up onto the gunwale and move out again to trapeze first from the gunwale, and then move further out across the water to trapeze from the other wing tip. This had become a complex, slow and very inefficient movement.

As wings grew wider, design developed in three stages.

By the mid-1980s, taut net was stretched across the previously void space. When this was taut enough, it became possible to run on it. Sometimes it wasn't. (Fig 1.33 of *Tia Maria* shows netted wings.)

Next, more reliable 'solid' wing surfaces were developed. A 1993 experimental Eighteen footer *Looney Tunes*, designed by Julian Bethwaite, was the first to introduce a number of ideas that would flourish in years to come – and one that did not. The rounded-down gunwales, the solid wings, the elimination of the draggy cockpit 'hole' by use of a continuous elevated deck, the extreme aerodynamic cleanness, the mainsail cuff to deck level, and the self-tacking jib were all years ahead of their time. The wishbone rig was one step too far. It worked brilliantly in some winds, but proved inconsistent.

From the ergonomic point of view, the principal one among a number of new features was the replacement of the low cockpit floor with a gunwale-to-gunwale slightly dished deck at the same level as the wing surfaces. For the first time, crew could unhook from trapeze at one wing tip and run across the intervening wing, the deck and the other wing without having to look at where they placed their feet, and hook up on the other wing tip after a faster, enormously simpler, wing tip-to-wing tip running movement than had ever previously been possible.

THE MECHANICAL FACTORS

9.12 ■ Gust response, the pre-load principle and rigidity

In Chapter 22, The Automatic Rig, we will discuss the very great increases in ease of handling and also in speed that flowed from acknowledging that the wind is never steady. To summarise the detail, the 1930s open boats flexed under rig load, so the more strongly the gusts blew, the more they flexed, the looser their shrouds became, the more their forestays sagged, and the fuller their jibs became and the slower they sailed. The advent of bendy rigs in the late 1960s exacerbated this, in that in stronger winds the mast was deliberately bent to flatten the mainsail, and this bending lowered the hounds with respect to the gunwale and slackened the shrouds even more. A very practical problem then developed in that beyond a certain slackness the big Eighteen footer rigs would begin to vibrate slowly, and this pulsing, if not immediately checked, quickly amplified and could destroy the rig. To fix this, by the mid-1980s top Eighteen foot skiff crews had started to use hydraulic rams to adjust their shrouds to keep them tight, whatever the mast bend. Inclusion of the hydraulics machinery made the boats even bigger, heavier, clumsy and much more costly.

Into this situation one designer introduced a breakthrough idea: do not vary the bend of the lower mast and, in this way, keep the shrouds and forestay tight for all of the time without hydraulics regardless of the wind or gust strength. Concentrate all of the bend in a new sort of topmast which would be more like a fishing rod. We will leave the topmast until later. Here we will look only at the rigid components.

Imagine an Eighteen footer with a fixed-bend lower mast sailing to windward in a moderate wind with harsh gusts. Consider what happens to the lower mast, shrouds and forestay gust by gust if the shroud tension is systematically increased. Let us start with the shrouds so slack that the leeward shroud is just taut in the steady wind. As each gust hits, the windward shroud and the forestay will stretch a little and the leeward shroud and the forestay will both sag and the jib will become fuller. As we tighten the rig step by step, the shrouds and forestay will be stretched – pre-stressed is the term – to the point where finally we have the rig so tight that the added load of the gust is less than the pre-load already applied. At and above this pre-load, the gusts will make no difference at all to the lower rig, so it will not go any slacker, the forestay will not sag, and the adoption of this pre-load principle was what made it possible to throw away the hydraulics.

My point in describing this in some detail is that in an Eighteen footer, the pre-load needed to achieve this is about 2000lb on each main shroud and 1000lb on the forestay. The lower shrouds and cap shrouds add another, say, 500lb each side, so the compression down the mast is about 6000lb or 3 tons.

It will be self-evident that for this principle to work every part of the system has to be adequately rigid. If either the mast bends (or alters its bend), or the shrouds are too stretchy, or the hull flexes, the high pre-load cannot be maintained and the forestay will sag. The classic open boat, even with a partner, is too flexible to handle stresses like this. The transverse frames of the framed and decked hull (Fig 9.3) are better, but do not support the chainplates in the right places.

Fig 9.4 shows the sort of immensely strong, stiff and light internal structure that has been developed by the skiffs. The total structure is really an elegant extension of the foam-sandwich principle. The horizontal section in Fig 9.4B represents the hull skin of the 49er, which has a gelcoat outer surface. (The Eighteens are usually laminated without gelcoat, and painted later, to save weight.) Gelcoat (a) is sprayed into the mould. A layer of very light cloth (b), which is woven for a smooth surface, is laminated onto the gelcoat, then a layer of strong cloth (c). At this point, straps of unidirectional (UD) carbon (d) (see page 144) – 300mm wide in the Eighteen footer (less in smaller boats) and 0.3mm thick – are laid into the laminate, as in Fig 9.4A. The foam (e) is then laid in and suction-clamped until the adhesive resin cures. Onto the foam a second identical strap (d) of the carbon UD is laminated, then another layer of strong cloth (f) of a weight and strength that 'balances' the strength of the light cloth plus the strong cloth on the outer surface.

The near identical deck has similar duplicated carbon straps.

A foam-sandwich 'X' frame centred on the carbon UD straps is added to the hull, as in Fig 9.4C, and attached as in Fig 9.4B. The foam (g), with a laminate of cloth each side, is glued to the bottom and 'tabbed' with tabs of light cloth (j).

When the deck is glued on, the straps in the deck match the X frame and lower straps to form four

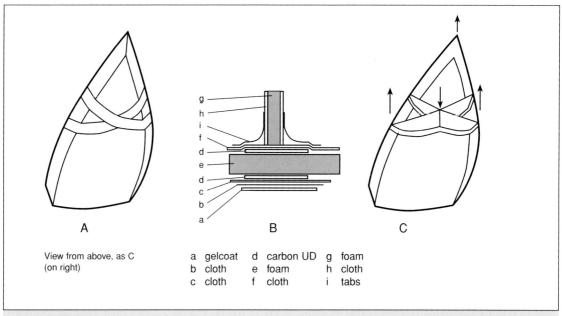

View from above, as C
(on right)

a	gelcoat	d	carbon UD	g	foam
b	cloth	e	foam	h	cloth
c	cloth	f	cloth	i	tabs

Fig 9.4 Skiff 'x' frame

I-beam girders in which the frame panels hold apart the flanges formed by the straps embedded in the hull and deck skins.

The mast is stepped on the centre of the 'X', the chainplates are attached at the ends of the aft arms of the X, and the forestay at the bow.

The design geometry is such that the duplicated carbon strap flanges each have a cross-section area of 0.31sq inches, and so an ultimate tension or compression breaking strain of about 62 000lb. The working load to carry the 2500lb upward tension at each chainplate is a horizontal compression force of about 5000 pounds from chainplate to mast and a tension through the hull skin of 5000lb, so the ultimate strength of the X frame is about 12 times the working load. Carbon stretches about 1.2% at failure, so under the working load of a pre-stressed Eighteen footer rig, the X frame stretches about 0.1%, or between 2mm and 3mm. In practice, this means that the mast sinks between the chainplates less than 5mm as the 3 ton pre-load of more than 30 times the hull weight is applied.

The carbon straps weigh about 7lb, the light foam-sandwich frame panels about 3lb, which gives a total of 10lb. This is a superb mechanical design.

The 49er is built similarly. It is a smaller, lighter boat and the pre-load is about 1 ton, not 3 tons.

A comment from left field. During one of the pre-Olympic regattas in Sydney in 1998 or 1999, an electrical storm swept over the fleet one afternoon and two 49ers suffered lightning strikes. One trapezing forward hand was thrown into the water some distance from the boat, but was unharmed. In the other (Ukrainian) boat, the lightning charge ran down one shroud and through the carbon strap of the outer skin to the water level. The momentary heating of the carbon blew myriad tiny holes through the outer laminates and the gelcoat over the strap. We found them another hull to use.

9.13 ■ Torsion (twist)

The problem of torsion has been around for a long time, but only recently has it surfaced as a serious design problem in high performance boats other than catamarans.

In the case of the pre-war displacement skiffs, big crews stacking on the gunwales certainly applied twisting loads, but the thick skins of the hulls acted like melon rinds (a scooped out melon with a thick rind is much harder to twist than the thin card of a shoebox), and, further, they always used running backstays to the aft windward gunwale to hold the masthead back, and this backstay carried much of the twisting load (Fig 1.5). Lightly built boats without decks, such as the English Fourteens, must have twisted significantly, but this would have been a part of the general flexibility and accepted as normal. The 1920s and 1930s New Zealand designs almost all followed the 'thin skins with frames and a deck' style, which behaved like a shoebox with a lid with a small hole in it (the cockpit); therefore they were structurally more rigid and twisted very little (Figs 1.29 and 1.30 and also Fig 9.3). The post-war Australian skiffs followed the same style.

Wings greatly increased the righting moment, but early wings were all 'flip-flop' wings hinged at the gunwales and supported at the fore-and-aft wing tips by 'wing wires' from the hounds (Fig 1.33 of *Tia Maria* shows hinged wings with the leeward wing flipped up and the windward wing flopped down). So while the design shift from trapezing against the gunwale of a 6ft-wide boat with the crew's centre of gravity displaced about 6ft from the centre of buoyancy, to trapezing from wings of nearly 18ft span, with the crews' centre of gravity displaced 12ft to windward doubled the twisting force. At first this did not affect the hull at all because the whole twisting load was taken by the wing wires.

In 1988 Julian Bethwaite's innovative B-14 was spectacularly successful, and he followed this in 1989 with the relatively tiny B-18 which was based on it. A major aerodynamic clean-up was one of the reasons why this small low-powered boat was able to sail faster than the previous mammoth designs. One part of this clean-up was to eliminate all unnecessary wires, so the wing-wings were eliminated and the wing structure became cantilever.

Suddenly, torsion became a major problem. For a few seconds following every tack or gybe there was a period when the sails were filling and the rig was twisting the forward half of the boat to leeward, and the crew were on the wing tip but not yet on trapeze, so their combined weight was twisting the aft half of the hull to windward, and the hull had to take the whole of this twisting load. At this point in the development process, torsional strength to resist twist suddenly became very important indeed.

If you roll paper into a tube and twist it, it will yield by the edge sliding. This demonstrates that torsion is a special case of shear. If you tape the edge so it cannot slide, the tube will fail not by the paper tearing in tension, but by the paper buckling inwards under compression. The three-dimensional curves of the hull stop its foam-sandwich skin from buckling inwards, but the flat deck needs help. In the modern Eighteen footer this is achieved by adding a second much lighter X frame between deck and bottom under the crew working area. This divides the hull and deck skins into a series of smaller triangular wedges. This design refinement makes the hull much more rigid and enables it to accept the high torsion loads easily.

9.14 ■ Summary

Prior to about 1950, all small sailboat hulls everywhere were built of timber, but over the period 1950–2000, both hull materials and design technology have changed rapidly. In Chapters 8 and 9 I have endeavoured to draw a broad-brush picture of the material, mechanical and dynamic forces that have driven the changes.

Chapter 10 • Hulls that Don't Baulk

10.1 ■ Background

I completed the manuscript of *HPS-1* in about 1991, and its content reflects the thinking of innovative sailors up to about 1990. By that time, the best of the three-hander Eighteen footer skiffs of Sydney were already demonstrating a performance level that separated them from all other sailboats. They were sailing faster than the wind as they tacked downwind, and they were sailing upwind at speeds faster than any prior monohull of similar size. This was the start of what we now call the apparent wind revolution. At the time I was too close to it all to appreciate what was happening from a broader perspective.

In the years since, of a number of new developments, two are of overriding importance. One of these has been the discovery that some hull shapes do not baulk as they sail progressively faster – that is, they have no 'hump' in their drag curve.

When I wrote *HPS-1*, I was unaware that among the Eighteen footer hull designs that then surrounded me, most of them created by the enthusiastic 'cut and try' efforts of gifted amateur designers and sailors, there might be some that could behave very unexpectedly; and that it was largely this strange property, which is even yet not properly understood, that has made possible the performance levels, first, of the new breed of apparent wind skiffs and, more recently, of the 'sportboat' keelboat genre that has endeavoured to copy as much as is possible of the skiff dynamics despite the handicap of keel weight.

In the light of what we have learned, it is appropriate to review what used to be regarded as the given wisdom about how a hull moves through the water, and then to present what we have learned since. The following notes summarise what we understand about the motion of the 'normal' hull, and then they present the evidence that not all hulls are 'normal'. In this way, we can better understand how strange are the new odd ones, and appreciate their near-unique advantages.

10.2 ■ The motion of a normal hull

The three inescapable factors in the total hydrodynamic drag of a hull from rest up to its hull speed are:

- Skin friction
- Form drag, *and*
- Wave-making drag.

10.3 ■ Skin friction

Skin friction is a complex subject because the friction depends on four different factors: speed, size, shape, and the smoothness of the surface. In the case of fast fish, a fifth factor – the strange properties of patterned roughness – may also be involved.

Speed

At very low speed the boundary layer – the slowed flow between the surface and the distance from the surface where the 'free stream' flows at undiminished speed – is governed by viscosity and is always laminar. This gives viscous drag only. As speed increases, at some point the shear force becomes greater than the viscous property can suppress and the boundary layer trips into turbulence. High-speed parcels of water momentarily scrub the surface and much increased shear (sliding friction) drag is developed.

At below the critical speed, flow is everywhere laminar. As the critical speed is reached, transition from laminar to turbulent flow occurs first at a distance downstream from the leading edge; as speed is increased, the transition zone moves upstream and approaches the leading edge more closely. A recent experiment was to coat a 49er hull with thick detergent and sail it at about 6 knots. Except for the 2–3ft just behind the bow, the detergent was scrubbed away quickly. This indicates that transition from laminar to turbulent at this speed occurs at 2–3ft behind the bow. But note particularly that centreboards and rudder blades with chord lengths (dimension leading edge to trailing edge in the direction of flow) of a foot or less can routinely run laminar, with very low drag.

Reynolds Number (RN)

Reynolds Number (RN) is the ratio of momentum to viscosity. Very simply, the greater the RN, the less is the influence of a fluid's viscous property. RN is the measure used by fluid dynamicists to define the scale of the flow.

In aeroplane terms, a 1ft chord propeller blade tip running at 500mph at ground level behaves exactly as does a 10ft chord wing tip at 50mph at ground level. At a height of 18 000ft where about half the mass of the atmosphere is below you, and the density is about half that at the surface, a 10ft wing tip at 100mph will behave as it does at 50mph at ground level where the density is double.

In sailing terms, we can assume that we are interested only in air at sea level density. A simple approach is to use the model aeroplane designer's VL (velocity times length) number of VL 1 = RN 4700, V = velocity in feet per second; L = chord in feet. Example: the sails of a 14ft dinghy, with mean chord (mean distance from luff of jib or mast to leech of mainsail in direction of flow) of 8ft, sails to windward in 10 knots of true wind at a boat speed of 6 knots. Apparent wind is 14 knots or 23.7fps, VL number is 23.7 x 8 = 189. RN = (189 x 4700) = 890 000, say, 1 million.

For water, multiply VL by 13. So the 1ft chord centreboard of the dinghy above at a boat speed of 6 knots or 10.56fps is running at VL of 1 x 10.56 x 13 = 137. RN = 137 x 4700 = RN 650 000. The 14ft hull is running at 10.56 x 14 x 13 x 4700 = RN 9 million approx.

A typical light aircraft with a wing chord of 6ft and a cruising speed of 100 knots (169ft per second) will run (at sea level) at RN (169 x 6 x 4700) = 4.75 million. A Jumbo will take off at about 30 million. Aeronautical engineers are not much interested in RNs less than 5 million. This is why the low speed aerodynamics appropriate to the scale of the sailboat has been so neglected.

Size

Size matters; there is a scale effect. The drag per sq foot of an aircraft carrier hull at speed is less than that of a small motorboat at the same speed. The principle involved is the ratio of viscous force to momentum. At very low speed and/or small scale, viscosity is dominant; in the extreme, this gives rise to laminar flow. As speed increases, viscosity remains constant but the momentum of each particle increases, so the viscous component becomes relatively smaller. This is why the drag of the 66-006 section (Fig 13.15) at Reynolds Numbers of 6 and 9 million is lower than that at 3 million, except in the laminar flow 'bucket'.

Shape

Flow over convex surfaces tends to remain laminar, so, for example, centreboards and aircraft wings can be shaped to retain laminar flow over distances from their leading edges that are not possible when the surfaces are flat. (This subject is touched upon in *HPS-1*.)

Smoothness

This is critical for two reasons. All tests show that the rougher the surface, the greater is the drag. And because roughness causes turbulence, laminar flow can never develop (at any practical speed) over a rough surface. The 'standard roughness' drag in Fig 13.15 shows no laminar 'bucket'.

Numbers

Fig 13.15 (from *Theory of Wing Sections* by Abbott and von Doenhoff) gives the shape and drag curves of a very thin NASA laminar flow section, 66-006 at RNs of 3, 6 and 9 million. In water, the RN of a 14ft dinghy at 6 knots will be about 9 million. The NASA sections are always highly polished for testing, except when they are deliberately blemished with 'standard roughness' grit for those tests.

This section gives a minimum drag coefficient in the laminar flow 'bucket' of about .003. This is for both sides of the section, so the drag coefficient for a single surface such as the bottom of a boat will be half – that is, .0015.

The formula is Drag (lb) = Area (sq ft) × Coeff of Drag × Density (water = 1 approx) × Speed (fps) squared. So the skin friction of a 59er hull with 42sq ft of wetted area at 5 knots (8.4fps) would be 4.45lb if the flow were everywhere laminar. But we have seen that except for the forward 2–3ft, the boundary layer will be turbulent at 5–6 knots. Fig 13.15 gives a drag coefficient of, say, .0055 for the turbulent boundary layer operating just outside the laminar flow 'bucket'. This is for 'both sides wet', so about 0.0028 for one side. So a realistic calculation of skin friction drag, which assumes that about 90% of the boundary layer will be turbulent, would be, say, 7.5lb. This would be true for a highly polished hull. NASA, though, are realists who understand that aeroplanes cannot always be clean and shiny, so they routinely do a run of measurements with the section coated with fine grit – what they call 'standard roughness'. This drag is given in the upper curve, its minimum is about .0083, and this suggests that the skin friction drag of a slightly gritty 59er at 5 knots would be about 12.3lb. Unpolished dinghies and yachts with marine growth do not win races. The higher the polish, the faster you sail.

The strange 'porpoise skin' factor

Porpoises can attain speeds of 40–45 knots for brief periods. Their skins are slightly rough. Some years ago a paper in the scientific journal *Nature* reported three principal facts:

- The first was the nature of the drag mechanism itself. At the microscopic level, vortices like tiny horizontal waterspouts form with their upstream ends attached to the surface, and for a while they live with their axes aligned with the flow and almost touching the surface. At the end of some lifespan, the downstream end suddenly rears up into the flow and 'bursts'. At this point the energy used to wind the vortex up is lost to the system in the general turbulence of the boundary layer and the energy used to wind up the next vortex appears to the system as drag. This process repeats many hundreds of times each second over every square inch of the surface.
- The second fact was that if the surface were roughened with tiny projections, the drag was normally increased by about 10%, as expected.
- But the third fact was that if the projections were arranged in a very particular pattern, the effect could be to 'organise' the turbulence in a way that increased the average life of each vortex, with the consequence that fewer reared up and burst each second, and that when the pattern was at its optimum the overall drag could be decreased by up to about 10%.

The problem was that the pattern was critical in the extreme and, further, that it was different for every change of speed and even for every different distance from the leading edge. It may be that the porpoise can feel what is going on and arrange its goose bumps second by second accordingly. We human beings are not nearly clever enough yet to do this.

10.4 ■ Form drag

'Form drag' is what we are thinking about when we sense, intuitively, that if we pull two shapes through the water at the same speed, one a 'streamline' shape like a slender fish, and the other a square brick of the same cross-section, surface area and volume, the streamline shape will disturb the water less as it slips through it, and so will be easier to pull. Why this should be so can be understood if we imagine them to be towed through a tube that is full of motionless water, as in Fig 10.1. As the fish shape is towed towards the left, the near-infinite mass of water ahead of it will not move, so the water around the front half of the fish has no option but to accelerate 'backwards' from the nose of the fish (Nose) to the maximum girth section of the fish's body (Max Girth) to pass through the restricted annulus between the fish and the tube wall on its way to fill the void that is continuously being formed behind the fish. From the forward point of the fish to the point of its maximum girth, energy is being expended to accelerate the water, and the pressure of the water drops. From the point of maximum girth to its tail (Tail), the process reverses – the water is slowed smoothly against the inert mass of water behind the fish, and as it slows and stops, its pressure rises and this increased pressure forces the tapered after part of the fish forward. In this way, the aft end of the streamline shape recovers almost all the energy that the forward half has expended in accelerating the water 'backwards'. The smoother the acceleration of the water and its return to rest, the less energy will be lost and the greater the proportion of it that will be recovered, and the less will be the total drag. This is what 'streamlining' is all about.

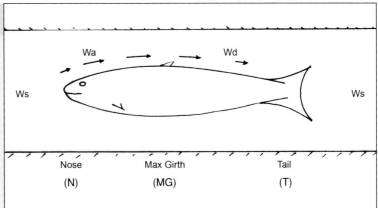

Fig 10.1 Fish in tube

Ws – Water stationary
Wa – As fish moves to left, water accelerates to right from N to MG
Wd – Water decelerates from MG to come to rest at T
The energy needed to accelerate the water from Nose to Max girth is returned to the system as the water decelerates and the pressure rises from MG to T.

When we tow a 'boxy' shape the situation is different. The square end of the box, as it advances, requires that the water accelerates with a great jolt, and also that it flows around sharp square corners smoothly at high speed. The water, very reasonably, refuses to do so. Instead it separates from the sharp corners with massive swirls and develops a thick turbulent boundary layer which slows the water and absorbs energy and degrades the area of low pressure. So when the back end of the box passes there is no pressure increase to drive it forward – there is no energy recovery. There are only more sharp corners, more turbulence, and more drag.

This situation will remain true regardless of the diameter of the tube, so we can think of the shores of the harbour or of the ocean as the tube walls. It will also remain true if we imagine the streamline 'fish' shape to grow downwards until it looks like a glider's wing or centreboard or a keel. The vital point is that whenever a moving body is completely immersed in a fluid, such as the centreboard or rudder blade in the water, or the spreaders in the air, energy must be expended to move the mass of fluid aside as the body passes, then to return it to its original state and position. The more smoothly this mass is accelerated and then slowed, the greater will be the recovery of energy, and this is what low drag is all about. Summed up, low form drag requires intelligent streamline shape.

10.5 ■ Wave-making drag

(Note that wave-making drag and wave-impact drag are different. Wave-making drag is present in flat water as well as waves because it represents the energy used by the boat to make the waves of its own wake. Wave-impact drag is due to waves not made by the boat and so is absent in flat water.)

When a body floats 'surface-piercing' – that is, only half immersed – a set of dynamics that are very different from the form drag of the fully immersed fish begins to run. Wave-making drag is the penalty we pay for playing on a fluid surface.

A typical rowing skiff can be up to 50 times as long as its waterline beam. This is so slender that for practical purposes it behaves as if it has no width and makes no waves as it passes. At its normal operating speed, it will develop skin friction drag, but almost no other hydrodynamic drag. Because of its extreme length it will be very hard to turn.

A typical yacht or dinghy hull short enough to turn quickly will usually have a length of between three and six times its waterline beam and an immersed volume sufficient to float itself and its crew. As the fore-body passes it necessarily moves water aside to admit its bulk, then the after-body closes the water behind it.

At very low speed the motion will be the same as that around a fully immersed streamline body such as the fish in the tube. But as speed increases, the wedge of the bow accelerates water sideways more forcefully and it heaps up against the topsides in the familiar bow wave. This heaped-up water immediately subsides to its original level; it can go only one way, away from the boat, and this continuous accelerate–heap up–subside process forms the familiar bow wave of the wake.

As the after-body approaches and passes, the process is reversed. The tapered shape of the after-body now calls for the water that has been accelerated away from the boat to reverse and flow back towards the boat. In

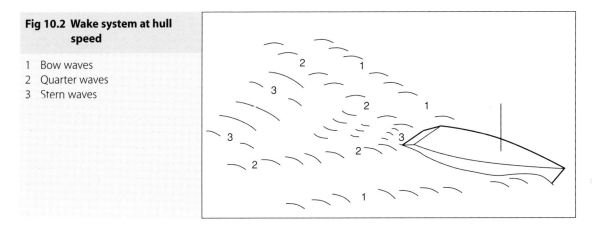

Fig 10.2 Wake system at hull speed

1 Bow waves
2 Quarter waves
3 Stern waves

practice what happens is that the water level falls and forms a trough at about the middle of the boat, and the higher water away from the hull accelerates 'downhill' into the trough back towards the boat.

This continuous process forms the familiar quarter wave of the wake. The inward wave motions either reflect from or cross under the boat and appear on the other side as the quarter wave that rolls outwards parallel to, and just inside, the bow wave.

A third motion is that the difference in level between the higher heaped-up water at the bow and the lower troughs on both sides towards the quarters causes the water under the boat to accelerate backwards. This flow starts the stern wave system, the transverse waves that appear between the diverging bow and quarter waves and that complete the wake system, as shown in Fig 10.2. Note that the heaped-up water at the bow is necessarily the first crest of the stern wave system.

The critical point is that the energy used first to heap up the water and force it outwards, and then to make the troughs that accelerate water inwards, and also to accelerate it backwards under the hull, has in each case been converted to, and is now conserved in, the orbital momentums of the bow wave, the quarter wave and the stern wave systems of the wake. It is lost for ever to the boat, has to be continuously replaced to keep the boat moving, and this energy demand is what we call wave-making drag.

Note that a hull will necessarily have form drag, in the sense that a square barge will drag more than a well-shaped hull of the same length and weight. But it will never be possible to measure it separately because the action of moving the hull will necessarily make the waves of the wake system and incur wave-making drag as well. What we can measure will always be the sum of the skin friction plus the form drag plus the wave-making drag. This is what we call 'hull hydrodynamic drag'.

Practical examples of form and wave-making drag would be well-shaped 14ft dinghies such as the 29er carrying two youths at about 450lb total sailing weight, the Tasar at about 500lb and the B-14 with a generally heavier crew at, say, 550lb all up. All have total hydrodynamic drags at 5 knots of about 17–19lb. As we saw above, skin friction will account for about 7.5lb of this, so the form drag plus the wave-making drag at 5 knots of the 450lb 29er will be about 9.5lb and 11.5lb for the 550lb B-14. Up to hull speed, this total drag closely follows the speed (squared) law, so at 2.5 knots it would be one-quarter its 5 knot value.

10.6 ■ The concept of hull speed

It so happens that 5 knots (4.95 knots more exactly) is hull speed for a boat of 14ft waterline length. This is the highest speed at which the hull can float 'level'. What happens at higher speeds is very different. To understand what hull speed is, and why the dynamics at all higher speeds are so different, we need to look first at the properties of wave systems that are not made by the boat.

The important point is that the speed with which the waves (in water) in any wave system will roll downwind will depend absolutely on the length of the wave – the distance between successive crests. In a system with crests 9ft apart, the waves will roll downwind at 4 knots. A system with a wave-length of 14ft will roll at 5 knots, at 20ft the speed will be 6 knots, and at 28ft the speed will be 7 knots. The formula is: wave speed (in knots) = 1.32 times the square root of the wave-length (in feet) (*HPS-1*, Chapter 13, covers this subject in more detail).

The converse of this is that a body such as a boat that moves across flat water will create a wake system in which the wave-length of the transverse stern waves will be proportional to the square of its speed, because it will be governed by the wave-length/wave-speed law above.

Given this knowledge, let us look again at what happens to our 14ft hull as it moves across flat water at knot speeds of 2, 3, 4 and 5, and then at 6 knots and 7 knots. At 2 knots the wave-length of the stern wave system is 2.25ft, so theoretically the bow wave will be followed by six stern wave crests along the length of the boat. Each would be likely to be only millimetres high, so they will not amount to much. At 3 knots and a wave-length of 5.1ft, there will be the bow wave plus two following crests; at 4 knots and a wave-length of 9ft, there will be the bow wave plus the second crest a little aft of amidships. At 5 knots the second crest of the stern wave system will lie exactly under the transom. This speed is called 'hull speed' and is critically important because this is the highest speed at which a 14ft hull can float 'level' with the water at the stern as high as it is at the bow. At this speed the hull will be subject to skin friction plus form drag plus wave-making drag, and nothing more. At 6 knots, the wave-length of the stern wave system will necessarily become 20ft, so the second crest of the stern wave system will have fallen back to being 20ft behind the bow wave and 6ft behind the transom of the 14ft boat. The transom will now be in the trough and floating on a water surface that is at a lower level than that at the bow. The result of this is that the boat will now be sailing uphill – up the receding face of the bow wave of its own making. Let us call this new component – this effort needed to force the boat up the slope – 'forced' drag. How significant can this be?

Every reader will be familiar with how easy it is to push a heavy vehicle on a flat surface, and how hard it becomes to push it up even the slightest slope. In the case of the boat, how steep can the slope be?

The slope is gentle at first, but quickly becomes steeper. What do we see in practice?

10.7 ■ Drag curves of non-planing sailboats

Tony Marchaz, in his *Sailing Theory and Practice*, gives the drag curves of *Gymcrack*, a small keelboat of typical yacht shape with a waterline length of 23.8ft and a weight of about 3 tons (6560lb). Its drag curves, both foul and clean, are given in Fig 10.3. This is an unusual diagram for a keelboat in that this boat was towed and the drags at increasing speeds were measured at full size (that is, the actual boat was towed in a canal; it was not a model towed in a tank and the readings then manipulated).

Note how rapidly the drag increases as hull speed is approached and exceeded. The increase of drag above hull speed is so great that for practical purposes heavy sailboats of this conventional shape have never been able to sail at speeds much faster than their hull speed.

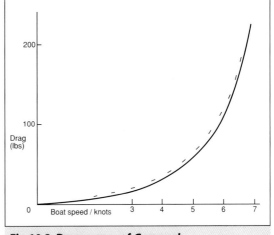

Fig 10.3 Drag curves of *Gymcrack*

Solid curve – Drag with clean bottom
Dashed curve – Drag with foul bottom
(Drags measured at full scale)
Waterline length   23.77ft
Weight   6560lb

10.8 ■ Drag curves of planing sailboats

Uffa Fox in England developed a series of planing sailboats in the 1930s. The best known of these were his International Fourteens, and his canoes. Fig 10.4 from Fox's 1936 book *Sail and Power* gives the lines of *Wake*, a state of the art design in its day. In about 1969, Tom Tanner, of the University of Southampton's Ship Science Dept, towed *Wake* at full size in the National Physical Laboratory's test tank. The drag curve is given in Fig 10.5.

Note how different is the shape of this curve from that of the heavy yacht. From rest to hull speed, the rate of increase is similar – close to speed (squared). As speed exceeds hull speed, the rate of drag increase at first starts to rise more steeply, exactly as it does with the heavier boat and for the same reason, but then

Fig 10.4 Lines of *Wake*

Lines of the sailing canoe *Wake* Length 17.5ft. Weight 453lb. Designer Uffa Fox. Lines from *Sail and Power* by Uffa Fox, 1936.

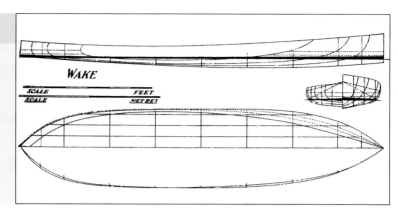

WAKE

Fig 10.5 Hull drag of the canoe *Wake*

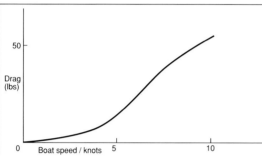

Drag measured at full scale in the National Physical Laboratory tank, at 453lb total weight, by Dr Tom Tanner.

it reverses as the lighter, flatter boat starts to plane over the top of the water.

In *HPS-1* I gave the drag curves of a number of the experimental NS14s that led to the Tasar. All these drag curves are broadly similar to that of the canoe. The drag curve of the Tasar is given in Fig 10.6. (For interest, I have added the drag measurements when a flap is added to the hull, and also when strakes are taped on. These are shown as insets of Fig 10.6, and photos in Fig 10.6A.)

The canoe is long and flat, and the NS14s and Tasar could also be regarded as not quite conventional by 1990s northern hemisphere eyes. The drag curve of a very conventional 'roundish' planing singlehander is given as Fig 10.7.

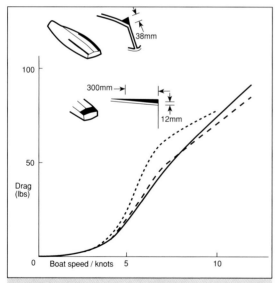

Fig 10.6 Drag curves of the Tasar

Solid line – Drag curve of standard Tasar
        at 500lb
Dashed line – Drag curve with strakes 500lb
Dotted line – Drag curve with flap 500lb

Fig 10.6A Strakes and flap taped to the Tasar

10.9 ■ Tow measurements – model and full size

A note about drag measurements in general is appropriate.

Big boats that are not yet built cannot be towed, and even if they had been built, they would usually be too big to fit into instrumented test tanks. So the published curves of almost all large boats are necessarily derived from models. The process of scaling up the simple drags of a model at model speeds to figures that relate to the expected drags of the full-size boat at higher speeds is complicated. Let us assume that a model had been made of *Gymcrack* with a 4ft waterline. The hull speed of that model would have been 2.64 knots, and the steep drag rise would have set in at about 2.7 to 3 knots. To arrive at the likely drag of the full-size boat, the measured drags would have been separated into the calculated skin friction and the calculated wave-making drag. The rest would be the form drag. The calculated skin friction and the calculated form drag would then be increased as the area or the mass and the square of the speed, and the wave-making drag as the square root of the waterline length – that is, as hull speed, and the square of the speed.

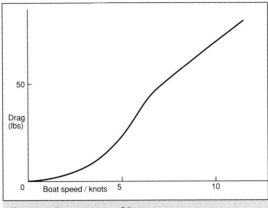

Fig 10.7 Drag curve of Byte

Total weight as towed was 275lb.

The three recalculated components are then added together to arrive at the final curve, but this curve can only be as good as the assumptions that have gone into the calculations. This is why 'the *Gymcrack* coefficients' have gone down in history as seminal. Because they were measured at full size, these – and these alone – were free from woolly assumptions and uncertainty.

10.10 ■ Full-size tow tests

Only on rare occasions have larger boats been towed at full size. Such tests are of unusual value because they are free of any question about the assumptions that have gone into the transformation calculations.

In this sense, all the curves given in this book are unusual:

- *Gymcrack* was one of those rare yachts to be towed full size.
- Tom Tanner measured the drag of *Wake* full size in the NPL tank.
- I have measured all the other hulls published here at full size.

10.11 ■ Our initial tow-test method

From the first tow tests in the 1960s and up until 1993, the test boat was fitted with a rudder to steer it but no centreboard. We ballasted it to the desired total fully rigged and crewed weight with water in plastic bags, and towed it behind the tow boat on a long light towline. We are fortunate in having the narrow waters of Sydney's Upper Middle Harbour (see Fig 1.22, inset) to work in. Early in the morning they are usually windless, traffic free and glassy. We used Northbridge Sailing Club as a base, and set up two flags at each end of the rigging deck to give two parallel transit lines. We measured speed by timing the interval between crossing these transits as we towed back and forth across them. We understood that a boat within the wake would at times be either assisted or baulked by the slope of the advancing or the receding face of one of the stern waves of the tow boat. We used a light tow boat and a long line to minimise this error.

The notes above, and the *Gymcrack* drag curves (Fig 10.3) with its very steep drag increase above hull speed, and the planing dinghy curves (Figs 10.5 to 10.7), all of which have pronounced humps, summarise what the world understood to be the way a hull moved through the water prior to one day in the early 1990s.

10.12 ■ The gem in the dross

One day we set out with high hopes to measure the differences in drag between two similar, but not identical, Eighteen footer hulls, plus one that we had modified by taping on strakes along the aft chines and a shallow flap across the bottom at the transom similar in principle to those added to the Tasar and shown in Fig 10.6A. My younger son Julian was enjoying his third year as Eighteen Footer World Champion, and we were looking for ways to make next year's boat even faster. The availability of hand-held GPS sets had offered a way of greatly simplifying speed measurement. Our object was to measure the fine differences between the three hulls at low speeds, then to measure the actual drag of a top-level Eighteen in the higher speed ranges.

As the day progressed, more and more things went wrong. The low-speed 'balance' method of comparing the drag of a test hull with the drag of a reference hull, which had worked so well in earlier years with smaller, lighter hulls, was unable to cope

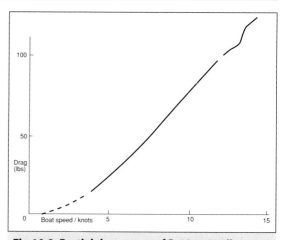

Fig 10.8 Partial drag curve of B-18 at 772lb

Angled hull without centreboard became unstable at speed.

with the greater inertia of the bigger heavier Eighteen footer hulls that were water-ballasted up to their fully rigged and crewed sailing weights of close to 1000lb. Further, a different tow boat threw more spray and this spray hit the towed boats. A longer beam was not strong enough and bent. And during a later, higher speed run, a hull (with no centreboard) became progressively more unstable in roll and yaw. At 17 knots, it suddenly pitched and rolled in a violent corkscrew motion twice, reared out of the water, and flipped upside down. The weak link we always put into the towline snapped and the day ended in disarray. When I roughly plotted the drag measurements we had secured up to that time, they did not even show the expected 'hump' in the curve above hull speed, and I set them aside in disgust and got on with something more rewarding.

Some weeks later I picked them up again and completed the analysis by adding in the corrections for towline angle and aerodynamic drag. The points then all fell on a smooth curve with little scatter *and no hump*. This is given in Fig 10.8.

An old research maxim runs, 'When all else fails, believe your measurements'. Suddenly, I recognised the gem – the impossible had happened. I was looking at what were perhaps the first ever set of drag measurements of a fast dinghy hull that was every designer's dream. This Eighteen footer hull had towed with no hump in its drag curve!

This recognition has changed Julian's and my attitude to everything. If this hull (one of his designs) had no hump, what about others? What was the error in the assumptions about hump outlined above? Could we design future boats with no hump? (We now think that the abnormal drag rise in the higher planing speeds on that day was due to the latent instability caused by no centreboard and towing at an angle.)

10.13 ■ Revised method and further measurements

Three more drag curves will show just how much this discovery has changed our approach.

At that time, the idea of a fast two-hander in the genre of an Eighteen footer was stirring. (This concept was destined to become the 49er.) We made a prototype and planned another tow-test day, but with two changes to the method.

The towed hull was again ballasted with water to the desired weights, but we made two changes. For stability at higher speeds, we towed it with centreboard as well as rudder in place. And, since we were going to use a centreboard in any case, we decided to try towing with the towed boat at an angle to the wake sufficient to place it on the flat undisturbed water outside the tow boat's wake. Both innovations have worked perfectly.

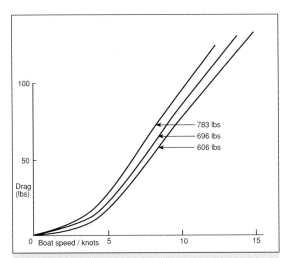

Fig 10.9A Drag curves of 49er, as measured in 1994

Drags of hull plus centreboard and rudder, towed at angle outside tug wake.

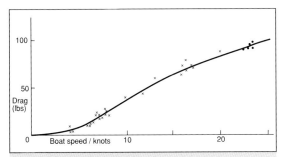

Fig 10.9B Detail of 606lb curve of Fig 10.9A

Original of 606lb (design weight) curve of Fig 10.9A; 1994 measurement technique; hull with rudder and centreboard towed at angle outside wake. System stable to 25 knots.

The method we now use is with a test team of four: the tow-boat coxswain (so far, it has always been my daughter Nicola); the towed-boat coxswain (to date, always Julian); a safety officer with a hand bearing compass; and myself as experimenter. We start with the test boat ballasted to the maximum weight at which we wish to tow.

The tow-boat cox has two GPSs that have acquired multiple satellites on the console in front of her, and establishes the rig on a line that will give a mile or so dead straight towards a distant aiming point on a ridge ahead and (a practical point) far enough away from northern ridges to ensure uninterrupted reception throughout the run of adequate GPS satellites.

The test-boat coxswain positions the test boat comfortably on the undisturbed water outside the bow wave of the tow boat. The towline angle varies from 30° to 35° at low speed to about 25° at higher speed.

When all is ready I ask the tug cox to establish at or close to a nominated speed. When she nods, I hand-signal and we all 'freeze' for ten seconds during which the towed-boat cox holds the towline angle steady; I note the minimum, maximum and mean towline tensions on the spring balance on my knee; the tug cox reads the actual speed during that period by GPS; and the safety officer measures the angle between the towline and the wake. When I have reliable towline tensions I hand-signal again, we relax, record the measurements above, then repeat. I repeat at least four times when all is steady, six or seven times if there is any unsteadiness such as small waves. Any wind is noted; we then move to the next speed. I usually call for runs at 4, 6, 8, 10, 12.5 and 15 knots.

We then dump a pre-measured mass of water from one or two garbage bags, and repeat the whole exercise at the lighter weight. In the case of the 49er hull, we borrowed a more powerful ski boat as tow boat for higher speeds and took it up to 25 knots. With this test method it was perfectly stable at this speed. We periodically re-test the Tasar as a warm-up to prove everything – on this occasion we took the Tasar to 22 knots, at which speed Julian advised that it was beginning to feel edgy.

The relevant drag figures for the 49er are given in Fig 10.9A, B, F, G and H.

To keep all these drag presentations in this chapter similar in appearance I have limited the boat speed axis to 15 knots (as Fig 10.9A). Fig 10.9B shows what we measured in 1996 when we took the 49er up to 25 knots – it gives all of our drag measurements for the 49er at that weight over the full range of speed from 4 to 25 knots, together with the 'best fit' curve. There is a change of slope at about 15 knots. I do not know what causes this, but it would be consistent with the scale effect that gives lower drag at higher RNs in Fig 13.15.

Note that by 'best fit' we are looking for both best fit and consistency between the three curves each from a full set of measurements at the three different weights. In this case we towed the boat at an unnecessarily high weight just to see what happened to the drag 'outside the square'.

I am fortunate in having the support of the experienced team above. The small scatter of the points attests to their steadiness.

Fig 10.9C Tug and 49ers

The complete towing system and crew on their way to the first trial.

Fig 10.9D Standard 49er on tow at 14 knots

Fig 10.9E Modified 49er on tow at 14 knots

Fig 10.9F Refinement of humpless feature

The 2007 refinement of the 1994 work: two 49ers towed abeam of tug outside the tug wake. Towline tension was measured by load cell and an electronic averaging device. Multiple configurations of weight, trim and heel measured at 1 knot intervals up to 18 knots. 'Humpless' drag curve was found to be a composite of the minimums of multiple drag curves at progressively higher bow-up trims. Courtesy of Simon Watin.

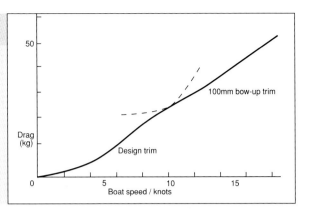

Fig 10.9G Refinement of fourth mode

The 2007 refinement of 'Fourth mode' technique (*HPS-1*, Section 20.11). Measured drags of 49er in three trim modes. Courtesy of Simon Watin.

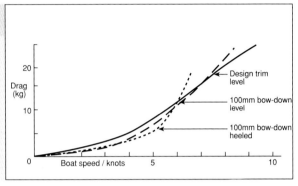

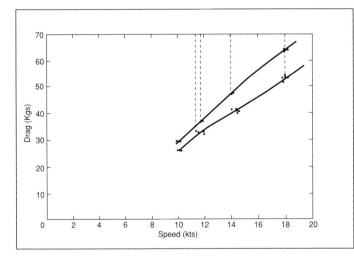

Fig 10.9H Differences in drag

Upper curve – Drag of standard 49er hull
Lower curve – Drag of 49er hull with
sharper chines.

In 1998 we made the 29er youth trainer. The object of this boat was to sail like a skiff to train for a skiff. My definition of apparent wind performance is the ability to win by tacking downwind in all wind strengths. No existing youth trainer could approach apparent wind performance in any wind. Conversely, if we could not achieve full apparent wind performance in all winds from a new small youth trainer there would be no point in making it. Julian suggested that I scale down one of the Eighteen footer hulls rather than the 49er. I lofted the hull, built the prototype, and as soon as it would float we towed it. At that stage the hull surface paint was undercoat, which we had dry-sanded with long sanding boards carrying 80 grit sandpaper, so it was fair but far from polished. Fig 10.10 gives the initial drag curve. The drag was higher than I expected, but the surface was not smooth. Above all, there was no hump just above hull speed, so we proceeded. A year or so later we towed a polished production 29er at two weights (the curves are given in Fig 10.10). These two sets of drag measurements give direct comparison between the drags of two near-identical hulls, one unpolished and the other polished.

Fig 10.10 Drag curves of 29er

Dashed curve – 29er prototype, fair, undercoated,
                    sanded 80 grit
Solid curves – 29er production, polished gelcoat.

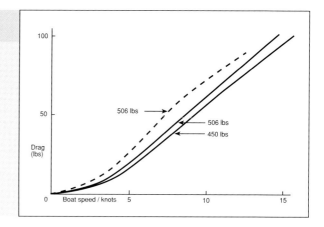

Fig 10.11 Drag curves of straked prototype 59er

A – Midship section as built. Drag curves probably
    as 29er, Fig 10.10.
B, B1 – As modified with strakes and false sides.
    Drag curves as above.
C – Midship section as rebuilt. Drag curves as
    Fig 10.12.

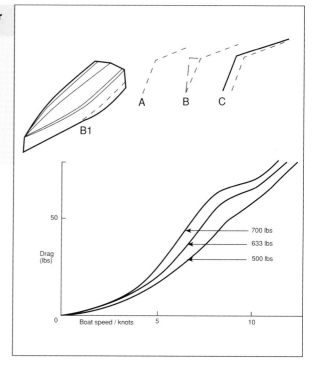

Another interesting set of drag curves is given in Figs 10.11 and 10.12 of the 59er prototype. To carry heavier adults, for the initial prototype I stretched the final 29er hull about 10% in length from 4440mm to 4800mm without any increase in beam or draught. The midship section below the chines was exactly as the 29er (Fig 10.11, inset A) and the maximum chine beam was 39in (991mm), so it is reasonable to expect that the drag curves, had we measured them, would have related closely to those of the 29er in Fig 10.10. The boat was quick, but when the wind stopped it rolled to windward too fast for the comfort of mature adults. In this design the chines lie on the waterline at design weight, so I progressively increased the chine beam pro rata with horizontal strakes at the chines and false topsides until the rate of roll was acceptable. The straked hull finished with maximum chine beam about 45in or 1143mm, as in inset B in Fig 10.11. It looked quite attractive. (The Tasar and Laser Two both have a maximum chine beam of 48in or 1219mm.) However, I sensed a difference when sailing it, so we towed it. Fig 10.11 shows its drag curves with the hull straked as described.

I rebuilt the bottom by padding it to the shape I would have built in the first place had I known that the wider chine beam was going to be necessary (inset C). As soon as it would float, I towed it with the rebuilt bottom. Fig 10.12 gives the drag curves of the rebuilt prototype.

The huge difference astonished us all.

Do not try to read too much into minor differences between Figs 10.11 and 10.12. A practical point is to look at the drag difference between the rough and polished 29er hulls in Fig 10.10. The rebuilt 59er bottom was much smoother than the dry-sanded 29er prototype, but far from the smoothness and polish of a production hull.

10.14 ■ No hump – the practical effect

Imagine two 59er type boats, identical except that one has the Fig 10.11 hull shape and drag curve, and the other the Fig 10.12 shape. Imagine further that these two boats, both crewed with heavy crews at close to 630lb total weight, sail side by side with the wind on the beam in a magic wind that cycles by rising smoothly to a gust peak just strong enough to give both boats a drive force of 70lb and a speed of 10 knots, and then falls smoothly to its lull minimum 25% slower, which will give both boats a drive force of about 40lb and a speed between 6 and 7 knots.

It is obvious from inspection of the drag diagrams that the boat with the hump will sail more than 10% more slowly in all wind strengths that give between 30lb and 70lb drive force. In practice, what happens is worse than that. As the wind dies, the boat with the hump squats, falls off the plane and slows to hull speed. It remains trapped there until the wind increases to the point where it is strong enough to push the boat over the hump to the point where it planes again. The crew of the boat with no hump have no idea whether their boat is planing or not; they are conscious only that their boat keeps moving well and their rival is behind and falling further back.

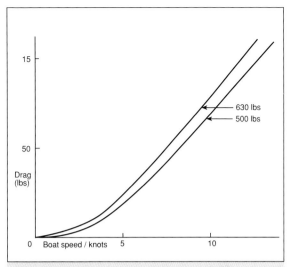

Fig 10.12 Drag of rebuilt 59er prototype

10.15 ■ No hump – the perceived effect

Martin Billoch is an Argentinian naval architect who among other talents was Optimist World Champion many years ago. His description is the best I have read:

> When I first sailed on a 49er, I had this strange feeling, that at that moment I could not explain, it was a feeling of not feeling the boat, I was not able to experience the feeling of starting to plane, it didn't feel right, and I thought that something was missing.
>
> Then some time later I learned from your articles in magazines that you were able to design dinghies that did not have a hump on the curve on the transition from displacement mode to planing mode … and then I saw the curve in one of your articles … and I said 'Oh, Oh, Oh now I understand that strange missing feeling … there was no extra HP required to jump from displacement mode to planing mode!!!'
>
> Before sailing the 49er, I was used to sailing 470 and Laser 5000 dinghies, boats that need lots of power to overcome the hump and start to plane, so you were able to feel that jump a lot.

10.16 ■ No hump – the observed effect

At the ISAF High Performance Olympic Dinghy evaluation event at Lake Garda, in September 1996, the familiarisation sailing was periodically stopped and a short two-lap windward–leeward race conducted. Of the 11 classes present, the 49er was not the longest, widest, or lightest – nor did it have the biggest sails. But in race after race the two 49ers finished together at the downwind mark at about the time that whichever boat was third was rounding the top mark in the four-leg races.

10.17 ■ Summary

In the years since 1990 one of the principal design advances has been first the recognition of the dynamically humpless hull – the realisation that hulls exist that do not baulk as minimum planing speed is approached – and then the exploitation of this understanding in the design of useful boats.

My position is that I did not invent the 'dynamically humpless hull'. I seem to have been the first to measure this property and recognise that it can exist in this kind of boat (ie not a wide ultra-light scow). Since we recognised it, Julian and I have created four hulls with this property: Julian designed his 49er and then his 29er, and I designed Mk 21, the last and best of my little High Speed Project experimental craft (covered in *HPS-1*), and more recently the 59er. The 59er is perhaps the most interesting in that this boat was very probably humpless as designed, then developed pronounced humpiness as I straked it for greater roll stability, then regained its humpless property with a conservative re-design.

This has been pure 'cut and try' development; I have no theoretical explanation for these extraordinary dynamic differences.

I have addressed a number of sailing science conferences and conducted seminars at leading national maritime colleges, displayed these 'no hump' curves, and invited discussion about them. As at 2006, none of the scientists nor naval architects present has had any more idea than Julian, Martin Billoch or me as to what may be the explanation.

10.18 ■ Postscript[1]

Between May and July 2007, just before *HPS-2* went to press, we combined two opportunities to conduct a further series of tow tests and other measurements on the 49er.

The first opportunity was created by the class itself, which has taken the deliberate decision to join with the designer and take a hard look at itself every 12 years (every third Olympiad) with a view to taking whatever steps are necessary to remain 'state of the art'. On this occasion, it was decided to look at the effects of:

- A more accurate hull shape.
- A change to all carbon spars and fittings.
- An even more automatic rig.

The second opportunity was created by Simon Watin, a French Naval Architecture PhD student from the Paris École Polytechnique, who had arranged with his professor and with Julian to conduct his thesis work in Sydney with us.

Between 1994 when I lofted and made the 49er prototype hull – which became the plug for the 49er moulds worldwide – and 2004 the cost of computer guided milling to an accuracy of about 0.1mm of large objects such as the external shape of a 5m boat has reduced from the astronomic to the affordable. My plug has turned out to be accurate within about +/– 1mm almost everywhere, but as with all handwork there are asymmetries. Some owners have had their hulls re-faired to correct discovered asymmetry to the extent possible with focused handwork. The practical question that now arises is 'Is there sufficient performance difference between a 1994 high-quality handworked shape and the more accurate computer-milled shape available in 2008 to justify the cost of the more accurate technology?'

We decided that potentially small differences would best be disclosed by towing two boats simultaneously. One would be a standard 'out of the mould' hull and the second would be a hull that had been modified.

Over the past 40 years, we have conducted four broad programmes of full-scale towing tests.

The first in the late 1960s employed:

• *Speed*	Timed transits.
• *Environment*	Boats towed in the wake of the tug.
• *Towline tension*	Mean tension estimated by me from reading an unsteady spring balance over about 6–10 seconds.

From this start we have systematically improved.

The second in the late 1980s and 1990 used:

• *Speed*	Twin GPSs.
• *Environment*	Boats towed in the wake of the tug.

---

[1] This postscript refers to hull shape. A second postscript in Chapter 22 looks at rig findings of particular interest.

• *Towline tension*	Mean tension estimated by me from reading an unsteady spring balance over about 6–10 seconds.

The third in the mid-1990s used:

• *Speed*	Twin GPSs.
• *Environment*	Boats with centreboards towed at angle on undisturbed water outside the wake of the tug.
• *Towline angle to wake*	Measured by hand-bearing compass.
• *Towline tension*	Estimated by me from reading an unsteady spring balance over about 6–10 seconds.

The fourth, in mid-2007, used:

• *Speed*	Twin GPSs.
• *Environment*	Two boats towed simultaneously, one from each end of an 8.5m beam so they were at all times on undisturbed water outside the wake of the tug (Fig 10.9C, D and E).
• *Towline angle to wake*	No longer relevant.
• *Towline tensions*	From load cell of accuracy 1 in 10 000, electronically averaged over five seconds.

The Woollahra Sailing Club's 'Rescue A' is 8m long, 2m beam, and is powered with an 80hp 4-stroke motor (Fig 10.9C). To measure small differences at full scale I sketched a new tow-test configuration, which Simon constructed and systematically improved upon. A transverse 8.5m beam well forward can tow two 49ers simultaneously, both of them on flat undisturbed water outside the tug's wake and spray. Fig 10.9C shows the tug, beam and 49ers, and Fig 10.9D and E (page 156) are near simultaneous pictures of the two boats under tow. Note the plastic bags full of water to ballast the two boats to the identical desired weight, and the tapes on the stem to adjust the fore-and-aft trim at the start of each run. This tug was able to tow the two boats at up to 18 knots. The boat to port with the marker tapes on the lower stem is the standard boat. The boat to starboard has been modified with a re-faired bottom and sharpened spray rails and chines.

On this occasion, to measure the towline tensions, in place of the earlier spring balance we used a load cell accurate to one part in 10 000 and an electronic device that averaged the towline tension over five seconds.

With this apparatus we were able to measure the drag of the standard hull and then the drag of the modified hull alternately every few seconds. In this way we could make far more measurements per hour, and far more accurate ones, than we ever could with the earlier methods. This increase in data acquisition speed enabled us to plan to measure the drags at 1 knot rather than 2 knot intervals – that is, we programmed to measure at 4, 5, 6, 7, 8, 9, 10, 12, 14, 16 and 18 knots. We set up the rig carefully and proved that everything worked properly in the wider but unsteadier waters of Rose Bay, adjacent to the workshop.

On a day when only light wind was forecast we started early and towed the whole rig 10 miles north into the narrow glassy waters of Upper Middle Harbour. On this occasion the team were: 49er helms Julian Bethwaite and Jason Griffith; safety and photography Tai Elliott; tug cox, the author; and experimenter Simon Watin. Over a long day on which everything performed flawlessly, we completed the whole programme of more than 500 alternate measurements of the two boats at different weights and fore-and-aft trims and angles of heel. At each measurement I called the speed to one-tenth of a knot. To arrive at the hydrodynamic drag, we recorded such wind as there was and corrected the towline tensions with the calculated aerodynamic drag appropriate for the apparent wind. As can be seen in Fig 10.9H, the scatter of the corrected points is miniscule.

The principal difference between the drags measured in this work and earlier work is that previously we towed hulls with both centreboards and rudders in place; the centreboards were fully down and were carrying a substantial side load. On this occasion the centreboards were removed and the slots taped over.

Three aspects of the hull drags obtained with this new approach are of particular interest.

Humpless drag curve

Fig 10.9F goes some way towards explaining the 'humpless drag curve' phenomenon. On this occasion we asked the two helms to adjust their ballast until their hulls floated, at zero speed, at 100mm or 50mm bow down, or at design trim, or at 50mm or 100mm bow up. During the ensuing run the helms did not move.

Fig 10.9F shows that the minimum drag as speed is increased occurs at progressively increasing bow-up trims. From this new knowledge we can infer that the drag curve shown in Fig 10.9B is really a composite of the low sections of a series of curves, as in Fig 10.9F. It is probable that Julian, who steered the towed boat in the 1995 tests, changed his position to optimise the attitude as the speed increased.

'Fourth mode' technique

Fig 10.9G on page 157 shows, for the first time, the extraordinary efficiency of the 'fourth mode' technique described in *HPS-1* (pages 270–271). When, at very low speed, these triangular hulls are trimmed bow down and heeled, the reduction of drag is remarkable. This is due to a combination of reduction of wetted area plus the reduction of the 'out of trim' wave drag of the flat aft bottom when there are small waves. Both the bow-down trim and the heel are essential.

When I looked at this graph I recalled an incident at the Hyama Tasar World Championships in Japan in about 1990. An earnest Japanese skipper with no more English than I had Japanese had discussed with me in sign language his problems in light air; put simply, he was sailing his boat upright and was finishing last whenever the wind died to near calm. Why? I tried to explain fourth mode, was not succeeding, so offered to show him my technique if, and when, the fleet waited for the wind prior to future starts. The next morning the opportunity presented itself: I found him pre-start and for 20 minutes I demonstrated the fourth mode technique upwind and downwind. He followed closely, imitating everything. Others joined in and we were like a comet with a tail. The breeze set in, we raced that day in breeze, and I forgot the incident.

The following day the breeze died and the race was shortened in the light air. I finished well. After the race I was startled when an excited figure suddenly joined the throng, burst forward and hugged me. 'Tirty places!!! Tirty places!!!'

Fourth mode worked for him; Fig 10.9G shows why.

'Sharp chine' effect

Figs 10.9C, 10.9D and 10.9H show a more subtle phenomenon. There is a small but constant difference in the drags of the two hulls up to about 10 knots. At higher speeds the difference in drag increases sharply, as is shown in Fig 10.9H. The photos show why. At planing speeds the dynamic pressure under the hull expresses the boundary layer diagonally outwards on both sides. This outward flow remains strongly attached as it flows around the rounder chines and up the topsides of the standard boat. In Fig 10.9D a substantial volume of water can be seen to be attached to the topside starting at mid-length and rising to its maximum height at the stern. A similar pattern shows with the 29er.

Fig 10.9E shows that the water is separating more cleanly from the sharper chines of the modified boat and that its topsides are much 'drier'. What is happening is that at low planing speeds each boat is carrying its own weight plus the extra weight of the water attached to its topsides. The standard boat is carrying much more of this extra weight (my estimate is 100–120lb extra), and this explains the rapidly increasing difference in drag in Fig 10.9H. At higher speeds, the topsides become dry and this difference will disappear.

Note that this measured difference in drag between sharper and rounder chines is repeated in Fig 10.6.

Another point of interest is the miniscule scatter of the drag measurements with the electronic averaging device. This is revealed by the points in Fig 10.9H. The GPS speeds occasionally jumped by 0.1 or 0.2 of a knot as the instruments lost and acquired new satellites over the nearby steep scarps. The speed of the rig was very steady and changed only slowly. I made no effort to average these tiny jumps, and called to Simon the speed displayed. This factor is reflected in the horizontal scatter in two of the clusters.

Chapter 11 • More Power – Trapezes and Wings

11.1 ■ The sliding plank

In the 1930s, a handful of canoes around the world were among the fastest and most innovative of sailboats. In my opinion the sliding planks that were used by these canoes were the first 'wings'. On them, the crews could move out to a position where only their feet touched the gunwale, or even beyond. In the twin plank canoe *Brynhilde*, Uffa Fox was able to reach 15 knots under sail. This was an extraordinary speed in an era when virtually no other small sailboat could much exceed its hull speed. Planks were surprisingly practical. In 1935 Uffa crossed the English Channel and cruised the Brittany coast of France in *Brynhilde*.

Planks were used worldwide; I used one on a modest canoe in the early 1930s on the Wanganui river in New Zealand.

Fig 11.1 shows a 1940s Australian Payne-Mortlock twin-plank canoe start. These were very fast craft; on occasion they were able to sail around a Manly ferry – which in those days steamed its 7 mile run at about

Fig 11.1 The sliding plank sailing canoe

In the 1930s, sliding seat sailing canoes were the fastest small sailboats. They were sailed in England, North America and Australia. This photo shows Australian Payne-Mortlock canoes racing in Adelaide. Courtesy of Peter Wilcox.

14 knots. When a strong sea breeze was blowing and the ferry's positions on its run from Manly to the city was exactly right, I am told by a friend who did it, Arthur Wild, that these canoes could start from astern of the ferry, overtake it to windward, and cross ahead.

The main limitations of these planks were that they were heavy and expensive, and no fore-and-aft movement of the crew weight was possible. But they worked well enough to make tiny canoes sail much faster than they could without them.

The sliding planks of the 1930s were almost completely eclipsed for the next 50 years by the simple, light and inexpensive trapeze. When the plank principle returned, it was in the form of wings.

11.2 ■ The trapeze – early development

The trapeze was first developed, almost simultaneously, in the late 1930s in both the UK and New Zealand. In the UK it was banned and in New Zealand it was ignored. It made no real impact until it was reintroduced 20 years later, after the 1939–45 war, as a European invention.

UK trapeze invention

Robin Elliott, a New Zealand yachting historian, writes:

Beecher Moore, an American who lived in England, came to prominence in the early 1930s (the exact date is obscure) when he attached knotted ropes, which he called 'bell ropes' to the hounds of his Thames 1 rater, Vagabond *[Section 1.6 and Fig 1.9]. His crewman was persuaded to hang out over the windward side of the boat clinging grimly on to the 'bell rope'. There was no harness. It was here that, for the British, the trapeze had its origins.*

Not until mid-1936 did it develop further. Peter Scott and John Winter had seen first hand the advantage Vagabond *obtained with her 'bell ropes' and they and Charles Currey (silver medallist in the Finn Class 1952 Helsinki Olympics) began experimenting in Chichester Harbour, using Currey's 12sq m Sharpie, with Currey's wife Bobby as guinea pig. A photograph taken at the time shows her swinging out over the side of the Sharpie, suspended from the trapeze wire with a loop of canvas uncomfortably high under her armpits. Another has her standing out from the hull, one arm dangling, the other to her forehead, as if to say, 'Why aren't the blokes doing this daft stuff?'*

Recently, Charles Currey wrote

We began playing around with the idea in 1936, at least 18 months before … the Prince of Wales Cup. We made two harnesses, one of which I still have, which were more like heavyweight military bras and were certainly very uncomfortable. They were made by the local tent maker at Emsworth. The whole development was kept as a secret and was not revealed on Thunder 'n Lightning *until after the start of the race for the POW. John wore the harness hidden under a jumper and the trapeze wires were camouflaged with blue and grey paint and tied to the shrouds with cotton stops. It was all great fun, and I well remember the faces of rivals when John first went out on the wire. Stuart Morris said it was 'most unfair'.*

The furore that followed that race in mid-1938, ensured that the new device was banned immediately.

New Zealand trapeze invention

Again, from Robin Elliott:

In New Zealand in 1936 Jim Frankham, the owner and skipper of the Eighteen foot M class Manaia, *was an inventive soul.* Manaia *already sported a continuous spinnaker halyard which looped both sides of the forestay and so made it quick and easy to hoist either to windward or leeward as desired. One day, to avoid a drenching during a waterfight between skylarking crews, Stuart Robertson, one of the crew of five, swung outboard on the halyard. The boat heeled to a surprising degree.*

Frankham decided that this was something not to be wasted.

The first weekend experiment was unfeeling; Stuart was asked to spend the windward legs 'swinging' in a rope loop. 'EXTREMELY uncomfortable! The marks in my backside lasted all week!' Frankham relented, and asked George Dennes to make a harness for Stuart based on the established 'parachute-harness-style' body harnesses which had heavy fabric down the lower back and straps through the crotch and around the thighs to carry the weight comfortably at the waist rather than under the armpits as in Scott's English 'bra' harness. [Fig 11.2 shows Robertson trapezing with this harness in Manaia, in Auckland, New Zealand, on the opening day of the 1937–8 season.]

From a historical point of view there is no question that this inventive New Zealand group developed a practical, secure and comfortable trapeze and harness technology and used it (Fig 11.3 is a 1938 photo which shows *Manaia* with three of the crew on trapezes). But unlike Scott and Winter, they did not make the corresponding mental leap and work out how to use it aggressively in their racing. Figs 11.2 and 11.3 both show the boat reefed, and with the non-trapezing crew 'sitting-in'. They did not win much, so there was no 'unfair' outcry. From a technical point of view, this may be understandable. A trapeze will make the greatest potential difference on the lightest boat, and least in the performance of a heavy one. 'M' class boats are not light, so it seems that they used it more as a frolic than a weapon.

In New Zealand the technique did not spread, and it lay dormant until it was reintroduced as part of the worldwide adoption of trapezes in lighter boats two decades later – in the 1950s.

11.3 ■ The trapeze era

From the early 1950s onwards, the use of trapeze by the forward hand became almost universal worldwide among dinghies designed for racing – such as the Flying Dutchman, 5o5, Fireball, 470, etc. A tendency towards crew specialisation developed in which small helms with bigger and/or taller forward hands enjoyed most race success.

Fig 11.2 Trapeze invention in New Zealand

Stuart Robertson trapezing in full body harness, Auckland, New Zealand, 1937. Courtesy of Robin Elliott.

Fig 11.3 Use of multiple trapezes in New Zealand, 1938

Multiple trapeze development – Jim Frankham sailing *Manaia* with three on trapeze. Courtesy of Robin Elliott.

Exceptions were classes where the user group expressed preference for no trapeze, such as the generally mature women forward hands for whom the NS14 and later Tasar was designed, or classes where use of a trapeze was inappropriate – such as the very light Moth.

An unusual national difference developed between Australia and the rest of the world subsequent to about 1975. An integral part of the design changes that were bringing much higher performance to the Eighteen footer skiffs at that time was that they were shifting from a crew of four with three on trapeze and the helm still on the gunwale, to a crew of three all on trapeze. This set the trend. Learning to helm from trapeze is a skill not easy to learn or to do well, and the smaller and more lively the boat the more skilful and agile does the helm have to be. Most helms worldwide, including Australia, elected to stay with their learned skills and remain on the gunwale where they could fiddle with a multitude of rig controls. In the Sixteen footer skiff class, which then sailed with a crew of four or more and a generally older helm, this was certainly true. But among the numerous Fourteen footer and Twelve footer skiffs, generally sailed by younger two-person crews, the new technique of helming from trapeze was enthusiastically adopted. This set an example eagerly followed by young Australian sailors in other classes to the point where helming from trapeze became, for a while, an almost uniquely Australian trait.

This led one designer to elect to specialise the other way. By 1987 the Eighteen footer skiffs had become raw, brilliant machines that tacked downwind at very high speeds. Julian Bethwaite sensed a desire by helms world wide to enjoy these new speeds in a compact boat, but without the need to learn the new skill of helming from trapeze. In his 1988 Exocet, now the B-14, he achieved this by giving it compact wings of a size such that when both helm and forward hand treated the wings as if they were part of the hull and body-hiked from the outer rails, their body positions and righting moment, etc were exactly the same as if they were both trapezing with feet on the gunwale. This boat flew fast both upwind and downwind, and remains popular.

Fig 11.4 Richard Court's sliding frame (beam view)

Photo: Photomarine, Perth.

But the adoption of the helmed-from-trapeze 49er as the Olympic high performance class in 1995 has introduced a strong worldwide trend towards helming from trapeze. This has reduced the previously unique appeal of the B-14.

11.4 ■ The beginnings of wings

In the mid-1970s Richard Court, who in the 1990s became Premier of Western Australia, reintroduced and improved on the sliding plank idea in one of his Eighteen footers. In a stroke of brilliant innovation, he combined the principles of both the sliding plank and the trapeze, and added the further ability to move crew weight fore-and-aft as needed for optimum trim on different points of sailing.

Figs 11.4 and 11.5 show his new arrangement. Instead of using three separate planks, his invention was a single rectangular 'rack' that could be slid from side to side. When it was slid to windward, the leeward fore-and-aft tube lay over the leeward gunwale and the windward tube was positioned far beyond the

Fig 11.5 Richard Court's sliding frame (stern view)

Photo: Photomarine, Perth.

weather gunwale. He and his crew then trapezed from this tube. The final refinement was that the outer bar was long enough fore-and-aft for all three not only to trapeze together, but to move fore-and-aft as far as was needed for longitudinal trim on different points of sailing. This was a brilliant innovation in that by combining the principles of the sliding plank plus the trapeze, he positioned his whole crew much further to windward than was previously possible. At the time of that World Championship regatta, the concept had not been sufficiently refined for it to work reliably all the time, but the potential speed advantage was clear for all to see. When everything worked properly, his was by far the fastest boat in the fleet.

It was from this beginning that wings originated, with progressively wider wings finally doubling the sail-carrying power without adding much to the total weight. As they did so, every other part of the boat and its rig needed first to be redesigned to make it strong enough to withstand this new power. (Richard Court's primary problem at the regatta above was that his rig was not strong enough and the topmast first bent and finally broke.) This greater sail-carrying power then needed to be blended with the greatest care into the changing dynamics of the progressively faster boats. When wings first appeared, the asymmetric spinnaker was still many years in the future.

At root, the first driver of the apparent wind revolution was the power of these new wings.

11.5 ■ Stub wings

The wings themselves have developed through five stages, and the re-start was modest. Over a period of about five years, Iain Murray dominated the skiff scene because he managed the changes better than anybody else. Fig 1.32 shows his first Eighteen, which had no wings. Over the following years the wings grew wider, the rigs grew bigger, new engineering was needed to accommodate the greater loads, and average speed around the course increased.

The first wings were fore-and-aft tubes mounted rigidly a few inches outside the gunwales. These stub wings proved light, simple, effective and completely reliable. As these proved their value, they grew, and the Eighteen footer skiffs started to sail faster, separated from all other sailboats, and changed forever.

As the rail moved away from the gunwale, boat speed increased, but at the expense of two problems. The first was that the gap between gunwale and rail became big enough to fall through if or when you slipped. The second was that the cantilever strength needed to support the weight of the crew at increasing distance from the gunwale was more than the existing hull design could bear, and beam and anchor point failures became common.

11.6 ■ Hinged wings

The solution to the cantilever strength problem was to hinge the wing beams at the gunwale, and support the outer rail at its fore-and-aft ends with 'wing wires' from the hounds. The arrangement was usually via a 'flip flop' strop such that as the crew weight forced the windward wing down, the leeward wing was pulled higher (Fig 1.33).

The solution to the gap problem was first to add an inner rail to the wing, and then to stretch taut net between the fore-and-aft beams and the inner and outer rails in the manner of a trampoline.

This solution was mechanically and ergonomically sound. There was now no mechanical limit to the wingspan, and the net made it practical for the crews. Up to that time, all experience had indicated that the wider the wings, the faster the boat would sail, so wingspan increased rapidly.

The story of the next few years was first of development and then of over-development, with ever-wider wings and ever-more-complex and expensive boats, until in 1987 the fleet hit a complexity limit, a cost limit, a manoeuvring limit and a drive-to-drag ratio limit all at once, and this line of development came to a sudden and unexpected end.

In what in retrospect was stage one of this process, wingspan grew until it reached nearly 30ft. Fig 1.33 shows Peter Sorensen's champion *Tia Maria*, with its 18ft wings temporarily increased during a particular regatta to a wingspan of 26ft. (Peter is lying on the wing netting.) He enjoyed a righting moment and drive force double that of an Eighteen footer without wings. This raw power opened a pandora's box of both benefits and problems. As the span increased, the problems began to outweigh the benefits. The detail of these problems will be discussed in the following chapters.

Chapter 12 • Handicaps, Performance Equalisation, and Turns per Mile

12.1 ■ The club environment

Sailing is a cultured art. For a few, enjoyment of sailing for its own pleasure is sufficient. These are the recreational sailors; they enjoy what is.

Other sailors look for more, and join clubs to find what they seek.

Of these, about half are busy professional, technical, academic, etc people whose lives are focused on their work, their families and their professional associates. They look for a weekend stimulus with a like-minded but different social group as well as the enjoyment of their chosen recreation. This is what golf clubs, tennis clubs and sailing clubs are about. In the case of a sailing club, the season's race programme, the start times and the start line are the club's way of encouraging its members to arrive, meet, prepare their craft, then start and sail and enjoy the trebled stimulus of sailing, of sailing with purpose, and of sharing the experience with friends in both your own boat and in the competing boats. After the finish, the shared race experience provides everybody with a ready-made subject to start the social conversation. This is a richer and more rewarding experience than sailing alone.

For many of these sailors this is what they want, and this is what they enjoy. Their life force is focused on success in their calling. To them, the social value of this different and essentially non-competitive recreational environment is priceless, so these organisation-effective sailors willingly accept office and donate their time and their talents to officering their clubs and their affairs.

My point is that for this large group of generally mature sailors club racing is in fact 'sailing in company', and is a means to a social end. As for sailing, technical adequacy to the point of competent control of the boat is all that they need. This level of skill never wins races; this they accept. For them, keeping score, and the score itself, is not important. For the other half of the club's sailors, the score *is* important.

Some will be learners, with high aspirations. They look to an improving score to attest progress.

Some will be mature sailors, as above, but with the added life view that whatever they choose to do, they will do it well; and whether it be skiing in the winter or sailing in the summer, they take pride in being among the leaders. They focus, analyse, practise, read books like this, and lift their game to sail in the lead group. They share in the wins.

Some will be younger sailors who have yet to establish their place within their peer group. For them, a club championship is a goal worth working for because it denotes superior technical and organisational skill and lifts their reputation several notches.

The occasional sailor will be driven by class, national, world or Olympic aspirations. The dedication, technical skill and prowess of these individuals puts them in a class of their own.

For all of these groups, the score is central, because their object is to score well.

12.2 ■ The two systems

A score is a measure of competitive success, and central to the philosophy of scoring is the dream that every one has an equal chance of winning. The key objective is that all sailors should have an equal chance of finishing well if they sail equally well. Any circumstance that will bias this expectation will destroy the basis of their pleasure. It will diminish everybody's self-respect, and diminish the respect for others.

In the case of sailing, scoring necessarily takes one of two forms, handicap or scratch ('all on equal terms, not handicap'). Let us look at handicap scoring first, because until there were one-design sailboats, all racing was necessarily handicap because no scratch racing was possible.

12.3 ■ Handicap racing

Handicap scoring itself takes one of two forms:

- *Absolute*   This is based on the technical criteria of the boat. Differences in personal skill are ignored (eg Sydney–Hobart, Fastnet and other ocean races).
- *Personal*   Differences in personal skill are also acknowledged (eg most club handicap systems).

Absolute

Early yachts were anything but one-design, and longer boats have always sailed faster than shorter ones because their hull speeds are faster, so early sailors who wanted to race 'on a level playing field' had no option but to agree to some handicap system that would penalise the faster boats. One way to do this was to create and apply an 'acceptable calculation' based on the critical dimensions of the boat. An example of this is that one of the early rules of the New York Yacht Club, formed in 1844, required each member to furnish to the club's measurement committee a model of his vessel which would become the property of the club. In essence, they had decided to use models to develop an absolute handicap system. The first Commodore was John Cox Stevens, and a model of his schooner *Gymcrack* was one of the first models. (The smaller *Gymcrack* mentioned in Chapter 10 is from the following century.) The technical aspiration of this approach survives as the modern VPP (Velocity Prediction Program). The 'acceptable calculation' expected from the original New York Yacht Club Measurement Committee is proving a little harder to write. The way the RORC, IMS, Harbour Adjusted etc systems replace each other every few years suggests that nobody has yet come close to a durable 'acceptable calculation'.

Personal

The object of the normal club handicap is that everybody within the fleet of that club, whether beginner or champion, should have an equal chance of winning. So this system has to include both whatever absolute technical differences there may be between the boats in the fleet, plus the changing differences in racing skill between the crews in that fleet. This is a problem to which there can be no exact solution. Many systems are used; all deliver approximate solutions. So long as they satisfy the sailors in that club, they are successful.

12.4 ■ Scratch racing

Equalising the boats – the One-Design concept

The idea of 'One-Design' class racing without handicaps was a creature of the mass production technology of the twentieth century. The concept was that if crews race in boats that have been made to the same plan and are therefore sufficiently similar so that performance differences between boats can be ignored, then all crews will have an equal chance of winning.

This looks simple, but it isn't, because the idea of 'One-Design' keeps fragmenting into finer and finer detail like a fractal pattern.

This concept has already passed through various stages – three 'boat' stages, and a further three 'personal' stages.

The three boat stages were:

1 Boats to the same nominal shape and weight, but of different performance by different manufacturers.
2 Moulded boats of identical shape and weight, but of rapidly changing stiffness and performance by the same manufacturer.
3 Moulded boats of identical shape and weight, and of unchanging stiffness and performance by different manufacturers.

The three personal stages were:

4 Moulded boats of identical shape, weight and stiffness as 3, but with ballast to compensate for personal differences in crew weight.
5 Moulded boats of identical shape, weight and stiffness as 3, but with ballast plus adjusted wing width to compensate for personal differences in both crew weight and also righting moment.

6 Moulded boats of identical shape, weight and stiffness as 3, but with ballast plus adjusted wing width to compensate for both personal differences in crew weight and also righting moment, plus a further adjustment to the ballast to compensate for the slower turning performance of boats with wider wings and the number of turns per mile anticipated.

1 Boats to the same nominal shape and weight, by different manufacturers

This was the beginning of 'One-Design'.

The initial concept was to define the basic shape by plan and require that every boat built worldwide be within a close tolerance of that shape, weight, etc. This approach led to the Herons and Mirrors, the Flying Dutchmen, Finn dinghies, Stars etc of the 1950s and 1960s. However, it did not work, for two reasons:

First, because while any two boats measured under the system of 'allowable tolerances' might both be within the tolerances and therefore be legal, there necessarily remained fractional differences in the final shape that were allowable within the tolerances. These fractional differences assumed grotesque importance in the minds of top sailors, who 'psyched' themselves into believing that if a Flying Dutchman built by one constructor had won at the previous Olympics, then only another boat from the same constructor could possibly win at the next Olympics. Whether this was true or not was never tested, but the perception was that the boats were not sufficiently 'identical', so the concept of 'equal chance of winning' was not accepted.

The second reason was that despite the rules there were sometimes real performance differences between two new boats of the same nominal weight and shape. In Section 9.4, I cite the 1971 situation where two new Starboats, one of 'solid' FRP and one of foam-sandwich construction, were not of equal speed when sailing to windward in waves because the topsides of one flexed under wave impact load much more than the other.

In this case, the concept that all crews would enjoy an equal chance of winning was not true because the class had failed to enforce its own rules to ensure that boats built everywhere in the world were technically identical.

The perceptions about tiny differences in shape plus the technical consequence of the real differences in stiffness brought this approach into general disrepute.

2 Moulded boats of identical shape and weight, but of rapidly changing stiffness and performance by the same manufacturer

In the case of the Star, the more flexible 'solid FRP' and the stiffer 'foam sandwich' boats as built by different manufacturers had been of different performance when new, regardless of any difference in shape.

The next step was 'Rigid Producer-Control One Design' as Hobie, Laser, etc, with all boats out of moulds taken from the same master plug. This technology did at last achieve the dream of true One-Design as regards shape and weight, but its Achilles heel was the rapid softening of the 'solid' FRP skin with use (Section 8.4), together with the fact that softer, more flexible boats sail more slowly through waves than rigid ones (as above). So in this case, while the boats were indeed of identical shape, weight, stiffness and speed as built, they lost performance with use so quickly that the policy of the best European coaches was to give their top crews two new 470 hulls every year, and another prior to any important regatta.

The One-Design dream was proving elusive.

3 Moulded boats of identical shape and weight, and of unchanging stiffness and performance by different manufacturers

This concept was at last achieved in 1975 with the Tasar, which was the world's first production dinghy to be fully cored, bottom, topsides and deck, with the then-new rigid PVC foam. Moulds in Montreal, Canada, in Banbury, in the UK, and in Sydney, Australia, all from a common master plug, ensured that all boats were of identical shape.

These rigidly cored hulls have proved immensely strong, stiff and durable, and they hold their performance. Hulls built in 1976 are still winning major races 30 years later in 2006.

This was a revolutionary technical advance. I designed the shape and the rig, and Ian Bruce was responsible for the great leap forward in hull construction.

Equalising the crews – performance equalisation

The dream that identical One-Design hulls and sails could deliver an equal chance of winning was already out of date by 1976. As hulls had approached One-Design, it had been observed that crews of different weights sailed at different speeds even when their boats were the same.

The result of this was that a second requirement – the concept of equalisation of the chance of winning as between crews of different weights – was added. From now on the demand would be:

- That the boats be technically identical, as in 12.4.3 above.
  - This is the One-Design concept as between boats.
- That further adjustments to compensate for personal differences in stature and weight as between crews should be agreed and enforced.
  - This is the performance equalisation concept as between crews.

Notes 4, 5 and 6 below trace the development of performance equalisation from its beginnings in 1972, up to 2007.

4 Moulded boats of identical shape, weight and stiffness as 3, but with ballast to compensate for personal differences in crew weight

In 1960 a new class of dinghy – 'a good boat for a man and a woman' – was born in my living room. The story of the NS14, the Nova and the Tasar is detailed in *HPS-1*, but as regards performance equalisation, the summary is as follows:

From 1960 to 1969 the various NS14 designs that were developed were moderate in most respects, except that all the hulls were much lighter than was then customary at the time and the resulting higher than expected performance raised eyebrows. Differences in crew weight did not seem to matter, and for nine years they were simply not an issue.

In 1969 an unusually fast and efficient fine-entry hull (designed by my elder son Mark Bethwaite) was rigged with my recently developed adjustable datum-marked wing mast rig of unusual aerodynamic efficiency. The result was a 'breakthrough' increase in performance.

It was soon found that this new design was sensitive as regards crew weight. In lighter winds, from calm to 7 knots (ie no planing), all crews of all weights in all boats sailed at about the same speed. But in winds of 8 knots and stronger, the lighter crews planed sooner and faster on the reaches and won by large margins (a 250lb 'man plus adolescent' crew finished ten minutes ahead of a 300lb 'man plus mature woman' crew in a typical 100 minute race).

Owners for whom the score was important began to sail with children selected for weight. The women for whom the class had been created were dismayed and began to leave.

My response was to create a new class, and in 1972 I re-rigged the 100sq ft NS14 with 123sq ft of sail. This was a sail area better suited to the now adjustable and lower drag wing mast rig, so the boat sailed much faster. But the key change was that I wrote a new rule – 'Everybody is welcome to sail with us, but if your total crew weight is less than 300lb, you will carry the difference in ballast.'

It seems that that was the world's first 'performance equalisation' rule.

It worked. It got rid of the 'man plus child selected for weight' crews, and the men and women for whom the class had been created kept on sailing together and enjoying each other's company. The Nova became the Tasar. I wrote the same 'crew rule' for the Tasar, because by then we knew that just having identical hulls was not enough to ensure that everyone would enjoy an equal chance of winning.

Half the crews want to win, and for 30 years the competition between them has been fierce and fair. The other half did not much care whether they ever won or not, but losing consistently to lighter youngsters was something else, and the 'crew rule' fixed that problem too.

5 Moulded boats of identical shape, weight and stiffness as 3, together with:

- Ballast to compensate for personal differences in weight, *plus*
- Adjustable wing width to compensate for personal differences in both the weight and the height of the crew (ie to equalise sail-carrying power).

The 1972 Tasar 'crew rule' focused the world's attention on the subject of performance equalisation.

In those classes that do not have such a rule, it was quickly found that there is an 'ideal crew weight' range within which it is possible for a skilled crew to win. In some classes, this weight range is very narrow indeed

– a matter of, say, plus or minus as little as 5lb from the ideal. Crews lighter or heavier than this narrow range are effectively excluded from such a class, because these lighter or heavier crews cannot win regardless of skill.

When analysed more closely, the Tasar 'crew rule' is seen to be a very blunt instrument as it focuses on the single factor of crew weight. What it did was raise the ideal crew weight for winning in a Nova or Tasar from 260–270lb to near 300lb. In this way it excluded for practical purposes the adolescent, lighter crews deemed undesirable by the generally 300lb approximately mature men and women crews who happened to be in charge of the class at that time. They took the view that lighter adolescents should compete against lighter adolescents, and not spoil the fun of mature adults.

But the rule did nothing to widen the weight range outside which it was not possible to win. Surely it was possible to do better than this. Indeed it was, and the development of wings that could be set at any selected wingspan up to a maximum opened the way.

A group of technically minded sailors who watered at the Warsash pub created a much better performance equalisation system. Their object was to give all crews 'of normal stature' – from normal light to normal heavy – an equal chance of winning. Under their system, all crews who are lighter than some maximum weight carry the difference in ballast, so the total weight of the boat plus crew plus ballast is always the same. At the same time, all crews who are heavier than some minimum weight are required to set their wing width to something less than the maximum, and in this way the righting moment – the boat's sail-carrying power – is also always the same. This two-factor system was a huge step forward in that it did, and still does, truly equalise the expected performance between crews of widely different weights – for as long as they sail in straight lines.

This was much better, but it was not completely right. For some reason, the heavier crews still seemed to win almost all the races, and it seemed that one more step was called for.

6 Moulded boats of identical shape, weight and stiffness as 3, together with:

- Ballast to compensate for personal differences in weight, *plus*
- Adjustable wing width to compensate for personal differences in both the weight and the height of the crew (ie to equalise sail-carrying power).

There was also a third 'turns per mile' factor:

- Adjustment of ballast to compensate for the fact that wider-winged boats tack more slowly so lose time on every tack, gybe and mark rounding.

It took a little while to work out why, despite having compensated for both the differences in crew weight and the differences in righting moment, the lighter crews with the wider wings never seemed to be there at the end of the race. Again, it was the vital Eighteen footer fleet of Sydney that alerted us to what was really going on with wingspan.

One year, the Eighteen footer fleet travelled north to a wide-open, steady sea breeze bay near Brisbane for their annual Australian championships. Some crews felt that in those unusually steady conditions in which they could make one tack per windward leg and one gybe per downwind leg, they could handle more power than their normal 17ft wingspan gave them. They set to work industriously and some boats grew their wings by a metre each night, until the widest spanned nearly 30ft. As the wingspans increased, the straight-line speeds increased. But there was a cost – the greater mechanical loads caused more and more topmasts, bowsprits/spinnaker poles and centreboards to break. One of these wide-wing boats won – it was the one that didn't break.

Fig 1.33 shows *Tia Maria* with its wings extended during this regatta. Both the normal wings and the temporary additions are clear to see. It was leading on points as it started the last race, but the bowsprit/spinnaker pole broke during the race and it finished the regatta in second place.

When the fleet returned to Sydney Harbour, with its narrower waters and less steady winds and 500 other racing sailboats sharing the water on Saturday afternoons, they were back in their usual environment where they had to tack more frequently in the narrower waters and duck and weave through the traffic. In these more variable winds and more crowded waters, the wider-winged boats finished not ahead of the boats that had chosen not to change, but a very long way *behind* them.

Why? They had overlooked the fact that a wider-winged boat has greater angular inertia, so it takes longer to turn. The crew have further to move, so it takes longer to move across the wider wings from tip to tip. The boat slows more during the longer turn, and it then takes longer to re-accelerate to its pre-turn speed.

A simple example gives the logic. If a tiny Optimist dinghy and a Tornado catamaran race around two marks set well apart, the Tornado that sails faster but turns more slowly will always win. But if the marks are set only a few metres apart, the Optimist that turns faster will win every time even though it sails more slowly. From this example we can understand why in crowded waters and/or unsteady winds, body-swung toe-strap boats that can turn and tack very quickly will often outperform normally faster trapeze boats and catamarans that may sail faster in straight lines but take longer to turn.

This realisation led me to understand a new design principle – that a third factor is involved in performance equalisation. Other things being equal, the fastest wingspan will depend on the expected number of turns per mile. The widest wings were fastest for the very long legs and small fleets (fewest turns per mile) of the Brisbane bay. Progressively shorter wings will be faster as the leg length becomes shorter and the fleet size increases and the expected number of tacks, gybes, turns and ducks and weaves per mile increases.

So, from a performance equalisation point of view, as between a heavy crew with no ballast and short wings and a light crew with lots of ballast and wide wings, the two crews will sail equally fast in straight lines. But every time they turn, the shorter-wing heavy-crew boat will turn more quickly and lose less speed and be back to target speed sooner.

The wider-winged lighter crew boat will take longer to accelerate in angular acceleration from 0 to about 30° per second and to arrest its turn from 30° per second to 0, so it will take longer to turn from its old to its new heading. During this longer time to turn, it will lose more speed. It will then need more time to accelerate from this lower speed and regain target speed. The crew will have further to move. For all these reasons, it will lose a little time every time it turns.

The more turns per mile, the greater will be the total time loss of the wider-wing crew per race. This is why the lighter crews were so seldom in the lead at the finish with the two-factor system.

To have an equal chance of winning, the lighter crews have to sail not at the same speed, but at a faster speed in the straight lines between the turns in order to make up for the time they lose in every turn.

The solution is simple. For a complete performance equalisation, it is necessary to make three compensations, not two:

1 Give lighter crews wider wings to equalise sail-carrying power.
2 Make lighter crews carry compensating ballast to equalise total weight.

This gives correct performance equalisation for straight-line sailing.

But when they turn, the wider-winged lighter crew will lose time on every turn, so a third 'turns per mile' adjustment needs to be added:

3 Reduce the ballast carried by the wider-wing, lighter crew so they can sail faster between turns to make up for the time loss suffered at each turn. The more the turns per mile, the greater will be the ballast reduction required to equalise their chance of winning.

This three-factor system of performance equalisation does at last give crews across a wide weight range an equal chance of winning. It was adopted by the 49er class in 1996, and used for the 2000 Sydney and the 2004 Athens Olympics.

A practical point is that the amount of ballast removed to compensate for the slower turns was nearly the same as the amount added to compensate for the lighter crews, so the boats in fact carried surprisingly little ballast.

Medical intervention

For the 2008 Beijing Olympics, a completely new aspect of scratch racing appeared. Some sailors in the 49er class crash-dieted pre-regatta to reduce their body weight by up to 10%. In this way they qualified for a wider-wing setting at their lighter weigh-in weight. Because of the point in the paragraph above, they carried little extra ballast. They then gorged to regain normal weight for the regatta, which they sailed with heavier bodies and the wider wings.

ISAF medicos have taken notice. They deem this practice to be a health risk, and in view of the 49er's remarkably wide weight tolerance without any compensation, have ruled that all performance equalisation requirements be discontinued for the time being.

12.5 ■ The measurer's methods

Starting from the New York Yacht Club's 'Every owner shall provide a model of his yacht', these methods altered little for a century, but have recently changed out of all recognition. The key steps have been:

1 The emergence in the 1930s of One-Design classes, with approved plans, and the measuring by ruler and scale of each boat (frequently amateur built) for conformity with that plan within acceptable tolerances.

2 The emergence with the 1969 Laser of the concept of the producer-controlled rigidly One-Design classes, and the measuring of each boat with ruler and scales for conformity with the standard product within much tighter tolerances.

3 The emergence of the policy of measuring not the boat but the constructor and his production tooling, and identifying the product from that tooling by embedded microchip.

As at 2007, the 49er expresses the most recent ISAF policy re eligibility for, say, an Olympic competition. This covers both hull shape and weight, and performance equalisation. The method is:

Hull and rig

- A master plug is identified and held in a safe location. A second back-up plug is held in another continent in the event of misadventure.
- Moulds from that plug are identified and licensed with approved manufacturers.
- Product from those moulds is identified by embedded chip with unique number and is registered according to a system jointly approved by the class and the ISAF.
- Eligibility of that hull is by identification of the unique embedded microchip number. Spot checks of weight and shape are carried out at key regattas.

Crew

- The three-factor performance equalisation system is used. Crew weights are divided into three bands. The system is that each boat carries a colour-coded wing width indicator, plus visible ballast beads.

12.6 ■ Summary

The dream is simple – that all crews should have an equal chance of winning.

The approach to that dream, though, has not been simple. The story above covers its growth from the models of the New York Yacht Club in 1844 to the third factor, in 1996, and to measuring the constructor and not the product in 2004, and to medical intervention in 2007.

The 'acceptable calculation' is proving to be a hydra-headed monster.

I have little doubt that sailing books of the future will describe and explain further factors and ploys yet to be revealed.

Chapter 13 • Sail Forces in Steady Airflows

13.1 ■ The wake-up call

In 1925 Manfred Curry conducted 'Experiments with Down' and published what he observed in his *Aerodynamics of Sails*. His apparatus was a long light fishing rod with a tiny feather attached to its tip by a fine thread. With this he was able to probe the flow over his sail, but only at one point at a time. His windward-side flow diagrams were strange. His leeward-side diagrams were not believable at the time – Fig 13.1 – so for another 40 years neither he nor anyone else took this work further. We can now see that his windward-side diagrams were accurate, but his leeward-side diagrams were trying to express unsteady separated flow around an over-sheeted sail in unsteady wind, and his single feather was inadequate for this task.

In the mid-1960s, sailors worldwide began to put tufts of light ribbon or wool on their sails. We were among the first to do so, and one of our early experiments was to put a pattern of ribbons on one side only of a mainsail and jib and sail it so that a low sun backlit the ribbons. This enabled us to see for the first time what was actually going on. Fig 13.2 shows what we saw. We looked in amazement at tufts that

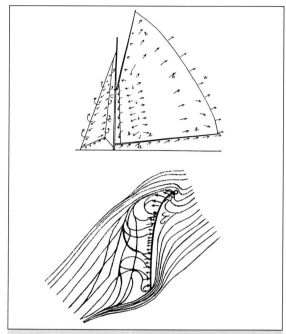

Fig 13.1 Manfred Curry's 'Experiments with Down'

Lines of flow observed by Curry in 1925. He used a light feather tied to the tip of a fishing rod. Diagram from *Aerodynamics of Sails* by Manfred Curry, 1925.

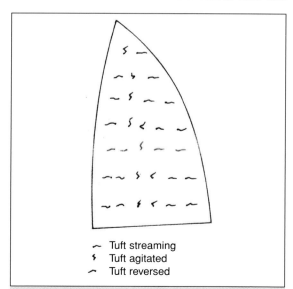

~ Tuft streaming
ς Tuft agitated
⌐ Tuft reversed

Fig 13.2 Tuft behaviour on lee side of sail

nonchalantly agitated or streamed the wrong way.

This was totally unexpected, and contradicted many of our assumptions about how lift and drag forces are developed. In particular, how could reversed flow occur over a sail when the wind was blowing the other way and the sail appeared to be performing normally?

The great advantage of many tufts attached to the sail, as compared with Curry's single tiny feather that could only be in one place at any one time, is that the tufts give a continuous indication of the whole flow pattern as it changes, often quite quickly, due to the wind's natural unsteadiness. This enabled us to see what was going on as a whole, and to believe it even though, at first, we did not understand it. Manfred Curry, for all his brilliance, was never able to see the whole picture.

13.2 ■ The 1966 to 1975 low-speed R and D work

Experimentally minded sailors were intrigued, and a core group formed spontaneously to find out more about these strange flows. They were Dr E J (Pat) Smith, a cloud and rain physics scientist; Colin Thorne, a structural engineer; Charles Mansfield, an appliance engineer; and myself – an aviator with an aeronautical engineering background who sailed for fun. All four sailed the then-new Northbridge Senior, later Tasar dinghies, and sailed them intelligently. Pat and I were both with the Australian CSIRO (Commonwealth Scientific and Industrial Research Organisation) and shared an office in a laboratory at Sydney University.

Much of the work noted below overlapped. In the broadest sense, it fell into five phases:

1 Development of the adjustable rig in 1965–8.
2 Basic flow observations and development of the wing mast rig in 1967–9.
3 Force measurements in 1968–70.
4 Smoke plume observations in 1969–71.
5 Confirmation by on-the-water trialling.

THE FIRST PHASE

13.3 ■ Development of the adjustable rig

We sailed, raced and watched the strange behaviour of our new tufts, and agreed on the following:

- The strange flows occurred on jibs as well as mainsails, so it was not just a mast problem.
- Fullness was a factor in flow steadiness; generally, the fuller the sails, the unsteadier the flow – particularly on the leeward surface.
- Fullness was a factor in speed; generally, fuller sails were faster, but only up to a point.

Sail fullness seemed to be a key to both steadiness and speed, so that became our starting point. This led directly to the adjustable rig.

Before 1965, our masts (in common with masts worldwide) had been stiff. Some of us had children who sailed Moths, and in about 1965 Moths started using 'bendy' masts with 'hockey stick' tops. About 1965, we too began to use lighter 'bendy' spars in our NS14s. Initially there were no adjustment controls. We found the more flexible masts to be a little faster than the stiff ones, but nobody knew why.

Then we fitted tufts, and saw what was going on. We noted that if we deliberately used extreme mainsheet tension to bend the upper mast back, this flattened the upper mainsail sufficiently to change the tuft behaviour. From this observation grew the desire to be able to control the tuft behaviour by changing the fullness of the whole sail.

From this starting point we moved quickly. We were using timber masts that we made ourselves so we could plane them to whatever flexibility we wanted. Soon we had developed mast, sail and batten combinations of sufficient flexibility, together with outhaul, downhaul and vang controls of enough power for us to be able to bend a flexible mast sufficiently to be able to set and sail with any mainsail camber we wanted between 0 and 16% camber almost regardless of sheet tension. We had reinvented and greatly refined the gaff rig capability of being able to set whatever fullness we wanted.

By experimenting with these new controls as we sailed and by comparing notes, we found that the fastest sail shapes were those that satisfied two criteria:

1 In all winds and on all points of sailing (except square run) – the fullest possible sails provided that the windward tufts streamed smoothly. (Fullest possible in this sense often turned out to be surprisingly flat.)
2 In stronger winds – flattened sufficiently so the crew could keep the boat upright.

Crews who used these new rigs and adjusted to these criteria sailed a two-hour race about 5 to 6 minutes faster than those who did not adjust. This sort of advantage repeated most regularly in relatively steady, moderate winds.

13.4 ■ The Datum Mark system

By this time, the NS14 class with its relatively inexpensive lightweight hulls, laminar flow foils, unusual speed and now its adjustable rig was attracting sailors from other classes and growing strongly. However, the adjustable rig was proving a two-edged sword. Only a year or two earlier no crews of any boats, anywhere in the world, had been able to adjust anything, because nothing had been adjustable. The thinking, the flexible mast technology and the controls had all been developed over about two years, and they called for new skills in racing these boats. For those crews who thought naturally in terms of airflows and forces, the new adjustability capability was heaven. As far as my wife and I were concerned, we simply repeated flatter upwind cambers and much fuller crosswind cambers, as full as we could hold upright, each fine tuned for the wind strength and tuft behaviour of the moment. Downwind, when running square, we set the sail flat again for maximum projected area. The boat flew. It all seemed so logical. But to those, particularly forward hands, who just loved sailing and whose special talents lay elsewhere, the adjustment controls were not only daunting, they were intimidating – because the fast combinations were not self-evident, and if you adjusted any of the three basic controls the wrong way, the boat sailed more slowly.

I became aware of this and sensed that an adaptation of the aviators' flight deck 'Drill of Vital Actions' might be helpful. A flight crew routinely adjust the camber of their wing for each segment of their flight. Flaps are extended (about 20% depending on the aircraft) for take-off; this is similar to sails nearly flat for sailing to windward in moderate winds. Clean wings (flaps and slats right in) for fastest cruise is similar to flattest sails for sailing to windward in strong winds. Flaps extended 50% for initial approach is similar to intermediate fullness for reaching; and flaps extended 100% for maximum lift maximum drag on final approach is similar to broad reaching. There is no aircraft equivalent to running square with separated flow.

I developed a Datum Mark system in which a knot in each of the outhaul, downhaul and vang control lines was set against a series of dots:

- When all three controls were positioned against one dot, both lower and upper mainsail set at 8% camber for sailing to windward in light air with the jib set 'open'.
- When all were positioned against two dots, the lower mainsail set at 4% camber for sailing to windward in moderate wind without back-winding behind a close-sheeted jib, and the upper mainsail set at 10% camber for optimum power.
- All knots positioned against three dots set it almost completely flat for sailing to windward in strong wind, as in Fig 13.3 (lower picture).
- With the outhaul positioned against a sharp arrowhead, the whole mainsail set at 12% camber for beam reach, as in Fig 13.3 (upper picture).
- And positioned against a blunt arrowhead, the whole mainsail set at 16% camber for broad reach.

This system eliminated all uncertainty and substituted simple and effective order. With it, all crews could repeat proven efficient sail shapes quickly and accurately, and it was adopted immediately and universally by the class. Fig 13.3 shows how it works on the Tasar. Experienced sailors who were newcomers to the class told me that this simple system enabled them to reach the front of the fleet in their new boats about two years sooner than they had anticipated from their experience with other classes. Old hands

Fig 13.3 The Datum Mark system in action

Top: Set to 12% camber for close reach.
Below: Set to 4% camber for close hauled in strong wind.

told me that they valued it because instead of looking at their tufts and responding with their rig controls, they could now set by numbers and get their eyes out of the boat again to look at what really mattered.

The first of the five phases of development was complete. It had needed only about two years to develop truly practical, reliable, repeatable adjustable rigs.

In hindsight we can now see that this work was important in not one respect, but in two. It led directly into the wind tunnel work in the years immediately following, and the development of the 'taut leech' aerodynamically efficient wing mast rigs that are so fast in steady air. And it also became the basis from which later grew the dynamically efficient automatic rigs which are faster yet in the more normal unsteady winds.

THE SECOND PHASE – FURTHER OBSERVATIONS

13.5 ■ Early experiments

By adjusting the fullness of our sails we were able to eliminate most of the agitating or reversed tufts, and as we did so we sailed faster. But there remained stubborn areas of unsteadiness behind the mast that we could not budge. Could we eliminate these and sail faster yet? What was causing them?

Our new tufts were close to the sail's surface, so were probably revealing what was happening within the boundary layer. What we then knew about boundary layers was very little, was primarily based on the thin high speed flows appropriate to aircraft, and nothing we knew suggested that they could flow the wrong way.

The standard aeronautical texts (eg NACA/NASA), together with my own aviation experience, was that:

- Flow over wings at high speed is always either fully attached or totally separated.
- Attached flow always flows from the leading edge towards the trailing edge.
- Separation when it occurs always starts at the trailing edge and flashes forward quickly.
- The separation process, once started, is near instantaneous and irreversible.

All sailing literature up to that time had suggested that the flow of wind over sails was broadly similar. But what we were observing from the behaviour of the tufts as we sailed were flow patterns that were completely different. The differences immediately obvious were:

1 Depending on sail shape:
   - Areas of unsteady flow appeared normal.
   - Areas of reversed flow appeared normal.
   - Reversed flow on the suction side appeared to occur first at the leading edge – just behind the wire luff of the jib or the mast of the mainsail – and from that starting point its aft edge moved aft progressively towards the trailing edge – that is, the leech – as we sheeted in.
   - This process was reversible; when we eased sheet, the aft edge moved forward again.
2 There was nothing in the given wisdom to suggest reversed flows, and there was nothing to alert us that the patterns of low-speed flows might be completely different.

It was time for us to have a closer look at the whole subject of low-speed air flows and, particularly, at low-speed boundary layers. So we started what became a series of progressively more controlled experiments to look at the pattern of wind flow over sails.

To provide repeatable conditions in which to measure, I made a flimsy wind tunnel, which was useful in both showing us how to make a more practical wind tunnel and also demonstrating what it could do. I then made a more durable and practical instrument, which gave good service for some years. This is shown as the lower picture on page 219 of *HPS-1*. Subsequent work was carried out using the superior equipment of the University of Sydney's Dept of Aeronautical Engineering. Fig 13.4 shows a model sail mounted on a sensitive balance in the university's tunnel. To develop the Tasar mast I made a third tunnel – the one shown in the upper picture in *HPS-1* page 219.

Within a few years we had looked at tuft behaviour as revealed by accurately repeated flows in wind tunnels, flow patterns as modified by different sail cambers, lift and drag forces as measured by strain gauges, flow patterns as revealed by smoke plumes, and the way different mast sections at different angles changed these patterns.

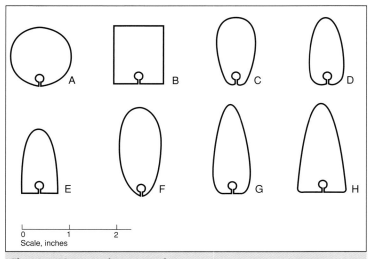

Fig 13.4 Test rig in wind tunnel

Fig 13.5 Mast sections tested

The 2ft x 2ft model rig and balance in the tunnel.

The mast profiles tested are shown in Fig 13.5. The round and square models are the benchmarks. The shorter streamline, ovoid and squareback sections were to whatever fore-and-aft dimension (usually about 70mm) resulted from planing the full-size hollow spruce mast until it bent fore-and-aft exactly as we wanted it to bend to control the sail camber. Of these, the profile D seemed marginally superior in the wind tunnel, was simple and inexpensive to make, and was fast on the water except that on occasion in unsteady winds (as in Fig 21.4C and D) it could lose flow completely, as in Fig 13.6, and it then seemed most reluctant to 'unstall' – that is, to re-attach the flow. This was the mast that either flew or floundered.

The longer streamline, ovoid and squareback sections in Fig 13.5 were all of the same general shape but were made as long as possible in the fore-and-aft dimension (the class rule at that time was that the mast must pass through a 4in ring). They were more expensive to make because they had a strong hollow nearly a square spruce 'core' that was planed flat on its forward face until the mast bent as desired, then a balsa fairing was glued on, the whole spar was shaped to the final profile desired (but to the 101mm fore-and-aft limit), and the final process was to cut the balsa fairing from the leading edge to the spruce core every 175mm. These cuts allowed the balsa to open like a crocodile skin and, in this way, the balsa acted as an aerodynamic fairing but did not affect the fore-and-aft mechanical bend. This shape was fractionally better in the tunnel, proved fast at all times on the water, exhibited none of the temperamental occasional separation characteristics of the type D shape, and was the shape of choice for many years until we developed a new profile for the alloy mast of the Tasar. Note the smaller leading edge radius of G as compared with D. At the time, we did not understand the importance of this.

At a point the smoke plume pictures became irresistible to the magazines, so we published what we were doing. Shortly thereafter, a seminal correspondence began to flow. Professor Arch Oliver (Professor of Engineering and Hydraulics, University of Tasmania) gave us an insight into the mechanism of 'the separation bubble' as a hydraulics phenomenon. He wrote:

The separated laminar shear layer at the mast is very unstable and rapidly starts to go turbulent in a very unsteady fashion with some very large eddies. We have measured a lot of ordered motion in the early stages as well as a lot of apparent disorder … The separated laminar shear layer can withstand almost no adverse pressure gradient but as soon as there are big waves or eddies in the flow there is an increase in pressure. My picture is of eddies combining to shoot bursts of low energy fluid into the free stream causing the free stream to slow down locally and the pressure to rise. This is very unsteady and takes some considerable time (ie distance of travel) to settle down into what is normally called turbulent flow. The eddies of the transitional flow of the free shear layer seem to be much larger and more energetic than those of turbulent flow. Transition is more violent in a separated shear layer than in one which is attached to a wall. The wall confines the eddies.

Fig 13.6 shows exactly this happening in the separated shear layer which is streaming back from the leading edge of a model aeroplane wing. Initially it is laminar, then begins to becomes turbulent, then starts to develop big eddies.

Professor Oliver again:

> *… in the turbulent shear layer all the eddies are spinning the same way and each is to some extent within the flow field of the adjacent eddies so the turbulent shear layer curves, always away from the higher speed flow, always curving inwards into the low speed fluid. In the case of the flow around your masts and sails the shear layer is curving until it re-attaches to the sail, and this mechanism is forming the separation bubbles you are observing.*

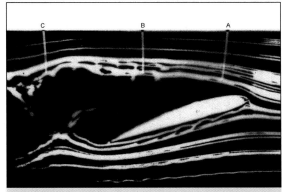

Fig 13.6 Completely separated flow —'stalled'

A   Shear layer still laminar
B   Shear layer becoming turbulent
C   Large eddies forming
From *Model Aeronautics Yearbook*, 1938, by Frank Zaic.

This explanation enabled us to understand what was going on, and clarified our ideas as to what we were trying to do. At root, we were trying to achieve the efficient fully attached flow around sails (Figs 13.7 and 13.8) with either small diameter wires or bigger masts at their leading edges (as in Figs 13.11 and 13.12). By about 1974, our overall view had developed as in Sections 13.6, 13.7 and 13.8 below.

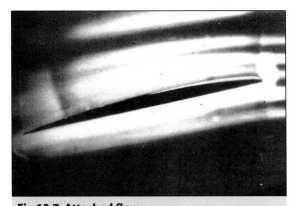

Fig 13.7 Attached flow

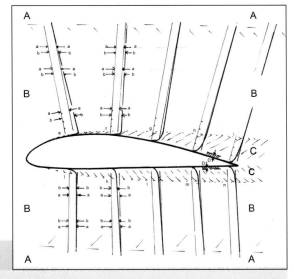

Fig 13.8 Detail of attached flow (right)

A–A, A–A	Undisturbed flow, ie the apparent wind
B–B, B–B	The free stream, between the apparent wind and the boundary layer
D and D	The boundary layer, to scale
C and C	The boundary layer, drawn with thickness magnified x 10
a–a, a–a, a–a	Speed of the undisturbed flow (apparent wind)
b–b, b–b, b–b	Speed of the free stream at that position

Note that the speed of the free stream:
• Is faster than the wind above the wing, ie on the lee side of the sail
• Is slower than the wind below the wing, ie on the pressure side of the sail.

13.6 ■ Laminar and turbulent flow

Laminar flow

If you put a dollop of a viscous fluid such as honey onto a glass plate and tilt it until the liquid moves, you can see the mechanism of laminar flow. The molecules that touch the glass do not move; those just above it move most slowly, and those at the upper surface move fastest. Flow speed increases with height from zero at the plate to fastest at the upper surface. Viscosity suppresses all turbulence, and for this reason there is no vertical mixing between the stationary honey on the surface, the slower-moving near-bottom layers, the intermediate layers, and the faster near-top layers. If the whole glass plate were smeared first with pink honey on the glass, and then blue honey over the pink honey, and you then tilted the surface and let it ooze down the glass for a week, the blue honey would still be on top.

The analogy of the way water flows in a stream is revealing. There will be pools where the surface is glassy and the flow is slow. A leaf dropped on the surface will drift downstream at a respectable speed. Waterlogged leaves in the flow near the bottom scarcely move; and waterlogged leaves lying on the bottom do not move at all. This indicates that only a trivial shear force is developed by the very slow near-bottom flow and the bottom itself.

Between the bottom where the flow speed is zero and the surface, each level (lamina) of water will flow a little faster.

This water is behaving in the same way as the honey. This is laminar flow.

Turbulent flow

Wherever the stream becomes narrow, the flow will become faster. At and above some critical speed, the shear stress between the water that touches and is momentarily attached at rest to the bottom, and the faster water just above it, becomes more than its viscosity can suppress, and the flow becomes a series of eddies as if you were running your hand over a number of round pencils that roll under your touch. In the case of a fluid, any two eddies that spin in the same direction and momentarily rub against each other will tend to merge and become one bigger eddy with the energy of both, so – unlike the pencils – some swirls can and do become very big. Smaller swirls embedded in bigger ones are swept from the bottom to the surface, and vice versa. In this way the bottom is continuously 'scrubbed' by parcels of water that are moving at full stream speed. Each parcel scrubs the bottom for a moment, and the molecules that touch the bottom come to rest. The shear between these and the fast-moving adjacent molecules is intense: the greater the speed difference, the more strongly the parcel sticks to the bottom. But this friction slows the parcel, so it is soon undercut by the next faster parcel and is swept up into the stream again. The intense mixing of the turbulence means that all of the water flows at about the same speed except for a relatively thin boundary layer close to the bottom, where the mean speed is an average between parcels at zero speed momentarily stuck to the bottom or leaving it, and those at full stream speed that are about to scrub the bottom.

In turbulent flow, waterlogged leaves at the bottom are scrubbed free and swept along as fast as those near the surface and, like the parcels of water, are swept from the bottom towards the surface and back again. This is turbulent flow. The surface reveals what is going on by becoming rippled.

Where the stream next widens, the flow speed will become slower. At the point where it falls below a critical speed, viscosity will take over and progressively slow and suppress the eddies. This will take time. The glassy surface further downstream will reveal the point where the flow has again become laminar.

If the transition from fast to slow takes the form of a jet of faster water flowing into a wider pool of slower water, a special sort of boundary layer, called a shear layer, forms between the faster and the slower water. The shear layer is a mass of eddies all spinning the same way, so every swirl is to some extent within the circulation field of the adjacent swirls. This causes the shear layer to curve always in the sense of curving away from the faster flow and towards, and reaching further into, the slower flow.

13.7 ■ Boundary layer flows around sails and foils

Around a wing, sail or centreboard, the boundary layer is necessarily different. In the natural wind or the stream the boundary layer has no unique starting point, so it will everywhere grow to its maximum thickness. But every wing, sail or centreboard has a leading edge, and that is where its boundary layer has to start.

The boundary layer always starts laminar and thin. If the speed is low enough, it will stay laminar indefinitely.

If the flow becomes faster, at some point the boundary layer will become turbulent as the wind does as it approaches 6 knots. In the case of a long flat surface, what happens is that the flow remains laminar for some distance downstream of the leading edge, then becomes unstable. The point at which it ceases to be laminar is called the transition point. Downstream of the transition point there is a transition zone in which the boundary layer becomes increasingly unsteady. At the downstream end of the transition zone, the boundary layer is fully turbulent. As flow speed is increased, the transition point and transition zone move forward closer to the leading edge. We saw in the case of the 49er hull covered with thick detergent that the transition point was 2–3ft behind the stem at 6 knots in water. What the undisturbed detergent tells us is that the skin friction under the laminar boundary layer is very small (like the waterlogged leaf lying on the bottom). The scrubbed-off detergent tells us that under the turbulent boundary layer the skin friction is significantly greater.

Laminar flow will last longest on a polished surface. NASA's 'standard roughness', or barnacles, or road grit after a long trip will all trip the boundary layer turbulent sooner and result in increased drag.

13.8 ■ The boundary layer, free stream and undisturbed flow

When air or water flows around a body, there are three separate and identifiable parts to the flow.

Closest to the body is the 'boundary layer' which is the fluid slowed by surface friction at and near the surface. The molecules that touch the sail or hull stick to the surface and stop momentarily. Those that are adjacent are slowed by viscosity. The boundary layer is this layer of slowed air or water. It may be either laminar or turbulent.

The distant part is the 'undisturbed flow' – that is, the natural wind, or the water of the harbour – which is sufficiently far away from the object so that the presence of the object makes no difference to its flow. In the case of Fig 10.1, the stationary water in the tube ahead of or behind the fish is the 'undisturbed flow'. In the case of a sail, the apparent wind beyond the boat's 'wind shadow' is the undisturbed flow.

The middle and most important part is the 'free stream' – the mass of air or water that lies between the slowed boundary layer and the undisturbed flow. Its trajectory is influenced by the shape of the sail or hull, but it is not close enough to be slowed by its skin friction. In Fig 10.1 the accelerated flow through the annulus between the fish and the tube between the fish's nose and tail is the free stream. The smoke plumes in Fig 13.20 on page 194 show how the free stream curves around a jib and mainsail.

13.9 ■ Tufts, leech ribbons and sail trim – summary

Apart from skin friction drag, all the lift and drag forces developed by a sail are generated by the difference between the free stream flow speed on one side of the sail and the free stream flow speed on the other. We cannot see the air, so to sail fastest we must trim our sails either by use of tufts and leech ribbons, or by feel when the tufts are stuck by rain, salt, spider webs or in very light air.

The fastest sailors will be those who can sense the difference between attached flow as in Figs 13.7 and 13.8, and Fig 21.1B, C and D (page 285); laminar separation as in Figs 13.9 and 13.10; and completely separated flow as in Figs 13.6 and 21.1E. So let us look at each of these.

Attached flow

When sailing to windward in moderate wind and flat water, the boat will sail fastest when the sail is as full as is possible provided that the windward tufts stream as in Fig 21.1B and C, the leech ribbons stream, and the leech is not 'hooked' – that is, the leech is approximately parallel with the centre line. The flow around the sail will be as in Fig 13.7, and the flow detail as in Fig 13.8, in which:

- A–A, A–A   Is the undisturbed flow – that is, the apparent wind.
- B–B, B–B   Is the free stream between the undisturbed flow and the boundary layer.
- D and D   These heavily hatched layers are drawn to scale to show the actual thickness of the upper and lower boundary layers at the trailing edge/leech.
- C and C   The lightly hatched areas C and C, bounded by e, f, g, h and i above the wing and j, k, l, m and n below the wing, are drawn with the thickness magnified ten times so as to show more clearly the way the boundary layer thickens, and the way the speed changes as the flow approaches the surface.

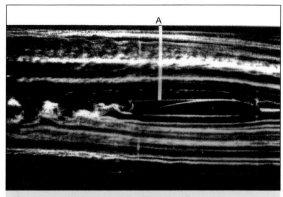

Fig 13.9 Laminar separation

A Laminar shear layer.
From *Model Aeronautics Year Book*, 1938.

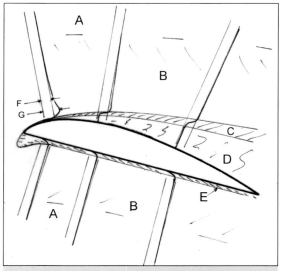

Fig 13.10 Detail of laminar separation

A   Undisturbed flow
B   Free stream
C   Laminar shear layer
D   Stagnant air
E   Boundary layer
F   Speed of undisturbed flow
G   Speed of free stream

Over the upper (leeward) surface it starts at a fraction of a millimetre thick at the leading edge, thickens to about 1mm thick at e, 5mm at f, 12mm at g, 25mm at h, and 36mm at i. It thickens slowly as it accelerates towards minimum pressure between e and f, then thickens faster as the air slows, to finish about 36mm thick at the trailing edge (leech).

Over the lower surface it thickens more quickly as it slows against the increasing pressure from j to k where it is already about 15mm thick, then thickens very little more as it accelerates towards the lower pressure at the trailing edge (leech) where it finishes at 16mm thick.

The constant spacing a–a, a–a, a–a between the pairs of lightly drawn parallel lines drawn perpendicular to the wing surfaces in Figs 13.8, 13.10 and 13.12 represents the speed of the undisturbed flow – that is, the speed of the apparent wind.

The changing spacings b–b, b–b, b–b between the forward lightly drawn line and the third heavily drawn line shows how the speed of the free stream changes between the undisturbed apparent wind to, and also through, the boundary layer.

Note how the free stream speeds are faster over the wing (ie on the lee side of the sail), and slower under it. This speed difference is strongly repeated in the smoke plumes of Fig 13.20 and the analysis of flow speed in Fig 13.21. The faster flow speeds over the top of the wing/the lee side of the sail give lowest pressure where the speed is greatest closer to the leading edge/mast, and the speed reduces as it approaches the trailing edge/leech. The slower flow speeds under the wing/on the windward side of the sail give higher pressure.

The pressure difference due to this flow speed difference is what supports the aeroplane in flight and drives the sailboat.

Fully attached flow, as in Figs 13.7 and 13.8, is possible only when the air at point e has sufficient speed to reach the leech at point i against the increasing pressure before it stops.

This flow pattern is indicated by all the tufts and the leech ribbons streaming steadily. If the windward tuft(s) agitate, the sail is too full. As the wind gets stronger, the windward tuft(s) will agitate unless the sail is flattened.

Completely separated flow

As the wind becomes lighter, the sail will be trimmed closer for more 'power'. Greatest power will be developed when the leeward tufts agitate and the leech ribbons start to 'pop in and out', as in Fig 21.1D. This leech ribbon behaviour indicates that leeward flow is still attached, but that trailing edge separation is beginning to occur.

If the sail is trimmed in further, the lee-side flow will separate completely, and the leeward tufts and leech ribbons go limp. This indicates that complete separation has occurred, as in Figs 13.6 and 21.1E. What happens here is that the lee-side air stops flowing faster, the pressure rises, and the sail's 'power' abruptly falls from point d to point e (Fig 21.1E).

In light air, it is *essential* to monitor the upper leech ribbons and upper jib leeward tufts to keep them 'alive'. Great twist will be needed whenever the flow becomes laminar and the velocity gradient linear, as is shown in Figs 3.14 and 3.15.

Laminar separation

With thicker model aeroplane wings and fuller sails, an intermediate separation can occur as the wind becomes lighter. This is called laminar separation and is shown in Figs 13.9 and 13.10. What is happening here is that feeble flow remains attached from the mast to the point of maximum depth of camber, then separates. Fig 13.10 shows how the flow speed suddenly reduces to nothing in the area D under the shear layer; the pressure rises, the 'power' falls to near nothing, and the boat slows.

It happens from time to time with fuller sails in unsteady light air, and is indicated by the leeward tuft near the mast staying alive but the leech ribbon going limp. To correct, ease the sail trim immediately until the leech ribbons stream to indicate restored, fully attached lee-side flow.

Laminar separation bedevils too-full sails in light air, and a slightly flatter sail will sail faster in light air. Eagles' wings are deeply cambered; dragonflies' wings are almost flat. Laser sailors will understand.

Reaching and broad reaching

When reaching and broad reaching, the sails can be made fuller to give more drive force and 'power'. Maximum coefficient of lift increases with increase of camber up to 16%. When broad reaching, every change of boat speed and boat direction, and every change of true wind speed and wind direction, will result in a change in the direction of the apparent wind. The practical result is that for maximum speed it is necessary to trim to the point where the leech ribbons are just 'popping in and out' (trim D and d in Fig 21.1), and then to monitor the leech ribbons and adjust trim and heading constantly in response to the constant small changes of apparent wind direction to maintain this maximum-power, maximum-speed trim. The sailor should be aware that complete separation will inevitably occur from time to time (leech ribbons will go limp), and unless constantly monitored and immediately corrected the boat will lose drive force and slow.

Practicalities

Particularly in light air and drizzle, when all the tufts and leech ribbons will be stuck, understanding of these flow patterns and constant attention to maintain 'maximum power' trim by intelligent 'feel' will be rewarded by consistent, higher speed.

13.10 ■ The separation bubble

As soon as the apparent wind speed exceeds about 3 knots the shear layer will trigger turbulent and curve inwards. To repeat Professor Arch Oliver: '… in the turbulent layer all the eddies are spinning the same way and each is to some extent within the flow field of the adjacent eddies. So the shear layer curves, always away from the higher speed flow, and reaches always further into the low speed fluid. In the case of the flow around your sails, this is the mechanism that forms the separation bubbles you are observing.'

Fig 13.11 (from *HPS-1*) shows this process in action. Unlike Fig 13.9 in which the exposure was short enough to 'stop' each eddy, the longer exposure time of Fig 13.11 reveals the eddy formation area as a time-lapse blur.

The sharp laminar shear layers flow near-straight until they begin to trip turbulent, at which point they begin to curve inwards strongly and re-attach to the model sail, to form two separation bubbles – one above and one below – the model sail.

Fig 13.12 shows the detail. A and A are the undisturbed flows, B and B are the free streams, C and C are the shear layers, D and D are the circulations within the bubbles, and E and E are the normal boundary layers that form behind the bubbles.

The way the flow speed changes between the undisturbed flows A, A through the free streams B, B to the shear layers C, C, through the bubbles D, D to the surface are shown in Fig 13.8 and Fig 13.10. 'F' in Fig. 13.10 is the speed of the undisturbed flow; 'G' is the speed of the free stream.

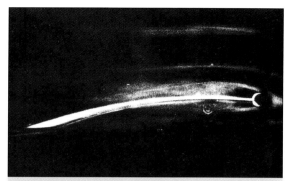

Fig 13.11 The separation bubble

Turbulent shear layers curve inward to enclose bubbles.

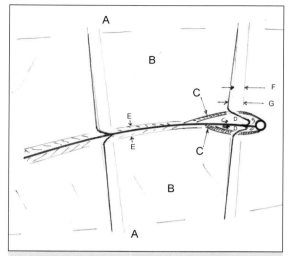

Fig 13.12 Detail of the separation bubble

A   Undisturbed flow
B   Free stream
C   Turbulent shear layers curve inwards and re-attach, to enclose bubbles
D   Separation bubbles
E   Attached boundary layer
F   Speed of undisturbed flow (apparent wind)
G   Speed of free stream (note that direction reverses inside bubbles)

The point of interest in this case is the way the flow direction reverses within each bubble. This is what causes tufts to stream in the wrong direction.

Within each bubble the air circulates. At the sail surface it flows forward from the higher pressure at the re-attachment point towards the lower pressure just behind the mast. It then rises from the surface and flows aft as the lower surface of the shear layer.

The upper and lower shear layers curve inwards and re-attach to the sail. Because the shear layers are themselves very unstable, their re-attachment points flicker back and forth over the sail. This is why tufts in the re-attachment area agitate at random.

Behind the re-attachment point a normal attached boundary layer, E, forms – similar to those in Fig 13.8.

Understanding the nature of the separation bubbles and the flows within them has explained the behaviour of tufts on the sail:

- Tufts within separation bubbles show reversed surface flow.
- Tufts in the re-attachment area agitate at random.
- Tufts in the boundary layer aft of the re-attachment point stream steadily in the normal manner.

13.11 ■ Leech ribbons

Leech ribbons serve a particularly useful function in signalling that the sail is close to its 'maximum power' trim. In Fig 13.18, as the sail with attached turbulent lee-side flow is trimmed in, the crosswind force (coefficient of lift) increases to 1.9 at 32°, then at about 34° the lee-side flow separates, all suction force is lost, and the total force reduces to the 'flat plate' value of about 1.2. In aeronautical terms, the sail has 'stalled'.

As the stall angle is approached, the attached boundary layer at the leech will slow to the point where it stops and begins to separate, as does the stopped water on the tumbler. At this point, higher pressure air from the windward side of the leech 'leaks' around the leech onto the suction side, as in the upper sail at 30° in the inset top left in Fig 13.18. As it flows around the leech it carries the leech ribbon with it. Because the aft-flowing boundary layer is turbulent, it does not split off as in Figs 13.9 and 13.10. Instead it sticks to the surface tenaciously, and the process is very unstable. But the fact that attached flow is faltering is signalled by the leech ribbons 'popping in and out' as the stagnant air tries to dislodge the attached flow. This 'popping in and out' indicates to the sail trimmer that he still has attached flow, but is close to the stall. The process is reversible. If the sheet is eased, fully attached flow will be restored, as in the sail trimmed at 22.5° in the inset in Fig 13.18. This is an invaluable trimming tool for reaches and broad reaches. (Refer also to Fig 21.1.) The ultimate use of this as a racing tool is the 'squeeze and ease' technique described by Emmett Lazich in Section 29.7.

This work led directly to the firm-leech, manually adjustable, aerodynamic benchmark rig of the Tasar in 1975, which summarised this line of thinking. This was about the stage we had reached by the mid- to late-1970s.

THE THIRD PHASE – MEASUREMENT AND ANALYSIS

13.12 ■ The standard texts

Most of us intuitively think of sails as wings, so let us look at the way the science of aerodynamics at aircraft scale presents its data.

Figs 13.13 and 13.14 are from NACA (National Advisory Committee for Aeronautics) report No 460 of 1935 on the characteristics of 78 related aerofoil sections. Fig 13.15 is from a later NASA (the NACA became the National Aeronautics and Space Administration) 1949 report. (These are American institutions, so the units are Imperial.)

Fig 13.13 and 13.14 show the way lift and drag measurements were published in the 1930s. The shape of the test sections was typical of the then-universal 'turbulent flow' school of thought. The test sections were surfaced to a standard high polish, and the variable density tunnel used compressed air to achieve a Reynolds Number of about 3 million. This is about the scale at which the wing-sail of Buddy Melges' iceboat would be working at 100mph (Fig 2.1). The lift over drag plot assumed an aspect ratio (span²/area) of six.

In Fig 13.15 the different shape of the 66-006 section generates laminar flow at small angles to the flow. The new 1949 presentation adds measurements of three properties not shown in Figs 13.13 and 13.14. The characteristics are now measured at RNs not only of 3 million, but at 6 and 9 million as well. And a further test is run with the surface deliberately blemished with a 'standard roughness'.

Together, these three figures form a useful starting point, for they are the closest that NACA came to single-surface sails at sailboat wind speeds. All three show the characteristics of thin aerofoil sections like a bird's wings, but in air flows much faster than small sailboats (other than iceboats) ever experience.

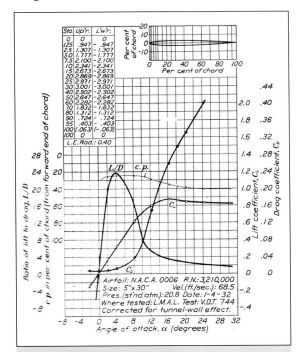

Fig 13.13 NACA 0006 section

Characteristics of NACA 0006 turbulent flow section.

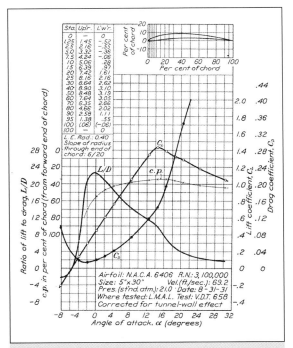

Fig 13.14 NACA 6406 section

Characteristics of NACA 6406 turbulent flow section.

13.13 ■ Simple lift and drag forces

In Fig 13.13 the 0006 section has a flat mean line, and the maximum thickness of 6% (the final '06' of the 0006) is at 30% of the chord (the distance between the leading and trailing edges in the direction of flow) from the leading edge. In the 6406 section of Fig 13.14, the mean line is curved at 6% of the chord (indicated by the first '6' of 6406), with the high point of the curve at 0.4 of the chord from the leading edge (indicated by the second digit '4'). Around this curved mean line is wrapped the same 6% thick envelope (the final '06') as in Fig 13.14.

The 66-006 section in Fig 13.14 is again wrapped around a flat mean line, but the envelope is different with the 6% maximum thickness now at 45% of the chord from the leading edge.

Figs 13.13 to 13.14 show the coefficient of lift (C_L), coefficient of drag (C_D), and lift over drag (L/D) curves of these sections at an aspect ratio of 6 and at angles to the wind from minus 8° to plus 32° as measured in a wind tunnel at RN about 3 million.

The reduced drag of laminar flow

Look now at Fig 13.15. The shape of this section is designed so that at small angles to the wind, the boundary layer flow over much of its surface will remain laminar. The practical result of this is the extraordinary reduction of drag at small angles to the flow which takes the form of a 'bucket' in the

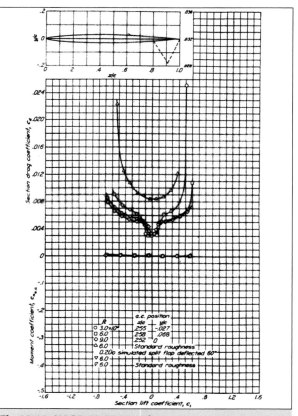

Fig 13.15 NASA 66-006 section

Characteristics of NACA 66-006 laminar flow wing section. (Note the low-drag 'bucket'.)
From *Theory of Wing Sections,* Abbott and von Doenhoff.

diagram. Why? Because a section surrounded by laminar flow will be 'cocooned' within a sheath of slow-moving air which exerts little shear force on the surface. Consider again the waterlogged leaf lying unmoved at the bottom of the laminar stream, and the glassy water under light air. At the scale of wings, centreboards and rudder blades, this property results in greatly reduced drag when the wings are operated at angles 'within the bucket'. At angles of attack 'outside the bucket' laminar flow is not achieved and the drag is about the same as that of the turbulent flow sections in Figs 13.13 and 13.14. The lift curve of Fig 13.15 (on a facing page in Abbott and Von Doenhoff and not shown here) contains no surprises.

The reduced drags measured at RNs of 6 and 9 million show that scale matters. Nine million is about the scale of the sails of an America's Cup boat sailing to windward in a wind speed of 40 knots, or the wing of a 737 at approach speed just before touch-down. Like the hull of the aircraft carrier, size makes a difference in the sense that bigger is more efficient. Look too at the reducing drag of the 49er hull when planing at higher speeds (Fig 10.9).

NASA are nothing if not practical, so they now run an extra test with the section deliberately blemished with a 'standard roughness'. In the case of this section, the standard roughness proves to be rough enough to prevent any laminar flow from developing at any angle and the drag at the 'in the bucket' angles has trebled. The drag has doubled at the 'not in the bucket' angles. The effect is broadly similar to that of small barnacles on a hull. Smooth and polished hulls sail fastest.

While laminar flow sections do not have much to do with sails, they have everything to do with centreboards and rudder blades. The astonishing performance of the modern skiff depends largely on its fine entry, low-wave-impact-drag hull and laminar flow foils.

Figs 13.13, 13.14 and 13.15 are typical of the formal data of aeronautical engineering.

13.14 ■ Sydney University wind tunnel measurements

The largest of Sydney University's wind tunnels in 1969 had a working section 7ft × 5ft. It was designed to run at aircraft speeds, but ran smoothly and steadily at 30ft per second. Its balances were designed to measure large forces, so we made a balance appropriate to measure the small forces we expected. Our model mounted on this balance is shown in the tunnel in Fig 13.4.

We used this facility to observe the tuft behaviour and to measure the associated lift and drag forces of all of the 32 different combinations of mast shape, mast angle and sail camber that we had earlier trialled in our 'car' observations. We used the same model and about the same wind speed as for the car work – 30ft per second, which is 20.44mph, RN ~400,000 – and measured the forces at angles of attack (angle between the chord and the apparent wind) from 0 to between 30° and 40°.

We first measured the drag and also the trivial lift of the frame without any sail or mast over the full range of angles of attack. We then measured the lifts and drags of 32 combinations of mast, mast angle and sail camber. The total forces measured, less the frame lift and drag previously measured, is given as solid lines labelled CL (coefficient of lift) and CD (coefficient of drag). No tunnel wall or other corrections have been applied. The tunnel was relatively large compared with the model, so whatever the tunnel wall corrections may be they will necessarily be small.

The 2ft square model sail necessarily has an aspect ratio of 1. The biggest unknown was the effect of the elliptical 2ft × 0.5ft ply end plates which reduce the tip losses. From previous work with model aircraft, I believe the effective aspect ratio would be approximately 1.3.

Figs 13.16, 13.17 and 13.18 have been repeated from *HPS-1*, except that I have:

- Redrawn them in the NACA format.
- Redrawn the top-left inset to a format that better conveys the behaviour of the tufts.
- Added as dashed lines the calculated coefficients of drag and the L/D ratios had the aspect ratio of the model been 6.

Fig 13.16 shows the characteristics of a sail with 7% camber at 0.5 of the chord from the leading edge to the trailing edge, and a round mast with a diameter of 5% of the chord.

Fig 13.17 shows the characteristics of a sail with 7% camber at 0.5 of the chord from the leading edge and wing mast type G in Fig 13.5, set at 30° to the chord.

Fig 13.18 shows the characteristics of a sail with 16% camber at 0.5 of the chord from the leading edge and a wing mast type G in Fig 13.5, set at 60° to the chord.

The NACA/NASA data present the raw data from models of aspect ratio 6.

In Figs 13.16, 13.17 and 13.18 the solid lines labelled C_D give the measured drags reduced to coefficient form. The dashed lines labelled 'C_D at AR 6' give the measured coefficient of drag corrected to represent its value had the model had an aspect ratio of 6.

The dashed line labelled 'L/D at AR 6' gives the ratio of coefficient of lift over coefficient of drag at aspect ratio of 6, and subject to the reservations stated is comparable with the NACA L/D curves in

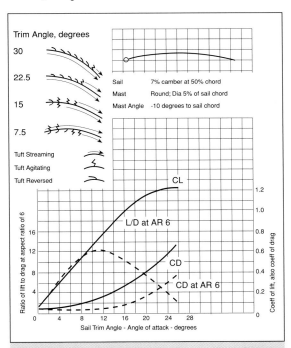

Fig 13.16 Characteristics of a 7% camber sail on round mast

Solid lines – Forces as measured from the rig shown in Fig 13.4
Dashed lines – Forces adjusted to the NASA standard aspect ratio of 6.

Figs 13.13, 13.14 and 13.15. The camber of the sail, the mast section and the angle of mast to the chord are given in the top right-hand panel.

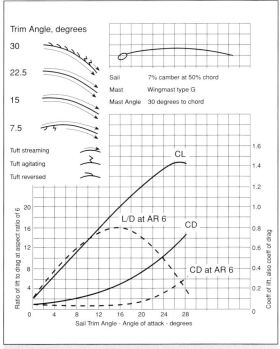

Fig 13.17 Characteristics of 7% camber sail on wing mast type G

Solid lines – Forces as measured from the rig shown in Fig 13.4
Dashed lines – Forces adjusted to the NASA standard aspect ratio of 6.

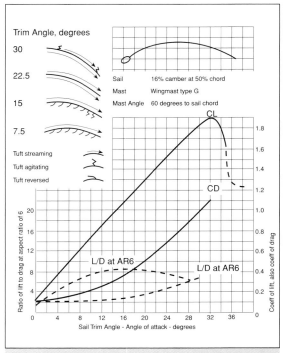

Fig 13.18 Characteristics of a 16% camber sail on wing mast type G

Solid lines – Forces as measured from the rig shown in Fig 13.4
Dashed lines – Forces adjusted to the NASA standard aspect ratio of 6.

The angle of attack between model chord and tunnel centreline is given across the bottom of the graticule. The solid lines labelled C_L and C_D, also the dashed line labelled 'C_D at AR 6', are read against the C_L, also C_D (coefficient of lift, also coefficient of drag), scale at the right-hand edge of the graticule.

The dashed line labelled 'L/D at AR 6' is read against the lift/drag scale up the left-hand edge of the graticule. The inset shows the behaviour of the tufts at angles of attack of 7.5, 15, 22.5 and 30°.

- Every tuft was deemed to be streaming, reversed or agitated.
- Streaming tufts imply attached flow.
- Reversed tufts imply a stable separation bubble above.
- Agitating tufts imply the zone in which the shear layer between the free stream and the separation bubble curves inward and re-attaches to the surface. This zone is mobile and extremely unsteady.

Crosswind force ('lift')

Let us for a moment ignore the RN scale difference and just look at the lift maximums and drag minimums of the two sections: one the 'flat' 0006; and the other the 'full' 6406.

To look at the difference in lift between flat and full let us imagine a dinghy on a broad reach with the apparent wind on the beam. If in a 20 knot wind we assume a planing speed of 13 knots, the apparent wind would be about 15 knots, and the 'lift' – the force at right angles to the apparent wind – would be the drive force. The coefficient of lift maximums are about 0.88 at 16° for the flat sail, and 1.43 at 14° for the full sail.

To arrive at useful force figures from these coefficients, the calculations are:

Force (lb) = 0.5 × Coeff of Lift × Area (sq ft) × Density × Speed (fps)^2

Standard density (mass per unit volume) of dry air at sea level 15°C and 760mm
Imperial units   SI units
0.002378lb/ft³   0.12497kg/m³

In this example the sail area is 150sq ft, the 'standard atmosphere' density of air at sea level is 0.001185 (0.002378/2). 1 knot = 1.69ft per second, so the apparent wind speed of 15 knots is 25.35ft per second.
The forces become:

- Flat   = 0.88 × 150 × .001185 × 25.35 × 25.35   = 100.5lb.
- Full   = 1.43 × 150 × .001185 × 25.35 × 25.35   = 163.3lb.
- The difference is stark. The full sail has nearly two-thirds more drive force.

This confirms what we know from experience: that deeply curved sails are fastest when the apparent wind is on or aft of the beam, and aerodynamic drag does not matter.

Drag

Let us assume the same dinghy sailing to windward at 5 knots in the 20 knot breeze – say an apparent wind of 23 knots.
The minimum of the coefficient of drag (C_D) curve of the flat section is about 0.0067 at 0°, and for the curved section about 0.0135 at minus 2°:

- Drag (lb) for the flat section   = .0067 × 150 × 0.001185 × 38.87 × 38.87   = 1.80lb.
- And for the curved section   = .0135   "   "   "   "   = 3.62lb.
- The minimum drag of the curved section is double the minimum drag of the flat section. The difference is 1.82lb.

Typically, the hull drag at a 5 knot boat speed of a Tasar or 29er is about 18lb, so if these were sails, the difference of 1.82lb between the aero drags of the flat sail and the fuller sail would be about 10% of the hydro drag. So this example again confirms what we know from experience: that it is slow to try to sail to windward in a strong breeze with full sails.

Observed flow and force differences

The key points from this work were:

Lift

As between sails with different masts:

- C_L max from the 7% camber sail with a round mast is 1.23.
- C_L max from the 7% camber sail with a wing mast is 1.44.
- The wing mast develops about 17% more lift at C_L max.
  C_L max is affected by the mast section.

As between sections of different camber:

- C_L max from the flat NACA section is 0.89.
- C_L max from the 6% camber NACA section is 1.43.
- C_L max from the 7% camber wing masted sail is 1.44.
- C_L max from the 16% camber wing masted sail is 1.90.
  C_L max increases with camber.

This change is shown as a curve in Fig 13.19A.

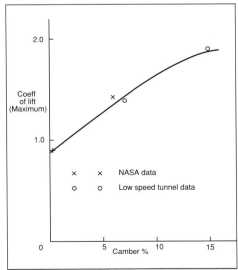

Fig 13.19A Change of C_L max and C_D min with camber

x x NASA data
o o Low speed tunnel data

Drag

As between the two NACA wing sections, and the two wing masted sails:

- C_D min of the flat NACA section is about 0.04.
- C_D min of the 6% camber NACA section is about 0.07.
- C_D min of the 7% wing masted sail is about 0.07.
- C_D min of the 15% wing masted sail is about 0.10.
  C_D min increases with camber.

This change is shown as a curve in Fig 13.19B.

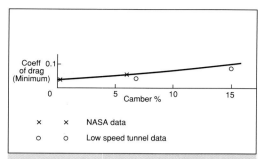

Fig 13.19B Change of C_L max and C_D min with camber

Note how simply Fig 13.19 explains why crews who adjust their sails win:

- If two identical boats race, both with the perfect camber for the wind at the start, and the wind does not change, they should finish together.
- But if the wind dies and one adjusts fuller and the other does not, the fuller sail will give greater drive and that boat must sail faster and win.
- If the wind freshens, and one adjusts flatter and the other does not, the flatter sail will develop less drag and that boat must sail faster and win.

Flow and forces at smaller angles of attack (trim angle)

- As between Figs 13.16, 13.17 and 13.18, the most obvious differences in flow are that behind the round mast many tufts are always unsteady at all trim angles, while behind the wing mast all the tufts stream more smoothly.
- At the C_L max sheeting angles used for reaching and broad reaching, greater lift, smaller drag and greater L/D ratios are always associated with the smoother flow of the wing mast. These rigs are convincingly faster for two-sail reaching and broad reaching.
- But, and surprisingly, at the smaller trim angles used when sailing to windward (up to about L/D max) the lift, drag and L/D ratios of the sail with the small diameter round mast are little different from those of the sail with the wing mast.
  - What seems to be happening is that with a small mast and at the small trim angles used when sailing to windward, the bubbles are small and present to the wind with a streamline shape that has the same power and no more drag than a solid wing mast.
  - But at the large trim angles used when reaching, the bubbles become very large and because of the reversed flows within them cannot develop high pressure differences. In these conditions the wing masts offer significantly higher performance.

It was not until very recently, when I corrected our 1969 measurements at an aspect ratio of 1 to the more realistic NASA aspect ratio of 6, and replotted them to the more revealing NASA format, that the lack of difference at the smaller trim angles became clear. This has explained a great deal.

THE FOURTH PHASE – SMOKE FLOW OBSERVATIONS

13.15 ■ Smoke plume apparatus

Up to this point, we had fitted tufts and found that they behaved in strange ways, had developed wing masts to smooth the flow, had tried the wing masts on the water and found them fast, particularly when reaching and broad reaching, and had repeated the tuft behaviour and measured the associated force differences in the wind tunnel. But as yet we could not 'see' what was happening. Flow visualisation by smoke plumes looked attractive, I had built a smaller tunnel of my own, so we set it up to give us smoke plume pictures.

The tunnel, which is the lower one on page 219 of *HPS-1*, was screened until the plume divergence was about the same as in a breeze. In light air the smoke plume from a cigarette drifts away as a filament. As soon as the boundary layer trips turbulent at 6 knots, the plume fans away as a cone. This is what we sail in, so it is sensible to duplicate about this level of turbulence in the tunnel. If a tunnel with a contraction ratio between intake and working section of four to one is run without screening, the air flows fast but is extremely unsteady with coarse turbulence (like the very rough flow from some water taps), even when the outside air is calm. If the entry is screened – I use multiple layers of mosquito netting, as shown in the upper photo on *HPS-1* page 219 – the flow becomes progressively slower and steadier until if you screen it enough it becomes laminar and the plume again flows as a filament. A screened filter on a tap works similarly. I found that three layers of netting steadied the flow until the smoke plume coned at about the same angle as in a light breeze.

We made smoke by putting briquettes glowing red hot into a jam tin full of sawdust. A second larger jam tin inverted over it kept the air out so it smouldered rather than blazed. This provided copious smoke for 2 or 3 minutes at a time. A tube from the cover tin ran to a register with the drinking straw nozzles. The suction in the tunnel caused by the flow speed and the screening was sufficient to suck the smoke through the nozzles.

Light from 1000W floodlights top and bottom was admitted as vertical blades through narrow slits, and these were aligned onto the smoke plumes. Everything in the tunnel was painted dark grey. We worked at night to reduce background light, and we routinely secured good photos. I used a polaroid camera for convenience, and to confirm as we worked that we had indeed secured a good exposure of every picture of a desired set.

The downside is that there were no negatives, and attrition to magazines, etc in the years since has decimated the original collections.

13.16 ■ The separation bubble

As soon as we put a model sail and mast into the smoke plumes, the mechanism of the separation bubble was revealed. Figs 13.11 (repeated from *HPS-1*) and 13.12 show the detail of this low-speed flow, which is described in Section 13.10 above.

The inward-curving mechanism of the shear layers enclose the bubbles into a type of streamline shape, so behind a small-diameter mast and at small angles of attack the dimension of the twin bubbles is small and the effect on the overall performance of the sail is limited. The effect of this is displayed in the re-plotted drag curves of Figs 13.16 and 13.17, where the difference in lift, drag and L/D ratio up to about 10° angle of attack between the round mast and the wing mast is trivial. This accounts for the observed windward-going performance of rigs with small-diameter round masts.

But as the trim angle is increased, the leeward bubble grows towards the leech – as is shown by the tuft behaviour in Fig 13.16. Within this large bubble what should be an area of high suction behind the mast is degraded by the forward-flowing air within the bubble. This reduction of suction leads to the loss of lift force and the higher drag between Figs 13.16 and 13.17.

What these smoke flows show is that the high-speed flow patterns described by the standard texts are correct, but only at flow speeds and angles of attack fast enough to keep all of the air (ie both in the free stream and in the boundary layer) everywhere moving towards the trailing edge. At lower speeds, this is no longer true, and different flow patterns emerge. As flow speed becomes slower, a situation will develop where behind some mast shapes and/or at some angles of attack, the surface flow can slow to the point where it stops and then reverses, and a stable separation bubble will then occur.

13.17 ■ Trajectory, speed and pressure

Smoke plume photos are useful in that they can give you a surprisingly complete picture of what is going on:

- As we have seen above, the visible plume trajectories show where the wind goes.
  In addition:
- The spacing between the plumes gives the flow speed – *and*
- The flow speed indicates the pressure.

Fig 13.20 shows the way a jib and mainsail on a close reach 'bend the wind'. Let us look at these three factors as they apply here:

Trajectory

The flow is everywhere attached, so flow direction is everywhere from right to left. (In the case of a complex flow such as a separation bubble, the direction of flow at any point may not be obvious from a still photo.)

Fig 13.20 Main and jib in smoke plumes

The local flow speed is proportional to plume spacing – the closer the plumes, the faster the flow and the lower the pressure. See also Fig 13.21. The mast is wing mast type G.

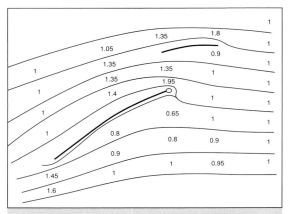

Fig 13.21 Change in flow speed in free stream

The speed of undisturbed flow (ie apparent wind) is 1.0. There is a change in flow speed in the free stream close to jib and mainsail. The higher the speed, the lower the pressure and vice versa.

Flow speed

The spacing of the plumes in this two-dimensional view gives the local flow speed at every point, as well as an indication of the local pressure. The spacing at the speed and pressure of the undisturbed wind is given by the plume spacing at the nozzles. If, in this two-dimensional flow, the spacing between the plumes reduces to one-half, this indicates that the flow speed has doubled, and also that the pressure there is substantially lower than at the nozzles, and vice versa. In Fig 13.21 I have repeated the plumes of Fig 13.20 in line form and added figures between the plumes to show how the free stream wind speed changes from point to point as it flows past these sails:

- The speed of the undisturbed wind at the nozzles is assumed to be 1.
- Where the plumes are closer than at the nozzles, the free stream speed is faster and the local pressure less than the undisturbed wind, and vice versa.

Local pressure

At subsonic speeds total pressure – that is, static pressure plus dynamic pressure – remains constant, so where the flow speeds up and potentially greater dynamic pressure is developed the static pressure will decrease.

Imagine a wide open tank full of water with a parallel open channel as an exit, and that the bottom of the tank and the bottom of the channel are level.

If the exit from the channel is blocked:

- There will be no flow speed anywhere (ie dynamic pressure will everywhere be zero) *and*
- The water surface will be level, so the hydrostatic pressure at the bottom of the tank and along the channel will be everywhere the same.

Now unblock the exit channel:

- As the water flows away from the tank and accelerates along the parallel channel, its surface level will fall as it accelerates. The faster it flows, the lower the surface level will become, so the hydrostatic pressure at the bottom of the channel will become progressively less under the progressively shallower and faster flow.
- If you momentarily block the channel at any point, the dynamic pressure developed by the speed of the water against the block at that point will heap the water up to the same level as the still water in the tank (apart from any friction loss).

This example shows that the total pressure – that is, the static pressure plus the dynamic pressure – remains constant.

If you bring moving air to rest, as wind against a spinnaker, increased dynamic pressure will be developed. This drives a boat on a square run.

If the apparent wind speed doubles, twice as many molecules will be slowed against the spinnaker, and each will develop twice the impulse as it slows from its doubled speed, so the dynamic pressure developed will become four times as great. If the wind speed triples, the dynamic pressure will become nine times as great – that is, the law is always 'speed squared'.

If instead of slowing the air you accelerate it to a higher speed, its pressure will decrease – as did that of the water in the channel. The pressure difference between the slower flow across the lower surface of a wing, or the windward side of a sail, and the faster flow over the upper surface of a wing, or the leeward side of a sail, develop the pressure differences that support an aeroplane in flight and drive a sailboat when sailing to windward.

These pressure differences can become surprisingly large. A fully loaded Jumbo-type aircraft may weigh 500 000lb and have a wing area of about 2000sq ft with flaps partly extended. At a speed of about 180 knots (300ft per second) it can develop a pressure difference of more than 250lb per square ft; this is sufficient for its wings to support its weight, and it can then leave the runway and fly!

Let us come back to sailboat practicalities. Sailboats work in slower apparent winds, and typically are designed on the assumption that their rigs will develop forces up to about 1lb per square ft (5kg/sq m) when sailing to windward in moderate winds. Fig 13.22 shows the way a jib and mainsail rig can bend the free stream when sailing to windward at a wind speed where the crew are 'looking for power'. Note the substantial area to leeward and behind the boat where the free stream is slowed and bent in an adverse direction. This is the area to be avoided at all costs by any rival.

Fig 13.23 shows that in stronger winds when the sails need to be eased (else the boat will heel too far or capsize) the free stream is much less affected. In strong winds a rival to windward can be ignored.

Smoke flow pictures can give a lot of information.

13.18 ■ The turbine blade principle

Fig 13.20 illustrates an important point that I have not seen referred to elsewhere in the literature. A wind machine – such as a bird's wing, sail, wing or a windmill blade – normally works in free air in which the speed and pressure of the air behind the wing is the same as that in front of it. In this mode of operation, cambers from flat to a maximum of about 16% seem to work best according to the particular circumstance. A camber of 16% 'bends the wind' between leading edge and trailing edge by about 65°. Birds' wings have evolved over millions of years and they all peak at about this camber range. But steam and gas turbine engineers use much greater cambers and 'bend the wind' by nearly 180° and achieve three or four times the 'lift' force per blade.

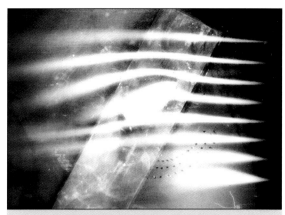

Fig 13.22 Flow pattern close-hauled: lighter wind

The flow pattern near a close-hauled sail in lighter wind. Slowed and adversely deflected flow aft and to leeward of sail greatly disadvantages any following boat.

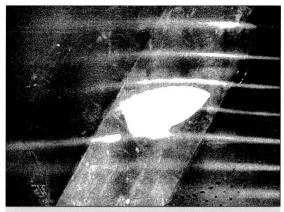

Fig 13.22 Flow pattern close-hauled: stronger wind

The flow pattern near a close-hauled sail in strong wind. In stronger winds a light boat cannot 'bend the wind' much without falling over. In strong winds, boats to windward can be ignored.

How do they do it? A feature of all turbulent surface flow is that for as long as it moves, it 'sticks', and the faster it moves the more tenaciously it sticks. A revealing kitchen experiment is to hold a smooth tumbler horizontally in a falling stream of water and see how far around the bottom and up the other side you can drive the falling flow of water from a tap. You will note that the flow always falls off at the point where it stops. (Try it around a rough-textured tumbler too. It always falls off at the bottom regardless of the flow speed.)

The point about the 16% or so maximum camber of the bird's wing is that this is the greatest practical curvature around which the air will keep moving and 'stick' right to the trailing edge on the suction surface. Greater curvature is counter-productive because the slowing air then stops and the attached flow falls off at some point forward of the trailing edge.

But if you arrange that the air at the trailing edge is at a lower pressure than the air at the leading edge, there will now be a pressure difference as well as momentum to keep the air moving, and with this device there is no limit to the curvature you can use. This is what happens in a turbine – the steam or hot gas expands a little as it passes through each stage, so the pressure at the trailing edge of each turbine blade becomes less than the higher-pressure air at its leading edge. This is the principle that enables turbine blades to be made with cambers so great that they turn the air almost 180° – and in this way achieve 'lift' efficiencies three or four times more than any bird's or aeroplane's wing can ever hope for.

Some sails are a bit special, too. Look again at Figs 13.20 and 13.21. Over the suction side of the mainsail and just behind the mast, the plumes are closer together. This indicates faster flow and lower pressure. From here the plumes diverge to the leech where the average spacing is the same as the spacing of the smoke nozzles, so the free stream speed is being slowed against the increasing pressure from the mast to the leech. But the jib is in a totally different situation. At the leading edge of the jib the smoke plume spacing is the same as that of the smoke nozzles and at the leech of the mainsail. But the leech of the jib is positioned just above the leading edge of the mainsail where the flow pattern around the mainsail is fastest and the pressure is lowest, so the jib exhausts into exactly this area of highest speed and lowest pressure in the flow around the mainsail. As a result, the jib enjoys the advantage of the turbine blade – it is working in a situation in which the pressure at the leech is less than the pressure at the luff. This enables the air around the suction side of the jib to flow at, and maintain, a much higher flow speed than it otherwise would. The plume spacing above the jib is about two-thirds the nozzle spacing, indicating a mean speed increase of about 1.5 – and 1.5 squared is 2.25. This is why jibs pull twice as hard, area for area, as mainsails.

This arrangement gives two great advantages over a single sail. First, the faster and sustained flow speed around the suction surface of the jib means that the jib will develop a much higher force per square foot than if it were working in isolation. Second, this faster exhaust from the jib will greatly improve the flow over the suction-side of the mainsail itself.

Fig 13.24 Wind flow pattern at start

The pattern of wind flow through the front line of boats at the start. Closely spaced sails form a cascade that turns the wind.

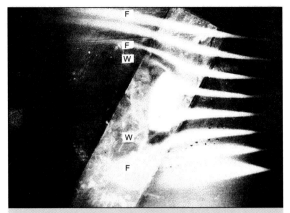

Fig 13.25 The flow pattern around sails on a square run

Ignore the orientation of the hull. The sail was glued to the hull, so it had to be placed crosswind to position the sail across wind to simulate a square run. The width of slowed air varies with wind speed. In light air it can be double the sail width. In stronger winds it reduces to little more than the sail width.

F Free stream
W Wake of slowed air

This advantage is not confined to small jibs. One of the practical surprises of apparent wind sailing is that you will sail faster and deeper downwind with the mainsail sheeted tightly, as if sailing to windward, rather than eased – as is normally fastest on a broad reach. If you think only of the drive force from the oversheeted mainsail this makes no sense at all. But if you think of the turbine blade effect of the more tightly sheeted mainsail over the whole of the big asymmetric spinnaker ahead of it, it makes a lot of sense.

Note that any overlap will reduce the advantage, and the work of those who spend millions of dollars looking for fractional advantage is worth observing. The well-researched slats and triple-slotted flaps of great aircraft, when right out, are arranged so that they match *exactly*, and nothing, repeat nothing, overlaps.

13.19 ■ Flow around sails of single and multiple boats

Fig 13.22 shows the flow pattern near, and downwind of, a single boat close hauled in wind speeds up to the design wind. A competitor who sails where the plumes are diverging will be in slower air; a competitor who sails where the plumes show changed direction will be headed to the extent indicated by the change of direction of the plume.

Fig 13.23 shows what happens in stronger winds. By definition, the design wind is the strongest wind in which you can keep the boat upright without easing anything. In stronger winds the eased sails cannot, and do not, bend the wind so much. In really strong winds you can almost ignore a boat to windward.

Fig 13.24 makes clear the full catastrophe of not being in the front row at the start. (The start is discussed in depth in *HPS-1*.) Fig 13.25 shows the flow around a boat on a square run. (The balsa sails were glued onto the model hulls, so to put the sails at right angles to the wind I turned the whole boat. Imagine the hull pointing to the left, with the sails still across the wind as when running square.) The width of the area downstream of the sails with slowed and disturbed wind is surprising.

The effect on each other of several boats that converge at a leeward mark in light wind and adverse tide can slow all of them to the point where none of the group can breast the tide, although each individually would have ample speed.

13.20 ■ Special application work

Most of the work noted above took place in the years 1968 to 1971. In practice, there had been initial competition between the simpler 'short' wing mast sections of type C, D or E in Fig 13.5, which were made from nominal 3in × 2in timber, and the longer sections of type F, G or H, which in practice needed glued-on balsa fairings and so were more expensive to make. In the steady wind of the tunnel, mast D was as good as any, but accumulating experience on the water was that in unsteady winds it could be disappointing. The longer section G was as good in the tunnel, and over the years proved more reliable on the water. As the class grew, we made a lot of timber masts of type G shape.

In late 1974 a new need arose. I was invited by Performance Sailcraft to join with them in creating a two-person boat for the world market based on my Nova, an NS14 re-rigged from 100sq ft to 123sq ft to take optimum advantage of both the sail shape adjustability and the wing mast efficiency that we had developed over the past few years. For One-Design uniformity, an alloy mast was going to be essential. With alloy it would no longer be possible

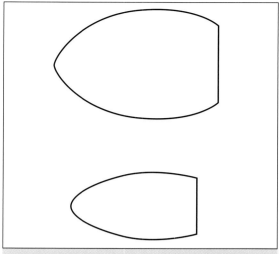

Fig 13.26 Efficient 'short' wing mast sections

to separate the mechanical and the aerodynamic properties – there could be no lightweight fairings. An inspired compromise was going to be called for.

I had given the tunnel to a university, so made another (upper photo, page 219 in *HPS-1*) for the specific purpose of developing a lower mast and a topmast section which, when extruded in alloy, would both flex adequately for adjustment and perform reliably aerodynamically.

What we found was that unsteady flow (such as C and D in Fig 21.4) tended to separate easily from the blunt leading edge of the type D mast, and once separated it was reluctant to re-attach. In unsteady wind this mast profile suffered from a narrow operating range. No such separation occurred with the type G mast, so that uncertainty was quickly resolved.

We systematically changed key properties of the type D mast, and found that the operating range was a function of the leading edge radius – the smaller the radius (but only to a point), the more tolerant it became. The sections of what became the Tasar lower mast and topmast are shown in Fig 13.26. They have given excellent wide-operating-range service.

THE FIFTH PHASE – ON THE WATER COMPARISON

13.21 ■ Experimental method

Whenever the model work suggested real improvement, we immediately made a full-size rig and sailed with it and developed it, usually by racing, to the point where it appeared to be performing about as well as could be expected. If after a few weeks of racing it still looked promising, we trialled it against a benchmark rig by boat against boat testing in as controlled an environment as we could select.

You cannot expect to measure small differences in unsteady conditions, so our method was to pick the situation that would give us the steadiest wind. Our steadiest local wind is the making sea breeze that flows along the east–west valley of Sailor Bay in Upper Middle Harbour. Fortunately, this flows past the Northbridge Sailing Club, which we used as a base. Two boats, identical except for the elements being tested, each towed two wooden clothes pegs on a thread. The first was at two boat lengths behind the transom, the second at four lengths. The two boats would take position with the leeward boat just moving and the windward boat taking station directly crosswind and with the midline clothes peg of the leeward boat abeam to leeward. When a suitably large area of uniform wind (either gust or lull) offered, they would accelerate together; at a call, stop-watches were started, the leeward boat sailed its best, and the windward boat sailed to keep the leeward boat exactly crosswind. Difference of speed was judged by reference to the towed midline clothes peg to leeward. The run continued until they reached the opposite shore (the bay is about 2km long and 400m wide), or either helm sensed that the wind had varied as between the two boats. They then tacked and exchanged windward/leeward roles for the next run. If there was sufficient time, the crews would switch boats. The test boat made systematic changes; the reference boat never changed anything. This method proved able to repeat gains or losses of one to two metres each run with surprising reliability. The photo on page 72 of *HPS-1* shows trialling in progress.

13.22 ■ Fleet comparison method

In the 1970s, Sydney conducted an annual 'Cock of the Harbour' event from the city – 7 miles to Manly and back, with a rounding mark deep in each of the bigger bays.

In 1980, 1981 and 1982 this event was replaced with a winter 'Two of a Kind' (2AK) handicap event in which the NSW State Champion and the Australian Champion of every class were invited to sail a three-race event around an equilateral triangle with 1-mile sides around Shark Island. The faster boats sailed three laps; slower boats sailed two laps. In 1980 variable winds averaged 5 knots; in 1981, again the variable and average winds were 4 knots (one race was abandoned); and in 1982 the average was 12 knots. Times were corrected on yardstick.

I used the raw uncorrected data to calculate average elapsed times.

If we use the internationally known 5o5 as a benchmark, the average elapsed times for the well-known boats for the eight races were:

Eighteen foot skiff	18% faster
5o5	Reference elapsed time
Sixteen foot skiff	1% slower
Twelve foot skiff	8% slower
Fourteen foot skiff	11% slower
Tasar	18% slower
470	23% slower
420	24% slower
Laser	31% slower

There are three lessons to be learnt from the above figures:

- It is obvious that the Eighteen foot skiff, which was sometimes unable to stay with a Flying Dutchman or 5o5 in the 1970s, had by 1980 become a much faster boat.
- The light airs and triangular courses were not kind to classes that relied on trapezes for upwind speed and on parachute spinnakers for downwind speed.
- The Tasar, a dad and mum, no spinnaker, no trapeze toe-strapper, consistently finished among or ahead of the smaller trapeze and spinnaker 'racing' boats such as the Fireball, 470, etc. It was by far the most adjustable boat, and by far the fastest two-sail boat in the race.

This data further confirmed that our work in making rigs both adjustable and efficient appeared to have achieved useful performance gains.

An amusing story relates to the Cherub. In 1976 my younger daughter Nicola, crewed by her younger brother Julian, had won the Cherub World Championship in her wing-masted, adjustable-rig Cherub (rig similar to a Tasar).

In the 1980 2AK races they were again together in her Cherub. In one race she made a brilliant pin-end start into a great header, tacked and crossed the fleet, and tacked to lay and round the windward mark which was not far distant. A Sixteen foot skiff converged from windward and astern and, in the manner of Sixteens in those days, shouted loudly for 'the kids' to get out of the way. Nicola held course. Julian, on trapeze, has a habit of doing the unexpected. He let the skiff's jib brush past him, then suddenly reached into the skiff and flicked its jib sheet out of its cleat. The skiff with three on trapeze flopped to windward, dunked its crew, and stopped. The tiny Cherub led the fleet around the first mark.

13.23 ■ Summary

This chapter has summarised what started as a gentle 1960 group dream of 'a good boat for a man and a woman', and the completely spontaneous but rigorously conducted R and D programme that developed and flourished until, with the launch of the One-Design Tasar in late 1975, my object and focus changed.

It represents a formidable body of work. It was practical and effective. Our 'dad' and 'mum', ultra light-weight, ultra strong and durable fully cored hulls, coupled with a new style of no spinnaker, no trapeze, aerodynamically efficient, high-lift, low-drag, adjustable, taut-leech rig, sailed as fast or faster than the trapeze and spinnaker racing boats of the same size of that time. Their adjustable feature in particular was widely copied and set a new trend worldwide. Those of us who had been involved were deeply satisfied that we had discovered and contributed new knowledge of value to the sailing community. We thought that with work as thoroughly conducted and rigorously cross-checked as this, that the results would apply to all sailboats everywhere. It turns out that they don't!

We now know that small-diameter round masts are efficient at dinghy Reynolds Numbers and small angles of attack (but not at large angles).

And we also now know that more flexible rigs that yield and recover moment by moment, and which work close to the optimum 'drive force to heeling force' shape for all of the time, are much more efficient in unsteady winds than taut-leech manually adjustable rigs that can only be approximately right for some of the time.

In reviewing this work with the benefit of 30 years of hindsight, I make three comments:

1 *Selected conditions.* We did not select our data any more than NASA selects its data. But by using only steady-wind wind tunnels in which to develop our rigs and selecting only abnormally steady real winds in which to cross-check our work on the water, we systematically avoided making realistic comparisons in the unsteady flows that are the normal state of the real wind. I now believe that everything in *HPS-1* and in this chapter is true, but only in steady flows.

2 *Creeping benchmarks.* In retrospect, the shift from stiff masts, to the beginnings of flexible masts that bent low down, to more flexible masts that were bent into circular arc curves by powerful controls, to rotating these masts (and these were the first wing masts that sailed fast on reaches) – all this happened over about one or two magic seasons. The serious work of refining the new wing mast technology then took over. The women for whom the NS14 and Tasar were developed had opted for no spinnakers, so our work was primarily directed to improving broad reaching downwind speeds. The huge increase in broad reaching drive force as between Figs 13.16 and 13.18 was our goal, and the downwind speeds demonstrated in the table on page 199 was its confirmation. We never thereafter developed nor sailed with, nor compared, slender fixed round masts with wing masts. So all our on-the-water trials were with progressively more refined wing masts against primitive wing masts, not against refined fixed masts.

3 *Changed priorities.* With the widespread adoption of the asymmetric spinnaker and apparent wind sailing, the function of the jib and mainsail on state-of-the-art skiffs has become to sail well to windward as part of a flexible topmast automatic rig, and to provide the 'turbine blade' boost to the non-overlapping asymmetric spinnaker on the downwind legs. Neither of these functions would now be much improved by use of a wing mast rig.

PART FOUR

Performance Advances 1991 to 2008

Chapter 14 • Evolution of the B-18 Marque

14.1 ■ Performance advances – overview

The manuscript of *HPS-1* was completed in 1991. An overview of sailing at that time was a scene of almost total conformity: dinghies, keelboats, monohulls and catamarans all sailed to windward at about hull speed; and most ran square downwind at a speed close to half wind speed or hull speed – whichever was the slower. The myriad sails on the world's waterways on weekend afternoons all moved at their measured and uniform pace.

As touched on earlier, at that time one class only in the whole world, the Eighteen foot skiffs of Sydney, were sailing at a performance level sufficiently faster than conventional to turn heads, and they had only just learned how to sail like this. My younger son Julian had become one of the active thinkers and doers in this innovative class. Through him I was a close observer of the Eighteen footers' turbulent progress from running square slowly to apparent wind sailing downwind at iceboat-like speeds.

I had worked out a way to measure, while they were racing, the actual speeds at which the best of the conventional boats, and also these new skiffs, sailed on different points of sailing and in different wind strengths, so was able to separate fact from hype. I was one of those who knew with certainty that these skiffs were indeed breaking out of the ancient mould (*HPS-1*, page 333). I was fascinated by their steadily increasing performance levels, but there were at that time about 50 (at most) such skiffs in the whole world, and most of these were in Sydney, so caution was in order.

HPS-1 reflected this environment: it was primarily a conventional book about conventional sailing. This was appropriate because at that time all sailboats everywhere, except for this one class, were still sailing as sailboats everywhere had always sailed.

In it I devoted a few pages to reporting the existence of, performance levels being achieved by, this one brilliantly innovative, non-conformist, 'cut and try' class. In retrospect, this was prophetic.

In 2008 the global view of sailing could not be more different. Whether it be big boats or little boats or the media or the shakers and movers of the classes, a revolution is underway. The skiffs' blazing speeds provided a new and compelling public spectacle. The Sydney harbourside audience increased sharply. The new spectacle was quickly recognised and brilliantly exploited by a sports producer to reach mass TV audiences first in Australia, and then to non-sailing audiences worldwide.

The modern Olympic Games is dependent for funding on spectacle and mass TV audience appeal, so the International Olympic Committee was quick to recognise the new opportunity and, through the International Sailing Federation, promote the new skiff spectacle to Olympic status and sailing mainstream. This has hastened the inevitable revolution and sharpened the differences between those who welcome the challenge and excitement of the new speed, and those who fear it.

Summed up, two huge changes have occurred in sailing in the years since *HPS-1* was written.

The first is the achievement, refinement and global acceptance of apparent wind sailing, and the 2008 world scene is of an as-yet small but growing number of these faster boats. America's Cup boats sail with apparent wind technique up to hull speed. Big 'water-bagger' or swing-keel Volvo-type monohulls routinely break the old records. Huge ultra-fast catamarans sail faster yet. Growing fleets of apparent wind dinghies satisfy sailors with a taste for real speed. All these are well served and reported by a vital section of the yachting media.

A mainstream of ageing classes are progressively adopting a siege mentality: this, though, is the classic pattern of the early stages of every technical revolution.

The second change is surprising and very recent. It is the emerging understanding that in adjusting our sail shapes manually and minute by minute, over the past 40 years we have been achieving only some small fraction of the total benefit potentially available. Rigs that flex automatically in a very special way are now sailing consistently faster than either rigid or manually adjustable rigs. The philosophy and logic of this very new performance advance is explained in the chapters ahead.

14.2 ■ Hull shape development

The Eighteen footer skiffs dominated the Sydney media from their post-war revival until they self-destructed in 1997 (Section 7.5). Bobby Holmes, David Porter, Iain Murray, Rob Brown, Julian Bethwaite and Chris Nicholson all earned their stripes and enjoyed in turn a few years at the top. The way they sailed and the rigs they used were all different. But one marque of hull that was designed and introduced in 1969, and is still the design style to beat, has contributed a stable reference line throughout, and so provides an appropriate starting point.

As a youth, my elder son Mark (see Chapter 29, Section 29.4) built and sailed Moths at junior national champion level, and at college sailed the then unusually slender fine-entry Lightweight Sharpie. From time to time he would borrow my Northbridge Senior (NS14) to sail with his girlfriends, and in 1969 he and a fellow student decided to build and campaign two NS14s to his design in the forthcoming 1969–70 Australian NS14 Championships.

By 1969 the NS14 had become highly developed, innovative, numerous and very competitive. Unlike the International Fourteens of the northern hemisphere, which were so expensive that there were never more than a few, the NS14s were a no-trapeze, no-spinnaker, low-cost, glued plywood boat of graceful shape – and about half the weight of all comparable conventional boats of that period. With their efficient rigs and very light weight (the fully rigged hull was required to weigh 140lb minimum), these 'mum and dad', no-trapeze, and no-spinnaker NS14s sailed rings around many of the conventional, heavier, trapeze and spinnaker 'racing' boats of their era. Their rigid, glued ply hulls held their speed for at least ten years. The class became very popular, and by 1969 numbered close to 1000. This depth of competition was the principal difference between this vital development class and the broadly similar, but hugely expensive, International Fourteen class of the UK and North America with its tiny numbers.

Mark's new hull design was decades ahead of its time, being innovative and logical. The principal difference was that the entry angle was unusually fine. The forward ends of the chines were straight lines, and developed their maximum chine beam much further aft than was customary, so the bottom and waterplane presented more as a triangle than the usual symmetrical lens shape.

On the water, this design offers three advantages:

1 In lighter winds and flat water their more triangular shape presents less wetted area, so they enjoy less skin friction and sail fractionally faster.
2 In drift conditions their triangular shape and flatter aft bottoms enable them to be sailed bow-down and heeled with even less wetted area and skin friction; we called this technique 'fourth mode'. When handled in this way, they dominated in drift (Fig 10.9G).
3 When sailed in waves, their finer entry bows made them a different animal. Whenever a mixed fleet started in flat water and then rounded a headland into waves, the new fine-entry boats simply ignored the waves and knifed through them at near undiminished speed while the blunter-bowed boats bucked and banged and slowed in the waves as they always had.

Mark called his boat *Medium Dribbly* and, in it, he won the 1969 Australian NS14 Championships.[1] In 1970 I put the design into production as the Dribbly Mk 1.

Mark had designed the flotation of Mk 1 to be 'right' for two fit, young students. However, it proved a little inadequate for heavier, older crews who sailed in inland fresh-water lakes, so late in 1970 I increased the keel spring (rocker) from 5in to 6in. This became Mk 2.

---

[1] For the record, he also won both the Sharpie and the Flying Dutchman Australian Championships that year.

I sensed that Mk 2 'squatted' more than it should as it moved from displacement towards planing, so in 1971 I slightly broadened and flattened the aft bottom to create Mk 3. This hull seems to have been the first body-hiked dinghy capable of windward planing, and in stronger winds this became routine for fit, skilled crews.

Larger numbers of heavier adult crews were by now joining and sailing in the class. So in 1972 I further rounded and re-faired the bottom between unchanged chines and keel line to increase flotation a little more. In this Mk 4 hull, everything seemed to become optimised in a compatible manner. In light winds it carried excess weight with negligible performance penalty. In moderate and stronger winds its performance, when crewed by crews of equal weight, was superior to any of the competing designs in this vital and creative development class. It immediately became the benchmark to be copied. Later, the bottom of this Mk 4 hull shape became the shape of the bottom of the Tasar. Fig 10.6A (page 152) show the bottom of a Tasar – in this case with strakes and a flap taped on for experimental towing.

Photos of the bottoms of Mks 1 and 3 and other NS14 designs of that era appear on page 251 of *HPS-1*.

My younger son Julian joined the Eighteen footer class, and after a few years of sailing as a forward hand, he built *Prime I* in the winter of 1982. This was the first of his three two-hander Eighteens. The hull of *Prime I* was the 14ft waterline Tasar shape stretched to 18ft without increase in beam or depth or any other modification. In it he sailed very fast, particularly in lighter winds, and won one heat of the 1982–3 season Eighteen footer World Championships.

The flotation of the stretched Tasar proved a little inadequate for the weight of an Eighteen footer with its much bigger rig and two-solid-young-males crew, so for his 1983–4 season in two-hander *Prime II* (Fig 1.34), he further rounded the bottom between keel and chines. This was the boat on which he trialled his newly invented asymmetric spinnaker rig. This boat and its revolutionary spinnaker system was worked up on a North American exhibition tour from San Francisco to Montreal, which included sailing in Newport, RI, immediately prior to the 1983 America's Cup series which was won by *Australia II*. Back in Australia, Julian sailed a 'steady' season, and again won one heat of that season's Eighteen footer World Championships.

For his 1984–5 season in two-hander *Prime III* (photo on page 161, *HPS-1*), Julian made an even finer entry hull by drawing the maximum chine beam slightly further aft yet, and he fractionally straightened both the aft topsides and the curvature of the aft bottom. This is a very important hull because, as we shall see, it is close to being the fastest Eighteen footer hull ever designed. Again, in it he won one heat of the Eighteen footer class of the 1984–5 World Championships.

All three of these two-hander Eighteen footers demonstrated extraordinary light-air performance. Often, they won their lighter-air races by margins of 10–15%. As they were systematically improved to increase their performance in stronger winds, this performance became a threat to the now-traditional three-handers.

The class responded by banning two-hander Eighteen footers.

Over the next few years the top Eighteens grew larger year by year. They added all manner of adjustment controls which made the boats more complex to sail. But principally, they added hydraulic rams to control their rig tensions, and these increased the total weight significantly. To float the added weight the boats became huge, heavy, bulky mammoths, and the cost spiralled upwards.

Julian understood very well what was happening. During those years he sailed as forward hand, with Rob Brown as skipper, on the gun mammoths *Goodman Fielder* and then *Entrad*. He helped with the rig design, and in the 1986–7 season they won the World Championship in Auckland, New Zealand.

The Eighteen foot skiff class virtually collapsed in the 1987–8 season (Section 14.4), and in 1988, disenchanted with the affairs of the Eighteens, Julian spent the year designing and building the prototype of the two-crew Fourteen footer initially called the Exocet. Following the Falklands war, the name was changed to B-14. For the hull, he scaled down the *Prime III* shape. From its launch in the winter of 1988, this tiny 14ft waterline, low-cost, small-rig skiff performed far above expectation.

The movers and shakers of the Eighteen footer class recognised the potential of the new dynamics, and encouraged Julian to 'give it steroids' to develop a low-cost, three-hander, Eighteen footer. They arranged for the donated full-page advertisement (*HPS-1*, page 177), and from this persuaded four businesses not previously involved with Eighteens to sponsor one boat each.

Julian borrowed the *Prime III* hull, which was still in good condition, modified the topsides by raking the bow forward to get a sharper entry angle at the gunwales, re-surfaced it to plug standard, and took a mould from it for his prototype B-18. In the pages ahead we will see that the fastest Eighteens ever sailed have been close developments of this hull.

Tow tests conducted on one of these boats in March 1993 were the first to reveal a hull drag curve with no hump at about hull speed × 1.5. (Fig 10.8), and in 1994 Julian asked me to size and loft a 5m hull to float a crew of two from the old *Prime III* shape – this has become the 49er. In 1997, I again worked from the *Prime III* shape in sizing and lofting the 29er prototype 1. (It subsequently progressed with minor changes through prototypes 2, 3 and 4, principally to increase flotation for today's heavier adolescents.) In 2001, my first 59er prototype was a stretched 29er.

Mark Bethwaite's innovative 1969 *Medium Dribbly* NS14 hull shape was at least 40 years ahead of its time, and is continuing to serve the sailing community well.

14.3 ■ The B-14 and its different rig

In 1988, Julian developed the first 'flexible topmast' rig, which he put into a 14ft prototype that has since developed into the B-14 class. We will look at this boat in the pages ahead, but this rig was seminal in that it was, almost accidentally, the first step towards the modern automatic rig. To put this into perspective:

- Up to the early 1960s, it was deemed, worldwide, to be the business of a mast to be stiff and to stay straight.
- Subsequently, masts were designed to flex – but only when bent by powerful outhaul, downhaul and vang adjustment controls, and even then they bent primarily in the middle.
- On the questionable logic that if a boat sails 5% faster with three adjustments, it should sail 15% faster with nine, this trend had developed to the point where the top conventional boats were equipped with up to 13 separate adjustment controls. The top Eighteen footers adjusted similarly, but found that when they bent their tall masts sufficiently to flatten their sails the height of their hounds lowered and their rigging went slack. To handle this problem they had found it necessary to go beyond pulley-hauley rope purchase systems and add hydraulic ram systems to adjust the lengths of, and to re-tension, their shrouds and cap shrouds when they bent and straightened their masts. This complex hydraulic addition had led to runaway weight, size, and cost increases which, together with other factors, had near-devastated the class in 1986 and 1987. Julian was dismayed by this trend, and, as previously mentioned, in 1988 took a year away from the Eighteen footer class to make the point that there were other and less expensive ways to make fast sailboats.

At root, adjustment of mainsail shape by bending the mast was desirable, but the problem had been that bending the lower mast affected stay tensions.

Julian's solution was to concentrate all of the flexibility and mobility in the topmast, and not to alter the bend of the lower mast at all. In this way the stays never went slack, so all the heavy and expensive stay adjustment machinery could be thrown away.

The rig he put into his new boat was a lower mast of stiff aluminium tube which was stayed so that it was bent to a fixed curve and held rigidly at that bend. The topmast was of flexible fibreglass which bent readily in the manner of a fishing rod; it yielded easily at the tip, and so in a gust the upper leech of the mainsail yielded first.

At a second level, Julian used this opportunity to achieve three design objects:

1 The first was to make the point that a light, small, very fast boat could be low in cost. Speed need not be costly.
2 Second, he wanted to offer, to the whole mass of weekend warriors worldwide, the breathtaking fun and excitement of skiff-style, apparent-wind, high-performance downwind sailing. Until then, this had been the province of a handful of elite Eighteen footer sailors in Sydney, plus a tiny scattering of innovative followers elsewhere.
3 Third, the boat should be easy to sail for northern hemisphere crews. Specifically, its helms should not have to learn the new skill of helming from trapeze, which was at that time almost unknown beyond Australia. To achieve this he fitted to the hull 'wings' of a span such that when fully body-hiked on the wings' outer rails the crews' weight distribution was the same as if they had both been trapezing from the gunwale of a hull without wings.

The B-14 prototype took to the water amid polite curiosity, but by the end of the first season its unexpected performance was commanding widespread respect (Fig 22.2).

I witnessed the first occasion of interest. This was a 'round the harbour marathon' race conducted by the Balmoral Sailing Club. The initial 2 mile upwind leg (from the bay NE of '9' to the shore SW of '1' in Fig 1.22) was into a making 7–10 knot NE sea breeze which is about as steady as breeze ever is. The club fleet was primarily Tasars, plus Lightweight Sharpies (the Australian College boat), Lasers and Lazy Es, etc – and the B-14.

As between the Tasar and the B-14, there was not much difference between hull size, hull shape or crew weight. The B-14 sets much more sail on a slender round mast; the Tasar sets less sail on a more efficient wing mast. In the lighter breeze, the B-14's wider wingspan was not relevant.

In the lighter wind I expected the B-14 to sail about as fast as the Tasar, or perhaps a little faster to windward. It didn't. The B-14 just sailed away from the Tasar fleet upwind. It pointed just as high, and sailed to windward with a speed advantage that surprised me. When we rounded the windward mark at Manly, it had tacked away downwind under spinnaker and was out of sight. It simply vanished.

A few weeks later it delivered a much more public and significant surprise when two skilled Eighteen footer sailors borrowed it. Because its performance was generating such interest, they requested and received a most generous invitation to join the Fourteen foot skiff class's Australian championship regatta as an exhibition entry to compare performance. The 14ft LWL B-14 is longer than 14ft overall due to its raked bow, so does not comply with the class's 14ft LOA rules. The B-14 has one rig that is about the size of the 14ft skiff's middle rig, so it was expected to finish mid to low fleet.

It didn't. On performance, in conditions that ranged from calm to gale, the B-14 sailed far above expectation, always in the lead group of the fleet.

Julian had designed a very quick boat indeed, one that clearly merited close observation and analysis.

14.4 ■ The B-18 marque: origins

Regular Saturday and Sunday afternoon races of the vital, spectacular Eighteen foot skiff fleet had first been engineered by Mark Foy in about 1900 (Section 1.6). For nearly 100 years (except in times of war) this spectacle had been a weekend focus for sailors, sponsors, punters, the media, and a large spectator public who followed the skiffs as a part of their harbourside enjoyment. The skiffs, already a Sydney icon (Fig 1.8), simply reinforced their status.

As described in Chapter 1, while the conventional mass of boats continued to plod at their traditional pace, and turned few heads, the skiffs had led the performance advances from moving-ballast displacement, to planing, to apparent wind sailing – and everybody looked. But by the 1987–8 sailing season, this Sydney icon was in trouble. Looked at from a broad technical level, the skiffs had reached a second peak in a post-war saw-tooth pattern, and needed to find a new direction.

Following the 1938 pre-war demolition of the Australian heavy, big-crew, displacement skiffs by the lighter, small-crew, 'seagoing' New Zealand planing Fourteens in Hobart in 1938 (Figs 1.29 and 1.30), the post-war fleet recovery started in the late 1940s as a surge of lighter, four-hander, planing Eighteen footers with three crew on trapeze and the helm on the gunwale. As the years passed, incremental 'improvements' to the overall design all had the effect of making the boats a little bigger year by year, until in the 1970s the whole heavy lot (the first peak of the saw-tooth pattern) were superseded by tiny, light, three-handers with better sail-carrying power to total weight ratios because all three crew were on trapeze in lighter boats (Fig 1.32).

The three-handers then repeated the folly. Initially compact and popular and fast and inexpensive and successful, over the years they grew bigger wings and bigger rigs and added hydraulics and multiple adjustments (*HPS-1* Fig 20.16, page 258). The size, weight and cost spiralled out of reach of traditional sponsors and crews. That was the second peak of the saw-tooth pattern.

Sponsorship dried up, no new boats were built. The class needed a new vision.

The basic problem was economic. In the early 1980s, the economics had shaken down into a stable mix. To have one of the five or six top crews carry their company logo on their spinnaker, Sydney businesses sponsored top crews at a going rate of about $20 000 per year, with lesser sums for those less likely to win. The whole thing was local to the cities with skiffs – the spectacle was on Sydney Harbour or Auckland Harbour or the Brisbane river; it was reported in the local media; the sponsorships returned good promotional value to the local businesses; and nobody else was interested.

In the mid-1980s the new spectacular downwind speeds of these first 'wet water' apparent wind sailboats attracted the attention of a sports TV promoter and a 'Grand Prix Sailing' programme was created. The cost of running special regattas structured for TV production was shared between 12 or 15 sponsors whose products were distributed nationally. The programme quickly achieved high prime-time ratings on national TV with its much wider audience reach. But the added 'TV Fleet only' televised regatta programmes were deliberately scheduled so as not to interfere with the established weekend harbour racing. So the 'normal' skiffs with their unchanged 'local business' sponsors, and the 'TV' skiffs with their 'national business' sponsors and higher costs, still shared the same start lines in the weekend club regatta and State championship and National championship programmes, and shared the wins. So far, so good. The addition of a 'TV' element at greater cost had not significantly changed the fundamentals. At the end of 1986, there were 25 to 30 Eighteens sharing the start line every Saturday and Sunday from September until April. Most were fully sponsored; they were top-of-the-range pieces of machinery, brilliantly handled by fit, athletic crews.

The next decision, to take the TV programme to the world, changed the foundations. In the 1986–7 season, the expense of the now-global TV campaign so escalated the costs that the Grand Prix fleet divided into five 'glamour boats' supported by wealthy sponsors with global products, and 'the rest', who were progressively abandoned by their local and national sponsors.

Therefore, the whole increasingly costly sailing and TV activity became skewed towards the 'internationals'. The local and national promotion component suffered, so the local and national sponsors withdrew. They had no interest in global product promotion and saw no reason to pay the very high 'global' fees for a programme with a wider reach than they could use. To add to the problem, it was at this time that the complexity, weight and cost of the mammoth boats spiralled to unsustainable levels.

The local and national sponsors withdrew throughout 1987, and the final blow was the failure of the promoter to achieve a critical mass outside Australia for his programme. Consequently, the global sponsors withdrew at the end of 1987, and no new boats were built for the 1988 season. The class was in disarray and lacked direction.

A cabal of skiff 'elder statesmen' emerged and started to look for some new direction in which to encourage the class.

Had any other class, skiff or conventional, been able to present fast spectacular sailing, this would have been their opportunity. But none were in a position to do so.

No conventional classes, monohull or catamaran, presented a performance spectacle, and particularly a downwind performance spectacle remotely comparable with the Eighteen foot skiffs. The table of relative performances in Section 13.22 gives the speeds of the different classes in the early 1980s, and in the years since the Eighteens had simply learned to sail faster.

With respect to the Sixteens – when the Eighteens were attracted to the main harbour by Mark Foy nearly 100 years earlier, the Sixteens became the creatures of the working-class upper harbour and riverside suburbs. From 1900 until the 1950s, the Sixteen footer clubs were sailing clubs that concentrated on sailing 16ft versions of Figs 1.5, 1.6 and 1.7. In the 1950s, relaxation of the NSW liquor laws saw most of the Sixteen footer clubs change focus. They adopted professional management, rebuilt their premises, and became popular local social watering havens, with strip artists being employed to draw crowds to boost bar patronage in the evenings. A gybe mark strategically placed outside the bar window was employed to boost weekend daytime patronage. The Sixteens' class rules were employed to encourage maximum family and friend bar patronage by insisting on four crew in every boat, no wings, and only two on trapezes. This recipe does not lead to spectacular speed, so up to the late 1980s technical development of the Sixteen foot skiff was inhibited by club management policy. (Starting in the 1990s, this attitude has changed dramatically. The inner suburbs have become 'gentrified', and a huge change in attitude has encouraged a similar change in skiff design. The Sixteen foot skiffs are now following the Eighteens, and have become featherweight three-on-trapeze machines with rapidly improving performance.)

The Fourteen foot skiffs and the Twelve foot skiffs were too small and too few, and not fast enough to command attention on a stage the size of the harbour.

In 1988, Julian withdrew, disenchanted, from Eighteen footer sailing and created the light, simple, inexpensive B-14. His object was to bring to the world's sailors the new breathtaking thrill of apparent wind downwind sailing in a light, simple, inexpensive, easy-to-sail boat. When the prototype performed far above expectation in Fourteen foot skiff invitational events (such as the Tyrrell's Classic which, by custom, has become the Australian Championship) and then knocked off the gun International Fourteen in UK, the movers and shakers of the Eighteen footer class found their new direction.

When he returned from the UK, they took Julian by the shoulder, pointed him at the B-14, and entreated him to 'give it steroids'. They encouraged four businesses who had never previously sponsored Eighteens to sponsor a run of four of the yet to be designed and built new breed at about $20 000 each, and advised the world that the Eighteens were back in business with advertisements such as that in *HPS-1* on page 177. This thrust got things moving again.

This was the genesis of the B-18, and it all happened with astonishing speed. The Eighteen footer class crumbled into disarray in the 1987–8 season. The B-14 was designed and built in the southern winter of 1988. Its unexpectedly high performance level became evident in the Tyrrell's Classic (the Fourteen footers' National Championships) in January 1989, and the UK B-14 activity occurred in the northern summer early in 1989. The B-18 was designed, and the first five boats were built during the southern winter in June to September 1989, and these boats led a revitalised Eighteen footer fleet in the September to April 1989–90 southern hemisphere season.

The fact that the 'budget boats' as launched were already close to the mammoths' best performance created renewed interest and excitement, and by the beginning of the 1990–1 season sponsors were again looking for good crews to sponsor.

The cabal of elders had done their work well.

14.5 ■ The initial B-18 design

Julian's thinking was governed by three overriding considerations in developing the initial B-18 design.

First, this was his opportunity to demonstrate in the Eighteen footer class what he had just demonstrated in the Fourteens – his vision that a lighter, simpler, less expensive boat could be faster than a mammoth. His first objective was to reverse the 'bigger and costlier is always faster' thinking that had led to the sawtooth pattern and its catastrophic peaks. (In 1938, the heavy, displacement, multi-crew moving-ballast 'rag carriers' were humbled by the tiny New Zealand planers. In 1975, the big four-hander Eighteens were beaten consistently by David Porter's tiny lightweight three-hander. In 1987, the costly complex mammoth three-handers had self-destructed.)

Second, the new design must truly be of low cost. The prior fleet had collapsed because it had priced itself out of the market.

The third consideration was a new one. Because of the circumstances of the moment there was no time to build and trial a prototype, so the initial design had to be as 'safe' as was possible.

Julian was in the fortunate position of having already put three years of thinking into lightweight Eighteens. These were his three two-handers: *Primes I, II,* and *III* of 1982–3 to 1984–5, and *Prime III* had been a very fast boat indeed. So he located *Prime III*, and found to his delight that it was still in surprisingly good condition.

Plumb-stem convention was thrown to the wind and the bow was raked to give the forward gunwales a finer entry angle. (A few inches were left vertical just above the toe of the stem to allow measurers the satisfaction of measuring a waterline length of not more than 18ft (Fig 15.2).) The gunwale height was lowered and the upper topsides were flared outwards a little. The *Prime III* hull, thus modified, was re-surfaced to plug standard and a mould taken from it, and from this mould the initial five B-18 hulls were taken. One was Julian's (ie ours), and the other four were to be owned by the sponsors. A deck with a crowned foredeck and dished after deck was built into the first hull laminate and a mould taken from that. The polyester/glass laminate, framing and bonding were based on the construction of my 1975 Tasar which was proving to be extraordinarily strong and durable. This approach to the hull offered the 'lowest risk' path to the hull of what was a revolutionary minimisation experiment.

The rig concept of rigid lower mast and glass fibre topmast was transferred from the B-14. The 'power' – the righting moment – of even this tiny Eighteen was more than double that of the B-14, so this was truly a leap in the dark. But Julian stuck to his guns. For the lower mast, he used an inexpensive piece of stock 8020 (80mm diameter, 2.0mm wall thickness) T6 temper tube in place of the exotic 96mm thin-wall high-temper units of vast cost that, up to then, had been deemed essential. This lower mast was stayed to be curved and to stay rigid at that curve. The specification of the flexible glass topmast laminate for this first Eighteen was inspired estimation.

He drew a sail plan of one rig only, with all three sails of modest area, and went sailing. The cost had been held to about $A20 000.

The new 'Budget Eighteens' had hulls that were smaller, lower volume, finer in line. They could be because they were so much lighter – about 300lb lighter. The complete boat weighed 300lb and was crewed by 450lb of crew – that is, 750lb total with a crew of three, all of whom trapezed from 14ft-span wings.

In contrast, the mammoths had become huge, heavy at 1100–1200lb (total of boat plus crew), blunter at the bow, and with 22ft wings. They cost close to $100 000, and as they sailed they pushed a lot of water.

14.6 ■ The B-18 marque, development

The B-18 became the vehicle for the first five years of a surge of technical development broadly similar to the Herrick Duggan years in Montreal and the Arch Logan years in Auckland nearly a century earlier.

The changes from conventional small-sail displacement sailing to big-sail displacement sailing with moving-ballast, from moving-ballast displacement to blow-downwind planing, and from blow-downwind planing to apparent wind sailing have been the three significant technical shifts in the art of sailing.

The first was a relatively slow process of setting and handling bigger sails which was achieved by years of cut and try development during the mid- to late nineteenth century and occurred almost simultaneously in New York and in Sydney.

The second was a decade of explosive development from 1895 to 1905, which occurred simultaneously in Montreal, in Quebec, and in Auckland, New Zealand. Thanks to the efforts of historians such as Robin Elliott we now know where and when these new techniques supplanted the older ways, and often where each breakthrough first occurred.

The third, the almost accidental attainment of apparent wind capability as a by-product of cut and try development to improve tactical performance when sailing the Eighteen footers' No 1 course on Sydney Harbour, appears to be unique.

From about 1970 to 1989, it evolved slowly within a relatively evenly matched fleet, and no one boat, no particular race, can be singled out as defining the moment of change. From 1989 to 1999, the rate of change became explosive. The first half of the movement was within the Eighteens; and the second half was the advent of the skiff-derived 49er and the youth trainer 29er into the world scene, the understanding of the critical ratios, and the development of the automatic rig.

From the 'safe design' budget B-18s of 1989 to the much faster purpose-designed boats of 1991 to 1994, the focused and well-funded 1989 to 1994 performance advances were developed almost solely within the Eighteen footers that sailed in the revived Grand Prix regattas. Often, a particular advance can be placed with a particular boat at a particular time.

14.7 ■ The first 'recovery' season: 1989–90

The new vitality of this class had encouraged a number of earlier boats – including three of the mammoths – either back onto the water or to stay on the water.

For the new B-18 crews and their sponsors, that 1988–9 season was a time of familiarising themselves with their new craft. The boats were potentially fast, but most of the crews were new to Eighteens, and the learning curve they faced was very steep indeed. A significant external factor was that almost all of the recent experience within the class had been that 'bigger is better', so there were plenty of 'experienced' armchair experts and observers always ready to advise with the message 'This boat is too small. Put on a bigger mast, bigger rig, bigger sails, bigger everything'. Some of the new crews listened and acted on this advice, and suffered poorer performance as a result. This was against the designer's advice, but there were no rules, and the owners owned the boats and could do as they liked. The irony was that the crews then usually sailed more slowly and turned back to the designer for help with their bigger sails etc, so he enjoyed very little peace that season. Despite these distractions, the new boats all put in a creditable season. The crews liked them; the sponsors were happy.

The designer was not. His approach was that the boats now existed, but that there was everything to learn about them before making any changes to the design. His first prototype B-18 had been purchased by a group of Swedish sailors and taken to Sweden.

So to enable him to make his point, we (my wife Nel and I who owned the company) built a second identical boat. Julian named it *Banana Republic*, and he set about experimenting with and developing better technique as opposed to changing the design (see Section 27.10). As experience was gained, small changes were made to sail shape, foils, systems and sailing technique, and the end result was a simpler, progressively more integrated boat and crew which sailed progressively faster.

At the end of the season, Julian took this stock, standard budget boat, with nothing at all made bigger, into the Eighteen footer 1989–90 World Championships on the Brisbane river. His diminutive boat cost one-fifth the cost of most of his competitors, had 14ft wings as opposed to their 22ft wingspan, and one rig only. Despite all this, halfway through the regatta he was leading on points and in grave danger of winning. Later in the regatta stronger winds and the progressively narrower waters (due to lower tides) revealed gybe technique problems, which were corrected quickly – but not quickly enough to retain the lead (Section 15.10) and he finished fourth – but the writing was on the wall.

The tide had turned. Fast Eighteens at an affordable price were back, and sponsorship of a skiff was a viable promotional decision for appropriate businesses.

14.8 ■ The European Exhibition Tour, 1990 BY JULIAN BETHWAITE

Following that season and the World's in Brisbane, we organised an exhibition tour in Europe for the B-18s. This enabled us to do a lot of focused development. While everyone else was sitting back going skiing or whatever, four of us went to Europe on exhibition and got a double season in which to develop and try out new ideas.

The key advantage of this tour was that four motivated crews with near One-Design boats were able to escape all the 'Too small; bigger is better' distraction of the Sydney scene and co-operate in a programme of experiment, measurement and comparison. We kept careful notes of everything we did. The abnormally steady winds of Lake Garda and the other mountain lakes of north Italy were an ideal locale for comparison work. The strong mistrals of the French Riviera ensured that everything remained practical (*HPS-1*, page 257). Some of the experimentation was planned. Some was accidental and revealed the unexpected. All was valuable. Examples:

Basics like rig tensions

In the earlier era of 'adjust everything because bending lower masts and flexible boats caused slack stays and hydraulic rams were needed to compensate', it was never possible to know what the tensions were at any time on the forestay, or on the main, cap or lower shrouds. The new mechanically rigid hulls and 'adjust nothing' rigs offered, for the first time, a platform on which the tensions would be stable, and thus the opportunity to measure with confidence and repeat known settings. So – surprisingly for so sophisticated a class – the first task was to establish what were the rig tensions we were actually using, and then to experiment and measure systematically and record until we had established the fastest rig tensions in light, medium and strong winds. Before long we had established the fastest tensions for everything with the rig set-ups we were using. This work was invaluable in providing a known starting point from which we have systematically improved in the years since.

Jib to mainsail area ratios

We had taken a stock of cast-off jibs of different sizes. I systematically tried these from the obviously too small to the obviously too large while the other crews changed nothing. This way, we were able to learn with confidence what were the fastest ratios. This led to understanding that:

- Jib/mainsail ratios of 30/70 and above were slow.
- Ratios of 28/72 gave good acceleration out of the tack, but poor higher speeds.
- Ratios of 27/73 emerged as optimum – *provided*
- Forestay height was set at 67%–69% of the *flexible* mast height.

Note: At the time of this work our boats were rigged with conventional vangs. These took the form of an adjustable tension system between the mast heel and a point on the boom about one-third of the way towards the clew. Tightening the vang pulls the clew down and tightens the leech to control mainsail twist independently of mainsheet tension.

In later years we developed a rig style that uses a 'ram vang' to perform the same function, but in this case it takes the form of a (compression) strut of adjustable length above the boom which attaches to the mast via a second gooseneck about a metre above the boom gooseneck. Extending the length of the strut forces the boom down – and also forces the mast forward. To counter this, lower stays are attached to the mast at the position of the ram vang gooseneck. The advantage of this system is that it creates a strongly stayed immobile point nearly 2m above deck level, and so allows use of a smaller diameter mast.

This change affects mast dynamics. In practice, in these later rigs the forestay is attached at 68% of the height above this immobile point, and for these higher jibs the jib/mainsail ratios needed to be reduced.

Once we got the ratios right I had local sailmakers fiddle first the roach and leech shape, and then the luff round, while I played with different cap shroud tensions to set different topmast bends. After this work, all the AAMI rigs in the years following were never maximum height or maximum area.

Centreboard wetted area

Previously we had just put the centreboard all the way down and forgotten it. We experimented by putting numbers on the backs of our centreboards so that we knew exactly how much was exposed under the hull, and systematically established what was fastest depth for the pre-start slow sailing and manoeuvring for when we were pointing high after the start, and for when we were free and footing for maximum VMG to windward, and also for when we were tacking downwind at maximum VMG. We just experimented, observed and measured, and recorded, refined and refined. The speed advantage achieved by using no more centreboard area than was necessary was sometimes surprising. Over the years, the work started here has developed:

- As we reduced the immersed depth, our top speed increased, but at the expense of poor acceleration from very low speeds.
- The limit was set by the rudder.
  - I needed sufficient 'power' from the rudder to tack the boat quickly enough, so we exited the tack still sailing at 6 to 7 knots.
  - I also needed to be able to steer for balance with certainty, and in particular to be able to turn sharply downwind when heeled by an unexpected bullet when sailing fast downwind.
  - A rudder blade immersion of 35in or 875mm gave this control. Less did not.
- As we lifted the centreboard, the boat sailed faster until the depth was about the same as the rudder. Lifting it further brought no extra speed gain and saw the start of control uncertainty.
  - Our practice settled on exposing only about 36in (900mm) of centreboard once we were able to sail at the speed we wanted.

The practical result of shortening the immersed depth in this way was to give these boats a new freedom to sail at whatever speed we wanted to sail. Upwind, it led to the sail flattening and drag reduction chronicled in the pages ahead. Downwind, it led to the realisation that smaller, flatter spinnakers sail faster.

Fastest spinnaker area

An accident – which in retrospect was fortunate – led to our learning that big spinnakers are not the fastest. That lesson was learned very quickly between David Witt and myself in an event in France. David blew out a big spinnaker. We had no spares. David asked if he could borrow one. I gave him the big one, which delighted him until in the next race, which was in light air, we beat him despite being a heavier crew. (Shades of the last race of the 1983 America's Cup.) For the next regatta we exchanged, and he then beat us. We altered the position of the tack and the sheet block until it set reasonably with exactly no overlap (like the flaps on a Jumbo when they are right out), and flattened the sail as desired by easing the halyard. It was rough and ready trialling, but it worked. Soon both of us could sail faster in all winds with the smaller spinnakers.

The experimental work we were able to complete on that tour was invaluable. But that tour did much more. We were invited to sail in many countries: at Sanary on the French Riviera; on Lake Garda in Italy; at Geneva; and the B-18 prototype ended up in Stockholm, Sweden, sailing on the weir outside the palace on Christmas Eve 1990.

As the tour progressed, top European sailors approached us. We invited them to sail with us whenever possible and appropriate, and in this way started a network of skiff enthusiasts and supporters which has just grown and grown over the years. It was the impact of that tour that established the Eighteen foot skiff class in Europe.

Further, we took a B-14 with us (*HPS-1*, page 332), and this boat created such interest that it, too, became the focus of a small European following. The effect of this was far-reaching, because it put the B-14 head to head with the Johnson J-14 which was also trying to break into the European market.

Author's note

As a consequence of this, Julian Bethwaite and Peter Johnston of Sunfish-Laser scheduled a lunch in Newport, RI, the following year to discuss this situation. The outcome was that rather than compete, they decided to co-operate in the development of a new and better boat. This was the concept that became the 49er.

We will look at these developments in the chapters ahead.

14.9 ■ The beginning of the 1990–1 season

Over the years, the Eighteen footer class had always lived a turbulent history, and the three years described above had seen yet one more self-inflicted threat to its survival. In this case the alertness, experience and spontaneous action of a cabal of elders, who identified and supported the vision of one designer, had created a new, tiny fleet of small, inexpensive, potentially fast skiffs of a new concept. These had begun to show their mettle through the 1989–90 season. How good would these new craft become? How good could they become?

At the beginning of the following season, 1990–1, the game was back to its customary uncertain 'normal'. These new craft, if well sailed and presented, offered the possibility of great promotional return for a modest outlay. This was the challenge and the opportunity faced by every potential sponsor who had a need for product promotion and a taste for picking a winner.

In the spring of 1990 the judgement of potential sponsors to this new situation was positive, and a number of new sponsors and crews formed liaisons. These new teams gingered up the older boats, and an impressive, taut, shiny fleet of 25 to 30 skiffs started each Saturday and Sunday afternoon. That there were so few stragglers attested to the skill of the crews and their intention to win. The spectators flocked back.

From here, and through Chapters 15 to 19, I will focus first on the story of the AAMI sponsorship, and then on the stories of the 49er consortium and of the 29er consortium. This is partly because I obviously know exactly what happened, but primarily because from the research, development, and outcomes point of view the work of this team has been the most innovative and successful, so it properly becomes the most appropriate vehicle to carry the story of the ongoing development thrust.

I would like to stress here that all of the other crews and sponsors were trying at least as hard, and all might well be able to write stories equally interesting.

14.10 ■ The Prime two-hander experience

As a background to what follows, it is worth noting that in 1982 Julian had approached Prime Computers and suggested to them that if he did his very best to develop fast two-hander Eighteen foot skiffs this would match Prime's marketing mantra that 'you can do more with less', and that this novel approach could well bring them significant promotion at relatively low cost. Prime liked the approach and agreed.

Julian's handling of that sponsorship was enlightened. Because his was the only two-hander, the media came to him for a story whenever other news was dull. When he invented the asymmetric spinnaker rig, his media profile blossomed. He worked closely with Prime's public relations people, and they managed to score about 40% of the yachting media column inches, despite the fact that he was not then one of the class's 'kings'. Concerning the effectiveness of the skiff as a promotional tool, it is a matter of record that the Australian 'Prime Computers' offshoot for a while outperformed the parent US Prime corporation.

When the class banned two-handers following the 1984–5 season, Julian advised Prime with regret that he could no longer present the innovative image that they sought and he enjoyed, and they parted on the very best of terms and with mutual respect. I mention this to make the point that a sponsor wants media exposure, that this can be achieved in more ways than winning, and that from the Prime Computers experience Julian was well aware of this. He had also earned a solid reputation for serving his sponsor well.

14.11 ■ The AAMI background

The prototype B-18 fleet had been launched in 1989, the crews had performed creditably, and the new sponsors were happy. During this season Julian had improved the boat and his sailing to the point where he had been competitive in the World Championships on the Brisbane river that year. During the Australian winter months, he developed his understanding of the boat further during the European exhibition tour.

Demographers have described Australia, correctly, as a series of isolated 'islands' (the capital cities), which happen to be joined together by relatively uninhabited land. Because of their isolation, each island has developed a different view of what life should be about, and these differences in attitude are sharp and fiercely defended. Not surprisingly, there is in free-trade Sydney a latent resistance for all things originating in protectionist Melbourne, and vice versa. A real problem for any business from one capital that seeks to expand into the other is how to present to the new market, ideally in a way which will be embraced by them as a new local enterprise that merits their support rather than alien culture to be resisted.

Brian Keane was CEO of Australian Associated Motor Insurance (AAMI), a Melbourne mutual motor insurance business that he had grown to the point where it enjoyed much of the Melbourne market. He looked at the bigger Sydney market, and asked his Sydney friends, 'What is the best way to put a Sydney face on a Melbourne company?' One said, 'Buy a local football team and have them run around in your colours.' Another said, 'Put an Eighteen foot skiff on the harbour with your logo on its spinnaker.' Brian Keane did both.

One afternoon shortly after his return from the European tour, I was with Julian as he was unrigging in Milson Park (the skiff rigging area adjacent to the Sydney Flying Squadron in Careening Cove) when a mutual friend approached and said, 'Julian, this is Brian Keane. I think it is time you two met.' Within ten minutes, Brian and Julian had shaken hands on a sponsorship deal. The way this worked for the next five years was:

1 Julian prepared a budget for the design, construction and campaigning of an Eighteen foot skiff in AAMI livery in every scheduled Eighteen footer race in both Sydney clubs and the NSW and the World Championships. The budget included appropriate salaries for the sheet hand and the forward hand, and not for Julian. The crew assisted in the construction and rigging of the boat and would be responsible for its repair and maintenance, and its preparation for sailing during the forthcoming season.
2 The sports TV *The Skiffs* Grand Prix programme had re-started and was becoming media dominant. Within a few weeks of their initial agreement, commercial logic drove AAMI to ask Julian to extend the deal to include sailing in the televised series. AAMI paid the appropriate fees and joined the sponsor group who, together with the producer (Bill McCartney), helped shape the way that the programme developed. With this development, the overall cost of the sponsorship increased from about $20 000 pa to $130 000 pa.

Following this development, Julian and AAMI jointly considered any other TV or media promotional opportunity that was offered, and usually took advantage of it.

An example of the way an unexpected opportunity was exploited occurred when the International Sailing Federation (ISAF) High Performance Olympic Dinghy (HPOD) Evaluation Committee invited 'Works Teams' to attend an evaluation event at Torbole, Lake Garda, in September 1996, with up to three boats. Julian suggested to Brian that this could become a major promotional opportunity if we took:

- One boat with just its '49er' sail insignia and its class number – that is, as in any normal club fleet.
- A second boat that would carry an insignia on its mainsail like Mark Foy's old Eighteen footers. In this way, the ISAF and everybody else could see what that element of the skiff approach would look like should they elect to follow it.
  - For Garda we put the biggest Australian flag on the mainsail that would fit.
  - This initiative has developed into the Olympic 'National flag' graphics on the mainsails or spinnakers of all classes, which now enables TV viewers to follow their nation's Olympic fortunes during the racing.
- A third boat which would be painted in full sponsor's livery as were the Grand Prix Eighteens. In this way, potential sponsors could see what their boat would look like should they elect to follow the highly successful Australian 'Grand Prix Sailing' sports TV precedent.

'Good idea. Thanks for the suggestion. AAMI will pay for the paint job.'
The promotional value of the pictures of the 49er in brilliant AAMI livery against the spectacular backdrop of the Lake Garda mountain walls would be hard to quantify.
3 At the end of each season, the boat became Julian's property.
4 In 1990–1 and 1991–2, Julian helmed and the AAMI skiffs won both the Grand Prix series and the Eighteen footer World Championship. In 1992–3 they won the Grand Prix series and the Australian (International entry) effective world championship. (In that year, the regatta for the J J Giltinan 'World

Championship Trophy', which was vested in the League, was the League's (closed entry) Club Championship sailed in One-Design slower boats and with entry from all other boats refused.)

5 Julian then retired as helm.

The promotional clout of the skiff was huge. AAMI sponsored a skiff for the five years from 1990–1 to 1994–5. A survey conducted in 2000 (five years after the last AAMI spinnaker sailed on the harbour) found that when asked to recall and rank their 'top of the mind' sporting images, the average Sydney sports supporter recalled even then the AAMI skiff in fifth or sixth spot.

All up, Brian Keane's decision to 'put an Eighteen foot skiff on the harbour with the AAMI logo on its spinnaker' would have cost AAMI about $150 000 per year over five years. For their money, AAMI were able to enter the Sydney market without resistance, and now enjoy perhaps a quarter of a market worth some billions of dollars per year.

It wasn't all due to the skiff, but it certainly helped.

14.12 ■ *AAMI I* – the 1990–1 season

Julian's account of this follows:

The AAMI sponsorship was an enormous relief in that it enabled me to focus again. I had done my best the previous year with the 'safe' initial B-18 design and it had delivered. We had had a mixed season in which I had been pulled in different ways by the new sponsors and their crews. I had not been able to devote nearly as much time as I wished to devote and should have devoted to our own boat, Banana Republic. *Despite this, we had learned to sail fast and had come close to winning or placing in the worlds. During the subsequent winter, the experimental and development work in Europe had been seminal in crystallising my understanding of the potential of this new design style and how best to achieve it.*

Brian's encouragement was 'To go for broke in a responsible way'. This was the answer to a dream. So the first and principal difference between the previous year in which I had been both learning how best to sail Banana Republic *and at the same time trying to assist several new B-18 crews, and my first year with* AAMI I, *was in clarity of thinking. I did not have to worry about anybody other than a sponsor whose ideas were as clear as my own.*

Brian's thinking was nothing if not positive and challenging. Within a few weeks of agreeing to sponsor me for $20 000 for the Sydney club races and the World Championship, the Grand Prix TV promotion became viable again and Brian immediately opted to enter. His sponsorship outlay increased from $20 000 to $130 000. Whatever I had thought would be my best, I determined to do better.

The hull shape of AAMI I *was unchanged from that of the B-18s, but the construction and materials were different. We opted for a painted carbon-epoxy hull and deck. The parts were laminated without gelcoat and were painted after de-moulding. The weight of a thin paint film is trivial compared with the weight of gelcoat. The epoxy resin is both stronger and much more elastic than polyester resin, and is completely impervious to water and water vapour. Carbon fibre is much stiffer than glass fibre (Chapter 8). The end product was a lighter, stronger and much stiffer hull.*

The hull framing was different in that we stiffened the bow. These boats routinely sail to windward through the harbour chop at 12 to 13 knots, and the impact force of every wave crest forces the topsides inwards just behind the bow. All of the B-18s had suffered some softening of the forward topsides and extreme forward foredeck from this flexing. To eliminate it, we fitted a long horizontal breast hook between the two topsides midway between chines and gunwale. This has completely eliminated the flexing, and so has both solved the mechanical problem and also increased the speed. (Anything that flexes will sail more slowly through waves, like the Flexi-Stars vs the Euro-Stars (Chapter 11).)

The centreboard was moved much closer to the mast. All the work on the rig, and the feel of the boat, suggested that the centreboard should go further forward. In recent years the position of the centrecase in typical Eighteens had drifted aft until it was up to 4ft aft of the mast.

Conversely, in recent years, I (FB) had put the leading edges of the centreboards of my NS14s, Cherub and the Tasar only 2–3in aft of the mast step, and the boats balanced beautifully. When you think about it, both positions were logical.

The NS14, Tasar, etc are designed with a compact rig, small jib, no overlap, and a relatively flat lower mainsail. This combination gives the maximum turbine blade effect (Section 13.27) to the jib, and a forward aerodynamic centre of pressure to the lower as well as the upper mainsail. The centre of pressure of the whole rig is just aft of the mast and that is where the centreboard is positioned for proper balance.

The progressively bigger Eighteens had set huge mainsails which had to be eased much of the time, so developed much of their drive nearer the leech. With little pressure difference near the luff, there was little suction to generate any turbine blade effect on the jib. To balance this force set-up, the centreboard needed to be positioned far aft.

Looked at from this perspective, Julian's 'miniaturisation' was also a return to a much more aerodynamically efficient rig, and the centreboard positions have simply marched forward to match the progressively more forward aerodynamic centre of pressure of the sails. This combination is one of the fundamental reasons for the increased speeds of the B-18 marque boats.

(An interesting historical note is that in the late 1950s John Spencer's tiny-sail NZ 12ft Cherub won the World Championships against the huge-sail 12ft skiffs, for exactly the same reason – the smaller rig was much more efficient and sailed faster upwind.)

Julian again:

AAMI I had three rigs. A separate mast was used for its big rig, and a telescopic mast plus strops on the stays for the No 2 and 3 rigs. A lever ram at the deck forced the mast back at deck level – this was before the days of ram vangs and lower stays. We found that cap shrouds which returned to the mast at the mast base made the boat feel 'wooden' and boats rigged this way sailed more slowly. 'Flying backstays' – cap shrouds that passed through the tips of upper spreaders and attached to the chainplates – resulted in a 'looser' feel and higher speed.

The stiff lower mast and flexi topmast was working well, and we were beginning to sense that the flexi tip rig was contributing more than we suspected. Throughout the season we kept refining shroud tensions and mast bends and the luff curves and the upper battens of our mainsails.

We finished first or second in every event that season, and had the TV Grand Prix Sailing series won with an event to spare.

Occasionally, a tableau presents that reveals unexpected factors, and the way they work – and the way they work together so vividly that watching it becomes a Eureka event that alters all future expectations. Such occurred in a race towards the end of that season.

Julian was sailing *AAMI I*. In the early Grand Prix regattas around Australia and New Zealand he had started well, and performed progressively better as crew co-ordination improved and they gained experience with their boat. As they lined up for the penultimate regatta in Sydney, *AAMI I* was ahead on points and would win that season's Grand Prix series unless the gun mammoth won both races of that regatta and also the final event.

The first race in late afternoon midweek (the midweek schedule was to avoid conflict with the programmed weekend races) was into one of Sydney's 18 to 23 knot 'black nor'easters' – strong sea breeze/funnelling winds. The tableau occurred during the last windward leg, just off a prominent vantage point (Bradleys Head, '12' in Fig 1.22) where several hundred spectators had gathered as usual.

The lead boats were the mammoth approaching from the south on starboard tack and *AAMI I*, which had just tacked and was sailing east on port tack. They converged close to the headland. As they converged, the point of interest was that the sheet hand in the mammoth was having to work far harder than I had expected. He was having to ease and recover about a metre of mainsheet every few seconds to keep his boat upright, while the sheet hand in the B-18 was freeing and recovering only a few inches and the boat was sailing noticeably more smoothly. A knowledgeable spectator commented on this to me. In the strong wind, both boats were sailing through the water at about 12 to 13 knots.

The mammoth tacked onto port tack about 30m directly ahead of the B-18. Julian immediately bore away to cut quickly through the mammoth's dirty air and by the time the mammoth had re-accelerated to target speed, the B-18 was about 20m directly to leeward of the mammoth. Soon it was hidden from view behind the mammoth's sails. About a minute later it emerged ahead and climbed slowly out to windward.

Through binoculars I watched both boats. By great good fortune, the low late-afternoon sunlight from the southwest was from behind the boats and along the plane of their mainsails. This angle of the light clearly revealed small changes in sail angle and shape as variations in brightness, and this enabled me to watch and compare the action of the two mainsails simultaneously for as long as both boats remained within the binoculars' 7° field of vision.

Over the next, say, two minutes, two or three gusts washed over the two boats. As each gust struck the B-18, the mainsail flashed bright first at the top as the upper leech yielded and the top of the sail flattened, then the brightness spread downwards as the sheet was eased to keep the boat upright.

One or two seconds later the same gust would wash over the mammoth. Its mainsail went bright first at mid-height as the mid leech yielded, then the brightness spread upwards and downwards, but it never reached the top.

The difference in the way the two rigs responded to changes in wind speed was stark.

A second surprise was that during each gust the top of the B-18's sail sometimes flickered darker then bright again several times each gust, as brief lulls within the gust washed over it and the springy leech closed momentarily, then it brightened again as the next 'mini gust' pushed the springy upper leech open.

In retrospect, those two minutes were a Eureka event for me. I was able to see:

- How a springy-topmast rig responds to quick changes in wind speed.
- How a bend-in-the-middle mast rig responds to the same changes.
- That there is a profound mechanical difference between the two responses, *and*
- That the wind speed changes significantly several times within a single gust.

It was this new knowledge, and the opportunities I sensed within it, that led directly to the work described in Chapters 5, 21 and 22.

Julian won that race and the series, and it was the first of his three consecutive Eighteen footer Grand Prix wins.

The spectator crowds were back on the foreshores; sponsors were looking for potentially good crews again; the rejuvenated sports TV programme *Grand Prix Sailing* was trending towards high prime-time ratings.

That season marked the end of the costly mammoths. Julian's new flexi-tip rig was beginning to yield results. Julian:

The AAMI sponsorship starting in 1990–1 led to an Australian season in which I and my crew had been able to focus on our own boat and learn how to get the best out of it. In winning both that year's Grand Prix series, and also the World Championship a few weeks later, we demolished for ever the myth that bigger and costlier is faster.

It had needed only two years to confirm the force of the 'smaller is better' credo that had driven first the B-14 and then the B-18 development. At root, this was the belief that a smaller boat will have less wetted area, and less skin friction, and so should sail to windward faster in flat water. The smaller finer-lined boat will have a finer bow wedge angle and so less wave impact drag, so should sail faster to windward through waves. And the lighter boat will have less planing drag, so should sail faster downwind.

All these points had now been proven. Nobody was ever again going to build another huge, costly, slower mammoth. All future boats would be B-18s or close copies, exactly as all Fourteen footers became Dribbly derivatives or close copies following the dominance of that marque after its 1969 breakthrough in the NS14 class.

All of this had happened where it mattered – on the water. The boat's fight for recognition against the established mammoths had been hard-earned, race by race, regatta by regatta. By the end of the season, the boat's reputation, and my own reputation as designer, had become secure.

It was time to move on.

For the next season's boat I was considering a number of modest innovations.

These are discussed in the next chapter.

14.13 ■ Truth and politics

This is a book about higher performance sailing. To keep focus on the performance advances I want to keep the environment within which they were developed simple, and for this reason will refer to the three years during which a number of extraordinarily effective detail developments were engineered in the new B-18 marque as AAMI year 1, year 2 and year 3. Those close to the Eighteens will know that the reality was more complex, so for the sake of completeness and accuracy let me describe the environment of that time once and not refer to it again.

The first point is that the performance of *AAMI I* so impressed one skipper that he implored Julian and AAMI to sell it to him mid-season. They agreed, and Julian built a duplicate boat, but in carbon epoxy (*AAMI I* was a glass/polyester hull), together with improved internal framing, and carried on with his racing and development in the new boat – which was technically *AAMI II*. In that boat, Julian and his crew won that year's Grand Prix series and later the World Championship.

The game then became Machiavellian. The Eighteen footer environment of the time was that the Sydney Flying Squadron (SFS) in Careening Cove (just off the picture to the left of '9' in Fig 1.22) on the north shore conducted the Saturday races, plus the NSW and often the Australian Championships. The League in Double Bay (between 5 and 6 in Fig 1.22) on the south shore conducted the Sunday races to an identical format. The J J Giltinan Shield had been dedicated as the World Eighteen footer Championship trophy and was vested in the League. Of a total fleet approaching 50 boats, about half were members of one club and the other half of the other. The management policy of both clubs was that members of either club were welcome to start with both clubs. On any day there were usually about 30 starters in these club races. Of the 50 boats, seven or eight, all SFS members, were also part of the Grand Prix Sailing TV circuit. Grand Prix Sailing events were scheduled either in photogenic distant locations, or if in Sydney were scheduled as midweek events to avoid any conflict with the regular programmed weekend races (as in the example above).

AAMI I's clean sweep of both the Grand Prix and the World Championship in its first year caused huge consternation among sponsors who had paid four to five times as much for their boats and participation. Lobbying by disgruntled sponsors resulted in Brian Keane and Julian being given the ultimatum: 'Sail solely with Grand Prix sailing or sail solely with the League'. An acute irony of this was that Julian was at that time, and had for some ten years been, Sailing Director of the League.

Giving ultimatums to Brian Keane was not a smart thing to do. AAMI was getting a huge promotional return from its skiff involvement, so Brian stirred the pot. In this progressively deteriorating situation, he doubled AAMI's exposure. His response to secure maximum media attention was to sponsor two skiffs, and immediately pulled the 'AAMI' Eighteen foot skiff out of the Grand Prix. He asked Julian to design, build and campaign a 16ft skiff, which became *AAMI III*, in the brilliant red, white and black AAMI livery, and sail it with the Manly Sixteen foot Skiff Club on North Harbour every Saturday as a stalking horse. The Sixteens had never attracted serious media attention, and nothing changed, but this exercise certainly drew attention away from the real player.

Brian asked Julian to carry on with his intensive Eighteen footer development with a new boat. This was Julian's next-generation Eighteen foot skiff, but it was painted in sombre black and grey, and named *All States*. 'All States' happens to be the name of a little-known AAMI subsidiary valuation company.

This boat, Julian and his crew sailed on Sundays. *All States* was a technically brilliant boat that suffered a horror year. It just made the cut into the Grand Prix Sailing finals event. In the days immediately prior to the Grand Prix final event, it was re-painted and re-badged as *AAMI IV* in the full brilliant AAMI livery, won the televised Grand Prix series, and went on to win the World Championship too for a second year. The media impact was huge. (The detail is given in Chapter 15.)

Along the way it posted, on one perfect day, the fastest time to complete the No 1 'round the islands' course ever sailed; 49 minutes and some seconds to cover the 15.4nm 'straight line from buoy to buoy' distance.

So much for the effectiveness of ultimatums. That one crumbled into irrelevance and no more was heard of it.

The following year, the third, saw Julian build and campaign *AAMI V*, and again win both the Grand Prix series and the Australian Championships which from that year on substituted for the World Championships.

This needs an explanation. Wherever there is fierce competition for great goals, there will always be politics – and Grand Prix sailing and Olympic sailing are no exceptions. A practical definition of politics is 'who gets what, where and when'. Sometimes, a grab for more power or influence can destroy the very thing desired. So it was with the crazy policy decisions of 1993.

The world situation at that time was that the Eighteen foot skiffs, with their unrivalled speed and spectacle, plus their highly developed and successful, high-rating, Sports TV *Grand Prix Sailing* presentation, were in a strong position to take this sort of sailing to the world.

Developments within the Olympic organisation strongly encouraged this. The Olympic Games were growing, event by event, into a sports TV extravaganza that was becoming so expensive that it could be paid for only by huge TV rights. The value to TV lies in spectacle. Of absolute importance was the fact that TV coverage of the sailing of the conventional Olympic class boats had been declining Olympics by Olympics, and sailing at the Olympics of 1992 had been so dull that it had generated near zero TV product. Both the International Olympic Committee and the International Sailing Federation were looking very hard at the contrast between the minimal and near financially worthless TV sailing outcome from the Olympic sailing in conventional boats and the high-rating Australian *Grand Prix Sailing* TV programme that showcased the spectacular speed of the skiffs. We will have more to say about this later.

Had the Eighteen footer class, the sponsors, the crews, the clubs and the TV producer all pulled together for a few more years, we would have seen Eighteen footer apparent wind skiffs worldwide by 1995 or 1996. But this was not to be. For whatever reason, one of the two Eighteen footer clubs, the League, chose to withdraw co-operation. A Sydney icon was threatened and the earth moved (Section 7.4).

The status quo had been established by 50 years of custom, not contract, so there could be no solution by recourse to the protest room or the law courts. Conflict resolution at the highest level was used, but to no avail. The League was adamant. The one trump card they thought they held was that the J J Giltinan Trophy, donated in the early 1900s and raced for as the World Eighteen Footer Championship ever since, was vested in the League. But even that did not work. When at the end of the season the League scheduled an 'Eighteen Footer World Championship' regatta, but with the same entry exclusions, it was correctly reported by the local media as a local closed-entry club championship and was virtually ignored by the foreshore followers.

From that point, on a new writ began to run. The Sydney Flying Squadron continued its Saturday club programme which culminated in the Australian Championships, open to any Eighteen footer from anywhere in the world. Within its programme it hosted the Grand Prix skiffs which contested not only the Club's events, but also an additional and completely separate series of televised regattas sailed at selected photogenic locations around Australia and New Zealand.

I have inserted this section both to explain exactly what happened, and to make clear that for simplicity from an 'Eighteen footer performance advances point of view', these three years will be described from here on as AAMI year 1 in 1990–1; AAMI year 2 in 1991–2; and AAMI year 3 in 1992–3.

In each of these years, Julian designed, built, managed, campaigned, sailed and won both the Grand Prix series and either the World Championship in years 1 and 2, or the Australian championship in year 3 (when the 'World Championship' had become a closed-entry club championship sailed in slower boats).

The top ten or so Eighteens were all trying just as hard. The Grand Prix scoring system was such that right up to the last regatta, the object was to qualify as one of the six in the final regatta. At the start of the final three race regatta, all boats started with zero points, so any one of the six boats that had qualified for the final regatta could win. In this way, uncertainty, continuing interest, competitive pressure and excitement were maintained right to the very end.

After these three years of designing, building, campaigning and winning in the fastest sailboats in the world at the time – the pinnacle level of this new sailing – Julian retired from helming Eighteen foot skiffs.

Chapter 15 • Design Refinement for Long-course Speed

by Julian Bethwaite

Author's note

This chapter has been written by Julian Bethwaite, apart from Section 15.11, which is by me.

15.1 ■ The second design revolution

In the 1989–90 season, the initial smaller lightweight 'Budget' B-18s – the prototype (which went to Sweden mid-season), plus the four others, then my *Banana Republic* – had sailed with the fleet and had performed creditably. The best of them was already near the top of the fleet. My season had been one of constant distraction, spent largely in responding to the calls of the new crews, encouraging, coaching, and helping in all ways possible.

The following month or two of concentrated development by a small, focused and co-operative group of sailors during an exhibition tour in Europe, particularly the weeks spent training in the mountain valley lakes of Italy with their fresh and abnormally steady winds, enabled this group of top crews to learn more about their new boats in a few weeks than had been possible in the whole of the confused Sydney season.

The following season, 1990–1 (AAMI year 1), became the year in which I was able to develop efficient handling and sailing techniques, and the performance we achieved demonstrated the full effectiveness of the superior 'power to weight' ratios that flowed from the move towards a smaller, lighter, finer-lined boat.

At root, this was the belief that a smaller boat will have less wetted area, thus less skin friction, and so should sail to windward faster in flat water. The finer-lined boat will have a finer bow wedge angle and thus less wave impact drag; and so should sail faster to windward through waves. And the lighter boat will have less planing drag, so should sail faster downwind.

The AAMI sponsorship starting in 1990–1 led to an Australian season in which I and my crew were able to focus on our own boat and learn more about how to get the best out of it. We won both that year's Grand Prix series and also the World Championship. This performance demolished for ever the myth that bigger and costlier is faster.

It had needed only two years to confirm the force of the 'smaller is better' credo that had driven first the B-14 and then the B-18 development. All the key points had now been proven. Nobody was ever again going to build another huge, costly, slower mammoth. All future boats would be B-18s or close copies, exactly as all Fourteens became *Dribbly* derivatives or close copies following the dominance of that marque after its 1969 breakthrough in the NS14 class.

All this had happened where it mattered – on the water. The boat's fight for recognition against the established mammoths had been hard-earned, race by race, regatta by regatta. By the end of the season, the boat's reputation, and my own reputation as designer, had become secure. It was time to move on. I began by considering a number of modest innovations for the next season's boat.

15.2 ■ The emerging promotional effect

At this point, the boat, the crew and I received a huge boost from an unexpected quarter. It turned out that the Eighteen was really beginning to work as a promotional tool for AAMI.

Brian Keane (CEO of AAMI) had bought a football team that was running around in AAMI's colours, and he had also sponsored the skiff. A football team is big-money sponsorship. The promotional returns were being monitored closely and at financial year end, the team was indeed achieving the expected promotional return.

But what had surprised everybody was that the same measurements revealed that the AAMI skiff was achieving greater – sometimes far greater – promotional returns than the football team, and for a fraction of the cost!

So Brian, in thanking me, encouraged me to think, not in terms of whatever I may have considered to be modest or reasonable development, but to 'go for broke in a responsible way' with whatever I thought might improve the skiff, regardless of whether others might think it responsible or not. Specifically, he encouraged me 'to spend what I deemed fit on any project I deemed worthwhile'. This encouragement changed my personal focus from one in which the sponsorship was a high-level recreation exercise, into one in which delivering best value to the sponsor became my primary object.

(I later learned independently that other sponsors had similarly been pleasantly surprised by the promotional return from their skiffs, and had similarly encouraged their crews to 'think bigger'.)

15.3 ■ Revised plan

After considering the possible options, I decided to embark on a broad series of programmes that would flow over the next few years. From these, and starting immediately over the winter ahead, I decided to pursue six primary technical thrusts:

1. Before designing and building a new boat, we would repeat a European Exhibition tour during the early Australian winter months similar to those we had found so advantageous in the years immediately prior. During this tour we would plan time for focused measurement, development and training in the steady-wind mountain lakes of Italy.
2. To use the then-new GPS capability to measure not only our best straight-line speeds upwind and downwind in different wind strengths, but to measure also the not-best speeds and find out why. Also, we would measure our actual tacking, gybing and mark-rounding performance.
3. To make use of this new GPS-derived knowledge, plus the training opportunity to develop better tacking, gybing and mark-rounding handling techniques, if these appeared possible.

These three thrusts should improve our understanding and handling of the present boat. In addition, we would:

4. Measure the hydrodynamic drags of the best hulls presently sailing.
5. Pursue in the new design a number of 'second order' efficiencies that I had been considering. Principal among these were to reduce aerodynamic drag to the extent possible, and also to pursue second-order weight reduction.
6. Equip the new boat with new equipment – specifically, the self-tacking jib and the spinnaker chute – and trial this and work it up.

These three thrusts had the potential to give us a better, faster boat.

I felt that this programme would be about the limit that we could handle properly in one year.

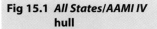
Fig 15.1 *All States/AAMI IV hull*

15.4 ■ Cosmetics

In addition to whatever I had been thinking, we were immediately asked to think in terms of a promotional goal that was being developed by AAMI's marketing group.

AAMI's marketing manager came to me and said, 'Julian, we need to change the face of the boat. AAMI is an insurance company and we want to soften our image and present as friendly. The skiff is working very well promotionally, but it looks brutal and a bit aggressive.'

We handled this in two ways:

From the livery point of view, we put the girl's face on the boat, and generated the word 'Lucky', which has become the hallmark of the campaign created at that time.

From the technical point of view, one of my objects was already to 'streamline' the hull and rig, and this dovetailed perfectly with the desire to soften the image. The more I worked to reduce aerodynamic drag, the smoother the boat looked and the happier the marketing people became (Figs 15.2 and 15.3).

That exercise in cosmetic styling led directly to the elegant styling of the 49er a few years later.

Fig 15.2 All States/ AAMI IV cosmetics

15.5 ■ 1991–2 – *All States/AAMI IV*, year 2 – design objects

In considering 'How to do it better', the primary object of Eighteen footer skiff design in 1991–2 was beginning to be dominated by the growing promotional success of the *Grand Prix Sailing* Sports TV programme, which was achieving high ratings in prime-time TV. Competitive and promotional success in the televised Grand Prix regattas was emerging as the overriding design object. Compared with this goal, success in Club, State and World Championships was becoming secondary.

Although the race environment was already changing, my conclusion was that the dynamic object remained unchanged. In the year ahead we would still be sailing copies of the traditional long Sydney courses. The Grand Prix events were programmed to be sailed in a series of photogenic locations around Australia and New Zealand, and some of the courses were beginning to become shorter for TV reasons, but it was to be another year again before this would affect design.

So in the simplest terms, the Grand Prix format would be one of high speed drag races in which the start and tactics counted for little, and the winner would be the boat that could sail fastest between the marks of long-leg courses. This was the design object.

15.6 ■ The European Exhibition Tour, 1991

In the early weeks of the 1991 southern winter, we repeated the learning and training technique of previous years, in which four crews and boats went to Europe for a four-week tour. We sailed intensively, shared knowledge, and used the then-new GPS. We measured not only the more flattering 'target' speeds upwind

Fig 15.3 *All States/AAMI IV* at Rottnest Island

and downwind in each wind strength when all was set and going perfectly, we also used them to find out what happened during a typical tack and gybe, and how long it took to accelerate back to target speed. In this way we were able to measure accurately how much speed and time we lost in tacks, gybes and re-acceleration as compared with a competitor who did not tack.

During this research and development, one of my basic rules was that in an Eighteen there are already enough variables so it is wise to keep one thing constant. In this case, we elected to keep the jib sheet tension as the constant. All our development was focused on keeping the forestay tension constant and engineering the rig for optimum mainsail response and to sail by steering and trimming the mainsheet on the basis of a jib that was set for the mean wind and not altered other than when essential.

15.7 ■ Tacking technique

The 'traditional' way we had been tacking in boats with separate port and starboard manually cleated jib sheets was as follows:

The forward hand's task was the most demanding. Two seconds before the tack, he would ease and recleat the jib sheet to take advantage of the circular air flow into the jib during the tack (Section 26.4). Between loss of power as the boat entered the tack and restoration of drive force, he had to unhook from trapeze, start to cross, uncleat the jib sheet, complete the crossing of 17ft wings, pick up the new jib sheet, and trim it in and cleat it at an exact position, hook onto new trapeze, and adopt trapeze stance on the new side. When re-accelerated, he needed to trim in the jib sheet.

The skipper's and sheet hand's tasks had been easier.

The skipper had moved the tiller smoothly to full deflection over about two seconds to start the turn and had simultaneously stood up, then unhooked, dropped the tiller extension, crossed, turned, picked up the new extension and arrested the turn smoothly prior to hooking up and moving onto the trapeze on the new side.

The sheet hand's task was similar, except that to maintain balance he followed well behind the forward hand and skipper.

Measurement

Our first GPS measurements of what we were actually achieving were so different from expectation that we found them hard to believe. While the GPS readout of rapidly changing speed necessarily lags by a few seconds, it was quite good enough to alert us to how much speed we were losing through the tack, and we were losing much more time and distance per tack than we expected. It quickly became the first priority to improve tacking technique to the extent possible. The measured figures were:

Speed at start of turn	13 knots, 22ft per sec, 6.7mps
Speed at end of turn	3.5 knots, 6ft per sec, 1.8mps
Time to turn 90° with smooth start and arrest	8.0 secs
Time from start of tack to regain target speed 13 knots	20 secs

If we assume straight-line deceleration and acceleration, mean speed is 8.25 knots, 13.9fps. So:

Distance sailed by tacker in 20 secs at 13.9fps	= 278ft	85m
Distance sailed by notional rival who does not tack	= 440ft	134m
Distance lost per tack	= 162ft	49.4m

On the Sydney Harbour No 1 course, there are a minimum of five tacks each windward leg if all goes perfectly and there is no awkward conflicting traffic, which is rare. Most races call for 20 tacks or more.

Twenty tacks at 50m lost per tack is 1000m lost per race in tacks. This was bad enough, but one of the things I had in mind for the next season's boat was to use smaller foils. Small foils do not work well at low speeds. That minimum speed of 3.5 knots did not look encouraging.

As soon as we realised how great were these losses, conservation of speed and minimising these losses became the overriding design and development object.

Analysis

The reduction in speed while tacking from 13 to 3.5 knots had to be due to the three big hydrodynamic drags – the straight-line drag of the hull, the added drag due to circular waterflow, and the drag of the deflected rudder – plus the generally smaller aerodynamic drag of hull, crew and rig.

We experimented to get a feel for the relative importance of the three big hydrodynamic drags by:

- Just letting the sheets go and measuring the rate of slowing without turning. This gave us baseline data on what to expect from the hull's momentum and its straight-line drag.
- As above, plus 'waggling' the tiller to add rudder deflection drag. The much more rapid slowing due to the deflected rudder was surprising.

- Turning progressively more tightly to understand the importance of circular waterflow drag. Up to a certain point, turning more tightly increased the rate of slowing but shortened the turn to a greater extent – so the speed loss became less. Beyond that point, the drag increased faster and the speed loss increased.

Change and trial

At this point, creativity, enthusiasm and a willingness to be different took over. The changes started by the work at Lakes Garda and Maggiore were continued following our return with the design and building of the new boat with its different equipment. Further on-the-water measurement of the performance of the new craft followed, and at that point we refined the new handling techniques further by adding the ooch and pump which had been made possible by the self-tacking jib. All this was completed in time to be competitive through the following season.

The crew tasks in an Eighteen see the forward hand as the most mobile body, so he is the balancer. If in a lighter unsteady breeze the boat begins to roll to windward in a lull, it is the forward hand who moves and runs across the wing as far as is necessary to keep the boat upright. For years it was a commonplace that as the forward hand ran, say, from left to right, his acceleration would drive the bow from right to left, and the skipper routinely applied the necessary helm to keep the boat straight.

Some lateral thinker came up with the seminal observation, 'If in a tack the forward hand were to move first, this would turn the boat into the tack without the need to deflect the rudder so much.' From this comment, a whole season of experimenting, trying new ideas, developing a new handling technique, developing new equipment design, and practising and perfecting new art began to flow.

When we thought about tacking in broader terms, we came to understand that the time-honoured 'standard' Eighteen footer tacking technique, in which the skipper always moved in first, had in fact been set partly by the optimum time the heavier hulls of earlier years had needed to turn through 90° (Chapter 26) which had been about 8 seconds, and partly by the time needed by the forward hand to complete all his previously essential tasks (and the time needed to trim in metres of sheet and then re-cleat it to an exact setting is significant). We realised that with our lighter, faster boats, plus a self-tacking jib, that a new technique might be faster, and over some weeks of experimentation (during which we had to imagine the self-tacker) we accomplished just that.

From first principles we theorised that:

- The forward hand and the sheet hand were furthest ahead of the rudder.
- If both were to accelerate hard across the boat, this would initiate the turn into the tack with greatest angular acceleration.
- This procedure would capsize the boat unless the skipper stayed on trapeze until the wind force increased from the new side.
- Therefore the skipper should logically move last.

We tried it. The helms found it a shock to the system to stay on trapeze and watch them go, but it worked! After a few days it began to feel natural, and we then set about improving it further.

The first improvement was again from theory. We reasoned that if the forward hand and the sheet hand were to pivot facing aft rather than forward as they turned prior to hook-up, the torque of their turns would increase the boat's rate of turn the other way.

We tried it, and it worked. We tried the skipper turning aft too. That did *not* work. The boat may have turned a little faster, but the skipper lost orientation momentarily, and the tacks became uneven. So we quickly rejected that as counter-productive!

The second improvement was from measurement. Once we were tacking well with the new technique, we measured what were the tack times and exit speeds: if we slowed a little prior to tacking; if we tacked at target speed; and if we accelerated to faster than target speed prior to tacking.

To our delight, we found that if we accelerated to about 2 knots faster than target speed prior to entering the tack, the optimum rate of turn became faster, the speed loss became less so the exit speed became greater, and the time to re-accelerate to target speed became the minimum.

Because the exit (minimum) speed was greater, we were able to pull the centreboard up a few inches more.

This was one of the key factors in increasing target speed to about 14 knots with the new boat, and the whole manoeuvre became tighter and faster yet.

The third improvement was unexpected and we did not grasp its potential until we were sailing the new boat with its self-tacking jib. Previously, the forward hand's need to pick up, trim in and cleat the new jib sheet had meant that he was preoccupied with these tasks as he approached his new trapeze position, so close co-ordination between forward hand and sheet hand was neither possible nor expected. But with the self-tacking jib all these extra tasks had vanished and forward hand and sheet hand found that they could co-ordinate in generating a great powerful impulse-pump.

It works like this:

The forward and sheet start running almost together; and the helm steers to spin the boat at the optimum rate of turn, and also to keep it level. As the forward and sheet hands grasp the trapeze handles and pivot aft to hook up, they let the boat heel a little, then together drive the wing down to flick the masthead to windward just as the mainsail fills with the circular air flow. At this point the sheet hand applies a mighty pump. This both stops the boat turning and shoots it forward. The rudder centres by itself. The skipper adjusts heading for acceleration mode, and a few seconds later, as target speed is regained, the jib and main are sheeted in and the boat is pointed higher for maximum VMG mode.

At the end of the development process, the measurements and sums with the new technique became as below. These assume the same 13 knot target speed in the same wind. In practice, by that time the target speed had become 14 knots:

Speed at start of turn	13 knots, 22ft per sec, 6.7mps
Speed at end of turn	7.0 knots, 12fps, 3.6mps
Time to turn 90° with smooth start and arrest	5.0 secs
Time from start to regain target speed	13 secs

If we assume straight-line deceleration and acceleration, mean speed through the tack is 10 knots, 17fps. So:

Distance sailed by tacker in 13 secs at 17fps	= 221ft	67.5m
Distance sailed by notional rival who does not tack	= 286ft	87m
Distance lost per tack with new technique	= 65ft	19.5m
Distance lost per tack with old technique	= 162ft	49.5m
Distance gain per tack between new and old technique	= 97ft	30m
Time gain per tack at upwind speed	= 4.5 secs	
Time gain per 20 tack race	= 1 min 30 secs	

This improvement had been achieved partly by use of a better tacking technique, and partly by fitting a self-tacking jib sheet system. (Section 15.7 details the technique, and Section 27.10 summarises it.)

That seminal comment by somebody at Garda – 'If in a tack the forward hand were to move in first ...' – had led to a most creative few months. What we had done, with the help of the new GPS measurements, was to develop a new three-part tacking technique that was very different from, and more efficient than, anything used previously:

- A 5-second pre-tack part in which speed was increased from 13 to 15 knots.
- A 5-second tack manoeuvre part in which, if the crew co-ordinated in a synchronised manner, the boat rotated through 90° and lost speed from 15 to 7 knots.
- An 8-second post-tack acceleration part in which the target speed of 13 knots was regained.

Of critical importance, we had realised that the crew could anticipate and synchronise if, and only if, the skipper turned the boat at the same rate of turn every time. If or when this did *not* happen, anticipation was impossible, co-ordination was lost, and the exit speed dropped to 2 or 3 knots. This is why the technique had not worked when the skipper tried facing aft when he turned. He had lost orientation and the rate of turn had become inconsistent. From this we learned that it was essential that the skipper face forward and retain uninterrupted forward vision and orientation throughout the manoeuvre.

15.8 ■ Eighteen footer racing tack

When I first started sailing Eighteens, the skipper used to go into the boat first and sit with his hand on the tiller ready to tack. By the end of the AAMI year 2, the skipper was the last person to go in. The actual process of a tack is that you have to sort things so that everybody knows that you are about to tack. Initially we used to do it counting down from five or three. Quite often on our boat, Andrew or David would call the tack. As skipper of an Eighteen in those days, you were just driving the boat as fast as you possibly could, and other than a call such as 'Julian, you had better look at this', I would not look beyond the bow, the next wave and the sails, so usually it would be the crew who would be calling the tack.

Once the call 'We've got to tack' was made, we would go into countdown procedure and put the boat through a tack. For a quick tack, the countdown was from two and there would be no pre-tack acceleration. Normally David would say 'Ten seconds to tack' and start counting.

At −5
The jib sheet would go out 1½in at the clew, and the mainsheet would be eased a similar amount. I would bear away about 2–3°, and the boat speed would increase.

At −1
The second change was to reduce the braking force of the deflected rudder as much as possible. So at countdown 'one', the forward hand stood up, and at 'Go' he started running across the boat. His mass accelerating across the boat forward of the slightly deflected rudder turned the bow into the wind. As he reached the other side, he grasped the trapeze handle and turned facing aft. His 'facing aft' body turn added further torque to the 'into wind' turn of the boat.

At 'Go'
At 'Go' – that is, one second later – the sheet hand stood up and started running a shade behind the forward hand. He similarly turned facing aft as he grasped his trapeze and hooked up.

The dynamic effect of the two bodies accelerating across the boat well forward was that the boat swung into the tack quickly and needed little rudder angle, so there was little rudder drag.

I stayed on trapeze, moved the tiller away slowly at first, but then firmly, and steered to keep the boat level as it turned. The rate of turn was always the same.

At about 3
As the boat reached head to wind, by which time the forward hand was already moving out on trapeze on his new side and the rudder was at full deflection, I stood up, dropped the tiller extension, and ran.

At about 4
As the boat neared its new aiming point, the mainsail would begin to fill in the circular air flow. The sheet hand and the forward hand would together 'ooch' the windward wing down to drive the masthead to windward and the sheet hand would simultaneously give a mighty pump on the mainsheet. The resulting impulse-pump of the mainsail into the circular air flow would convert the angular momentum of the turning boat into a solid impulse of forward thrust to start the re-acceleration process. In doing so, it would arrest the turn and the rudder would centre naturally.

By 5
The skipper had by this time grasped the new tiller extension and immediately adjusted the heading for optimum acceleration. Sometimes he would miss his hook-up, in which case he would simply steer while swinging by hand. As the boat settled into its acceleration, the sheet hand would reach aft and lift him to facilitate the hook-up.

At about 13
The boat would be up to target speed, and all three of us would co-ordinate to trim in jib, and trim in mainsail, and steer higher for maximum VMG mode.

The big difference in technique between the earlier and later tacks was that originally the skipper went in first. By the end of our 'tack technique for self-tacking jib' development I went in last, always, even in what we called safety tacks.

The difference in performance was that with the new technique the boat regained target speed 6.5 seconds sooner; the time lost per tack compared with a boat that did not tack was about 4 seconds less.

15.9 ■ Eighteen footer safety tack

The tack described above was the racing tack. In the 1% situation where in the last race all we had to do was finish, or if it really was blowing at 25 to 28 knots and we had to finish or had to get into a breakwater or similar, we did have what we called a safety tack – which was pretty basic.

We kept the sequences, the co-ordination and the synchronism the same, but backed off on the dynamics:

- We did not increase speed pre-tack.
- The skipper would stay on the wire and turn the boat as in the racing tack, but the turn was more deliberate.
- The boat was held level throughout the tack.
- There was no effort to ooch or pump.
- The boat was deliberately turned a little too far.
- The forward hand uncleated the jib sheet and held it by hand.
- All three crew hooked up and settled. Only then did they sheet in.

This was also a safe and useful technique in big waves.

A summary of the movements of the racing tack and the safety tack above appears in Section 27.10.

15.10 ■ Gybing technique

Improving our gybing technique was something that required about two years to get right. There were three stages:

Stage 1

Our starting point had been the 'classic' Eighteen footer 'blow-downwind' handling technique in which the gybe is completed as quickly as possible. In this technique, as soon as the gybe is called, the boat is turned with a high rate of turn, all three crew complete their tasks as it turns, the skipper reverses the helm as the boom goes across, the boat is steadied on its new heading, and brought under control with steer-for-balance and smart trapezing and sail handling. We now see this as a 'synchronised co-ordination' manoeuvre in which all three functions of steering, sail trimming and balance, by all three crew members, occur as one synchronised and co-ordinated burst of activity while the boat turns.

Because it is easier for the skipper to change hands on sheet and tiller extension if he faces aft as he turns, this was traditionally the standard practice. The skipper would call the gybe, start the turn, move quickly across the boat facing aft changing hands as he went, and in this way be already in position to exercise firm control by reversing the helm by the time the boom swung across.

As the fleet moved from blow-downwind to tack-downwind dynamics, and then to lighter, more slender boats, there had been so much else to learn and do differently that it had not occurred to us until the end of year 1 with *Banana Republic* to question the basics of the gybe manoeuvre.

Our handling of gybes that year, primarily in Sydney Harbour, had been adequate, with few swims. But the World Championships on the Brisbane river were a different story. The early races were in moderate winds and flood tides with a wide waterway. Halfway through the regatta we led the scorecard, but with lower tides and stronger winds later in the regatta, the river channel became narrower and called for larger numbers of gybes as we tacked downwind. We started capsizing and lost the lead.

Stage 2

Urgent crew discussions brought a critical factor to light – that the way I was turning the boat in the gybes was so inconsistent that neither the sheet hand nor the forward hand could anticipate and so could not co-ordinate with me or with each other.

This accusation of inconsistency stung, because I was conscious that it was true. I knew that *whenever I faced aft in a turn I lost orientation*, and had already been concerned because I knew that I was unable to steer for balance during a critical part of each turn. Now I was being told that the crew couldn't do their job either because I was not delivering a fixed rate of turn every time.

We changed technique mid-regatta. I forced myself to face forward as I turned.

It worked like magic. Prior to each gybe I assessed the conditions of the moment, called the gybe, forced myself to turn facing forward and so retained uninterrupted forward vision and orientation as the boat turned. The boat turned at a fixed rate of turn every time, and I could steer for balance within and throughout the whole turn. The crew rapidly developed co-ordination, and the capsizes ceased.

It was too late. We had lost the lead, then the kingplank and foredeck softened and we lost rig tension, and *Banana Republic* finished fourth. But better gybes were a 'work in progress'.

It was because of this experience that we had immediately identified the cost in inconsistency when the skipper tried facing aft when tacking. Facing aft was fine for the forward hand and the sheet hand, *but we had learned that the price of the skipper facing aft in any manoeuvre is too high*.

Stage 3

This was the ability to use the GPS to measure what was really going on in the gybes as we had in the tacks. Because the entry speed, deceleration and subsequent acceleration are so much higher in the gybe than in the tack, the lag in GPS readout introduced more uncertainty, but there was no doubt that our minimum speeds were much lower than we had previously imagined. This suggested that we should take a whole new approach to handling technique in our search for ways to do it better.

15.11 ■ The environmental factors BY FRANK BETHWAITE

Author's note

Sometimes, the outsider can see more of what is going on…

Julian Bethwaite, in creating the tape from which this chapter was written, used a strange 'verbal shorthand' to describe the effects of factors that had not yet crystallised in his mind – for example:

There are two types of gybe. There is the gybe you do because you can do it, and there is the gybe you do because you want to do it. Far too many people gybe because they can do it in a spot where they want to do it. The really good people can gybe wherever and whenever they want to. Further, there is a right time to gybe and a wrong time to gybe. A very good skipper can gybe at the wrong time and survive. Unless you are very good you have to gybe at the right time, or accept the probability of capsize if you must gybe at the wrong time. The only way you can become good is by practice in which you pre-set your gybe time or position and gybe at that time or position regardless of the wave state and/or wind state at that instant.

Charlie McKee (Olympic Bronze Medal in the 470s at Atlanta, plus a second Olympic Bronze in the 49ers at Sydney 2000) used the same sort of verbal shorthand in one of his 1998 'McLube Reports' in which he describes a strong-wind 49er regatta: '… they showed why they were World Champions. They gybed where they wanted. We gybed where we could …'

I suggest that both Julian and Charlie are expressing the effects of three interrelated factors that are now better understood than they were 10 or 15 years ago:

1 The difference between perception and reality in ideal conditions.
2 The difference between perception and reality in real wind and waves.
3 The difference between the 'synchronised co-ordination' that is fastest for all tacks, mark roundings and

conventional gybes, and the 'sequential execution' that is both fastest and safest for apparent wind gybes (Section 26.5).

1 In ideal conditions

The perception of a gybe in any conventional 'wind from behind' boat is:

A The gybe is quick.
B There will be no significant loss of speed.
C There will be a significant sudden reversal of heeling force as the boom cracks across.

In this case, there is no difference between perception and reality.
The perception of a gybe in any 'wind from ahead' apparent wind boat is:

A The gybe is quick.
B There will be no significant loss of speed.
C There will be no sudden reversal of heel force.
In this case, all three perceptions are wrong. The realities are:

A Quick

Wrong   All tack-downwind gybes must involve a turn through generally 70–90° (followed by a bear-away as the boat accelerates). At a rate of turn of, say, 30° per second with a smooth entry and exit, this will typically take about 5 seconds. During this period, there will be no drive force, or it will be negligible.

B No speed loss

Right   But only for a heavy keelboat that is sailing at hull speed or less. These boats carry their way because their momentum is huge and their low-speed drag is small.

Wrong   For all light skiffs with trivial momentum that enter the gybe sailing fast. We have seen above that the speed loss measured by GPS during an Eighteen footer tack was from 13 knots at entry to 7 knots at exit 5 seconds later.

If we look at the gybe dynamics of a 300kg 49er in a wind of 12 knots, we see:

Table 15.1 Speed loss in turns

At boat speed	Hydro drag	Added drag of circular waterflow plus rudder deflection (say 30%)	Total drag	Deceleration
17 knots	71kg	21kg	92kg	2.5 knots/sec
13 knots	55kg	18kg	73kg	2.05 knots/sec
9 knots	30kg	9kg	39kg	1.1 knots/sec

From inspection, a light skiff will lose on average about 2 knots per second as it turns, so will exit the gybe at about 7 to 8 knots. This is the price it pays for being light. This calculation is also consistent with the GPS measurements of the more leisurely tack, and the GPS indications through the gybe.

C No sudden reversal of heel force (in ideal conditions)

Wrong   We see in B above that the apparent wind will be from behind in the later stages of a moderate-wind gybe, even in the ideal case.

Light   In 6 knot winds, a 49er will enter the gybe at up to 12 knots, exit at about 6 knots, and there will be no reversal. In light winds this is, in any case, of little significance.

Moderate   In the 12 knot example above, there will be an apparent wind from aft of about 5 knots at the end of the gybe.

Strong   In 20 knots, the boat will enter at about 24 knots, exit at about 10 to 12 knots, and there will be a strong reversal of heel force.

2 In real wind and waves

The wind factor

Wherever there is breeze, there will be gusts and lulls, so the reversal of force will be greater for 50% of the time, and less for the other 50%.

The wave factor

Whenever there are significant waves, the boat will be slowed by the receding face for at least 50% of the time; this will cause a stronger apparent wind from behind and so a greater reversal of force. Also vice versa when the boat accelerates down the advancing face of a suitable wave.

The combined factors

For 25% of the time, there will be a much stronger reversal of heel force, and vice versa.

Summary

Contrary to expectation, the apparent wind boat that gybes will sometimes – but not always – experience significant wind from behind and so will experience the same sudden strong reversal of heel force that the wind-from-behind boat always experiences. This is the reality that Julian and Charlie are describing.

In its favour, the skiff is very much faster, and so can be kept upright through anything by steer for balance provided adequate speed is preserved and the technique focuses absolutely on firm steer for balance (no facing aft, and no changing hands when there are more important things to do).

3 The difference between the 'synchronised co-ordination' manoeuvres and the 'sequential execution' of the apparent wind gybe

One of the defining characteristics of lead-group sailors of both wind-from-behind boats and apparent wind boats is that their tacks and mark roundings and the wind-from-behind gybes are all executed with synchronised co-ordination. A perfect example of this is the Eighteen footer racing tack described above, in which over a period of five seconds as the boat turns all three crew members 'do their thing' in a synchronised, co-ordinated manner.

The defining characteristic of the typical follower is that he/she and their crew tend to execute their manoeuvres in a sequential manner – for example, in a mark rounding they will first steer round the mark and the boat slows; they then sheet in and it moves but heels; they then hike and ultimately regain target speed.

It is hardly surprising that the approach of the lead-group sailor to the apparent wind gybe was to regard it as another manoeuvre that is best executed in a synchronised manner.

Life is not that simple. They learned quickly that the apparent wind gybe is the exception. Its essentials are:

- Gybes cannot be avoided. If you elect to tack downwind, the boat has to gybe, and frequently. So it is essential to develop a safe, consistent gybing technique.
- Only when it has turned far enough on the other gybe will the spinnaker fill. This will usually require a turn through 90° or more before the spinnaker fills, inflates and begins to pull hard, followed immediately by a deliberate turn downwind as the boat accelerates. These turns take time, and cannot be rushed without stopping the boat.
- During the turn it will be necessary to steer for balance, particularly to counter any sudden reversal of heel force from the mainsail cracking across (as 2 above).
- Once the sails unstall they will heel the boat. This has to be controlled by steering downwind for equilibrium.
- Once the sails are trimmed the boat will accelerate strongly, and as it accelerates the apparent wind will both become stronger and will swing forward, and during the seconds of acceleration while curving downwind the boat will need firm and precise control in all three elements of steering for balance to keep it upright, sail trimming in the rapidly changing wind, and sailing at the stability limit for fastest acceleration and highest ultimate speed.

Put bluntly, there is a general tendency to take the attitude 'The sails are full. The gybe is over. I can now relax and change hands.' Those who take such an attitude pay the price by capsizing in strong wind and waves. The apparent wind gybe is *not* complete until the full sequence has been completed, and:

1 The boat has turned.
2 The sails have filled.
3 The boat has completed the re-acceleration and bear-away process to its new speed and heading.
4 The boat is steady at target speed and on its new course.

Trying to change hands during segment 3 above is an invitation to momentary loss of control and capsize.
   Either change hands very early, or after you have reached '4'.

End of author's note

Julian's account continues to the end of the chapter.

15.12 ■ Eighteen footer racing gybe

The difference between the right and the wrong time to gybe reflects the basic point that the ideal is to have the lowest apparent wind speed over the boat during the gybe. So the object is to start the gybe at the moment of highest boat speed possible. So exactly as we sailed low for a few seconds to accelerate a little prior to entering the tack, we sailed high for a few seconds prior to the gybe so as to enter the gybe with higher boat speed. This enables you to execute the gybe with as little interference from the apparent wind and waves as possible because if you have enough boat speed you can steer it without difficulty through any waves as you turn.

When to gybe

If you are on a big ocean swell, the worst time to gybe is when you are overtaking the swell and sailing up the receding windward face of the wave. If in 20 knots you *must* gybe, find yourself a wave to surf, accelerate down the advancing leeward face, and then gybe. This is true of Eighteens, of yachts, of anything. The second worst time is right in the middle of a lull because then you have the least boat speed with rising wind imminent. At these times the boat is sailing at its slowest. This is not quite as bad as gybing at the beginning of the gust when the boat is slow and the sails load up in the gust, but it is almost as bad.

In big ocean swell, the best time is when you are sailing down the advancing, leeward face of the wave. The boat is being accelerated down the wave by something other than the wind, so there will be less pressure in the sails which makes it easier. In a gust, the best time to gybe is just after the peak of the gust has gone past and the wind is abating. The first 20% of the gust is when the wind is increasing and reaches its strongest and will have accelerated the boat to its highest speed. As soon as you feel the pressure back off, that's the time to gybe. The boat will be at its fastest with least load in the sails through the gybe. It does not *look* easiest – it looks as if you are still in the gust – but it is normally the best time to do it.

The mechanics of the gybe

Because the skipper's consistency is so important it is proper to expect him to steer accurately through the gybe, and do little else. At root, the new technique was placing a new responsibility on the skipper – to repeat the rate of turn so reliably that each crew member could rely on it to anticipate and so synchronise his movements smoothly with the whole manoeuvre. And central to reliable repetition of rate of turn was that the skipper should look ahead throughout the gybe and never lose orientation even for a moment.

We are talking here of three-hander Eighteen footers. The two-hander Eighteens were closer to the 49er – they were much more lively, so were more of a challenge. But in principle they were identical.

Practical 49er racing gybe

The skipper runs through literally a metre behind the forward hand. He will have accelerated the rate of turn to its maximum, the rudder will be well deflected, and the dynamics of his running across aft of the centreboard will keep the boat turning fast. He will drop the tiller extension and run through to the other side. If the boat is well balanced it will continue to turn, and he will end up doing a funny little movement where he turns facing forward and hooks up and moves out onto the wire at the same time as picking up the new tiller extension. At the appropriate time and heading he will steer the boat out of the turn onto the optimum heading for acceleration, then do the big bear-away as the boat regains speed. As the sails load up, the sheet hand moves onto the wire. This is a much quicker manoeuvre, with far more room for error, but it usually works.

15.13 ■ Eighteen footer survival gybe

In the old days – and even now in strong winds – you send the skipper in so he can steer from a secure position, look forward, identify what he is going to do, and decide when. This applies to the situation where you have to gybe, but do not have the speed as in the ideal situation.

Immediately prior to the gybe, the skipper will take the mainsheet from the sheet hand, move in to sit in the boat on the windward side with his hand on the tiller, scan forward, decide the moment, call the gybe, and start the turn. The first movement is that the sheet hand will stand up and run somewhat forward into the middle of the boat. As he moves, he takes the old spinnaker sheet from the forward hand, and trims it in quickly and hard. This counters to some degree the loss of pressure in the spinnaker due to the adverse circular airflow and so either accelerates the boat or at least delays the slowing due to loss of drive force. The sheet hand moving forward early allows the skipper to move across in front of the tiller later, and also allows the sheet hand to concentrate on what is happening with the spinnaker.

The forward hand runs between the skipper and the sheet hand and out onto the other wing, and normally will hook up and go immediately out onto the wire and be on the wire by the time the boat is passing through the straight downwind heading. By this time, the sheet hand has picked up the new spinnaker sheet in his other hand.

At about this time the skipper moves across facing forward, grasps the new tiller extension, and moves quickly into the netting of the new windward wing with his foot against the inner rail. He still has the mainsheet. Throughout this process, the skipper has been facing forward, controlling the rate of turn and steering for balance through the turn.

If the boom has cracked across he will have reversed the helm momentarily as in a conventional gybe to keep the boat upright, then continued the turn (Section 27.10).

At this point, the new apparent wind will begin to press the spinnaker against the jib. The moment this happens, the sheet hand will drop the old spinnaker sheet, and start pulling in some 5m of new sheet to draw the spinnaker clew around the forestay. At the same time he moves onto the wing and out onto the wire. As the spinnaker fills he trims it for both drive and balance as the boat stabilises and starts accelerating on its new heading.

When the boat steadies, he passes the spinnaker sheet to the forward hand. As soon as the boat is comfortable, the skipper makes his way out, passes the mainsheet to the sheet hand and moves onto the wire – if he needs to be out there.

That is the mechanics of a three-hander Eighteen footer survival gybe. (These techniques are summarised in Section 27.10.)

We now take the view that if you capsize in the gybe, it is all the skipper's fault. Given adequate speed at entry, the skipper should be able to keep the boat upright with steer for balance even if the crew falls over and does a cockroach on the floor.

It was primarily during the relatively private, concentrated practice and development sailing in the reliable steady winds of the Italian mountain lakes during the European Exhibition tours that we were able to focus on our emerging problems from a 'basic objects and first principles' approach. The tack and gybe examples above attest the value of taking a fresh look on occasion, no matter how strong the tradition.

15.14 ■ The 1991–2 boat

On our return to Sydney, my design approach to the 1991–2 season was that four areas looked promising:
1 To exploit a second-order weight difference that was emerging.
2 To reduce aerodynamic drag.
3 To try a spinnaker chute on an Eighteen.
4 To fit a self-tacking jib to try to minimise speed loss through tacks.

In the event, three further unexpected areas emerged:

5 Flatter sails, *also*:

6 Helical twist, both of which occurred by accident.

7 Stiffer lower masts; these were engineered deliberately.

All of these reinforced one another and increased speed.

I elected to design for maximum VMG, with a bias towards boat speed rather than pointing.

The biggest change in the design thinking between the Eighteen footers *AAMI I* and *AAMI II* of 1990–1, and *AAMI IV* of 1991–2 (*AAMI III* was the Sixteen footer), was the realisation that we had come to the end of the massive reductions in hydrodynamic drag that flowed from creating a lighter boat. From the prototype and *Banana Republic* to *AAMI I* (the one we sold mid-season), and *AAMI II* (the replacement boat), we had made detail changes in hull materials and internal structure. Glass/polyester had been replaced by carbon/epoxy. Long horizontal breast hooks had been added between the topsides forward to stop them from flexing inwards when driven fast to windward through the oncoming wave crests. A full-depth I-beam X-frame girder with strong unidirectional carbon top and bottom flanges (Fig 9.4) now carried the mast compression and stay tension loads, and a duplicate X-frame under the mid-cockpit floor carried the twist load of the cantilevered wings. Each hull had been lighter, stronger, stiffer and faster than the one before. Other designers were now copying the shapes, weights, structures and ratios of the B-18, and it was time to move from big changes in ratios and to look for more speed and steadier speed from focused refinements.

The start point was to make best use of the European Exhibition tour plus the then-new GPS speed measurement capability to establish the actual speeds at which we were sailing and manoeuvring. We had done this.

We used a new tow technique to establish base-line data about the hydrodynamic drags of the hulls we were sailing. From this came the realisation that some hulls at less than some critical weight have drag curves without the characteristic 'hump' just above hull speed (Chapter 10).

15.15 ■ Second-order weight reduction

We started the refinement process by further exploiting weight advantage in a different way. To defend against flimsy hulls such as those that failed to survive the elimination series in the 1898 Seawanhaka Cup challenge (Section 1.9), the class had agreed on a minimum hull weight of 72kg. But while all crews now sailed hulls of this weight, the old writ of 'bigger is better' was slow to die. All the armchair experts still advocated 'biggest possible for everything', so – not surprisingly – the new small hulls were usually equipped and rigged with bigger and heavier gear. We realised that the potential differences in equipment weight were so great that they added up to a significant difference in total weight. Big centreboards weighed 12kg; ours weighed 6.5kg. Big rudders weighed 7kg; ours weighed 4kg. Their alloy lower masts were big; ours were 1m shorter and smaller in diameter. Their booms were huge; ours were modest. They used 3.2mm wire for their cap shrouds; we used 2.5mm. All told, we realised that *AAMI IV* could finish about 40kg – about 10% of total weight including crew – lighter than most of the other B-18s, and the new 'B-18 copy' designs were generally using gear that was bigger and heavier yet.

We felt that this anticipated weight difference was big enough to justify a different design approach based on an assumption of increased windward-going boat speed of about 5%. This gave an apparent wind increase of about 2.5%, from which we could get the same drive force from sails and a rig 4% smaller, which helped make it all smaller and lighter. *AAMI IV* was designed around this assumption. Centreboard and rudder were smaller in area, and biased towards finer leading edge radii and laminar flow sections. Smaller diameter masts carried slightly smaller sails, and slightly lower rigs and slightly shorter centreboards gave increased sail-carrying power and increased drive force from the same righting moment. The end result of the slightly greater drive force and slightly smaller total weight was that the 'drive force to total weight' ratio became significantly greater.

---

[1] Adrienne had a reputation among her crews as one of the rare helms who could take a boat 'to the very edge' and hold it there at maximum speed without periodic disaster. A decade later it was Adrienne who navigated *PlayStation* to its world-record 24 hour run, skilfully keeping it in the favourable quadrant of a co-operative Atlantic low which was going the same way. Later she repeated the effort in a more complex environment, navigating around the world in record time. Skiff sailors seem to develop a sense of what makes a boat go fast.

With the skiffs *All States/AAMI IV* and *Ella Bache*, Adrienne Cahalan and I had teamed up as training partners. I had designed a fractionally smaller rig for Adrienne[1] (page 232) as was appropriate for the slightly lighter weight of her crew. The two boats were near identical in ratios and speed. They sailed midweek, sometimes alone, sometimes in company with half the fleet, as the different developments and changes were systematically incorporated, trialled, and fine-tuned. It was an exciting and turbulent year.

15.16 ■ Aerodynamic drag reduction – the hull

We looked carefully at all the drags that, until then, had been considered 'not significant' – that is, the airflows over the hull, wings, crew and rig.

We started with the hull. If you put a three-dimensional cubic brick in the middle of a wind tunnel it will have a coefficient of drag of 1.05 (Hoerner). If you put it between two walls, the coefficient of drag in the two-dimensional flow increases to 2.05. So, if we ignore the velocity gradient (Fig 3.23), the coefficient of drag of a brick-like hull floating on one wall (the water) would be about 1.55. If the brick were to become a long open-top shoebox with a huge square open cockpit, the coefficient of drag would logically double to about 3.0. If we make a conservative estimate of the drag coefficient of 'square' hulls with high sides, sharp gunwales, square cockpits and vertical transoms – I am thinking of shapes like the 420, Enterprise and Star – it would have to be about 2.0.

The calculation of the aerodynamic drag of an Enterprise hull in an apparent wind of 20 knots, approaching from 25° off the bow, will be:

Drag = 0.5 × density (slugs/cu ft) × projected area (sq ft) × coefficient of drag × speed in fps (squared)

Density of the standard atmosphere at sea level is 0.002378 slugs/cu ft at 14.7psi and 15°C. By convention, the density is multiplied by the 0.5 term to give 0.001189. For practical purposes, we will use 0.0012.

Area will be the dimension projected across the apparent wind times the height – ie:
Beam = 5ft, plus (length × sin 25 = 14 × .42 = 6) so effective width = 5 + 6 = 11ft
Height   = 2ft
Effective area   = 22sq ft

The effect of the turbulent velocity gradient will reduce the effective speed of the apparent wind to, say, 0.7, so speed will be about 20 knots = 33.8fps × 0.7 = 23.7fps.

So the aerodynamic drag will be about 0.0012 × 22 × 2.0 × 23.7 × 23.7 = 29.6lb.

This looks and feels real. If you have to hold an Enterprise-size boat without sails slightly crosswind in the water in a 20 knot wind, this is about the force with which it will try to pull away from you. A Star-size hull with its longer length and higher sides would need two people to hold it.

These are the sorts of forces that used to be regarded as 'not significant'!

Beginning with *Prime II*, we started a trend that leads directly to the present 49er, 29er and 59er hulls. The key differences are the lower freeboard, the rounded-down gunwales, the elimination of the near-vertical sided and ended cockpit, and the elimination of the vertical transom. If we compare the aerodynamic drag of the 59er with the similar-size Enterprise:

- The projected 'across the apparent wind' dimension will be the same at 11ft.
- The height is lower at 1.5ft, not 2ft, so the projected area becomes 16.5sq ft.
- The velocity gradient correction for the lower hull will reduce from about 0.7 to, say, 0.6.
- The elimination of the square-sided cockpit restores the 'sharp-edge brick' drag from 2 to 1.55.
- The elimination of the 'base drag' of the vertical transom further reduces it to, say, 1.45.
- But the huge difference comes from the rounded-down gunwales. A rounding of the edges with a radius of 10% of the dimension reduces the drag coefficient of the brick in the wind tunnel in three-dimensional flow from 1.05 with sharp edges to less than 0.1 with rounded edges (Hoerner).

So we can replace the coefficient of drag of 1.45 with a new value of 0.145, and calculate the aerodynamic drag of the 59er hull in a 20 knot apparent wind as:

$16.5 \times 0.145 \times 0.0012 \times 20.3 \times 20.3 = 1.18$lb (and this is about what it feels like).

This shows what a little 'streamlining' can do. There can be no better example of detail refinement than this.

15.17 ■ Aerodynamic drag reduction – wings, crew and rig

Wings

Reduction of wing aerodynamic drag was a step-by-step process. First, we fitted cantilever wing beams and discarded the four 'wing wires' from the hounds to the forward and aft outer corners of the wings. This not only eliminated the drag of 40m of 2.5mm wire, but at a second level it also gave us an enormous advantage in pre-start manoeuvring. Wings started as stubs, then quickly became 'racks' hinged at the gunwale and supported at their outer corners by wing wires from the hounds. Wingspan increased to the point where they were invariably called 'wings'. One consequence was that the aft wing wires held the boom and mainsail within a restricted arc between them, and the practical effect of this was that the minimum circle of a gybe became quite large. Without wing wires, the boom could be let go right to the shrouds and the boat could again gybe in a pirouette.

The B-18s and *AAMI I* had generated two 'bumps' forward on each gunwale – the forward bump was the forward wing beam and aft of that was the chainplate with its cluster of shrouds, cap shrouds and lower shrouds attachments. Each bump created significant interference drag. Starting with *AAMI II*, we moved the forward wing beam aft to the shroud position. (This is shown in Fig 15.2.) Later we attached the shrouds to the top of the cantilever wing beam stub a few inches outside the gunwale width, which made one smoother gunwale 'bump' in place of the previous two. The wider staying base enabled us to use lighter, smaller-diameter stays. The aft movement of the forward beam reduced the area of high-drag net. So that the forward hand could trapeze in the same position, the length of the outer rail was not changed and the forward end of the rail now projected forward of the forward beam.

In an Eighteen made after the *AAMI* series, we substituted 'solid' smooth low-drag panels for the high-aerodynamic-drag net – this reduced the aerodynamic drag substantially, and led directly to the 'solid' low-drag wings of the 49er.

Crew

There was little we could do about crew drag other than dress as smoothly as possible, and be very conscious of trapezing with our bodies aligned so that the oncoming apparent wind 'saw' only one body.

Rig

Everything here was directed towards smaller weight and drag; wing wires were discarded. Smaller-diameter stays were set from a wider staying base, and the masts were shorter and of smaller diameter. The sails were smaller and in fact flatter, and this flattening resulted in significant drag reduction (Fig 13.19B). A mainsail of 400sq ft that is 2% flatter will develop 4lb less form drag in 18 to 20 knots of apparent wind. The smaller sails of *All States/AAMI IV* featured the cut-away leech profile now seen in the 49er sport sails.

These design changes to reduce drag were all incremental refinements. Together with the second-order reduction of weight referred to above, their combined effect helped create the fastest Eighteen foot skiff ever to sail (Figs 15.1, 15.2 and 15.3).

15.18 ■ Spinnaker chute

In that second year, we built in a spinnaker chute. This was an unbelievably potent tactical advance.

Without it, the spinnaker drop and slow sailing started 20 seconds prior to mark rounding. With it, we sailed at full downwind speed almost to the mark, rounded and sailed away at 70% speed with two on the wire for, say, 10 seconds, while the third hand reeled it in; he then joined us on the wing for 100% upwind speed.

If we calculate the advantage in distance and time as between two Eighteen footers, one with and one without a spinnaker chute, the sums look like this:

Table 15.2 performance advantage of spinnaker chute

Assumptions

Wind, true	12 knots		
Speed downwind	with spinnaker	20 knots	33.8ft per sec
Speed downwind	no spinnaker	10 knots	16.9ft per sec
Speed upwind	100%	12 knots	20.3ft per sec
Speed upwind	70%	8.4 knots	14.2ft per sec

Start point	Both boats	338ft, 103m, from and approaching the leeward mark.
End point	Both boats	142ft, 43m, from the leeward mark after rounding.

Boat without chute

Twenty seconds to drop and stow:

Start to start plus 20 secs	10 knots	16.9fps	338ft – rounds mark

Seven seconds with three on wire at 12 knots:

Start plus 20 to plus 27 secs	7 secs	20.3fps	142ft

Boat with chute

Carries spinnaker at full speed for 8.5 secs longer:

Start to start plus 8.5 secs	20 knots	33.8fps	287ft

Drops spinnaker:

Start plus 8.5 to plus 11.5 secs	3 secs	16.9fps	51ft – rounds mark

Forward hand stows spinnaker; boat sails more slowly with two on wire:

Start plus 11.5 to plus 21.5 secs	10 secs	14.2fps	142ft
Thereafter sails to windward at		20.3fps	

Boat without chute arrives at position 142ft upwind of leeward mark in	27 secs
Boat with chute arrives at position 142ft upwind of leeward mark in	21.5 secs

Advantage of chute per leeward spinnaker drop	5.5 secs
Advantage of chute per leeward spinnaker drop in three-drop race	=16.5 secs or 558ft

The first Grand Prix Sailing event that year was at Hayman Island, and we won it. The boat was fast, and the advantage of the chute helped us 'clear out' and sail our own races. The spinnaker chute worked brilliantly, but mechanical failure was to prove costly.

The second event was at Townsville. There, the spinnaker chute split open. It was a FRP top hat section inverted with a flat top glued on, and was positioned from bow to stern under the deck and cockpit floor. The boat nose dived, the dynamic pressure split the top off the flanges, water entered and filled the buoyancy cavity between cockpit floor and hull, and we nearly sank. We missed races while we drained the boat and sealed the ends of the tube, and then suffered equipment failure in the last race. At the end of that second regatta, we lay last in the series score. Despite its very great advantages, there was not enough time between events to open the boat up and rebuild the chute, so we closed it up and sailed without it for the rest of the season.

From that disaster we worked out what we had to do to achieve a place in the finals. We could not afford even one single added bad placing, so we sailed very conservatively in Melbourne in very rough water and at all the following events. It was just a question of starting well, of not taking flyers, and of being conservative on the racetrack. I am sure that the other competitors realised what we were doing and exploited our conservatism to their sometime advantage, but we had a job to do, kept at it, and did it.

As the last of the qualifying events, which was in Auckland, New Zealand, approached we were close to, but had not quite secured, a place in the final six qualifiers, so we were driven to taking a chance with another technical change to lift our performance.

15.19 ■ Conservation of speed

What had happened between the disaster at Townsville and the final elimination in Auckland was a cascade of consequential factors, all of which interacted favourably.

We put the self-tacking jib on and the boat went faster through tacks. Because it went faster through tacks it slowed less and exited the tacks faster, so we could pull the centreboard up more. Because we could pull the centreboard up more, we ended up sailing faster to windward with flatter sails. This increased the apparent wind, so we then reduced the sail area. Therefore we ended up with smaller sails, and smaller drag, and the boat went faster again. So the tacking technique altered. Prior to entering the tack we eased the jib sheet a small and very precise amount – 1–1½in at the clew. This both enabled us to accelerate a knot or so prior to starting the turn, and opened the jib sufficiently to allow us to use the circular airflow going into the tack. Above all it meant that all the forward hand had to do was to run from one side of the boat across the 17ft wings to the other side of the boat and get onto the wire just as quickly as was possible. This enabled me to swing the boat faster. For a little while we had to alter rudders because, at the higher rate of turn I was looking for, the rudder tended to stall as I drove it into the tack. We were already using twin tiller extensions, but we went into every detail, and if we could find a quarter-second improvement we went for it because the cumulative effect was significant around the course.

With these techniques we slowed less, so we were able to make the centreboard shorter (and lighter). With the shorter board, our windward-going target speed became faster. This in turn enabled us to move the centreboard further forward, then to make the sails flatter, which reduced the drag more and increased windward target speed. But the forward centreboard also allowed us to use a flatter spinnaker, so our target speed downwind increased as well.

15.20 ■ Flatter sails

Because the boat exited tacks faster, the apparent wind at the start of the post-tack acceleration was stronger so we were able to make our sails smaller and flatter and masts shorter and of smaller diameter. This reduced weight and drag.

The way we were moving was going to call for flatter sails at some point, but an unexpected consequence of sailcloth development triggered us into using flatter sails sooner than we had intended. What happened was that Mylar® sailcloth with a diagonal reinforcement of Vectran® thread, in addition to the normal warp and weft reinforcement threads, became available. The sails with which we started our second year were computer-designed to give us the fullnesses when sailing we had found fastest the previous year, but were built from a lighter cloth with the new diagonal thread.

They set flatter!

Both the sailmaker and ourselves were initially at a loss to understand this, but very soon we understood that the technical quality of sailcloth really had improved by another notch. Up until that time, all sail panel design had included a factor to allow for the property that even Mylar® has some diagonal stretch, and this stretch will increase the fullness of a sail under wind pressure by some small amount. The new diagonally braced cloth was different in that it simply did not stretch diagonally and so set at its design fullness. So the difference was that the previous stretch allowance could now be discarded.

Our initial reaction was that we should recut or replace with fuller sails, but before we made any move we found that we were in fact sailing faster. The higher speed out of tacks meant that we no longer needed the fuller sails for low-speed acceleration. The flatter sails developed less drag in the gusts, and these sails meshed with all the other design refinements we were experimenting with. So instead of reverting to fuller sails, we 'grew' into and used the flatter sails as a part of the ongoing refinement work.

15.21 ■ Centreboard flow-on effects

A consequence of the smaller, flatter sails was that the position of their centre of pressure moved well forward. Big full sails used for quick re-acceleration from low speeds need easing at target speed; when so eased, they 'catch the wind' only in their leeches with consequent far aft centre of pressure. When smaller, flatter sails are sheeted more efficiently, the centre of pressure moves forward, so we were able to move our centreboards forward by up to 300mm to a more normal position closer to the mast. This made the boats much better balanced upwind, and more controllable when tacking downwind under spinnaker. (The lee helm of the big mammoths downwind under spinnaker had sometimes been so great that a light skipper was in danger of being lifted off the wing rail.)

Because the boat speed stayed higher, we could make our centreboards shorter and lighter. In practice, our centreboards, which were of the minimum practical area for satisfactory low-speed handling on approach to the start line, were about half the weight of those of some of our competitors. Further, as noted earlier, we put numbers down their trailing edges, and pulled them up to an exact depth as soon as we were clear of the start line and up to speed. The combination of lower rig and shorter centreboard gave us increased drive force through waves and/or target speed at a higher pointing angle in flatter water.

15.22 ■ Acceleration consequences

A consequence of the flatter sails and tiny centreboards was that our initial acceleration from zero to about half speed was slower than boats with fuller sails and bigger foils. From half speed to full speed, it was faster. We needed to plan our starts very carefully. In our favour were the advantages that our lighter boat, which had no wing wires, was much more manoeuvrable than our rivals', and we could gybe in a pirouette and they could not. Our plan – which almost always worked – was to manoeuvre by 'snaking' to maintain adequate room to make a run at the line over the last few seconds and hit it with at least half speed. When we could do this and keep our nose clear for the next few seconds, we were away and clear. Whenever this ploy failed we immediately hung back, tacked for clear air, and used our speed clear of the fleet while most of them were still holding each other high and slow.

15.23 ■ No 1 course record sail

By the end of that season we had shortened the centreboards to 1700mm and lightened them to 6.5kg. Both the lighter-wind and the stronger-wind boards were near identical in area, but the lighter-wind board used a leading edge radius of about 0.7% of the chord, while the stronger wind board used about 0.4%. We had shortened the rudder to 850mm (immersed depth), the sails had been cleaned up and flattened, and masts were bending where they should and the ratios were just about perfect.

Confirmation that these design and handling refinements had been worthwhile and really worked was affirmed in a very satisfying way. Later in that season, in one heat of the World Championships, we sailed a race in which, for us, all the factors 'came right'. As explained in detail in Chapter 29, we covered the 15.4nm buoy-to-buoy-in-a-straight-line No 1 course in a few seconds less than 50 minutes. This was substantially faster than the previous record, and as of mid 2008 it still stands (see Section 29.3 – Eighteen foot Skiff: No 1 Course Record Sail).

15.24 ■ Mast stiffness – distribution of flexibility

This was a strange one. We had suffered the mechanical failure of the spinnaker chute during the first race of the second regatta of the 1991–2 Grand Prix series at Townsville. We missed three races and lost points while we drained the boat and carried out emergency repairs. As a result, at the conclusion of that regatta we were scored a very bad last and were playing catch-up for all of the rest of that season. As we approached the final elimination race, we had improved our position from impossible to insecure – but we still needed something special to make the cut into the six-boat fleet that would contest the 1992 Grand Prix finals. So for the final elimination races – to be sailed in Auckland, New Zealand – we had to find that something extra.

In our drive to save weight and reduce drag we had fitted lower masts of yet smaller diameter. These were meant not to move. In practice, they did move more than I liked, and with the diagonal rigidity of the new sailcloth all movement was undesirable, so I reasoned that if we could immobilise them further this might be the 'something extra' we were looking for.

We fashioned a set of stiffening plates from round tube 2mm thick which mated the forward side of the masts and tapered from about 25mm wide at the hounds, in a long diamond shape to a maximum mid-length width of about 75mm, to 25mm again about 600mm below the lower spreaders. These 'balanced' the alloy sailtrack on the aft side. The lower masts felt noticeably stiffer ashore and the topmasts visibly curved more when we played with the sheet, so we crossed our fingers and went sailing.

The boat was instantly dubbed 'The Auckland Express'. Upwind it just flew faster, and was unbeatable. We made the cut. Once we had qualified for the finals, which was our objective, there were no longer any constraints to be conservative, and we could race as we pleased. We sailed carefully, but were able to take what risks seemed prudent.

At Rottnest Island, off Perth in Western Australia, we won the 1991–2 Grand Prix, and a little later we won the World Championship – both for the second time.

Over the next few years, as is described in Chapter 16, development of the Grand Prix racers shifted towards higher-pointing, faster accelerating, more manoeuvrable boats better suited to the shorter courses that were being called for by TV considerations. The design object became 'First at the windward mark', because whoever first established a lead was unlikely to be passed. The boats began to be designed for faster acceleration off the start line and higher pointing, and to be faster through tactical manoeuvres, but they did not have the raw speed of the long-course 'drag racers' of the 1990–1 and 1991–2 seasons.

Author's note

This was one more straw in the wind about the strange speed of a rig that flexes primarily at the top. What they seem to have done in this case by stiffening the lower masts was to so concentrate the bend in the upper masts that, to quote Julian again, '... beyond a critical increase in sheet tension the leech laid open and the sail flattened at the top, the rig held the forestay tight, and the boat dropped drag, and pointed higher, shooting forward with every gust'.

Chapter 16 • Design Refinement for Short-course Manoeuvrability

16.1 ■ The development of the skiff TV spectacle

Bill McCartney was the brains and producer behind the *Grand Prix Sailing* Sports TV programme. Towards the end of its run, the development of the format that best showcases fast skiffs on the TV screen was almost as creative as the skiffs themselves.

From the mid-1970s until about 1984, the Eighteen foot skiffs, and only the Eighteen footers, developed iceboat-like wet-water downwind speed. During this time, while the rest of the sailing world kept sailing sedately downwind in their traditional wind-from-behind processions at half wind speed, the Eighteens began to radiate a new spectacle of downwind sailing at three times the speed through the water, diverging and converging as they tacked downwind, sailing with knife-edge balance, and on occasion when things went wrong, their disasters were at speeds that sometimes saw bodies flying through the air on the ends of trapeze wires, or falling or diving from wing ends often 4m above the water. The harbourside audience numbers exploded.

As discussed previously in Chapter 14, TV coverage started modestly in 1983, and immediately attracted a loyal and growing audience. The focus of the top Eighteens shifted from winning the Club, State or World Championships to winning the televised Grand Prix series. But in 1987 the TV producers overplayed their hand, tried to go international too soon, failed to achieve critical economic mass, and their promotional failure led to a local collapse in 1988 of Eighteen footer sponsor support, club management, vision and sailing.

There was no such collapse in the technical innovation driven by the class culture of 'give it a go', and the sheer merit of the new lower-cost higher-speed B-18 'budget boats' reasserted itself in increased fleet strength by about 1990. The harbourside audience grew even larger.

TV coverage began again with a greater depth and quality, and governance of the next year's arrangements was co-operatively agreed at the end of each season at meetings between the interested stake-holders – the TV producer, the designers, the sailors, the sponsors and the clubs. Clips of the previous two seasons' sailing were compared: how high the spray was thrown last year as compared with the year before, what changes might lead to better spectacle, etc. At the end of this process a consensus was reached. From this, the invitations to participate in the following season's Grand Prix were issued, and these included, for example, 'for boats with wingspan no more than 5.3m'. This was solid common sense in action.

For the three seasons – 1990–1, 1991–2 and 1992–3 – the racing arrangements were changed little and the programme's ratings increased.

The televised Grand Prix events were rotated between Australian and New Zealand capital cities and photogenic resorts. At first the race format mimicked the long courses enshrined in the Sydney Eighteen footers' No 1 course, but soon both the leg lengths and the race length began to be shortened for several reasons.

Video footage was gathered from three sources:

1 Helicopters were used for both wide and close aerial shots.
2 An innovative fast camera boat was developed which made almost no wake at speed. We designed and made the first one in 1993–4 from two Tornado hulls with 500mm of freeboard added and a low cockpit forward in each hull. In between was a platform with a high, centrally mounted camera with unobstructed 360° view. With two small outboard motors, this machine was faster than the fastest skiff, threw no spray, and made almost no wake. It was always crewed by a cox in one hull and lookout in the other who were themselves Eighteen foot skiff skippers, and so could anticipate the racing crews' manoeuvres and quit position instantly when a skiff helm glanced at them and nodded for room to tack or gybe. They were able to position themselves close alongside a racing skiff for close-by shots without creating waves or wind shadow or interfering with that boat's, or any other boat's, freedom to manoeuvre.
3 Head cameras and microphones were used for onboard atmosphere. At the start of each regatta, the crews drew straws to determine which skipper would wear the head camera for which race.

239

From the wealth of footage generated from these three sources, skilled production and editing missed nothing as they cut and mixed to satisfy the rule that the average attention span of the TV audience is 17 minutes. Periodic clips explaining various points – for example, the port and starboard rule – enabled a non-sailing audience to better understand the action. Umpires were introduced to enforce the rules with on-course penalties; and in this way, protests were eliminated and the first boat across the line was the winner. This satisfied non-sailing viewers who did not understand the logic of post-race protest proceedings. The whole enterprise put to air a professional action-packed colourful spectacle easily understood by a growing non-sailing TV audience.

This was the environment that generated the extraordinarily fast machines such as *All States/AAMI IV* (which was later dubbed 'Auckland Express' – this is the boat on the jacket of *HPS-1*, and the 2003 and 2007 reprints). The impact of the national TV promotion in Australia was huge, and during the 1990–1, 1991–2 and 1992–3 seasons, sailing became an active spectacular sport followed by a large non-sailing TV and harbourside audience, as opposed to its traditional status as a dull and uninteresting pastime to watch.

Contrast this with the fortunes of sailing on the other side of the world. TV coverage at Olympic events had been progressively declining, and TV footage of sailing from the Olympics prior to and including Atlanta was virtually zero. The Olympic TV producers dismissed sailing footage with indifference because it offered no spectacle of interest to the non-sailing public.

From the Eighteen footer Grand Prix producer's point of view, the format that had been developed up to 1992–3 presented the boats massed on the screen at the start, and often at marks, and pairs or threes routinely conflicted between marks. Sometimes they suffered spectacular disasters at speed. Always they sailed at speeds utterly unknown in sailboats previously. While this had attracted an initial large TV audience that had grown year by year, by the fourth year realpolitic began to set in, and it was time to change.

16.2 ■ Development of the shorter-course format

The driving factors were, first, the growing success of other TV formats in other sports; second, the growth of the 'hospitality' component of the TV promotion; and, third, the desire of venues with smaller waters to host the events.

The 'more-on-screen' factor

Worldwide, both golf and soccer are hugely popular, but far more people watch soccer on TV than watch golf. A single golfer making a swing cannot compete with the colourful spectacle of two dynamic teams all on screen, wheeling as they co-ordinate in attack and defence. So a lesson was learned from soccer – more competing boats on screen means more viewers.

The hospitality thrust

In Sydney, ferries have followed the skiffs for more than a century, and sponsors and their guests used ferries for the initial years. But ferries offer good views to only a limited number of passengers because the apparent wind skiffs now outrun the ferries and vanish – and in any case the ferries at speed make too much wake to be welcome anywhere near racing sailboats. So the idea grew of having a large hospitality barge moored adjacent to the start–finish line and having the boats race around it.

The smaller-waters thrust

This is self-evident in that these programmes strongly promote resort venues, so resorts bid generously for the privilege of playing host. Smaller courses opened the possibility of hosting to more resorts.

Over the next three years, by logical steps, the race format changed from long-leg to short-leg racing. Before long it had stabilised into a compact format driven not by the image of the long No 1 'round the islands' course in Sydney with its 2nm windward–leeward length, but by the 25 minute tape life of the Beta-cam equipment used.

After his third Grand Prix win, Julian retired as a helmsman, and was immediately co-opted as Race Director by *Grand Prix Sailing*, and helped develop the essential elements of the short-course race arrangements of the later years. The whole exercise was ultimately driven by the 25 minute tape life just mentioned.

The format was as follows:

- The distance between the windward mark and the leeward mark was set according to the wind speed, and was adjusted race by race as the wind strength changed so that the race time from start to finish would be a little less than 25 minutes. Typical would be a windward–leeward leg length of 900m, which implied an average VMG between marks of 15 knots.
- The Committee Vessel was moored at one end of the Start–Finish line, which is also the gate, about 300 to 400m upwind of the leeward mark.
- The angle of the windward to gybe leg was set to showcase the skiffs' maximum speed when tacking downwind.
- The angle of gybe to leeward leg was set 15° deeper than the skiffs' fastest downwind VMG angle, and so provided options for each boat and some opportunity to pass.
- A large hospitality barge with two decks was moored adjacent to the Committee Vessel. The lower covered deck was furnished and was for food, wine and relaxing between races. The upper deck was a completely clear surface some 6m above the water and was an ideal platform from which the whole race could be viewed.
- The course was from the start, twice around the windward, gybe and leeward marks, and upwind through the Start–Finish gate each lap, with a final windward and return loop for a fast-moving downwind finish.
- The season's regattas acted as elimination races so that the number of starters in the final races was six.

This format concentrated the fleet so that all the boats, or most of them, appeared on screen in any wide-angle helicopter shots. Closer shots showed more boats on screen than in the past and there was more mark-rounding action and more tactical confrontation between them. This pleased particularly the non-sailing audience, which increased in numbers yet again, so the producer was happy. The sponsors and their guests loved it because the boats were always in sight as they raced around them, so their favourite could be followed through the whole race. The smaller water required opened the possibility of hosting the event at a larger number of resorts, so different backgrounds began to appear.

Thus this was the format used until the whole Grand Prix culture was abandoned in 1997 following the selection of the skiff-derived 49er as Olympic and the collapse of the Eighteen footer promotion culture.

Its dynamic essentials were used as the model for the four compact courses within Sydney Harbour which were used so successfully at the Sydney 2000 Olympic Games.

16.3 ■ The different tactical demands of the shorter courses

The tactical consequences of the changes above were profound. The shorter the legs, the harder it is to pass. So the object in short-leg racing is to be first at the first mark, and then defend your position.

If a boat sails at 12 knots through the water and tacks through 90°, it will take 16 minutes to cover the 2.3nm from Clark Island to the Sow and Pigs Reef in Sydney Harbour, assuming no tidal current. An Eighteen footer with a long bowsprit/spinnaker pole is nearly 30ft long, so to pass it from close astern to clear ahead needs a gain of, say, 50ft. If we assume a speed difference of 2%, or 0.25 knots or 0.4ft per second – which is a substantial difference – it will need 2 minutes to gain 50ft. Given a long course there is time and to spare to do so, and so for years the Eighteens focused on raw speed.

But with the short courses no leg is longer than 750m – 2500ft maximum – and upwind a boat sailing as above will cover the distance from leeward mark to gate or gate to windward mark in less than 2 minutes. In these conditions the ability to pass with slight extra speed within the length of a leg is marginal at best, and impossible otherwise.

Conversely, if a boat is designed for tactical advantage – faster acceleration, ability to point higher even though at slower VMG, and ability to tack more quickly – with these tactical advantages it can dominate lower-pointing, but potentially faster, boats over short legs. One classic technique is to make a leeward-end start, accelerate more quickly off the start line to get 'nose in front', then by pointing very high and so 'holding them up' deny boats to windward the clear air and room they need to sail free and develop their best VMG. In this way the slower top-speed but higher-pointing boat can soon get into a position from which it can tack and cross all the starboard tackers it has held up.

These performance characteristics became the design object as the courses shortened.

16.4 ■ Hull design

In the practical sense, the B-18 Eighteen footer hulls developed through three marques.

The shape of the original B-18 of 1989–90 was that of *Prime III* of 1983. This was not altered and remained dominant through 1990–1 (AAMI year 1) and 1991–2 (AAMI year 2).

In preparation for the 1992–3 season we undertook a major development programme. We knew the total weights of our boats and crews, so we flooded the moulds with that weight of water and in this way established exactly what were the 'at rest' waterlines and immersion depths of these remarkable hulls.

We also knew which were dominant when racing on the water, so we conducted tow tests to find out exactly what were the hydrodynamic drags of these hulls plus their centreboards and rudders. This work revealed the astonishing 'no hump' property which has changed the whole basis of our thinking since that time. We now realise that Eighteen footers and similar skiffs probably have more in common with iceboats and catamarans than with Cadets and 470s.

Despite this, our approach remained very cautious. All the top racing teams were now using our hulls and rigs. We took the B-18, extended the bow 75mm and cut 75mm off the transom, re-faired the whole wetted surface, took a mould off it, and called it the B-18 Mk 2B. Two years later we repeated the process to make the B-18 Mk 3C. This became the dominant hull shape until, in 1997, the TV-driven *Grand Prix Sailing* circuit was discontinued.

16.5 ■ Rig development

The fastest long-course boats had used flexible masts, with luff round curves of 5.5–6% of the luff length. For faster acceleration the masts became progressively stiffer, with curves reducing to about 3.2% of the luff length.

The long-course boats had spent most of their time at high speed, and surprisingly small centreboards proved big enough to win. Further, these boards used very fine leading edge radii of about 0.7% for the lighter-wind board and 0.4% for the strong-wind foil. For the serious business of baulking other boats by pointing high at lower speed with little leeway, or matching and over-running a boat trying to do just this, larger centreboards with LE radii of about 1% are found to be better.

At these lower speeds, the apparent wind was not so strong. Sail area increased. At a later stage (following the appearance of the radical wishbone-sail *Looney Tunes*), a cuff on the mainsail was used to extend its working surface down to deck level. This gave a big increase in speed, and was helpful in carrying the rigs across a wider wind speed range.

Surprisingly, the asymmetric spinnakers became substantially flatter. The long-course boats had used a curve as for an 18% uniform camber at their leading edges, and the flatter curve of a 12% camber towards the leech. As the short-course boats developed their fastest sails, the curves became 13% forward and 7.5% towards the leech. (The 49er has continued this trend.)

These boats could accelerate fast and point high, they reached the first mark initially by employing short-course tactics, and generally went on to win. But already they were slower around any long course than the long-course drag racers of the early 1990s.

With the termination of the Grand Prix programme in 1997, the primary motivation to strive for higher speed was removed, and all Eighteen footer development ceased. At this point, the third era of the Eighteen footer skiffs as a 'no rules' development class ended. To summarise:

- The first era was the 'bigger sails' of 1800–1900 (see Chapter 1, Figs 1.5, 1.6 and 1.7).
- The second era was 1900–38 with regular-programmed, highly visible weekend racing that elevated the big-crew displacement skiffs to iconic status.
- The third era was 1945–97, in which light skiffs first brought the performance of the planing sailboat to a new level, then carried right on to develop very fast apparent wind downwind capability.

The League One-Design Eighteens still sail, but the One-Design rules block all development. They are easier to sail, and they get people onto the water – but it is now all very ho-hum compared with the R and D ferment of the class's glory days when the Eighteens' passion for yet higher speed attracted a huge public and media following as they showed the world the way to sail faster.

Chapter 17 • The 49er

17.1 ■ Concept and origins

In late 1993, about the time Julian was sailing his second and third year *AAMIs* faster than anyone had ever sailed skiffs before, he suggested 'the time is ripe for a good two-hander in the genre of these new Eighteen footers'.

The seminal idea had been hatched by Julian and Peter Johnson of Sunfish Laser over a lunch in Newport. They had discussed the potential conflict between Julian's 1988 B-14, which was growing in Australia, Japan, Canada and England, and Peter's J-14, which was growing in the USA and Scandinavia, but having difficulty moving further afield. They concluded that one way to avoid continuing conflict would be to join forces and make use of the recently developed Eighteen footer technology to make a new boat that was better than either of the existing boats.

Julian asked Takao Otani (of Performance Sailcraft, Japan) if he would like to join a consortium to develop the proposed new boat. Takao's answer was, 'I'll be in if it will be less than 5 metres long.' (This was due to a punitive Japanese import excise on sailboats longer than 5m – which has since been discarded.) Julian's response – 'That's easy. We will make it 4.99m long' – was to give the new concept its ultimate name: 49er.

We started to sketch a new 4.99m two-hander.

17.2 ■ New factors

Three recent developments drove our thinking in a new direction:

1 The new Eighteen footer technology

The detailed developments outlined in Chapter 15 had achieved speed increases relative to the fleet. That these were real had been proven by the No 1 course record sail late in the 1992–3 season. These provided a new and solid technical base for an innovative approach to a two-hander.

2 Helming from trapeze

Seven years earlier, in 1987, the B-14 had expressed our very best technology plus vision. Its primary object had been to bring ice yacht-style apparent wind downwind sailing performance in a small, inexpensive boat to northern hemisphere crews who at that time did not helm from trapeze. This it had done, but by 1994 the worldwide culture had changed. The *Grand Prix Sailing* TV footage was distributed globally, and young helms worldwide were by the early 1990s beginning to copy the Australian 'helm-from-trapeze' technique as the new 'fun buzz'. So there was no longer any need to position the helm other than on trapeze.

3 *Looney Tunes*

In 1992, a senior Time-Warner executive had asked Julian to design and build him the most future-oriented Eighteen footer that Julian could responsibly conceive. This boat was called *Looney Tunes*. This was a seriously interesting boat, a huge departure from the step-by-step cut-and-try development of the mainstream.

Its hull incorporated low-drag rounded-down gunwales, and new low-aerodynamic-drag and ergonomically efficient 'solid' wings. The rig was revolutionary in that it used a wishbone set-up, with the wishbone attaching to the mast at height, and a mainsail luff cuff around the mast base all the way down to deck level.

Looney Tunes joined the 1993 European exhibition tour, with Julian and Raimondo Tonelli sailing with Graham Bird, the owner, and teaching him how to handle the skiff. The jump from college sailing in heavy, slow dinghies 30 years prior to one of the world's hottest skiffs was a very steep learning curve indeed. *Looney Tunes* didn't win anything that year because of the training obligation, but this experience was exactly what the owner wanted so everyone was happy.

Looney Tunes' performance pattern was interesting. It had the usual Eighteen footer wardrobe of two rigs (recently reduced from three), and at the design wind speed for each rig, the boat was significantly faster to windward than its 'conventional' rivals. As the wind became stronger, the wishbone rig became progressively less efficient and the speed advantage reversed, because the wishbone set-up lacked the sophisticated and increasingly automatic adjustment technology that had been developed in conventional rigs over recent years.

Three factors were interacting:

1 The high attachment of the wishbone to the mast supported the mast from buckling backwards when a flogging spinnaker snapped the masthead forward. This permitted a smaller-diameter mast, and was a positive.

2 The mainsail cuff to the deck had been added solely to keep the spinnaker from wrapping around the lower mast and getting caught on the gooseneck, but the boat speed jumped when it was added and this was a positive (we did not understand why until some years later). So at the design wind speed for each rig, where the mainsail was exactly the right shape, the boat bolted.

3 But the wishbone arrangement could not both flatten the upper mainsail and simultaneously free the upper leech to match a stronger unsteady wind, and this proved a big negative.

As always, we needed time to separate and analyse the three factors and their effects, and to understand exactly what was happening.

Julian comments:

Looney Tunes *is the most seminal godparent of the 49er because on it we trialled most of the things which subsequently turned up on the 49er – fabric external spinnaker chute, self-tacking jib, a cuff on the mainsail luff to deck level at the mast, solid wings and wishbone rig. These all showed up first on* Looney Tunes, *and all except the wishbone rig were extremely successful.*

Because of three recent factors – the availability of faster B-18 style technology, the new willingness of non-Australian crews to helm from trapeze, and the lessons learned from the cutting edge Looney Tunes *– we were now in a position to design a helm-from-trapeze two-hander very much faster than either the B-14 or the J-14.*

17.3 ■ The initial English input

In early 1994, as the 4.99m two-hander began to crystallise from a sheaf of calculations into sketches, an English entrepreneur quite independently approached Julian with a request that he design a fast two-hander for a proposed English sports TV production along the lines of the Australian Eighteen footer *Grand Prix Sailing* programme.

The English entrepreneur dreamed of very fast boats racing in close company with the inevitable inadvertent collision and damage, so his aim tended towards expendable hulls of very low cost.

To eliminate the high labour cost of hand-laminated hulls, he suggested to us that the hulls be vacuum-stretch-moulded from point-and-area-reinforced plastic sandwiches by the thermoform process. In this process, multiple layers of plastic, each about 1.6mm thick, are pre-glued in a flat sheet by industrial process to form a sandwich. Strong dense outer skins were separated by sheets of lighter foam, except that strong reinforcement could be added wherever desired and to whatever extent called for. The advantage is that the material from which the flat sandwiches are assembled can be cut and stacked by computerised process and so each flat foam panel can be assembled relatively inexpensively if the batch size is sufficient. The boatbuilder then heats each sheet in an oven until it is sufficiently plastic, transfers it quickly onto a platen, the edges are clamped, an inverted hull mould is lowered over it, and a high-volume suction is applied quickly. This draws the sandwich up into the mould. After a few minutes' cooling, the part is rigid enough to be separated from the mould. Products such as Canadian-style canoes are routinely made in this way, are robust and perform well over long lives. This process gives a hull that is strong enough to bounce off rocks without damage in white-water sports, but that lacks the rigidity needed to set up and maintain the high rig tensions needed by fast sailboats.

The emerging design of our proposed boat meshed closely with what the English entrepreneur was looking for as regards performance. I visited the UK to check the thermoform process as developed to that stage, and concluded that it would be satisfactory at the level we were aiming for.

17.4 ■ The consortium

By mid-1994 the four interested parties – Julian, Peter Johnston, Takao Otani and the UK entrepreneur – all agreed that it was time to go ahead, so we formed a consortium.

From that moment I accepted two new responsibilities, the first of which was administrative. I became the one who defined the long-term and the short-term goals, developed the next three months' plans, estimated the costs, reported progress week by week by correspondence and photos, called for the contributions, got them, and kept the books. In the end, there were seven phases:

1 To agree the mission object.
2 To design, build, sail and develop a prototype, and measure its performance.
3 This was triggered by the ISAF's 'High Performance Olympic Dinghy' – HPOD – criteria which was published in mid-1995. This called for a change in mission object; the consortium unanimously voted to 'go for it'.
4 To build a second prototype to the new design object, and sail and prove it.
5 To present the new design as well as possible at the ISAF's High Performance Olympic Dinghy Evaluation Event which was conducted at Torbole, Lake Garda, in September 1996.
6 This phase was the period of intense lobbying between the Evaluation Event and the ISAF meeting in November 1996 at which the 49er was selected as an Olympic class. Up to this point, the whole project was held together by nothing more than correspondence and consensus. Along the way, significant sums of money were transferred. Both at the time, and in retrospect, it was a most unusual and successful management effort.
7 To hand the new 'mission accomplished' class over to an ISAF-approved class organisation for long-term class management within the ISAF.

My second responsibility was technical. Our small staff were fully occupied making our usual products, so when we had decided the mission object and the design object, and Julian had decided the broad design parameters, it fell to me to complete the detail design and make it.

17.5 ■ Design objects and details

Design

The design objects were agreed as:

- B-18 style very high apparent wind performance in a One-Design two-hander.
- Best possible performance from 0 to 25 knots with one rig.
- Length to be 4.99m or less.
- Hull to be a non-load-bearing thermoformed laminate.

Details

Over a period of a few weeks, Julian summarised his thoughts on the design details:

The big thing by the time we got to the 49er was that we had two new beliefs – we didn't at that time understand the mechanisms or why they worked, but from our own experiments and observation of all of the Eighteens we sensed that there were two new factors at work in the fastest boats.

The first belief was that some of the Eighteen footer hull shapes seemed to sail without baulking at the speed where all theory suggests, and all previous experience had confirmed, that there should be a 'hump' in the drag curve.

Figs 10.3, 10.5 and 10.6 are examples of this 'conventional wisdom' with its humps. Fig 10.8 is the plot that I put aside for some weeks because at first I did not believe that it could be true.

Julian comments again:

In retrospect, the hull which to me felt more 'free' on the water than any other was Prime III. [Prime III *was the third of Julian's two-hander Eighteen footers.*]

We will use the Prime III *hull shape as our starting point. The new boat will be an updated 4.99m version of the 5.49m* Prime III, *transformed in section to float a crew of two.*

The second belief was that in these boats we were also gaining experience with fast 'bow down' non-planing sailing. In the past the normal practice had been to sail bow-up and start planing as soon as the boat was moving fast enough to plane cleanly. But we had found that if we kept the new smaller finer-entry Eighteen footer hulls bow-down and in the water they sailed faster and pointed higher in the 12 to 14 knot boat speed 'sailing to windward' speed range, particularly through waves. Obviously, a hull will lift bodily to some degree, so we will make use of that too by making the boat smaller and sharper yet. The new boat will sail at about 300kg total, so we will design the flotation to displace 280kg and let the dynamic lift (with the bow low) do the rest. The splash rails along the forward chines which we used first on Looney Tunes *have helped achieve this lift without throwing water. We will copy that feature.*

As an example, the present League One-Design Eighteens are rounder in the bottom and have more volume under the mast, but they jump out of the water too soon, which is safe but slow. They are coming out of the water way too early, which is easier to sail and good for survival, but bad for maximum speed.

We will design the new boat to stay in the water for longer and then come out in a controlled manner with the bow still low at very high speed. If we let it come up too early, all we will do is limit the top speed.

We now know a great deal more about rigs. The big difference between the new boat and the Eighteens on which we have done all the recent development is that the new boat will have one rig only and this rig will have to sail fast across the whole wind speed range from 2 to 25 knots. This will mean a longer and more flexible topmast than we have ever used, much more development to get it right, and it will be an interesting exercise to work through.

All the work we have done with foils will be valuable in choosing the fastest shape, area and leading edge radius.

17.6 ■ The prototype design

For greatest accuracy and fairness I set up a drawing surface full size, and on it transformed the lines of the 5.5m *Prime III* into a 4.99m '49er' which would displace 280kg when immersed to the point where the horizontal chines just touched the water. From these lines I cut and set up the keel line and frames, skinned these with 9mm balsa, skinned the balsa inside with strong glass laid in epoxy, faired the outer surface with great care, and then glassed that, and within a few weeks we had our prototype hull. The deck was built similarly. The 49er prototype deliberately duplicated the thermoform approach. It was given no strong frames – nothing beyond the natural rigidity of the balsa-glass-epoxy sandwich.

As soon as the boat was smooth and waterproof we towed the hull and foils at different weights (Fig 10.9) to see whether we had a flyer or a lemon. Within a few weeks, Julian had rigged it and started sailing. At that point it ceased to be 'Frank's project'. I was swept aside by an army of younger sailors who simply could not leave it alone – which is exactly as it should be.

17.7 ■ The prototype rig

The prototype hull and deck were deliberately made 'soft' to duplicate the dynamics of a thermoform structure. To carry the rig loads, Julian designed a light alloy space frame that attached to the hull at the stemhead and the two shroud positions. The mast step did not touch the hull. This frame accepted the shroud and forestay tensions and the mast compression load of about 1 tonne, and performed with every success for close to a year.

Julian comments: 'In the 49er we had to take the skiff rig to extremes. The 49er topmast bends a long way. This exposed it to the idiot factor, but we had no option. The boat had to sail with the same rig from 2 to 25 knots, which is an enormous range – and it does.'

To get the sort of bend and rig dynamics that Julian sensed would be needed, we had our mandrel makers come up with a most unusual mandrel: it was 4.25m long and slightly barrelled. Around this the laminate was wound, baked and separated. This tapered tube was sleeved into a 4.2m small-diameter alloy lower mast, and two spreaders and three stays held the lower mast rigid at whatever curve gave the lower mainsail the fullness desired for the day. The upper mast yielded to flatten the upper sail and free the upper leech in the gusts. Julian decided to stay with the wishbone rig trialled on *Looney Tunes*.

The initial rig was astonishingly good. The sail area chosen – main 15sq m, jib 6.5sq m, spinnaker 38sq m – was right in the sense that it was practical for two people to handle, and from the first sail proved blindingly fast.

The first topmast invited stiffening a little here, softening there. The second was very close to ideal. The third – the Rev 3 – was dynamically perfect and these dynamics have never been changed since. What *has* been changed are the mechanical arrangements, of which more later.

17.8 ■ The ergonomic revolution

In the virgin-new 49er Julian was able to express to the ultimate his revulsion against the Eighteen footer mammoths with their hydraulics and the over-gadgeted 5o5s, 470s etc, with their 13 separate and demanding adjustments. While these represented the traditional industrial design ergonomics of their day, he understood full well that they simply kept crews so busy focusing inside the boat fiddling with their gear that they had no time to look outside the boat to see, plan, and use the changes and gusts that more successful sailors saw and exploited on their way to winning.

About this time I was writing 'If a boat needs to be constantly adjusted as it sails along, the designer has not finished his job.' Fig 17.1 says it all. The absolutely clean deck under a near-automatic rig, and the total absence of all unnecessary adjustment gadgets, is as revolutionary as the skiff-derived design itself.

Fig 17.1 also shows a second revolution: the deck and wings form a continuous surface across which the sailors can run quickly from side to side without needing to look to see where they put their feet. Compare this with the tedious task of the sailor of any boat with pipe racks – he needs to cross the gap between pipe and gunwale, unhook, step down onto the cockpit floor, cross to the other side, hook up, mount the gunwale, and negotiate the other gap. And do it all with appropriate care, otherwise he falls through the gap into the drink.

What we see with the 49er prototype is the beginning of a new style of skiff design in which the boat itself is designed with fast ergonomics as opposed to the adequate but slower ergonomics of the conventional boats

Fig 17.1 49er general arrangements

of the mid-1990s. This approach had its roots in the year when Julian started this process by reducing the tacking time of *AAMI III* from 20 seconds to 13 seconds (Section 15.7).

In Section 17.16 we will see that when put to the test, the 49er delivered a level of performance much faster than would be expected from simple consideration of its length, wingspan, sail area, and weight. The point I wish to emphasise here is that the features that made this performance advance possible – the technology advances that flowed from years of experience with the revolutionary Eighteen foot skiffs – were designed into the concept from the beginning, and were then further refined as the prototype was developed.

As launched, the prototype was already the fastest skiff on the harbour except for the top Eighteens. Over the next few months I measured its performance in different wind strengths, and we were all very happy to see that the unusual 'no hump' drag curves had contributed to a performance with unusually high windward-going speed. We had always been confident of good downwind speed, and that was there too.

With development, this performance level simply became available over a wider range of wind speed.

17.9 ■ The test pilots

During that era, the practice was growing for top overseas crews to visit Sydney for the Eighteen footer season, and be provided with a sponsorship and the best of last year's boats that were still available. This suited the programme producer because it gave an international flavour to what would otherwise have been a purely Australian activity. It suited the sailors because it gave them a near-zero-cost way of coming to grips with the revolutionary Australian Eighteen footers and the compact circle of designers and sailors who designed, built and sailed them. Because of Julian's several prior European tours, he enjoyed personal friendships with most of the sailors and was naturally their initial contact. Our small company often seemed more like a league of nations than a boatbuilding business. At first they all floundered towards the back of the fleet, but before long they became competitive and to be reckoned with. Charlie and Jonathan McKee from Seattle (both Olympic medallists), Anders Lewander and Peter Mikos from Stockholm, and Tim Robertson from the UK, were typical of these regular visitors.

The 49er has been international in both design and development from its inception. The design inputs are noted above.

The prototype was first sailed from Balmoral (the bay NE of '9' in Fig 1.22) one blustery afternoon, crewed by Julian and Charlie McKee. From then on, whoever wanted to sail it only had to ask, and if they came from the other side of the world so much the better. All we asked in return was an honest assessment. The opinions of all who sailed it were recorded, read and valued; we regarded criticism by the widest possible circle of test pilots as essential, and the boat's very thorough working over from the beginning by this fortuitous international panel of sailors was a critical step in its development. It accumulated hours on the water at a very high rate. In general, they asked for no major change other than to question the controllability of the wishbone rig in strong winds. But they made many suggestions for small changes, all of which were tried and many adopted.

17.10 ■ 'Bye-bye wishbone'

The wishbone rig did not survive, though we gave it our best shot. Julian tried a number of different geometries. Some were better than others in different wind speeds, but as the wind became stronger and gustier, the wishbone was simply not as controllable nor as efficient as the best conventional rigs developed on the top Eighteens, and therefore not as fast.

In place of the wishbone, Julian fitted a boom and ram vang arrangement that we had trialled some years earlier and that preserved most of the mechanical and ergonomic advantages of the wishbone rig. The attachment point of the vang strut was kept relatively high. This created a stable point between the hounds and the deck where the strut held the mast forward, and lower stays attached at the same point held it back. This allowed the use of a smaller-diameter lower mast, which was a very important aerodynamic advance.

The lack of obstruction below the boom enabled the forward hand to move more quickly from side to side, so retaining this vital ergonomic advantage.

The extension of the luff by a cuff to deck level had been added to *Looney Tunes* initially to stop the spinnaker from getting caught around the gooseneck, but the unexpected performance advantage was so obvious that it was unthinkable not to retain it.

This new rig called for a further surge in trialling and development, and testing relative to known boats established that Julian had designed well. The new rig was as fast in lighter winds as the wishbone, and in stronger winds was both faster and properly controllable.

17.11 ■ Three steps along the way

While the on-the-water development of the prototype was progressing well, three unexpected events were to redirect the whole enterprise. The first two caused the project to mark time for a few weeks:

1 The UK proposal to create a 'UK Grand Prix' style sports TV programme based on skiff spectacle did not proceed, so that particular market, and the UK consortium partner, vanished.
2 One of the remaining consortium partners withdrew his preference for the thermoplastic hull manufacturing method, and opted instead for roto-moulding. He argued that the then-new roto-moulding technology of a dense thin outer skin backed by a thicker, lighter, foamed inner skin would be of acceptable weight and rigidity and less expensive than the thermoform process. This may or may not have been true. The practical difficulty was that at that time there was not a roto-moulding oven in the world big enough to accept a 49er mould. The other consortium partners became increasingly concerned as to what he proposed to do about this small problem. While we were awaiting his solution –
3 The International Sailing Federation (ISAF) promulgated its High Performance Olympic Dinghy (HPOD) criteria in 1995.

17.12 ■ The ISAF HPOD criteria

In early 1995 the International Sailing Federation published its 'High Performance Olympic Dinghy' (HPOD) criteria, and circulated copies to all builders of small sailboats worldwide. The background to this document goes back to the revival of sailing after the 1939–45 war 50 years earlier.

In the late 1940s and the 1950s the new affordable glass fibre sailboats with their revived trapezes were providing excitement by performing above expectation. Sailors were flocking to sailing in large numbers, and the sport enjoyed both a large share of the recreational market and also substantial media coverage. We called those years 'the dinghy boom'.

The IYRU, now ISAF, knew a good thing when they saw it, so they made sure in their 1950s reorganisation that nobody could spoil it by changing anything too easily. In institutionalising this 'no change' policy, they were brilliantly successful. In the Olympic classes, for example, the classes of boats have occasionally changed, but there has been no significant change in the appearance of the boats nor their performance levels for over 40 years.

Unfortunately for the ISAF, their ability to deny change within their compass was unable to save them from the wider effects, because they were unable to prevent the rest of the world from changing. The belief that if you change nothing you will be safe from change is as flawed in sailing as it is in all other walks of life. The world itself changes, and as it changes, expectations change. The ISAF's pinnacle Olympic 1950s and 1960s style sailboats are now regarded as dull and stodgy, sailing's share of the recreational market has collapsed, and with it so has media coverage. The TV coverage of sailing at the Atlanta Olympics was virtually zero.

This was bad enough, but while this decline in the reputation of sailing as an exciting contemporary recreation was going on, the International Olympic Committee has progressively turned the Olympics into a global TV sports spectacular which is now so expensive that it can be paid for only by massive fees for global TV rights. TV pays for visual spectacle; to justify inclusion within the Olymics, every sport must now present with spectacle sufficient to attract its share of the TV audience. The consequence is that all sports that are not, or cannot become, TV spectaculars are now candidates for exclusion from the Olympics and sailing is no exception.

Following the pre-Atlanta Olympics, the IOC approached the ISAF with the blunt message 'Either lift your game and become TV spectacular, or get out of the Olympics'. When the ISAF looked for spectacle in sailing such as would attract a regular mass TV audience, there was nothing, nothing at all within establishment sailing anywhere in the world.

But in the skiffs it was there, and up in neon. The Australian skiffs had already developed and proven the full package – the new apparent wind downwind performance was fast, exciting, and spectacular to watch.

Regular TV programmes based on these skiffs attracted a mass non-sailing audience sufficient to achieve high prime-time ratings. Brilliantly liveried boats raced tactically over short courses laid out in photogenic locations. The best excitement, spectacle and uncertainty comes from relatively small, evenly matched fleets, so prior elimination races limit the starters in the final televised races. A mass audience does not understand the rules detail of any sport, and for TV spectacle and audience satisfaction, protest proceedings held after the race are unthinkable, so umpires must penalise infringements on the water and the first boat over the line is the winner. This sort of package attracts and holds a mass TV audience.

If the ISAF had been able to put Eighteen footers into the Olympics, they would presumably have done so. But at one extreme the anarchic 'no rules' skiffies wanted nothing of the ISAF and its rules; at the other extreme, an Olympic medal is meant to be equally available to a sailor from Botswana or Berlin. This would not work with Eighteens, because skiff construction culture was based on only one city, and the hometown builders were so far ahead they would be hard to beat. So a different approach had to be devised.

The approach decided upon by the ISAF was intelligent and effective. It was decided to create a new One-Design class in the image of the Eighteen foot skiffs – that is, with a level of performance capable of generating TV spectacle, but with an administrative class structure that could exist within the ISAF and the Olympic environment.

The first step in this process was for the ISAF to empower a committee to draft, agree and publish 'High Performance Olympic Dinghy' (HPOD) criteria, and send it worldwide to all manufacturers of small sailboats. In essence it stated that:

- The ISAF wished to see developed a class of boat that did not at that time exist.
- They had in mind a One-Design two-hander which would sail with a level of speed and performance that would deliver visual spectacle similar to that of the Eighteen foot skiffs.
- It was intended that an Evaluation Event would be held in about a year's time at which builders who so wished would be invited to present their boats for evaluation.

17.13 ■ The consortium's response to the criteria

We received a copy of the HPOD criteria, and I circulated it to the consortium.

Julian and I together considered the criteria. Not surprisingly, our skiff-derived two-hander fitted the HPOD criteria closely. On the positive side, the prototype had already been sailing for nearly a year. It had been unusually well tested by a wide range of sailors from many countries and their responses had been uniformly enthusiastic. We had already developed it beyond its original concept by, for example, the change from wishbone rig to boom plus ram vang mainsail control. It 'sailed like a skiff', was unquestionably fast, and was already delivering the spectacular performance desired by the ISAF and the IOC.

But neither of the intended low-cost construction technologies for the hull could possibly be available and developed within the one-year time frame available, and the only way to produce a superior boat within the time frame specified would be to use the best existing construction technology. This would apply equally to everybody else, so it represented a change rather than a negative. And since we were routinely making the world's lightest, strongest and fastest skiffs year by year, on balance this had to be an advantage for us.

Julian thought about this for a few days, and stated that:

- He could redesign the hull as a load-bearing structure within a short time by using present Eighteen footer hull construction technology.
- The performance of such a boat would be higher than that of either the prototype or the proposed production boat because of the anticipated lighter weight plus the greater rigidity of the hull.
- The visual appeal of the boat he had in mind would be of a new order.
- The consortium's design object would need to be changed from 'best available performance at minimum cost' to 'best possible performance at acceptable cost'.

I advised the consortium, and set up a meeting to consider the matter. The consortium unanimously opted to change the design objects as suggested and to proceed with the suggested boat with a view to presenting it for HPOD evaluation. This decision was taken in early to mid-1995.

A critical consequence of the change to conventional construction was that David Ovington of Ovington Boats in the UK, who was building our Eighteen foot skiffs under licence and so was familiar with our construction technology, would become a consortium member and our UK constructor.

17.14 ■ The 49er final design

Julian had recently produced a formidable output of very fast skiffs, and the 49er prototype was at least as fast as we expected, so we considered that the superior performance desired by the ISAF had already been achieved. This left Julian free, in approaching the new challenge, to make the most of his recent work in both responding to the AAMI marketing request to make the AAMI Eighteen footers more visually appealing, and also the request to think outside the box in the design of *Looney Tunes*.

He dreamed for a few days, then astonishingly quickly produced the working sketches of a gracefully styled boat that looked like nothing else built at that time. It combined visual grace and beauty with hard-nose practicality. The hull is light, stiff and durable. The boat's dynamic efficiency and advanced ergonomics give it a sheer speed on the water which puts it into a class of its own. The graceful styling was unique, and the astonishing thing was that he did it so quickly.

Our approach to this opportunity over the next few months was fast, efficient and professional. We decided not just to build a prototype for the evaluation event – instead, we decided to put the new boat into production as soon as we could.

We were confident of the growing international reputation of the Eighteen foot skiffs, and were extremely fortunate that skiff crews from all over the world had been sailing the prototype for many months, and that they had reported its outstanding performance worldwide to the point where we were already receiving enquiries and potential orders. So the 4.99m skiff-derived prototype already commanded a potential global market, and an established class with numbers of boats already sailing worldwide could only improve its appeal to the HPOD Evaluation Committee.

We did not touch the bottom of the balsa-glass-epoxy prototype below the chines. It was fair and stiff and it sailed fast, and that proven shape would be the shape of the production boat. We modified the topsides and deck. We increased the gunwale freeboard 50mm, took a mould from what was now a plug, built the first production hull in it, and into that built a deck to the new design. This became the production prototype. We took a mould from that, and proceeded step by step with the internal framing in the same way until we had moulds for everything and plugs for all the moulds.

Meantime, the new production prototype had been rigged and was sailing hard. Again we welcomed the opinions of all who asked to sail it, and if they came from Ukraine or South America so much the better. So it was routinely and extensively sailed not only by us, but by crews from all over the world. It proved a little faster than the original prototype, and nicer to handle because of the added freeboard – and particularly the improved ergonomics of the 'solid' deck plus wing surface. It was lighter, the shallow dished deck, sloped transom and 'solid' wings all had less aerodynamic drag, and the smooth continuous dished deck and wing surface presented greatly improved ergonomics for the crew to run across, so we expected it to be faster, and it was.

17.15 ■ Global spread

The overview of what had happened was that, because we had started our two-hander project 18 months prior to the release of the HPOD criteria, we found ourselves with a contender fully tested and proven, and not only sailing fast but in production in both Australia and the UK many months prior to the Evaluation Event. This had all happened within a few months of the release of the HPOD criteria.

Very quickly, sailors and builders around the world took a view that looked at the here and now and had little to do with a future evaluation event yet to be announced. What they saw was a new style of two-hander straight from the lineage of years of cutting edge development of the fastest of the Australian Eighteen foot skiffs. The new boat mirrored the skiffs' uniquely fast performance. They saw a boat that had for the past year been transparently worked up and developed by being sailed by crews from all over the world. These crews had reported that this boat was like no other.

Not surprisingly, builders worldwide did not wait for the Evaluation Event. They approached us for the right to build the 49er, and the tooling to do so. By the time the Evaluation Event was conducted at Torbole,

Lake Garda, in September 1996, the 49er was in production in Australia, the UK and in the USA. The world fleet was 168 boats which were sailing in Australia, New Zealand, the USA, Canada, the UK, some countries in Europe, in Japan, and in South Africa.

17.16 ■ The evaluation event

The approach of the Evaluation Committee was intelligent and effective. The mechanism was to publish in 1995 the 'High Performance Olympic Dinghy' (HPOD) criteria. Those who responded were later invited to attend an Evaluation Event at Torbole, Lake Garda, which was conducted by the ISAF Evaluation Committee on 6–10 September 1996.

Eleven 'works teams' representing either manufacturers or classes accepted the invitation, each with up to three of their boats. The boats were: OD-14, Flying Dutchman, Mach 2, 5o5, Int 14, ISO, B-14, Jet, BOSS, L5000, 49er. The Mach 2 was a Flying Dutchman hull with a larger rig and sails and two on trapeze. It proved difficult to right following capsize. The Jet was a smaller boat designed specially for the event.

We attended with three 49ers. As mentioned earlier, the first carried only the 49er class insignia and its sail number. The second carried the biggest Australian flag that would fit on the mainsail, so that everybody could see what the boat would look like if the ISAF chose to go that route. (This initiative has developed into the stylised national flag livery on mainsails and spinnakers now used for on-the-water identification.) The third was given full 'Grand Prix' sponsor's livery on hull and sails, as are the top Eighteens, so that this approach too could be looked at and considered.

At the Evaluation Event, the contenders were evaluated in four ways:
1 ISAF technical officers checked the 11 designs for compliance with the HPOD criteria. Not all complied.
2 Twenty experienced but generally younger sailors, seventeen men and three women, helms and forward hands, had been chosen by the ISAF from the many around the world who had offered to be their countries' 'test pilots'. These became the 'National Authority' (NA) sailors who sailed the boats and ranked them for handling, performance and desirability as a potential Olympic class.
3 From time to time, familiarisation sailing was interrupted and short races were conducted both to establish that these boats did in fact deliver higher performance than the existing Olympic classes and, at a second level, to ascertain which of them was fastest.
4 The generally older ISAF Evaluation Committee members observed everything and wrote their report in the following weeks.

The format was that the first and second days were for familiarisation sailing during which every NA sailor would sail every design. The third and fourth days were to be given to formal evaluation work.

On the first day, the morning northerly blew at 5 to 10 knots before it faded about noon. The afternoon southerly set in and built to about 15 knots with stronger gusts. The second day started with an early morning breeze of 14 to 16 knots, with gusts to 20, but mist then enveloped the mountains and the wind died and stayed calm for the rest of the day.

The individual sailing was periodically interrupted for racing – four-leg windward–leeward courses of about 30 minutes' total duration were sailed. The Evaluation Committee ruled that no more than two of each class should start. For optimum and consistent performance, the initial races were crewed by 'works team' sailors. In our case, the helms were Julian, and Jonathan McKee from Seattle; and the forward hands were Abby Parkes from Sydney, and Peter Mikos from Sweden. Abby owns and helms her B-14; Jonathan is a Gold Medallist in the Flying Dutchman class, and a very good Eighteen footer helm.

Two races were sailed the first day and one on the second. A consistent pattern established in which the two 49ers finished close together in a downwind finish with the third boat, whichever it was, usually just rounding the windward mark. As an example, the elapsed times for the second race were 27 minutes plus or minus 2 seconds for first and second, and 31 minutes 30 seconds – that is, 4 minutes 30 seconds or 17% slower – for third place.

Both Julian and I were astonished at this difference in raw performance. On paper, our 49er was a very average boat. It was not the longest, widest, or lightest – nor did it have the biggest sails. I expected it to sail well, but I expected all the other boats to sail well too. I had expected the boat speeds to be close, and still expected the outcome of the Evaluation Event to be close. But from the very first race, and regardless of the wind strength, the two 49ers simply separated from the fleet within seconds of the start and consistently finished about one downwind leg in front of whichever boat was third in the four-leg windward–leeward races. It is clear that simple statistics of length, beam, sail area and weight bear surprisingly little relationship to performance with boats of this nature.

As the Evaluation Event proceeded, I sensed that four factors were emerging as critical – performance; styling; lineage; and an advanced but rational performance equalisation system (Chapter 12).

With respect to performance equalisation, the 49er was the only boat to offer complete compensation – wider wings for the lighter crews, but with a ballast penalty to keep heavier crews happy, plus then a reduction in ballast to compensate the lighter crews for their slower tacking in their wider-winged boats.

Of the four factors, the most obvious was the large and consistent performance difference. This called for response, so a whispering campaign was put around that yes, the 49er was fast, but it was so difficult to sail that only a handful of sailors worldwide could possibly sail it – therefore it could not be considered as a practical boat for merely Olympic-level sailors.

Julian's response was direct and effective. As the afternoon ora (southerly lake breeze) started to blow up the lake after the noon calm period on the third day, he set off singlehanded. In the rising wind he sailed offshore upwind on port tack, tacked, sailed back to close inshore upwind of the club, executed a bear-away and gybe hoist, and swept fast downwind past the club under spinnaker at full stretch on trapeze, executed a perfect gybe drop while steering with the tiller between his knees, and sailed upwind back to the ramp. No sailor from any of the other teams was game enough to attempt to repeat this singlehanded effort in any other boat. That was the end of 'the 49er is too difficult to sail' whispering campaign.

The background to this was again the Eighteen footer European tours. While waiting for the wind, crews had been in the habit of amusing themselves by sailing Eighteen footers singlehanded, and seeing if they could hoist a spinnaker, sail with it, and drop it, before the boat fell over. In comparison with an Eighteen, the smaller 49er is relatively easy to sail singlehanded, and several other helms have since demonstrated their ability to sail the 49er singlehanded.

As the Evaluation Event progressed, we were asked first if we would accept NA sailors as either helms or forward hands, and later the 49ers were by committee request raced solely by NA sailors.

The third and the fourth days were given to evaluation. Every NA sailor sailed every class in a fixed exercise: launch, and when ready cross the start line, sail a short four-leg upwind/downwind race, cross the finish line and return to shore, where he or she then retired and completed a questionnaire in private. The final three questions were 'What do you think of the xxx as a boat?', 'Would you buy one if you could afford it?' and 'Should the xxx be in the Olympics?' An 'exit poll' suggested that the NA sailors' opinions were as convincing as the performance differences. The 49er scored 17 out of 20 on two of these questions and 16 on the third. The most scored by any other class was 4 or 5.

On the fifth morning the Evaluation Committee asked to borrow four boats for a closer look at HPOD criteria detail such as whether ballast carried by light crews for performance equalisation purposes could affect, say, the difficulty of righting following capsize. (It did affect it critically with one boat – a light crew of two women were unable to right a heavily ballasted boat from the inverted position.)

The Evaluation Committee, under the chairmanship of Mike Jackson, was thorough with its planning, its technical approach and its execution, and I am delighted to record above how well they planned and carried out their task. Their report favoured the 49er, and the rest is history.

My thanks go further, because historically my view is that the ISAF has not been good at making sound technical decisions, as opposed to questionable political ones. As an example, a similar evaluation three decades ago favoured the Etchells, but when it came to implementing the change, national politics reigned supreme and the European Soling was substituted regardless of the evaluated superiority of the American Etchells. With this example as our warning, it was hard to see how anybody could get an Australian upstart through a rigid Eurocentric bureaucracy. But it happened, and I thank those who put technical superiority ahead of political expediency.

Subsequent note regarding performance

The surprising performance difference between the skiff-derived 49er and the next fastest dinghies first evident at the Evaluation Event has been confirmed year by year in the Portsmouth Yardstick numbers. For example, the 2004 PYN of the 49er is 747, of the Laser 5000 and the Boss is 846 and 847 respectively – 13.4% slower. All other boats are slower again. Skiffs tend to sail downwind twice as fast as upwind, so a difference of 16.6% will see the faster boat finish a four-leg race downwind as the follower rounds the top mark. Julian and Jonathan McKee were both very experienced, very fast Eighteen foot skiff sailors. None of the other helms at the Evaluation Event enjoyed anywhere near their level of skiff experience. That probably accounted for the other 3%.

17.17 ■ Refinements

Topmasts

As numbers of 49ers began to race closely, the topmast came in for criticism on two counts:

- Its stiffness changed with time, *and*
- It broke too often.

Opinion focused on the carbon/glass mix as the culprit. In Chapter 8 the differences between carbon and glass are described. Carbon is stiff, but tends to be brittle. Glass is flexible, elastic and tough, but has its problems when laminated with polyester resin. If they are mixed with care, the result can be the stiffness and lightness of carbon with the toughness of glass. But if they are mixed without due care, it is possible that light carbon filaments can occasionally be over-stretched and fail progressively, and in this way the stiffness of the laminate can change with time. As I saw it, there were three possibilities:

1. The carbon-glass mix could be wrong, leading to progressive failure of the carbon.
2. The polyester-carbon-glass laminate could be being over-stressed, leading to progressive softening of the glass-polyester laminate, like a Laser or a 470 hull.
3. It could be something else.

I did not think that it could be 1 or 2, because we had designed the laminate with a 100% safety margin. But – as always – I went back to basics to get the facts. As a starting point, I conducted two tests.

The first was based on the fact that a fibre-reinforced-plastic laminate always makes a noise when it fails, and generally the noise starts some time prior to the point of catastrophic failure. My first object was to measure how far a topmast could be bent before it started to make a noise.

When the 49er topmast is bent to extreme to flatten the sail in strong wind, the axis at the top is bent backwards through 30° as compared with the axis at the bottom (of the topmast). I set up a topmast laminate (with no sailtrack) by tying the bottom and the forestay attachment point to strong points, and pulling the tip back progressively with a spring balance to measure the force.

At 30° bend, there was no noise whatever. As we bent it through 40°, then 50°, and released the tension and re-applied it, there was no noise, and it returned to its original straightness and needed the same force to bend it the same distance. At about 57°, the crackling started, and Fig 17.2 shows this bend. The photo is taken from the roof looking vertically down the corner of the building (the white bit). Because the plane of

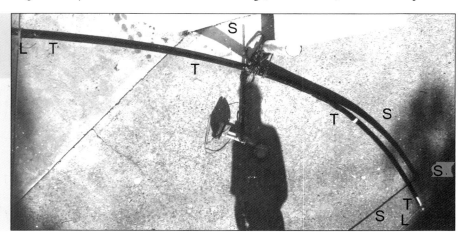

Fig 17.2 A 49er topmast undergoing bend test

T Topmast
L Ropes
S Shadows

Fig 17.3 A 49er topmast undergoing fatigue test

The topmast is clamped at the bottom, supported at the forestay attachment point, loaded (approx 25kg) at tip to bend 30°. Added tension at tip oscillates the tip through 150mm at 50 cycles per minute. No change was detected after 250 000 cycles.

the pavement changes from slope on the right to level on the left, the shadow from the low sun does not repeat the curve of the topmast. To avoid confusion I have identified the shadows. We pulled harder still and it broke at about 58°. This confirmed that our designed 100% safety margin was real.

The problem was not progressive failure of the carbon at 30° bend.

To see whether it could be the sort of glass-polyester fatigue softening described in Section 8.4 (called creep), I set up a test rig on which the topmast was secured strongly at its base, supported with a pad at the forestay position, bent 30° with about 25kg of weights tied to the tip, and flexed through 6 inches 50 times per minute. Fig 17.3 shows this apparatus. Each test occupied several days, and we left it running overnight. We stopped the test morning and evening – about every 30 000 to 40 000 cycles – and measured the absolute deflection between the original position of the tip unloaded, the present position unloaded, and the original and present positions when loaded with a fixed weight. Fairly soon a trend appeared. In the cooler mornings, the deflection of the 8.25m topmast was a few millimetres less than in the warmer afternoons. What was happening was that we were measuring the slight differences in stiffness due to temperature, and the huge number of cycles under extreme working load was having no effect whatever on the stability of the laminate. After three days and a quarter of a million cycles of this punishment, the absolute deflections were unchanged. I decided that enough was enough.

The problem wasn't softening by creep.

It is so easy to overlook the simple things. An alert sailor mentioned that the rivets holding the alloy sail track to the FRP laminate were working loose at the ends. When we checked, we found three facts:

1   The stiffness of the FRP laminate plus the alloy track was 40% greater than the stiffness (rate of spring) of the FRP laminate alone.
2   The rivets worked loose with use, starting at the ends.
3   As they worked loose, the alloy sail track started to slide over the laminate, and in this way the mast-plus-alloy-sail-track assembly became softer.

Our response was not to improve the riveting, but to remove the problem completely by designing and sourcing tough high-molecular-weight plastic sail track, which we now glue on. This plastic track stiffens the topmast by 1%, not 40%, so we developed a stronger FRP topmast so that the new Rev 9 topmast plus the new plastic track finishes with exactly the same bend properties as the Rev 3 topmast with its alloy track.

A second major advantage of the 'glue on' method is that the sharp rivet shanks protruding into the mast cavity were eliminated. These had both increased the friction when hoisting the spinnaker and damaged the halyard, and eliminating the rivets cured both of these problems.

At root, the 49er calls for its topmast to bend much further than had been customary with any boat in the past. One consequence was that normal riveting yielded, and we fixed it by removing the rivets. That has solved the softening problem.

Finding out what was causing the random breakages came out of left field. A sharp-eyed forward hand racing on Lake Garda happened to be watching the boat ahead. Its spinnaker flogged and the topmast failed. What he saw in that split second was that as the spinnaker flogged, the upper spreaders twisted far out of line and then the mast failed.

Of course! Again, this was due to the unusual degree of backward bend. On a yacht mast that stays straight, a sideways pull creates no twist force. But on a mast that is bent far back, a sideways tug on the tip by a flogging spinnaker will twist it unless it is designed to resist twisting. As the upper spreaders are twisted out of column, a point will be reached where the shrouds can no longer support the topmast adequately and it buckles sideways under the reduced moment and greatly increased tension of the twisted stays.

We redesigned the laminate schedule so that carbon tapes now spiral around the laminate both ways between lower and upper spreaders: there is no more excess twisting; no more spreaders going out of line; no more of those breakages.

It is called development.

The terms of acceptance of the 49er by the Evaluation Committee wisely foreshadowed a year to tidy up whatever was deemed necessary prior to freezing the 49er design as 'formal One-Design'. The topmast work above fell into this category. I think it took a little longer than a year, but we were transparent about what we were doing, we were obviously making solid progress, and the final Rev 9 mast plus plastic sail track has given excellent service since it was introduced ten years ago.

Two further changes have been adopted by the class.

Rudder stock

Following the development some years later of a light, inexpensive, practical and strong cast alloy rudder stock for the 29er, the 49er class has opted for a similar cast alloy rudder stock.

Performance equalisation schedule

Following three years' successful experience, 1997–2000, with a four-step performance equalisation rule, the class eliminated one step and adopted a simpler three-step rule after the 2000 Sydney Olympics (see Chapter 12).[1]

---

[1] A very recent development has been the ruling by the ISAF that this form of performance equalisation should be abandoned on medical grounds (see the note at the end of Chapter 12).

Chapter 18 • Transition Years

18.1 ■ The big changes

The asymmetric spinnaker first flown on *Prime II* was an extremely successful experiment. Its primary object was to reduce the workload on the forward hand of a two-hander Eighteen footer. Even in its initial form the system was unexpectedly efficient in that not only was the spinnaker much easier to set and drop than with the conventional gybing pole system; further, once set it sailed about as fast as the best conventional gybing pole spinnakers of the day.

From the practical point of view, it was a very good first trial.

From the philosophical point of view, it was revolutionary. It was revolutionary because the principle of the new rig bypassed the previous limit on downwind speed.

If your vision is to waft downwind with the wind behind you, it is self-evident that you must always sail downwind at a speed slower than the wind. But if you think in terms of tacking downwind like an ice yacht, much higher speeds are possible. This new principle opened the way to speeds on the water that previously had been unattainable.

So the important contribution of the new rig was not so much the convenience of the simpler system, nor the faster sets and drops, nor the speeds initially achieved – it was the promise of speeds progressively faster than had ever previously been contemplated. The effort to achieve these higher speeds has fuelled a development surge that continues to this day.

Note that not one but two fundamental principles have been changed.

The first change is that the apparent wind when sailing downwind has moved from behind the beam in the case of the conventional boat to ahead of the beam in the case of the apparent wind boat.

The second change is that the change of speed of the apparent wind with change of boat speed has been reversed. In a conventional boat, the faster the boat sails downwind, the lighter the apparent wind becomes. If a boat surfs a wave, the apparent wind can become zero. In an apparent wind boat, the faster it sails, the stronger the apparent wind becomes. If the boat surfs a wave and accelerates, the apparent wind just gets stronger.

18.2 ■ Spinnaker size

As previously discussed in Chapter 14, in the early 1990s an annual 'circus' developed in that a container full of three or four Sydney Eighteen footers was invited to a mini 'circuit' of demonstration sailing at European resorts for a month or two each northern hemisphere summer. There the boats and crews sailed for demonstration or race. The unique performance level of these boats drew big spectator crowds and in this way promoted both the resorts and the boats themselves. These forays were run on a shoestring. Each boat had its three rigs, but otherwise there was minimal spares back-up. It is a great credit to these remarkable boats that they kept on sailing reliably even when 10 000 miles from their usual support bases.

As noted in Section 14.8, one year a big spinnaker blew out and shredded. From that point on, one of the boats would have to be without a big spinnaker in the lighter winds. Julian Bethwaite elected to be the one to do without.

He experimented, on the assumption that with a smaller sail the optimum downwind VMG would be achieved with a faster boat speed. He sailed a little higher and pushed the boat faster. As the apparent wind went forward beyond a certain point, the relatively full asymmetric spinnaker collapsed at the leading edge. The fix for this, 10 000 miles from home, was to flatten the sail by easing the halyard. As the sail sagged to leeward, it tended to assume the shape of a horizontal semi-cylinder, and the further it was allowed to sag, the flatter it became in the luff-to-leech direction.

Julian experimented systematically. He flattened the spinnaker until it was exactly right for the higher speed; he then lifted the centreboard further and shifted the tack of the spinnaker back a little along the bowsprit, to optimise balance. He adjusted the sheet block position for optimum trim and angle of the flattened sail. With a big spinnaker, the blanketed mainsail becomes so ineffective that it was normally just sheeted tight to act as a backstay, and otherwise ignored. With the smaller spinnaker and higher speed and closer pointing, the big mainsail began to enjoy useful wind and contribute drive force again, and accurate mainsail trim began to be rewarded with a stronger turbine blade effect, giving extra drive force from the smaller spinnaker and better balance. This extra force enabled the faster-sailing boat to sail lower while holding its higher speed.

The astonishing result of this episode was that the smaller-spinnaker boat began to beat its big-spinnaker rivals downwind, even in lighter 'big-rig' weather. The short-term result of this was the beginning of the 'smaller spinnakers, not bigger ones, are faster downwind' design trend. The longer-term result shows in rigs such as those of the 49er and 29er. From the aerodynamic point of view, their spinnakers are relatively narrow, relatively flat blades of moderate area with not an inch of overlap. (It is interesting to look at the slatted and triple-flapped high-lift array of a 747 wing on final approach with flaps fully extended – everything mates exactly and nothing, *repeat nothing*, overlaps.)

From a handling point of view, the spinnakers have become aerodynamically almost balanced around their pivot axis from tack to head. This design development has the advantage that they can be controlled in trim angle with surprisingly light sheet loads.

18.3 ■ Automatic response

The forerunner to the modern Eighteen footer was Julian's B-14. All the 'smaller and lighter is faster' dynamics were there – elimination of vertical bulkheads, static lower mast, flexible topmast, unstayed flexible retractable spinnaker pole. Why unstayed? Look again at the point above re control of fullness by easing the halyard. This leads to another story.

When the B-14 was first introduced into the UK, a major yachting magazine offered to conduct and publish a boat test. Julian was asked to sail at Queen Mary reservoir with a test skipper nominated by the magazine. When they launched, Julian was surprised – but on further thought *not* surprised – to see an International 14 launch from further down the shore. Boat tests are usually an objective stand-alone test of a particular boat. This one was apparently to be a comparison of the antipodean upstart with a British icon. So be it.

My point in relating this story is twofold. First, it is nice to be able at last to report the presence of the International 14 that day. The fact that no word of its presence appeared in the published article attests the opinion of the magazine staff of the relative performance of the two boats under test conditions.

Second, I know no better example of the advantage of the automatic rig. What Julian recalls is that the boats sailed upwind, crosswind and downwind for some hours under test conditions in winds of varying strength. The International 14 may never have got ahead, but it either stayed abeam or close astern when conditions were relatively steady, so there was little difference in speed in steady conditions. But when conditions changed quickly, significant differences appeared. As an example, on one particular leg both boats started at the windward dam wall. The International 14 had borne away, set spinnaker and was planing fast across the dam. The B-14, following, planed at about the same speed in the same wind, which was relatively steady for the first part of the leg. Then both boats entered a patch with unsteady wind. The International 14 staggered and slowed. The B-14, with its rig flexing nicely, maintained its speed and shot past.

What was happening in those gusts was that with each gust onslaught it was not only the B-14's flexible topmast that yielded. The flexible spinnaker pole also yielded, and in yielding it momentarily flattened the spinnaker towards the fastest shape for optimum drive force and least drag in the momentarily stronger apparent wind of the gust peaks. This momentary yielding both preserved or increased the boat speed through the rapidly changing conditions, and it gave the crew enough time – probably about half a second – to begin to accommodate to the new wind with sail trim and tiller.

Whatever was happening on the International 14 with its rigidly stayed bowsprit/spinnaker pole was not so kind to the speed of the boat.

18.4 ■ The apparent-wind-angle (beta) limit

If you compare pictures of the fastest mid-1980s skiffs with present state-of-the-art boats like the 49er, the big difference is not so much the smaller sails and more flexible masts as the enhanced sleekness of the modern designs. In place of the pipe and net wings are sleek surfaces with about one-tenth the aerodynamic drag. Gone are the high, sharp gunwales and the multiple vertical bulkheads and transom. In their place are low topsides, rounded gunwales, flush decks and sloped transoms. Gone, too, are all the knobbly bits of the rigs that used to catch the air. It all looks so much better. But the drive for these changes has been perform-ance, not appearance.

For as long as sailboats sailed downwind with the apparent wind behind them, drag necessarily added to their downwind speed. But with apparent wind sailing, the apparent wind is always from ahead, so drag always reduces speed. The faster a boat wants to sail, the more essential it becomes to focus on lower drag rather than higher power to get that speed. The example of the ice yacht shows just how true this is at the extreme of presently achievable performance.

When I was writing *HPS-1* 20 years ago, the people at North Sails, then based at Peewaukee, who knew about iceboat sailing advised me that the best speed they could expect from a top Skeeta was then about five times the wind speed.

In the years since, the leading iceboat designers have improved on that five to one ratio. Fig 2.1 shows Buddy Melges sailing a sleeker Skeeta at about six times wind speed (77mph in 10–14 mph of true wind). Fig 18.1 shows the vectors, the 10 knot (average) true wind to scale; the iceboat's track and 67 knot ground speed tacking downwind, and the 60 knot apparent wind. The important fact in this diagram is the angle of 7.5° between the iceboat centreline and the apparent wind.

If you turn the thinking in Fig 18.1 around, what it is telling you is that when sailing fast the apparent wind will always be strong, so the drive force will always be limited by the boat's sail-carrying power – that is, by its stability. In this situation what matters is the drive force to drag ratio. Because the drive force is necessarily limited, the only way to sail faster is to reduce the drag. This has the effect of reducing the 'pointing angle'. A skiff that sails crosswind at twice wind speed will be sailing with the apparent wind 27° off the bow. An iceboat that sails at six times wind speed will sail with the apparent wind 9.5° off the bow, and 7.5° when tacking downwind. Until you can sail closer to the wind than 7.5°, you will never be able to tack downwind at more than six times wind speed. So it turns out that the limit to speed is not so much the power that the sails can generate, it is the drive force to drag ratio. If your drive force is already at the stability limit, you can get this ratio higher only by reducing the drag. This is what the increased sleekness of the modern skiff is all about. The fast foilboats of the future will need to be very sleek indeed.

The facts of life of the fastest ice yacht, the Skeeta, are given in Chapter 2. If you head it crosswind in a 10 knot breeze, get in, and sheet on, nothing happens. If you push and run until it is moving about 10 knots crosswind, jump in and pump efficiently in the 14 knot apparent wind, you can just accelerate. Once you have a speed of 15–20 knots, the whole thing begins to work, the speed winds up towards 50 knots (whether upwind or downwind does not much matter), and at this speed the 70sq ft of sail area is far too big and the boat would sail faster with a smaller sail. But if you use a smaller sail, you cannot get it started! So the maximum drive force is determined by other factors, and the top speed is determined by that 7.5° angle. If you could halve the drag and work at 4° or less, you could sail at ten times the wind speed, not six! So in the case of this extreme apparent wind sailboat, the top speed is determined, in the end,

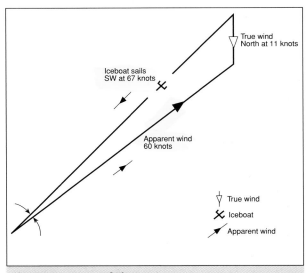

Fig 18.1 Vectors of Fig 2.1

not by the 'power' (drive force) available, but by the drag. The only way it can sail faster than six times wind speed is to reduce the drag.

18.5 ■ The practical speed increases of the skiff revolution

Figs 6.1A and 6.1B give the performance envelopes of the 5o5 and the 49er, and show the astonishing increase in the efficiency of the sailboat as a wind machine which has been achieved over the past three decades.

About 25 years ago when speed attempts across the Weymouth speed circle were an annual fete, I recall that Rodney Pattison, the Flying Dutchman gold medallist, achieved a maximum average speed of about 12 knots in his Flying Dutchman in a wind of about 12 knots, which is consistent with the 5o5 envelopes in Fig 6.1A. So as a starting point we can assume that the fastest of the conventional boats of the 1970s could achieve at best a boat speed of about wind speed.

In 1983 I published performance envelopes based on the measured performance when racing of a number of the top Eighteen foot skiffs of the period. (These are shown in *HPS-1*, Fig 24.1.) The best ratio of boat speed compared with wind speed is 10.6 knots in a 6 knot wind which occurs on a close reach. This is a speed of 1.76 times the wind speed.

Fig 6.1B shows the performance envelopes of the 49er. The best ratio that this more modern wet-water boat can achieve is 12.35 knots in a 6 knot wind when tacking downwind – that is, a speed of 2.06 times the wind speed.

Postscript

In Section 3.8 I give an example of abnormal 59er boat speeds observed in wind speeds in the 5–7 knot range. On that occasion I discarded the observed speeds as accurately measured but unbelievable.

One morning on a weekend many years earlier (in about 1996) a fleet of 49ers were practising short windward/leeward races. The wind was generally light air, but with patches of 5–6 knot wind. On that morning I repeatedly measured downwind boat speeds of 12–13 knots in wind speed measured at eye level of 5–7 knots, no more. My 49er performance diagrams reflect those measurements.

In Section 10.18 I describe the circumstances of a recent more on-going measurement programme, in which two 49ers were sailed extensively with onboard GPS and an observer in a chase boat measured wind speed and direction. The expected scatter of points giving boat speed and direction every two seconds is greater in the 5–9 knot winds than in stronger winds. My speed observations from 11 years ago fall within the upper part of this scatter.

I now believe that this greater scatter is partly due to the naturally greater variability of lighter winds, plus the added variability of the different forms the boundary layer can adopt in 5–9 knot winds, which are discussed in Section 3.6. At root, if an observer measures a wind speed of 6 knots at eye level, a well-sailed 49er can be expected to sail anywhere between about 10.5 and 12.5 knots depending on the shape of the boundary layer at the time.

These ratios of about 1.0 times wind speed for the best 1970s conventional boats, about 1.76 for the early 1983 apparent wind skiffs, and 2.00 for the current pinnacle Olympic skiff, attest the astonishing performance increase achieved by the skiffs in recent years. They have doubled the maximum wind speed/boat speed ratios, and can now sail nearly twice as fast in the same wind as any popular wet-water boat could sail as little as 30 years ago. But we still have a long way to go before we can approach the iceboat's ratio of six times wind speed.

In the years immediately ahead, a new generation of skiffs based on the technology of the foil Moths should be able to sail at speeds intermediate between the present skiffs and the iceboats.

The three factors noted above –

- that smaller sails are faster,
- that rigs that flex in the right way are faster, *and*
- that less drag and not more power is the key to yet faster speeds in the future

– are three of the principal fields of development that have opened up since the advent of *Prime II*'s revolutionary rig in 1983.

Chapter 19 • The 29er

19.1 ■ The properties of a skiff

The apparent wind 49er was selected as an Olympic class in 1996. The performance level of the 49er skiff, as compared with all previous Olympic sailboats, is revolutionary. It achieves this performance by combining sailing characteristics, boat handling skills and race tactical skills that have been either unknown or not previously used by sailors of conventional sailboats. Owners of early 49ers faced a very steep learning curve indeed. The principal differences were:

1 It routinely sails to windward at speeds well in excess of hull speed.
2 It tacks downwind faster than the wind with the apparent wind forward of the beam.
3 It is helmed from trapeze.
4 It has a wing-like asymmetric spinnaker which calls for a different handling skill from handling a parachute spinnaker.
5 Assessing larger areas of distant wind – for example, picking which will be the stronger-wind side of the course downwind – has become a critical skill. This is a different skill from chasing nearby local gusts close to the rhumbline.

This list is seminal, because by definition these are the five new skills that sailors need to master before they can win in fast apparent wind craft such as the 49er.

How can young sailors learn these skills? When looked at in this way, the list above becomes:

• A checklist by which to select an existing trainer, *or*
• The design objects for modifying an existing trainer, *or*
• The design objects for a new boat.

I know something about youth trainers because nearly 25 years ago I designed the Laser Two, which quickly became one of the world youth trainers (see below). At that time it was the best there was. So my first approach was to look at the Laser Two in this new light.

There was, however, no hope there. That late 1970s conventional design cannot train in even one of the five new skills. Further, no other youth trainer available in 1996, nor since, is any better. Following the selection of the 49er many new designs have appeared. Superficially they all look like a cross between a brick and a skiff, because to look something like a skiff is what they were designed to do. But at the performance level, none of them could tack downwind faster than they could run square in most winds. Except for one or two, these boats have failed to achieve. They cannot deliver fast, reliable, apparent wind sailing, and to contemplate using this sort of contraption as a serious youth trainer was irresponsible.

I was asked if it might be possible to modify the Laser Two – to make it an apparent wind trainer by giving it a new rig? I looked first at the true apparent wind boats that we knew well: my better High Speed Project experimental boats, Julian's two-hander Eighteens, then his Exocet B-14, then his world champion B-18 Eighteen footers, then the 49er. Against these I sketched potential rigs on the Laser Two hull that began to look more and more like a Twelve foot skiff, but that still would not do the whole job. So the answer had to be that modifying the Laser Two (or any of the other popular youth trainers) could never be more than a partial solution.

This left only one conclusion. A new youth trainer was needed – one that would be designed from the outset to sail like a skiff to train for a skiff.

We decided to develop such a boat.

19.2 ■ Earlier work – the Laser Two

It was my privilege to design the Laser Two youth trainer in the late 1970s. (My approach to the 29er was necessarily coloured by this earlier work.)

The Laser Two project was triggered by the conviction by Ian Bruce and the Performance Sailcraft (Montreal) board that there was an opening in the market. In Europe, about 100 000 young sailors outgrew their Optimists, etc each year, and most moved into one of four youth trainers. All four were too heavy to roof rack, all were pricey; and despite their price, some went soft quickly so they rapidly lost speed and became uncompetitive. A market survey that canvassed the opinions of parents, and those who advised non-sailing parents, concluded that, 'If we could design a youth trainer that was light enough to roof rack and strong enough to last, we could expect to enjoy a substantial share of that market.'

In retrospect, I find it revealing that it was only the parents who were asked. Nobody thought to ask the young sailors what they wanted.

Eight other subsidiary requirements were added – for example, the boat must float upright at a dock; the basic boat must present 'clean as a hound's tooth' on the showroom floor; all spinnaker gear must be an optional add-on; all trapeze gear must be an optional add-on; eight must fit into a 20ft container, etc.

We set the crew age limits as the post-puberty adolescent at the lower end and the college student at the higher end. I turned to the then current Pharmacia Upjohn medical data for average weight at various ages. As each child approaches puberty, his/her weight and growth pause, then their limb length spurts, then they pause again. The increase in limb length in the growth spurt is where they outgrow their children's boats. The pause in weight post-puberty becomes the logical lower crew weight design limit for an adolescent's boat. I noted that the mean weight post-puberty of both boys and girls was 45kg (100lb). Girls then grew until, at age 17, primary growth ceased. Boys grew slightly more slowly, but continued growing for another two years until, at age 19, their primary growth ceased. From this data I sized the Laser Two for crews who would weigh, dressed for sailing, from 100kg (220lb) to 125kg (280lb).

At that time I had designed a string of 14ft waterline boats – NS14s and the Nova and the Tasar. Their hulls weighed 140lb, and they were routinely roof-racked. All delivered exceptional performance. In the smaller 12ft Cherub class my design was the current world champion.

The shape of the Laser Two hull developed between these various design streams and I managed to get it right first time. Ian Bruce's forte is industrial design and visual appeal, and he called for some cosmetic changes. His approach to rig size was to repeat his Laser formula 'Sailors get bored with small sails – try bigger and bigger sails until they are obviously too big, then cut them back one notch'.

This approach created a design that, over the next 30 years, has given tens of thousands of young sailors a lot of pleasure.

19.3 ■ The 29er – the cut and try approach

What became the 29er proved a much more complex project. At the time we commenced work on the new boat, Julian was preoccupied with 49er growth in demand, growth in class administration as it spread across the world, and the political problems that always accompany change. So it fell to me to get the project underway.

The object was beautifully simple. This boat was to be a youth trainer that would train in all five properties noted above. Put simply, its job was 'to sail like a skiff to train for a skiff'. Re feedback, Julian and I were agreed that on this occasion we would not ask the parents. Instead, we would ask the young sailors themselves what they wanted and what they thought of our emerging prototypes.

Practical points were international co-operation and also funding. The 49er had been developed and jointly funded by a consortium of a Japanese, an American, a Brit, and ourselves. This policy had worked superbly. The global input throughout the project made the developing design truly international and, even more importantly, made it immediately *acceptable* internationally. A new consortium was eager to contribute ideas and advice to the new project and, for the second time, this policy of accepting international advice during the conception, design and development stages has proved invaluable in creating a boat that could be accepted worldwide on its merits rather than being resisted by the customary 'not invented here' prejudice.

A number of factors made it not appropriate at that time to repeat the group funding arrangements, so my wife Nel and I elected to fund it.

It is self-evident that Julian has developed a unique 'feel' for skiff dynamics. The 29er is his design, and my role has been to interpret his ideas. He opted for his B-18 Mk IIIC hull as the model. After nearly 15 years, this is still the world's fastest Eighteen footer hull, and he thought that its form when scaled down would serve the lighter youth sailors better than a scaled-down 49er shape.

My Laser Two approach to crew weight had given the right answer in 1979, so I looked out my 1975 data on adolescent weight and limb length. The wing width – the maximum gunwale beam – was set by the Japanese Roads and Traffic Authority's maximum towing width.

Once the key factors of underwater shape, flotation needed, maximum wing width and minimum limb length were decided, I transformed the Eighteen footer underwater shape and lofted the new hull to float the same crew weight as in my 1978 Laser Two. This proved to be my first mistake.

The 29er deck design was an interesting exercise. The Eighteens and the 49er had become wide-winged craft in which the sailors needed to shift their weight over substantial distance by running. Their decks had developed into relatively flat unobstructed surfaces without cockpits, over which the sailors could run without need to look where they placed their feet.

The 29er was to be a youth trainer that would be crewed by a forward hand on trapeze and a helm sitting on the gunwale, so a cockpit was needed for the helm's feet. The question was, 'How deep should the cockpit be?' I wanted to keep the freeboard and profile low for least aerodynamic drag, but a too-shallow cockpit is uncomfortable. I checked existing designs and observed that an 8in depth was regarded as acceptable by young crews.

I lofted a deck form to match the hull which was suitable for separate moulding. These original strip-planked parts became a hull part and a deck part with a 9in deep self-draining cockpit and side decks spaced about 2in above or in from the hull laminate.

This project was to pass through four prototypes before we got it exactly right.

19.4 ■ 29er Prototype Mk I – May 1997

As soon as the hull would float I towed it to find out whether, at this smaller size, we still had one of these strange shapes that sail with no hump in its drag curve. At this point, the hull's outer surface was being faired by sanding high-build undercoat with long, slightly flexible boards to which 80-grit sandpaper was glued, so the shape was already fair but the surface far from polished. To my delight, while the drag was much higher than I would have expected from a polished hull, there was no hump at 7–7.5 knots of the nature of Fig 10.5 (a late 1930s Uffa Fox canoe) and Fig 10.6 (my 1975 NS14-derived Tasar). Fig 10.10 shows both these initial drag measurements and the much lower drags measured on a polished hull of slightly different shape two years later.

We rigged it with an old B-14 small rig from many years earlier, and went sailing. It was immediately apparent that we had a boat with the performance level we wanted. In strong winds and big waves, it handled truly and did not bury its bow. When sailed in winter light airs against a benchmark Tasar fleet, it held its place upwind and vanished at speed as it tacked downwind as soon as there was wind enough to inflate the spinnaker. It performed well even when crewed far above its design crew weight. In strong winds it handled well and sailed fast in both flat water and waves. The cockpit was deep enough for comfort.

On the negative side, the side decks were too high, and there was far too much flotation when capsized. That 2in gap between hull and deck gave the crew an uncomfortable impression that they were sitting *on* the boat rather than *in* it. When capsized, it inverted quickly – which is safe – but when on its side during right-ing it floated with the centreboard about 1ft above the water. At this height it was too difficult to climb onto it. A minor point was that it carried too much lee helm with the spinnaker set.

(At this point it is proper to point out that Australian designers design their boats to invert, and quickly, when they capsize. In pre-1960 days, timber boats swamped when heeled too far, then lay on their sides and floated low, and safety was not an issue. But with the advent of Moths with closed decks, then Lasers, etc, all of which float high when on their sides, it was soon found that in a strong wind a high-floating boat on its side will blow downwind faster than a sailor can swim. In Melbourne the configuration of Port Phillip Bay, and in Adelaide the configuration St Vincents Gulf, are both such that a sea breeze that starts onshore will back as it strengthens until it is blowing offshore with respect to some of the shorelines within the bay or gulf. (Figs 9.5, 9.6 and 9.7 in *HPS-1* explain this mechanism.) A fatality did occur in Melbourne many years ago in which a Moth on its side blew away from a young sailor in an offshore sea breeze. The sailor drowned. The cure is to design the boat to invert; in this way, the sails act as a sea anchor, and the sailor can swim to his boat without difficulty.)

What we learned from prototype Mk I was that we could indeed get true apparent wind performance from a smaller boat, and we could build and shape a small hull that sailed without any hump. These were solid starting points; it was now time to refine the detail.

19.5 ■ 29er Prototype Mk II

We made a second prototype. For this Mk II hull we took a mould off the external hull of Mk I, and in it made a foam-sandwich hull laminate with topsides strong enough to carry the weight of the crew.

The shape of the deck was different in three respects:

1 The deck topsides above the cockpit floor were simple, thin wafers of laminate that glued directly onto the strong foam-sandwich hull laminate – that is, without internal framing. This made the wings 50mm thinner, so the crew now sat on a surface 2in lower.

2 The fact that the side deck was now 50mm lower raised the question of cockpit depth and comfort. Julian was undecided whether the shallower cockpit that would result from a (higher) self-draining cockpit floor would be comfortable and practical, or whether a deeper cockpit with a lower non-self-draining floor and a transom would now be needed. So we put in the cockpit floor at the very lowest level for a self-drainer so that we could experiment.

3 We set the centrecase a little further forward to better balance the helm feel under spinnaker.

This gave us a light, stiff hull that was fully cored – that is, all the working surfaces were of foam sandwich. This, in a youth trainer, was as revolutionary as the dynamic design, and has cost-effective economic consequences – the logic of which has still not been grasped some ten years later.

19.6 ■ The durability revolution

Look at it this way. Prior to the 1980s, most popular dinghy classes were made of thin glass fibre skins that quickly softened and progressively lost speed because of the properties described in Chapter 8. The economic result of this method of construction is a high level of demand. A perfect example is the comment to me by a head European coach in 1979, the year prior to the Moscow Olympics: 'We find that xxx hulls soften and lose their speed very quickly. To enable our top teams to perform with peak performance, we give them two new xxx hulls each season, and another just prior to any major championship.' So sailors who wanted to remain competitive had to buy a new hull each year. The discarded boats remained intact and floated, but because of softening and speed loss could not win against new, stiffer boats. So they are sold second season as near-new boats for less than new price; the third year the price drops a little more, and so on. Under this system a class with 10 000 keen sailors will demand 10 000 new boats each year. This is exactly what was happening with the Laser class in the 1970s, with the Montreal and the Waterford plants each making 6000 new boats every year. In this scenario, providing 30 new boats for a world youth championship involves providing 0.25% of annual production and is easily accommodated within a common sense promotion budget.

Contrast this with Ian Bruce's 1975 fully cored (ie all foam sandwich) structure that he devised for my Tasar design. These hulls are light, but so stiff and strong that even now, in 2007, hulls built 30 years ago – in 1976 – compete and finish well in world championships of 130 boats. They remain as fast and as competitive as the most recent 2007 product. This is the advantage of foam sandwich, done well.

The consequence of this superior construction technology is reflected in a huge difference in demand. To stay on top, the owner of a non-cored boat needs a new hull every year. To stay on top with a fully cored 49er, 29er, B-14 or Tasar, the hull may need to be replaced every 10 to 20 years. So the demand generated by a notional group of 10 000 owners may be as little as 500 each year, not 10 000.

Now that one of the world youth designs offers this sort of durability, the expectation that 30 new boats be provided at no cost – that is, between 5% and 10% of annual global production – is totally unreasonable. It is long overdue that expectations for the provision of boats at the world youth championships are brought into line with the economic reality of these more durable hulls.

19.7 ■ Mark II hull, statics and dynamics

Mk II was rigged with its 'proper' youth trainer rig, and launched in about September 1997. We were delighted with all the changes. The lower side decks now 'felt' right. When on its side, being righted after capsize, the hull floated lower with the centreboard only a few inches above the water, which was ideal. With the new rig and the new centreboard position the boat now balanced perfectly. Performance, both upwind and downwind, and in all wind strengths, exceeded expectation. This boat did truly 'sail like a skiff to train for a skiff'.

As an experiment, the very low cockpit floor in this boat was logical, and with it we were able to learn everything we needed to know about both possible options for the final design. In practice, the cockpit depth proved more than adequate for comfort, so we quickly took the decision to raise the cockpit floor in the final boat about 30mm and make it a self-drainer. Meantime, we fitted a temporary transom to keep the water out when the wind fell light, and got on with the development work.

The fact that the hull handled weight so well made us think in terms of two models: a smaller-rig youth trainer for adolescents, and a larger-rig 'sport' boat for young adults. So we developed two rigs, a simple single-spreader small rig, and a larger rig with two spreaders to carry a masthead spinnaker and two trapezes.

This boat did truly 'sail like a skiff to train for a skiff', and we were all impressed with the boat that was emerging. Takao Otani visited from Japan more than once, spent a lot of time in it, and offered many suggestions. He was the one who found out, from hard experience one day, that if he capsized in light wind, the entrapped water was near impossible to clear. That settled that question – we fitted the temporary transom.

I set about measuring its performance in different winds and with both rigs and found, to nobody's great surprise, that in the fresher breezes the smaller rig was the faster.

We also took very seriously the business of finding out what young sailors thought of it. We are fortunate indeed in the level of co-operation we enjoy. Several clubs offered to co-operate – typical being the Kembla Sailing Club in Wollongong on Lake Illawarra about an hour's drive to the south of Sydney. They offered to help and asked for the boat for a weekend. From volunteers, they selected seven young crews of varying age and weight and experience and ran a near-military operation. On the first day the boat was rigged with its small rig. Each crew launched, capsized and righted the boat in front of the club, then sailed it out into the lake to play upwind and downwind for half an hour with a coach watching. Where both were helms and each took his/her turn at the helm, they sailed for longer. On return they all completed sail reports that included their age, weight and experience, the boat they dreamed about, and their impressions of *this* boat. The next day they repeated the whole exercise with the bigger rig. Winds on that weekend varied from 6 to 16 knots. From this sort of work from the Kembla, Hunters Hill and Northbridge Clubs, and the Royal Sydney Yacht Squadron, we learned all sorts of unexpected detail, and progress could not have been more positive.

It is hardly surprising that this new craft was by now attracting a very great deal of attention worldwide. Towards the end of our programme of performance measuring and evaluation by young crews, we were asked to urgently airfreight the prototype to the UK for display at the Paris and Dusseldorf Boat Shows for marketing purposes. We sent it, with the temporary transom removed for cosmetic appearance, and the very clear instruction 'Do not under any circumstances sail this boat publicly unless you first refit the transom, else it will swamp with a hefty crew in drift conditions'.

The boat was shown as planned, and aroused much interest. Then came the disaster. For whatever reason, and directly contrary to our advice, the boat was sailed at a very public winter showpiece regatta, without a transom, without the cockpit floor being raised, and crewed by a solid crew, on a cold, grey drizzly winter day with little or no wind.

The boat swamped, exactly as it had with Otani.

Our American consortium partner walked away; our British partner stepped back. The date was December 1997.

19.8 ■ 29er Prototype Mk III

Back in Sydney, my wife Nel and I, who were funding the project, understood exactly what had happened. During the weeks that followed there were noises from the northern hemisphere that we should forget about real apparent wind performance for a training boat. After all, it was only for kids, they said! It was suggested that we make Mk III a bigger, more tubby boat – give it an asymmetric spinnaker that would look like a skiff certainly, but be satisfied with a fat, blunt hull that would float in all conditions, even if it would not sail like a skiff.

My wife and I rejected this suggestion and stuck to our guns. We did not like the term 'kids' and the implication that poor technical quality is good enough for young sailors. Our strong view is that young people are important, and worthy of our best efforts.

The disaster had been caused by the stupidity of those who would not listen to our advice, and was not due to any technical incompetence. Our conviction remained that this boat must 'sail like a skiff to train for a skiff', or it was not worth doing. We started again.

We were convinced that the international approach during the design and development phase, which had worked so well with the 49er, was too valuable to allow to lapse. So I invited Ian Bruce, of Laser fame, with whom I had worked with the Tasar and the Laser Two 25 years earlier, to listen to what we believed in, assess what we were doing, look at what had happened in the UK and why, and let us have his opinion as to what he thought would be acceptable in North America. He came, looked, and joined us without hesitation as our new North American partner.

I set about designing Mk III. Whereas Mk II had been experimental in the sense that we were uncertain about the cockpit floor height and transom configuration, Mk III had no such uncertainties. We had made the boat available to as many young sailors as possible. From their sail reports we learned that their weights for their ages were considerably heavier than I had anticipated from the 1975 medical data from which I had designed the Laser Two. I looked out more recent data (Pharmacia Upjohn) and, sure enough, today's adolescents are heavier. The average weight at the post-puberty pause has increased from 45kg in 1970 to 50kg in 1995. They have been increasing in weight by about 2kg per decade during recent years due to better nutrition. Asiatic adolescents seem to be increasing even faster due to more protein in their diet. It was Takao Otani who said, 'Even in Japan they are not now as small as that', so with the next boat I increased both the total flotation as well as the buoyancy under the cockpit floor.

I modified the shape of the bottom to increase flotation by about 15kg. I worked out a height for the cockpit floor so that the boat would carry two solid adolescents plus an adult instructor. We moved the rig and partner forward a little for better forward hand comfort in light air, and we increased the sail area of the smaller, simpler rig to match the increased design crew weight. This boat became Mk III. I worked quickly, and by late January 1998 Mk III was sailing.

The open transom deck configuration presented one final problem. Like the 49er, when the boat righted following capsize, the cockpit drained quickly and the feather-light boat then tended to 'take off' at speed and was sometimes difficult to hang onto. So we fitted a low transom with big scuppers so that when righted it would initially carry sufficient water to make it docile and easy for the crew to re-board. Within 30 seconds, all the water drains out and full performance is restored.

Mk III was so successful that by the end of February 1998, Takao Otani from Japan, Ian Bruce from Canada, and David Ovington from the UK spent a week sailing it, evaluating it, and deciding the next step.

We decided that there should be one more prototype.

19.9 ■ 29er Prototype Mk IV

Mk IV had fractional changes to overall length and chine detail aft which improved stability in gybes. Changes to the partner, to the gunwale line forward of the stub wings, to the transom and to the scuppers finally got the hull cosmetics right. While Mk III had sailed very well initially with its bigger rig, we found that what we had learned about adolescents being heavier now than they were 30 years ago also applied to their parents, and even the slightly larger hull was not now truly big enough for two solid young male adults. This realisation made two rigs a nonsense, and Mk IV became solely a purpose-built youth trainer with one rig, and everything proportioned to be the correct size for adolescents of today's average weight. The transparent sails were near-invisible, so we decided to pipe them with fluorescent orange to make them conspicuous and recognisable at a distance.

At the end of April 1998 the principals again met in Sydney, sailed and evaluated Mk IV, approved what we had done and cleared it for production. We named it the '29er'. Julian's later opinion was: 'I think we finally got the 29er hull correct. I am not sure whether it is big enough, but it appears to be pretty good. The only thing I would change if I had another chance is to make the foot of the jib a little shorter. That's just a

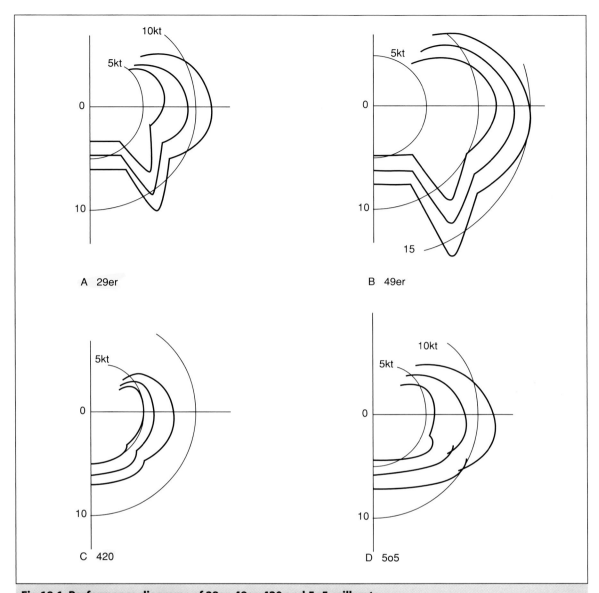

Fig 19.1 Performance diagrams of 29er, 49er, 420 and 5o5 sailboats

The four performance diagrams are all to the same scale.
The inner, middle and outer bold curves are the performances in true winds of 6, 9, and 12 knots.

personal feeling. In terms of simplicity and usability, it is another step up from the 49er.'

The performance envelope of the boat we had created is shown in Fig 19.1A. Its performance is utterly unlike that of any other youth trainer. Why we had done it is shown in Fig 19.1B, C and D. Fig 19.1B shows the performance diagram of the Olympic 49er. This is quintessentially the diagram of the apparent wind skiff. The whole point of Fig 19.1A is that it is so strikingly similar to Fig 19.1B. The five new skills outlined in Section 19.1 that are needed to sail a skiff well are the skills needed to sail the 29er well. This boat does indeed sail like a skiff to train for a skiff.

Fig 19.1A and 19.1B are both completely different from Fig 19.1C and 19.1D. Fig 19.1C repeats the performance diagram of the 420; those of the Laser Two are similar. Fig 19.1D repeats the performance diagram of the 5o5; those of the Flying Dutchman and 470 are similar. Fig 19.1C and 19.1D are broadly similar, and both are essentially different from Fig 19.1A and B.

19.10 ■ Acceptance and spread

The judgement of the world seems to be that young people now want to sail with the speed of a 49er (Fig 19.1B), and that a really fast youth trainer like the 29er is a good place to start.

Within a year, the 29er was being made in six countries: Australia, the UK, Canada, New Zealand, South Africa, and Argentina in South America. In 1999, it won the USA Sailing World 'Boat of the Year' Award; in March 2001 it was selected by the Canadian Yachting Association, and immediately confirmed by the International Sailing Federation, as the new two-handed youth trainer to be used by both boys and girls at the Youth Worlds sailed at Lunenberg, Nova Scotia, in 2002.

The Sydney skiffs had developed their blazing speeds by cut and try development in a fiercely competitive environment that was free from restrictive rules.

The 49er is a cut and try development from the Eighteen foot skiffs by a designer and design team with a unique feel for this way of sailing. It was good enough to merit immediate Olympic selection.

The 29er is a cut and try development of the 49er by the same designer and team. It has proved good enough to be selected as the world youth training boat in an amazingly short time.

Cut and try is usually the fastest way to proceed in the early stages, but sometimes there can be other and better ways later on. In the next chapters we will look at some of the insights that further measurement and analysis have been able to offer.

Author's note

I would like to acknowledge the input of Takao Otani from Japan, Ian Bruce from Canada and David Ovington from the UK with regard to the 29er design. It has been their experienced guidance and advice to Julian, my wife Nel and myself that has enabled the prototypes to be regarded as a truly global effort as they developed, and for the final product to be accepted on its merits worldwide, and so quickly.

Chapter 20 • The Critical Ratios

20.1 ■ Smaller is harder

All credit must go to the Eighteen foot skiff class for the breakthrough from conventional, slow, 'blow-down-wind' sailing to modern, fast, 'tack-downwind' sailing. These particular skiffs developed into long, feather-light craft with big sails, wide powerful wings and fit, athletic, alert and anarchic crews who viewed restrictive rules with contempt and who were always trying something new. As far as the Eighteens were concerned, the invention of the asymmetric spinnaker and the associated development of the ice yacht-like apparent wind downwind sailing technique was just one more first that worked, and it was then time to focus on the next possible way to sail a little bit faster.

The Eighteen foot skiffs' speeds aroused excitement, envy and both the IOC's and the ISAF's interest and action. At first sight, the 49er looks like a straight 'special purpose' evolution of Eighteen foot skiff technology by the pre-eminent Eighteen foot skiff designer of that time – one who happened to have an earlier background in both three two-hander Eighteens and, more recently, the 14 footer B-14. Because the size and dynamics are so similar, it does not seem surprising that the 16½ft 49er 'sailed like a skiff' so well from the outset. It is only when you look again and see what is *not* there, that the full impact of yet another advance between the Eighteens and the 49er becomes clear.

The skiffs, for all their speed, do not in fact have much tolerance for change of wind speed. They get around this by each having a wardrobe of three rigs (recently reduced to two), and the key pre-race decision each race day is whether to put up the big, or the No 2 or the small rig for best performance in the anticipated race-time wind. In this contest there are no second prizes – those with the wrong rig up become the stragglers in the fleet.

When compared with this, the ability of the 49er to deliver very high performance with its single rig across the whole wind speed range from calm to a near gale 25 knots is nothing short of remarkable. The key advances here have been the reduction of weight, and particularly of aerodynamic drag in both hull and rig, and the development of an unusually flexible rig that yields in a very particular way.

The smaller (4.44m) 29er proved harder to get right. At the time I thought that this was because we were receiving and responding to a stream of critical input from our global partners that just kept on flowing in. The 49er project had in its final year worked to the ISAF 'Evaluation Event' deadline, so the period during which we could respond to critical input was limited. Beyond a cut-off date, it was too late for further change. The 29er project had no deadline, so was more relaxed with respect to time. But in retrospect I now see that what happened with the 29er was our first encounter with a new phenomenon – that these new 'apparent wind' boats are harder to get right as you go smaller and/or reduce the sail power.

The example of the 49er, and later of the 29er, led to a crop of asymmetric 'me too' skiff copies. Some of these were adaptations of existing boats, and examples within Australia that I know well and have sailed against are the Cherub and the Manly Graduate. My observation of both these classes, when fitted with asymmetric spinnakers, was that in stronger, steadier winds both of these boats could tack downwind and vanish into the middle distance at impressive speed. But in lighter or unsteady winds they were dreadful. They flopped around, reaching back and forth at the back of the fleet and often finished last. After these races I listened to mutterings of 'I wasn't tactical enough'.

Descriptions of new asymmetric dinghies that called themselves skiffs in northern hemisphere glossy magazines all looked attractive, but again in the chat pages on the web the phrase 'In some winds you have to be tactical' soon appeared. My curiosity was aroused.

Table 20.1 The critical ratios

Extended critical ratios

	Sail area (sq ft)	Wet area (sq ft)	Total wt (lb)	Crew wt (lb)	Half beam (ft)	Arm horiz (ft)	Right mom (lb ft)	Mast above sheer (ft)	Depth hull (ft)	Cp C'bd (ft)	Arm vert (ft)	SCP (lb ft)	A SA/WA	B SA/TW	C SCP/TW
Laser	70	40											1.75		
NS14	100	40											2.50		
Tasar	123	42											2.93		0.27
Tasar X	240	42	500	300	2.75	3.55	1065	18	2	1.3	7.80	136.54	5.71	0.48	0.27
29er	290	39	500	280	2.75	4.72	1322	20	2	1	8.00	165.20	7.44	0.58	0.33
59er	400	41	550	330	3.33	4	1320	21.3	2	1	8.33	158.56	9.76	0.73	0.29
49er	600	43	600	350	5	8	2800	26.9	2	1.2	9.93	282.12	13.95	1.00	0.47

Ratio A SA/WA	governs VMG D/wind at Vb up to hull speed	<2.75	run square fastest
		>2.75 to <5	tack D/wd with Wa aft faster
		>5	AWS faster
Ratio B SA/TW	governs VMG D/wind at Min Planing speed	<0.52	Run Sq faster
		>0.53	AWS faster
Ratio C SCP/TW	governs		
1 Up/wind	Ability to windward plane	<0.3	unable
2 D/wind	Ability to maintain performance in stronger wind	0.27	OK

20.2 ■ The experimental Tasar

At about this time, interest in the addition of an asymmetric spinnaker emerged in the Tasar class. As designer, and also because of my technical interest in the genre, I offered to develop and trial such a rig and report on it, and in 1999 the class requested me to proceed.

The Tasar topmast is slender. Calculations suggested that it could carry a spinnaker, but not from the top of the mast. I drew up a simple hoist and retractable bowsprit system and designed the biggest spinnaker I thought safe. Julian helped with advice. The total sail area was 123sq ft main and jib, plus 117sq ft spinnaker or 240sq ft (22.1sq m) total. This was 80% of the area of the 29er's 27.5sq m. Simple performance calculations suggested that this sail area should be big enough to make the Tasar perform satisfactorily downwind. We put it together, it all worked well ashore, so we went sailing and tried it.

At first we sailed boat against boat with other Tasars at the club. In stronger winds it performed as expected. It planed fast as it tacked downwind; it gybed through 90° or less. In these winds when two boats started a downwind leg together, it routinely sailed downwind with a VMG very much faster than the boat that ran 'square' or nearly so.

In lighter winds it was very different. In drift conditions from calm up to about 2 knots it could sail fast, but only when close to a beam reach, otherwise the bottom of the spinnaker fluttered. In these drift conditions a boat without spinnaker that ran square, or nearly so, would always move ahead. This problem is common to all apparent wind sailboats. As soon as a boat on a broad reach develops significant speed in drift conditions, the direction of the apparent wind through the lowest few metres necessarily blows from near ahead, while the direction at the masthead blows from the beam (the ribbons in Fig 3.14 show this). This enormous twist in the apparent wind is more than any rig can cope with efficiently. In these conditions it is faster for both the conventional and the apparent wind boats to sail directly downwind without spinnakers: the conventional boat because the spinnaker collapses in drift, and the apparent wind boat because it cannot handle the twist in the apparent wind developed by its own speed. In a narrow range between about 3 and 5 knots it then sailed well, performed with authority, and usually finished well ahead of the reference boat(s).

We were not very confident of these drift and light air measurements, because during the month or two over which we were evaluating this rig we never did get light air conditions steady enough to be confident that the boat(s) that were running square or nearly so, and the downwind tacker that necessarily swept widely from side to side of the rhumb line, were sailing in the same wind. But in the 3 to 5 knot winds it usually won, so the calculations seemed to be accurate.

The mid-range winds were altogether different. When we raced we sailed fast, but no matter how hard we tried, we could not sail at angles low enough to stay with, or beat, boats that were sailing straight downwind as fast as they could with poled-out jibs. In these conditions we *always* fell behind the rest of the fleet.

After a little while I realised that this was exactly what I had seen a year earlier when I had on several occasions raced my conventional Tasar against Cherubs and Manly Graduates. (The Manly Graduate is an NS14 – prototype Tasar – fitted with a spinnaker. The class had recently opted to permit an asymmetric spinnaker.) At that point I realised that something other than 'not being tactical enough' was going on, and decided to set up a programme of formal measurement.

I will always remember a seminal afternoon some weeks later when everything, experimentally, went exactly right. I had asked Ted Hamilton, one of the most technically knowledgeable sailors I know, to assist me. Ted attached a GPS and Turbo Meter to his anorak and slipped waterproof notepaper and a pencil under a shockcord holder. On this afternoon we sailed in the tideless flat water of North Harbour (between '1' and '8' in Fig 1.22). A SSW gradient wind blew unobstructed and clean from Clark Island (11) to Manly (7), so was as steady as a gradient wind can ever be. It started at 12 knots and died slowly to about 7 knots over two hours. We sailed about a mile upwind and downwind many times. With a little practice, we were able to get the boat up to its best speed quickly; I then steered with one hand and held both the spinnaker sheet and the mainsheet in the other while Ted measured and recorded the steady speed and direction from the GPS.

Immediately after each reading we gybed, accelerated and stabilised; as soon as we were up to speed, Ted read and recorded speed and direction again. We usually made four or five gybes each run. At the beginning and end of each run we hove-to briefly and measured the true wind speed. In this way we were very confident of the three critical numbers – the true wind speed, the boat speed, and the gybing angle (ie the difference between headings before and after each gybe).

It became obvious to us while we were sailing that as the wind became progressively lighter, our sailing angles were getting closer to a beam reach and our gybing angles were getting progressively closer to 180°. At worst, all we were doing was reaching back and forth and approaching a notional downwind mark progressively more slowly. We found that in order to 'keep going' we needed to sail at a relatively unchanged boat speed through the water. We tried to sail 'deeper', but all that happened was that we confirmed again what every apparent-wind sailor knows – that a very sharp 'cut-off' develops. Above the cut-off speed and heading, we sailed at about 7.5 to 7.7 knots (which happens to be the Tasar's minimum planing speed at the weight at which we were sailing), with the apparent wind just forward of the beam. As soon as we bore away at all, the apparent wind decreased, the boat stopped planing, and the boat

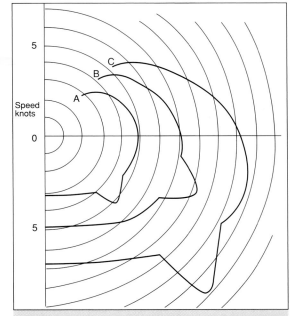

Fig 20.1 The performance of the experimental Tasar with asymmetric spinnaker

A Performance in true wind of 4.5 knots
B Performance in true wind of 7 knots
C Performance in true wind of 12 knots

speed abruptly fell to about its hull speed of 5 knots initially, and to 4 knots in the lighter wind later – that is, to about the normal 'run square' boat speed in that wind strength. There was nothing in between, nothing at all.

I analysed the measurements and drew Fig 20.1. This is accurate, but is unsatisfying in that it does not well convey the dramatic loss of relative performance in the mid-range winds.

So I tried a different approach and drew Fig 20.2, and suddenly the whole problem came to life. Fig 20.2 shows exactly the same information as Fig 20.1, but the presentation of downwind speed (VMG) against wind speed shows the frustrating loss of performance as the great dip in the curve that dominates the diagram. I thought about this for a while, then advised the Tasar class that the addition of an asymmetric spinnaker to the Tasar would not lead to performance that would make people happier. I discontinued the trial.

20.3 ■ The shape of the problem

Fig 20.2 is one of the most useful diagrams I have drawn. True wind speed is given across the bottom; downwind VMG (velocity made good towards the downwind mark) is given up the side. For interest I have put in a line + + + + at 45°. This is the locus of downwind speed equal to wind speed. Performance curves above this line indicate downwind VMG faster than the wind.

To give overall perspective, I have added the downwind performance of some well-known conventional boats and some apparent wind sailboats:

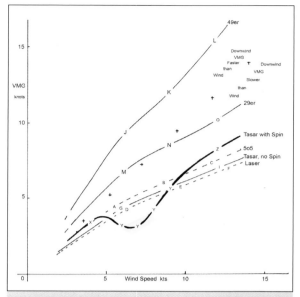

Fig 20.2 The downwind performance of six sailboats

- The curve of the 5o5, one of the faster conventional boats, is given as A–B–C. It sails straight downwind, or nearly so, at about three-quarters of the wind speed up to its hull speed, and at about half wind speed when it is planing in stronger winds.
- The curve of the popular Laser is given as D–E–F. This sails in the same way, but slightly slower.
- The curve of the standard Tasar (no spinnaker) is given as G–I. This whole line of enquiry has been driven by the difference between curve G–I and the strange curve X–Y–Z.
- The curve X–Y–Y–Y–Z is the performance of the experimental Tasar.

All of the conventional boats sail downwind heading either directly, or nearly directly, towards the downwind mark, so there is little or no difference between the boat's speed through the water and the downwind VMG.

- The performance of the apparent wind 49er is given as J–K–L. Point J shows that the 49er approaches the downwind mark at 9.2 knots in a 6 knot true wind. To do this, it sails at 12 knots through the water and gybes through approximately 78° (Fig 6.1).
- The performance of the 29er – 'must sail like a skiff to train for a skiff' – is given as M–N–O. It delivers!
- The performance of the best Eighteen foot skiffs (with big rigs up in lighter winds and smallest in strong winds, etc) will be a little faster than the 49er.

Do not get too carried away by these apparent wind performances. The performance curve of the iceboat in Fig 2.1, at five to six times wind speed, will lie somewhere off the top of the page. We still have a long way to go before we should be satisfied.

Fig 20.2 states the apparent wind revolution simply and forcefully. Over the millennia, since the days of the Phoenicians until 30 years ago, no sailboat ever even *approached* the + + + + line at 45°. Now even a good youth trainer lies above it in some winds! The sailing world has much for which to thank the skiffs of Sydney.

20.4 ■ The beginning of wisdom

The great dip in X–Y–Y–Y–Z in Fig 20.2 accused me. My simple sums had been good enough to get points X and Z reasonably right, but had failed utterly in not warning against point Y. I spoke with my naval architect and academic friends; they wrung their hands. The performance of light, fast, unballasted sailboats in unsteady winds has never been studied in depth (who would pay for such work?). Established performance prediction programs all relate to sailboats with heavy keels, or to power-driven hulls that assume steady state, and until recently they gave nonsense answers when applied to skiffs (though at least one naval architect who has focused on this problem in recent years now seems to be achieving useful results).

But overriding all of this was a deeper question. The well-established performance prediction programs all tend to take the known properties of the boat plus the assumed relationships between those properties and solve for the likely performance of a boat that has not yet been built.

My situation was the reverse. With respect to the 49er, the 29er and the experimental Tasar:

- I knew the design factors.
- I knew the measured performance. I have been able to measure the actual performances achieved by many dinghy and skiff classes on the different points of sailing and in different wind strengths, while they were racing. The method is simplicity itself. A colleague and I use a light inflatable and 'formate' closely on a lead boat for long enough to read our steady speed and direction by GPS. We stop quickly, measure true wind speed and direction, catch up with another lead boat, and repeat this sequence perhaps 50 to 60 times in a race. When possible, we follow through tack or gybe, and so obtain very accurate tacking and gybing angles. In this way I have accumulated sufficient measurements to be very confident of their accuracy. For this I have to thank the many crews and race officers who have allowed me to make these measurements over the years.
- What I did not know were the relationships or the logic between the design factors that gave such unexpected differences in the performances of the 49er, the 29er and my experimental Tasar.

If I were to learn more from this situation, I knew I would need to take a new approach. So my object became to find out what were the relationships between the design factors. I was in an almost unique position.

Re hydrodynamic drag, we have measured the drags of a number of hulls plus foils at relevant speeds and different weights by towing at full scale, almost always on flat water and usually in no wind. Of the greatest importance, by towing at full size we have bypassed – and so have completely eliminated – the usual scale effect uncertainty. We know the drags of these hulls and foils exactly.

Re the aerodynamic forces, I am fortunate in that my background is aerodynamics, particularly low-speed aerodynamics, and I sensed that the unknown factors that led to the strange performance such as X–Y–Z might well be aerodynamic.

And as noted above, I know the performance on all points of sailing exactly.

In this new light I looked again at my simple sums to see if they could be made more useful. I set myself the task of trying to find a consistent set of equations that would predict from the known design data the nine measured boat speeds and downwind VMGs in true winds of 6, 9 and 12 knots – that is, points M and N and O; and P and Q and R; and X and Y and Z in Fig 20.2. In essence, I set out to create a useful VPP (Velocity Prediction Program) for the downwind performance of high performance dinghies and skiffs.

It needed half a year's spare time, and the sums are not simple any more, but they have indeed become useful. The work involved three stages:

20.5 ■ Analysis – step one

The first step was to develop a calculation string – a program – that gives the drive force, the total drag, the heeling force and the righting moment of each of the three boats at every wind speed, boat speed and downwind sailing angle. The string differs from the earlier simple calculations in that it now includes every known property of every boat down to the most minute detail, and calculates every individual force that I can identify. In essence, I wrote a new sort of VPP, one that is relevant for fast apparent wind skiffs.

The analysis takes the following form: I start with a true wind speed – say, 6 knots – and initially assume a boat speed that is obviously too slow – say, 6 knots – and apply the calculation string to the first of five different sailing angles, which is 110°, or 20° below a beam reach. The second is 120°, and so on to the fifth, which is 150° or 30° above a square run. Each calculation yields two pairs of key numbers:

- The first pair are the total drive force from the sails and the total drag force (ie both hydrodynamic and aerodynamic) at the assumed wind speed, boat speed and sailing angle. Both of these change as the sailing angle changes. At 110° the drive force is usually greater than the total drag; at 150° it is almost always less. At some sailing angle between these two, the drive force will equal the drag, and that is the deepest sailing angle at which the boat can sail steadily in that wind at that speed according to the assumptions in that string – provided that the boat can be kept upright.

- The second pair are the total heeling force and the righting moment. The righting moment is fixed – it is the maximum the hiking and/or trapezing crew can do to keep their boat upright and it does not change. The heeling force is least at the sailing angle nearest the square run and increases progressively as the boat is assumed to sail closer to a beam reach. The sailing angle at which the heeling force equals the righting moment is the highest the boat can sail in the assumed conditions without easing sheets – that is, it is the stability limit.

The process is repeated at an assumed boat speed two knots faster, and the VMG is usually greater. The process is repeated at progressively increased boat speeds until the VMG peaks and starts to decrease. From this mass of calculations the boat speed and sailing angle that give the fastest downwind VMG can be identified. Sailing at this speed and angle will be the quickest way to the leeward mark at that true wind speed as predicted by that string.

Fig 20.3 is an example from 49er calculations that shows the sort of information this approach reveals. Points A, B, C, D, E, F and G represent the calculated performance if we assume that the boat is sailed in an 8 knot wind. At point A, the drive force and the drag of the 49er in 8 knots of true wind when sailing at 10 knots are both 96lb. At point B, the heeling force and the righting moment are both 2800lb/ft. The heavy solid arc at 10 knots radius between A and B shows the sailing angles at which a 49er can sail at 10 knots in an 8 knot wind. If it tries to sail lower than point A, there will not be enough power and it will slow, so point A represents the drive force limit. If it tries to sail above point B, it will fall over unless sheets are eased, so point B represents the stability limit.

Points C and D show the same information, but when the boat is sailed at 12 knots in the 8 knot wind. In this case, at point C, the drive and drag are both 140lb. At point D, the heeling force and the righting moment are both 2800lb/ft.

Point E on the 14 knot radius is where the drive and drag would be equal if the boat could be kept upright. But point F is where the heeling force equals the righting moment at 14 knots. Since the heeling force is greater than the righting moment at point E, the boat cannot be sailed at 14 knots.

The locus A C E represents the drive force limit. The locus B D F represents the stability limit. The point at which they cross, G, at about 13.5 knots and 143° – that is, luffed 37° above a square run – is the fastest the boat can sail downwind at 13.5 knots of boat speed in an 8 knot true wind according to these assumptions and calculations.

Points H, J, K, L and M and the hatched loci repeat the information of the earlier points, but with the assumed true wind increased to 10 knots. The hatched lobe H, K, M, L, J is the fastest the boat can sail downwind in a 10 knot true wind according to these calculations.

For interest I have added the lobe O, P, Q and R – which is the measured performance diagram of the 49er when racing in a 9 knot true wind – as a dashed line.

These calculations were beginning to be accurate enough to be useful.

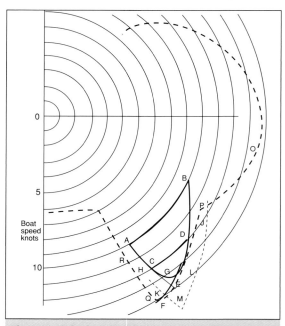

Fig 20.3 Calculated and observed performance of the 49er

Lobe A C G D E – Calculated performance in true wind of 8 knots

Lobe H K M L J – Calculated performance in true wind of 10 knots

Lobe R Q P O – Observed performance in true wind of 9 knots

The entire process is then repeated with the second boat, and again with the third. The critical point is that it is exactly the same calculation string that is applied to each boat.

At the end of this process I held the predicted downwind performance of each boat in each wind from 4 to at least 12 knots of true wind according to the assumptions written into that string.

As I progressed and refined this work, the prediction of the measured performance at seven of the nine points became more accurate – that is, the three 49er points and the three 29er points in 6, 9 and 12 knots true wind speed and the performance of the experimental Tasar in 12 knots. But the string still did not predict the dip in the Tasar's performance between 6 and 9 knots.

20.6 ■ Analysis – step two

The second step was to accept that I had done the best I could with most of the factors. There is little in this world that we can know exactly, but we can know most things well enough for practical purposes. When I looked at my calculation string, all but two areas of the core data came from standard NASA or fluid dynamics texts, or from Hoerner's *Fluid Dynamic Drags*, or from my own measurements.

There were two areas that were uncertain. The first was interference. The second was what was the nature at atmospheric scale of the transition from laminar to turbulent flow in the surface boundary layer at wind speeds from 5 to 10 knots. I felt it proper to try the effect of varying both of these over the range of values that could be justified by observation or common sense.

20.7 ■ Interference

This is a mystery area; I will quote just one observation.

If you take a particular sail area – say the total sail area set by an America's Cup yacht when tacking downwind in 6 to 7 knots of true wind – and hoist and set and trim the mainsail, the jib and the spinnaker as best you can, you will enjoy a particular drive force and boat speed and VMG downwind. Now if you lower the jib, and sail with just the mainsail and spinnaker set, all evidence to date is that you will sail faster despite the fact that the total sail area without the jib is only, say, 90% of the total area with everything set.

One way of expressing this real-life observation would be to assign an interference factor of, say, 1.0 to the main and spinnaker only configuration, and a factor of, say, 0.85 to the 'everything set' main plus jib plus spinnaker configuration where each of the three sails is set closer together and necessarily interferes with the flow over the adjacent sail to a greater extent.

It seemed to me from these sorts of observations that the interference factor could lie anywhere between 1 and 0.8, so I tried 1, then 0.9, then 0.8. In the end, I found that a value of 0.9 gave the best 'fit' between calculated and observed speeds.

20.8 ■ Transition from laminar to turbulent flow

I began to look much more closely at the way flow changed from laminar to turbulent in nature. In writing *HPS-1* in the 1980s, I knew that the transition from laminar to turbulent flow was abrupt at both laboratory scale and at aeronautical wind tunnel scale. I conducted the experiment with 1g ribbons, which is repeated in Figs 3.14 and 3.16 of this book, and from this information drew Figs 3.8 and 5.1 in *HPS-1*, on the assumption that abrupt transition would apply at all scales.

On further consideration I realised that at the enormously greater scale of nature, two extra factors – change of surface temperature and change of surface roughness – must both necessarily be involved. Fig 3.19 from Alan Watts's 1965 *Wind and Sailing Boats* considers both water and dry-land surfaces, and suggests that there is usually a lot less wind at 1, 2, 3 and 4m above the surface than one would expect if the boundary layer were fully turbulent all the time. Another realisation was that since my 1g ribbons streamed horizontally in winds of 5 knots, all that Fig 3.16 is confirming is that the wind is more than 5 knots. How much more we cannot know from ribbons as light as these. I needed much more definite information about the transition from laminar to turbulent flow between 5 and 10 knots.

So I conducted the experiment with the 20g windsocks that is described in Section 3.5 and Figs 3.20 to 3.22. As a result, we now have a much more complete and complex picture of how the wind that affects our sails changes its speed with height over the water:

- When the surface is glassy smooth and the air is warmer than the water, the change of speed with height in light air of 3 to 4 knots can be linear, as in Fig 3.23B – that is, 1 knot at 1m, 2 knots at 2m, to 5 knots at 5m – and this linear pattern blends smoothly towards, and finally reaches, the fully turbulent boundary layer pattern at about 10 knots or possibly more.
- But when the water surface is rough (small waves) and the water is warmer than the air, the speed change can be completely different, as in Fig 3.23A. In these conditions, light air of nearly 3 knots at 1m can already be completely turbulent.
- While Fig 3.19 has more to do with dry surfaces, the overall message is the same.
- Both sets of data indicate that for much of the time, the wind speed at 1, 2, 3 and 4m above the water will be less than previously assumed on the understanding that the boundary layer would be fully turbulent in all winds of 6 knots and stronger.

The practical result from this work and this line of thinking is that because the wind near the surface is not as strong as I had assumed it to be, the total drive force from the lower sails in winds from 6 to 10 knots is normally only about 0.7–0.8 as much as I originally believed. So in place of the knife edge change in the boundary layer from laminar flow to turbulent flow implied by Fig 3.23A, I tried smoothing the transition between 3 and 10 knots in the manner of Fig 3.23B. This was the key that worked!

When I applied an interference factor of 0.9, and smoothed the transition from laminar to turbulent over the wind speed range from 3 to 10 knots, my calculation string then correctly predicted all nine observed speeds, and mimicked the great dip in Fig 20.2.

It was a supremely satisfying moment.

20.9 ■ The third step – the critical ratios

All of this had occupied many months of spare time and much machine memory and much paper. Over these months of work, I had been so close to the detail that I had not appreciated the more general value of what I was doing. It required some weeks of doing something else before the new idea emerged that provided the key to the wider puzzle.

I had until then looked at the curve X–Y–Z as a 'flawed continuum' – that is, as a line that should have been reasonably straight, like M–N–O, but wasn't because of some flaw in the boat's design. Then one day I suddenly realised that the factors that the program suggests are more important at low wind speeds are different from those that dominate at higher speeds. This prompted me to look at the curve X–Y–Z in another way.

What if the curve X–Y–Z was in fact a relatively short low speed lobe X–Y on the left and a quite different high speed lobe Y–Z on the right, and these two lobes did not quite overlap?

What if what looked like a dip in one line was not a dip at all, but a gap between two different lobes? Curves M–N–O and P–Q–R could equally well be looked at as the tops of two different lobes that happened to overlap.

A little more thought suggested that there are not two lobes, but three:

- The first covers the boat speed range from rest to hull speed, in which the drag of the hull is small.
- The second covers the boat speed range from hull speed to minimum planing speed, in which the drag of the hull increases rapidly.
- The third covers the boat speed range from minimum planing speed to limit of control, in which the planing drag increases linearly.

Looked at this way, the dip in the curve X–Y–Z is caused by some inadequacy of the second lobe, not by any inadequacy of the first and third lobes.

This approach led me to a new view of downwind dynamics. The factors that are critical in giving superior speed when tacking downwind in a lighter wind are not the same as those that are critical in a mid-range wind. In stronger winds, yet other factors become critical, and in very strong winds a different writ runs again.

I now think that the following approach explains what we observe. The key observations are:

- All sailboats can run straight downwind with the apparent wind aft of the beam at some speed slower than the wind. This is conventional blow-downwind performance.
- The essential dynamic of apparent wind sailing – the ability to tack downwind with a faster VMG than blow-downwind sailing – is that the boat must be capable of sailing at least half as fast again when broad reaching as when running square.
- Some sailboats can do this, but only in some winds. These boats have limited apparent wind capability. I call these boats marginals; my experimental Tasar was one. (My UK proofreader advised me that the English term is 'soaks'.)
- A small but growing number of sailboats follow the lead set by the iceboats and the Eighteen foot skiffs (and now the foiler Moths) and can tack downwind faster than they can run square in all winds. These are the true apparent wind sailboats.

This thinking leads to the concept of the critical ratios. Given equal excellence of design, it is the critical ratios that govern the ability to deliver true apparent wind performance in each of four dynamic regimes. These and the approximate ratios are:

Regime	Critical ratio
1 From rest to hull speed	Sail area/wetted area
2 From hull speed to minimum planing speed	Sail area/total weight
3 From minimum planing speed to stronger winds	Sail – carrying power/total weight
In strong winds	The rig's handling properties

20.10 ■ The first critical ratio – sail area to wetted area

From rest up to hull speed, given equal excellence of design:

- At the same speed
  - The drive force will vary as the sail area.
  - The drag force will vary primarily as the wetted area.
- And at different speeds
  - The drive force will vary as the square of the apparent wind speed.
  - The drag force will vary as the square of the boat speed.

If in any boat in a steady light to moderate wind you set a tiny sail and run straight downwind, the boat will sail at a slow speed. If you then broad reach, the speed will not much increase. At that slow boat speed the apparent wind will not be significantly different, so the drive force from the sail will not change much and the boat speed will remain slow.

If in imagination you double or quadruple the sail area, the speed when running square will increase, but because you can never sail directly downwind faster than the wind it can only increase a little (Figs 1.6 and 1.7). But if with these bigger sails you now broad reach, the higher boat speed will bring a much stronger apparent wind onto the beam. In this stronger apparent wind the drive force from the sails can double or quadruple, and speed can increase dramatically (Fig 1.34).

So up to hull speed, it all depends on the sail area.

The 29er is probably the smallest true skiff. For interest, the sail area to wetted area ratios of the 29er, 59er and 49er are 7.43, 9.75 and 14 respectively. Boats that have demonstrated their ability to win by tacking downwind in all winds, such as the Laser 5000, the Topper Boss, and the RS 800, all have ratios greater than 6.

At the other end of the size spectrum lie the America's Cup boats. In light winds, their performance dynamics are identical with the 29er. In the 7 to 8 knot winds in San Diego, the IACC boats routinely tacked downwind at about 9 to 10 knots boat speed. They were able to do this because their hull speeds were about 10 knots, and until hull speed is exceeded they are very low-drag boats despite their great weight. The drag curve of *Gymcrack* (Fig 10.3) reveals why it is that, given sufficient sail area, heavy yachts can tack downwind to win in winds that drive them no faster than their hull speed.

At near-drift wind speeds, the reduction of wind speed in the lower few metres so twists the apparent wind (Fig 3.15) that the drive force from the lower sails when broad reaching becomes negligible, and the faster the boat sails the more severe is the loss. In these conditions, apparent wind sailing ceases to be efficient.

20.11 ■ The second critical ratio – sail area to total weight

This is the most difficult ratio to satisfy. From hull speed to minimum planing speed, and given equal excellence of design:

- At the same speed
  - The drive force will vary as the sail area.
  - The drag force will vary as the total weight.
- And at different speeds
  - The drive force will increase as the square of the apparent wind speed.
  - The drag force will increase according to the boat's hull design –
    As the fourth or fifth power in the case of the yacht (Fig 10.3).
    As about the third power in the case of the conventional dinghy with a hump in its drag curve (Fig 10.6).
    As about the speed increase in the case of the skiff with no hump in its drag curve (Fig 10.10).

Fig 10.3 shows why heavy round yachts tack downwind only when they are sailing at less than their hull speeds. The extra drive force needed to sail 50% faster at higher boat speeds is prohibitive.

Figs 10.9, 10.10 and 10.12 demonstrate the most favourable situation. These relatively straight drag curves show that these boats need only 50% more drive force to sail 50% faster. With good design, sufficient added sail area is not difficult to provide, it can be held upright with trapezes and wings, and this arrangement gives the performance between hull speed and what would normally be minimum planing speed shown by the curves J, K, L and M, N, O in Fig 20.2.

Figs 10.5, 10.6 and 10.7 show the drag curves of a canoe and two more normal dinghies, and the curve X, Y Y Y, Z in Fig 20.2 shows the performance of my experimental Tasar which did not have quite enough sail area to tack downwind efficiently in winds between 5 and 10 knots.

Every figure in these diagrams is reliable. Julian and I have been living and breathing these apparent wind boats for very many years. What is so fortunate for the reader is that the experimental Tasar so accurately represents the full catastrophe of so many of the 'skiff copies'.

Keith Melvin, a Tasar sailor from Edinburgh, now resident in Norway, has a turn of phrase that sums it all up: 'In the afternoon race in PA1s [popular asymmetric 1], we rounded the windward mark and set off, keeping our air clear like you should. Funny thing – one crew had trouble hoisting, ran straight to the downwind mark without spinnaker and beat us all' (from *Minorca Sailing*). And from *Minorca Sailing* again: 'They had just acquired a 29er. We all had a sail. I am much too big for it, but downwind, despite my weight, it just went ballistic.' And two years later: 'First race of the season. Windward/leeward course near the Forth Bridge, wind 12 knots against tide. Fleet a Rockport skiff, two RS800s, eight PA1s, two (smaller), PA2s etc etc. The skiff and the RS800s enjoyed apparent wind sailing. The rest of us didn't. I was crewing in a PA1. We were the first to stop tacking downwind, pull up the board and crab downwind. The other PA1s all followed to cut their losses. The two PA2s were amazing; long after we finished they were still reaching back and forth trying to get downwind against the tide.'

We are fortunate that the 29er and my experimental Tasar X are so accurately documented. The detail differences between their sail areas (29er 300sq ft; Tasar X 240sq ft), sailing weights (29er 475lb; Tasar X 500lb) and drag curves are small, yet the difference between the measured performances M, N, O and X, Y Y, Z in Fig 20.2 are very large in the 5 to 10 knot wind speed and 5 to 7.5 knot boat speed range. The 29er delivers, and we put it into production. The Tasar X did not deliver, and I terminated further experiment with the asymmetric rig and did not put it into production.

The critical sail area/total weight ratio for the hull speed/minimum planing speed range clearly lies between these two examples.

20.12 ■ The third critical ratio – sail-carrying power to total weight

In progressively stronger wind and rougher water, a point will be reached at which, even by reducing the apparent wind by steering downwind, the boat will become overpowered with firmly trimmed sails and it will be necessary to sail with eased sheets. At or a little before this point, a skiff with three suits of sails will sail faster with a smaller, lower, more compact rig, so it is obvious that sail area no longer has anything to do with the ability to deliver apparent wind performance. The ability to sail upright and under full control when technically overpowered is now the overriding requirement.

I express this capability as 'sail-carrying power', and the critical ratio becomes 'sail-carrying power to total weight'. It implies good righting moment, and the ability to steer quickly and accurately with light control at high speed through progressively rougher water. Once the boat is planing cleanly, all the dynamic difficulties of the 'hull speed to minimum planing speed' regime reverse and become favourable.

In stronger winds, if a crew hold their heading, as the wind speed increases, the apparent wind increases broadly similarly. As the apparent wind increases, the drive force from the sails will increase as the square of the apparent wind speed. So a 10% increase in wind speed will give about a 21% increase in drive force.

The drag curve for almost all planing sailboats at planing speeds is close to a straight line. So a 10% increase in wind speed will give a 21% increase in drive force and the speed will increase by about 20%.

This increase in boat speed will then swing the apparent wind forward, so in order to keep the angle between the apparent wind and the boat about the same, the boat must be steered more downwind.

This combination of steering more downwind and at a higher speed is the factor that gives the huge increase in downwind VMG. In Fig 20.2 the slopes B–C, E–F show that blow-downwind boats gain about half a knot extra VMG with every extra 1 knot of wind speed. The slope of the curve K–L shows that the 49er gains about 1.3 knots of downwind VMG for every extra 1 knot of wind speed.

This is the area that was so well researched and developed in the mountain lake work reported in Chapters 14 and 15, and that was confirmed so dramatically in the record sail that is reported in Section 28.3.

20.13 ■ The fourth critical ratio – the rig's handling properties

As the wind becomes stronger yet, the vital factor for control becomes the handling characteristics of the hull and rig. In the real world, the general roughness of the wind and the size and roughness of the waves (eg whether regular or chaotic) and the skill of the crew will determine the limit of control. This is not really a ratio at all, but it is so intimately tied up with the ability to deliver authoritative apparent wind performance across the wind speed range that I always include it as if it were.

At root, the second ratio will always call for a lot of sail. When the wind kicks in, you have to be able to handle that sail:

- Rigs that are stiff and unyielding are difficult to control and fall over first.
- Rigs that are flexible, but yield in the middle, fail next.
- Rigs that both yield and flatten from the top down, and fill up from the bottom up, enable crews to retain control in the strongest winds. (See Fig 22.4. This leads to the automatic rig, which is described in Chapter 22.)

An extreme example of controllability occurred at a 49er World Championships in Bandol. The mistral set in and blew at 30 knots, with gusts to 40 knots. Sailing was cancelled. One crew, for fun, rigged with the standard 49er rig, but were not quite able to hold it, and were bowled over.

Julian was carrying a prototype smaller rig for inspection and consideration by the 49er World Council. Chris Nicholson and Gary Boyd borrowed it, put it up, and were able to control it. In their favour was that in the offshore wind the water close to shore was absolutely flat. Julian, armed with two GPSs and a wind gauge, borrowed a Club Med speed boat and, with a group of interested race officers and sailors on board, formatted on the 49er. Chris repeatedly accelerated to and sailed steadily at 32 knots for half a minute at a time in the gusts, and held about 28 knots in the lulls. As Chris sailed back to the dock area, Julian stopped periodically and measured the wind – the gusts did indeed routinely touch 40 knots.

This was the fastest reliably measured open water speed that I was aware of at that time (about 1997). It may well have been exceeded in the years since by the big 25–30m catamarans such as *PlayStation* which now use skiff ratios to chase world records.

20.14 ■ Summary

Fig 20.2 shows the full force of the apparent wind revolution, together with the consequences of failing to satisfy the critical ratios. If you think of all sailboats as a spectrum, with children's trainers, Lasers, 420–470-style dinghies and most yachts at the conventional performance end, the downwind performance of the classic 5o5 A–B–C is about the best downwind performance to be expected from conventional blow-down-wind sailing.

As a group, all of these boats respond in a broadly similar way to a common handling technique and a strategy that is narrowly focused, and to tactics that are close, and these subjects are the stuff of sailing literature up to the present.

At the other end of the spectrum, the iceboats have been lonely and supreme for 100 years. They have now been joined by boats like the Eighteen foot skiffs, 49ers, the re-rigged Tornados, the B-14, L5000, Boss, 29er and RS800, and more recently by the water-ballasted and swing-keel big-boat designs, and even more recently by the foil Moths. The downwind performances of the 49er and 29er are given by curves J–K–L and M–N–O in Fig 20.2.

From the notes above we can now see that the ability to deliver winning apparent wind performance downwind in all wind speeds up to the maximum safe wind speed is due to no single design breakthrough. Three separate ratios – sail area to wetted area, sail area to total weight, and sail-carrying power to total weight – and then a special blend of handling characteristics with an automatic rig all needed to be identified, and then satisfied, and then matched within an appropriate design before it became possible to tack downwind with authority in all wind strengths and win.

We have had to crack all four parts of a complex four-part password before we could understand the full logic. Perhaps it is not so surprising that it has taken us 100 years to begin to catch up with the ice yachts.

PART FIVE

The Automatic Rig

Chapter 21 • The Evolution of Manual Adjustment

21.1 ■ The drive for adjustment

Slow change of sail area in response to slow change in wind speed has been a part of sailing for millennia. Faster 'peak the gaff' and 'ease the sheet' manual change in sail camber, trim and twist has been employed since the adoption of the fore-and-aft rig with a lateen sail in the East, and the fore-and-aft rig with a sprit or gaff mainsail in the West.

The development in the 1960s of the flexible Bermuda mast and dedicated adjustment controls enabled crews to reset the shape of their sails quickly enough to adjust to individual gusts and lulls.

Developments from the 1960s to about 1990 were driven by six assumptions.

With respect to wind *speed*, that:

1 For each wind speed there will be a fastest sail shape.
2 By using manual adjustment a crew can adjust to that shape.
3 It is the business of the crew to adjust to that shape.
4 The rate at which the wind speed changes will allow crews time to adjust to the fastest shape.

And with respect to wind *direction*, that:

5 It is the business of the helmsman to steer his boat to the wind when sailing to windward, or for the crew to adjust sail trim when sailing offwind.
6 The rate of change of wind direction will allow the helmsman to steer his boat to each change of wind direction, or for the crew to adjust sail trim downwind.

Recent research has shown that assumptions 2, 4 and 6 are false:

• Assumption 2 is false because adjustment technique that depends on stretching the sail under tension cannot provide the twist frequently demanded by assumption 1.
• Assumptions 4 and 6 are false because we now know that substantial changes in both the speed and the direction of the real wind occur every few seconds – that is, at a rate much faster than it is possible to respond to with any manual adjustment technique.

The automatic rig (Chapter 22) is the new technology that has evolved in response to these revised facts.

21.2 ■ Slow adjustment through the ages

The Chinese junks of antiquity shortened sail efficiently and intelligently. Their sails were fully battened with horizontal bamboo battens. As the wind speed increased, they both reduced their sail area and lowered the height at which it was set by progressively lowering the upper spar and collapsing the lower battens and the sailcloth between them into a roll at the bottom of the sail. Nothing to catch the wind other than the bare mast was left above the upper spar, so the aerodynamic drag was progressively reduced and the junks continued to sail efficiently in stronger winds. This was adjustment by slow change of sail area, without significant change of sail shape.

The great clipper sailing ships of the early nineteenth century were equally efficient in shortening sail, but not so intelligent. To keep every sail within the capacity of a relatively small crew to handle, they divided their total sail area into multiple 'square' sails, each set on a yard and trimmed by four ropes. As the wind speed increased, the sails were furled and lashed to their spars, starting from the top and working down, one by one. This both reduced the sail area and reduced the height at which it was set. But in this case the spars with their furled sails and all of the ropes and rigging remained in the wind and caused massive aerodynamic drag as the wind speed increased. Hal Wagstaff, for many years the ISAF Vice President for Australia and New Zealand and adjacent parts of the world, sailed as a youth as a seaman on one of these vessels, to find out how they worked. He recollects:

> *Crosswind and downwind they were fine. As the wind increased we shortened sail; the drag aloft didn't matter and they continued to sail well at good speed.*
>
> *Upwind was a different story. In lighter winds, with everything set and drawing its best, they sailed to windward surprisingly well. But as the wind speed increased and we shortened sail, the drag of all the bare spars and furled sails and rigging aloft increased as the square of the (apparent) wind speed, and it quickly became so great that to maintain reasonable speed through the water we had to sail progressively closer to a beam reach. So as the wind became stronger, their ability to sail to windward became progressively less until in really strong winds they could not sail to windward at all. This was not intelligent.*
>
> *That experience enabled me to understand why so many had been wrecked on lee shores.*

21.3 ■ Unintentional slow adjustment technique

In the nineteenth century and up to about 1920, almost all yachts and dinghies used gaff rigs. These, by their nature, were fluently adjustable, because tightening the peak halyard raised the gaff and tightened the leech and necessarily made the upper mainsail fuller. Easing it made the upper mainsail flatter. But nowhere in the literature of the 1920s do I remember reading anything about adjustment of camber or the effects of adjustment. Rather, there was constant admonition to 'peak the gaff' regularly because it was the nature of halyards to stretch.

The background to this is that all cordage in those days was made from either hemp or cotton, and ropes spun from both of these fibres tended to stretch under tension. So during any race it was natural and expected that the peak halyard – the longest rope in the rig – would stretch a little and the gaff would sag. This would make the upper mainsail flatter and allow the upper leech to twist to leeward. So it was an accepted part of sailing that normal stretch in the longest halyard would make the rig lose both 'power' and pointing ability. Alert sailors therefore 'peaked the gaff' regularly to restore the shape of the rig to what 'looked right and felt right'.

It is inevitable that what looked right and felt right would have been fuller on a quiet day and flatter on a stronger day. But they seem never to have thought of it that way, and what they wrote suggests that they believed they were simply compensating for undesirable and unavoidable stretch in their halyards. I think we would now say that they periodically adjusted upper mainsail fullness to what looked right and felt right as the wind speed slowly changed as they sailed.

21.4 ■ Rigid rigs, and manually adjustable rigs

Rigid rigs

Starting in the 1920s, there was a great change from the heavier, more costly mast-plus-gaff rig to the simpler, generally lighter and less costly 'Bermuda' (one-piece, no-gaff) rig. From the 1920s until the mid-1960s, all these masts were rigid, because it was believed that the business of a mast was to stay straight and stiff, and not to change unintentionally as the gaffs had done when the peak halyard stretched. 'Adjustment' for strong-wind and light-wind days was to have two suits of sails, one fuller and one flatter.

At that time, wind seems to have been considered to be a uniform flow. Reports of America's Cup races in the 1930s report tide and current differences in detail, but make no mention of the wind. The concept that there might be advantage in 'working the shifts' had not yet appeared in the media or on the helmsman's radar. Since the rigs of those days had no capability of flattening sail on a gust-by-gust basis, there was simply no consciousness of adjustment as a subject for discussion.

These rigid rigs survive in boats with masthead forestays. In these rigs, sheet tension controls twist; and outhaul controls fullness of the lower sail. Fullness of the upper mainsail cannot be adjusted by bending the mast (with normal rigging).

Manually adjustable rigs

In the 1960s, it was found that rigs with masts that bent a little were faster than rigs with rigid masts. From this limited flexibility, the manually adjustable rig was developed.

It was my privilege to be at the cutting edge of this. In 1960 we started what became the NS14 (ie Northbridge Sailing Club, Seniors' Dinghy, 14ft long). The first thing we got right was to create a non-one-design (ie development) hull of a comfortable size and sensible underwater shape for body-hiking by two adults. The key difference was that we built them with the then-new waterproof plywoods and waterproof glues and used aircraft construction technology rather than traditional boatbuilding methods (Fig 9.3), so they weighed about half the weight of the typical hulls of that era, and these light plywood boats stayed stiff and held their speed for at least ten years. What we had done, unwittingly, was to provide a very good R and D platform.

About the mid-1960s, the Moth class found that masts that bent a little sailed faster than those that stayed straight. I was one of those who helped my elder son build his first Moth. I planed the first mast too enthusiastically, found that it bent a bit, and promised to make him a better, stiffer one next week. But he won his first race at the adjacent Moth club, then won the race the following week. Those of us at the Northbridge Sailing Club where the parents were sailing the new NS14s, and our children were sailing Moths at the adjacent Seaforth Moth Club, all sensed that something strange was going on. We played with our children's mainsheets with new interest, watched the Moth mainsails flattening as we pulled, and began to think new thoughts about what we might do with this capability. The rapid development of tuft technology and flexible wing mast rigs and adjustable sail shape, and then the datum mark system to repeat efficient sail shapes quickly, is described in Section 13.4.

What was happening was that the concept of sail shape adjustment each minute or so to match the gust and lull wind speed changes was being born. Our mental picture was that the gust/lull sequence looked like the dashed square-wave-form line in Fig 26.10A. At that time we knew that boats with full sails staggered and sailed slowly in strong gusts, that when we flattened our sails they did not stagger and we sailed faster, and from this thinking the technique of flattening and restoring fullness on a gust/lull-by-gust/lull basis was born.

Design consequences

The sail area originally chosen for the NS14 in 1960 was 100sq ft – 9.3sq m. With the relatively full sails typical of the early 1960s set on stiff round masts, this area proved exactly right for a 300lb average-weight body-hiking man and woman crew in Sydney's 12 knot average summer afternoon sea breezes.

In the early 1970s we began to use our new ability to 'depower' in stronger winds as a design factor. Flattening sail in stronger winds both reduced drag and reduced the heeling force as well. We realised that by turning this thinking around we could justify bigger sails to start with and so sail faster in the lighter winds, then flatten to depower when the wind speed increased. In 1972 I designed a new 123sq ft rig for the NS14 hull and called the new class the Nova. I was a little startled by the 'Windward Planing Superboat' headline of a subsequent magazine boat test, but this boat was certainly quick. It became the 1975 Tasar. With this boat we took this new technology to the world as a cutting edge example in the global trend towards the capability and practice of sail shape adjustment.

Use in practice

In view of the developments over the next 30 years it is important to be clear about what these manually adjustable rigs can, and cannot, do. As a general rule, they have masts that can be bent sufficiently to allow any desired sail camber (fullness) to be set by appropriate use of outhaul, downhaul and vang or backstay controls, but the control forces needed are so great that no automatic response to wind speed change is possible nor expected.

If we take the rig in Fig 13.3 as an example, Fig 22.7 shows the mechanics. The sail is built to the shape shown by the solid outline and the cambers drawn and noted at each height. This is the fastest shape from calm up to the design wind of 11 knots, except that in light air the clew outhaul is eased to set the lower sail at nearer 10%. This movement does not affect the upper sail, which stays at 10% camber.

Up to 11 knots, the vang is not touched. As the wind becomes progressively stronger increasing vang tension is used to bend the mast. By 20 knots and at a tension of 400lb, the mast bend matches the luff curve of the sail, with the result shown in Fig 13.3B.

This is efficient adjustment of camber. Sailing for the last 40 years has been largely using such rigs to match sail camber to wind speed as we sail; but note that to achieve this flattening, the sail is stretched so tightly that it cannot yield much nor twist much to small (5–10lb) changes in aerodynamic force at the leech.

In the case of larger rigs, and particularly those with stiff topmasts, manually adjustable rigs tend to take a characteristic shape, which is well demonstrated in Fig 11.5. The lower mast bends forward, the sail flattens behind the bend, a kink forms in the leech, and the upper sail between the stiff topmast and the taut leech above the kink does not twist nor flatten much.

There are two consequences to this manual adjustment approach:

- The first is that these rigs behave like a stick-shift car. They hold whatever sail shape the crew set, almost regardless of subsequent change in wind speed. In the extreme, a sail flattened as in Fig 13.3 for strong winds stays flat even when the wind goes calm. The corollary is that, like the car, they confer no advantage until the crew 'changes gear' and does in fact match the sail shape to the wind of the moment. Note that this means 'powering up' for every lull as well as flattening for every gust. The more diligent the crew and the more frequently and accurately the crew adjust, the faster the boat sails. But there is a limit to what even the best and most diligent crew can do.
- The second is that the tension down the leech needed to bend the topmast back in this manner severely limits the sail's ability to twist. So when significant sharp wind *direction* changes occur, the crew need to ease a lot of mainsheet to let the whole sail out, rather than ease only inches to let the top twist off (as in Figs 22.5 and 22.6). This explains the difference in the behaviour of the two sheet hands described in Section 14.12.

In 1972, Professor Mike Lucas built a copy of our adjustable wing mast rig and used it in his Moth on Tuttle Lake, Kansas. In the relatively cool and steady-wind mornings, the wing mast rig was significantly faster than his previous whippy bamboo stick, to the point where the Moth became the fastest boat on the lake. But the 'ka' in Kansas means 'south wind' in the local Indian language; Topeka Airport records prevailing 25 knot southerlies on hot summer afternoons, and in these hot strong southerly winds the gusts took the form of multiple harsh gust peaks with lighter mini-lulls between them, more like the trace in Fig 21.4D.

Mike had no hope of adjusting to depower every few seconds to each quick gust peak. At a second level, his tightly stretched sail could not twist and blow off at the top, so Mike was forced to yield and recover yards of mainsheet every few seconds.

Despite the sophistication of his rig, his Moth staggered and sailed slowly, but when he replaced his manually adjustable wing mast with his old whippy bamboo stick that yielded like a fishing rod, he sailed smoothly again and regained his superior speed in the strong, rough winds.

One weekend in 1972 I sailed with him, and thought that Kansas must have a private rough-wind factory all of its own.

21.5 ■ The calculated speed gains

As Julian's B-14, B-18 and 49er rigs started to sail with magic speed 20 years later, I remembered those quick harsh gusts, and the response of the bamboo stick, and have tried to analyse and blend modern technology with practical sailing to achieve both the speed that rewards accurate adjustment in lighter winds with the yield dynamics that are faster in stronger winds such as Mike Lucas's bamboo stick:

- Fig 21.1 summarises Figs 13.6 to 13.18 in a practical way.
- Fig 21.2 extends Fig 13.19 in a useful way.

- Fig 21.3 is based on Figs 21.1 and 21.2. It shows the fastest we can expect to sail in notionally steady winds –
- If we trim best possible in an 11 knot lull.
- If in the following gust
  - We do not adjust.
  - If we adjust best possible with the manually adjustable rig.
  - If we adjust to a theoretical best with a new kind of rig.

To make the calculations I created a notional boat something like a 29er sailed by adults with a slightly bigger sail. Total weight (boat 200lb and crew 300lb) is 500lb (227kg). The righting moment with the helm body-hiking and the forward hand on trapeze is 1425lb/ft. The hull drag is that of the 29er (Fig 10.10). The rig of 140sq ft (13sq m) is proportioned such that when sailing to windward at 6 knots in an imaginary, magical, steady 11 knot lull, the heeling force from the firmly sheeted sails is equal to the maximum righting moment exerted by the crew of 1425lb/ft – that is, the design wind is 11 knots.

The next step was to flesh out my recently drawn maximum lifts and minimum drags of Fig 13.19 into Fig 21.2A which is a family of curves of the lift coefficients at different angles of attack expected from sails that are flat, or of 5% camber, or of 10% camber. Fig 21.2B is a similar family of curves of drag coefficients. These represent about the mid-ranges of all the standard-text and private-study data available to me.

The next step was to develop an appropriate calculation string. This has been interesting to develop and has proved illuminating. I started with the calculation string I had developed for downwind sailing (Section 20.5). While that had proved seminal in first explaining the 'dip' in the downwind VMG diagram of the experimental Tasar, and then in revealing the critical ratios, I quickly found that it was inadequate for sailing to windward, because of the difference in the nature of upwind from downwind sailing. As an example, if when sailing downwind you change your heading, this will change the apparent wind speed and direction and the drive force and the drag force, but will not affect the trim of your sails because the calculation assumes that it is the sailor's job to keep the sails at their optimum trim regardless of change of heading.

But if when sailing to windward you change your heading, this will affect every – repeat *every* – other factor, without exception. So I extended my downwind program into a new and different

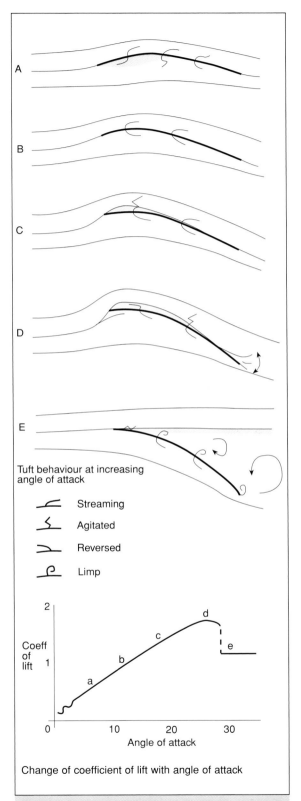

A

B

C

D

E

Tuft behaviour at increasing angle of attack

⊂ Streaming

ᐳ Agitated

ᐳ Reversed

ᒪ Limp

Change of coefficient of lift with angle of attack

Fig 21.1 Tuft and coefficient lift behaviour

upwind calculation string that accommodates all of the upwind facts of life.

This one is used in this way. I start with the maximum righting moment of 1425lb/ft, which is fixed. I assume a true wind speed, a boat speed, and a boat direction relative to the true wind. To the extent possible, I have linked every other factor to these three variables. Along the way I have applied the corrections I thought appropriate – for example, that the 'turbine blade' effect would increase the speed of the apparent wind over the jib by 10%, and that the deflection of the wind direction by the jib onto the mainsail behind it would be half the angle of attack of the jib. An important refinement was to divide the sails into four horizontal panels, each of 35sq ft. The practical effect of this is that the lift and drag contribution of each of three levels of the jib and four levels of the mainsail – seven in all – can be separately calculated and totalled to arrive at the final drive, drag and heeling forces. This enables the program to calculate the effects not only of twist and flattening of each sail, but of different amounts of twist and flattening as between the jib and the mainsail as well.

The program is tremendous fun to play with. You start by setting the basics – the true wind speed, the boat speed, and the heading (relative to the true wind). You then trim your sails – you adjust the camber and set the trim angle (the angle between the sail at that level and the boat's centreline) at three levels for the jib and four levels for the mainsail, in the manner of Fig 21.1. The program then gives you

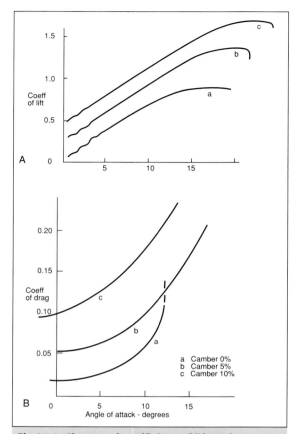

Fig 21.2 Change of coefficient of lift and coefficient of drag with camber

the angle of attack (the angle between the apparent wind and the sail) at each of these seven stations. From Figs 21.2A and 21.2B you enter the lift coefficient and the drag coefficient for that angle of attack and camber at each station – and, presto, the program then gives the heeling force, the drive force, and the total drag.

If the heeling force is greater than the maximum 1425lb/ft righting moment, you ease your upper sails a little on the next try; if the drive force is greater than the drag, you try pointing a little higher; you adjust everything a little bit and do it again. Before long you will have tweaked the program so that the drive equals the drag, and the heeling force equals the righting moment, and that is the highest you can point in that wind at that boat speed. Boat speed times the cosine of the pointing angle gives VMG.

You then try the whole thing again at a slightly higher boat speed; the VMG may increase a fraction. You try faster again; the VMG stays flat or decreases a touch, and the string with the highest VMG is close to the best you can do. You then try twisting the upper jib a shade more or a shade less, and tweak another one or two degrees better pointing angle at the same speed. It is just like sailing, and all the responses are astonishingly realistic – other than that you do not get wet.

The calculated performance from different techniques in steady winds

I analysed six scenarios. True wind direction in each case is assumed to be 000°.

Case 1   is a crew who sail to windward in an imaginary steady 11 knot lull.

Case 2   is a crew who in a following imaginary steady 15.4 knot gust ease nothing and luff to stay upright.

Case 3   is a crew with a manually adjustable rig (like Fig 11.5 or Fig 13.3) who, in the same gust, hold their heading almost steady and flatten as best they can and ease sheets to stay upright.

Case 4   is a crew with a more automatic rig, like Fig 22.5, who in the same gust hold their heading and ease sheets and flatten, and free their upper sails to stay upright.

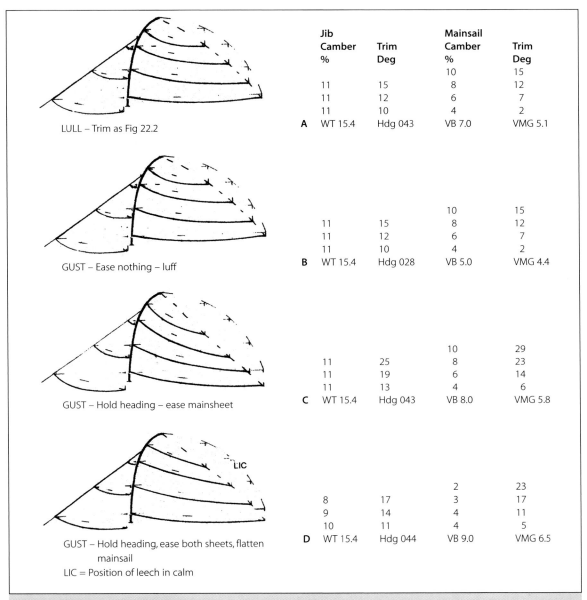

	Jib Camber %	Trim Deg	Mainsail Camber %	Trim Deg
			10	15
	11	15	8	12
	11	12	6	7
	11	10	4	2
A	WT 15.4	Hdg 043	VB 7.0	VMG 5.1
			10	15
	11	15	8	12
	11	12	6	7
	11	10	4	2
B	WT 15.4	Hdg 028	VB 5.0	VMG 4.4
			10	29
	11	25	8	23
	11	19	6	14
	11	13	4	6
C	WT 15.4	Hdg 043	VB 8.0	VMG 5.8
			2	23
	8	17	3	17
	9	14	4	11
	10	11	4	5
D	WT 15.4	Hdg 044	VB 9.0	VMG 6.5

LULL – Trim as Fig 22.2

GUST – Ease nothing – luff

GUST – Hold heading – ease mainsheet

GUST – Hold heading, ease both sheets, flatten mainsail

LIC = Position of leech in calm

Fig 21.3 Effect of sail trim on speed

Case 5   repeats Case 3 but in 20 knots.
Case 6   repeats Case 4 but in 20 knots.

The calculated performances are given in Table 21.1, overleaf.

The calculation looks about right. The fact that the boat sails to windward almost no faster in 20 knots than 15.4 knots indicates that the greater drive force from twisting the upper sails more is being absorbed by the greater aerodynamic drag of the stronger wind, and suggests that the whole boat would sail faster with a smaller, lower rig. This is exactly what we observed in the 20–25 knot winds of the San Francisco 2005 USA 29er Championships near Treasure Island, and the subsequent World Championships in the 'Gate'. The 29er rig is slightly lower and smaller (130sq ft) than that of my notional boat. There the lead boats were sailing to windward at a measured 11 knots, so my calculations look to be either realistic or a shade conservative.

Fig 21.3 displays the sail shapes of Cases 1, 2, 3 and 4 in Table 21.1.

Table 21.1 Differences in VMG performance

Case	Wind speed	Technique	Performance		
			Vb knots	*Hdg*	*VMG knots*
1	11 knot lull	All sails sheeted firmly	7.0	043	5.1
2	15.4 knot gust	Ease nothing. Luff to stay upright	5.0	028	4.4
3	15.4 knot gust	Hold heading. Ease and twist	8.0	043	5.8
4	15.4 knot gust	Hold heading. Ease, twist and flatten	9.0	044	6.5
5	20 knot gust	Hold heading. Ease and flatten sails	8.0	043	5.9
6	20 knot gust	Hold heading. Ease, twist and flatten	9.0	043	6.6

Case 1 in Table 21.1, Fig 21.3A and Fig 22.2 all show the shape that sails fastest at the design wind. The fall of the light in Fig 22.2 shows that the jib and the upper mainsail are both trimmed to and are working at about the same angle of about 10° off the centreline at the foot of the jib and behind the hounds of the mainsail. The lower mainsail is trimmed to near 'boom along centreline' to avoid being backwinded by the jib, and at this trim is not contributing much drive, but is contributing greatly to the turbine blade effect on the flow over the jib. Vang is slack. This is all standard stuff with no surprises.

To set the slightly smaller mainsail in Fig 13.3 to this 10° twist with no vang requires a mainsheet tension that gives 90lb of tension down the leech.

Case 2 in Table 21.1 is also shown by Fig 21.3B. Since nothing has been eased, the sails have not changed shape. All that has happened is that the whole boat has been pointed higher to avoid being blown over. The slower boat speed and slower VMG show that this is not the way to win races.

Case 3 in Table 21.1, which is shown in Fig 21.3C, is interesting, in that it is the best I could do when assuming a 'manual adjust' technique. As the wind speed increases, the ideal technique is to follow the skiffs and replace the bigger rig with a smaller, lower rig. Another good way is to follow the Chinese junk and lower the whole sail and furl the unwanted area at the bottom, as in normal reefing. But if you cannot lower your sail but can adjust its shape, the logical approach has to be to twist off the now unwanted upper area of the mainsail and flatten it completely so that it contributes as little capsizing force as possible.

Herein lies the difficulty. To completely flatten the sail in Fig 13.3 needs a leech tension applied by the vang of about 100lb. If in imagination you set the traveller far to windward so that the mainsheet pulls the boom sideways and not downwards at all, you still have that 100lb of leech tension applied by the vang, and the sail will not twist as you want it to. If you ease both vang and sheet, the sail then twists and goes full – so will not point. In practice, an intermediate setting with sufficient vang to preserve pointing gives best and respectable speed on the water and also proves to give the fastest calculated performance. But particularly with bigger rigs, this results in the characteristic shape shown in Fig 11.5 with the sail more flattened in the middle and the upper sail neither much flattened nor twisted. So Case 3 is a practical and useful compromise which would work reasonably well if the basic assumptions about how often a crew should adjust were true.

Case 4 in Table 21.1, which is shown in Fig 21.3D, gives the calculated performance if the upper sail is both twisted and flattened until it contributes no drive force and – because completely flattened – minimum heeling force. We will discuss this in Chapter 22.

What we see in the comparison of Case 3 and Case 4 is the first of the two intrinsic limitations of the manually adjustable rig – that is, that it cannot provide both appropriate flattening and appropriate twist simultaneously.

So far, we have been looking at the sail shapes that sail fastest in notionally steady winds, with the object of doing the best we can with manual adjustment through the minute-by-minute gust–lull cycle. Since the invention of the manually adjustable rig 40 years ago, the basic concept for the lead-group sailor has been that, to win, a crew should respond to the wind's minute-by-minute gust–lull cycle by applying vang sufficient to preserve pointing and easing sheet enough to stay upright in each gust, and easing vang and tightening sheet again to restore speed in each lull. And that their reward for doing this will be to sail to windward faster than crews who do not adjust.

This has been true, but the rewards have been small. Why?

288

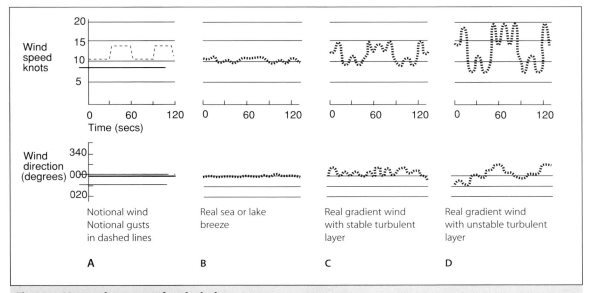

Fig 21.4 Unsteady nature of real wind

If the wind blew in a series of neat parcels in which steady lulls of 11 knots were followed half a minute later by steady gusts of 15.4 knots, sailing would have been simpler, and the rewards greater. But what Figs 3.6 to 3.11, 3.33, 5.1 and 5.2 all tell us is that the wind does not blow in neat 30-second steady-gust and steady-lull parcels. Fig 21.4 more accurately represents the speed and direction changes in the real wind.

When looked at in this way we can see that what we have really been doing for the past 40 years is adjusting every minute or so to the average gust speed and the average lull speed of the notional wind, and we have been missing all of the potential advantage we could have enjoyed had we been able to adjust more accurately and more quickly. Within the more 'spiky' environment of the real winds of Fig 21.4C and D, the actual performance advantage we have enjoyed has been much less than the theoretical advantage potentially available.

What we can now see is that if we could adjust our sail shape every few seconds so that the shape would at all times be optimum for the wind speed of the moment, we would be able to sail very much faster. To do this manually would mean making two or three significant adjustments not every minute, but every few seconds. This is beyond the capability of even the most diligent crew. This is the second limitation of the manually adjustable rig. Can it be done automatically? This leads to Chapter 22.

Chapter 22 • The Automatic Rig

22.1 ■ The seminal change

The reasons

Julian's three two-hander Eighteens in 1983, 1984 and 1985 had revealed that two pairs of hands could not do all that was expected from a competent crew in an Eighteen foot skiff with a conventional rig. The year with *Prime I* was an ongoing struggle for Ian Hobbs as he wrestled with a 12ft long gybing spinnaker pole.

The primary drive for the invention of the asymmetric spinnaker with its fixed bowsprit/spinnaker pole that was fitted to *Prime II* was to reduce this workload. The new rig sailed faster downwind and, with the shorter leg times, there was then insufficient time to complete all the desirable adjustments.

In the rig design of *Prime III*, Julian began the shift towards what has flowered into the automatic rig with its minimal adjustments. By today's standards it was primitive, and it had an alloy topmast, but even in that early state it worked in the sense that it was so much simpler to handle that Julian and Michael Wilson could focus on their sailing, and it was so much faster in stronger winds than the preceding two-handers that it threatened the three-handers. As described in Section 14.2, the class lost patience and banned it.

Over the next two years the slack-stay problem surfaced with boats such as *Entrad* (Fig 22.1). In Chapter 14 I have described how the adoption of the more flexible masts needed for manual sail shape adjustment in the tall-masted Eighteen footer skiff class led to 'loss of rig tension' problems. When they bent their lower masts by up to 6% of the mainsail's luff length, the lower mast became shorter and this caused the primary rigging to become unacceptably slack. The response to this problem by the top Eighteen foot skiffs was to add hydraulic rams to adjust and control their shroud tensions. In 1987 the flow-on effects of the greatly increased weight, complexity and cost of this development had temporarily devastated the class.

Unusually flexible topmasts were first used as a solution to this mechanical problem, but Julian's response in 1988 was to invent a different sort of rig which was simple, low in cost and light in weight. He set the lower mast to a fixed bend that was never changed. That solved the slack shrouds problem, so he was able to discard the hydraulics and all their complexity, weight and cost. He then concentrated all of the flexibility in the topmast. This was an extension of the *Prime III* thinking, but this time it was made possible in flexible glass due to a co-operative association we had developed with the glass fibre tube makers. They had no hang-ups about what a mast should or should not look like, nor what it should be made of. So when Julian provided them with a new mandrel and asked not for a 'stiffest possible' carbon topmast, but for a flexible all-glass topmast with a particular rate of spring and distribution of flexibility, their first attempt was close to the mark – and by the third try we had exactly what we wanted. This approach was trialled in a 1988 boat that has become the B-14.

The rig of that boat was the starting point for a revolutionary line of development that has matured into faster, more automatic rigs that are based on a different dynamic system.

The broad history

Dated pictures give the broad sweep; we will look at the finer detail later:

- In the 1930s, sliding seat canoes such as *Wake*, Fig 10.4, were deemed to be the fastest small sailboats in the world. Their masts were stiff.

- In the late 1930s, Australian design followed Fox's design closely. The Payne-Mortlock canoes in Fig 11.1 were the only sailboats fast enough to 'sail around a Manly ferry' steaming at 14 knots. Their masts remain stiff to this day.

- Figs 11.3 and 11.4 of an Auckland 'M' class, *Manaia*, in 1937 and 1938, similarly confirm that in that era masts were meant to be stiff.

- Fig 1.32 of Eighteen footers in the late 1960s shows that not much had changed in 30 years.

- Fig 13.3 shows a very good example of the manual adjustment technology we had developed in the NS14 class in the late 1960s. To flatten the sail as shown requires a leech tension approaching 100lb, so that the sail can neither respond to small differences in aerodynamic force, nor can it twist much. Once set, this rig will hold the shape set until it is reset to some other shape.

- Fig 11.4 from the early 1970s shows the Fig 13.3 manual adjustment technology as first adopted by the Eighteen footer class. What we see is a 'tight-leech' manually adjustable rig in which, when the vang is tightened, the lower mast bends, the sail flattens in the middle with the characteristic kink in the leech, the topmast is still stiff, and the upper mainsail will neither flatten nor twist much.

- Fig 22.1, from 1986–7, shows one of the five top manual-adjustment-with-hydraulics skiffs of that era sailing in extreme conditions in Auckland, New Zealand. In view of the text at the top of page 294, it is interesting to note that the skipper is Rob Brown and Julian Bethwaite is handling the spinnaker.

- Fig 22.2 from 1988–9 shows the revolutionary B-14 rig. In this 'to windward in the design wind' picture it does not look very different, but the key changes – the fixed-bend lower mast and the flexible topmast – are there.

Fig 22.1 *Entrad*, 1985

Big, manually adjustable Eighteen foot skiff.

Fig 22.2 B14, 1988

B-14 in design wind.

Fig 22.3 AAMI I, 1990
Fig 22.4 AAMI IV, in a strong gust (inset)

- Fig 22.3 of *AAMI I* from 1990–1 shows that the topmast has become noticeably more flexible.
- Fig 22.4 of *AAMI II* from 1991–2 shows the very different way that these new, more flexible rigs yielded in very strong winds. Compare the mast bend in Fig 22.4 with the mast bend in Fig 22.1, also in very strong wind.

Fig 22.5 49er

49er in 15–7 knot gust. Rig as in Fig 21.3D

- Fig 22.5 shows a 49er (designed in 1995) sailing in about the 15–16 knot gusts assumed in the Table 21.1, Case 3, calculations. Note the very different way in which the upper mainsail has automatically flattened and twisted freely away under the aerodynamic load of the gust, as compared with the upper mainsail in Fig 11.5.

The observed difference

In the tableau described in Section 14.12, Rob Brown, the defending champion, was sailing *Prudential*, a development of *Entrad* (Fig 22.1). Julian was sailing *AAMI I* (Fig 22.3). In the lulls, both rigs looked like Fig 22.2. In the gusts, *Prudential*'s mainsail flattened first in the middle and looked like Fig 11.5 and was static between adjustments. *AAMI*'s mainsail flattened and opened first at the top like Fig 22.5, and 'flashed' as in the quick mini-gusts and lulls it flattened and then 'filled up' quickly and near-automatically.

22.2 ■ The consolidation years

In earlier chapters, I have described the swift progress by intensive cut and try development from the prototype B-14, to the B-18, to *AAMI I* and the tableau above, to the intensive 'improve everything' year with *AAMI II*, which culminated in the astonishing performance of the record sail (Section 29.3). For a few more years, so much else was happening that it was not until some time later that the opportunity presented itself to reflect and analyse what we were doing.

I sensed that the previously unexplained speed of the B-14, and now the B-18s, could be due in part to five previously unconsidered factors – all of which were working together in these new rigs in a particularly efficient way:

- The first was that the new distribution of flexibility – a stiffer lower mast and a much more flexible topmast – enabled the upper leech to open and the mainsail to flatten from the top down in a way quite different from, and much more efficient both dynamically and aerodynamically, than the conventional 'low-bend' manually adjustable rigs with the kink in their leeches. (Case 4 of Table 21.1.)
- The second was that the rate of spring chosen by Julian was dynamically only just stiff enough to hold the upper leech firm up to the design wind. In stronger winds it was soft enough to allow the added force of the gust to start opening the upper leech automatically, from which point only a small subsequent easing of the mainsheet by the sheet hand was needed to keep the heeling force in the gust balanced with the righting moment of the trapezing crew.
- The third was that the 'tension the cunningham' method now being used to flatten the sail added no leech tension, so the leech remained free to twist.
- The fourth was that the real wind was a much more complex flow than I had previously thought it to be. Until then, I had believed the wind to be relatively simple 30 second gusts and 30 second lulls in the wind speed, with only trivial fluctuations during the gusts and the lulls (*HPS-1*, Chapter 5). Instead it now appeared to be both these gusts and lulls together with a superimposed pattern of smaller, quicker but still significant gust peaks and gust lulls. In addition, there were also significant quick direction changes. Chapter 5 (of this current book) touches on these, and Fig 21.4 represents the more complete present view of the wind.
- The fifth was that these quicker changes of speed and direction repeated far too frequently for any crew to respond to all of them efficiently, so only some fraction of the potential benefit from adjustment was being achieved from any manual adjustment rig. By way of contrast, the new rigs were flexing fluently to every change, and so achieving a far higher 'strike rate'.

Summed up, these rigs were faster than the earlier rigs in two primary respects:
1 They were intrinsically more efficient, and so were naturally faster in stronger winds.
2 They flexed automatically and quickly, and so delivered all of the potential advantage suggested in Table 21.1 rather than only some of it.

What we had developed was a rig that yielded near automatically, near instantaneously and in a remarkably efficient way. This approach also explained why the whippy bamboo stick in Mike Lucas's Moth had performed so well in the rough air on Tuttle Lake in Kansas 18 years earlier.

Fig 22.6 Byte C2

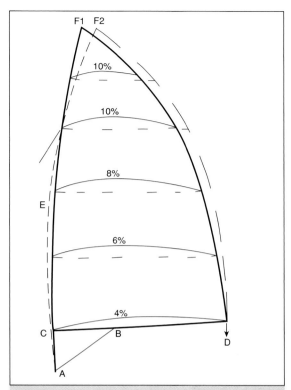

Fig 22.7 Mechanics of manual rig adjustment

Solid outline – Sails natural shape
Fastest from 0 to 11 knots

Dashed outline – Sail flattened for 20 knots
400lb tension applied between A and B
Lower mast forced forward at C and E
90lb leech tension applied at D
Masthead drawn back from F1 to F2
This flattens sail, as in Fig 13.3.

22.3 ■ The mechanics of the manual and the automatic rig

Why did these new rigs adopt the Fig 22.5 shape which looks like a young dragonfly's wing in flight, while the old ones adopted the Fig 11.5 shape which looks like the wing of a grumpy dragonfly with constipation?

The primary reason is that the mechanism used to flatten the sail adds no leech tension.

The manually adjustable rig

Fig 22.7 shows the mechanism of the manually adjustable rig. The solid outline and cambers show the natural shape of the sail, which is like Fig 22.2. This is the shape the sail and upper battens adopt when hoisted in calm air on a mast that typically has a fairly stiff topmast. The manual adjustment rig will hold this shape unchanged regardless of wind strength until it is adjusted. Normal practice is to leave the sail at this shape up to the design wind. (The design wind is that wind strength at which the boat can just be held upright, without easing anything, by a crew that is fully hiked or trapezed.) The concept is discussed in *HPS-1*, pages 224, 225).

In stronger winds vang tension between A and C is applied in the gusts. This is the primary control. The clew outhaul is used to progressively flatten the foot, and the downhaul (cunningham) to smooth the diagonal wrinkles. In, say, a 15 knot gust, 200lb of tension will apply 165lb forward thrust at the gooseneck C, and a downforce of about 40lb at the clew. The forward thrust bends the lower mast forward at E. The added 40lb of leech tension applies about 20lb aft force at the head, which bends the topmast back about 50–60mm from F1 to F2, and the sail is smoothly flattened to about 5% camber above and behind the hounds and pro rata down to the foot. For 40 years sailing has been applying appropriate tension to flatten thus in the gusts, and easing to restore fullness and power in the lulls. At these modest tensions it all works quite well.

But when the lulls become stronger than the design wind, the dynamics become different. In gusts of 20 knots and more, the sail should be both flattened and twisted off at the top. A vang tension of 400lb will, through the leech tension, bend the topmast back about 150mm and the mast bend will then match the luff curve of the sail which will then become almost completely flat, as in the dashed outlines and cambers of Fig 22.7 and shown in Fig 13.3 lower. But the cost is the added 80lb of leech tension; this prevents the sail from twisting off at the top until it generates almost no heeling force. Because the sail will not twist sufficiently, to keep the boat upright the sheet hand has to ease the boom a long way each gust to let the whole sail out to a smaller angle to the wind. This is the compromise that is necessary on the water, which is accurately reflected in the calculations of Table 21.1, Cases 3 and 5, and shown in Figs 21.3C and 11.5, and observed in the tableau.

The automatic rig

Fig 22.8 shows the mechanics of the automatic rig. In the dinghy park and from a distance, there is no difference. The hoisted sail looks like Fig 22.2, because this is the quintessential shape that sails fastest upwind in light and moderate winds. On the water it will hold this shape from calm up to the design wind.

Closer inspection reveals the three key differences between the Fig 22.7 manual-adjust rig and the Fig 22.8 automatic rig:

1 The topmast is between two and three times springier in the automatic rig than the typical topmast in a manual-adjust mast.
2 There are two sets of spreaders in the automatic rig
  • The stronger lower shrouds run from the forestay attachment point (the hounds) through the tips of the lower spreaders to the chainplates on the gunwales. They are tensioned until the forestay is at the tension desired for the expected wind.
  • The springier topmast is supported sideways by lighter independent cap shrouds which run from the masthead through the tips of the upper spreaders to the chainplates on the gunwale.
3 There is a powerful downhaul (cunningham) purchase system.

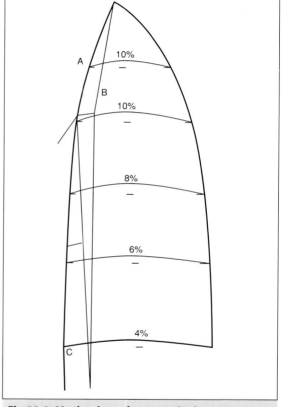

Fig 22.8 Mechanism of automatic rig

A   Flexible topmast
B   Cap shrouds
C   Downhaul

The mast-sail-batten combination of the upper mainsail is designed to give the Fig 22.2 shape when sailing in all lighter and moderate winds. A small but precise tension on the cap shrouds is applied to bend the topmast back to give the upper sail fullness desired. (The cap shrouds also support the topmast when the masthead spinnaker is set.) The topmast is now a pre-loaded spring which will remain at that bend until the leech tension becomes greater than the pre-load. This is the break-out point. At greater leech tensions, the mast – as a spring – will then respond to the aerodynamic forces.

If in imagination we sail to windward in a wind that builds from calm to the design wind, increasing mainsheet tension will be needed to hold the Fig 22.2 trim as the increasing wind force tries to blow the upper leech to leeward. At the design wind (11–12 knots) the rig becomes 'balanced' at the breakout point, with the springy masthead now held back solely by leech tension and the windward cap shroud. At the design wind the leeward cap shroud just becomes slack. The job of the windward cap shroud is to ensure that the masthead when it bends further flexes aft – which will flatten the sail – and not sideways to leeward.

The way the light is falling on the sails in Fig 22.2 shows ideal design wind trim. The jib and the upper mainsail are both at about the same fullness and the same angle to the oncoming apparent wind, while the lower mainsail is progressively both flattened and twisted towards the centreline, to avoid being back-winded by the jib, until the classic 'boom along centreline' trim is reached. The job of the lower mainsail is primarily to provide the turbine-effect boost to the flow over the lee side of the jib (Section 13.18).

Up to this point, the mainsail has been trimmed and the boat steered for optimum 'power' – as in Fig 21.1D in drift, as in Fig 21.1C in light breeze, and as in Fig 21.1B at the design wind. The centre of pressure plot in Fig 13.14 shows how the centre of pressure remains relatively steady at about 30%–35% of the distance from the leading edge (from mast to leech) at all higher angles of attack, and also demonstrates how quickly it moves towards the trailing edge (the leech) at the smaller (stronger-wind) angles of attack. This is obvious when you think of trying to sail to windward in a blow with a too-full sail – the forward part of the sail flutters, the wind 'hits' only the leech, and the far-aft centre of pressure makes the boat want to round up.

As the wind speed increases above the design wind, the angle of attack moves towards A in Fig 21.1, the centre of pressure moves towards the leech as in Fig 13.14, and this aft movement of the centre of pressure alters the springy balance and pulls the easily yielding topmast back a little further. (It cannot yield sideways because of the windward cap shroud.) It is this aft movement of the springy topmast that both flattens the upper mainsail and allows the leech to twist to leeward. This starts at the top; the more strongly the wind blows, the more the topmast flexes aft and the further down the sail the flattening and twisting proceeds. If you ease the sheet a few inches, the flattening and twisting spread down another metre or two. As the gust fades into the lull, the topmast springs forward to restore the Fig 22.2 shape. Because the vang does not need to be touched, there is none of the added leech tension which prevents the sail from twisting in the manually adjustable rig. Figs 22.4, 22.5 and 22.6 show automatic rigs at work.

If on strong-wind days you want to set a flatter sail, you tighten the cap shrouds ashore to pull the topmast further back. This flattens the upper sail to the shape you want, but does not apply any tension to the leech, so the behaviour above remains unchanged.

22.4 ■ The variables

To cope with the normal variables of sailing – heavier and lighter crews, the need to pinch and point higher off the start line to hold tactical position, or to make the rig yield more easily in the choppy air near a windward mark under a weather shore – the downhaul comes into its own as a tuning device to adjust the balance point.

Normal design – that is, the 49er – is to combine topmast, sail and batten design to provide a breakout point powerful enough for a heavy crew to pinch off the start line without the rig yielding. Such a set-up will be, by itself, too stiff to yield automatically at the balance point appropriate for a light crew.

If progressively higher tension is applied to the downhaul, the sailcloth nearest to the mast is tensioned and stretched from tack to head. The battens hold this taut sailcloth away from the mast, and this tensed panel bends the topmast backwards. If you apply enough tension you can bend it to the point where the cap shrouds go slack. This function enables the crew to set and reset the breakout point at any time. When racing in Rose Bay in an easterly, our practice was to leave the downhaul slack for the start and until we were clear; then to hike to extreme and adjust downhaul so the sail stayed 'filled up' in the lulls and it just opened and flattened as desired in the puffs. As we approached the Dover Heights shore and the gusts near the hills became sharper and choppier, a little more downhaul gave earlier quicker automatic yielding and a smoother, faster ride.

The automatic rig works because the topmast is designed to bend from the top like a fishing rod, and to be just strong enough to hold the Fig 22.2 shape at the design wind; the rig is designed to leave the leech free to twist; and the breakout tuning system – the downhaul – is also designed to work without loading the leech.

Two points of interest:

Never make the mistake of thinking that only the stiff can be strong. Springy can be strong too. A 49er returning from practice at dusk capsized off the club and stuck its topmast and sail into the ooze. The crew were unable to right it and swam ashore. Next day they were shocked to find the inverted hull almost airborne at low tide. An hour's steady pulling from the gunwale of a stout motorboat on a rope tied around the spreaders finally got it out. Apart from the black ooze, it was none the worse for its ordeal (see Fig 17.2).

The thin line that is the centre of pressure plot in Fig 13.14 may not shout 'force' at you, but that is what it means. A story from 60 years ago, when I was test pilot at a major air force repair base, is interesting. Sometimes a tricky problem presented. One such was a bomber that had suffered a fire on the ground at a forward Pacific island airstrip. For a time the flames engulfed one wing just outboard of the engine. The ground crew managed to extinguish the fire, but not before the metal had been scorched. The aircraft was nursed back to the repair base in New Zealand. The question for the engineers and test pilot – was the scorched wing still airworthy? I suggested that a key consideration would be whether the temper of the alloy skin had been degraded by the abnormal heat, and that this would be relatively easy to find out by comparing the behaviour of the suspect wing with the undamaged wing by applying both gentle upward acceleration and twist. My idea was accepted, and I flew with the engineers at dawn on a cloudless morning. Flying straight down-sun I slowed the aircraft until it began to tremble and shudder as it approached the stall (leech ribbons just popping in and out). At that light weight, the speed with flaps up was 90 knots. I accelerated to 99 knots and eased firmly back on the yoke until it began to tremble again. For work with fighter aircraft I had had a little accelerometer made, which I routinely clipped onto the top of the instrument panel. At this speed and angle of attack it showed 1.2 × gravity. The wings bent up a little under this added 20% bending load, and at this lowest speed and greatest angle of attack the upward force was acting with the centre of pressure at its forward extreme and so was both lifting the wingtips and twisting them up at the leading edge. The near horizontal light revealed the way the upper skin of the undamaged wing 'quilted' between the ribs and frames, as was normal under the compression caused by the gentle upward bending, and it revealed too the diagonal tension lines that developed from the leading edge just outboard of the engine to the trailing edge at the wingtip as the forward tip was twisted upwards by the forward centre of pressure. The scorched skin of the suspect wing stayed flat and lifeless and looked like soft lead rather than spring steel. The watching engineer officers expressed alarm. I then put on power and shallow dived to 200 knots, again straight down-sun, and again eased back on the yoke to apply a 1.2g upward acceleration load, but this time at a very small angle of attack at high speed and with the centre of pressure towards its aft extreme (as in a full sail in a strong gust). Again the good wing 'quilted', but at this higher speed the wingtip was being twisted down by the aft centre of pressure and the diagonal tension lines revealed by the low sun ran from the trailing edge near the engine to the leading edge at the wingtip. Again, the appearance of the skin of the suspect wing was 'dead' and very different. The engineers needed no further persuasion. The temper of the alloy skin had been unacceptably degraded by the fire, and we fitted a new outer wing.

The twist force I used to reveal the damage to the bomber's wing is the twist force we use in the automatic rig to initiate the aft flex from the balance point.

Consider a 49er sailing like Fig 22.2 in an 11 knot lull. The mainsail will be generating about 200lb of cross-wind force, with the centre of pressure at about 40% – Fig 13.14 – that is, 1m behind the mast at sail mid-height. At this, the design wind speed, the rig is balanced at its breakout point but nothing has yet moved.

The boat enters a 15.4 knot gust. The angle of attack decreases to about half (the V2 law); the centre of pressure moves aft 10%–20% (Fig 13.14); and the topmast is suddenly pulled aft by the same leech tension, but it is now acting from a point 10%–20% further aft than in the lull. If you calculate and resolve the forces, the aft force on the topmast in the design wind speed lull is 52lb, and this is the design breakout point; in the gust it increases to 63lb because of the aft movement of the centre of pressure. This extra 11lb bends the springy topmast further aft, and in so doing it begins to flatten the upper sail and allows the upper leech to open. Note that all of this initial flattening and yielding happens instantly and completely automatically.

What follows is that the sheet hand will probably ease the mainsheet a few inches to keep the boat upright through the gust. The effect of easing the sheet with the automatic rig is to allow the boom to rise and the upper sail to twist further open. This further reduces the angle of attack of the upper sail so the centre of pressure moves further aft still, and further flattens the upper sail as in Fig 22.5, rather than the boom move out and the upper sail not twist nor flatten as in Fig 11.5.

Fig 22.6 shows this thinking applied to the single-sail rig of Ian Bruce's C2 Byte. This is the revival of Mike Lucas's whippy bamboo stick, but this time at exactly the correct springiness for the average-to-heavy Byte sailor. (C2 means 'Carbon', 2-piece.) The rig was developed in Sydney. First we trialled a series of progressively springier topmasts until the upper sail twisted and flattened with a solid crew as we wanted. Then we trialled progressively springier lower masts until the heavier crews using no downhaul still had all the power they wanted, and the lighter crews used adequate downhaul to adjust the rig so that it yielded at the right point for their weight.

Julian took the rig to Canada. Ian Bruce is a practical sailor, and one afternoon he gathered together at Hudson on the Ottawa river between Montreal and Ottawa a standard Byte, a Laser Radial (which usually sails faster than the Byte), a Europe Moth (which usually sails faster than the Byte), the new C2 Byte, and four young women of about the same skill and weight. It mattered not which sailor sailed which boat, or whether the wind was fresh or light – the C2 Byte always sailed away from the others.

Fig 22.6 shows a relatively light woman sailing comfortably at good speed in a fresh breeze with the upper sail twisted and flattened so it develops minimum heeling force. In this situation, almost all of the drive is being contributed by the lower sail.

22.5 ■ Postscript – a more automatic rig in action

The automatic rig is a concept in which greater boat speed is sought by designing for elastic mechanical response of the sails and spars to the unsteady turbulent flow of the real wind. The design objects are not easy to define, and differences in response and performance have not in the past been easy to measure or quantify or demonstrate with certainty.

A recently conducted series of parallel simultaneous measurements represents a major advance in research technology in that this method can reveal clear differences in boat performance between rigs of different elasticity.

In Section 10.18 I have described the circumstances that led to two months of experimentation and measurement of the hull, spar and rig properties of the 49er in mid-2007. One of the three questions asked by the 49er class was, 'What would be the effect of moving to lighter all-carbon spars and an even more automatic rig?'

Two rigs were developed with all-carbon spars and more square-top sails. Fig 22.9 shows a standard 49er mainsail laid on top of one of these, with the luffs and clews of both sails aligned. The experimental sail calls for a mast about 220mm higher, and the extra chord and area of the squarehead is clear to see.

A comprehensive programme was set up to compare each of the new rigs with the standard rig when sailed in close proximity by near identical crews of different skill, different weight, and in different wind strengths.

One of the measurement methods employed was to

Fig 22.9 Standard and squarehead sails

Standard 49er mainsail, and experimental square-head mainsail.

have the standard boat, and one of the boats being evaluated, sail a series of windward and leeward legs in close company while a chase boat measured the wind and photographed the rigs. Each 49er carried an onboard GPS programmed to record speed and direction every two seconds.

Figs 22.10 and 22.11 show, from each of the two boats, the scatter diagram of the 60 approximately two-second-average speed and direction points measured by their GPSs while they sailed the same (of many) 2-minute tacks – this one on port. The mean wind direction measured by the chase boat during the period of each tack was assumed for these analyses. The wind direction at either boat at any time will have been slightly different due to the wind's normal short-term variation and longer-term oscillation, and this factor will account for some of the scatter in direction. (Because the readings were adjacent and simultaneous, this will not affect any difference as between the two boats.)

Fig 22.12 is repeated from *HPS-1* and shows the scatter diagram of the speeds and directions of 24 gusts and lulls over a 30-minute period. In this case, I have printed it inverted to better show its similarity with Fig 22.11.

Just from inspection of Figs 22.10 and 22.11 it is clear that:

- There is an obvious difference between the scatter pattern in the two diagrams.
- This experimental method can detect difference.
- The observed difference is that the squarehead rig with the 'softer' leech develops two much more concentrated scatter clusters based on the gusts and the lulls than does the standard rig. Fig 22.11 is much more like Fig 22.12 than is Fig 22.10.
- There is a real difference between the performance of an existing highly developed automatic rig and an even more automatic rig deliberately designed so that the leech twists open with a lesser force.
- The smaller scatter implies that the even more automatic rig sails more steadily through the unsteady wind.

Further:

- The combined evidence from all the data acquired during the measurement programs shows that both of the more automatic rigs sail a little faster than the standard rig.
- Crew evaluation was that the more automatic rigs were easier to sail in that they would reach and hold maximum speed more easily than the standard rig.

What these experiments reveal is that there seems to be a particular 'in tune' flexibility of the leech at which the rig responds in a particularly efficient way to the wind's quick variations of speed. The Fig 22.11 rig consistently drives the boat faster in the gusts and quick gust peaks than in the lulls. The response of the standard rig is more blurred and without clear gust/lull discrimination.

One of the consequences of the Fig 22.11 pattern is that with such rigs we need to accept that in the future there will be *two* target speed ranges, not one fixed target speed.

After 40 years of being at the cutting edge of first the adjustable rig and then the automatic rig, it is gratifying to be able to present such convincing evidence.

Fig 22.12 Gust/lull scatter diagram (right)

Scatter diagram of mean wind speeds and directions in sequential gusts and lulls, from *HPS-1* (page 35). The diagram is inverted for better congruence with Fig 22.11.

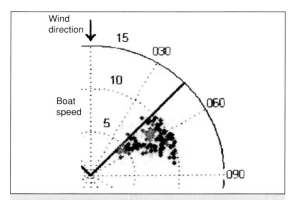

Fig 22.10 Scatter diagram of standard rig

Each darker point represents the boat speed and direction over a two-second period (the lighter points are those of the adjacent experimental rig).

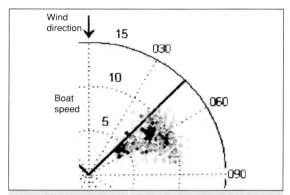

Fig 22.11 Scatter diagram of squarehead rig

As Fig 22.10, but here the dark points in Fig 22.10 are lighter, and vice versa, to show the scatter diagram of the experimental squarehead rig. Note how these points lie in two more compact groups. This rig is self-adjusting automatically to the quick gusts and lulls. Note the similarity of this pattern with the gust/lull pattern of Fig 22.12.

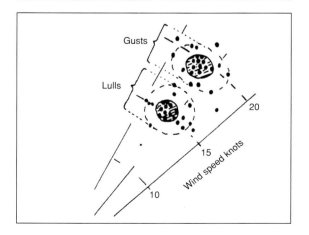

PART SIX

The Sailing Simulator

Chapter 23 • The Evolution of the Sailing Simulator

23.1 ■ Similarities with the flight simulator

Over the past 50 years the flight simulator has developed from being a relatively inexpensive substitute for a plane into being an indispensable tool that can do much more than any plane can do, and at a much lower cost and in safety.

The sailing simulator is new, but it already has so many similarities with the flight simulator, and its usefulness appears to be developing along lines so similar to the flight simulator, that a quick overview of its forebear's history is a good starting point.

23.2 ■ Flight simulator development – substitution

In 1945 the world's future great airlines started as a group of what would now be regarded as underfunded fringe operators. Within 15 years, we had put the ocean liners out of business.

Central to that success was safety and all-weather reliability, and central to that ability was the world's first primitive simulator – a gimballed instrumented box with a seat, control column, rudder pedals, flight instruments and a hood. It was driven by pushrods, valves and bellows and called a Link trainer. On an adjacent table was a map of the airport of interest, complete with its long-range radio-navigation 'beams' for approach from distance, plus the then developing short-range localiser and glide slope aids that led us through low cloud towards the runway threshold. Over this a crawler crawled at representative speed. An operator at the table interpreted what radio signals would have been received by a pilot at the position of the crawler, and fed these signals to the pilot who was flying 'blind' (under the hood) in the box.

That Link enabled us to practise the new art of locating, bracketing and flying along and down these radio beams with increasing familiarity and accuracy. In the Link we rehearsed, time and again, the triple arts involved in approaching an airport in foul weather. We started with the approach to the airport along one of the 'beams' of the long-range radio navigation aid. We then transferred from the long-range aid to bracket and centre on the local blind landing aid for the duty runway, and finally 'flew' the precise descent down the localiser and glide slope to the runway threshold. Over and over, we did this in the Link until we were skilful enough, and always in-practice enough, to use the aids confidently 'for real' whenever the weather turned foul. It was because of the Link that we could descend through low clouds, confidently and routinely, to the point where we were close enough to see the runway approach lights, cross the threshold, and flare for touchdown.

The value of that simple Link trainer was that it substituted for a whole fleet of expensive training planes that the airline did not have to buy nor maintain. As a training tool it was primitive, limited and inflexible. All it could do was allow us to practise radio navigation approach patterns at one approach airspeed, but that property alone proved enough to make airline flight schedules reliable.

That late 1940s Link trainer, which substituted for the plane, was the start of today's high-technology simulation.

23.3 ■ Flight crew emergency training

In the following decades, two huge changes have driven the status of the flight simulator from substitute to indispensable.

The first change was inherent in the growth of air travel. Aircraft became progressively bigger, faster, more expensive. But, above all, they became so reliable that 'in flight' emergencies became a rarity. A training system was needed to ensure that flight crews could handle any emergency when it did arise. This led to the periodic check system. Look at it this way:

- Passengers see flight crews as smartly dressed officers who fly their schedules.
- Flight crews see their aircraft as an assembly of systems: control, power, fuel, hydraulic, electrical, pressurisation, communication, navigation, etc.
- Check captains see flight crews as technicians who can deal safely with random system malfunction or failure.

Through the 1950s and 1960s the 'check' system was instituted. Usually just after an aircraft had arrived from a scheduled flight and been unloaded, a check captain, a skipper and a first officer would take it and fly the empty plane for an hour or more. This happened once every six months, and during this hour we practised all the things we hoped would never happen. It was torrid, exciting and rewarding in that both the checkers and the pilots being checked learned so much and also came away knowing that we could all still do it. But, to be good, the check captain had to push the limits all the time, and we had to be very careful, because occasionally things could and would go wrong. One example was a check captain who, in a big three-engined aircraft, simulated the failure of a wing engine during the take-off roll. This is a routine exercise, but on this occasion he made a tiny mistake – he pulled the throttle back 10mm too far and inadvertently selected idle reverse instead of idle forward. The aircraft had ample power from the other two engines to accelerate to take-off speed, and the directional control of the wheels still on the runway and the rudder was sufficient to keep straight. But following lift off, at that low airspeed the rudder alone was unable to keep it straight in flight because of the small but critical reverse thrust from one wing engine. It slewed, stalled and crashed in front of the control tower, killing all three. During those decades this sort of thing did happen occasionally around the world. They were accepted as 'training incidents', no passengers were hurt, and they seldom made headlines.

23.4 ■ Flight simulator development – extension

The second change was the development of the computer, and the addition of the power and flexibility of the new computer to the primitive Link trainer. This created in the 1970s and 1980s the modern flight simulator, which quickly developed into a training aid so realistic that anything that can be done in a plane can now be done in the simulator, and done, with near-total realism, at a fraction of the cost and in safety. At root, the aircraft designer's performance program is loaded into the computer memory, and this program is accessed through the manipulation of the simulator controls. The resulting performance is displayed as moving graphics on a computer screen.

Realism at this level invited a huge change in training culture. The same flight training manual could now be used for training or checking regardless of whether the exercises were carried out in a plane or in the simulator. This soon led to the near total integration of in-flight training and simulator training. From this new start, decades of co-operation between both military and civil training directors, aircraft designers and simulator designers have developed a flight training culture in which simulator training and checking and in-flight work are fully integrated.

Note that in this sense the simulator has not become 'as good as the plane for training'. It has become much *better* than the plane. Its training efficiency is formidable. You can practise six bad-weather approaches and landings at six airports around the world without the need to take off even once. This represents a huge saving in crews' and instructors' time and in training aircraft utilisation cost.

In the realm of emergency training, the flight simulator has introduced a new era. Instead of practising emergency procedures in a real plane, always skirting warily and always close to danger as in the example above, the check captain can now simulate one system failure, then another on top of it, then throw in a distraction, and deliberately load the crew to breaking point. The cryptic comment 'OK, I think we'll stop it there – you have ten seconds to live' says it all.

Once the shock wears off, the simulator can re-play the lead-up segment by segment; the crew's thinking and actions can be discussed and analysed, and the crew can see where it was that they failed to keep focus on the critical priority and let control of the plane slip away from them. This sort of training delivers crews who are better trained in emergencies, more knowledgeable, more confident, safer – and still alive.

These two examples, typical of all the other training areas, show how the flight simulator is no longer substituting for the plane. Its usefulness now extends far beyond what any aircraft can do.

The flight training culture of simulator training, now totally integrated with in-flight training, is the result of 50 years of co-operation. Its reward is better training at lower cost in greater safety.

This, then, is the ultimate goal of the sailing simulator. It is equally useful, and will be similarly accepted, but it will take time.

23.5 ■ Sailing simulator origins and development to date

In the following sections we will see how quickly the sailing simulator has already moved through an object for amusement and substitution, to the point where it is already delivering, in an extension role, results that cannot be achieved in any boat.

Handling a sailboat well is a complex art form, and to impart the skill, instructors use words, sketches, models and demonstrations. Some put a child's trainer on a tyre or pivoted platform ashore and move the boat while the student manipulates tiller and sheet. Others extend the physical training function of a hiking bench with a rope to pull and a tiller extension to grasp. Some computer games have realistic graphics on their screens. All of these are useful, but prior to the late 1990s none simulated the interaction of a sailor sailing a real boat in real wind on real water.

The idea of a realistic sailing simulator was born during a discussion about sports physiology at the University of Southampton in the mid-1980s. To study the performance of any athlete it is necessary that he/she exercise in a laboratory adjacent to whichever instrument measures the function being studied – heart rate, blood pressure, oxygen uptake, etc. A treadmill adjacent to the measuring instrument can be programmed to simulate the marathon at the Beijing Olympics, and exercise bikes can be programmed to simulate the Tour de France; thus the mechanics of measuring a runner or cyclist under working load are relatively straightforward. To answer the question 'How do we miniaturise and waterproof whole laboratories of measuring instruments so they will fit into the pockets of a Finn or a Laser sailor?', one lateral-thinking student, John Harrison, volunteered the suggestion, 'It might be more economical to make a marine treadmill for use in the laboratory and use the standard instruments, rather than try to miniaturise and waterproof them all.' Harrison carried the concept forward in Southampton to the extent possible without substantial funding. The idea stuck in the mind of one of the staff, Dr Norman Saunders.

Ten years later, as Professor of Anatomy and Physiology at the University of Tasmania in Hobart, Saunders set up a sports physiology research project to study the physiology of sailors. A 'marine treadmill' based on Harrison's idea was to be a key part of the project. Modification of the concept, further development and then construction were undertaken by Ross Brown and David Lovell. A first trial used moving weights to simulate sail force. The second design took the form of two tubular pyramidal frames such as one sees in children's playgrounds to support the beams to which the swings are attached. In this case, the high pivots supported the ends of a steel hammock that carried most of a Laser. It was proposed to drive the hull with pushrod, valve and bellows technology similar to that of the Link trainer.

Halfway through the project, Dr Tim Gale looked at what was going on and said 'If you complete what you have in mind, you will have one boat which will sail in one way in one wind speed. I think I can write a computer program based on flight simulator technology which would drive pneumatic motion equipment which is already developed and available. It would have an added link to measure the sailor's hiking effort and a loop to include that as a factor in the heel and speed calculations. This approach would offer very much greater flexibility, eg the ability to select any of a number of different wind speeds, as well as greater accuracy and realism of response.'

The computer approach was adopted, it was soon working properly, and the world's first interactive sailing simulator began to be used to study the physiology of sailors when they were sailing their hardest – but it was in the laboratory and adjacent to the measuring instruments instead of on the water. It was huge and clumsy, but it worked brilliantly. Word spread – dinghy sailors and yachtsmen became interested, sailed it, and were amazed at its realism.

A formal experiment with dinghy sailors was then set up. The top 20 Laser sailors on the Tasmanian State list familiarised themselves with the simulator, then sailed their fastest around a series of standard short races. The result astonished everybody. The simulator rankings matched the State list exactly, sailor by sailor.

The date was the mid-late 1990s. Subsequent development was initially glacial, then rapid.

An approach to the Institute of Sport at the apex of the sporting pyramid was probably a little too soon. Only sports physiology was discussed; there was no experience of substitution and nobody had considered extension. The Institute of Sport directors were not sufficiently impressed.

Saunders sought other opinions, and this was when I became involved.

My philosophical view, coloured by my flight simulator experience, was that something that the simulator could already do much better than any boat would be to train novice sailors at the base of the pyramid. Sail training is always beset by problems with weather, darkness and season, and a simulator could offer instruction and coaching to the many who aspire to sail well. It could do this reliably and efficiently and economically. Above all, it held the promise of being able to deliver superior training by competent instructors rather than indifferent training by enthusiastic amateurs.

I suggested that if a sailing simulator could be produced in compact and portable form, this could revolutionise sail training. I believed it should be possible. The flight simulator has no wings and tail – the sailing simulator needed only the cockpit, no bow nor stern, no sails. A light, compact, affordable simulator could be used at clubs, taken to young sailors in schools, used at winter adult evening learn-to-sail classes in warm buildings when there is snow outside, and taken to the water's edge in summer.

23.6 ■ The first generation

We were joined by an engineering design group, who undertook to design and build a compact and commercially viable development of the laboratory simulator. I very quickly realised that this, too, was probably a little ahead of its time because while everything – program, sensors, motion machinery and the design itself – was good enough to work reliably in skilled hands, it soon became clear that these factors were all just short of reliability when faced with the rigours of field operation.

The designers were ships' engineers who were accustomed to huge marine machinery, so it is hardly surprising that their ideas as to what was light and compact were relative. The generation-1 design was a strong steel frame which supported a whole Laser in a cradle that rolled. It was necessarily bulky, heavy and costly, but the primary problem was that the electronics were marginal. The program was at that stage inflexible because it was not modular, and the sensors were electronically delicate in the way they meshed with the program and the motion equipment.

The end result was that this simulator was technically brilliant for its time, but was too big and clumsy to be readily portable, and proved electronically 'delicate'. Around the world a number of them performed reliably in skilled hands in promotion and demonstration roles, but the electronics proved insufficiently robust to achieve reliable, everyday operation in the more demanding environment of field trials run by sailing instructors in real sailing schools with real student sailors.

A few of these simulators moved around the world, but they were used only for prestige by elite institutions, or as boat-show draws by big marketers. None of these generation-1 simulators were ever used for the simulator's primary purpose – routine teaching of students to sail.

23.7 ■ The second generation – technical development

The marine engineers withdrew. It was time to start again with a more determined thrust towards my original idea of a compact, portable and affordable simulator.

What we had learned from the generation-1 machines was that in many ways they were like the early Link trainers in aircraft. They were good enough to reveal small differences in skill between 20 good Laser sailors, all of whom sailed with good technique in the middle of the performance envelope, but they gave very mixed signals to a youngster in trouble at low speed in irons towards the edge of the performance envelope. For example, in light wind and at low speed the feel of both tiller and sheet became heavy instead of light.

The design objective of the generation-2 simulator in 2002 was that it should be smaller, lighter, portable and much less costly. It needed to be physically and electronically robust, faster in response, and to respond realistically over as wide an area of the performance envelope as possible.

The very substantial development in the power and speed of personal computers, programming and sensors in the years between the design of the generation-1 simulators and the second generation-2 machines made it all so much easier.

I worked out what length of cockpit was essential for sailing hard, and cut off all of both bow and stern not needed. The new simulator suddenly became compact, lighter, less costly.

Within the Australian Maritime College we found motion equipment engineers and technicians and programmers who understood the value of both modularisation and electronic reliability. Dr Jonathan Binns completely rewrote the program in a more robust and faster language, and in modular form so that it could accept future extension.

The earlier slow-response linear sensors and long-stroke machinery for roll, steering and sheet trim were replaced by light-actuated near instantaneous rotary sensors and short-stroke machinery, which was itself modularised and redesigned to give more accurate simulation.

These design developments gave the generation-2 machine faster response with more realistic simulation over more of the performance envelope. A sailor using the simulator can now inch towards the start line at half a knot with light fingertip control of sheet and tiller, then suddenly accelerate hard over the final seconds, and it all feels just as it feels on the water.

Chapter 24 • A New Way of Thinking

24.1 ■ Sailing – the sportsman's view

Sportsmen and sportswomen who enjoy popular recreations such as tennis, swimming, golf, cricket, etc, know that if they apply themselves and employ a good coach they can expect to reach whatever level they want to achieve (consistent with their physique).

This belief is justified because in these sports there is an unbroken correlation from beginner to world champion in the sense that the basic skills initially learned remain unchanged as the sportsman lifts his game. Improvement is achieved by a combination of practice to reinforce learned techniques, and coaching to acquire further skills at progressively more advanced levels.

Because of this unbroken correlation between acquired skill and performance, participants in these sports present as a mobile continuum from beginner to champion. Put simply, if two adolescents reach mature strength and one does nothing, he/she will not improve. If the other commits unlimited time, motivation and funds to engage first-class coaches, there is nothing to stop him/her from going right to the top – and some do. The pattern of mobility within this continuum is characterised by the acceptance of the status quo by most, improvement to some higher level by a few motivated players, and the swift rise to the top by a small number of highly motivated new champions, alongside the progressive decay with age of the old ones.

An interesting related statistic is that the Sydney *Yellow Pages* lists pages of swimming and tennis coaches, and columns of golf and cricket coaches. Clearly, in these sports, the services of practical, helpful coaches are sought and used by the players who want to improve, and the coaches are effective in helping these players lift their game. As a result, cadres of competent coaches make a living because they deliver value for money. This is the recreational norm.

When we look at sailing, at first glance a similar continuum seems to be there. Club handicap systems based on observed personal performance are universal, and they work consistently and well. But when we look more closely, nothing quite fits. The normal unbroken bottom-to-top, beginner-to-expert mobility pattern is not there. What we see in sailing is different:

- A few sailors at the top always lead. These few share all the wins.
- The great majority of sailors always follow. None of these followers ever lead or win.
- No established follower ever seems to become a leader, no matter how motivated he may be.

A significant observation from left field is that:

- The *Yellow Pages* directory of Sydney, a great sailing city, which lists so many coaches from other sports, *lists not a single sailing coach*. The same is true of Auckland.

This does not mean that there are no sailing coaches. Weekend mornings at most sailing clubs ring to the shouts of young sailing instructors in inflatables yelling at confused students. The more experienced sailing instructors call themselves coaches.

What the absence of listing by any sailing coach means is that no sailing coach is confident that he/she can lift a motivated sailor's performance from follower level to lead-group level.

So while, in other sports, confident effective professional coaches assist their students to improve their game and reach top level, in sailing there is no cadre of coaches who are confident that they can provide this service. Why this difference?

The simplistic belief system that has grown over time to explain this situation is that all sailors initially learn to sail in about the same way. All sailors then improve and sail progressively faster as they gain experience. So the accepted belief is that all experienced sailors finish up being able to sail more or less equally fast.

From this it follows that the observed differences in speed, week by week, must be due to the fact that leaders lead because they sail faster boats, and followers follow because they sail slower boats. This sort of pseudo-logic is obvious rubbish. From time to time, the experienced follower buys the leader's boat. The result? He *still* follows. But these consistent contradictions have not to this time shaken the core belief that all experienced sailors sail equally fast, and it is the boats that are different.

A more objective analysis runs as follows. The simpler the sport, the fewer are the areas that really matter, so the easier it is for a coach to focus on the one or two areas of importance, to detect error, correct the error, and in this way improve the athlete's performance. As an example, track and field runners have no equipment other than a few grams of clothing, so success depends almost entirely on fitness, their running technique – that is, how they handle their bodies and limbs – and motivation. In these sports, coaching can be concentrated on these few areas that matter.

At the other end of the scale lie the sports with complex equipment, such as the equestrian events and sailing. As the complexity of the equipment increases, so does the number of factors that contribute to success.

In the case of sailing, success at high level is possible if, and only if, the boat itself is technically flawless, and in addition the sailor has complete knowledge and adequate skill in every one of many areas – that is, the handling skill of manipulating the controls; the sailing skill of steering to the wind; the technical skill of optimising sail trim and adjusting sail shape to the changing wind and sea-state conditions; the strategy skill of identifying then exploiting approaching opportunity; the tactical skill of matching determined opponents, plus motivation – to name only the obvious ones. In a more complex sport such as sailing, success is possible only if the athlete is near-perfect in *every* area that is important. But it is obviously much more difficult for the sailor to be self-critical in every detail, or for a coach to probe and analyse every area for possible weakness. Further, it is very easy for a subtle near-universal weakness to remain unidentified.

In this chapter I suggest that such a weakness may have been lying, unidentified until now, in our understanding of the art of boat handling, and that failure to recognise this weakness has crippled the performance level and pleasure of generations of sailors.

24.2 ■ Sailing – the simulator's view

In recent years, access to the sailing simulator has been like being able to look through a microscope where previously the view has been through frosted glass. This property reaches its peak with the simulator printout (Chapter 25). As is usual, it has taken a little while to analyse what we see and so understand what is going on.

Over the past few years, progressively more focused work with this new sail training tool has enabled us to see and understand what is really happening, and where and why the established belief system above is false.

The core discovery has been that because sailboat handling is a more complex art form than, say, track and field, swimming and ball games, the great majority of sailors initially approach sailboat handling not in one way, but in one of *two* slightly different ways.

As a result, because sailors are using one or the other of these two slightly different skill patterns, what looks like the normal all-embracing single continuum of the sport turns out, in sailing, to be not one continuum but two – *natural* and *fast*.

Natural handling technique

One approach to learning to handle a sailboat is to adopt the simplest, most consistent, and easiest way to learn: I call this '*natural* handling technique', and refer to those who use this technique as 'natural' sailors. It is easy to understand why the great majority of sailors learn to sail this way, because it is so obvious and consistent, and therefore much quicker to learn. Usually sailors who sail this way are completely unaware that any other method exists.

So what we see when we look at sailing as a whole is primarily the very normal beginner-to-expert continuum presented by the great majority of natural handling technique sailors. It is only when we know what to look for that we see that this continuum does not and cannot reach right to the top, *so not one of this great majority of sailors can ever win even one serious race.*

Fast handling technique

The other approach to handling is near identical except that in four key respects it is more efficient and therefore faster. I call this '*fast* handling technique' and refer throughout to those who use this technique as 'fast' sailors:
So what we see when we look at sailing as a whole is not one continuum, but two:

- Almost invisible, except at the very top, is the bottom-to-top, beginner-to-expert pattern of the few fast technique sailors. These are the ones who are competent in all the skills that are important where they sail. The very few sailors at the top of this continuum are the ones who always lead, and between them they share all the wins.
- Superimposed over this pattern, but not reaching quite to the top, is the pattern of the ten or twenty times more numerous natural handling technique sailors. Because it is denser, this pattern almost obliterates the pattern of the fast sailors – except at the top. The sailors at the top of this continuum are just as motivated, their boats are equally fast, and they are just as skilful in all the areas of importance in sailing, *except handling*, as are the fast sailors, but because they are (quite unconsciously) using a less efficient and slower handling technique than the fast sailors, they are never in the lead at the finish of the race.
- Because handling, once learned, becomes automatic and subconscious, both groups are unconscious of the detail of what they are doing with their hands and bodies as they manipulate their controls. Neither group has any idea that the way they handle their boats is different from the way their friends and rivals handle their boats.
- And because handling, once learned, becomes automatic and subconscious, it becomes ever more deeply embedded with experience. For this reason, natural sailors *do not sail faster with experience*. And this is why club handicap systems work so well.

Because natural sailors do not know why they sail more slowly than the leaders, and there are no listed coaches who know why either, and to date no body of literature to alert them, this whole population of sailors follows in races for life regardless of how brilliant they may be in other walks of life.

This view of sailing seems to explain, simply and logically, everything that we observe, and the story of this journey of discovery is given in Sections 24.3 onwards. The present position is summarised in Section 24.13 onwards, and leads to the remaining chapters of this book.

24.3 ■ The journey of discovery

It was immediately obvious that the generation-2 prototype simulator was a very different piece of machinery. First and foremost, it was electronically and mechanically robust and proved itself to be completely reliable. We quickly forgot all about the vexing temperamental tantrums of the earlier machines, and came to respect generation-2's flexibility, its crisp response, its unexpected realism, its general user-friendliness. It was compact and portable enough to be carried upstairs and downstairs by willing hands. So we were able to put it to work without delay at what these simulators should have been doing for years, but in fact had never done before – the routine teaching of students to sail, or coaching of experienced sailors to sail faster. Nobody had ever used a sailing simulator for serious student training before, so we set about finding out what it could do, and how best to use it. This has become an illuminating journey towards a very new way of thinking.

The starting point was well summarised by a senior academic student's recollection of his father's comments many years earlier: 'This is your first boat. It will take you a year to learn to sail it, a year to learn to race it, and a year to learn to win in it.' This neatly encapsulates the conventional wisdom – that experience is rewarded by competence, safety and speed, that only with experience can you expect to sail fast, and only with experience plus speed, plus looking after your boat well, can you expect to win. This was the view from which I had written *HPS-1* in the 1980s, and why the advice in it is all about 'sailing' – that is, what to do with sail trim, etc to make your boat set-up faster – and not about 'handling' – that is, how to move the tiller, the sheet and your body to handle the boat efficiently and so sail it faster.

24.4 ■ Initial use

Many visitors to the factory sailed the simulator. Some were just curious, but some sensed opportunity and asked for help. School sailing groups began to use it on days too windy for on-the-water sailing. Back-markers sailed it; we saw their obvious problems, commented, helped them, and back on the water they sailed more confidently and faster. Most had never suspected that they had problems with their handling techniques in the first place. Most of them loved it for identifying and curing their problem, but some hated it for disclosing that they *had* a problem. I sensed that adult resistance to learning was alive and well, and that we might sometimes have a greater problem with this syndrome than with a student's faulty technique.

Respect for this strange machine began to take root, and soon we scored a spectacular success. A very experienced boat chandlery proprietor who routinely sails both dinghies and yachts was finishing last in a hot 25 Laser twilight fleet. He said that he felt he could match anybody for speed straight-line, but was losing so badly on the tacks and turns that he was finishing last, and could I help?

He was right! I asked him to tack. He used a strange, slow inconsistent face-either-way technique, the boat stopped after he centred his tiller, then he picked up the sheet, re-trimmed his sail and began to hike. He took an age to get going again and regain target speed. We changed places, and he watched as I first repeated his technique and then demonstrated the synchronised co-ordinated technique used by champion sailors. He was astonished at the way the faster technique 'flowed'. We discussed what he had been doing and what I felt would be faster, and set to work. He was motivated and intelligent, and focused on accuracy, confident that speed would follow. As his fluency and consistency improved, he began to think ahead and his exercise performance times improved dramatically. He commented later that what we had done that morning was far more than he had expected or believed possible.

The following evening on the water he improved from his customary twenty-fifth place and last, and finished the evening at lead-group level. The following week he phoned with delight to let me know he had scored his first-ever win. A few months later we met again and he commented that by applying the same principles to his yacht sailing, he had become a regular lead-group performer in yachts as well.

I mentally gave the simulator a tick, and looked forward to more successes when the experts took over. But life isn't that easy.

After a few weeks of faultless trial operation I deemed the simulator to be ready for more public exposure. As a retired pilot, I am aware that flight simulator technology and culture has been driven by the vision of the military and airline training directors rather than the marketing thrust of the simulator constructors, and I assumed that the same drives would operate with the sailing simulator.

Therefore I loaned it to three 'expert' sail-training institutions. The first was a great school with 150 students who sail for their recreation. The next was a big established sailing school at the height of its busy season. The third was an innovative sailing club which runs an annual 'Live-in' – an intensive week-long sailing instruction 'camp', which that year was for 70 children. All three institutions said 'Thank you' and used the simulator exactly as if it were just one more boat. I felt that this was a bit short-sighted, but at that stage did not know enough to assert otherwise. And so the results, not surprisingly, were exactly as if they had used just one more boat. I sensed that we could have done so much more.

At the factory we had used the simulator in the intimate, hands-on, one-to-one compare-this-way-with-that-way and look-at-the-difference technique of the flying instructor. We had discussed what we proposed and why we thought it better, and then coached our occasional students movement by movement until they were fluent. This way had produced solid results.

All three of the institutions I had approached or worked with had adopted an 'Instructor talks and student listens' approach. They had each sat the student in the simulator, said 'Like this' (and the instruction was poorly prepared and the demonstrations were inconsistent between instructors), then it was, 'OK, you've learned that. Time's up.' It was hardly surprising that the potential results had been no better than the students normally achieved.

I thought about these differences in approach for a while. Up to this point I had believed that it would be these expert sail training institutions that would have the culture and the skill and the vision to recognise the potential of the simulator, and pick it up and run with it in the same way as the military and the airlines have run with the flight simulator. But none of the three had shown any willingness either to recognise the simulator's potentially unique advantages or to change from their established ways.

I concluded that the strong safety and economic drives that motivate the military and the airlines towards flight simulators do not apply to the training institutions that service the recreational sailing market. If the simulator had potential, it was not going to be the sailing schools who would take the trouble to discover it. They were too fixed in their ways. This left no alternative but for those of us who were going to work with simulators to find out for ourselves what simulators could really do.

24.5 ■ Overview of the task

My objective became to understand better what this new tool could do and how best to use it. As we have gained experience, this objective has expanded to include a new view of the nature of sailing itself. In view of the story that unfolds in the pages that follow, the skills I was able to bring to this task are fortunate.

In the early 1930s I had learned to sail (primarily self-taught) and as an adolescent had built two sailing canoes and then an Idle Along (Fig 1.28) in which I won the New Zealand Junior Championship just prior to joining the New Zealand Air Force early in the 1939–45 war. I designed, built and flew model aircraft, so developed a feel for low-speed aerodynamics. I studied formal aerodynamics and aeronautical engineering and, in 1938, learned to fly.

My flying career from 1938 until 1968 was unusual in scope. I flew for two years as an Air Force flying instructor, then for nearly two years as a test pilot. This was a most intense period of learning about the fine detail of the performance of the aircraft that had been assembled, repaired or rebuilt, and that it was my job to check and certify. Then followed three tours of operations that were gung-ho stuff. The following years of airline flying in the rapidly expanding technical environment of the post-war years was in effect a return to both the high flying standards of flying instruction and the high technical standards of the test-pilot years. For a final eight years I managed a small fleet of aircraft and crews for a great scientific organisation, flew with my crews frequently, but spent most of my time analysing the cloud- and rain-related data our projects were researching.

It is appropriate to note that flying an aircraft demands simultaneous co-ordination in four dimensions. Whether the task is a pinpoint carrier landing or a night approach to touchdown in a brutal gusty crosswind, the pilot must control the pitch, roll, yaw and speed of his craft simultaneously, accurately and without hesitation. Either you co-ordinate fluently, or you don't fly.

Handling a sailboat safely and fast requires exactly the same co-ordination of steering, sail trimming and balance (yaw, pitch, roll and speed) in a much more unstable environment and through a much greater range of wind speed (the sailboat wind speed range starts from calm) and a much wider range of wind angle (the aircraft never runs square).

There is no question concerning human beings' natural ability to co-ordinate. That everybody has learned to co-ordinate fluently and well early in life at the unconscious level of the infant is attested every time he/she stands balanced on two feet, or walks or runs. Most adolescents and adults welcome the challenge to learn further co-ordination skills – such as cycling, skiing, skating, riding surfboards or sailing. The gain is that with every advance in co-ordination, a higher performance level opens up.

To date, the way we have used this new tool has enabled us to make several huge strides in understanding the nature of sailing itself.

WORKING WITH CHILDREN

24.6 ■ First trial with beginners – unsupportive environment

The first simulator training notes were written prior to the 'Live-in' week of intense sail training at the sailing club. In that year's camp 70 children were assigned in groups of five to 14 instructors, and each day was divided into two morning and two afternoon sessions.

The original intention was that I instruct the instructors, so I wrote up appropriate training notes to provide a consistent reference of scope, sequence and method that each instructor could read and agree to, and from which he/she could work with their students on the simulator during the simulator sessions.

In the event, not only was no time planned for me to instruct the instructors, it turned out that the system called for each instructor to instruct his students with his own handling technique. Not surprisingly, these proved to be very different as between instructors. For example, one or two still believed that beginners should face aft when tacking 'because that way is easiest for beginners'. At a second level, the children learned so fast on the simulator that they frequently overtook their instructor who was left flat-footed as the youngster exceeded what the instructor thought they could learn. So I found myself locked into an inflexible system with short sessions, too many students each session, plus an instructor who knew nothing about simulators, who sometimes had a very different idea from mine about the best handling technique to teach, and who was often outpaced by his students and had to be rescued.

Each day brought its surprises. Problems arose; unexpected opportunities developed. Each night I wrote a 'patch' or patches either to correct the problem, or to better exploit the opportunities. In the weeks following the 'Live-in', I re-wrote the initial training notes to integrate all the patches into an improved 'Sailing Simulator Sail Training Manual'.

In the subsequent post-course session about how to do better next year, we all concluded that the way we had handled the simulator trial that year was not an efficient way to use the simulator. But by documenting an efficient and proven method, that initial Training Manual has proved to be an invaluable starting point.

24.7 ■ Second trial with beginners – supportive environment

From that rather inauspicious beginning, work with children developed in a way that has surprised us all.

Our design office, in which I kept the simulator, and our workshop below is now situated in the premises of one of Sydney's great sailing clubs. The resident sailing school at the other end of the building catered, among other interests, for the mid-week and weekend school sailing needs of several secondary or high schools.

One spring weekend morning I happened to be at the office when the weather was too wild for novice sailing. Alert young faces appeared at the door, I welcomed them in, word spread, and as I invited the first of the students to sail, and showed him how to start and run the simulator, the master in charge, Tony Sear, plus one or two parents, appeared. I was startled to hear the shock in Tony's voice: 'But you can see *everything*.'

The first student wavered uncertainly. I showed him how to tack. The next student's first tack was a tangle of crossed arms and legs, so I said, 'Perhaps I should show you how to tack'. Again I was surprised when Tony cut in with a terse and authoritative 'I think you had better show *all of them* how to tack'.

The discussions became more serious. As the children sailed, I showed Tony my training notes, and discussed the organisational problems caused by the 'rigidity of approach' that had led to the difficulties at the 'Live-in' (of another club) some weeks prior. I said I would welcome the opportunity to work with a group of children, and that my object would be to try the one-to-one approach of the flying instructor. This was a method with which I was well familiar and that I had always used on the water with good results. I felt it would be very efficient if adapted to the simulator. I offered to instruct one or two groups for a few sessions so that we could all observe how my training notes worked, how the simulator worked as a sail-training tool, how the one-to-one instruction technique worked, and also to compare the results from simulator instruction with those from the established on-the-water instruction method. Tony had vision, agreed enthusiastically, and offered me a group of four beginners from nine o'clock to ten-thirty and another four from ten-thirty to twelve for the next four Saturday mornings.

In these sessions the learning curve became very steep for all of us. Both children and parents were surprised at the efficiency of simulator instruction, the precision of the techniques taught, and the children's speed of learning.

What they were accustomed to was a regime in which every lesson had some components of changing into sailing clothes, rigging the boat, launching it, sailing out through the moored boats to clear water, and then doing all this in reverse at the end of the lesson. Only the relatively short time in clear water in between could be used for direct instruction. All too often this opportunity was spoiled by wind that was either too strong or too light. Frequently, too, there were communication difficulties because the meanings of particular words were not understood, particularly if they were shouted across the water by an instructor from another boat. So their experience was that progress was always uncertain, always glacial, and almost never systematic.

The simulator presented differently. The four children walked in the door, sometimes with the school sailing coach, put down their gear, kicked off their shoes, and we set to work. No time was lost in peripheral activities.

Children are a delight to work with in that they co-ordinate naturally, and have no prior perceptions to hold them back. If we were working on tacking, I would put props under the simulator gunwales so it could not roll, and leave the program off and the screen blank. I then described and demonstrated the handling routine of the three foot and body movements, the routine of the three hand and arm movements, then how these two routines are co-ordinated and synchronised to mesh together, and finally the routine of the three change-hands movements that follow (Chapter 26). They sailed in turn, with each student practising the first routine, then the second, then co-ordinating them, then the whole tack. While each 'sailed' the simulator, the others watched and learned. I was standing close alongside, could see everything, encouraged good technique, and corrected error before it could become entrenched. By this time the questions were flying, with each question being heard by everybody. Every question was answered fully, quietly and completely with the opportunity for everybody to listen and for anybody to ask follow-up questions. Up to this point, the simulator was still on its props with the screen blank.

When they thought they were ready – not when *I* thought they were ready – I invited them to switch it on and run the program. Almost all children today are fluent with computer games and so are already skilful at handling computers and interpreting moving images on a screen to orient themselves in virtual space. A key aspect of my approach is that, from the outset, the students run the simulator. They are in charge, and my role is simply to advise and encourage.

I left the props in place and had them select the slowest boat and the lightest wind (Optimist in 8 knots). At this stage they began to watch the screen and synchronise their routines and movements with the boat as it turned, and to centre the tiller when the boat on the screen reached the chosen aiming point and the sails filled. As they gained fluency, I removed the props so the boat could roll, and they started, almost unconsciously, to synchronise and co-ordinate steering with sail trim and balance as they tacked.

Again, I encouraged them to ask any questions they had, and to ask them at the relevant time. If they were sailing, I encouraged them to reach for the mouse and pause the program, which stops the action and freezes the image on the screen, and then to ask their question. In this way we could all hear the question and all share in the answer, then with 'Play' the paused boat moved on. Before long we added random gusts to make the wind more realistic, then selected the Byte, then the Laser Radial for the bigger students, and increased the wind strength from 8 knots through to 10 knots, to 12 knots. By the end of the session they were having tremendous fun handling what felt like a real boat with real speed in a real gusty wind, and generally doing it well and controlling the boat to keep it level as they tacked. (The mechanical stops limit the simulator's roll to 15° each way.) All this had taken just 90 minutes.

What impressed their coach was that the students sailed in exactly the same way on the water an hour later.

In subsequent sessions they learned equally quickly how to gybe and round marks and to sail fast in straight lines. (The detail is given in Chapters 25, 26 and 27.)

I have described this typical session because it shows up so well some of the differences between the simulator and a boat, how different teaching is with a simulator from teaching in a boat, and why beginners can learn so much faster and so well on the simulator:

- No time is lost in peripheral activity; 89 minutes of the 90-minute session were spent sailing.
- The students learn the very best, fastest, synchronised, co-ordinated handling techniques right at the beginning. The techniques taught are those that are used by Olympic medallists and world champions, and there will be no need for these students ever to unlearn sloppy uncoordinated technique later.
- Every student could watch every demonstration closely, could hear every word, so each understood exactly what he or she was meant to do and how to do it. I encouraged them to ask any question when it was relevant to ask it, not at the end of their sail.
- Communication was perfect, because I had them stop the simulator whenever they wanted to ask a question. While it was stopped, there was no responsibility to control a moving boat, so the sailor could focus on the discussion and the answer without distraction. Everybody listened to each question, to the answer, and joined in any discussion.
- The simulator enabled us to be systematic. We started with the lightest wind and the slowest boat, and progressively worked up to more challenging conditions – but only when each student was ready.

Beginners have nothing to unlearn, so there was no resistance to learning. Given the near-ideal environment described above, it is hardly surprising that they acquired good technique much faster than all on-the-water experience suggests is possible.

The Master in Charge, the parents and the school coach were impressed.

24.8 ■ Third trial with beginners – using the new opportunity

Some of the children I had been instructing were unquestionably 'beginners' in their sailing capability, despite having been sailing for some time. At this point I became much more interested in the school sailing scene, watched what was going on at the other end of the club, and came to realise that all five of the schools who use the facilities of the club and its associated sailing school operated in broadly the same manner.

A relatively small group of children reach the level at which they can sail respectably and can handle themselves on a start line and around a race course. These sailors become the school sailing team, and get most of the coach's attention. These young sailors are easy to manage because they enjoy their sailing, they are motivated, they learn, they have fun, and do not drop out.

All the other children float around for their hour or two on days when the wind is not too strong, and are shepherded to keep them from straying by people who are shepherds rather than instructors or coaches. They learn very little, they remain almost permanently at 'beginner' level, they don't enjoy it much, they don't have much fun. Not surprisingly, many of these drop out.

A parent confirmed that this approach was much wider than school sailing: 'I arranged some extra coaching with a [different] sailing school. They floated around, he was shouted at a couple of times during the hour, and that was the sailing lesson.' I thought about this, and how quickly and well our test group had learned. It seemed to me that with the simulator it might be possible to change the whole pattern of school sailing for the better.

Towards the end of the spring school term, I put a proposal to the masters in charge of sailing at two schools:

'What I see are smaller groups of students who are sufficiently competent to race. These enjoy the fun of sailing in company and racing with purpose. They are motivated, they are enthusiastic, and they are easy to manage.

'I see larger groups of beginner-level students who spend a year or two being "shepherded", who are not yet competent to race and sail with purpose, who are approaching that level, but approaching it very slowly. These students are not much motivated and do not have much fun and learn little.

'Based on how fast and how well the first trial group learned on the simulator, I think it would be possible to instruct students, in groups of not more than four, from "complete beginner" to "competent to race" level, on the simulator in a short course of about five 90-minute sessions.

'If this proves true, school sailing could be changed into an activity in which *all* students could quickly learn on the simulator to sail well enough to start racing in light winds. In this way all would be able to enjoy the fun of sailing in company and racing with purpose. As competent racing sailors, they would be easier to manage, motivated, more enthusiastic, more satisfied, fewer would drop out.'

It is hardly surprising that it was Tony Sear who consulted his school, St Ignatius' College at Riverview (one of Sydney's great schools), and his students' parents, and they were the ones who said 'Let's try it'.

I rewrote my Training Notes and divided it into an initial very comprehensive 'Handling with Competence' level, and then a following 'Handling with Speed' level.

In the following (autumn) term two groups, each of four beginners, came for simulator lessons each Saturday morning for five weeks. As soon as they could sail around a short course we made it fun by using the 'save the last sail' and 'add a competitor' functions.

The first four minutes of any sail with a start and a finish can be saved to the computer memory as a file that starts from the beginning of the pre-start countdown (we usually use one minute), and so includes the first three minutes of the race. We save as initials/month/date/sail number (first, second, third, etc sail that session), so any sail can be recalled when wanted. Any saved sail can be repeated on screen as an individual sail for study or discussion, or added as a competitor, or printed out for permanent record as in Chapter 25. What happens when the sail is added as a competitor is that it repeats its sail synchronised with the start time of the present race, so the sailor and the added competitor(s) start together. The image of the present sail is always red. The colour of the added images is green on the overhead view.

The effect of saving the last sail then adding that sail as a competitor is that a 'ghost' fleet grows as the exercise progresses. Let us say we start with a Laser Radial in 8 knots of wind, with gusts but no shifts at this stage. The first student sails, notes his time (usually about three and a half minutes), saves the sail, and then adds this saved sail as a competitor. The next student sails, but in addition to his own red image on the screen there is the green image of the previous boat which repeats its sail. On the horizontal view the screen shows any added boat within the forward field of vision. In these short-course races with typically 40 seconds between start and first mark, the course becomes too crowded to apply 'keep clear' rules, and in any case the 'ghosts', which are blindly repeating, nonchalantly sail through each other and through you. By the time each of four students has completed two sails the last race is sailed as one of a fleet of eight, one of which is your own last sail. Fig 24.1 shows the screen with such a fleet.

These ghosts are motivating in the extreme, as a blunder sees the whole fleet move ahead of you. A moment of poor technique sees the nearest boat glide half a length

Fig 24.1 Simulator screen

The horizontal view shows:
Starboard end start mark. Port end mark under boom of third boat.
Wind arrows on water show wind direction.
Tuft streaming upwards shows sails undertrimmed.
Overhead view shows:
Start line, and windward gybe and leeward marks.
Fleet of four at start.
Speed dial (lower right) shows boat speed at 4.8 knots.
Direction gauge (top right) shows boat pointing a little low. (Wind direction is down screen.)
Countdown and elapsed time dial (top left) shows fleet 1.9 seconds into race and the "NOT STARTED" shows that the sailor was OCS on this start.

ahead, but a good mark rounding moves you a length ahead of the three boats that were previously about level. Fast acceleration to target speed moves you ahead of an adjacent rival, and benchmark (champions' time) in 8 knots is about two seconds less than three minutes. Each race takes students at this level between about 3½ to 4 minutes, plus the saving and adding, the change-over and a 1-minute countdown to the start, so eight races take about 45 minutes. We take a break, clear all competitors from the screen, and do it all again, but at 12 knots.

Towards the end of the course the beginners were handling slow sailing and time and distance control well on their approach to the start line, starting accurately, were thinking ahead and planning and executing their tacks and gybes and mark roundings well, and were repeating the short course exercises consistently at about 85–90% of a champion's speed.

At this point, another of the simulator's unique advantages showed through. On the water, beginner-level students never learn stronger-wind sailing, and steering for balance and apparent wind sailing remain mysteries to them, because they are simply not expected, nor allowed, to be on the water when the wind is strong.

On the simulator, as soon as these students became consistent with their boat handling and racing in light and moderate winds, I was able to expose them to progressively stronger winds. We put them in boats that developed real speed downwind, explained steer for balance, demonstrated it, and showed them how it works – and then watched as they mastered it and used it to sail downwind with increasing confidence in even the strongest winds.

On the water their sailing became more confident; these students will never feel insecure in strong winds.

314

As a fitting end to this series of five sessions I had them select the 29er, and they had tremendous fun in racing windward–leeward courses, sailing it downwind under spinnaker, learning the feel of an apparent wind skiff in a breeze, using steer for balance to control it as they turned downwind for equilibrium, then searched for and found the fastest angle to steer, and learning the difference between a conventional gybe (apparent wind from behind) and an apparent wind gybe (apparent wind from ahead). They started in 8 knot winds, and I left it to each of them to increase the wind speed when he or she felt ready. Most found that about 12 knots of true wind plus gusts was as far as they cared to go at that stage.

These were beginners who had been sailing the simulator for just 90 minutes a week for five weeks!

Tony had also arranged simulator coaching for his more advanced school team, and was rewarded by his school winning the inter-schools championship that year, for the first time. It looked as if a quiet revolution had begun.

Winter and winter sports intervened, but we all looked forward to the next season. Our vision was to carry the established efficiency and quality of simulator training and coaching onto the water by blending the simulator and the on-the-water Training Notes, increasing the quality of the on-the-water coaching, and using the simulator for revision, check and back-up.

It was not to be. Tragically, Tony Sear suffered a fatal heart attack during that winter. Leaders with his vision are rare.

WORKING WITH ADULTS

24.9 ■ Development of the benchmark technique

The first few months of coaching experienced adult sailors on the simulator were turbulent months, because adults come with a belief system firmly in place. What has been accepted as wisdom for generations runs something like this:

- Wherever sailboats race, a few sailors lead and share all the wins.
- Most sailors follow, and never win.
- As they gain experience, all sailors sail more safely and faster.
- So all experienced sailors sail more or less equally fast and handle their boats similarly.
- So leaders lead because their boats are faster.
- And followers follow because their boats are slower.

As we gained experience with the simulator, a very different picture began to emerge. What we were looking at was the contradiction of the old way of thinking; the beginnings of a new way of thinking; and a glimpse at the reasons why. Our early work necessarily started from our experience with instructing on the water, where the coach says, 'This way works. Do it like this'. 'Like this' in sailing has always meant 'as close as you can to what I have shown you' because that was all a coach could say. No coach has ever had any basis for saying anything different.

Note the difference between sailing and other sports such as track and field, swimming or cycling. In these sports a coach will say, 'Do it like this, and expect to do it in xx seconds'. Why the difference? Because on the water both wind and water are naturally unsteady (Fig 26.10), and it is not possible, and never has been possible, to measure accurately in unsteady conditions. So no sailing coach, ever, has been able to measure accurately nor compare one sailor's performance with another's.

The simulator is different. It is a precision measuring device, and can repeat steady, standard conditions, and in these it can measure and record performance. So, on the simulator, two performances can be compared, and the differences revealed with certainty. This has led to one of the seminal differences between simulator coaching and on-the-water coaching, and progress has been swift.

At first we simply looked at the time the student took to complete one of the standard short-race exercises, and improving personal performance was reflected in shorter times. The student's question became, 'What is a reasonable time to aim for?' The answer to that one was, 'Faster than you sail now'. Soon came the second question – 'What is the best possible?'

At this point simulator training diverged for ever from on-the-water work. World champions and Olympic medallists have sailed the simulator to the best of their ability, and we observe that they all use the same handling technique, and they have recorded times within a second or two of each other in the same wind. These we accept as 'best possible' or 'benchmark'. Suddenly, a new picture emerged:

1 Every student knew what he could do now.
2 He knew that if he made no significant mistake he could repeat that performance on the simulator.
3 He knew that if he applied himself to mastering and using faster manoeuvring and straight-line handling technique, and reinforced this with practice, he could improve on what he could do now.
4 He also knew what the best sailors could do, and therefore knew exactly where his present performance stood with respect to the world's best.

It has never previously been possible to know even one of these four facts.

As students worked to improve their times, we necessarily focused on each manoeuvre. I developed a 'session pro forma' that enabled us to set standard times within which each routine of each manoeuvre should be completed.

Somewhere during this process, I recalled that the original laboratory simulator prototype had had a printout function, and asked the programmer if this could be adapted and added to the capability of the new machine. He responded, and printouts such as Figs 25.1 and 25.2 can now be printed after any sail with a start and a finish. Each printout shows, on a second-by-second basis for four minutes, eight critical traces:

1 The wind speed.
2 A snail trail of the boat's track around the course.
3 The sailor's steering input.
4 The sailor's sail trimming input.
5 The sailor's balance (hiking) input.
6 The boat's heading response.
7 The boat's speed response.
8 The boat's roll response.

The printout is discussed in detail in Chapter 25.

With these 'record, reveal and compare' developments in simulator coaching technology, sailing has ceased to be an uncertain 'touchy feely' exercise in which nothing can be measured, nor performance described accurately. Instead, it has become one more sport in which an athlete's performance can be measured, recorded, analysed and compared with his last week's performance or the world's best sailor's performance.

We call it 'the benchmark technique'.

24.10 ■ The benchmark technique at work

The following description of a session shows how this works. My students on this occasion were two highly motivated very senior engineers; both had been sailing at follower level for many years. We met 7pm to 10pm Friday evenings when all of us were in town. There had been a three-week gap since the second session, so we started with revision, in which the two students alternated to sail three races each in 8 knots of wind. At the finish of each race each student saved his sail to the computer memory, then added it as a 'ghost' competitor that repeats the sail on the screen as a green image which begins at the start signal. In this way, each student's sail became a race against both his own and his training partner's previous sails, so by the sixth sail there was the sailor's red image plus a realistic fleet of five green ghosts.

The effect as the ghost fleet grew was that each student ceased to sail at his previous level. Instead, he began to react to the fleet and lifted his level as he became determined not to be passed. Both of their times decreased by 2–3% each race, except when they made a blunder. When they made even a slight error, this was instantly penalised by an adjacent ghost which glided another length ahead.

We then cleared all the 8 knot ghosts and did it again with four races, each in 12 knots. The fleet of the sailor plus seven ghosts in the last race was impressive.

During this exercise lightning struck twice. Each student, at a different time, sailed his first race ever with fast technique and with no significant error, and in this way each achieved benchmark speed. For both of them, their delight knew no bounds; they had proved they could break their previous mould.

We then repeated the routine with six races in 16 knots. Both started with blistering races, then began to fade. By this time, nearly two hours had passed and they were approaching overload.

So we took a break. I brewed strong coffee and we talked about real racing and the need both to sail fast and also to scan and look for options while you continue to sail fast. We decided to remove first the speed dial, and then both the speed dial and the wind direction gauge. The object was to encourage 'sailing by feel' with eyes 'out of the boat'.

My previous experience from single-session coaching suggested that the removal of these instruments would result in better 'feel' but at the expense of less accurate sailing and slower times. But these students were now much more experienced in the simulator than my previous single-session students, and better prepared to sail 'by feel'. These two finished their evening with each sailing three races without the aids. Each race was either at the same speed or slightly faster than the mean time they had achieved with them.

From this we learned that there is a progression – the beginner, when learning, both needs and consciously uses every aid. But later, when his reactions have become automatic and he is sailing more by feel, simplifying the screen can lead to faster sailing.

Note the training technique – the simulator 'short-course' exercises put a huge premium on both manoeuvring with minimum time loss, and also on accurate acceleration to regain and then hold target speed.

Note the personal improvement – these two, and others like them, had started their sessions with a handling technique that, once they had familiarised themselves with the simulator, gave at best race times about benchmark plus 30%. By the third session they had changed to efficient synchronised co-ordinated handling technique and were achieving mean times of about benchmark plus 2–3%.

Note the logistics – these two had kicked off their shoes that evening at 7pm. By 10pm, they had sailed 28 fiercely competitive races, had each proved to himself that he could indeed sail error-free and so achieve benchmark speed, and had further proved that he could now start to look out of his boat as he sailed without losing speed. It was a memorable evening.

These two sailors had for years been sailing in a fleet of 14 to 15 boats in a strong club and finishing about fifth and tenth. The following season, the faster one won the club championship, and the slower improved from tenth to third with an occasional win.

Over the first year, simulator training technology with adults had reached this level.

24.11 ■ Delegation and attempted integration

The following winter the training captain of Concord and Ryde Sailing Club (an innovative upriver club), who had been following my school sailing work, floated the idea of coaching for all of his club members who were interested. The idea grew, and he asked me to what extent I would like to become involved.

My response was that I thought that the time had come to delegate the simulator coaching, and also to initiate follow-up with integrated on-the-water coaching in the same way that airline and military simulator programmes are followed up with in-flight work:

- I offered to coach the training captain's coaches.
- I offered to make the simulator available at his club – with its membership centred 10 miles up the Parramatta river from our situation near the Heads – for the months needed.
- I suggested that, for best value for his students, simulator training should be alternated and integrated with on-the-water training.

We set up a programme with three stages:
1 The first was three three-hour winter evening coaching sessions in which I coached the training captain's four senior coaches.
2 The second was 12 three-hour sessions that followed in which each of the senior coaches themselves coached assistant coaches. I sat in on these sessions, kept quiet and hands off except that I joined in the post-sail discussions, and occasionally suggested a different approach.
3 The third was with the simulator at their club, with their programme under the control of his coaches, who from then on would also control the integration of the on-the-water coaching with the simulator work.

His four senior coaches are superb, and two of them in particular have a common background. They sailed dinghies in youth, both then became active and very successful in major ocean racing events for 20 years, and both have returned to dinghy sailing to sail with their children and their children's friends. The approach of one of these coaches was revealing: 'I have sailed a great deal and have enjoyed a lot of wins. But have never really known how to tack well. Thank you for showing me how it should be done.'

The shore programme ran without a hitch, and I kept in touch by offering to stand in and substitute when needed. I was impressed with the enthusiasm of the coaches, and the attitude of the sailors: 'My husband and I find this wonderful. Can something similar be run for my son and his friends?'

But on this initial trial of simulator plus integrated-on-the water coaching, the planning for the on-water work did not achieve seamless continuity. A completely different approach and method was used on the water, the students became confused, and the exercise tapered off inconclusively.

Post-course analysis suggested that the most experienced (the coaches) and the very inexperienced (the near beginners) got a lot out of it, but for the mid-fleet sailors it proved ho-hum. Once more, I found myself asking 'Why?'

24.12 ■ A World Championship

At this time we enjoyed another huge win. Peter Heywood has been sailing Lasers and Tasars, and sailing them well at club and state championship level, for 20 years. In addition, for some years he had been finishing mid-fleet at the annual Laser Masters World Championships.

Prior to the 2005 Laser event in Fortalesa, Brazil, he asked if he could practise on the simulator. This became interesting. He is both experienced and good, and his manoeuvring was excellent, but initially he could not get close to benchmark times. From the printouts we analysed it as a straight-line sailing problem: insufficient attention to acceleration to target speed, insufficient attention to holding target speed. He thought about this, was somewhat surprised, but changed his approach and his technique, and soon was turning in consistent champions' times.

At Fortalesa he found himself again sailing mid-fleet, but this time with a difference:

The ocean waves were refracting around a headland so on one tack we were sailing more into the waves and on the other tack sailing more along them. On the along-wave tack we were sailing as any normal experienced sailor does; ie sailing as close to the wind as one can sail with advantage. Normal wave technique calls for bearing away a little in the troughs and luffing through the crests, but in the bigger ocean waves the crests were so big that the boat stopped if you luffed much. Sailing in this way the whole fleet was making dreadfully slow progress upwind.

As I sailed I developed a vivid mental picture of a simulator printout of the most unflattering kind. Anything would be better than this, so I began to experiment. I tried sailing wave by wave, bearing away in the troughs with technique so extreme that I thought it must fail. Instead it proved a little faster. So I kept experimenting to the point where I was pulling away to an outrageous degree in the troughs, almost reaching, almost planing, and using the speed to luff firmly and sail more quickly over the long crests.

I found that in those conditions the more outrageously I steered low along the troughs, the better the boat felt and the further I sailed ahead [HPS-1, Fig 22.21.3].

Peter won that World Laser Radial Grand Masters championship with a score-line like 4, 8, 1, 1, 1, 1, 1, 1, and the remark on return: 'Thanks. It was the simulator work that did it.'

My comment would be that the simulator simply revealed to him the fundamental importance of good straight-line technique and holding target speed, and that it was Peter's intelligence in adapting this principle in the unusual circumstances of the refracted waves at Fortalesa that did it.

24.13 ■ Pilot group 'simulator plus on-water trial'

By this time, the simulator score-line appeared as follows:

- With experienced sailors, high-level performance achieved on the simulator is followed by improved performance on the water without on-water coaching.

- With school sailing, integrated simulator coaching and on-water coaching leads to faster training to desired standard and higher overall group sailing-skill level.
- With mature sailors who sail at follower level, high-level performance achieved on the simulator is not usually followed by similar improvement on the water when no effective on-water coaching follow-up is provided.

Why?

A few months later I was approached by another club who were aware of the Concord and Ryde Sailing Club work the previous season. We discussed what could best be done to coach the club's follower-level sailors in view of the strengths, weaknesses and conclusions from previous work, and particularly the Concord exercise.

My concern was that while all students made big gains in handling performance on the simulator and some went on to sail much faster on the water, there were other students who did not. My view was that something important was happening that inhibited the transfer of skill to the water, something which we did not yet understand, and that it was this that had led to the ineffectiveness of the Concord exercise. I felt that the most important next step was to find out what this was.

We agreed that on this occasion the quickest way forward would be to conduct not a whole-of-club programme, but a small pilot group experiment to identify what were the problems encountered by simulator students when they 'went to water', what was causing these problems, and how best to coach to solve them. I offered to coach such a group with the proviso that on this occasion I would move to the water with them.

We invited interested sailors to meet and discuss. Eight generally very inexpert adult sailors accepted, and others joined later. Most had been crewing yachts, and in one case helming yachts. All aspired to the livelier, more participatory and more rewarding fun of sailing fast dinghies. All owned, or part-owned, Tasars. All were sailing at tail-end-of-fleet performance level. All aspired to sail at lead-group level. All were highly educated, highly intelligent and highly motivated professionals.

Two had made serious efforts to become proficient, and one had paid to learn to sail with the sailing school at the other end of the club. She had enjoyed one session about theory, and for four sessions she had floated around four-in-a-boat in light wind being shouted at. At the end of the course she was presented with an impressive peak-body-approved glossy certificate that stated that she had completed the course and had learned to sail. Her opinion was different. As far as she was concerned, she had learned little of value. Whenever the wind exceeded 11 knots, she and her husband found themselves upside down and discouraged.

The other had learned from committed voluntary instructors at a highly organised club in Perth, nearly 3000 miles away at the other end of Australia. He had experienced much the same fare, but this time dispensed by earnest club elders who assured him: 'Everybody learns to sail this way. As you gain experience, you will sail faster.' He too was critical of what he had been taught, because whenever the wind became fresh he found himself woefully slow and near helpless.

The objective of these participants was to learn to sail at lead-group level, and my object was to find out what had blocked previous sailors in this category from improving their on-water performance following simulator training.

Simulator work

They set about learning to sail the simulator with enthusiasm, and this proceeded well. Within a few weeks, all were sailing within 10% of benchmark performance, with one or two even better.

At that point we went to the water in the strong unsteady 12 to 15 knots (with gusts to 20 knots) winds typical of Sydney in spring – that is, like Fig 21.4C and D. I sailed in the boats with each pair.

On-the-water work

Within a few minutes of beginning to sail in a breeze with the first crew, I realised that we had found what had inhibited previous simulator students from sailing fast when they had moved to the water.

For them, it was an error in assumption.

- They had assumed
  - That they could sail.

  – That their problem was that they could not sail fast.

As a result, we had focused on the detail of faster manoeuvring technique.

- What I observed was
  – They could sail with control in the lighter winds, but could *not* yet sail with control in stronger winds.
  – Their problem was not that they could not sail fast.
  – Their problem was that they could not yet sail with confident control of their boats in any winds much stronger than the design wind. This was surprising because many of them had had years of experience in sailboats, but not as helmsmen or helmswomen.

All of them were completely unprepared for the fresh unsteady winds, and unable to control their boats well in such winds even in straight-line sailing. In addition, all of them were overwhelmed by the quickly repeating unsteadiness. The fact that they continued to execute their tacks and gybes well was irrelevant in the stress of trying to sail with control in very ordinary conditions that were beyond their capability.

From my point of view, the next few weekends were both a steep learning curve and one of the more rewarding experiences of my life, because by sailing in their boats with them I was able to look at the situation through their eyes and their experience.

I asked them to sail me upwind and crosswind and downwind, so that I could see exactly what they were doing with their hands, bodies and eyes (and therefore their brains). It was from this observation that I was able to identify what I now call '*natural* handling technique' (see page 323), and to see where this comes from, and what its strengths and weaknesses are.

As soon as they had sailed sufficiently for me to see and analyse their technique, I had them heave-to; we then discussed what they were doing and why they were having trouble, and I suggested a better way of doing it. We changed places.

Upwind, I repeated what they had been doing:

- They had all been using the tiller, and only the tiller, for everything. As they became more stressed, they clutched the sheet immobile and luffed for equilibrium. In the gusts they luffed higher. None had been encouraged to think of co-ordinating two controls.
- In prolonged gusts they luffed very high, and the boat nearly stopped, so losing effective steerage way. Because they no longer had steerage way, the 'use the rudder for everything' technique ceased to work. At that point they lost effective control, their anxiety levels became extreme, and sailing ceased to be fun.

I then demonstrated 'fast handling technique' (see Chapter 26):

- In every gust I continued to hike as hard as possible, *did not luff* (other than to follow the wind's normal direction changes), but held heading with tiny movements of the tiller, and eased the sheet independently as much as was appropriate in each gust, and recovered it as the gust eased.
- The result was the boat sailed upright, under control, and it flew.

We could all see exactly what were the differences in technique, and the differences in control, and the differences in performance.

When reaching and broad reaching, I again repeated what they had been doing:

- They had been luffing for equilibrium in the gusts, clutching the sheet, and then using extreme body movement both ways to retain balance of the crosswind boat as the quick gust peaks and quick lulls washed over it.

Again, I demonstrated fast technique:

- As the gusts hit, I did *not* luff. At each gust onslaught I *turned smoothly downwind and eased sheet* until the boat was in equilibrium.

- I then steered for balance to keep the boat upright.
- In the quick lulls between the gust peaks I *did not move my body*. When the wind lulled and the boat started to roll to windward I luffed (still steering for balance) to increase the apparent wind, which both increased the heeling force to restore equilibrium and also maintained speed.
- In the quick gust peaks I turned downwind again for equilibrium.
- This way, the boat followed a 'snaking' course, up a little in the quick lulls and down in the quick gusts, at full 'power' and at high speed for all of the time. Throughout, we all kept our bodies still. The boat sailed upright, under control, and it flew.

Again, we could all see exactly what were the differences in technique, the differences in control and the difference in performance. Over the next few weekends, these sailors' lives changed for ever:

'The time I spent with you in the boat in fresh wind was probably the most challenging and rewarding of my sailing life. On the following weekend, in strong wind (at another club), my sailing was unlike any earlier sailing. We found ourselves in complete control, competitive upwind and now able to pass boats as we snaked downwind.'

'Prior to the group coaching, my outlook on sailing was not ambitious nor exciting. I expected to "muck around" with only limited expectations of improvement due to what I knew was poor technique. The impact on me of the recent simulator plus on-the-water coaching has been profound. I feel that I now have a platform from which to really practise, and drastically improve and enjoy my sailing for the rest of my life.'

'In yesterday's very strong and difficult conditions, I mastered steer for balance downwind and simultaneous independent co-ordination upwind. It was a coaching session of absolute enjoyment and fun in which, for the first time, I enjoyed complete control of the boat.

'There's a long way to go but I feel like we've broken the back of the journey. Prior to the group coaching, sailing was pleasurable but it was frustrating due to not knowing what I didn't know, – eg why the leaders sailed faster.

'I feel we now know why and how the fast sailors sail fast, and more importantly we now know the techniques they use which we can now use to make us sail fast too.

'I now also realise that it really is easier to sail using co-ordinated fast technique than uncoordinated natural technique.'

My response

I added appropriate straight-line exercises in upwind and downwind strong-wind control to the simulator part of the work, and now make a practice of sailing with my students for their first hour or so when they return to the water in stronger winds. The result is that when they go to the water now, mature students welcome the opportunity to play in the stronger winds, and delight in their new ability to control their boat and sail it fast.

With this addition of strong-wind, straight-line fast handling technique, both upwind and downwind to the simulator program, and the realisation that it is either helpful or essential to accompany students and sail with them in their boat for their first hour on the water in stronger winds, we seem at last to have arrived at a reliable, efficient and effective sail training method.

A recent visit by a senior (retired, voluntary) club training officer from the Wanganui Sailing Club in New Zealand is a copy-book case. A current Yachting New Zealand plus Sailing Clubs sail training initiative had reached the point where an improved youth training approach was being considered, and the use of a simulator had been floated. His club has a highly developed sail training facility based on a nearby lake, and it provides a sail training service for both its own members and for a number of schools from both the city and from outlying districts. He was aware of my simulator work, and enquired, and then we corresponded. I invited him to visit Sydney and see for himself what was going on.

He and I spent Tuesday morning introducing him to the simulator. He had never played computer games, so needed a while to accommodate to the simultaneous horizontal and overhead graphics presentation on the screen and to become fluent in orienting himself in virtual space. On Wednesday, we changed his manoeuvre technique from sequential execution to synchronous co-ordination, and he began to shorten his exercise times. On Thursday, we altered his straight-line technique from luff-for-everything to simultaneous independent co-ordination of tiller and sheet upwind, and from luff-for-everything to steer for balance downwind. This was a huge day for him.

By Friday, I introduced him to our training boat, a Tasar. By good fortune the wind was fresh and gusty so this sail quickly became a practical demonstration of how effective the fast techniques are in controlling the boat. On Saturday, the wind was still fresh and gusty. We clipped a GPS that displays speed in large easy-to-read numbers to the forward coaming, and he refined his use of the new techniques by making the sail a continuing and increasingly successful practice at rapid acquisition and consistent holding of target speed. On Sunday our luck ran out when the wind became light and variable.

Back home, he had been accustomed to finishing second or third in his fleet, but since returning from his visit he has won his races by substantial margins: 'We are not sailing any faster. We are just keeping the boat moving fast for all of the time.'

From my point of view, the end result is that we have at last developed a practical, efficient and effective coaching technique that can lift the performance level of the natural handling technique sailor to that of the fast handling technique sailor.

His club, and his National YA, are rethinking youth training.

24.14 ■ Objective achieved

In 2003 I set out to find what the simulator could teach, and how best to teach it. It has been a longer journey than I expected because it has covered so much new territory.

The present well-established flight simulator activity had its origins as an industry when the primitive Link trainer proved that it could train pilots in instrument flying approach technique when using the then-new radio aids, better and more economically than was possible in flight.

I think that the situation we have now reached with the sailing simulator is comparable. Like the Link, a simulator is not essential, but the simulator has now proved that it can deliver practical effective sail training at a much higher level of quality and in a tiny fraction of the time that is needed by on-the-water training. For this reason, its use will grow.

In years to come, the present simulator will be regarded as primitive. It will be further developed in the same way as the flight simulator has been developed over the years.

24.15 ■ A new way of thinking

At about this stage I sensed that I was looking at a consistent pattern. Three separate groups had all experienced broadly similar difficulty in either controlling their boats or in sailing their boats at respectable speed:

- Motivated, mature, experienced sailors in both the UK and Australia had found themselves unable to control the 59er at speed.
- In the evolving simulator work, a few champion sailors proved able to sail the simulator fast from the outset, but most experienced sailors needed half as long again to sail a very short race which is all tacks and gybes and mark roundings and acceleration, and with not much straight-line sailing between the manoeuvres.
- In the more recent simulator-then-on-the-water work, highly intelligent and motivated (but generally less experienced) sailors were unable to control their boats on the water in unsteady conditions in stronger winds.

These three groups, by definition, were among the most motivated of sailors – they were the ones who dreamed either of sailing a faster boat, or of sailing their present boats faster, and were prepared to do something about it. The four common threads were:

- They all used a common, simplest possible, 'use the tiller for everything, and co-ordinate nothing' handling technique.

- They all believed that the handling technique they had been taught was the best there is.
- They were completely unaware that any other handling technique existed. They had never considered, nor had it ever been explained to them, that the sailors who lead, and sometimes win, use a handling technique that superficially looks identical, but that on closer examination has critical points of difference, all of which involve co-ordination.
- Their common simple technique was intrinsically slower than the fast technique used by the sailors who lead and sometimes win.

In thinking about this pattern, it occurred to me that if I looked at 'sailing' from a new starting point – that is, that sailing is a complex sport in which two well-established and broadly similar handling techniques coexist below the conscious level – the whole previously inadequately explained picture became logical and explainable.

As explained earlier, one technique I call 'natural', and the other I term 'fast'. This thinking, when developed, leads to the analogy of the two coexistent continuums mentioned in Sections 24.1 and 24.2. One of these does not – and *cannot* – reach right to the top, and it is this new realisation that explains the whole complex picture.

24.16 ■ Natural handling technique

Let us once more be specific. The great majority of sailors learn to sail either by imitation (crewing), and/or from books, or from club training schemes, or from commercial sailing schools:

1 Whichever approach is used, it is logical and natural to adopt the simplest, most consistent technique to do the job.
2 There is a natural desire, while learning, to execute the different steering, sail trimming and balance movement routines one after the other. This 'one after the other' sequential execution enables each routine to be learned and mastered by itself.

Natural handling technique satisfies both 1 and 2 above, so it is near-universally adopted because it is easiest to learn and fastest to teach. The end result of this process is a handling technique that looks like this:

A Natural tack, gybe and mark rounding technique

These all involve manipulating three separate controls in a precise way. The tiller is moved to turn the boat and arrest the turn on a new aiming point. The sheet is moved to trim the sail to the new apparent wind, and the body is moved to balance the boat.

If you learn to tack and gybe and round marks by first turning the boat onto its new heading, trimming the sail just right as in all the best books (ie as Fig 21.1), then moving the body into a hiking position to keep the boat upright, and you change hands on sheet and tiller somewhere in the middle of the manoeuvre, this will work safely every time – until the wind gets stronger. This is *sequential execution* – the simplest way to accomplish a series of tasks, so it is the quickest and easiest way to learn and to teach.

B Natural straight-line sailing technique

In light and moderate winds – that is, up to design wind strength (usually about 11 knots when sailing to windward) – a boat can always be kept upright by hiking, so roll control is never an issue. In all stronger winds, the heeling force from the sails can always be reduced by luffing (turning into wind). So the simplest way to sail straight lines is:

In lighter winds:
Upwind   Steer to the wind, trim sail and hike as necessary.
Downwind   Steer to the mark, trim sail and hike as necessary.

In stronger winds:
As above, plus luff as necessary. In stronger gusts, luff higher.

This is the 'use the tiller for everything and luff for everything' approach – what I call the 'natural' handling technique.

Once these simple and consistent techniques are mastered, they enable a sailor to launch, sail up and down the harbour with confidence on a good afternoon, race in company, and return to the jetty or launching ramp in safety. People who can do this can call themselves 'sailors', and this is how the great majority of sailors sail for life. With experience, they learn to judge the weather better and so sail more safely.

But with this technique, these sailors can never match the sailors in the lead group for overall speed. In lighter winds they sail no faster in straight lines and they lose a few seconds every tack, gybe or mark rounding, so at the end of the race they are never in the lead. In all stronger winds, they are slow for the reasons described above.

They do not sail faster with experience because of a subtle near-universal weakness that, until now, has remained unidentified. It is this – with accumulating experience, the initial 'simplest to learn' technique becomes automatic, slips below the conscious level and becomes embedded in the subconscious, so these sailors continue to sail in exactly the same way. This is the reason why they do *not* sail faster as they accumulate experience. (This is why handicap systems work so well.) A practical point is that in lighter winds they can sail just as fast as the leaders (except when accelerating and turning) so they think they are sailing with the best and fastest technique.

Because of these intrinsic disadvantages, natural handling technique sailors cannot match the race speed of fast technique sailors, so they follow for all of their sailing lives. The four points of difference between natural and fast handling technique are covered in Section 24.17.

24.17 ■ Fast handling technique

A Fast manoeuvring – tack, gybe, and mark rounding

The object of the fast sailor, when manoeuvring, is to lose least time with respect to a rival who continues in a straight line – that is, a rival who executes no manoeuvre. The fast sailor does exactly the same things that the natural sailor does, but he/she does them at different times.

The natural sailor performs each of the three routines, plus changing hands, in sequence (sequential execution). In contrast, the fast sailor completes the three essential routines together *within the time it takes the boat to turn*. The change-hands routine is delayed until the boat has completed the manoeuvre and is accelerating strongly on its new heading. This is *synchronised co-ordination*. The details of this technique are given in Chapters 25 to 29.

The advantage can be seen in the difference in time to regain target speed and time to the first mark between Figs 25.1 and 25.2.

In Fig 25.1 the leader regains target speed in 9–10 seconds, so loses about 5m or 2 seconds, or one length per tack, as compared with a competitor who does not tack. In Fig 25.2, all four of the followers' tacks show the follower regaining target speed about 20–30 seconds after the start of the tack, so each of these tacks loses about 15m or 6 seconds, or three lengths, as compared with a competitor who does not tack.

The difference between the leader's synchronised co-ordination technique and the follower's sequential execution technique is a loss of about 4 added seconds per manoeuvre, so in a 50-tack-plus-gybe-plus mark rounding, race the natural sailor will finish about 200 seconds, or 3½ minutes, behind the leader just by using the slower natural handling technique to turn his boat. Yet again, this is one of the reasons why followers follow.

B Fast straight-line sailing

A key difference between the natural and the fast sailor when sailing straight lines is that the natural sailor uses a simple single-mode technique, whereas the fast sailor uses a two-mode technique.

Single-mode technique

When sailing to windward, the natural sailor tends to apply maximum VMG sail trim and boat set-up (ie 'by the book') at all times, regardless of whether he is sailing fast or not.

After every manoeuvre he will necessarily be sailing slowly. Maximum VMG set-up will get him to target speed eventually, but at the cost of slow acceleration.

Two-mode technique

The fast sailor uses a two-mode approach for all straight-line sailing. When not at target speed, for whatever reason:

- He will point a shade lower (say, 5° or 10° in light air) and free sheet a little, and so sail in acceleration mode for fast acceleration to acquire or regain target speed quickly.
- When, and only when, he is at target speed, will he point higher with tighter sheet and sail in maximum VMG mode.

A good analogy is freeway driving at the foot of a long hill. If two cars are baulked to low speed by a truck ahead, and when free to pass and accelerate, one changes to a lower gear and the other does not, the car that does not change gear will accelerate uphill but slowly. It will regain freeway speed eventually, but by that time the car that changed to a lower gear, and accelerated fast uphill to regain speed, will be out of sight.

The practical consequence of being acutely conscious of target speed, and of using two-mode straight-line handling technique, is that the fast sailor sails at target speed for more of the time than the natural sailor. Peter Heywood's 'World Championship' note above is a good, if extreme, example. (Peter won the Laser Radial Grand Masters division World Championship for a second time in 2007.)

C Fast straight-line handling technique – to windward (see Chapters 25 to 29)

The object of the fast sailor when sailing straight lines is first to acquire target speed and then to maintain it. From calm up to the design wind, both the natural and the fast sailor will steer to the wind, trim sail and control roll by body movement (hiking). Up to the design wind, there will be no significant difference in straight-line speed.

When sailing to windward, a discontinuity appears in control of roll at the design wind:

- In stronger winds, the natural sailor avoids co-ordination so he grasps the sheet immobile and uses his tiller for everything. This is the 'luff for everything' technique.
  - As the wind speed increases, he luffs for equilibrium. In the gusts he luffs higher.
  - In the stronger wind of the gust, the aerodynamic drag increases. Because he does not ease his sheet, the drive force does not increase. As a result, the boat sails more slowly.
- In stronger winds, the fast sailor continues to steer to the wind, hikes to extreme, and controls roll by *simultaneous independent co-ordination* of sail trim (sheet) with tiny co-ordinated movements of the rudder.
  - Because he eases his sheet and twists the sail, the boat sails faster.

The practical advantages of the fast sailor's technique when sailing to windward are given in Fig 21.3. The starting point in this diagram is that in the 11 knot lull wind, both the natural and the fast sailor sail equally fast with a VMG of 5.1 knots, as in Fig 21.3A.

In the 15.4 knot gusts, if the sheet is held and the boat is luffed (as in Fig 21.3B), the boat will sail at a VMG of 4.4 knots. This is the 'co-ordinate nothing, and use the rudder for everything' natural handling technique in action. But if the optimum heading is held and the sheet is eased to control roll, as in Fig 21.3C, the boat will sail at a VMG of 5.8 knots. And if the heading is held and the sheet is eased to control roll and the sails twist and flatten by good automatic rig design (as in Fig 21.3D), the boat will sail at a VMG of 6.5 knots, or about 50% faster than the 'luff and luff higher' natural handling technique. This is fast handling technique, plus the automatic rig in action.

The advantages of fast technique are that the boat stays under control, and sails very much faster, as demonstrated in Fig 21.3. This is the fast simultaneous independent co-ordination handling technique in action.

Therefore Fig 21.3 shows why it is that the natural sailor can stay with the fast sailor in the lighter winds, but suddenly becomes uncompetitive when the wind becomes stronger.

The frontispiece shows fast technique in action. The 29erXX, crewed by the 1996 29er World Champions Silja Lehtinen and Scott Babbage, is sailing to windward at a boat speed of 10–11 knots, VMG about 7.5 knots, in a true wind of about 18 knots.

D Fast straight-line handling technique – offwind (see Chapters 25 to 29)

Because the apparent wind becomes less when sailing straight downwind, the design wind when sailing downwind for all boats without spinnakers will always be much stronger than when sailing upwind. But apparent wind skiffs broad reaching with big spinnakers at wind speed or faster create their own much stronger apparent winds, and this factor – coupled with the size of their spinnakers – often means that they can be fully powered downwind (ie sailing in their design apparent winds) in surprisingly light true winds. Fig 2.1 is the extreme example.

When reaching and broad reaching downwind in stronger winds, a second major discontinuity appears in the control of roll and speed of a fast light sailboat. From light air up to the design wind, both the natural and the fast sailor will steer to the mark, optimise sail trim, and control roll by body movement (hiking). Both will sail at about the same speed. But in stronger winds when gusts heel the boat, the natural sailor will control roll by luffing (turning upwind) for equilibrium. This again is the 'luff for everything' natural handling technique in action. Its simple appeal is that the same technique (luff for everything) always works (up to a point) regardless of whether the boat is sailing upwind or downwind. What happens next is that the crew find themselves leaping in and out to maintain balance as the quick gust peaks and lulls wash over the crosswind boat. While this is going on, their boat is both heading in the wrong direction (away from the mark), and not sailing fast at steady speed, so this technique wins no races at all.

In these stronger winds, the fast sailor controls roll by *turning the other way*. This is the discontinuity. The fast sailor uses the *steer for balance* technique at all times when he is sailing, other than when sailing to windward. Particularly in the stronger winds, this technique is not only efficient – in very strong winds it is the *only* technique that continues to work.

When the boat is heeled by a gust, the fast sailor turns downwind, not upwind. This is simply the technique of steering the hull under the rig. Whenever the boat rolls to the right– that is, the mast and sails start to move to the right – he steers to the right, and vice versa. The dynamics are identical with riding a bicycle, and again – like the bicycle – once the technique is mastered it is executed with small, almost imperceptible movements of the tiller exactly as, when riding a bicycle, the beginner uses gross movements, but with practice they become tiny.

When hit by a normal strong sustained gust with several short gust peaks, the fast sailor uses three variations of steer for balance – first to establish equilibrium at gust onslaught, next to maintain balance in the stronger wind, then to maintain full 'power' for steady maximum boat speed through the unsteady, quick gust peaks and intervening quick lulls:

- At each gust onslaught he establishes longer-term equilibrium in roll in the stronger wind by turning downwind as far as is necessary and easing sail. Turning downwind reduces the apparent wind. Also, when running square there is no heeling moment, so at some heading the reducing heeling moment of the wind must equal the fixed righting moment of the boat, and the boat will then be in equilibrium. This is normal steer for balance, but with the variation of a longer turn downwind due to the gust onslaught. Fig 22.4 is an extreme example.
- Once equilibrium is established, he uses normal steer-for-balance for short-term control of roll.
- As each lull between the quick gust peaks occurs, the boat will necessarily start to roll to windward and slow a little. In these quick lulls, instead of sitting up, he and his crew continue to hike to extreme. He controls the roll by turning upwind (luffing) as far as is necessary to re-establish equilibrium. The luff – the turn towards the wind – both steers the hull under the rig, and it also increases the apparent wind which increases the wind's heeling moment, so at some heading the increasing heeling moment must equal the boat's fixed righting moment and the boat will again be in equilibrium. This is normal steer for balance, but with the variation of a longer turn upwind due to the lull.

This technique of 'snaking', of controlling the heeling force by sailing as high as he can without heeling, always lower in the gusts and higher in the lulls, enables the fast sailor to sail steadily at full 'power' and at maximum speed through the unsteady gusts, lulls and quick gust peaks of even the strongest winds.

His reward is to sail steadily at maximum speed a little more downwind than the rhumb line. This keeps him in the gust for longer (he does not sail out of the side of the gust). When the gust dies, he then needs to sail a little higher to regain the rhumb line – and so again enjoys a faster point of sailing than his natural technique rival.

The advantages of this are twofold:

1   The first is that the fast sailor keeps sailing at maximum speed and under secure roll control on a heading towards, or a little below, his mark (Figs 15.3 and 22.1 and 22.4).
   –   The 'luff and luff higher' natural sailor can control roll only by luffing progressively higher and sailing away from his mark. Sailing in the wrong direction wins no races. It also means that the natural sailor will usually sail out of the side of the gust, and will then have to sail more downwind on a slower point of sailing for a longer time in the adjacent lull to regain the rhumb line.
   –   The fast sailor tends to remain within the gust and so sails faster and more directly downwind and for a longer time in the stronger wind of the gust. To regain the rhumb line as the gust dies, he will then sail a higher heading on a faster point of sailing as he regains the rhumb line.
   –   The practical speed difference in favour of fast technique is huge.
2   The second advantage is the practical point that the righting moment provided by steer for balance increases as the square of the boat speed. So to control the boat in really strong winds and at really high speeds, steer for balance works brilliantly and nothing else works at all. At the speeds of Fig 15.3 and 22.1 and 22.4, the boat speeds are far beyond the point where moving a body will make any significant difference. If a sailor wishes to sail at these speeds, he/she has no option but to stop luffing and learn to turn downwind for equilibrium and to steer for balance.

24.18 ■ The four key differences

The simplified scenarios above indicate that there are only four significant differences between the fast handling technique of the champion and the natural handling technique that traps the follower. They are:
1   Use of *synchronised co-ordination*, in place of *sequential execution*, for the tack, gybe and mark rounding manoeuvres.
2   Use of *acceleration mode* then *maximum VMG mode*, in place of *maximum VMG mode* only, in all straight-line sailing.
3   Use of *simultaneous independent co-ordination*, in place of *luff for everything*, when sailing upwind in straight lines in stronger winds.
4   Use of *steer for balance*, in place of *luff for everything*, when sailing downwind in straight lines in stronger winds.

The detail of these fast handling techniques is given in the chapters ahead.

24.19 ■ Summary

The object of the 2006 and 2007 Pilot Group exercises was to find out why earlier simulator-trained groups had not sailed with superior performance when they moved back to the water. But the end result has been to go much further than this.

We have discovered that the overarching sailboat handling environment is not, as is generally believed, a single homogeneous system. Instead, it is a more complex environment in which two parallel and broadly similar handling systems coexist at the subconscious level. The simpler 'natural' system used by the great majority of sailors is intrinsically slower than the 'fast' system used by the few. This discovery accurately describes the real sailing environment we observe and live in.

The origin of the many natural sailors lies in the attractive simplicity of natural handling technique, together with a general unawareness that it is intrinsically slow, and a similar unawareness that any other handling technique exists (eg no significant media discussion of handling as a subject, and no sailing coaches listed in the *Yellow Pages* – true in Auckland as well as in Sydney).

The origin of the few fast sailors appears to be that either:

• They learned or were taught fast technique in the first place. This would explain why sailing fast and well runs in small clusters and families.
• They shifted from natural to fast handling technique by some process not yet generally understood.
   –   An interesting observation is that in medical schools it is noted that a small number of students excel at the 'fuzzy logic' of diagnosis, and one theory is that this may be an expression of unusually

> fluent intuition. A process such as this may be equally relevant in sailing. Whatever it is, it exists. Fast sailors have always been with us, but they have always been thin on the ground.

In general, fast sailors are not consciously aware of why they sail fast. This is because handling, once learned, all happens at the subconscious level. We do not think about, therefore we do not talk about nor discuss, how we move our legs when we walk, or how we move our hands when we eat or write. So club champions give countless talks, and sailing instructors and coaches exhort, but few touch on what matters. As a result, even the most highly intelligent and motivated followers continue to follow, and they become increasingly frustrated. This is 'sailing' as we see it.

In years past the existence of and the differences between natural and fast handling technique have not generally been identified and therefore not understood. My object with this book is to describe what we have discovered and to make a difference.

The primary benefit that will flow from this discovery will be in youth training. No enlightened parent will in future want their child to be trained to follow for life, and never to lead. It is just as easy to teach fast handling technique as it is to teach natural handling technique.

For present sailors who want to lift their game, the key to moving from the slower natural handling technique of the follower to the fast handling technique of the leader is understanding – understanding that the two systems coexist. Comprehending that both systems are subconscious, so can never be changed until we lift discussion into the conscious, talk consciously about the different techniques and the differences between them among ourselves, and deliberately decide to adopt, practise and perfect the fast techniques. Nothing will change unless and until we decide that we want to change and are prepared to do something about it.

It has been my privilege to spend half my life in flying, starting with in-depth experience in flying instruction and the beginnings of the flight simulator. The other half has been spent in learning more about how small, fast sailboats work and how best to sail them, and more recently in working to find how best to blend the unusual properties of the new sailing simulator with established sail training and flying instruction practices to help those who want to sail faster to lift their game.

This background has given me a much clearer appreciation of what matters – of what is important to mature motivated sailors who now follow, but who want to lead, and to parents who want their children to be taught to lead rather than always to follow.

Thanks to the precision of the sailing simulator, in Chapters 25, 26 and 27 I am able to describe and demonstrate the detail of fast handling technique much more exactly than has ever previously been possible. I have included all relevant detail presently available to me so that alert and motivated sailors, either individually or in co-operative groups, will be able to read, understand and work on each of the four critical areas of difference.

In this way, motivated sailors will at last be able to lift themselves out of the slow trap of natural handling technique and lift their game to the performance level of the lead-group sailor who uses fast handling technique, as have the students above.

The week-by-week reward to the present natural sailor who changes to fast handling technique will be the fierce personal challenge of knowing that he can now contest the lead, and of sailing to this new level. It will be the sheer fun of actually contesting the lead, and the deep satisfaction of the occasional win. The longer-term reward will be the increased self-esteem that flows from walking tall in your chosen recreation.

In the remainder of this book I touch on what really matters to those who want to lift their game and sail well.

Chapter 25 • The Simulator Printout

25.1 ■ The critical difference

The critical difference between the simulator and a boat is the simulator's ability to repeat standard conditions, to measure accurately, to record, and to compare small differences with certainty.

It can save to memory everything about the first four minutes of any sail that includes a start and a finish (ie the printout includes the pre-start manoeuvring), and can record and display this as a printout. This printout shows the sailor's steering, sail trimming and balance (hiking) inputs, and the boat's heading, speed and roll responses on a second-by-second basis. This enables us to look at the detail of a champion's or a student's technique in a way never previously possible.

Fig 25.1 shows the printout of a short race sailed by Julian Bethwaite. The boat is a standard Laser in a wind of 12 knots, and the printout takes a standard form of eight separate displays, which I have labelled A to H from the bottom of the page upwards.

A is an overhead view of the course, in this case a triangle. The three round marks are the windward, gybe and leeward course marks. The two triangular marks are the start and finish line. The scale of this display is given in metres by the 25, 50, 75 markers along the extensions of the start line. The start marks are 30m apart. The true wind blows from the top of the page downwards. A snail trail which assumes no current shows the boat's track.

Time is given by the minute markers −1, 0, 1, 2, 3 just below the wind velocity plot (plot H). The heavy vertical line through 0 represents the start time in each plot. The light vertical solid or dashed lines below the minute markers, −1 to 3, show the flow of the time from 1 minute pre-start to 3 minutes into the race. In this case, the race was completed in about 2½ minutes.

Plots B, C and D record the sailor's steering, sail trimming and hiking inputs. Plots E, F and G show the boat's heading, speed and roll responses.

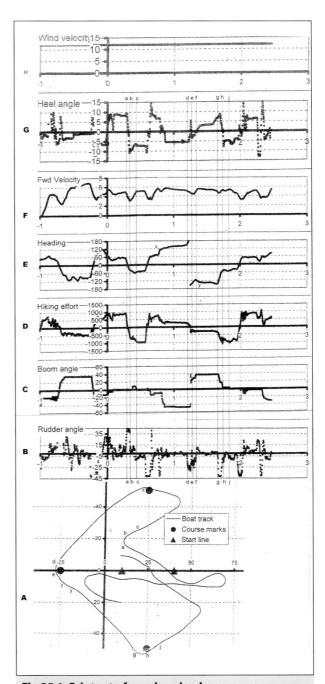

Fig 25.1 Printout of race by a leader

Each element is measured many times each second. The rudder angle and boom angle are in degrees relative to the boat's centreline. The hiking effort is in newton metres (1 newton metre is 0.74ft/lb). Heading is in degrees from the direction of the true wind. Speed is in knots, and heel angle is in degrees (the simulator is mechanically limited to +/– 15° of roll). H is the wind speed selected for this sail. Both gusts and shifts can be added; whether or not they have been added is not shown on this trace.

The plots show the sailor's control movements and the boat's response as it sails through the manoeuvres of the race.

25.2 ■ The leader's technique and the boat's response

A The tack

Let us look at the detail of this sailor's printout. The boat is a standard Laser and the wind is 12 knots. Target speed to windward in the Laser in this wind is about 4.8 knots, and a shade faster in the gusts. I have added the light vertical lines a–a, b–b, c–c etc as event markers in traces B to G, and as position markers in the over-head view A.

The sailor crosses the line at time 0 sailing at 5.5 knots (plot F) – a little fast. For the first 7 or 8 seconds, he points a little high to wash off speed (plot E, heading, and also the snail trail at s+5 in A, the overhead view). At about 8 seconds, he adjusts heading to maintain a speed close to 4.8 knots. The adjustment to heading shows on plots E and A, and the stabilised speed shows on plot F. Note that he pointed a shade too high at about 7 seconds and the boat rolled to windward (plot G) and he hiked slightly less forcefully for 2 or 3 seconds (plot D) to restore equilibrium.

At 16.1 seconds after the start (event marker a–a), he applies 45° of helm (plot B) to start his first tack. This is the moment of Figs 26.1A and 26.2A in Chapter 26. He pauses momentarily to roll the boat firmly to windward (plot G), then starts to move his body. At 20.6 seconds, 4.5 seconds later (b–b), he centres the helm on the new heading (plots B and E, b–b). During the turn the boat loses speed from 4.8 knots to about 2.9 knots (plot F, at b–b), and during the tack he moves his body quickly so he is already hiking strongly on the other tack as he centres the tiller (plot B, at b–b) to arrest the turn. At this point he starts to roll the boat more upright (plot G), eases the sail 5° (plot C), steers a little lower (plot E, also A), and as a result accelerates very quickly to regain target speed of 5 knots at c–c (plot F) and c (plot A) 26.4 seconds after the start, 10.3 seconds after starting the tack, and 5.8 seconds after centring his tiller.

At c–c he has regained target speed (plot F); at this point the boom comes in (plot C) and he points higher (plot E, also A) – as high as he can point and hold his target speed 4.8 knots (plot F).

Note that:

- He turned the boat through about 90° in 4.3 seconds.
- He was already almost at full hike as the sails filled – that is, he both synchronised his movements perfectly to match the boat's dynamics as it turned, and he then anticipated the roll to leeward as the sails filled by hiking earlier and in fact rolling the boat to windward as the sails filled. Both the moment of minimum speed and the moment of the start of the new acceleration – both of these occur at the instant the sails fill as the tiller is centred to arrest the turn.
- All subsequent tacks repeat this technique exactly.

This is the classic efficient tack and post-tack acceleration of the 'synchronised co-ordination fast handling technique' of the lead-group sailor.

In view of Section 25.3 below, note that he had rounded the windward mark and had steadied on course for the wing mark at 'x', in plot E, and also at x in plot A, at 47.7 seconds after the start.

B The conventional gybe

The sailor positioned his boat so that he would just skim past the mark at the mid point of his turn. (From here on, I will refer to this technique as *apexing* the mark.) Event markers d–d, e–e and f–f at 70.5 seconds, 74.4 seconds and 78.7 seconds respectively after the start refer. He moved the tiller about 25° (not to the normal 45° full excursion) to starboard (plot B) and, as the boat turned, he started to move his body towards the port side, plot D. At e–e the boat has turned beyond the straight downwind direction and is running about 25–30° by the lee. At this point, his body was mid-movement (Fig 26.3D). At this instant he gave the sheet a sharp tug to make the boat gybe when he wanted it to gybe, not when the *boat* wanted to gybe, and simultaneous with the tug he both moved his body quickly to the new side (Fig 26.3D) and he momentarily reversed his rudder (the spike at e–e in 25.1, plot B). It is this momentary rudder reversal that stops the boat from rolling further to starboard. The left-hand rising side of the roll trace spike between d–d and e–e (plot G) shows that the boat began to roll to starboard as the boom flicked to starboard (Fig 26.3C). But at this instant the sailor reversed helm and the boat immediately rolled the other way as shown by the right-hand side of the spike. With the boat upright and under smooth control, he completed his turn and accelerated to target speed on the next broad reach. Note that the very fast acceleration to regain target speed from f–f to y was achieved by pointing higher from f to y (plots A, E and F). Note how little he moves the rudder (plot B) on the broad reaches prior to and following the gybe.

C The leeward mark rounding

I have drawn in event markers g–g where the rudder is deflected to start the rounding at 99 seconds after the start; h–h at 103.4 seconds where the tiller is centred 4.4 seconds later; and j–j at 109.4 seconds, 6 seconds later, where target speed has been regained and the sheet is trimmed in and the boat pointed higher 10.4 seconds after the start of the rounding and 6 seconds after the start of the post-rounding acceleration.

The individual traces reveal superb technique.

In the rudder angle trace, g–g in trace B, the trace is curved at g–g as it flows from rudder centre to rudder deflected 44°. The curve reveals that the tiller movement started slowly and accelerated as the excursion increased. The rudder was centred at h–h with the boat pointed a little low (plots E and A), the sheet eased (plot C), and the boat was pointed higher and the sail sheeted in 6 seconds later at j–j when the boat had regained target speed.

The boom angle, trace C, shows that the boom was trimmed in while the boat was turning. The pause in the movement is where Julian took another grip on the sheet as he drew it in. The boom was trimmed in, but only as far as he wanted it in by the time he centred his rudder – that is, the sails retained optimum trim and full drive force throughout the turn, and were not sheeted right in as he started his post-turn acceleration.

The hiking effort, trace D, and the heel angle, trace G, show that the boat was sailed heeled slightly to windward on the broad reach as it approached the mark. During the turn, the body was extended to hike hard to keep the boat flat as the sails were sheeted in. The speed trace F shows that there was minimal loss of speed during this turn.

As an illustration of 'How to do it right', this example – indeed the whole sail – would be hard to beat.

25.3 ■ The typical follower's technique

Fig 25.2 shows just the boat speed (fwd velocity) traces of two very different followers. One is a veteran of more than 20 years of regular club sailing, and the other is a young sailor who recently 'learned to sail' at a sailing school.

The point of interest is that the traces are broadly similar because they both use much the same technique. Both sail well to the point where they start their first tack at a, and both take longer than they should to complete their limb and body movements, thus losing more speed than they should between a and b. What happens is that at the point where they arrest their turn, the sails are not yet in and they are not hiked, so the boat keeps on losing speed from 2.9 knots to 2.0 knots at point b. Therefore they are sailing more slowly than they ought to be as they start accelerating at b.

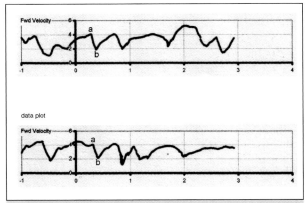

Fig 25.2 Part printout of race sailed by two followers

Both then adopt their best 'sailing to windward' datum mark technique, pointing high with sheet in hard, and so both accelerate much more slowly than the leader. Both take about 20 further seconds to regain target speed, instead of the leader's 5.6 seconds. By the time they approach target speed, it is time to tack again and they repeat the whole catastrophe.

The first follower has rounded the windward mark and is steady on course for the wing mark at 69 seconds after the start. The other is slower. In Fig 25.1 the leader reached this point in less than 48 seconds. At this difference, if the leader finishes a race in 60 minutes, the faster follower will finish in nearly 90 minutes.

This is exactly what we see on the water whenever a lot of manoeuvring is called for – that is, in big fleets, at congested marks and in fickle winds. In more open situations the followers sail at about the same straight-line target speed as the leaders, so the differences due to poor handling through manoeuvres affect their times to a lesser extent.

It is relevant to note that we are not here discussing familiarity with the simulator. One morning I was about to begin a session with a mature sailor when Julian and Chris Nicholson walked in. Chris's long cv includes three 5o5 World Championships, two Eighteen foot skiff World Championships, and three 49er World Championships. He had never previously sailed the simulator. Julian asked if he could use the simulator for a few minutes, said, 'Look, Chris, like this', and sailed a short race as in the printout at champion's speed. Chris – first time ever in the simulator and with no more familiarisation than observing Julian's sailing plus the 1-minute countdown pre-start – sailed the same race in the same wind and matched Julian's speed.

When you are as good as that you can sail anything fast first time, including the simulator.

Many other medallists and world champions have sailed the simulator and, after a short while, they all sail the standard exercises within two or three seconds of each other. To date, every one of them has used an identical technique – the one I call 'fast handling technique'.

The comparisons above of the techniques and the performances of the leaders and the followers are stark, but they are entirely typical.

25.4 ■ How the leader thinks

Let us be practical and start at the beginning by asking ourselves, 'How does a leader think? What drives him?' Look again at Fig 25.1. There are four key points:

1 *The precision of the pattern of the snail trail in the overhead view.* This sailor thinks ahead, plans, manages according to plan, sails accurately, does not sail an inch further than essential.

2 *The strong near-continuous horizontal line formed by the fwd velocity trace.* This sailor thinks target speed, and his whole race is driven by the determination to sail at target speed for as much of the time as possible. Tacks become minor dips in the strong line.
   - Look at Fig 25.2. The followers' traces do not even begin to develop a horizontal line.

3 *The solid regularity of the hiking effort trace.* This demonstrates focus and simplicity of control. This sailor drives his boat steadily, controls balance with sheet and tiller, never sits up.

4 Look at how little the rudder moves between manoeuvres. This shows clear thinking, focus, anticipation and certainty. Tiller-waggling indicates uncertainty – there is no uncertainty here.
   - Note that this is the antithesis of 'natural handling technique' in which the rudder is used for everything.

It is interesting to consider that the quite substantial first half of Chapter 26 is devoted to ensuring that the segments a–b, d–e and g–h can be so small that they interrupt the fwd velocity (target speed) trace so little. There is a lot of information in Fig 25.1.

In this and the following chapters it is my privilege, and the privilege of my contributors, to introduce to the reader the fast handling technique used by world champions at this new level of detail.

PART SEVEN
Handling

Chapter 26 • Fast Handling Technique

26.1 ■ Foreword

Of the many new factors that have emerged since I wrote *HPS-1* in the late 1980s, three are critical. They are:

1 A much more accurate appreciation of the wind's differing degrees of unsteadiness (Fig 21.4), and the observation that it is the degree of unsteadiness rather than the wind speed that distresses many sailors.
2 The realisation from simulator teaching, and confirmed by on-the-water coaching and observation, that the great majority of sailors use the natural 'sequential execution' technique for their turning manoeuvres, and the natural single-control 'luff for everything' technique to control heel when sailing upwind and downwind in straight lines – often despite long experience of sailing without competitive success.
3 The observation that those few sailors who lead, and sometimes win, all use a different and faster handling technique.
    In their turning manoeuvres
    • They use a 'synchronised co-ordination' technique at all times.
    In their straight line sailing
    • At all times and in all winds, they use a two-mode technique –
        acceleration mode when not at target speed, *and*
        maximum VMG mode when at target speed.
    • Upwind in stronger winds, they use a 'simultaneous independent co-ordination' handling technique.
    • Downwind in stronger winds, they use the 'steer for balance' handling technique.

In my 1992 edition of *HPS-1* I described how the wind works, how the waves work, how the boat works, and why and how to shape the sails and set up the boat for best speed in different winds and waves. At that time I thought that all experienced sailors handled their boats with about equally good technique, and that advice about the optimum shape at which to set adjustable sails in the different conditions was the best way to help them sail faster.

This 'sailing' advice remains accurate but, for the reasons given in Section 24.15, I now realise that it did not go far enough. So my objective in this book is to pass on to sailors who want to sail faster the actual detail of the handling – the why and the how of the way the champion sailor thinks, and moves her tiller, sheet and body to sail at lead-group speed and enjoy her share of wins. This is the stuff of Chapters 25 to 29; this handling advice blends with, and adds to, the sailing material in *HPS-1* Chapters 22 to 25.

We will start with the turning manoeuvres, because they remain constant regardless of whether the boat is a blow-downwind boat or a tack-downwind boat, and regardless of the unsteadiness or otherwise of the wind.

In the descriptions of the manoeuvres that follow, the sequence, co-ordination, excursion and time of every movement of each manoeuvre is described and depicted with an exactness that has never previously been possible. This is pure simulator technology, but as *HPS-2* goes to press, sailing simulators are still very thin on the ground worldwide. So it is a valid question as to why I should consider it relevant to refer to simulators in this book at all.

My response is that the simulator is proving itself invaluable as a research tool, as well as being efficient beyond all expectation as an instructing and coaching tool. At the research level, it has been access to the sailing simulator that has provided the detailed information that has enabled us to identify both the 'natural' and the 'fast' handling techniques as coherent entities, and to do this with a precision sufficient to be able to identify the critical differences between them. At the instructing and coaching level, no simulator is necessary to achieve the results described below. Fast sailors have always been with us. But it is just so much easier, and so very much faster, if you have access to a simulator.

26.2 ■ Turning manoeuvres

DEFINITIONS

Circular airflow	The curved airflow that envelops any rig that turns.
Circular waterflow	The curved waterflow that envelops any hull that turns.
Target speed	The speed that, in the present conditions, will get you to the next mark most quickly.

A Circular airflow

Imagine that a very long boat has a flag at the bow and another at the stern. If the boat is at rest in a calm, both flags will be limp. If in a calm the boat rotates to the left under engines at zero forward speed, the flag at the bow will indicate an apparent wind from the left, while the flag at the stern will indicate an apparent wind from the right. This is the ultimate circular airflow.

If we now imagine that we set a jib right forward and a mainsail right aft and sail to windward on port tack in a straight line in light wind, the flow of the apparent wind over jib and mainsail will be from the same direction. But when we tack, the bow swinging to the left will 'feel' an apparent wind from the left due to the turn, so the jib will stay full of wind long after the boat has passed through head-to-wind. At the stern, the mainsail that in the turn will be working in an apparent wind, which is now from the right, will flutter immediately the boat starts to turn, and then fill early from the right. This is the practical effect on a rig of the circular airflow induced by a turn.

B Circular waterflow

The same considerations apply to the hull. If a 4m boat that is sailing at 4 knots (2m per second) turns, say, to port at 30° per second, the flow at the bow will come from 30° to port of the centreline, and at the stern will be from 30° to starboard of the centreline. These flows across the hull greatly increase the drag.

I have not yet worked out how to measure this increase, but a useful analogy is to think of the difference in drag between towing a straight banana in a straight line, and towing a banana curved at 60° in a straight line. The flow over a straight boat that is sailing in a curve will be broadly similar to the flow over a curved banana that is being towed in a straight line. In both cases, the flow at the ends will be across the bottom instead of along it and will be thoroughly disturbed, and the greater the bend or the tighter the turn, the greater will be the angle and the disturbance and the drag. In the case of the boat, the deflected rudder adds further drag. Rolling the boat as in a roll tack will further disturb the flow and further increase the drag.

The balance between the boat's momentum, which keeps it moving, and all the extra turning drags that slow it as it turns leads to the concept of the optimum rate of turn (see Sections 15.7–15.13).

C Optimum rate of turn

When tacking, drive force from the sails will necessarily be lost, so a boat that turns very slowly as it tacks will stop mid-turn. The lighter the boat the less will be its momentum and the sooner it will stop. So turning too slowly will win no races.

If it turns very quickly, as in a crash tack to avoid a collision, the fully deflected rudder plus the extreme drag of the small-radius circular waterflow will virtually stop the boat. It will then have to re-accelerate from near zero speed. This will take much time, so turning too fast will win no races either.

Between these two extremes there will necessarily be a rate of turn when tacking that will lose least time with respect to a rival who does not tack (Section 15.7). In practice, a rate of turn of about 30° per second appears to be near optimum when tacking for most light dinghies of between 3.5m and 5m in length (except at low speed – ie in light airs).

When rounding either a wing mark or a downwind mark, drive force from the sails will be retained by a wind-from-behind boat, so despite the extra drag the boat will keep moving reasonably fast. But precisely *because* it is moving fast, if it is not turned reasonably smartly it will sail a much longer distance than necessary. So both observation and experience suggest that about the same 30° per second rate of turn is also fastest when executing mark roundings that do not involve tacking, and also gybes (again except in light airs).

D Optimum time to turn

Tacks, and roundings of windward and wing and leeward marks, and gybes of apparent wind skiffs, all involve turns through about 90°, and 135° from run to close hauled. A turn through 90° at 30° per second will nominally take 3 seconds. But in practice it is faster to use the rudder gently and ease the boat both into and out of the turn, so the observed times of the fastest tacks and mark roundings are about 4.0–4.5 seconds for smaller boats, and 4.5–5 seconds for the larger boats, between tiller 'down' to tiller centred. In light air it will be longer.

Optimum time for a downwind gybe (ie no mark rounding included) in a conventional (wind-from-behind) boat will be about half that (ie about 2 seconds).

These logically derived optimum rates of turn and times to turn become the key to a logical definition.

> **DEFINITION**
>
> *Efficient handling technique* This is one in which all the essential hand, limb and body movements needed to steer, trim sail and balance the boat are completed within the optimum time required by the boat to make its turn.
>
> *Note*: In the special case of the apparent wind gybe – special because it is necessarily a sequential execution manoeuvre – we need to add 'and to regain target speed'.

E Time measurement

Encouragement to complete a tack or mark rounding within so many seconds calls for a way of measuring times of the order of a few seconds. A simple and adequate and surprisingly accurate method is to practise carrying in your mind a cadence of three beats per second – that is, *nought* da da *one* da da *two* … For obvious reasons, always start with 'nought' or 'go', never with 'one'. To keep the energy pulses crisp and even, reduce all the single-digit numbers to one syllable – that is, 'nought' or 'go' for zero, 'for' for four (fower), 'sev' for seven. Try it looking at your watch until you get the cadence, then practise until you are accurate within 1 second in 20. This method is easy, useful and quite accurate enough for the work ahead.

F The body and stick diagrams

The Section 24.11 exercise in which I coached the coaches led to a request for diagrams of each movement of every routine, so I drew the stick figures. These in turn had some coaches' students asking how the human body should best deliver these movements, so I asked Nicola Bethwaite[1] to model. As the course progressed, coaches advised that both the clarity of the stick figures and the integrity of the sailor performing the manoeuvres both contributed strongly, so Nicola and I produced a second set of pictures which are technically better and which better integrate with the written descriptions and the stick figures.

These pictures are not static-posed. They are dynamic – that is, they are taken as she performs each manoeuvre in a simulator simulating the dynamics of a standard-rig Laser in 12 knots of wind.

---

1 Nicola (with Julian sailing forward) won the World Cherub Championship in a strong-wind series in Adelaide in 1976. She finished second in the prior light-air Worlds at Torquay in the UK. In 1988, she represented Australia in the 470 Women's class at the Seoul Olympics, represented once more in the Yngling class at the Athens Olympics in 2004, and was selected to represent again at the Beijing Olympics in 2008 but broke both arms in a cycling accident and had to withdraw.

G Horses for courses

The *principles* of fast handling technique never change – everything is focused on least loss of time with respect to a boat that does not tack, gybe etc. The *detail* of the handling movements for, say, a tack will necessarily be very different as between a Finn dinghy with no trapeze, a short tiller extension and a deep cockpit in which a sailor needs only to rise slightly, pivot on his feet and sit on the other deck; and a 49er with twin trapezes, long twin tiller extensions and a flat wings-and-deck surface 10ft wide, over which the crew must run from gunwale to gunwale during a tack or gybe.

All my on-the-water experience and the recent years of simulator coaching suggest that the critical factor that triggers sailors into thinking about tacking, etc differently is whether the sailor uses a single tiller extension short enough to move from side to side with her, or uses one or the other of long twin extensions, each of which always stays on the same side. I observe that all sailors who are accustomed to a single short extension that they move from side to side do not react to – and do not usually even mention – the differences between boats like the Laser with its narrow shallow cockpit and wide side decks, boats like the Heron, Pacer or old International Fourteen with their wide deep cockpits and narrow gunwales, and the 'generic' simulator with its deep cockpit and comfortably shaped 'Rogge'[2] style side decks.

In the sections that follow I will describe how champion sailors handle their sailing, and what the simulator printouts tell us about the times and motions of their technique. For completeness in this and Chapter 15 and Chapter 27, I have asked champion skiff sailors to describe the different techniques they use in order to handle the wider wings and long twin tiller extensions of the bigger and faster skiffs, and the different techniques called for in practice by stronger winds. In Chapter 28, Rohan Veal describes the completely new art of handling, sailing and winning in foil Moths.

H Options

Minor options are simply not relevant. When sailing a boat with a deep cockpit and flat decks, it is easy to pinch the tiller extension momentarily under the thigh or buttock. With a shallow cockpit like the Laser, the knees stay high so the thigh cannot lie flat on the deck to pinch the extension. With narrow gunwales there is no deck. Minor adjustment of technique is called for to accommodate these variations.

Another option is whether to carry the tiller extension in front of or aft of the body. Beginners find that holding the tiller extension aft of the body enables them to use a direct push and pull on the tiller with the extension across the boat and that this method of steering is simpler for them in the early stages. Many experienced single-tiller-extension sailors prefer to carry the extension in front of the body; others find the aft-of-body method faster. Skiff sailors with long twin extensions simply cannot carry the extension in front of the body because it both interferes with the freedom of movement of their forward hand or crews, and in any case it traps the helm behind the extension when he/she wants to tack or gybe. So both the slowest and the fastest sailors hold the extension aft of the body in a 'saucepan' grip. Many others prefer and use the 'in front of the body' or 'reversed dagger' grasp. It simply does not matter – both groups sail equally fast.

Adapt the detail to what is simplest for you in your boat. Stay with the important principles.

26.3 ■ THE TACK

The fast sailor's objectives are:

- To turn the boat at the rate of turn that will steady on the new heading with least loss of speed and time as compared with a rival who does not tack.
- To complete all the necessary hand, arm, body and foot movements within the 4 seconds or so that the boat needs to turn *and, without delay,*

---

[2] When Jacques Rogge, the present International Olympic Committee supremo, was a Finn-sailing medical student he put electrodes into the thigh muscles of his Finn-sailing fellow students to study the ergonomic efficiency of:
- The Elvstrom 'droop' hiking stance used in Finn dinghies (possible only in boats with adequate freeboard).
- The Laser straight-legged hiking stance (necessary in boats with low freeboard).
- Hiking Soling style with boots tied to the deck.

His conclusion was that the 'droop' stance delivered about the same righting moment as the Laser straight-leg style, but with only two-thirds of the energy expenditure. The Soling method uses much more energy for less righting moment, so forget it.

- To accelerate strongly to regain target speed.

Let us look at each of these factors in turn.

The leader's movements and times

The tack proper has two co-ordinated routines, each of three movements, followed by a three-movement 'change hands' routine later. These blend into one smooth manoeuvre that gives you both the fastest tack and immediate post-tack acceleration, as well as continuous control of the boat throughout and following the tack.

The hand, arm, body and leg movements are shown by the photos of the sailor performing the movements (Fig 26.1, A to G) and the matching stick figures (Fig 26.2, A to E). The time and excursion of each tiller, sheet and body movement and the boat's speed and orientation are shown by the leader's printout, Fig 25.1.

The points at which each sequence starts are (Figs 26.1 and 26.2):

A Prepare to tack. At about start of tack minus 5 seconds. Select the new aiming point at which you will arrest the turn. Shift the grip on the tiller extension to hold it at or near its end – *and* disengage the aft foot from under the swing strap (Figs 26.1A and 26.2A). (Note: If you sail a two-crew boat, warn your forward hand 'Tacking in *two* de de *one* de de *go* …')

B Start the tack (time 0). Move the tiller extension smoothly, initially to leeward, slowly at first then with increasing speed for rudder deflection about 45°, and simultaneously put your aft foot across to the lee side of the cockpit. For minimum hydrodynamic drag, start the tiller extension movement slowly and accelerate it as you approach full excursion. (Figs 26.1B and 26.2B (start).)

C Within half to one second of Go, start to swing the tiller extension not only away from you, but in a horizontal arc forward. This makes room for your body. As soon as there is room to move, start to move so that your body follows the tiller extension closely. Transfer your weight towards the new windward side in a movement in which you rise slightly. Pivot on the balls of your feet in a crouching stance, facing forward, and place your buttocks on the new deck 2–2.5 seconds later (at time 3–3.5 secs after Go). Keep your head down, so it will not be hit by the boom. Do not allow the tiller extension to rise, or the boom will knock it out of your hand. (Figs 26.1C and 26.2C show the mid position of this movement.)

D This shows the end of the pivot movement. The tiller is still fully deflected with the turning boat approaching its new aiming point. (Figs 26.1D and 26.2D.)

E About half a second later, as the bow approaches and reaches its new aiming point and the sails fill, make three movements smoothly and simultaneously – centre the tiller smoothly to arrest the turn, extend your body to hike hard, and ease the sheet slightly for fast acceleration. (Figs 26.1E and 26.2E.)

This completes the tack, and you are into the post-tack straight-line acceleration to regain target speed. Note particularly that at this stage you have *not yet changed hands* with the sheet and tiller extension. Changing hands is *not* essential to the tack, and is not a part of the tack proper. Steer with your arm behind your back until the boat is accelerating strongly.

When convenient (usually after one to two seconds, but it does not matter):

F1   Pinch the extension lightly under your thigh (Fig 26.1F).
F2   Change hands on the sheet (26.1F) and, with the now free aft hand –
F3   Pick up the tiller extension (Fig 26.1G).

G   Sail in acceleration mode to regain target speed quickly (Fig 26.2G).

Then adopt maximum VMG mode – sheet in slightly and point as high as is possible while maintaining target speed (Fig 25.1). The difference in heading between acceleration mode and max VMG mode is usually 5–10°, and never *more* than 10°. One hand at arm's length subtends an angle of 10° (ie each finger subtends 2°). For a roll tack, pause between B and C, then move faster to D and E.

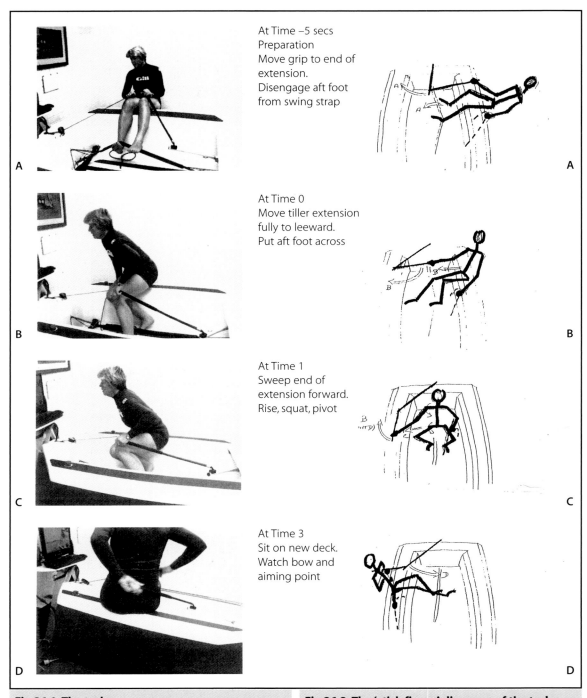

At Time –5 secs
Preparation
Move grip to end of extension.
Disengage aft foot from swing strap

At Time 0
Move tiller extension fully to leeward.
Put aft foot across

At Time 1
Sweep end of extension forward.
Rise, squat, pivot

At Time 3
Sit on new deck.
Watch bow and aiming point

Fig 26.1 The tack

Fig 26.2 The 'stick figure' diagrams of the tack

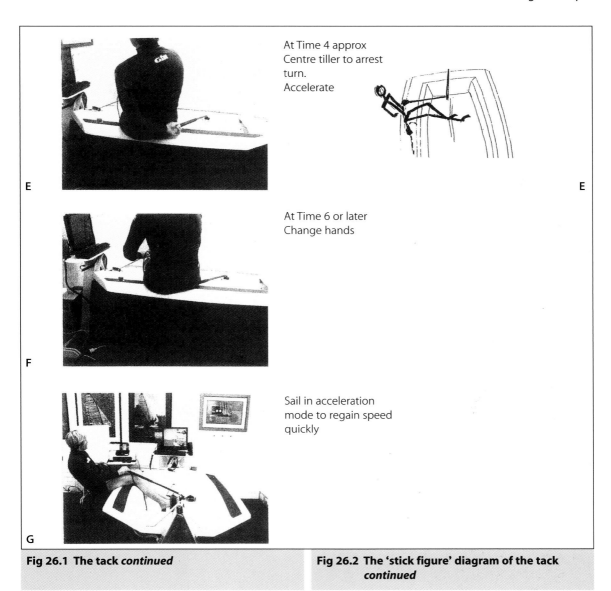

At Time 4 approx
Centre tiller to arrest
turn.
Accelerate

E

E

At Time 6 or later
Change hands

F

Sail in acceleration
mode to regain speed
quickly

G

Fig 26.1 The tack *continued*

Fig 26.2 The 'stick figure' diagram of the tack
continued

The boat's response

At this point let us look again at Fig 25.1 and at Section 25.1A.

At 16.1 seconds after the start (event marker B–B), Julian applies 45° of helm (plot B) to start his first tack. This is the moment of Figs 26.1B and 26.2B. He pauses momentarily to roll the boat firmly to windward (plot G), then starts to move his body through the Figs 26.1 and 26.2C and D positions. At 20.6 seconds, 4.5 seconds later (E–E), he centres the helm on the new heading (plots B and E, at E–E). This is the moment of Fig 26.1 and 26.2E position. During the turn the boat loses speed from 4.8 knots to about 2.9 knots (plot F, at E–E). During the tack he moves his body quickly so he is already hiking strongly on the other tack as he centres the tiller (plot B, at E–E) to arrest the turn. At this point he starts to roll the boat more upright (plot G), eases the sail 5° (plot C), steers a little lower (plot E, also A), and as a result accelerates very quickly to regain target speed. Only when he is accelerating strongly does he change hands (Fig 26.1F). At time 10.3 seconds after starting the tack, and 5.8 seconds after centring his tiller, he has regained target speed; and at that point he sheets in a little further and points higher (as in Fig 26.1G).

Note that:

- He turned the boat through about 90° in 4.3 seconds.
- He was already almost at full hike as the sails filled – he synchronised his movements perfectly to match the boat's dynamics as it turned. Note that the tiller is centred to arrest the turn, the boat is deliberately rolled to windward as the sails fill, and the moment of minimum speed and start of the new acceleration all occur at the same instant.

Training notes

For readers who wish to acquire and practise this technique, I suggest:

- Practise your counting seconds until you can rely on it.
- Put pads under your boat and tie it firmly so that you can hike to extreme both ways with confidence.
- First practise the individual routines –

Prepare

Hike to extreme. Start counting down from, say, 5. At 3 or 2 –
1 Select the aiming point on which you will arrest your turn.
2 Disengage your aft foot from under the swing strap.
3 Shift your grasp of the tiller extension to the end.

The first routine is three foot and body movements. Practise these at first without the extension:
1 Put the aft foot across to the lee side.
2 Rise slightly, pivot 180° on the balls of the feet in a squatting stance, facing forward as you pivot. As you pivot, the toe of your aft foot should slide under the swing strap on the new side. Do not raise your body. Keep your head down else it will be hit by the boom.
3 Sit smoothly on the opposite deck. There should be no thump. Practise until you can do this smoothly in 3–3.5 seconds.

The second routine is three hand and arm movements:
4 Start by moving the tiller extension smoothly fully away from you – slowly at first, then faster – this starts the turn.
5 As a continuous movement, sweep the tiller extension in a horizontal arc forward – this makes room for your body. Keep the tiller and rudder fully deflected as you do so.
6 Look forward to see where you are going. As the boat notionally approaches and reaches its new heading and the sails fill, arrest the turn by smoothly centring the tiller and hike strongly in anticipation of – ie, slightly prior to – the roll to leeward.

Note that up to this point you have retained your grasp of the end of the tiller extension. To retain this grasp as your body pivots requires that your arm wrap behind your back. (Look at the photos and diagrams in Figs 26.1 and 26.2, C, D and E.)

To become comfortable with this, practise the 1, 2, 3 routine again, but this time place your aft hand on the opposite deck, *and leave it there without moving its position* while you rise, pivot and sit. As you pivot, your arm will wrap behind your back and you will finish the routine sitting in front of your hand. Keep doing this until it feels natural, then pick up the tiller extension and put it all together. The sequence of the starts of each movement takes the order 1, 4, 5, 2, 3, 6.

The third routine is to change hands on sheet and tiller extension (Figs 26.1 and 26.2, E, F and G):
6 Pinch the tiller extension lightly under your thigh.
7 Change hands on the sheet.
8 With the now-free aft hand, pick up the tiller extension.

Now put 1, 2, 3 and 4, 5 and 6 together. They become –5 to 0 (prepare), then at time (seconds):

    0   Put the aft foot across to start the 1, 2, 3 routine. Rise, squat and start pivoting.

0	Simultaneously, start to move the tiller extension smoothly all the way to leeward. This makes room for your body to begin to move, so always start by moving the extension and follow the extension closely with your body.
0.25	Immediately begin to sweep your hand with the end of the extension in a horizontal arc forward to make more room for your body. This gives your body room to complete the 1, 2, 3 routine.
0.5 to 3.5	Move through and complete the 1, 2, 3 routine. Hold the tiller fully deflected. Do not lift your head or the extension, or the boom will hit either or both.
3.5 to 4	Sit on the new deck and start to hike. The rudder is still fully deflected. As the bow approaches and reaches the chosen aiming point and the sails begin to fill, and not until then, centre the tiller smoothly, hike hard, and ease the sheet a touch.

In this position you can steer, even though your hand is behind your back. You can hike hard on one leg if necessary because one toe is under the toe strap. You still have the sheet in your other hand, so you have retained full control of your boat throughout the tack, and still have full control of it. You do not need to change hands before you start accelerating hard to regain target speed.

When convenient – usually after a second or so, but never until you have started to accelerate strongly – complete the last three movements of the routine (Fig 26.1):

7 Sit lightly on the extension to steady it momentarily (rudder is straight, so the boat will sail straight).

8 Change hands on the sheet.

9 Pick up the tiller extension with the now-free aft hand.

Practise the whole manoeuvre until it 'flows' in about 4 seconds for the tack, and with the change hands routine at about 6 seconds. When practising, deliberately pause for a second or two, and work your sheet and extension as if sheeting and steering, before changing hands.

The most common errors are:

- Slow and/or inefficient body and arm movements.
  - Sailor starts the tack, but does not complete all the movements prior to the boat reaching the new aiming point, so the boat turns too far.
  - Sailor starts the tack, moves slowly, arrests the turn on the aiming point, but then completes moving body and/or changing hands. Does not start accelerating until some later time. This gives the Fig 25.2 result.
- Slow acceleration due to:
  - Complacency, no appreciation of the target speed.
  - Adoption of one single 'point high, sheet tight' mode of sailing to windward.
  - 'Sitting in' and pointing high, and not hiking until the apparent wind builds to the expected force with even slower acceleration (Fig 25.2 again).

Guard against these.

Technique with twin tiller extensions

For completeness of description for both high performance and apparent wind handling techniques, I have asked Julian Bethwaite to describe the techniques used when tacking a big skiff with twin tiller extensions. (Refer to Section 15.7 *et seq*, and Chapter 27.)

26.4 ■ THE MARK ROUNDING

Hull dynamics and tracking

The fastest mark rounding will involve hull dynamics (optimum rate of turn), tracking technique to apex mark (current will make a difference in light winds) and handling technique. We will assume that a rate of turn of 30° per second is optimum, and that there is no current nor conflicting traffic so apexing the mark will always be fastest.

The most complex and difficult mark rounding is from run to close hauled. This involves a change of heading of 135°, which will occupy about 6–7 seconds, during which all three handling factors – steering, sail trimming and balance – will be changed simultaneously through their maximum excursions.

The fastest way to round any mark is to 'apex' it. The boat should skim the mark halfway through its turn.

A turn of 30° per second at 5 knots (2.5mps) describes a circle of about 5m radius. Unless there is current and/or competing traffic, to apex a mark during a 90° or 135° turn the boat should approach the mark about 3m clear of, and parallel to, the ray between the last mark and the mark about to be rounded. When the bow of the boat is about 3m to windward of the mark, it should commence its turn. The gunwale or the crews' heads should skim the mark mid turn and the turn should be completed a shade below the close-hauled heading for fastest acceleration to regain target speed.

The leader's movements and times

The hand, arm, body and foot movements are shown by the photos of the sailor performing the movements in Fig 26.3A to D and also the stick figures in Fig 26.4A to E. The times are shown by the leader's printout (Fig 25.1).

The points at which each sequence starts are (Figs 26.3 and 26.4):

Prepare for the mark rounding as you approach the mark:
A Steer towards the start-of-turn point. Select the aiming point on which you will arrest the turn. Prepare to hike hard without delay – slide the buttocks out as far as possible and jack-knife the torso inwards to preserve balance.

Draw in sheet as much as prudent without a detectable loss of speed (Figs 26.3A and 26.4A).

When the bow reaches the start-of-turn point:
B Start the rounding (time 0 seconds). Move the tiller extension smoothly to leeward sufficiently to start the turn at the rate of turn desired. At full reaching boat speed, the optimun rate of turn will usually call for less than full deflection of the rudder.

Start to move your body towards full hike as soon as the boat begins to turn. Keep moving your body outwards in anticipation of a roll to leeward. Do not wait for the roll to develop prior to hiking hard (Figs 26.3B and 26.4B).

Either:
C1 As soon as you are confident of the rudder angle, sit lightly on extension (time 1 second). Draw in the sheet with two hands; maintain sail trim for maximum drive force throughout the turn. Adopt and hold full hike. Complete the trimming in of the sheet (time 4 seconds).

D1 Pick up extension (time 4 seconds). (This technique is shown in Fig 26.4C, D and E.)

Or:
C2 Hold the tiller extension in front of your body. Draw in the sheet with your other hand; grasp the sheet with the thumb of your tiller hand between pulls. Maintain max drive sail trim. Complete trimming in of the sheet (time 4 seconds). (This technique is shown in Fig 26.4B and C.)

When bow reaches the aiming point – at time about 6 seconds:
E Maintain full hike. Centre the tiller (Figs 26.3E and 26.4D).

The boat's response

Let us look again at the fast sailor's printout, Fig 25.1. The event markers g–g show where the rudder is deflected to start the rounding at 99 seconds after the start; h–h at 103.4 seconds show where the tiller is centred 4.4 seconds later; and j–j at 109.4 seconds into the race show where the sheet is trimmed right in and the boat pointed higher 10.4 seconds after the start of the rounding and 6 seconds after the start of the post-rounding acceleration.

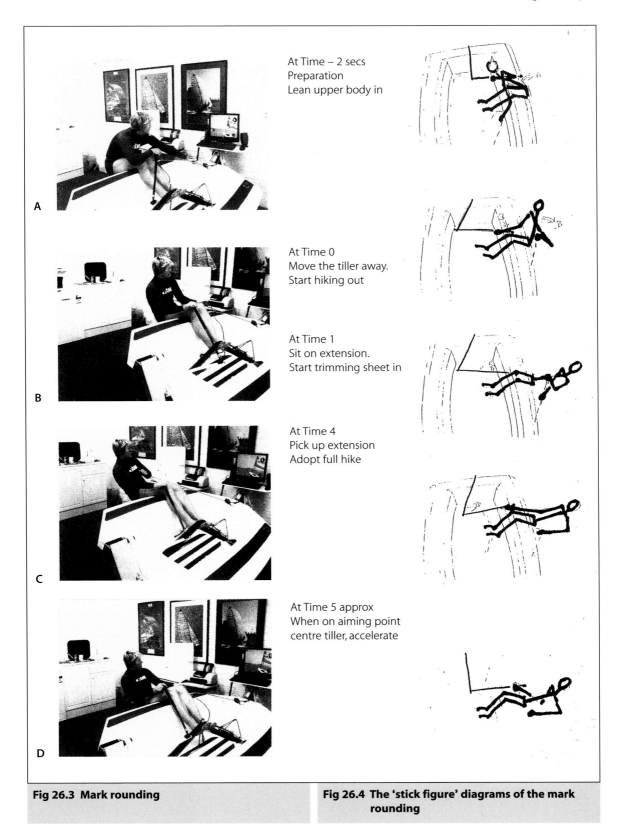

At Time – 2 secs
Preparation
Lean upper body in

A

At Time 0
Move the tiller away.
Start hiking out

At Time 1
Sit on extension.
Start trimming sheet in

B

At Time 4
Pick up extension
Adopt full hike

C

At Time 5 approx
When on aiming point
centre tiller, accelerate

D

Fig 26.3 Mark rounding

Fig 26.4 The 'stick figure' diagrams of the mark rounding

Training notes

The key requirement for any mark rounding is that all of the necessary movements should be performed efficiently within the time that the boat needs to turn. For readers who wish to acquire and practise fast technique, I suggest:

- Pad and secure your boat firmly so you can hike strongly both ways.
- Practise the individual routines and times –

Prepare

- Slide the buttocks outboard to extreme.
- Lean upper body inwards to extreme to preserve balance.

Rounding

Body

1 Extend the body progressively from leaning in to full hike in 2 seconds.
2 Maintain full hike.

Either – Option 1: Efficient with Rogge-type side decks and gunwales

Tiller extension

3 Move tiller to leeward	Start to 1 second
4 Sit lightly on the extension	At 1 second
5 Pick up the extension	At about 3 seconds
6 Centre the tiller	When the bow reaches aiming point, at 4 to 5 seconds

Sheet

7 Trim the sheet in with both hands as the boat turns, between 1 and 3 seconds

Or – Option 2: More efficient with shallow-cockpit boats

Tiller extension and sheet

Hold extension in front of the body.
8 Move the tiller to leeward (time 0)
9 Draw the sheet in with free hand (time 1–3.5 seconds). Hold the sheet between pulls with the thumb of the tiller hand.
10 Centre the tiller when the bow reaches aiming point, at time 4 to 5 seconds.

Whichever method is used, the sail should be trimmed accurately to the changing apparent wind during the turn.

Putting it together

The key to a minimum-time rounding is anticipation – start to do everything about 1–2 seconds before it becomes necessary:

- Prepare for the rounding as you approach the 'start of turn' point by trimming in the sheet as far as is prudent without loss of speed. If you approach a little wider and 'come up' a few degrees in the final seconds as you approach, this will bring the apparent wind forward and hold speed and enable you to bring your sheet in some way in anticipation.
- At the start-of-turn point, move the tiller extension to leeward, not all the way, and simultaneously start to hike, and start to trim in the sheet. It does not matter if the boat initially heels to windward a little.
- Steer to apex the mark. Hike to extreme. Trim the sheet right in then ease it 100–150mm.
- Arrest the turn 10–5° below close hauled.

- Sail with maximum acceleration to regain target speed before hardening up to VMG maximum trim at target speed.

Most common errors
- Not co-ordinating.
- Not apexing the mark; sailor sails to the mark, then starts to turn.
- Not hiking while rounding.
- Not trimming to maintain full sail drive while rounding.
- Sequencing – the most common error of all
  - Sailor steers to the mark, then starts to turn.
  - Sailor steers round turn, then the sails flap, so the sailor sheets in.
  - Then the boat heels, so the sailor starts to hike.

By the time this follower's boat is up to target speed, a notional lead-group sailor – who was abeam the follower approaching the mark, but apexed the mark and used synchronised co-ordinated technique, so started accelerating 4 or 6 seconds earlier – would be 10–15 seconds or 5–6 lengths ahead.

26.5 ■ THE TWO GYBE MANOEUVRES

Figs 26.7, 26.8 and 26.9

To illustrate the critical dynamic differences between the wind-from-behind gybe and the apparent wind gybe I have drawn the boat tracks of the Laser gybe in Fig 26.7, the 49er lighter-wind gybe in Fig 26.8, and the 29er strong-wind gybe in Fig 26.9.

In each diagram, the true wind blows straight down the page – that is, notionally from the north (360°).

Diagrams labelled 'A' in Figs 26.7, 26.8 and 26.9

In each of these figures the inset diagram 'A' shows the performance envelope of the boat in 6, 9 and 12 knots of true wind. In the case of the 29er, because we carried out much of the prototype testing in winds in the 17–22 knot range, I am able to add a very confident 20 knot performance envelope. This is fortunate in that it correlates directly with the strong-wind 29er USA and World Championship regattas in San Francisco in 2005 (Section 27.11).

Diagrams labelled 'B' in Figs 26.7, 26.8 and 26.9

These are 'snail trails', to the scale of the A diagram, of the boat's track across the water (assuming no current) from the commencement of the gybe to the point where the boat is on its new heading and up to speed and the gybe manoeuvre is complete:

- The segments labelled 'Y–0' indicate that the boat is sailing at target speed and heading as it approaches the start of the gybe at time marker '0'.
- Marker '0' indicates the position and time at which the tiller is moved to start the gybe.
- Markers 1, 2, 3, 4 etc indicate the positions reached by the boat 1, 2, 3, 4 etc seconds after the start time 0.
- The boat will lose about 13% of its speed every second as it turns due to the increased drag as a result of circular waterflow and the deflected rudder and the loss of drive force. This progressive slowing is shown by the progressively shorter segment-vectors 0–1, 1–2, 2–3 etc, and the speed at key points is noted to the left of the segment.
- The sequence of the skipper's tasks 'S', the forward hand's tasks 'F', and the boat's responses 'B' in each segment as the gybe progresses is given in the text below.
- The segment 'X–Z' indicates that the gybe is complete, and the boat is established in straight-line sailing at target speed. Y–0 and 8–Z or 9–Z are mirror images of each other.
- In the case of the wind-from-behind Laser, the gybe manoeuvre is complete when the boat is established in straight-line sailing on target heading. As it accelerates to regain target speed, very little changes, so it is safe for the change hands routine to take place at any time after 4.

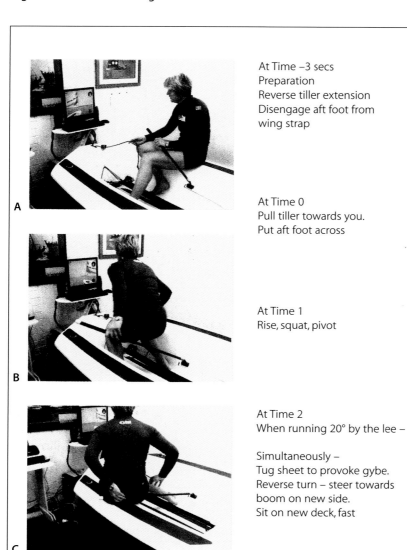

At Time −3 secs
Preparation
Reverse tiller extension
Disengage aft foot from
wing strap

At Time 0
Pull tiller towards you.
Put aft foot across

At Time 1
Rise, squat, pivot

At Time 2
When running 20° by the lee −

Simultaneously −
Tug sheet to provoke gybe.
Reverse turn − steer towards
boom on new side.
Sit on new deck, fast

At Time 2.5 to 3
Centre tiller
Steer for balance

At Time 6 or later
Change hands
Steer for balance

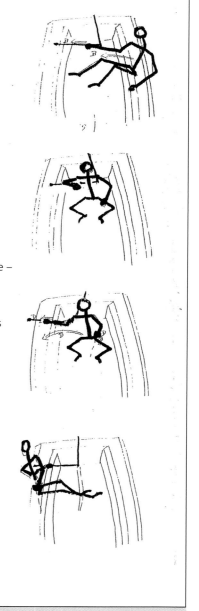

Fig 26.5 The gybe

Fig 26.6 The 'stick figure' diagrams of the wind-from-behind gybe

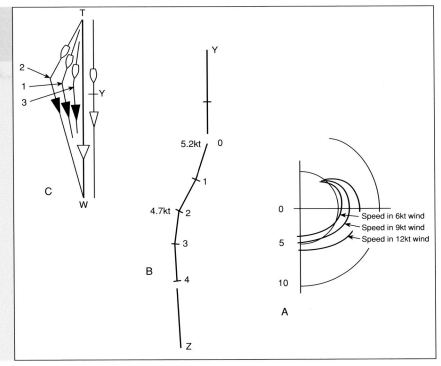

Fig 26.7 Dynamics of wind-from-behind gybe

Laser gybe in 12 knot wind.

- In the cases of the 49er and 29er apparent wind boats, it is inherent in the crosswind acceleration process from the low speed at which the boats exit the turn that as the boats re-accelerate the apparent wind will go forward and increase so the boat will need to be controlled with care as it is driven at its stability limit and steered to curve downwind and the sails are trimmed as it accelerates around the curve. Not until this re-acceleration and curving downwind process is finished is the gybe manoeuvre complete.

Re changing hands, there are three safe options:
1 The skipper moves early and quickly, and changes hands *before* the mainsail goes across. The forward hand delays moving, to balance the boat.
2 The skipper moves her body, *but does not change hands* until the gybe is complete.
3 The boat is equipped with twin tiller extensions.

(Note: To change hands *during* the gybe manoeuvre is not a safe technique. It inevitably invites the troubles noted in Section 27.11 (San Francisco 29er Worlds).)

Diagrams labelled 'C' in Figs 26.7, 26.8 and 26.9

These are drawn at twice the scale of diagrams A and B. They show how much the apparent wind changes during the apparent wind gybes, and how little it changes in the wind-from-behind gybe:

- The bold vertical line with the open arrowhead is the true wind, from 360° (N).
- The two vectors labelled TY with the open boat symbol (drawn close alongside TW in the Laser diagram), and the associated vector labelled YW with the solid sharp arrowhead, represent the speed and direction of the boat, and the speed and direction of the apparent wind as the boat sails segment Y–0 at target speed and heading.
  - Similarly, the vector labelled T1 with the boat symbol represents the boat speed and direction, and the associated vector 1W with the sharp solid arrowhead represents the apparent wind speed and direction as each boat sails segment 0–1 and approaches marker 1 at 1 second after the start of the gybe at time marker 0.

– Vectors T2 and 2W represent the boat speed and direction, and the apparent wind speed and direction as each boat approaches time marker 2, and so on throughout the gybe.

26.5.1 ■ THE 'WIND FROM BEHIND' GYBE

Dynamics

The controlled gybe in conventional boats is governed by the dynamic that the apparent wind is always from astern. Particularly in stronger winds, the boom and mainsail will reverse sides forcefully with a strong instant reversal of both heel force and turning moment. The key to safe, controlled gybes is to divide the gybe into three parts:

1 The first part is a deliberate preparation so you can make the sail gybe when *you* want it to gybe, rather than at some uncontrolled time when the sail wants to gybe.
2 The second is a short burst of intense activity in which you force the sail to gybe, apply a sharp downwind turn which is exactly synchronised with the gybe, move your body to the new side, then cancel the sharp turn.
   • This technique enables you to apply a momentary equal and opposite heeling and turning force which balances the reversed heel and turn forces as the boom changes sides. This balancing of forces keeps the boat upright and under confident control.
3 The third part is the post-gybe tidy-up of adopting the desired heading, and changing hands on sheet and tiller when all else is complete.

This fastest and safest of gybes has almost the same three movements: body, hand and arm, and change hands routines as the tack, but the preparation, the way the movements are co-ordinated, the dynamics and the speed of execution are very different.

The modern technique in Finn- and Laser-type boats of running by the lee means that in these craft the helm may sit or crouch on either the opposite side or the same side as the boom, so while the principles of the gybe always remain the same, the detail of the movement routines in particular boats and with particular techniques will and must change. This means that no standard description can be written to 'fit' all boats and techniques.

For this reason, the description below will assume a conventional boat that sails downwind slower than the wind and in which the helm sits on the side opposite the boom when running.

The leader's movements and times

The sailor's movements are shown in Figs 26.5 and 26.6 A to D, the times of the movements in Fig 25.1, and the boat's track in Fig 27.5.

The dynamics are to steer the boat towards the boom until you are 'running by the lee' by about 20°. Then:

• Give the sheet a sharp tug – this will trigger the gybe, *and*
• Simultaneously both reverse the turn to turn downwind momentarily.
• (Also simultaneously) complete your body movement to the new side.
• Immediately thereafter centre the tiller.

The key to control in a strong-wind gybe is the sharp synchronised but brief turn downwind towards the boom's new side as the boom cracks across. It is this momentary turn that keeps the boat upright and under control.

The sequences are (Figs 26.5 and 26.6):

Preparation at –5 seconds

1 Select the aiming point at which you will arrest the turn. This will depend on whether you are gybing during a run, or gybing around a mark. For this example we will assume a gybe during the run – that is, one which finishes on the same heading, as in Fig 26.8.

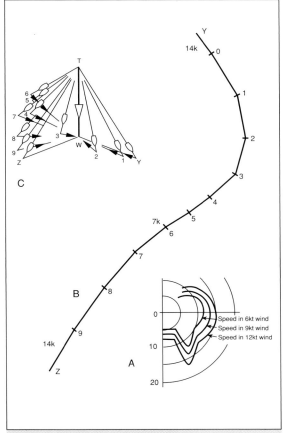

Fig 26.8 Dynamics of apparent wind gybe in moderate wind

49er gybe in 9 knot wind.

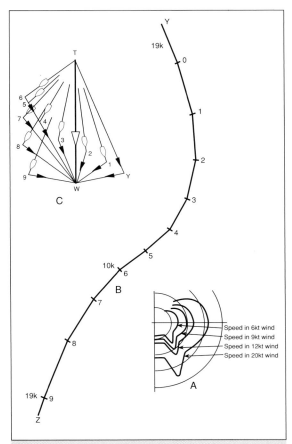

Fig 26.9 Dynamics of apparent wind gybe in strong wind

29er gybe in 20 knot wind.

2   Reverse the tiller extension – lay it to the side away from your body, and hold it as far along its length as you can conveniently reach.

3   Free your aft foot from the swing strap. These movements are shown in Fig 26.5A and 26.6A. Fig 26.5A shows Nicola using the 'tiller extension in front of the body' grasp.

At time Go (0 secs) simultaneously

4   Put the aft foot across.

5   Move the tiller towards you to start the turn.

6   Rise and start pivoting (Fig 26.5B and C).

Note that in this case the tiller extension does *not* make room for your body. You have no option but to move and pivot forward of the tiller (so it had better not be too long).

When the boat is running by the lee about 15–20° and is ready to gybe, simultaneously

7   Tug the sheet sharply to trigger the gybe.

8   Reverse the turn – steer sharply towards the boom on its new side.

9   Move your body very quickly to sit on the new deck.

10 Almost immediately after 8 above – centre the tiller, and steer for balance as in Figs 26.5D and 26.6C and D. In Fig 26.5B the boom has just gybed from port to starboard; note that the tiller is momentarily to port as the sailor steers sharply towards the boom on its new side.

At this point the gybe is complete, with the boat under control. It all happens very quickly.

Note that if the sail 'beats you' and gybes before your tug at 7, simply accept it and proceed immediately with 8, 9 and 10.

11 Steer towards the new aimimg point.

When convenient and the boat is under secure control

12 Sit on the extension.

13 Change hands on the sheet.

14 Pick up the extension.

The boat's response

Between them, Figs 26.5 and 26.6, and the printout in Fig 25.1, show every detail of the leader's technique. The boat's response is described in Section 25.1. Fig 26.7 shows that the apparent wind does not change much in the wind-from-behind gybe. There are no surprises.

Training notes

The preparation is different. In the tack, the tiller and extension move away from you and in so doing make room for your body to follow. But in the gybe they move towards you and crowd you, so the most sensible technique is to make room for your body and tiller before you start by getting the extension out of the way. So, at:

5 seconds before the start reverse the tiller extension and grasp it as far away from you as you can.

The first routine is the same three foot and body movements as for tacking, but with a slow start and a very fast end to the movement:

1 Put the aft foot across to the far side. Rise slightly, pivot 180° on the balls of the feet in a squatting or kneeling stance, and facing forward as you pivot. Keep your head down, otherwise it will be hit by the boom.

2 The boom will gybe when you are midway across the boat. At this point, deliberately stop moving. Instead, move very quickly from wherever you are to a position where you have three-point stability with your buttocks sitting securely on the new deck and both your feet on the floor.

The second routine is four hand, arm and body movements, all performed very quickly:

3 Move the tiller extension towards you to steer the boat towards the boom. This starts the turn.

4 When the boat is running by the lee 15–20°, do four things very quickly:

- Give the sheet a sharp tug to trigger the sail to gybe.
- Simultaneously move quickly to the new side.
- Also reverse the turn to steer the boat momentarily towards the boom on its new side. (For practical purposes, you do this by carrying the tiller extension with you as you move your body quickly.)

5 After a brief moment, centre the tiller.

The third routine is to steer towards the new aiming point and later to change hands on the sheet and tiller extension:

6 When the boat is steady, steer towards the new aiming point.

7 When convenient, pinch the tiller extension lightly under your thigh.

8 Change hands on the sheet.

9 With the now-free aft hand, pick up the tiller extension.

First practise 1, 2 and 3, but this time the timing is different:

- Put the aft foot across.
- Rise slightly, pivot 180° on the balls of the feet in a squatting stance, facing forward as you pivot. (In heavier boats, kneel to give yourself three point stability for a stronger tug.) Move smoothly and deliberately. Keep your head down or otherwise it will be hit by the boom.
- Then move very quickly from mid-position to sit on the new deck.

Put it together like this:

- Reverse the tiller extension.
- Put the aft foot across.
- Move the tiller extension towards you to steer the boat towards the boom. This starts the turn.
- As the boat turns, rise and pivot deliberately.
- When the boat is running by the lee 15–20°, do three things simultaneously and another almost immediately after –
    1 Give the sheet a sharp tug to trigger the sail to gybe.
    2 Move the body very quickly from mid-position to the new deck.
    3 Reverse the turn sharply. Steer the boat towards the boom on its new side.
    4 And then, almost immediately, centre the tiller.

The first priority is to control the roll caused by the gybe, and this is done by reversing the turn as the boom gybes. Then almost immediately thereafter, centre the tiller, and then resume the turn towards the new aiming point.

As soon as convenient following the gybe, change hands.

Timing

The gybe is quick. In strong winds the sail will exert big sudden reversed forces, and firm decisive control is essential. How long? An initial modest rate of turn will give surest control, say, 15° per second, so the gybe goes like this:

- Start the turn.
- Judge when to tug.
- Do 1, 2 and 3 simultaneously, and 4 immediately thereafter, and that's it.

Once you tug, it is all over. Total time, downwind, is 3 to 4 seconds.

The appearance of the ideal gybe is a single flowing manoeuvre in which the boat turns until 1, 2 and 3 all happen simultaneously, followed almost instantly by 4, and it's finished. The subsequent changing hands with the boat under secure control is almost an anticlimax.

(Note: If the sail gybes sooner than you expect, simply accept it and immediately carry on with 2, 3 and 4.)

The conventional gybe, the follower

There is no typical follower's gybe. The key difference between leader and almost all followers is that the follower tends to wait for the gybe to occur, and then adopts crisis management and works his controls one at a time without co-ordination. This leads to a wide variety of outcomes – none of which win races.

My experience over the past few years is that nobody has previously encouraged the typical follower to think any manoeuvre through in a logical manner, and to point out how much easier it all becomes if you co-ordinate your steering, sail trimming and balance movements efficiently.

The most common errors are:

- Indecision – reluctance to start the gybe.
- Indecisiveness – waiting for the boat to gybe, rather than making it gybe.
- Not co-ordinating – doing only one thing at a time.
- Not steering for balance following the gybe.
- Reluctance to steer with your arm behind your back until the appropriate time to change hands offers.

All other problems flow from these five.

26.5.2 ■ THE APPARENT WIND GYBE

Dynamics

The gybe of an apparent wind sailboat is different from all the other turning manoeuvres, because by its nature the gybe is necessarily a sequence of events, and so cannot be regarded or handled as a short burst of synchronised co-ordinated activity. The self-evident difference between Fig 26.7 and Figs 26.8 and 26.9 shows just how different these dynamics are.

A second difference is practical. Up to this point this chapter has described the techniques of the helm of a singlehanded dinghy. If the crew is more than one, this technique may change not at all if the extra person is a passenger, and much more if the forward hand is a skilled co-ordinating sailor who shares the tasks.

But apparent wind sailing by its nature implies an asymmetric spinnaker and a forward hand who knows what he/she is doing. Two people can share a sequence of tasks in more than one way. As an example, the tack and gybe sections of Chapter 15 describe the extraordinary evolution of very different sequences and task-sharing as one alert crew sought to develop more efficient overall manoeuvring techniques. So this section and those that follow will discuss what needs to happen and why and when, but will not try to prescribe *who* does what. How they co-ordinate is up to the crew.

The iceboat gybe

Fig 2.1 shows the situation prior to the simplest apparent wind gybe possible. In this photo the iceboat is tacking downwind on starboard gybe at about 60 knots or more, in a true wind of about 10 knots. If the wind is northerly it will be heading about southwest. (The vectors are too long to draw to scale on a page this size, so we will use words.)

An iceboat gybe will involve a skater's curve from southwest through south to southeast. Skeetas are strongly built and quite heavy – about 600lb I understand – so it will have lots of momentum. Friction drag of the runners on the ice is minimal, and aerodynamic drag is small. So the boat will be moving at about 50 knots as it passes through south, and still be sailing at about 40 knots as it passes through a southeast heading and approaches east to bring the apparent wind to the left of dead ahead by a useful angle. At this point, appropriate tugging on the sheet will 'pop' the wing mast (and the battens) to the right angle and shape for port tack. From this position, the boat can accelerate again to its target speed of 60 knots or more as it bears away to a heading about southeast.

The iceboat travels so much faster than the wind at the start of the gybe that throughout the gybe the apparent wind will remain strong and from near straight ahead. Prior to the gybe, the heeling force was from the right (in the photo the starboard runner is off the ice). Following the gybe, it will be from the left. During this sort of gybe there is only one reversal of heeling force. It can be sudden as the mast 'pops' and efficient flow attaches. The control response is to turn instantly downwind to steer for balance, for otherwise a capsize can occur. This is why iceboat rules give right of way to the *windward* boat, for safety reasons.

The 49er lighter-wind gybe

The bigger skiffs (and now the foil Moths) have some of the dynamics of the iceboat in lighter winds.

Fig 26.8C shows that a 49er tacks downwind at 12 knots in a 6 knot wind, and at 14 knots in a 9 knot wind. So in lighter winds it can enter the gybe sailing substantially faster than the wind, like the iceboat, and the apparent wind will blow from ahead – like the iceboat at the start of the gybe, and not from behind like the Laser.

Fig 26.8B shows the S-curve typical of every apparent wind gybe. The boat is sailing at target speed and heading in both segment Y–0 and mirror image segment 9–Z. But if in turning from Y to Z the turn is arrested between 3 and 4 on the heading of TZ in diagram A in Fig 26.8C, the spinnaker will not be full with attached flow, and the boat will sail slowly indefinitely on that heading. Only by turning to segment 5–6 in diagram B, and T6 in diagram C, can the spinnaker be filled with attached flow. When this happens, substantial drive force is regained and the boat will accelerate as it sails along the curve 6–7, 7–8, 8–9 to regain target speed at segment 9–Z in diagram B. Note in diagram C how much the apparent wind swings forward from 6W through 7W, 8W, 9W to ZW as the boat accelerates, and how much the boat bears away from heading T6 through T7 etc to TZ as it accelerates to stabilise and sail steadily along segment 9Z on heading TZ, which is the mirror image of TY.

The inset diagram C in Fig 26.8 shows how the 49er and the apparent wind behave in a gybe in a true wind of 9 knots (the diagram format is as in Fig 26.7):

- TW is the 9 knot true wind to scale.
- TY is the boat speed and direction, and YW is the apparent wind speed and direction at target speed (14 knots) as the boat approaches the start of the gybe at 0 along segment Y–0.
- T1, 1W, T2, 2W and T3, 3W show how the boat slows; the apparent wind decreases from port, and falls to almost nothing but is still from ahead as it changes from port to starboard between 2W and 3W.
- In such a gybe the mainsail will waft lazily from starboard to port. In the near calm there can be no force from the sails, so there can be no sudden significant reversal of heel force.
- From T3, 3W to T6, 6W the boat continues to turn and slow to a little less than 7 knots as the apparent wind increases from starboard. During these seconds the asymmetric spinnaker is handled and trimmed until it fills on the new tack between T5 and T6. See D1 and 2 below.
- When the spinnaker fills with attached flow, drive force approaching one-quarter to one-third of the boat's weight develops abruptly and the boat accelerates strongly. Initially it sails in the direction of the segment 5 to 6.
- The vector triangles T6, 6W, T7, 7W, T8, 8W and T9, 9W show how the acceleration of the boat from 6.5 knots at T6 to 14 knots at TZ causes the direction of the apparent wind to swing from near NE at 6W to near ESE at Z–W. During this acceleration period of about 5 seconds, the skipper:
  - Will be sailing the boat at its stability limit – that is, as close to the wind as is possible so as to sail in the strongest apparent wind in which he can keep the boat upright. This will give him the fastest acceleration. So the length of the apparent wind vectors 7W, 8W, 9W etc – that is, the speed of the apparent wind – is governed by what the boat and crew can stand without heeling significantly.
  - Will be steering for balance as he probes and sails at the stability limit.
  - Will be bearing away as the apparent wind goes forward from 6W to Z–W.
- Point Z is the mirror image of point Y and is the 14 knot target speed and direction in a 9 knot true wind. Only when the crew reach this point, and not before, is the gybe manoeuvre complete.

Crew tasks and handling technique

The essential tasks of the helm, the forward hand, and the boat's response are:

Table 26.1 Crew tasks in lighter wind apparent wind gybe

Time from start	Segment task	Crew member
0 to 3	Start turn towards new aiming point	Helm
0 to 2–3	Hold old spinnaker sheet	F/hand
3–4 to 5–6	Trim in new spinnaker sheet	F/hand
3–4 to 5–6	Continue turn, plus steer for balance as new spin sheet is trimmed in	Helm
5–6 to 9–Z	Fill spinnaker, trim for maximum drive force	F/hand
5–6	Sudden heel force	Boat
5–6	Reverse turn, then steer for balance	Helm
6–7 to 9–Z	As boat accelerates –	
	Probe and sail at stability limit for fastest acceleration	
	Trim sails for maximum drive force	
	Steer for balance	
	Bear away as apparent wind goes forward	Both crew busy
9–Z	At target speed and heading on new gybe	Gybe complete

This gybe is typical of the dynamics of all apparent wind gybes in lighter winds. Time and distance lost per gybe in the 49er in a 9 knot wind: 3 seconds, 18m, 3.5 lengths.

Practical points

The optimum rate of turn from 0 to 6 will be governed by the dynamics of the boat. Too slow a turn and the slow turner will see a faster turner accelerate and enjoy target speed sooner. Too fast a turn will see the boat near stopped by 6. Whatever rate of turn is found fastest, it is critical that the skipper then repeat that rate of turn consistently so that confident, efficient crew co-ordination based on anticipation of a fixed rate of turn can develop. (See Sections 15.10 and Sections 27.10 and 29.11.)

There are two very good practical reasons why it is faster to delay the handling, setting and trimming of the asymmetric spinnaker rather than rush it.

1 Spinnaker 'wineglass'

In any gybe in which the apparent wind is from behind at any time, if both spinnaker sheets are allowed to run free the leech of the asymmetric spinnaker can blow forward of the luff. When this happens, a 'wineglass' is likely to occur on a proportion of occasions, and wineglasses take a long time to unravel.

The technique to avoid a wineglass is to tighten the 'old' spinnaker sheet as the boat enters the gybe, and hold it taut until the spinnaker just begins to press against the forestay in the apparent wind from the new side. Then the new sheet is drawn in as fast as possible. This involves pulling in some 4–5m of sheet to draw the spinnaker clew forward about 2–2.5m to and around the forestay, then aft to trim and set the spinnaker in the new apparent wind. In practice, this task cannot be completed in less than about 2 to 3 seconds.

2 Spinnaker 'flog'

As the wind speed increases, there will be a speed at which the natural frequency of a fluttering spinnaker (or flag) will synchronise with the eddy formation of the air (the Karman trail) and at this wind speed the spinnaker, if uncontrolled, will flog in a sequence of oscillations in which the crosswind drag will change rapidly from almost nothing to great yanks that will threaten to capsize the boat. In the stronger winds in which this can happen the technique to avoid this is to hold the spinnaker clew for a little longer on the 'old' side – that is, until some significant pressure builds – then draw the clew around the forestay with care.

This results in a predictable build in pressure and heeling force as the spinnaker is held, followed by a period in which the heel force reduces but the spinnaker never flogs as the clew is drawn forward to the forestay, the heel force increases as the clew is drawn aft, then there is a great surge in heel force and also 'power' as the spinnaker fills and unstalls. In practice this adds another second or two to the time between when it is safe to start pulling in the new sheet and the time the spinnaker is trimmed in, fills, and the boat starts accelerating. The benefit is that the boat can be controlled with certainty in stronger winds because the big spinnaker never flogs.

The 29er strong-wind gybe

Given equal excellence of design, smaller boats sail more slowly than larger boats. Further, a property of all boats is that as the wind becomes stronger, the boat speed to wind speed ratio becomes less. Inset diagram A in Fig 26.9 shows that in a 6 knot wind the 29er can tack downwind at a boat speed of 9 knots – that is, at a boat speed to wind speed ratio of 1.5 – while in 20 knots of wind it can sail at about 19–20 knots, a ratio of 1. In practice, this means that the smaller skiffs will have some of the gybe dynamics of wind-from-behind boats in stronger winds.

Fig 26.9C shows the effect of this. A 29er that gybes in a 20 knot wind starts from a target boat speed about wind speed, and as it turns and slows the boat speed becomes progressively slower than the wind speed. In this situation, the apparent wind must blow from behind as it changes sides, and the mainsail will gybe with a substantial reversal of heeling force, exactly as in any other wind-from-behind boat. At T1–1W the apparent wind is 6 knots from just aft of the port beam. At T2–W2 it is 5 knots from near astern, at T3–W3 it is 8 knots from near the starboard quarter, and at T4–W4 it is 13 knots from near the starboard beam. The mainsail will necessarily gybe between 3 and 4.

In all other respects, this gybe will be identical with the wind-from-ahead gybe of the faster 49er in lighter wind illustrated in Fig 26.8. So the practical consequence is that the tasks and responses in the Fig 26.9 stronger wind gybe will be identical except that there will be one added event – the heel force will reverse when the mainsail gybes (as well as when the spinnaker fills later) – and one added task – to reverse the turn then steer for balance following the mainsail gybe (as well as following the subsequent spinnaker fill).

Crew tasks in strong-wind gybe

In stronger winds and/or smaller boats the crew's essential tasks and the boat's response become:

Table 26.2 Crew tasks in stronger wind apparent wind gybe

Time from start	Segment task	Crew member
0 to 2–3	Start turn towards new aiming point	
	Change sides quickly, change hands	Helm
0 to 2–3	Hold old spinnaker sheet	F/hand
3 to 4	Mainsail gybes; sudden reversal of heel force	Boat
3 to 4	Reverse turn, then steer for balance	Helm
3–4 to 5–6	Trim in new spinnaker sheet	F/hand
3–4 to 5–6	Continue turn, plus steer for balance as new spin sheet is trimmed in	Helm
5–6 to 8–Z	Spinnaker fills, trim for maximum drive force	F/hand
	Sudden heel force	Boat
5–6	Reverse turn momentarily, then steer for balance	Helm
6–7 to 8–Z	As boat accelerates –	
	Probe and sail at stability limit for fastest acceleration	
	Trim sails	
	Steer for balance	
	Bear away as apparent wind goes forward	Both crew are busy
8–Z	At target speed and heading on new gybe	Gybe complete

This more complex sequence is typical of the dynamics of apparent wind gybes in stronger winds. Time lost per gybe: 3.5 seconds, 22m, 4 lengths.

Apparent wind gybe notes

For practical purposes, the faster the boat and the slower the apparent wind, the easier the gybe. The irregularity of wind and waves can be used by skilled crews to make life easier. Where there is an option, the best time to gybe will be at the peak of a gust when the boat is sailing fastest and the wind speed is decreasing, and when surfing a big wave. The worst time will be in the increasing wind at the beginning of a gust, or when blocked by slow waves.

As an example, look at what Scott Babbage says about waves in Section 27.10. The big rolling waves near Treasure Island were not a problem. With the long fetch of the 20 knot wind across the bay from the Gate, the waves would have been rolling at, say, 12–13 knots. There was no tidal current near Treasure Island, so the speed of the waves over the bottom would also have been 13 knots. The boat's best speed midway through a gybe is about 13 knots, so the boats were not baulked by the waves. The apparent wind would have been 6–7 knots from behind, and in these conditions the first reversal of heel force as the boom swept across created no significant problems.

But off St Francis YC, the fetch was shorter so the waves were shorter and slower – let us guess, say, 10–11 knots. This is the wave speed through the water. Now subtract the speed of the ebb current through the gate of, say, 5–6 knots, and these waves roll at about 5 knots over the bottom. Here you suddenly have the situation where the boats are blocked at perhaps 5 knots 'speed over the bottom' in a 20 knot wind. This gives an environment with an apparent wind from behind of 15 knots in waves that are steeper and irregular due to the wind-against-tide effect.

In this situation the 29ers had exactly the same 'reversal of heel force during the mainsail gybe' problem as any wind-from-behind boat would have had, plus the need to control the boat through the second spinnaker-fill reversal a few seconds later. Skippers who chose to try to change hands on sheet and tiller late in the gybe were unable to steer for balance with authority in a complex situation, and in consequence suffered control problems and capsize.

At the World Championships at Weymouth a year later, the winds late in day two were just as strong as at San Francisco, but the problems had vanished. A more efficient gybing technique had been substituted. Silja Lehtinen started by reversing her tiller extension pre-gybe to pre-empt any mid-gybe tangle with the sheet, and proceeded with a measured, consistent rate of turn with continuous steer-for-balance control throughout the gybe. Whether she changed hands early or late I do not know and it does not matter. What is critical is that she did not change hands mid-gybe.

Note how Julian Bethwaite in Section 15.10, Scott Babbage in Sections 27.11 and 29.6, and Rohan Veal in Section 28.8 (page 406), all emphasise the need in the gybe for:

- Consistent rate of turn.
- Continuous steer-for-balance control.
- In addition, they are unanimous in the exhortation 'Don't interrupt vital control sequences by changing hands mid-gybe. Change early if you can, otherwise don't change until the end, when it is safe to do so.'

G.1   Apparent wind gybe summary – skipper

- Scans wind, and wave pattern immediately ahead.
- In unsteady conditions, considers increasing speed prior to gybe.
- Calls gybe.
- Always looks ahead and turns at consistent rate of turn to enable crew co-ordination to be based on anticipation.
- Moves to new side early.
- Changes hands early – prior to any mainsail gybe.
- Steers for balance with uninterrupted authority through 'busy' part of gybe.
- Steers firmly under rig when mainsail gybes, and again when spinnaker fills.
- Does all this well; does little else.

As Julian says, 'If the boat capsizes, it is the skipper's fault.'

G.2   Apparent wind gybe summary – forward hand

- Stays on old windward side early to balance early cross to new side by skipper.
- Trims in and holds old spinnaker sheet until spinnaker presses against forestay in new apparent wind; then either:
  - Trims in new spinnaker sheet as quickly as possible to fill spinnaker, *or*
  - In stronger winds, pauses briefly and moves onto trapeze early, then trims in new spinnaker sheet deliberately to maintain heeling force without spinnaker flog to balance against through the trim-in process.
- Trims spinnaker for maximum drive force through acceleration and bear-away process.

26.6 ■ STRAIGHT-LINE SAILING

DEFINITIONS
I will use the term 'clock' to mean a short-term clockwise change in the wind direction, and 'back' to mean a short-term change in an anticlockwise direction. The meanings of 'veer' and 'clock' are identical in the northern hemisphere, but the meaning of veer – 'change direction (esp. of wind) sunwise' – alters with the hemisphere. The meaning of clock remains constant.

Basics

Straight-line sailing covers everything in sailing other than the tack, gybe and mark rounding turning manoeuvres described above. In Fig 26.11 it is divided into its four dynamically different arcs:

Arc I   is sailing to windward.
Arc II   is close reaching.
Arc III   is the reaching and broad reaching arc.
Arc IV   covers running.

Straight-line sailing at target speed is the most important and the most difficult of all manoeuvres to perform consistently and well. This is because it is in itself a continuing series of small manoeuvres in response to three destabilising factors: the natural unsteadiness in both speed and direction of the real wind; the increased drag due to 'bad' waves, both natural and man-made; and tactical interference by other boats.

These notes discuss the handling techniques, and waves are discussed in *HPS-1*, Chapters 13, 14 and 15. There are many good books about tactics.

The basics of straight-line sail trim are described in *HPS-1*, Chapters 22, 23, 24 and 25. This material remains accurate, so will not be repeated here.

In winds from calm up to the design wind, roll can always be controlled by body movement, so there is never any problem with roll control in winds up to about 11–12 knots. This is why the 'luff for everything' technique can deliver acceptable straight-line results in light to moderate winds.

To better understand the wind's roughness, I went back into the Kingston tower traces (the source data for Figs 3.4 to 3.11), the Dynes data of Figs 3.33 and 5.1, and the windsock data of Fig 3.22, but looked at the extremes instead of the means. For reality, I took a turbometer out to the end of the local jetty on some 'rough wind' days and listed the gust maximum and lull minimum speeds, and the clock and back maxima. All the data confirmed what the Dynes traces show: that individual 'gust max to lull min' ratios of 4, 5, and 6 to 1 in wind speed, and surprisingly big clocks and backs, are commonplace when the wind is rough. From this I have drawn Fig 21.4B, C and D as useful and relatively conservative traces of the extremes through which the sailor must at times control her boat.

26.7 ■ Arc I: To windward

A The leader's basic technique

When sailing upwind, in Arc I in Fig 26.10, in the real, unsteady wind:

- In winds from calm up to the design wind, the leader controls her boat by using both of her hands and her body
  - She steers with one hand.
  - She trims sail with the other hand.
  - She moves her body.
- Her reward is to sail to windward (in the notional boat of Fig 21.3) and an 11 knot wind at a VMG up to 5.1 knots (Fig 21.3A and Table 21.1).
- In all stronger winds her body is assumed to be at full hike, so cannot move further; therefore to control her boat she uses both hands
  - She steers to the wind with one hand.
  - She trims sail to control roll with simultaneous but independent adjustment of the sheet with the other.
- Her reward is to sail to windward at a VMG up to 6.5 knots (Fig 21.3D).

B The follower's technique

When sailing upwind, in Arc I in Fig 26.11, in the real, unsteady wind:

- In winds from calm up to the design wind, the follower tends to control her boat by using one hand and her body
  - She steers with one hand.
  - She holds the sheet immobile with the other hand.
  - She moves her body.
- Her reward is to sail to windward in an 11 knot wind at a VMG up to 5.1 knots (Fig 21.3A).
- In all stronger winds, her body is assumed to be at full hike, so cannot be moved much, so she uses one hand
  - She steers with one hand. She luffs as necessary to keep the boat upright.
  - She holds the sheet immobile with the other hand.

- Her reward is that she does not need to co-ordinate the movements of her two hands.
- But the cost is that with this technique she sails to windward at a VMG about 4.4 knots (Fig 21.3B). This is about two-thirds of the leader's speed. This is why she follows.

This pattern, in which all sailors tend to sail at about the same target speed in lighter winds, though huge differences in performance open up as soon as the wind becomes rougher or stronger, is exactly what we see on the water, so let us have a look at the two techniques: why the follower sails as she does, and why the leader's technique is so much faster.

Let us start with the follower.

C Typical follower history

This is discussed in Section 24.13. Most sailors are self-taught, or imitate and learn by crewing for others who are self-taught – or learn from instructors who are not themselves fast sailors.

At this stage in her career, the sailor's objective is control, and specifically to control roll to keep the boat upright. Her first survival lessons are:

- That up to a certain wind strength the boat can be kept upright by body movement.
- In stronger winds this is no longer possible.
- In stronger winds gusts heel the boat.
- If the boat heels too much, it can always be brought upright by luffing (turning towards the wind).

What happens when a boat turns into the wind and the sail trim is not simultaneously trimmed in is that the angle of attack of the sail to the apparent wind is reduced as Fig 21.1 from D towards A, and the sail's coefficient of lift and crosswind force from d towards a in lower diagram to the point where the heeling moment becomes less than the stability of the boat. At this point equilibrium is restored.

The technique of hiking plus luffing is efficient in bringing the boat upright, particularly when sailing to windward, and it is simple, but for the reasons given in Fig 21.3A, B and C and Table 21.1 it is slow, so it wins no races.

Consider the situation in which a novice sailor enjoys practising in lighter winds. Gusts heel the boat most when sailing to windward, but in winds up to the design wind (10–11 knots) she can control roll by hiking. She can read about how to set efficient sail shape, and with this technique, plus practice, she can sail almost as fast as anyone else, so she has 'learned to sail'. In stronger winds luffing is most effective when sailing to windward, so in winds up to the design wind and a little stronger, the boat can be kept under adequate control by hiking plus luffing in the gusts, and she can trim sail between gusts. When sailing downwind the apparent wind is much lighter, so problems with roll occur less frequently.

This one-handed 'control roll by luffing' technique presents as simple and consistent. It requires no co-ordination, it enables the novice sailor to learn quickly and become progressively more confident in light winds, and unless very strong reason is advanced for doing something else, this is the technique that becomes embedded and that the great majority of sailors then use for life.

As we have seen, when racing they can sail almost as fast as anyone else in winds up to about 10 knots. In 12 knot unsteady winds this technique becomes noticeably slower, and in stronger unsteady winds they cease to be competitive and begin to have real difficulty in remaining upright.

This is the history and profile of the typical follower. There are a lot of them. Their most revealing trait is that in a gust, they work the tiller extension furiously with one hand and clutch the sheet immobile with the other.

D Leader's detail technique – direction

The leader's first point of departure from the follower is that she wants to win, so she starts with two objects, not one:

- Her first object is to sail fast.
- Her second object is to control her boat efficiently so she can sail fast.

She knows that all winds are unsteady in direction – sometimes very unsteady, as in Fig 21.4C and D. She knows that she will sail fastest to windward if she sails her boat at the best angle to the wind, so her first objective is to hold that best angle as accurately as possible by steering to follow the changes in wind direction. This task occupies the hand with which she holds the tiller extension.

She knows that all winds are unsteady in speed (Fig 21.4 again), and that when the wind is strong this unsteadiness will roll the boat. Unlike the follower, she takes this in her stride by taking the sheet in her other hand and with it she trims sail independently – that is, she eases sheet as necessary in the gusts and recovers it in the lulls to keep her boat upright whatever the wind strength.

At root, when sailing to windward:

- The follower uses a 'steer only' uncoordinated one-control-at-a-time technique. This is simple in that it needs no co-ordination, but the price is poor performance and loss of control in stronger winds.
- The leader uses a more efficient 'steer plus trim sail' simultaneous independent co-ordination two-control technique. Her reward is to sail faster and in control in all winds.

E Wind direction and steering

As wind direction changes, the direction from which the apparent wind approaches the luff of the jib changes about twice as much as at the masthead (*HPS-1*, Section 22.5). So while responding to the tufts is a case of 'fuzzy logic' and responding to running averages, in practice it is extremely sensitive and accurate. Tufts stream as Fig 21.1B only in the smooth flow of a wind tunnel. In the real wind they always flick occasionally, so the behaviour of the leeward tufts in the progression from 21.1A through B to C is almost never flicking at 21.1A, periodically flicking at B, and agitating at C. The unsteadiness of the windward tufts goes the other way.

The leader's first focus is to steer her boat accurately to the wind, and to do this she watches her jib tufts. She corrects any change in tuft behaviour by steering the bow away from the tufts which are fluttering more than they should. The quick mnemonic is 'move the tiller extension towards the fluttering tufts' – that is, if the leeward tufts flutter more than they should, move the tiller extension to leeward for the correct turn.

This is the technique that becomes embedded in her subconscious.

Tufts can stick to the sail due to rain, salt, cobwebs, etc. When this happens, the leader's technique from the days before tufts were invented (in about 1965) is a good fallback. We used to sense the optimum VMG pointing angle by feel, and sailed at that angle, but did a little 'wriggle' every few seconds which was a quick but smooth luff to the point where either some part of the jib went 'soft' and indicated 'too high', or the boat began to roll to windward, and we immediately bore away to return to the fastest angle.

Particularly in the lighter winds when the sails can be trimmed close to point D (Fig 21.1), the sail force does not change much when the wind 'lifts' in direction, nor is there any visual indication, and a sailor who was sailing solely by feel often would not realise that the wind had lifted and she could point higher without loss of speed.

By using the test-wriggle technique every, say, 10 seconds, we were often pleasantly surprised at how far we could luff. We then fell back only through the minimum angle and in this way detected and enjoyed more lifts than our non-testing rivals.

F Leader's detail technique – roll

Concerning wind speed, the leader is very conscious of the complex way in which the wind speed changes (Fig 21.4) with its slower gust and lull pattern plus superimposed quick gust peaks. But, like the follower, she realises that there are better things to attend to than try to respond to every change of wind speed.

The practical thing to do is to respond only to roll, because, other things being equal, provided the crew are at full hike and the boat is correctly trimmed and upright it will be sailing its fastest.

So the leader's second focus is to keep her boat upright, and to do this she senses its roll. She corrects any departure from upright by adjusting sail trim to restore the mast to the vertical.

The quick mnemonic is 'move the sheet in the same direction as the masthead' – that is, if the masthead starts moving to leeward, move the sheet hand to leeward to ease sail.

This is the second part of the co-ordinated technique that becomes embedded in her subconscious.

G Co-ordinated technique

The nature of the apparent wind coupled with the dynamics of the boat invite a beautifully simple technique to handle an otherwise complex situation. This is the logic:

Fig 21.4 shows that the speed and direction of the true wind both change irregularly and are not correlated. When measured as true wind at a stationary point – for example, the anchored committee vessel – speed and direction will combine momentarily in any one of nine permutations that are random. That is:

Table 26.3 Behaviour of apparent wind, to windward

Wind speed		Wind direction	
	Backs	No change	Clocks
Decreases	Decreases and backs	Decreases and no change	Decreases and clocks
No change	No change and backs	No change, no change	No change and clocks
Increases	Increases and backs	Increases and no change	Increases and clocks

But from the point of view of the leader who crosses the start line adjacent to the committee vessel at target speed, the addition of her boat speed to the true wind generates an apparent wind that is much more orderly. Let us assume that she is on starboard tack, and consider the four extreme permutations.

Decrease in speed and back in direction

- Decrease in true wind speed will swing the apparent wind more towards the boat's centreline, so the back in direction will be accentuated.
  - Windward tufts will agitate. Boat will start to roll to windward. The helm will bear away to correct. The hand with the tiller extension will initially move towards the body (ie towards the fluttering tufts), and in the direction in which the masthead is moving.
  - Back in direction will reduce the angle of attack of the wind on the sail, and the boat will roll to windward. The helm will tighten the sheet to correct. The sheet hand will initially move towards the body.
- Total initial response. The tiller hand moves towards the body. The sheet hand also initially moves towards the body. *Both hands initially move the same way* (towards the fluttering tufts in lighter winds, or in the direction the masthead is moving in stronger winds).
- Subsequent response. The tiller hand will arrest the turn at the point where the tufts stream as desired. The sheet hand will independently optimise sail trim at that heading and wind speed by adjusting the sheet.

Decrease in speed and clock in direction

- Decrease in true wind speed will swing the apparent wind towards the boat's centreline. This will oppose and so reduce the clock in the true wind direction.
  - Leeward tufts will agitate. The helm will luff to correct. The tiller hand will move away from the body.
  - Clock will increase the angle of attack of the wind on the sail, and the boat will roll to leeward. The helm will ease the sheet to correct. The sheet hand will initially move away from the body.
- Total response. The tiller hand moves away from the body. The sheet hand initially moves away from the body. *Both hands move the same way* (towards the fluttering tufts, and in the direction the masthead is moving).
- Subsequent response. The tiller hand arrests the turn. The sheet hand will independently optimise sail trim with the sheet.

The 'increase and back' and 'increase and clock' permutations reach the same conclusion. On port tack, the whole pattern is repeated as the mirror image.

So it turns out that the leader's technique of continuously controlling both heading and roll calls for no black magic, because whatever sheet movement is called for by trimming accurately to follow the boat's roll, an initial movement of the tiller *in the same direction as the masthead is moving* will almost always be the correct initial movement to make to correct the associated change in apparent wind direction.

Therefore the control response to the wind's random unsteadiness when sailing to windward turns out to be much simpler than at first appears. The random true wind has become an orderly apparent wind. That is:

> • Whenever a change in wind speed and/or direction causes the boat to start to roll, *start* the correction by moving *both* hands in the same direction as the masthead is moving. (In lighter winds, move the hands towards the fluttering tufts.) This is quick, automatic, and requires no consideration.
> • Once the correction is started, the hands then move independently and deliberately.
> – The tiller hand moves delicately as it follows the tufts in responding to the new apparent wind direction.
> – The sheet hand moves quickly as far as is necessary to stop the masthead moving away from the vertical, then immediately starts a slow return to mid-excursion in a slow control movement which returns the mast smoothly to vertical over the next few seconds if no further change occurs meantime.

H Control dynamics

In my flying instruction days we used the terms 'ballistic' and 'feedback' with special meanings:

Ballistic control was to sense error, apply a big correction, wait until the error is not only corrected, but over-corrected to the point of over-shooting the other way, at which point a second big correction is applied the other way – and so on, like a child learning to ride a bicycle. Ballistic control with its brief wait between each sudden control movement leads to oscillation.

Feedback control is to sense the error (the masthead moving away from the vertical), apply an initial quick correction big enough, but only big enough, to stop it moving away from the vertical, then immediately – that is, in anticipation, without waiting – reduce the correction slowly and control it so that the masthead returns to the vertical slowly and under control, and never over-shoots.

In practice, the easiest way to apply feedback control is to use a 'quick then slow' saw-tooth technique; sense the error, make the initial correction quickly, then immediately start to return the control towards its mid-position. The immediate application of the slower reducing control before the masthead can begin to accelerate the other way is the key to suppressing potential oscillation.

To show how it works we will look at two examples. In both cases we will assume the notional boat in Fig 21.3 and Table 21.1 to be sailing close hauled, port tack, in the unsteady wind of Fig 26.4C – that is, at and above the design wind so body movement can be ignored.

First example

• Boat at target speed in an 11 knot lull is hit by a 15 knot gust and back in direction.
• Inputs – helm observes leeward tufts agitating indicating back, and feels boat begin to roll sharply to leeward.
• Initial responses (simultaneous)
– Small tiller movement to leeward to start luff to correct for change in wind direction.
– Big quick sheet movement to leeward to correct sharp roll to leeward.
• Further responses (independent)
– Tiller is centred when tufts indicate that correct angle to wind has been restored.
– As masthead stops moving to leeward, the hand with the sheet immediately starts a slow return movement towards mid-position. If a second gust peak rolls boat further to leeward, sheet is again eased quickly, then the slow recovery is immediately resumed. The ideal is that the hand with the sheet (or traveller) will return to its mid-position (ideal sail trim) as the masthead resumes the vertical some seconds later. In practice, the next unsteadiness in the wind will probably have occurred before then; for example, if the next roll is to windward, both hands will stop whatever they were doing about the previous roll to leeward and both will make a quick movement to windward to stop the windward roll, then the sheet hand immediately starts its slow movement towards the mid-position.

Except for unusual peaks or lulls, the body is held steady.

Second example

- Boat on port tack at target speed in a 15 knot gust enters an 11 knot lull and clock in direction.
- Inputs – helm observes windward tufts agitating indicating clock, and feels boat begin to roll sharply to windward. In this situation of pointing too high and with reduced drive force, the boat will lose speed at the rate of about 15% per second, so prompt decisive action is called for.
- Initial responses (simultaneous)
  - Big tiller movement to windward to bear away quickly to correct for change in wind direction.
  - Quick sheet movement to windward to oversheet momentarily to correct roll to windward. (This will also increase the turbine blade effect on the jib, and reduce the speed loss.)
- Further responses (independent)
  - Tiller is centred when tufts indicate that boat has turned through optimum VMG angle and is at acceleration mode angle to new wind.
  - As masthead approaches and reaches vertical, hand with sheet moves quickly to leeward to 'acceleration mode' trim.
- Boat sails in acceleration mode for some seconds to regain target speed.
- With target speed resumed, helm points higher and sheets in to resume maximum VMG mode.

Note: If the end of the gust is obvious from the marks on the water (often it isn't), a third, even more efficient, technique is to bear away in the last of the gust as you approach the lull; in this way, you avoid losing speed when you enter it. (See Lazich in Section 29.7 – 'If a lull is coming and you don't know about it ...')

There is no black magic in the simultaneous independent co-ordination close-hauled techniques above. The mental picture ceases to be a crew who sail stop-start with their bodies bobbing in and out of the boat, and becomes a crew who adopt a body position of less than full hike in lighter winds, full hike at and above the design wind, and who sail smoothly with sheet hand moving fluently, tiller hand moving almost imperceptibly (Fig 25.1 between manoeuvres), and bodies moving not at all other than smoothly to adjust to the slower changes in wind speed.

The rewards for sailing like this are substantial. The notes above, and Fig 21.3 and Table 21.1, show that:

- In winds from calm up to the design wind
  - The follower can sail as fast or almost as fast as the leader. (The follower's coarser rudder movements hold her back.)
- In all stronger winds
  - The follower with her 'steer only' technique sails progressively more slowly and with progressively more uncertain control.
  - The leader with her 'steer plus trim sail' technique sails progressively and substantially faster (leader VMG 5.8 knots, follower VMG 4.4 knots) and retains secure control in all winds.

The different dynamics of different boats

As soon as the inefficient technique of 'luff for everything' is replaced by the efficient technique of 'steer to the wind, and play sheet to stay upright', the sailor has the basis for the fastest straight-line sailing possible from his boat.

While a technique of 'steer at a constant angle to the wind – ease sheet to stay upright' will always give fastest speed when reaching straight for the next mark, a refinement of the technique according to the dynamics of the boat will usually give a yet faster VMG when sailing to windward. The extremes are the yacht and the iceboat.

When sailing to windward in a keel yacht with a speed-limiting drag curve such as Fig 10.3 (ie Soling, Etchells, Yngling), the practical situation is that in the stronger gusts, provided that the sails are eased and flattened appropriately, the fastest VMG will be achieved if the boat is sailed almost at a constant speed. To do this will mean pointing higher in the gusts. Mark Bethwaite, World Soling Champion in 1982, found it fastest to point about 10° higher on average in the gusts than in the lulls in typical conditions.

When sailing a typical skiff such as the notional Table 21.1 boat, or an Eighteen foot skiff, the heading for fastest VMG in both gust and lull varies very little – only between 43° (in the lull) and 44° (in the gust) – so the hand movements on the tiller extension will be subtly different as between the yacht and the skiff.

When sailing a craft that is not speed-limited by its drag curve, such as the iceboat in Fig 2.1 or the foil Moth in Fig 28.1, it will probably result in a faster VMG if the boat is pointed a little lower and sailed much faster in the gusts. The iceboat, for example, may sail to windward in the 10 knot lull on good ice at about 30 knots. In the gust it will achieve a faster VMG if pointed a shade lower and accelerated to about 40 knots, and then driven at that speed through the gust.

26.8 ■ Arc III: Reaching and broad reaching

A The follower's technique

The really big differences in handling technique between the typical follower and the skilled apparent wind leader occur offwind.

On a broad reach, the follower's 'luff for everything' technique enables her to sail towards the mark and control the boat efficiently in lighter winds. But as the wind becomes progressively stronger, two problems arise.

The first occurs when the wind first becomes strong enough to heel the boat. The helm controls roll by luffing and sailing more crosswind. This has two disadvantages:

1 She is no longer sailing towards the mark. Sailing in the wrong direction wins no races.
2 The boat, now headed crosswind, is subject to the quick gust peaks and lulls, and the crew tend to leap from side to side of the boat to control its roll, rather than getting on with their race and sailing steadily towards the next mark.

The next problem is more serious. In the stronger wind, the boat begins to move fast. A situation is soon reached in which, if a fast-moving boat that is heeled by a gust is turned towards the wind at speed, the turn itself will roll the boat further to leeward, and the combined rolling moments of both the gust and the turn lead to capsize. Fig 22.4 is an extreme example. If, at that speed, the boat were to be luffed (turned sharply to the left) it is obvious that it would simply roll uncontrollably to the right and capsize.

So, in the end, the follower's 'luff for everything' approach is not efficient, in that it cannot even assure control in stronger wind, let alone speed.

B The leader's technique

In the gusts the leader turns the other way. Summarising the technique from Chapter 24:

- As the gusts hit I did *not* luff. At each gust onslaught I turned downwind and eased sheet until the boat was in equilibrium.
- I then steered for balance to keep the boat upright.
- Through the quick lulls and gusts I *did not move* my body.
- Whenever the wind eased I luffed a little (still steering for balance) and trimmed in the sheet. This increased the apparent wind which both increased the heeling force to restore equilibrium and also maintained or increased speed.
- When the next quick gust peak pressed the boat, I again turned downwind for equilibrium.
- Handled in this way the boat followed a 'snaking' course, up in the quick lulls and down in the quick gusts. Throughout, we all kept our bodies still. The boat sailed upright, under control, and flew.

This is 'steer for balance' in action. Its advantage is that it delivers both speed and secure control.

C Training notes

Beginners will have no problems here; they have nothing to unlearn. Some lifetime followers merit sympathy, because the subconscious forces that resist change are sometimes so very strong. The sticking point seems to be the requirement that the boat be turned downwind – with both the slow turn downwind method and the steer for balance method – when the boat heels to leeward. In introducing some sailors to the 59er I sometimes encountered resistance to the point where one follower said, 'I see it and feel it and I understand the physics and see how it works. I admire how you do it, and am certain that I could learn to do it if I had to.

But the difficulty of bringing myself to turn "the wrong way" is so great that I find that I just don't want to. Let's go in…' Most others made the leap, and were soon revelling in a new world of secure control at speeds they had previously only dreamed of.

The key to both understanding and 'feeling' how every factor works is to try each method by itself and learn to use it in isolation – that is, in lighter winds and while very deliberately *not* using any other method. This way, you can observe what happens, accommodate to it, and progress at your own pace. When ready, you can put the factors together with simple, co-ordinated hand movements, and enjoy speed with increasingly certain control.

Start by trying each of these methods on days when there is not too much wind.

D The four methods of roll control

(a) Trimming sail

Easing sheet will always reduce sail heeling force (except when running square). Throughout this exercise move only the sheet.

Head on a close reach. Trim the sail as in C Fig 21.1. Select and sail straight towards an aiming point. Hike as necessary to sail upright, and thereafter *keep still*.

Whenever the wind speed changes, make a quick firm movement of the sheet in or out to correct the roll error.

The nmemonic for initial direction of movement is 'move the sheet hand the same way as the masthead is moving'.

Make the initial excursion proportionate to the error; for a tiny movement of the masthead, likewise make a tiny movement, and bigger for a bigger movement.

The dynamics of the control technique are always a saw-tooth pattern of 'quick then slow', an initial quick ballistic movement to arrest the increasing error, then immediately begin a deliberate slow return movement for 'feedback' return to upright without over-shoot. If you make a big quick movement to correct the roll, and then wait, the masthead will begin to move quickly back towards upright and you will have to make another big quick movement to stop it over-shooting. This way leads to oscillation.

The most practical way to avoid this is to start the slow recovery movement immediately, with no delay at all. So in a short puff, yield quickly then immediately begin the slow return towards the mid-point of the control excursion. In a prolonged ragged gust it may be necessary to yield several times. So be it, but always start the slow recovery immediately after each yield.

A useful technique is to sail always with your sheet and tiller extension arms bent, with your elbows near your hips. This has two advantages:

1 You can ease or trim in the sheet without changing your grip.
2 As you sway from the hips as you hike, you do not alter the position of either sheet or tiller.

Imagine the boat to be a skiff Moth with almost no beam and no stability of its own. Practise control of heel *both ways* with smooth sheet movement. *Do not move body/bodies.* Repeat the exercise until the sheet control movement has become fluent, smooth and accurate and is beginning to be automatic.

(b) Making a slow turn into wind

If the helm luffs (turns into wind) far enough, heeling force will be reduced, as described above. (This is the follower's method.)

To practise this, sail as above. Start by sailing on a beam reach; trim sail as B or C in Fig 21.1. For this exercise, adjust body position(s) so boat is heeled slightly to leeward.

Turn slowly to windward. At some point the boat will roll upright. Arrest the turn. From this point, bear away or luff to control heel by adjusting heading to sail upright as wind speed and direction change. *Do not move sheet or body/bodies.* As the boat rolls to windward or leeward with changes in the wind speed, move the tiller extension with the quick then slow technique to arrest increasing error quickly, then return slowly to sailing straight line on whatever heading gives equilibrium at that wind strength. If necessary, deliberately sail heeled slightly to windward, then to leeward, for the exercise. Again, continue until smooth fluency is developed.

(c) Making a slow turn downwind

A boat that runs square does not heel. Appreciation of, and use of, this fact is the first huge point of difference between leader and follower. What happens when a boat turns downwind is that the crosswind component of the apparent wind and the associated heeling force fall from a maximum when close reaching and beam reaching to zero when running square. If the helm bears away (turns downwind) far enough, at some point the heeling moment must reduce to less than the boat's stability, and equilibrium will then be restored.

Every sailor knows that if you turn a boat towards the wind without trimming the sails, at some point the sails will lose their angle to the wind and stop heeling the boat and it will come upright.

The purpose of this exercise is to demonstrate, very consciously, that the boat will come upright just as surely if you turn downwind far enough – but you have to turn 'the other way'.

The reasons why it comes upright are different. The downwind turn reduces the speed of the apparent wind. And as the boat approaches the square run, the crosswind component of the apparent wind reduces towards zero.

Repeat as in exercise (b) above. Start by sailing on a beam reach, then trim sail as B or C in Fig 21.1. For this exercise, adjust body position(s) so boat is heeled slightly to leeward.

Turn slowly downwind, and *do not move sheet or body/bodies*. At some point the boat will roll upright. Arrest the turn and from this point onwards control roll by adjusting heading, but this time as the boat heels to leeward *turn downwind* to bring it upright. As it heels to windward, turn upwind.

This will be new territory for many sailors. Not only are they turning 'the wrong way', as the boat turns three factors are combining to change the roll force:

1 The first is that as they turn downwind the apparent wind becomes weaker, so there is less wind force to heel the boat, and the faster the boat the greater will be the difference in apparent wind and heel force caused by a change in heading.
2 The second is that a wind from the beam will heel the boat to leeward, while a wind from directly behind will not heel it at all, so regardless of the apparent wind strength the boat will come upright as it approaches a square run (Fig 22.4 is an extreme example).
3 The third is the 'steer for balance' effect – that the boat at speed rolls away from the turn (next section).

The combined effect of these three factors is that quite small changes of heading make a surprisingly big difference to the roll force. This is why the apparent wind skiffs can carry such big spinnakers – their crews control the speed of the apparent wind they sail in. This is what apparent wind sailing is all about.

The key point of this exercise is to demonstrate to the student that if a sailboat is heeled by too strong a wind on a beam reach, it does not matter whether it is turned upwind or downwind. A turn either way will bring it upright. So to someone who has never done it, a new logic opens up:

- *To reduce the heel force*
  - When sailing upwind, turn upwind.
  - When sailing downwind, *turn downwind. Forget all about turning upwind.*

(d) Steering for balance

Traditionally, large sailboats have carried lead and/or other forms of ballast for static stability, so have characteristically been heavy and had drag curves like those in Fig 10.3 and their maximum speeds have been modest.

Until recently, the smaller dinghies and catamarans have all run square when sailing downwind, so have similarly been limited to modest maximum speeds. At these modest speeds the dynamic forces in turns have been negligible. As a result, the dynamic technique of steering for balance in the manner of a cyclist has never been a core subject in either sailing tuition or the sailing media.

Over recent decades, some small sailboats have trebled their downwind speeds. Increasing numbers of big water-ballasted or swing-keel monohulls and catamarans have adapted skiff technology and are now sailing very fast.

This trebling of speed has elevated steer for balance from a technique 'of negligible importance' to a technique which, at these higher speeds, becomes absolutely dominant. Very simply, at high speeds, 'Steer for balance works brilliantly. Nothing else works.'

Some years ago I coached many mature experienced sailors on the 59er, and was astonished to find that so many were unaware of steer for balance. More accurately, most thought that they knew what it meant and that they would be able to use it naturally if and when it became necessary; but when faced with real speed, they turned the wrong way and simply 'lost it'.

Recent experience with larger numbers and a wider age and experience range of sailors on the simulator has confirmed this. Only a tiny handful of experienced sailors know how to control a sailboat at speed and how to get peak performance from it. Significantly, many lead-group sailors believe they know what 'steer for balance' is and believe they can do it, but when put to the test they do not know and cannot do it. Virtually all followers do not even know what it is.

Like turning downwind for equilibrium, steer for balance is simplicity itself. If a boat that is sailing with centreboard down is turned sharply left, it will roll to the right, and vice versa. This property enables a crew to steer for balance with a technique identical to that of the cyclist – that is, if the boat rolls to the left, a turn to the left 'steering the hull under the rig' will bring it upright. This is the second major point of difference between follower and leader.

This property is dynamic and increases as the square of the speed, so it is trivial at low speed, becomes significant at modest speeds (say, 10 knots), and becomes absolutely dominant and overrides all other forces at high speeds.

A corollary of this is that it is when she is sailing fastest in the strongest winds that the leader has the most secure balance control of her boat (eg Fig 22.4).

This is exactly when the follower has least control, or has already lost it.

E   Steer for balance – the dynamics

Imagine that you are looking, from astern, at a light outboard motorboat moving away from you at speed, as Fig 26.10Ai. If the coxswain turns sharply left, the hull will slide across the water to the right, as Aii, and water will heap up under the starboard chine and the boat will roll to the left as in Aiii.

If a sailboat sailing fast with no centreboard is turned similarly, it too will roll to the left, as in Fig 26.10B.

But if the crew put the centreboard down, it will roll the other way. In Fig 26.10Ci and ii, the centreboard turns with the hull and develops a strong force to the left. This force to the left acts some feet below the water through the centre of pressure of the centreboard. The boat's centre of gravity is at about the level of the crew some 2ft above the water, and this mass, at speed, wants to go straight ahead. Therefore the boat is being accelerated to the left at low level by the centreboard, while inertia at a higher level is resisting the acceleration with a force to the right, so a turn to the left will roll the boat to the right.

Use of this principle is steer for balance.

At the 4 knot speed of the trainer, and the 6 knot speed of the conventional dinghy and yacht, this roll force is negligible, so in the example above where the boat is heeled by a gust and rounds up automatically but at low speed, the roll force causes no problem. But at the 15–20 knot speed of the apparent wind skiff, it will be about ten times greater (the roll force increases as the square of the boat speed) and will have become dominant. Look at Fig 26.10 again, but this time imagine that it is a skiff sailing away from you at 20 knots in a breeze, that the crew are hiking or trapezing to extreme, and that it encounters a gust that heels it to the right despite the sheets being eased, and that further action is called for to survive. At this point, look at Fig 22.4.

Option 1 is to do the conventional thing and turn left and round up. This is what the great majority of sailors do. This course of action has three problems:

1   The first is that any turn to the left at this speed will roll the boat further and strongly to the right, and in Fig 22.4 this would certainly capsize the boat.
2   The second is that any turn to the left will be a turn upwind which will lead to a stronger apparent wind, and even further heeling and potential capsize troubles.
3   The third is that if this is a race situation and the mark on a broad reach is ahead and somewhat downwind, any turn to the left will be a turn away from the mark and will win no race.

Option 2 is to turn to the right. This has three *advantages*:

1   The first is that a turn to the right at speed will roll the boat strongly to the left, and this will quickly bring the heeled boat upright, which is exactly what is wanted.
2   The second is that by turning downwind the apparent wind will be reduced, so the cause of the problem will be lessened.
3   The third is that the boat will still be sailing fast, under control, directly towards the mark.

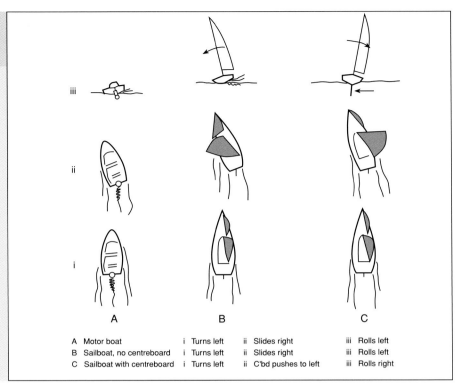

Fig 26.10 Dynamics of steer for balance

A	Motor boat	i Turns left	ii Slides right	iii Rolls left
B	Sailboat, no centreboard	i Turns left	ii Slides right	iii Rolls left
C	Sailboat with centreboard	i Turns left	ii C'bd pushes to left	iii Rolls right

Option 2 is called variously 'steering for balance' or 'steering the hull under the rig' or 'when sailing downwind, turn downwind in the gusts'. They all mean the same thing.

If you are one of the many sailors who has never thought about this, and/or have never done it (and most sailors haven't) think about it and decide to give it a try, because the advantages are enormous.

This technique is the key to control of any fast boat downwind, and particularly to the art of tacking downwind in an apparent wind skiff.

F Training notes

The ideal way to learn steer for balance is to sail in a breeze in a fast boat with somebody who can do it and have him/her coach you until it becomes an automatic response, like riding a bicycle.

If this is not convenient, you can learn to do it yourself by approaching it logically. It really is simplicity itself, in the same way that riding a bicycle is simplicity once you master it. The problem is that you need to overcome established habits at two levels as you learn.

The quickest way to learn is to use the technique to roll the boat. The roll stabilisers of ocean liners are trialled by reversing the connections and making the boats roll alarmingly when steaming at high speed through flat water. This is astonishing to watch. So:

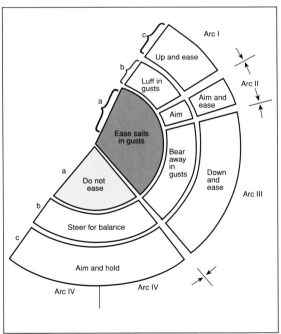

Fig 26.11 Fast handling techniques in each arc

a Sail trim response at gust onslaught
b Steer response at gust onslaught
c Co-ordinated response at gust onslaught
As wind dies, reverse response.

- Set up on the heading on which you can sail as fast as possible. In lighter winds, this will be on a beam reach. In stronger winds it will be on a broad reach. Trim sail to maximise speed.
- Turn abruptly downwind 10° (one hand at arm's length subtends an angle of 10°). The boat will roll to windward. There will be a time delay that becomes shorter with increasing speed.
- Turn upwind, then downwind, through an arc of 15–20° centred on the aiming point. It will quickly become apparent what is the frequency, the rate of turn and the amount of turn that gives the greatest roll in that boat at that speed. If you waggle the tiller quickly, nothing will happen. But when you combine the optimum frequency to turn back and forth with the most effective rate of turn and amount of turn, you can roll a fast boat at speed in a strong wind to the point of capsize.

As you become fluent, you can sail faster yet by adjusting your sail trim to keep it at point D in Fig 21.1 despite the turns. To do this, ease your sheet as you turn downwind, and vice versa. In practice this means that you will work your hands in opposite directions. As you pull the tiller extension hand towards your body to turn downwind, your sheet hand moves away from your body to ease the sail, and vice versa. (*Note: This is the reverse of the sailing to windward technique, in which both hands initially move the same way.*)

As soon as you become familiar with this new technique, stop for a moment and think about what you are now doing:

- Each time the boat rolls to leeward, you are steering to leeward – downwind – to roll it upright.
- So next time when, on a reach or broad reach, the boat is rolled to leeward by a gust, and not by you, try steering sharply to leeward, and the boat will roll upright. It is as simple as that.
- It works equally well the other way. If, when sailing fast, the boat rolls to windward in a sudden lull, a sharp turn to windward before it loses speed will bring it upright.

This is the art of steering for balance.

(*Critical note*: If the centreboard is raised to extreme or removed, the *roll developed by steer for balance reverses*! At speed, a sailboat hull without a centreboard will behave like the motorboat, which rolls the other way. At low speed, steer for balance does not work either way, so to avoid this trap (eg when approaching a beach in an onshore wind), sail very slowly after you lift your centreboard.)

G Co-ordination of slow turn downwind, steer for balance, and luffing for speed

When reaching and broad reaching in even the strongest and roughest wind, the boat can be sailed at full 'power' and full speed, with the crew at full hike and sails trimmed for maximum coefficient of lift as D in Fig 21.1, by using a combination of steer for balance and luffing to the stability limit. Heel is controlled through the quick gust peaks (Fig 21.4C and D) and intervening quick lulls by steer for balance. The sail is trimmed as the boat turns both ways by moving the hands in opposite directions, and the crew *stay on trapeze*, or *do not sit up*.

When the next strong gust arrives, the crew simply turn downwind and ease sheet as far as necessary to reduce the apparent wind and the heeling force until the boat reaches equilibrium and sails upright. Through the short-term unsteadiness, the skipper steers for balance. As the gust fades, the crew do not sit up; the skipper simply luffs a little higher to increase the apparent wind and sheets in until the boat is again in equilibrium and fully powered – and still sailing fast – more crosswind in the lighter wind of the lull. In this way, by steering as low as is necessary for equilibrium in the gusts and as high as is necessary for full power in the lulls, they keep sailing fully powered and at constant high speed for all of the time. This is how the leader sails steadily at high speed through unsteady wind downwind.

Fig 22.4 is a good example. The Eighteen footer, broad reaching for a mark, has been hit by a very strong gust. The helm's response has been to bear *away with a slow turn downwind until the boat reaches equilibrium and rolls upright. He is holding it upright with steer for balance.* When the gust passes, he will turn upwind a little to resume his heading for the mark. This technique calls for sailing a little above the aiming point in the lulls and a little below it in the gusts.

Shape and trim sail as in Fig 21.1D. Sail shape should be as full as possible provided the leeches are not hooked and the boat can be sailed upright. In lighter winds, the fuller the sails, the deeper the boat can sail with sails operating at maximum coefficient of lift as in Fig 21.1D. As the wind speed increases, a boat with full sails will quickly be overpowered if it attempts to sail more crosswind. In practice, a shift in sail shape from 'fullest possible' to 'flattest possible' occurs quite quickly in increasing winds on broad-reaching legs. This is particularly true with boats that sail fast when reaching; the reason is that their speed first pulls the apparent wind forward of the beam and then increases it as they sail faster – even though they are sailing downwind.

26.9 ■ Arc II: Close reaching

Offwind, for fast boats, steer for balance works brilliantly when all else has ceased to be of any use. The faster the boat sails, the better the control. Slower boats can be controlled without it but at the expense of poor performance and progressively more uncertain control as the wind strength increases.

All sailboats sail more slowly as they approach close hauled, so the effectiveness of steer for balance will reduce as the inverse of boat speed (squared) and become negligible at close-hauled speed (except for iceboats, foil Moths and very fast skiffs).

As the point of sailing approaches close hauled the boat speed will reduce, so the dynamic roll force of steer for balance will reduce. At the same time the apparent wind will increase and the rate at which a heeling force is developed by bearing away (as occurs when sailing close hauled) will increase sharply.

For the reasons above there will always be 'changeover' heading for all 'normal' sailboats between close hauled and beam reach at which the diminishing effectiveness of steer for balance will equal the increase in heel force due to bearing away. At this point of sailing neither method will work. This is shown as Arc II in Fig 26.11.

In this range, roll control becomes very simple. Aim straight for the aiming point; do not turn either way. Control heel solely by independent adjustment of sail trim (Section 26.8A above).

26.10 ■ Arc IV: Running square or near-square

As the boat is sailed progressively further downwind towards a square run, a point must be reached at which the flow over the mainsail will separate and become like Fig 21.1E or Fig 13.25. All suction force is lost. What was a coefficient of lift (crosswind force) of 1.6 to 1.8 for a wing mast mainsail or an asymmetric spinnaker of 16% camber becomes a coefficient of drag (downwind force) of about 0.9–1.0. Whether the sail is cusped or flat makes little difference, so it should be flattened so as to present the greatest possible projected area. In this situation the wind force will be perpendicular to the sail's surface, there is no roll force, and to control the random roll forces in strong unsteady winds and waves, steer for balance is used.

Lighter winds will present no control problem. As the wind becomes progressively stronger, if the mainsail is sheeted in towards the centreline the wind force – perpendicular to the sail, and particularly the upper sail – will try to roll the boat to leeward.

If the sheet is eased all the way and no vang is applied, the upper leech will blow forward of the mast, and the boat will roll to windward.

Between these two positions there will be a point where the upper sail lies square across the boat, the wind force will be straight along the boat's centreline and the boat will not want to roll either way. In a strong wind, the sail will twist so the boom will need to be drawn in to keep the upper sail trimmed square to the centreline. The lower sails can be ignored; the upper sail will have the dominant effect. Fig 22.4 is a good example. In a very strong gust the crew have eased the sheet and turned downwind to the point where the boat is no longer rolling to leeward. The upper sail has been eased almost square across the boat and eased no further, otherwise the boat would roll to windward. In all the instability of a severe gust, this boat is in equilibrium in roll and under secure steer for balance control as it tears downwind.

This is steer for balance at work near the run.

Practical advice from a multiple Laser World Champion: 'When running in a Laser, sail a course "anywhere but square". Deep broad reaching and running by the lee are invariably faster than square.'

26.11 ■ Stop–start sailing, and snaking for steady speed

The nature of the wind's flow is to alternate between about 30 seconds at lull (gradient wind) speed and about 30 seconds at a gust speed 30–40% stronger. Quicker gust peaks and lulls are superimposed on this basic pattern (Fig 21.4). If you release a toy balloon onto the water and motor downwind alongside it, it will dart ahead, then slow and fall behind, in a stop–start manner. The motion of slower and heavier sailboats tends to be smoothed by their momentum. Light dinghies that run square sail stop–start. The skiffs and the fastest and lightest dinghies have found new ways to sail more steadily and faster on average when reaching and broad reaching.

Yachts and heavy dinghies with drag curves like Fig 10.3 tend to sail easily up to target speed but then to sail no faster, so their performance envelopes tend to be circular.

Most planing dinghies with drag curves like Fig 10.7 need a good shove to get them up and planing, so tend to plane in the gusts on reaches but not upwind nor downwind. Their performance envelopes tend to be more elliptical – wider in the reaching and broad reaching directions, but no faster upwind and downwind.

The 'shove' needed to get them planing tends to form a 'step' in the performance envelope. As an example, the Tasar (Fig 10.6) sails easily to about 5.5 knots, planes freely at and above 7.5 knots, but in dying wind 'falls off the plane' at 7.5 knots and immediately settles back to about 5.5 knots, so almost never sails steadily between 5.5 and 7.5 knots.

These performance and planing dynamics, coupled with the way the apparent wind becomes stronger when a boat sails 'higher' and becomes weaker when it turns more downwind, combine to make possible the technique of sailing at a near-constant and faster average speed by 'snaking' – sailing lower in the gusts and higher in the lulls when reaching and broad reaching:

- In unsteady lighter air, sailing low in the puffs gives the ability to sail high enough to maintain useful speed in the intervening light patches.
- In moderate wind, it is often possible to stay on the plane by sailing higher through the lulls and then sailing lower in the gusts to get back below the rhumb line but still on the plane. In the case of the Tasar, this way can give a steady boat speed of 7.5 knots and an average speed of 7.2 knots in place of the straight-line speeds of 7.5 knots through the gust, then 5.5 knots through the lull at an average of 6.5 knots. (Heading variations of not more than +/–15° away from the rhumb line are assumed.)
- In strong winds this technique meshes with slow turn downwind for equilibrium then steer for balance in enabling the boat to be driven at its maximum speed more downwind in strong gusts, and then luffed for more apparent wind to maintain a steady high speed through the lulls. Fig 22.4 is an extreme example.

26.12 ■ Summary of fast technique

The handling technique of fast sailors is characterised by:

- *When manoeuvring*
  - Use of synchronised co-ordinated technique for least loss of time in turning manoeuvres.
- *When sailing straight lines*
  - Use of acceleration mode to acquire target speed quickly.
  - Focus on maintaining target speed throughout race.
- *When sailing to windward*
  - Accurate steering to the wind.
  - Use of simultaneous independent co-ordination to steer and trim sail(s) for:
       Maximum boat speed and VMG,
       Control of roll.
- *When sailing offwind*
  - Control of roll in strong gusts by use of slow turn downwind to establish equilibrium.
  - Use of steer for balance for quick control of roll in all winds, but particularly in stronger winds and waves.
  - Use of luff to stability limit to maintain power and speed through quick lulls, which leads to a 'snaking' technique to maintain steadier apparent wind and steadier speed and higher average speed through the quick gusts and lulls.

Fig 26.11 summarises the way the co-ordination of the movement of the sheet and tiller extension hands changes as the boat sails on different points of sailing in stronger winds:

Segment **a** is what you do with the mainsheet when the gusts hit.

Segment **b** is what you do with the tiller.

Segment **c** shows how the co-ordination changes in each of the arcs.

In Arc I (Close hauled, and near close hauled)

At gust onslaught:

- The boat will heel, so ease sheet simultaneously and independently, sufficiently to keep boat upright (usually a big movement).
- The apparent wind will lift (move towards the beam), so luff a little to follow it (tiny movement).
  – ie both hands move together, in the direction the masthead is moving, ie away from the helm's body.
- When the wind eases, do not sit up. Bring both hands back towards body to restore power in lighter wind.

In Arc II (Close reaching)

At gust onslaught:

- The boat will heel.
- Ease sheet sufficiently to keep boat upright (usually a big movement).
- Aim for aiming point. Do not luff nor bear away.
- When wind eases, recover sheet. Do not sit up.

In Arc III (Reaching and broad reaching)

At gust onslaught:

- The boat will heel.
- Ease sheet to maintain optimum trim.
- Bear away (turn downwind) until boat comes upright in equilibrium.
- Then steer for balance.
- In quick lulls, luff and sheet in for power and speed. Do not sit up.
  – At all times, hands move in opposite directions.

In Arc IV (Run and near run)

At gust onslaught:

- Boat will accelerate.
- Hold sheet (*do not ease*). Adjust to trim upper sail square across boat. (In boats with 'springy' masts – eg Laser, Finn – this may mean sheeting the boom closer to compensate for the extra sail twist in strong gusts.)
- Steer for balance.

Training aids

The recent development of GPS-based instruments that display either speed or VMG in big characters has opened the way to useful and accurate on-the-water training in the skills above.

We are finding that skiffs and dinghies tend to sail within surprisingly narrow speed ranges. This is making possible a training technique based on:

Unit in Speedo mode

• Not at target speed for this wind	Why not?
• Too slow out of tacks, gybes	Why?
• Too long getting back to target speed	Why?

(Note from Fig 22.11 that boats with no hump in their drag curves (eg 49er) sail at higher speed in the gusts than in the lulls, so to windward they have two target speeds, not one.)

Unit in VMG mode
Use to progress to higher levels: handling, picking lifts, scanning.

26.13 ■ The scan

There is much truth in the benediction 'Here is your first boat. Enjoy it. It will take you a year to learn to sail, a year to learn to race, and a year to learn to win.'

In greater detail, what is being said is:

- It will take you a year to learn to control it.
- It will take you a year to learn to sail it fast.
- It will take you a year to learn to sail it fast in the right direction.

A note about scanning will help those sailors who want to sail in the right direction and win.

Scan principles

Before you can sail intelligently, you need information. Scanning is the technique used to acquire information from a number of different and changing sources and to assemble it into one mental 'picture' adequate for the task at hand.

An everyday example is driving a motor vehicle. To drive safely in city traffic a driver needs information from six different sources: the road ahead, the three rear-vision mirrors, the blind spot either side prior to changing lanes, the speedometer, the traffic lights and critical traffic signs, and other conflicting vehicles or pedestrians that may be approaching, merging or crossing. It is self-evident that you cannot get information from all six sources by looking in one direction.

To drive not only safely, but in the right direction, you had better look at the extra destination signs, too – otherwise you may find yourself driving fast, but down the wrong road. It happens. It happens in sailing too.

The technique of scanning is to look at each source in turn for long enough – but *only* long enough to find and interpret the critical information, then move to the next source. This process, constantly repeated, forms and continually updates an integrated mental picture that the driver carries in his brain. He then controls his vehicle more by reference to this mental picture than by what he is looking at at any one moment.

The fast sailor's scan
To sail fast on the water a sailor needs to scan, keep in mind, and continuously update four sets of information:
1 Wind immediately approaching.
2 Wind here.
3 Navigation factors.
4 Traffic.

With these four, the good boat handler can sail as fast as any other sailor in the fleet, and often wins when conditions are reasonably steady, or when they repeat in predictable ways – that is, when 'local knowledge' can be relied on.

But she seldom wins in the more normal and unpredictable unsteady conditions in which options occur. This is because she does not look for options, so does not choose the faster tack or gybe when choice offers because either she has not seen it, or has seen but not recognised the implications of what she has seen. As a result, she often sails fast but in the wrong direction. This wins no races.

The winning sailor's scan
To race a sailboat *and win* in the more normal, unsteady conditions, a sailor needs to scan and continuously update two extra sets of information:

1 Wind at distance and emerging options, *plus*

2 Gusts.

This sailor has learned to sail as fast as the 'fast' sailor but uses less of her attention to acquire and hold target speed. She uses the rest of the time to look further ahead and identify options as they emerge; to consider these options, to decide which is the fastest path from where she is to the next mark, and to replan to sail accordingly.

This is a management skill; to manage she needs information, and the scan is the way to get the relevant information.

Method of scanning when sailing upwind

- A long look, 1000–2000m upwind and ahead for emerging shift, and surge and fade options.
- A shorter look, 200–500m, upwind and ahead for accessible (within 60 seconds) gusts.
- Traffic, laylines, imminent gusts and lulls.
- Sail trim, tufts, leech ribbons.
  – Repeat. *Scan continuously*.

Method of scanning when sailing downwind

- In wind-from-behind boats – look 100m astern +/– 30° for imminent gusts when running downwind slower than the wind.
- In apparent wind skiffs – look 500–1000m cross-and-slightly-downwind *both ways* for surge and fade options when tacking downwind in fast apparent wind skiffs.
- Then look at the layline, traffic, sail trim elements.

What to look for

- In Chapter 29, champion sailors discuss *where* they look, and *what* they look for.
- Sections 6.4, 6.5 and Fig 6.2 discuss where to look downwind.
- Section 3.17 discusses the flow patterns within gusts.

There is always pattern to the day's wind, and what the experienced winner is alert to is the first sign of a change in this pattern. For example, a reduction in wind speed frequently precedes a change in direction, and that change can sometimes be seen by looking harder further upwind (flags, smoke, other boats).

Divergent flow within gusts can be used to advantage in three ways:

Upwind

1 Any gust will give a 'lift' if accessed anywhere along the gust front, then sailed in the direction away from the axis.
- eg If you can reach the left-hand side of an approaching gust, adopt starboard tack at the gust front and take the lift from the clock on the left of the axis.

2 Any gust that can be accessed at the gust front near the axis will give a lift in either direction.
- As above, but in this case you can choose and take the lift towards your preferred side of the course.

Downwind

3 Any gust accessed from the side will give a header that will enable you to sail downwind at broad reach speed as you sail in from the side of the gust towards the axis.

Fast handling technique, plus intelligent scanning, is the combination of skills that wins most races.

Chapter 27 • Handling an Apparent Wind Skiff

27.1 ■ The contributors

These notes describe how to handle and race a high-performance apparent wind skiff which tacks downwind at high boat speed like an ice yacht, rather than blowing downwind at lower speed like a conventional sailboat. I understand that the ISAF now prefers the terms 'Contemporary' and 'Corinthian'.

Sections 27.1 to 27.9 describe the general principles and the techniques that work best in light and moderate winds. Until very recently, I enjoyed racing in these conditions and can write about these with confidence.

Due to age I have never sailed the bigger Eighteens and the 49er, so I have asked Julian Bethwaite to write Section 27.10 which describes the handling techniques used to control these bigger and more powerful skiffs.

In more recent years, while I have greatly enjoyed racing the 59er, due to failing strength and agility I have deliberately avoided racing in strong winds.

Scott Babbage is a skilful and articulate young 29er and foil Moth sailor mature beyond his years, who as forward hand supported David O'Connor to finish second in strong winds and waves in the 2005 San Francisco 29er World Championships. His contribution in Section 27.11 brings a younger group's focus to the reader.

The following year he supported Silja Lehtinen to win the 2006 29er World Championships at Weymouth with a textbook work-up and regatta execution. His description of that regatta appears in Chapter 29.

27.2 ■ Seamanship

As compared with yachts and conventional dinghies, skiffs as a group are light in weight, narrow on the waterline, and have big sails. On the water, because of their narrower beam and light weight they invite the approach to balance of the cyclist or the skier rather than that appropriate to a tricycle or trolley. The reward is control of a sensitive and responsive instrument with a very high performance level.

Care of a skiff ashore

Ashore, never walk away from any boat with its sails up, because an unexpected gust can blow it over – and this applies particularly to a light skiff. Lower the sails or tie it down firmly into a substantial trolley before you walk away from it.

Preparations and adjustments

With a stable boat, you can launch it and then eat your lunch, fiddle the adjustments, look up the tide tables, etc while afloat. With the skiff, it is better to do ashore everything that can be done ashore, prior to launching. In particular:

1 Adjust swing straps in or out for personal leg length and tighter or looser for optimum comfort when fully hiked. 'Optimum comfort' tends to be looser for spine horizontal in stronger, steadier winds, and tighter as the spine tends to be more angled for quicker movement inwards in lighter and/or unsteadier winds. Similarly, adjust trapeze height.
2 In body swung boats (B-14, 59er), adjust swinging handle position for optimum comfort while sailing; again, spine horizontal with boat upright in stronger, steadier winds, shoulders higher in lighter and unsteadier winds.
3 The forward hand's head and body should always be an inch or two lower than the helm's so as not to block the helm's forward field of vision (as in the frontispiece of this book).

Launching and returning ashore

Holding the boat in shallow water

Hold the boat at the shrouds, and turn it away from the wind by lifting your hand and heeling it to leeward. Turn it towards the wind by lowering your hand and pulling the rig over you.

If you hold a narrow light skiff at the bow with its sails up in any breeze, you cannot control it. If you have to hold it momentarily at the bow, lift the bow to make the wider stern carry more of the weight. This will help steady it a little.

Moving offshore – beach or ramp

The boat will sail to windward with negligible leeway with only a little centreboard down and will steer well with only a little rudder down, provided sheets are slightly free *and it is sailed upright.*

When ready to move offshore from beach or ramp, the forward hand stands thigh-deep and holds the boat at the shrouds on a close-reach heading. The helm boards, inserts and lowers the centreboard and rudder blade as far as is possible, then, holding sheet and tiller, moves to leeward to balance the boat as the forward hand boards over the wing. Sail with foils half down until clear of moored boats etc, then lower foils fully. (Note: *If you forget to keep it upright and let it heel with only half rudder down, it will turn away from the curved immersed side, overpower the rudder and round up.*)

Returning ashore

Reverse the sequence above when returning to beach or ramp. Raise foils halfway before you sail between the moored boats, and sail upright with free sheets to the ramp.

In any wind that allows an approach to a ramp even slightly into wind, no problem arises. But when a fresh breeze blows directly onshore, it is necessary to handle the boat firmly in order to lose speed in an orderly manner. There are three options:

1 Simplest

- Round up beyond the moored boats.
- Lower the mainsail. Sail in under jib alone. The 49er, 29er, 59er et al will all sail upwind, crosswind and downwind under jib alone.

2 Easiest for non-experts

- Approach with foils half up and converging with the shoreline.
- The forward hand sits by the windward shroud, grasps the jib sheet painter at the jib clew, pulls the clew to the windward gunwale and holds it down firmly to pull the whole jib leech to windward of the mast.
- He/she also drags both legs in the water as a brake.
- The helm kneels or stands upright to leeward and moves as appropriate to balance the boat.
- This 'hove-to' configuration allows an approach at controlled speed to the point where the boat can be abruptly rounded up and the forward hand can slide off into the water and either stand on the bottom holding the shroud, or can act as a sea anchor at the bow to hold the boat head-to-wind (the skipper is still aboard and balances it) until the boat blows ashore to the point the forward hand secures footing.

3 Elegant (but needs practice)

- Approach converging with the shore, with foils half up and free sheets. In any breeze, the boat will be moving fast despite the free sheets.
- The forward hand raises the centreboard almost completely, and simultaneously the helm turns the boat more into wind to adopt a near close-hauled heading. With the centreboard almost right up, the boat will drift sideways – ideally along its previous track. The direction of drift will depend on the amount of centreboard exposed by the forward hand (this is the practice bit). A final turn of the hull to near head-to-wind will spill all wind from the sails and the boat will stop and become docile. Given practice and the necessary co-ordination, this technique gives safe, slow, controlled approaches – even in difficult conditions.

(Note: Never remove the centreboard from its slot until one crew member is on the bottom and holding the boat at the shroud, otherwise the bow can blow downwind of the rudder, the sails will fill, and the boat will then accelerate on a broad reach and converge at speed with the shore or other boats.)

When departing from or returning to a deep-water dock or pontoon, none of the above shallow-water techniques will be necessary.

Righting after capsize

The boat will invert unless a crew member gets onto the centreboard quickly. This is a safety design feature to prevent a boat on its side from blowing downwind faster than a sailor can swim.

Never endeavour to right the boat with the spinnaker hoisted. In a breeze it is not possible. In lighter wind it *is* possible, but the boat will then sail straight over the spinnaker and it will wrap around the bow. It is then almost certain to be torn in the attempts to clear it.

Larger crew member

- Swim over the leeward wing, stand up, grasp the tip of the centreboard, lean back, roll the boat, preferably with the mast to windward.
- As the mast approaches horizontal, climb onto the centreboard, and grasp the jib sheet.
- Wait for a smaller crew member in the cockpit to lower the spinnaker, if hoisted.
- Stand on the end of the centreboard. Lean back on the righting line. As the boat rights
  - if the mast is to leeward – pull the wing down by 'climbing' the righting line.
  - if the mast is to windward – move aft along the gunwale and board over the stern, or hold the centreboard and go under the boat with it as the boat rolls (Laser and Moth technique) and board over the windward wing.

Smaller crew member

- Swim into the cockpit.
- Lower the spinnaker if hoisted. Locate and uncleat the halyard, and lie back in the water with feet against the cockpit floor and pull to lower the spinnaker, which will resist threading through the throat because of the entrapped water, so expect to do it steadily and slowly. Call 'stowed' to crew on the centreboard.
- Stay in the cockpit.
- As the boat rights, be 'scooped up' and simultaneously move to the windward wing to prevent the wind from capsizing the boat to leeward.
- Grasp the tiller extension and apply the lee helm while larger crew member moves aft and re-boards. If this is not done, the bow can be blown downwind of the larger crew member (whose body acts as a sea anchor), the sails will fill and the boat can 'take off' and be difficult to control and board.

(Note: All skiff-type boats are difficult to sail at zero speed. The two objects when righting are first to right the boat and re-board, then to regain some boat speed for steer for balance control as quickly as possible.)

27.3 ■ Explanation of Figs 27.1 and 27.2

Because performance diagrams are symmetrical it is usual to draw only one side of the diagram. One-sided diagrams are fine for leisurely armchair analysis, but drawing only half the diagram tends to mask the profound difference in the fundamental downwind properties between the wind-from-behind type of boat and the apparent wind boat, and the effect of this difference on the way their crews need to think.

For this chapter, I have drawn Figs 27.1 and 27.2 two-sided. Both diagrams are to the same scale. For readers who may not be familiar with polar diagrams, let me explain exactly what you are looking at in Figs 27.1 and 27.2.

Imagine that you are in a hovering helicopter at height directly above a moored start boat at O and that an unusual race is about to start. A number of 420s (Fig 27.1) or 29ers (Fig 27.2) are tethered by the stern to the start boat; the wind is 6 knots from the north.

At the instant of start the tethers are released simultaneously, and the 420s or 29ers all sail as fast as they can directly away from the start boat, each in a different direction. Before they vanish, you take a photo. Later, you draw a line through all the boats.

You have just drawn the 6 knot curve in Figs 27.1 or 27.2.

The speed of each boat on each point of sailing in a 6 knot wind is given by the distance it has sailed away from the start boat in the interval between the start and when you took the photo. If the wind had been 9 knots, the boats would have sailed faster and so sailed a little further, and you would have drawn the 9 knot curves. In 12 and 20 knot winds, they would have sailed faster yet, and you would have drawn the 12 and 20 knot curves. These diagrams are called 'polar graticule performance diagrams', or just 'performance diagrams' for short.

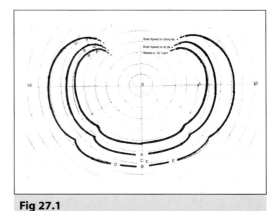

Fig 27.1

Two-sided performance diagram of 420 in 6, 9 and 12 knot true winds.

The shape of the performance diagram of all blow-downwind boats without spinnakers is shown in Fig 26.7, which gives the speed of the Laser on all points of sailing in winds of 6, 9 and 12 knots.

When a blow-downwind boat hoists a spinnaker, the added speed adds a bulge to its 'no spinnaker' performance curve as in shown in Fig 27.1. As the boat sails faster, the apparent wind becomes lighter, so the speed increase is not as great as is usually imagined.

The shape of the performance diagrams of notional apparent-wind craft with small spinnakers is given in Fig 20.1. Small bulges appear on the 'no spinnaker' curves in strange places.

The shape of the performance curves of both the smaller skiff-derived apparent wind boats and the recent bigger or huge swing-keel or water-ballasted monohulls, or the even faster multihulls, is shown by the diagram of 29er performance, Fig 27.2.

A new genre of even faster apparent wind boats that fly on foils will explode in the years immediately ahead.

As between Figs 27.1 and 27.2, it is clear that there are relatively small but significant differences between the upwind parts of the diagrams. But the important point about these two-sided diagrams is that they reveal so starkly the huge difference between the downwind dynamics of the wind-from-behind gybing spinnaker pole Corinthian dinghies and the Contemporary apparent wind skiffs with their asymmetric spinnakers.

Note the factor common to all the apparent wind boats – the spinnaker adds nothing to the speed at and near the square run.

Fig 27.2

Two-sided performance diagram of 29er, in true winds of 6, 9, 12 and 20 knots.
Drawn to the same scale as Fig 27.1.

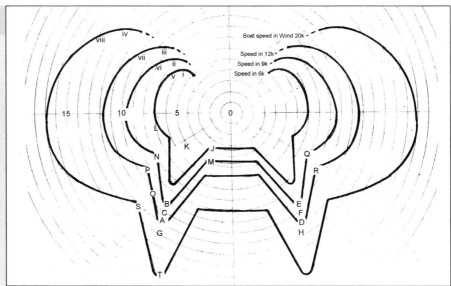

27.4 ■ The dynamic differences upwind

Flexibility

Because it has a hump in its drag curve (Chapter 10), the conventional boat baulks at a speed just above its hull speed. This limits its flexibility within this just-above-hull-speed speed range.

The peaks P and Q in Fig 27.1 on the 6 knot and 9 knot performance curves are 'pointy', and the steep downward slopes of the curves from P to R and Q to S indicate that any attempt to point low and 'foot' in lighter winds will result in poor VMG because the boat baulks against the hump in its drag curve. In light and moderate winds, this boat has a narrow 'groove'.

Not until the speed is up to 7–7.5 knots, and the trapeze-powered boat is windward-planing cleanly in winds of 12 knots plus, does the curve T to U slope downward less steeply. These boats have a wider 'groove' in stronger winds than in the lighter airs.

The tactical consequence of a narrow groove in the lighter winds is that if a windward and a leeward boat are both sailing at target speed, the windward boat cannot sail much faster by sailing a little lower. All that happens is that the windward boat falls down onto the leeward boat without moving ahead freely.

The strategy consequence is that if there is stronger wind 'over there', it cannot be reached more quickly without severe penalty by sailing a little faster, particularly in the lighter winds. Pointing just 4° higher or lower incurs a 3% VMG loss in the lighter winds.

Fig 27.2 shows that, because it has no hump in its drag curve, the skiff has relatively flat tops to its windward-going performance curves. The peaks i, ii, iii and iv are not 'pointy'. The slopes i to v, ii to vi, iii to vii and iv to viii are not as steep as P to R and Q to S in Fig 27.1. Fig 27.2 shows that the 29er has a surprisingly wide 'groove' in all wind speeds, and because of this it can be pointed or footed as desired in both lighter and stronger winds with little penalty. The 29er can point 7° higher or lower in the lighter winds, and more in the stronger winds, with no more than a 3% VMG loss.

The consequence is that the wider-groove boat is tactically much more mobile. This will logically lead to more fluid and aggressive tactical attack and defence. (See Scott Babbage's comments in Section 29.6 about how Silja Lehtinen used this 'wide groove' feature to deadly tactical effect in the 29er World Championships at Weymouth.)

The strategic difference is small, but the ability to reach better wind a little more quickly is probably enough to tip the balance in marginal cases.

Relative advantage of sailing in stronger wind

The velocity made good towards the windward mark (VMG) of the 420 dinghy in 6, 9 and 12 knot winds (points P, Q and T in Fig 27.1) is given in Table 27.1, together with the similar points i, ii, iii (and iv for 20 knots) from Fig 27.2 of the 29er.

VMG/wind speed difference, upwind

Table 27.1 shows both the absolute advantage and the relative advantage to be gained from sailing in stronger wind upwind.

Table 27.1 VMG/wind speed difference, upwind

Wind true, knots	6	9	12	20	Increase in VMG per knot of increase in wind	
VMG upwind 420	3.2	3.75	4.4		= 1.2/6	= 0.20 knots
VMG upwind 29er	4.1	5.05	6.05	7.75	= 1.95/6	= 0.35 knots

Both boats sail faster in stronger wind, but the skiff has no hump in its drag curve, and gains nearly twice as much advantage as the 420 in speed and VMG from sailing in stronger wind.

The practical result of this is that the 420 will gain more from 'getting the shifts right', and the 29er will gain more from 'getting the gusts and the surges right'.

Momentum and static and dynamic balance

Momentum is not revealed by the performance diagrams. Because of its lighter weight, the skiff will slow and stop more quickly than a heavier boat. Its crew will therefore be more motivated to keep it moving, even if this means pointing lower when the wind dies to drift.

The primary difference between handling a light, narrow skiff and a more stable boat such as a wider, flatter dinghy or catamaran or yacht, is that the skiff needs to be balanced all the time, like skis or a bicycle, while the wider boats do not.

At rest and at low speeds, the statically stable boats are easier to balance. But as speed increases, the static stability factors remain constant while the dynamics of steer for balance increase as the square of the speed (Chapter 26), so, before long, steer for balance becomes dominant, nothing else will work, and the habit of the stable-at-low-speed boats to roll uncontrollably when pushed too fast downwind – unless steered for balance – attests their problem.

Conversely, while the narrow, light skiff is harder to balance at low speed, it is easier to keep upright like a bicycle by steering for balance at all times while it is moving, and the faster it sails the more stable it becomes.

27.5 ■ The dynamic differences downwind

Decision-making

When racing upwind in light and moderate conditions, the apparent wind boat is different – but not *very* different – from a wind-from-behind boat.

Downwind, it is a different animal. Let us start with the race plan options as each of our four sailors (Section 27.6) approaches the windward mark to round and race downwind to the leeward mark in a moderate breeze.

The factors that will be most important in governing who will reach the leeward mark most quickly will be:
1 The performance potential of each boat. These are displayed in Figs 27.1 and 27.2.
2 The skill with which this potential is utilised.

The wind-from-behind sailor has to tack to reach a mark upwind, but on all other points of sailing he/she can routinely head straight for the mark (see Fig 27.1). So when heading downwind, where the biggest potential gains or losses are to be made (Chapter 29), the wind-from-behind crew need make no immediate decision.

All observation and experience is that most do indeed make no decision and routinely sail downwind 'in procession'. This is a comfortable approach in that this 'no decision' strategy will also minimise the probability of significant loss.

The apparent wind sailor has to tack both upwind and downwind. Only when the next mark is near crosswind can he head straight for it (see Fig 27.2). So when faced with every downwind leg, the apparent wind sailor has no comfortable, minimum-risk, 'no decision needed' refuge. He has no option but to choose left or right, and this unavoidable need to choose makes every downwind leg a challenge that is subject to major potential gain or loss.

This is territory natural to a leader who is always looking for options and has already scanned and seen reason to prefer one side.

It is *not* comfortable for the inexperienced follower who has not yet reached the level at which he can both sail fast and at the same time scan, observe, analyse and decide.

Relative wind speed/VMG difference downwind

Table 27.2 shows both the absolute advantage and the relative advantage to be gained from sailing in stronger wind downwind.

Table 27.2 VMG/wind speed difference, downwind

Wind true, knots	6	9	12	Increase in VMG per knot of increase in wind true, 6 to 12 knots	
VMG downwind 420	5.2	6.3	7.4	= 2.2/6	= 0.37 knots
at Vb (boat speed)	5.2	6.3	7.4		
VMG downwind 29er	6.3	8.1	9.9	= 3.6/6	= 0.60 knots
At Vb knots	8.9	11.4	14.0		

The dinghy that runs square is stuck against the hump in its drag curve, so gains 0.37 knot of boat speed and VMG per 1 knot of added wind speed.

The skiff that is broad reaching develops much greater drive force, planes cleanly, and gains an extra 0.6 knots of VMG for every 1 knot of wind speed.

If we accept my estimate of 20% as the typical difference in wind speed as between surge and fade (Chapter 6), then the reward for choosing the surge side of the course rather than chasing individual gusts will be up to (20% times 0.6) = 12% at best (when it applies over the whole leg and the other side is all fade), and probably better than 6% in the more usual case where the new surge takes its time to form.

This sort of advantage is huge as compared with the 3% difference between F and C in Fig 27.1, but is altogether consistent with both my earlier and more recent observations.

The practical effect

In Chapter 1 I noted that there was an explosion in the size and excitement of the harbourside audience as the Eighteens began to tack downwind in the early 1980s. In place of the drear, slow 'run square' processions in which nothing ever changed much, the skiffs were suddenly moving at exciting speeds, and as soon as they split tacks downwind nobody knew which boat would be ahead at the downwind mark nor by how much, nor why they gained or lost so much. The fans and the punters loved it.

From 2000 to 2003, I enjoyed several years racing in a good, relatively evenly matched fleet of 59ers, B-14s and 29ers (the well-handled 49ers were much faster), and we all became acutely aware that the race results were usually dominated by the crews who picked the better sides downwind, and that the gains from 'getting it right' were usually of the order of hundreds of metres rather than tens of metres.

It was this very practical and exciting 'hands on' experience that has led to my interest in surges and fades, and the measurements and exactness of these notes.

27.6 ■ Planning and handling – upwind

Let us look at the differences in the dynamics, the thinking, the scanning and the handling when racing these twenty-first-century apparent wind skiffs as compared with racing the wind-from-behind boats that led the fleets in the last century.

To do this let us look at and contrast the thought processes and then the handling techniques of four notional sailors as they race around a course.

The first and second sailors are an inexperienced follower and an experienced leader, both of whom sail a wind-from-behind boat such as a 420, classic 5o5, etc.

The third and fourth sailors are again an inexperienced follower and an experienced leader, but these sailors sail apparent wind craft such as the 29er, 49er, etc.

Let us follow the thinking of the four sailors as they start a second upwind leg in light to moderate wind. We will assume that the fleet has spread to the point where each sailor can sail wherever he wants to:

- The wind-from-behind follower will focus on sailing at target speed. He will probably respond to gusts by pointing higher at the same speed.
- The wind-from-behind leader will scan to track both shifts and also existing and forming gusts, will endeavour to position himself to take advantage of the divergent flow within gusts, and will tack as

necessary to sail in stronger wind and on the advantaged tack for longer than his opponent. To do this he will sail at the boat's lower target speed in the lulls and its slightly higher target speed in the gusts.

- The apparent wind follower will sail in much the same manner as the gybing pole follower, except that he will increase his target speed a little in the gusts for better VMG.
- The apparent wind leader will scan more widely, will track not only the shifts and local gusts, but also the wider and longer-lasting surges and fades, and will be generally more mobile in using his higher speed and greater flexibility to position himself on the side of the course advantaged by stronger wind and on the advantaged tack for more of the time than his opponent.

Handling upwind – in light air

Like bicycles and skis, skiffs develop a 'solid' feel with movement, and when sailing to windward in light air this is reinforced by the stronger apparent wind caused by their inherent speed. The corollary is that in those lulls that are light enough and that last long enough to significantly reduce speed, the effect on balance of loss of apparent wind and sail force is greater. When in a lull the wind drops from, say, a useful 5 knots to a very light 1 or 2, the light rig can roll quickly – so be prepared to move in fast until you get the feel of the more mobile boat and can anticipate its behaviour with smooth movement.

Ergonomics

In unsteady light winds, fastest VMG is achieved by steering a little low to maintain ample boat speed and apparent wind speed through the lulls. In these conditions the fast body-swung boats (eg B-14 and 59er) can be roll-tacked with advantage in the quicker changes. In moderate and strong winds, these simpler skiffs lack the raw power of the wider-winged and trapeze-powered skiffs and their fastest VMG is achieved by pointing high at modest boat speed (about 8 knots) with a surprisingly taut mainsheet. Many crews report that fluent easing of the jib as well as the main in the gusts improves speed and control. These slender boats are unusually quiet through the water. To check speed, glance at the wake.

The helm, who necessarily has both hands full, should not need to make quick changes of body position. He should adopt a comfortable stance, either sitting on the flat area of the deck, or in stronger winds hiked with the thighs over the gunwale. Apart from oscillating infrequently between these two positions, the helm in lighter winds when sitting on the deck should sway from the hips to co-ordinate smoothly with the forward hand's wider movements in preserving balance.

The forward hand should be smoothly mobile and move as necessary across the full width of the boat if necessary, to maintain balance to the extent that body movement is appropriate. He should move with sufficient fluency so that the helm does not have to change position other than when the wind does something unexpected. Movements should begin with swaying of the shoulders and upper body, with the buttocks following the shoulders when a major change of position is necessary. Aim for smooth movement with shoulders leading and buttocks following, rather than smaller jerky movements of the buttocks with the spine vertical.

Sail trim, tufts and leech ribbons
Mainsail and jib (see Fig 21.1)

In all light air and light/moderate winds (ie up to the design wind), the crew will be interested in trimming for maximum 'power' from their mainsail and jib – that is, the closest trim at which the leeward-side airflow remains attached. This sail trim is indicated by the behaviour of the tufts and the leech ribbons.

At small angles of attack the leeward-side tufts on the jib, and the leeward-side tufts and the leech ribbons on the mainsail, will all stream.

As the jib is trimmed in or the boat pointed lower, the leeward-side tufts will stream, then begin to agitate, then will go limp:

- Agitation of leeward-side tufts indicates jib trim close to maximum 'power' (leading edge separation is beginning to occur).
- Limp tufts indicate that flow has separated, with loss of lee-side suction and much lower power and much higher drag.

As the mainsail is trimmed in, the leech ribbons will stream, then 'pop in and out', then go limp:

- 'Popping in and out' indicates mainsail trim close to maximum 'power'. (Trailing edge separation is beginning to occur, as in Fig 21.1D.)
- Limp leech ribbons indicate that flow has separated, with loss of lee-side suction, loss of 'power' and much higher drag, as in Fig 21.1E.

Light air (surface glassy), sail trim
1 Ease outhaul for 9–10% camber at foot.
2 Ease downhaul completely for 9–10% camber of upper mainsail.
3 Main trim. Ease mainsheet until upper leech ribbons stream. *This is essential.* Trim to keep them 'just popping in and out'. In light air this will call for unusual twist.
4 Jib trim. Sheet close at the foot with slack sheet, for twist. Trim the jib sheet so the *upper* leeward jib tufts stream, and occasionally agitate.

In light winds the lowest 2–3m of air move very slowly. Focus on the upper sails; these are working in stronger air and will be providing most of the drive force despite the smaller sail area.

Light air demands and rewards constant scanning for best air to windward, and constant scanning of the upper tufts and leech ribbons to keep them alive. (Hint: If in a near-calm patch the leech ribbons collapse, try easing the sheet a long way momentarily to restore flow, then trimming in again with the flow attached. It sometimes works!)

Tufts work best when they are clean, salty tufts stick. Cobwebs also stick tufts in some localities in some seasons, so always hose or wash the tufts and ribbons after sailing to keep them clean and salt-free.

In rain and drizzle tufts do get wet and stick. At such times, revert to the 'continuous test' technique used for centuries before tufts were invented in the 1960s. Luff gently until either some part of the jib indicates that the boat is pointing too high, or the boat is sensed to begin to roll to windward. Note the heading against a shore feature, and immediately bear away about 5° (one finger at arm's length gives 2°; four fingers plus the thumb, together, give 10°). Note a feature ahead and aim for it for, say, 10 seconds, then test again, and keep on testing. The luff and bear away should be smooth, but quick enough so that the boat does not lose speed.

The advantage of the continuous test technique is that when the wind direction changes in the direction that frees the boat (ie when it 'lifts'), the helm who tests continuously will detect this lift and adjust heading to sail pointing higher at the same speed through the water for the duration of the lift. His rival who does not test will not detect the lift (without tufts) and will continue to sail on a heading some degrees lower than optimum.

Light air, hull trim
If you can hear water chuckling at the stern, the boat is out of trim stern down. Sail it upright (except in light air) and move forward and it will become quieter, and you will sail faster.

For fastest trim of a triangular skiff-style hull in light air, heel the boat until the wing or gunwale skims the water, move forward until the wake becomes quiet, and then move a little further forward yet. This light-air trim gives least wetted area, it twists the upper sails to leeward a little by gravity, and the 'Vee' shape of the chine skimming the water aft gives less drag in any waves than the flatter aft bottom presented by upright trim (see Fig 10.9G).

Light-air steering
Following tack or loss of speed, first acquire desired speed, then point higher:
1 In light air, point about 10° low with slightly eased sheets and leeward tufts just agitating until target speed is acquired.
2 As soon as target speed has been acquired, systematically point higher and tighten sheets until speed loss is sensed.
3 Bear away slightly to hold the highest pointing angle and sheet tension that gives target speed.
4 Whenever speed loss is sensed, revert instantly to acceleration mode (1 above) to re-acquire target speed quickly.

In light air there is very great advantage in 'keeping going'. Whenever pressure is lost, endeavour by all means possible to maintain some respectable speed as you sail towards the nearest stronger air. Even sailing near crosswind at some speed towards faster moving air is better than sitting immobile in nothing at some higher pointing angle, waiting, and with the whole acceleration process to go through before you enjoy useful speed again.

Handling upwind – in breeze

For as long as the wind is light and the water surface glassy, sail heeled and bow down (Fig 10.9G), twist the upper leeches to leeward, and sail the nearby lines of stronger air.

As soon as the water surface becomes rippled by the breeze, the very great increase in wind speed over the lower sails as the boundary layer trips turbulent (Fig 3.23) gives a most recognisable surge in 'power' and drive. When this occurs (but not until), sail more upright, pick up speed, sheet more firmly and point higher.

Shift your scan from nearby to distant. As the turbulent boundary layer thickens, the gust/lull mechanism will establish, and there will be an advantage in sailing into and staying within gusts for as long as possible. As the turbulent layer approaches its full depth, the roll mechanism will phase in, and the wind direction will begin to oscillate. Often the oscillations are quick at first, which makes it easier to identify and 'hook into' the wind shift pattern.

In these 7–11 knot breezes it is usually fastest to sail a shade free with slightly full sails, particularly when the wind shift pattern is easy to read and the boat is usually sailing the lifted tack.

Making adjustments

As the wind speed increases and the boat begins to feel over-powered in the gusts:

- First flatten the lower mainsail progressively and completely. You no longer need the extra 'power' provided by camber, and the more you flatten the sail, the more you reduce the aerodynamic drag.
- Then apply downhaul. This will both flatten the upper mainsail and open the upper leech, and at the same time make the upper leech open in the gusts more freely.
- If a moderate wind becomes choppy, as when the windward mark is close to an elevated shore, applying a little downhaul to a fuller sail can make the upper leech open more freely in the choppy stuff without sacrificing the power of the fuller lower sail in the lulls.

In essence, the crew of an automatic rig skiff set their sails to the mid-range of the conditions they are sailing in, and leave it to the rig to respond instantly and automatically to the quick gust peaks, gusts and lulls as they sail.

This is a critical change. After decades of first developing adjustable rigs and then labouring diligently as I sailed my adjustable NS14s, Novas and Tasars to keep the rigs adjusted to the normal 30-second (approximately) gust then 30-second lull pattern, it was a shock, but a most pleasant shock, to try progressively softer topmasts in the 59er prototype and in this way logically approach and settle on an automatic rig that did it all so much faster and more accurately than any crew could do it manually.

My subsequent years in the production 59er have simply confirmed that this is a much more efficient, pleasant and faster way to sail.

Slender skiffs sail in a quiet 'effortless' manner. This actually presents to the crew as an unusual problem – the slender hulls give only the most muted audible signals of speed, particularly in flat water, and even the most experienced crews will need to learn to assess speed visually by looking at the wake rather than by listening to the customary rising pitch of the splash and gurgle. (The foil Moth sailors now have the same problem – their boats are almost completely silent.)

Fastest sail trim in gusts

As between feathering, easing only main in gusts, easing only jib, easing both, and easing both but with the jib eased more than main, the technique 'ease both, but ease jib more than main' appears to give faster VMG to windward than any of the other techniques in the smaller lower-powered skiffs.

Further, the consequence of the apparent wind boat's 'no hump' and the wider groove is that the target speed in the gust will be substantially faster than in the lull (Figs 22.11 and 22.12).

If we consider a continuum that runs from hull speed-limited boats such as the Soling, J24 etc at one extreme, and iceboats at the other:

- The target speed of the *Gymcrack*/Soling genre is inflexible, so except in lighter winds it has no option but to sail at the same speed in the gusts as the lulls, and to do this it must luff at gust onslaught and 'feather' to hold the same target speed at the higher pointing angle.
- The target speed to windward for the iceboat in a 10 knot lull may be 30mph, and in a 14 knot gust may be 40mph, so the fastest technique of the iceboat sailor will be to bear away briefly at gust onslaught, accelerate from 30 to 40mph, then point at about the original pointing angle, or possibly a little lower, but at the higher target speed of 40mph while the gust lasts.

Powerful skiffs such as the early 1990s Grand Prix Eighteens were probably closer to the iceboat than the Soling in their windward-going dynamics.

A recent surprising observation is that the small sail area of main and jib on the 29er – deliberately small as is appropriate for a youth trainer – is almost exactly right for very high speed in skilled hands in stronger winds. In 1998, when we were developing the final rig for the 29er, we sailed on many autumn days when Sydney's 17–22 knot 'black nor'easters' blew, and in these I was able to measure these speeds in strong winds on repeated occasions. This is where the 20 knot curve in Fig 27.2 came from. At the 2005 29er USA Championships and the World Championships in the Golden Gate's strong winds (Section 27.11), the lead 29ers routinely sailed to windward at boat speeds of 11–12 knots, and at up to 22 knots for prolonged periods downwind.

These are astonishing speeds for a youth trainer. But the 1980s big skiffs each had three rigs, and the smallest rig was quite small. The 29er's single small rig happens to be about what one would expect to be the optimum size for maximum speed in strong winds.

David Hall, of Ovington Boats, UK, has contributed the following on this subject:

I have demonstrated the 59er nearly every week this year. It never ceases to amaze me how many incompetent sailors are out there – I guess I take our skill levels for granted. [Reading between the lines – sailing with natural handling technique and unable to control with steer for balance at high speeds.]

Sailing upwind in winds up to 10 knots the boat can be worked hard and is as fast as the B14, Laser 4000, and 5o5 etc. Sometimes you can feel the boat just sailing on the foils like a hydro foil at 90° – I hope you can understand what I mean there.

Once the breeze is up it is very hard to keep the bow down to keep planing freely.

Letting the sails out in the gusts is a must – feathering and luffing must be a last resort. The boat is so light that it just stops instantly.

We sailed in a crazy wind at Queen Mary and found that raising the centreboard 300mm helps. The boat slides sideways instead of getting blown over.

Even with the jib open, cunningham on and mast tip over the side, it still needs some serious weight over the side to keep it driving.

To sum up – all the 'upwind' differences between conventional and apparent wind techniques noted above are, at root, differences of degree rather than differences of kind.

27.7 ■ Downwind – scanning and planning

Racing techniques downwind

These start with the thinking you need to do as you approach the windward mark. Let us assume that our four notional sailors approach the windward mark in a 9 knot wind with 12 knot gusts:

Conventional follower

The wind-from-behind follower knows that by rounding and simply heading straight for the downwind mark he will always be sailing the 'least-risk' course. So he will focus on the mark-rounding technique and spinnaker hoist immediately following, then sail towards the downwind mark at the speed of point A (no gust) or B (gust) in Fig 27.1. During the downwind leg he will expect to enjoy his share of gusts, so will also expect to sail the leg at a mean speed of about C.

Conventional leader

The wind-from-behind leader will focus on improving on the 'least risk' course. When sailing downwind in both light air and breeze, he will deliberately scan at two ranges.

In light air (from the N) he will scan the nearby water surface close behind his boat, ie 'up the apparent wind', to the north, NNE and NNW for lines or areas of stronger air. (Note: in *HPS-1* I stated that in heated light air a hexagonal pattern of 100–200m diameter could be expected in some conditions. In the years since we have seen and sailed these patterns not infrequently, so do not be surprised if you see them in your area too.) He will respond to these immediately accessible local small-scale differences as opportunity offers.

In breeze he will scan at the 100m range through the arc NW, N and NE for existing and forming gusts, and will gybe and angle to reach and sail in such stronger air as is accessible (see Chapter 6 re the scan sweep area).

In all winds he will scan for surges. These will develop, live their longer lives and vanish. Usually they will be too distant to access – 'There's more pressure over there but it's a bit too far away'. Only when a surge occurs close by will he be able to access it. These occur, but not often.

So his experience will be primarily that runs are where he heads towards the leeward mark, observes gusts that form close behind or close alongside his boat, accesses those that are near enough to offer advantage, and in this way inches ahead of his rivals length by length. Usually, when he sails in surge his rivals will be in surge too:

- So as he approaches the windward mark he will track the existing and forming gusts to windward of the mark, decide where the stronger wind will be over the 2 minutes immediately after he rounds (longer for a forming gust and/or stronger wind), and decide whether the fastest technique will be to
  – Round, hoist and broad reach to the nearest gust, then run at D.
  – Round, hoist, and run at B.
  – Round, gybe, hoist and broad reach to the nearest gust, then run at E.

In this way he will expect to start the downwind leg at either D, B or E. During the downwind leg he will be diligent in scanning for potential stronger wind, in planning to exploit it, and in handling to lose least speed and distance as he angles and gybes to position the boat in the strongest wind he can find. In this way he will expect to sail at average speed about F, a little closer to B than C, and about 3–4% faster than C. This is the skill of the leader, and this is his reward. The regularity with which he leads attests that this reward is real. The drear spectacle of the downwind procession attests that the reward is small.

Apparent wind follower

The apparent wind follower will focus on what he can see, and from this decide which side to sail. As he approaches, he will track the existing and forming gusts near the mark, decide which gybe will lead into the best available gust, and decide whether to:

- Round, hoist and sail at A in Fig 27.2 until he runs out of that gust, when he will sail at B.

OR:

- Round, gybe and hoist, to sail immediately at D, later at E, at an average speed of about F.

Either way he will expect to sail the leg at an average speed about F or C.

Two-mode sailing – acceleration technique

The apparent wind follower crew may start by 'being conservative' and sailing as close to a run as they can with the spinnaker full at point M in Fig 27.2. Their speed will be 5 knots.

Their apparent wind leader rival will sweep by, sailing the same heading but twice as fast through the water at 10 knots, at point B. How does the apparent wind follower get from M to B?

Just continuing to point in about the same direction as the apparent wind leader will not do it. The true wind speed, boat speed and apparent wind speed vectors are given as points 4 for the follower at half speed and point 9 for the leader at full speed in Fig 26.9C. The wind speeds in that figure are different, but the principles are the same. At point 4, the apparent wind is aft of the beam, flow over the sails is separated, there is no lee-side suction, the coefficient of lift of the whole rig is about 1.0, the total drive force is the same as the drag of the whole boat, so everything is stable and no acceleration can occur.

The technique to accelerate is to luff until the boat is at or close to its stability limit at point 6. Only by turning crosswind far enough to unstall the sails can the acceleration process be started. As the boat is turned more towards a reach, the apparent wind increases in strength from 4–W to 6–W and moves forward, the sails unstall (lee-side flow attaches and suction develops) so the coefficient of lift of the rig increases from about 1 to 1.6 to 1.8, and the drive force (the product of the apparent wind (squared) times the coefficient of lift) increases about fourfold. The boat accelerates strongly, the apparent wind swings forward from 6–W to 9–W as the boat speed increases, and the boat has to turn downwind to stay upright. (Fig 26.8 shows this lighter wind situation more accurately, but with a different boat.)

The N to B and Q to E edges of the lobes in the 9 knot curve in Fig 27.2 represent the stability limit with the spinnaker up and trimmed in 9 knots of true wind. The boat cannot sail any higher than N or Q with the spinnaker trimmed in, or it will heel despite the crew hiking to extreme. So the fastest way to access points B and E in a 9 knot wind is to luff until you are at the stability limit, hike to extreme, and as the boat accelerates to bear away as the apparent wind goes forward but only as much as is necessary to stay upright. This is 'probing the stability limit', and will give the fastest acceleration. As the boat approaches B or E, the hull drag will increase and the drive force from the sails will reduce until they balance, and that will be point B or point E (Fig 26.8C and 26.9C give another look at this process).

Apparent wind leader

The approach and scan of the apparent wind leader will be utterly different. It will reflect the differences in dynamics and thinking referred to above:

- He has no option but to broad reach SE or SW and to sweep widely across the course.
- The N true wind will become an apparent wind from ESE or WSW in lighter winds, or from E or W in stronger winds (Figs 26.8 and 26.9), so his two scan areas of interest are to the E and ESE, and to the W and WSW, and not to the N.
- The speed of his boat is such that he not only *can* access surges, he *must*. In a 12 knot wind he will be sweeping crosswind at about 500m each minute, so at any instant if he carries on he will be 500m further, say, southeast of his present position in 60 seconds' time, but if he gybes he will be 500m to the southwest of it. At these speeds gusts of, say, 200m diameter have become small beer, except to the extent that they can be used to advantage (next section); the differences that now matter are at the scale of the surges and fades.

As he approaches the windward mark he will be thinking 6–7 minutes ahead. Except in light air, the average upwind leg of a mile or so takes about 10–12 minutes, and the average downwind leg for an apparent wind skiff takes 5–6 minutes. Before the race, he and his forward hand will have timed such surges and fades as offered for observation and in this way formed an idea of the mean surge life in that day's wind (Chapter 6).

As he sailed upwind he will have deliberately scanned both sides of the course, noted which side had the stronger wind (and probably sailed in it), but he (and his crew) will also have kept track of when that stronger wind appeared. So their thinking as they approach the windward mark will be to assess whether the surge they have just sailed through is likely to last another 6 minutes, or whether on balance it is due to die, in which case the other side of the course is more likely to enjoy the next surge.

So their decision, if confident of their surge observations, is:

- To round and hoist and sail for the surge they expect on the left side of the course (looking upwind), and expect to sail on average at G.
- To round, gybe and hoist, and sail for the surge they expect on the right side, and sail on average at speed H.

Or, if not confident:

- To look to see which side offers the stronger air as they approach the mark, sail initially for that, but then gybe back and forth in it down the rhumb line until the larger-scale surge situation clarifies with the next developing surge.

Once established, the apparent wind leader's scan technique becomes:

- To scan the water 300–600m to the east, then to the west, alternately and repeatedly, compare the estimated wind speeds both ahead and the other way, keep track of his position and try to keep track of time.
- If he is satisfied that the wind where he is and ahead is as strong or stronger than anywhere else, no change of plan is called for.
- But if the water ahead, say, to the west suggests that the wind is beginning to look softer than that behind and to the east, then any decision to gybe must take into account
  - The difference between the anticipated wind speed ahead and the observed wind speed, and the rate at which the change is occurring the other way – that is, is it yet significant?
  - Probability. Is this an expected change that is occurring a little early? Or is it an unexpected change that should be verified further prior to any gybe?
  - How close is the lay line?

Half the brain is tied to the optic nerve, so how you scan will determine how you sail. Nothing posits the difference between blow-downwind sailing and apparent wind sailing more clearly than the notes above.

27.8 ■ Use of gusts

The way the surface flow diverges within gusts is described in Section 3.17.

Because the added surface wind speed within gusts makes the advancing faces of the waves steeper, and the steeper faces reflect less light, the areas of gust in the air reveal themselves clearly and immediately as darker areas on the surface of the water below.

The effect of this mechanism together with the divergent flow mechanism is to provide a unique exception to the principle that because the air is transparent and invisible, none of the patterns within its flow can be seen, so all need to be inferred by other means. Because both the darker water surface below the gust, and the divergent mechanism within it are constant, the flow pattern within every gust can be anticipated with confidence.

When sailing upwind in the Fig 21.3 situation in an 11 knot gradient wind, the numbers would be that the speed of closing with its 15.4 knot gusts would be boat VMG 5.1 knots or 8.6 feet per second (fps) plus gust speed 15.4 knots, or 26fps: total 34.6fps, or 2080 feet per minute (fpm) or 633 metres per minute. So if a forming gust is identified half a kilometre upwind and smart decision and action are taken to enter the gust front at the gust axis one minute later, the helm can elect to take a certain lift on his preferred tack for a further minute (or more) within the gust. This is a very powerful strategic tool with which to approach the windward mark efficiently in otherwise difficult conditions.

If it is not possible to reach the gust front at the gust axis, a certain lift can still be enjoyed, but only on the tack that sails away from the gust axis.

When sailing downwind in a blow-downwind boat that runs at about half wind speed, the situation is broadly as shown in Figs 6.2A and 6.3A except that the distances are expanded about 25% because we are now considering an 11 knot gradient wind with 15.4 knot gusts rather than a 9 knot wind with 12 knot gusts.

But when tacking downwind in an apparent wind boat such as a 29erXX with an upwind performance in an 11 knot wind about that assumed for the notional boat in Fig 21.3, and a downwind performance in a 15.4 knot gust somewhat faster than the mid points between the 12 and the 20 knot curves of the 29er in Fig 27.2, substantial advantage can be enjoyed from a gust if it is approached intelligently.

The 11–14 knot gusts in 8–10 knot winds tend to be about 200m wide. The 15–20 knot gusts in stronger winds tend to be about 500m wide. My estimate of the crosswind dimension of the generally 16 knot gusts that Mark and I measured in Section 3.17 was about 400–500m – that is, each of us was about halfway between the gust axis and the side of the gust.

So an apparent wind boat that enters the side of a gust can expect to bear away at least 10°, and probably more when at the edge of the gust and opposite the body of the gust (as opposed to nearer the gust axis). The effect of this will be to sail almost directly downwind at full boat speed and so at a greatly increased VMG for as long as the situation persists. And because the boat speed will be greater than, but not *much* greater than, the gust speed, the situation can persist for the remaining life of the gust.

Julian advises that in the days of the 'drag racer' Eighteens they would, on occasion, sail thus down the side of a gust and turn to sail along its gust front. The trick then was to gybe to clear the gust well before crossing the gust axis, otherwise the heading would be lifted away from the downwind mark – and while the boat speed would remain high, the VMG would become progressively less. In those days we all thought that this was the function of the 'fan' (*HPS-1*, page 39). We now realise that the divergent flow is intrinsic within the gust mechanism and is not merely an edge effect.

27.9 ■ Downwind – handling

The single-line spinnaker system

Most apparent wind skiffs now use the single-line hoist and drop system which, I understand, was initially invented by the International Fourteens and has subsequently been refined in detail.

When the spinnaker is not set it lies in a chute under the deck, or in a fabric sock that lies on the deck and that is attached at its forward end to a smooth throat through which the spinnaker exits from and is drawn into the sock.

The spinnaker pole lies in guides, retracted so that its forward end does not extend forward of the bow.

To hoist a spinnaker

A single halyard runs from the head of the spinnaker (in the sock), out through the throat and up to and through the masthead block, then down to the base of the mast (usually internally). It exits the mast running forward, passes through an idler block, runs aft through a cleat, then through the forward of two stand-up blocks, both on the cockpit floor. The two stand-up blocks and the sock can be seen in Fig 17.1. The spinnaker pole is hidden by the sock.

A line from the idler block runs through a fixed block near the bow and back to where it is attached to the aft end of the spinnaker pole. So when the forward hand pulls the halyard to hoist the spinnaker, the first action is to draw the idler block aft – which draws the spinnaker pole forward to its extended position.

A separate line attached to the tack of the spinnaker (in the sock) runs through an exit block at the forward end of the spinnaker pole, aft through the pole, and is attached to a fixed point. When the pole is drawn forward, this line draws the tack of the spinnaker forward. The line length is such that the spinnaker tack is drawn to the forward end of the pole when the pole is fully extended.

To hoist the spinnaker, the forward hand stands up, grasps the halyard aft of the forward stand-up block, and pulls as fast as he can.

The idler block is drawn aft, the spinnaker pole extends forward, the tack of the spinnaker is drawn to the forward end of the pole, then the load comes on as the head of the spinnaker is drawn out of its sock and up to the masthead and the body of the spinnaker follows.

The skipper who is some metres aft of the mast can see the progress of the hoist better than the forward hand who is more under the spinnaker, so normally calls the hoist 'Halfway', 'Another metre', 'You're there'. A texta mark on the halyard that stops adjacent to the cleat when the spinnaker is fully hoisted adds a second level of certainty.

The halyard is being drawn through the cleat so it cleats automatically.

To drop a spinnaker

The other end of the halyard runs aft through a second stand-up block, then often through a 'gobbler' block on light shock cord which draws the slack in the halyard over the aft deck. This prevents the slack in the halyard from bunching and tangling at a block at the aft end of the sock. The halyard then runs forward through the sock and throat and either to a big eye in a strong pull-point in the middle of the spinnaker, or more generally through the eye in the lower of two pull-points then up to the eye of the upper pull-point. A stopper knot is tied in its end. The pull-points are positioned so that the distance from one pull-point to the most distant edge of the spinnaker is nowhere longer than the sock.

To drop the spinnaker, the forward hand stands up, picks up the halyard between the two stand-up blocks, and pulling forward (in fact upward) through the aft block takes up the slack in the gobbler and the free line from the throat to the lower pull-point. He then 'fires the halyard' (lifts it out of its cleat) and pulls as fast as possible. The halyard pulls the two pull-points together, and in so doing folds the big spinnaker into a 'W' shape with the two pull-points at the bottom and all the edges at the top, and this is the way the spinnaker is pulled in through the throat and aft into the sock. He keeps pulling until the pull-points appear at the aft end of the sock, at which point all of the spinnaker is within the sock. As the tack is drawn into the sock, it draws the spinnaker pole back with it into its retracted position.

It is a very clever system, and it works reliably and well. The key to clean hoists and drops is to check first that all of the halyard is clear and free, then hoist and drop fast. Any slowness or delay sees the bulk of the big spinnaker 'beat you' and drop into the water and wrap around the bow. This wins no races at all.

A practical point is that the spinnaker halyard should always be grasped between the two stand-up blocks, and for both hoisting and dropping. Never hoist nor drop the spinnaker by pulling from the cleat – this will simply cut through the top of the plastic guide.

Rounding the windward mark

In the case of the bigger, more powerful skiffs in all winds, and the smaller ones in strong winds, the speed with which the boat accelerates, and the apparent wind increases and changes direction, and the sail forces change as the boat executes its downwind turn create an astonishingly powerful 'micro-dynamic' which makes this turn a manoeuvre that requires very firm handling to retain control. At root, the boat needs to be steered for balance skilfully and forcefully as it sails and accelerates around the turn.

Leeward and windward hoists and drops

Most apparent wind skiffs carry their spinnakers in a chute or sock, and in most the throat of the chute or sock is aft of the forestay. So the asymmetric spinnaker must necessarily be rigged to hoist on one side or the other of the forestay. If the spinnaker is rigged to hoist to port of the forestay, it will blow to port of and hoist clear of the forestay when the boat is on a starboard gybe – that is, the apparent wind is blowing from starboard to port across the boat. This is called a leeward hoist (and drop), and leeward hoists and drops are simpler and faster.

In the case of windward hoists and drops, care has to be taken not to foul the spinnaker around the forestay. With smaller boats, this involves running near square for the few seconds of the hoist or drop. In larger boats (49er, Sixteen and Eighteen foot skiffs), the boat is deliberately steered under the spinnaker as it is hoisted or dropped.

Gybe, hoist and accelerate, or hoist, gybe then accelerate

In the adjacent sections I imply that crews who wish to sail immediately to the right-hand side of the course (looking upwind) will 'round, gybe and hoist'. Because a leeward spinnaker set is simpler and faster, many apparent wind crews prefer to reverse the order – that is, they find it faster to round, hoist, gybe immediately, and then accelerate. This is a matter of preference.

Hoist technique
Helm

For a leeward set	–	Steer between a broad reach and a run.
For a windward set	–	Steer directly downwind. 49er and Eighteen footer helms deliberately steer the boat under the spinnaker as it hoists.

Forward hand
Ease jib sheet one foot, no more, and cleat. Hoist the spinnaker. A person who is standing can hoist faster and more easily than when seated. In detail, the hoist falls into two parts. The first few metres of hoist see the pole extend, the spinnaker tack goes to the end of the pole, and the spinnaker head begins to rise. Then there is a

moment when the bulk of the spinnaker pops out of the throat. Once this happens, it is essential to hoist very fast, otherwise the spinnaker can fall into the water and stop the boat.

Drop technique
Helm
Steer a little low. This will zero the apparent wind for a few seconds while the boat slows. For a windward drop – where the spinnaker needs to come to windward of the forestay as it moves into the throat – run square for a few seconds and steer the boat under the spinnaker to keep it from wrapping around the forestay as it drops.

Forward hand
As with the hoist, the drop falls into two parts. The critical object is to drop fast enough through the first part to keep the bulk of the spinnaker from falling into the water.

Stand up. Pick up the spinnaker halyard between the two stand-up blocks. Pull through the aft block to take up the slack from the gobbler – then release the forward part of the halyard from its cleat, and simultaneously pull the aft end of the halyard as fast as possible until the bulk of the spinnaker is at the throat, then give an extra tug to pop it into the throat. The object is to have the bulk stowed in its sock before it can fall into the water.

Keep pulling until the spinnaker cloth appears at the aft end of the sock. At that point the whole of the spinnaker will be stowed in the sock.

Handling downwind – in light air
In wind too light to lift and inflate the spinnaker, the fabric will hang vertically. This will prevent any organised flow over the mainsail, so in very light conditions, a skiff, like any other boat, will sail faster without the spinnaker.

As the wind speed rises from 1 knot to near 2 knots, it can lift and inflate the spinnaker and you can sail fast on a reach but the extreme twist in the apparent wind (Figs 3.14 and 3.15) makes it impossible to tack downwind at an efficient angle, so in drift conditions never try to tack downwind at wide angles. Sail as deep as you can with the spinnaker still full.

David Hall again re the 59er: 'Downwind in light winds you can ghost down going as deep as you dare. Only when there is enough breeze for both to sit on the side is it worth going for it – then heat it up and get the speed up as soon as possible. The rest takes care of itself.'

In light and moderate air
In light air of 4, 5 and 6 knots, you can sail where you like with spinnaker up within the range of about J, K, L in Fig 27.2.

As the wind speed increases, the range within which you can carry your spinnaker efficiently decreases through M, N until at about 10–12 knots you have no choice and are committed to 'following your spinnaker' at B.

Sail trim
Expect to ease the mainsheet about one foot, no more. The tighter the mainsheet, the deeper and faster the boat will sail (provided the leech ribbons are streaming or 'popping in and out') due to the turbine blade effect of the mainsail on the spinnaker (Section 13.16). Trim the mainsail in until the upper leech ribbons just 'pop in and out'. Expect this trim to be surprisingly close to its normal close-hauled position.

Ease the jib until it *just* does not flap. Trim the spinnaker so that the luff is just on the point of curling. Observe constantly, test by easing, and re-trim continuously.

When sailing downwind like this, every change of wind speed, every change of wind direction, and every change of boat speed and direction will all appear as a change in the speed and direction of the apparent wind, so this will almost 'ripple' with short-term changes, and the forward hand's trimming of the spinnaker will reflect this by being always 'fluid' as he keeps the luff just on the point of curling.

The handling technique used by the fastest crews in this situation is to luff to accelerate, choose the speed and depth they think will give fastest downwind VMG in the average wind speed expected immediately ahead, adopt the body position that will give them that speed, and then keep their bodies still.

The helm steers for balance and the forward hand adjusts spinnaker trim to every minor change by keeping the spinnaker luff just on the point of curling. This technique will maintain optimum speed and VMG in that wind.

Whenever the wind speed changes perceptibly, they adjust their boat speed by changing their body positions – with bodies further out for a wind angle a little deeper and faster in the gusts and through the surges, a little further in to sail higher and closer to a reach to maintain optimum boat speed and angle through the lulls.

So, for maximum average speed – keep still and steer for balance as described in Sections 26.8D and E. The end result is that you will 'snake' slightly as you sail downwind. In stronger wind, to sail faster and deeper, sit further out and bear away as the boat accelerates and the apparent wind goes forward with the higher speed. Keep still and steer for balance until the puff dies. In the next lighter patch, anticipate the slowing and move bodies in slightly and luff a little to increase the apparent wind and maintain optimum boat speed through the lull, and keep bodies still and steer for balance until the wind speed next changes.

Adjust your body position to get what you deem the best speed/depth combination in the wind of the moment. Keep still, control your depth by adjusting where you sit as the wind speed changes, and steer for balance. This is the technique of the leaders.

Handling downwind in breeze

As the wind speed approaches, typically, about 12 knots, your choice of heading vanishes. The increasing wind makes a 'stability limit' wall which limits your ability to luff further with the spinnaker trimmed. This is the stability limit. These are the lobe edges P–A, R–D, S–T in Fig 27.2. You still steer for balance, and you can still bear away to keep upright. But you cannot sail higher than the stability limit and stay upright with the spinnaker trimmed in. The stronger the wind, the deeper you have to sail to stay upright – note how points K, B, A and T form a curve downwind. Provided the designer and the sailmaker have both done their job well, the angle at which you need to sail is also the boat's fastest angle in that wind. This is the price you pay for the new speed – you have no option but to sail the boat as it was designed to sail.

This has always been true of every sailboat when sailing upwind. It has now become true of the fast apparent wind skiffs when sailing downwind in stronger winds. The good news is that the stronger the wind, the faster you will sail, and the faster you sail, the more stable and controllable the boat becomes.

27.10 ■ Handling the larger skiffs   BY JULIAN BETHWAITE

Author's note

Julian invented the asymmetric spinnaker, has been one of the central figures in bringing about the apparent wind revolution, was World Eighteen footer champion three years running in skiffs of his own design, and has since designed the 49er, 29er, SKUD, 29erXX, etc.

Eighteen footer – racing tack (see also Chapter 15)
Preparation

- Communicate by countdown so that the whole crew know that you are about to tack.
- For an emergency tack, the countdown starts from 2.
- Normally it was 'Tacking in ten', then countdown through 5.

Forward hand

- At countdown 5 to go, ease the jib sheet 25–40mm at the clew.
- At countdown 1, stand up.
- At 'Go', start to run to new side.
- From about 2 to 4, with the boat through the wind, grasp handle, turn facing aft, hook up as you turn and trapeze to keep boat flat. Swing by hand if not yet hooked up. Control the boat's attitude – keep it dead flat.

- Approaching 6, as boat nears new aiming point and together with the sheet hand, allow boat to heel slightly then apply a powerful impulse to roll the boat and drive the masthead to windward as the sheet hand applies a pump to arrest the turn.
- At 12 to 14 seconds after commencing tack, sheet jib in to optimum VMG (target speed) trim.

Sheet hand

- At countdown 5, ease mainsheet 50–75mm.
- At 'Go', stand up.
- At 1, start to run to new side.
- At 3 to 5, turn facing aft and hook up and trapeze to keep the boat flat. Ease sheet.
- Approaching 6, as boat nears its new aiming point and together with forward hand, allow to heel slightly then apply a powerful impulse to roll the boat and drive the masthead to windward and simultaneously apply a single powerful pump to the mainsail to arrest the turn and start to accelerate the boat.
- At 12 to 14, sheet in to target speed trim.

Helm

- At countdown 5, point 2–3° lower to increase speed. Stay on trapeze.
- At 'Go', start the tack gently. Increase the rudder deflection progressively until it is fully deflected at about 2. Stay on trapeze. Observe forward and sheet hands going across. Steer for balance through the turn to keep the boat flat.
- By 3, with boat about head-to-wind and turning at maximum rate of turn and with rudder fully deflected, stand up, drop extension, run to other side.
- At 5 to 6, as boat approaches new aiming point grab handle, turn facing forward and hook up with your forward hand as you turn, grasp new extension with aft hand. If you miss the hook-up, swing by hand.
- Rely on the sheet hand's pump to arrest the turn. This will near-centre the tiller.
- Give the boat a last small 'kick' with the rudder if necessary to bear away onto the new heading if the pump with the main has checked the whole turning process a shade too soon. Steer a slightly low heading appropriate for fastest acceleration.
- Accept lift by sheet hand for hook-up if necessary.
- At 12 to 14 as target speed is regained, steer higher for maximum VMG mode at target speed.

Eighteen footer – safety tack

In the 1% of situations where it is justified, such as big waves or squall, use the safety tack. The sequence remains exactly the same, but:

- Slow the pace. Slow the boat down and take it through the tack carefully.
- Turn a little too far.
- Ease both sheets and hold jib sheet in hand.
- Forget the pump and the impulse.
- Allow time for all three crew to hook up and settle.
- When settled, trim in carefully, and together.

49er tack

In the 49er, the skipper generally holds the jib sheet and the crew holds the mainsheet. The crew on a 49er works a lot harder than the crew on an Eighteen, and the 49er is in fact a much harder boat to sail than the Eighteen, especially the present, more stable One-Design Eighteen, because the 49er is so much more lively. The old Eighteens were terrifying, but they were big pieces of machinery and responded more slowly than the lighter 49er.

You can push a 49er a lot harder because you are not going to get hurt – much – but more importantly the 49er is all within your capacity, whereas the Eighteen is quite daunting if or when the power comes on the wrong way.

Preparation

Communicate by countdown.

Forward hand

The tack process is the same as the Eighteen. Quite a lot of 49er crews do now play jib sheet when sailing upwind.

At countdown 5, ease the jib at the clew 15–40mm.

The crew always goes first on the 49er, and the skipper crosses just behind him. The biggest issue on the 49er is that the crew tends to come back too far into the skipper's area. He should come back only sufficiently to lift the bow a little.

If you tack with the bow in, it drags through the water and the greater drag of the circular waterflow (Section 26.5) slows the boat more than if you hold the bow a little higher and 'skim it'. With the Eighteen, the rudder is big enough to make the boat do what you want it to do.

Some crews have the lower 18in (450mm) of the trapeze system rigid; this enables them to hook up one-handed.

Helm

In the 49er you rely far more on the skipper steering the boat out of the tack. Quite often you will have the situation of the skipper steering while hanging from the handle, and at some appropriate stage the crew will hook him up.

In either case, arrest the turn pointing a little low for acceleration; only when target speed is attained, point higher and sheet in both jib and mainsail for optimum VMG mode.

49er safety tack

As with the Eighteen:

- Slow it down.
- Turn a shade too far.
- Ease both sheets.
- Hold sheets in hand.
- Allow time to hook up and settle.
- Trim in together.

Eighteen footer gybes

There are two types of gybe. There is the gybe you do because you can do it, and there is the gybe you do because you *want* to do it. Far too many people gybe because they can do it in a spot where they want to do it. The really good people can gybe wherever and whenever they want to.

Further, there is a right time to gybe and a wrong time to gybe. A very skilled skipper can gybe at the wrong time and survive. Unless you are very good, you have to gybe at the right time, or accept the probability of capsize if you must gybe at the wrong time.

The only way you can become good is by practice of the sort where you pre-set your gybe time or position and gybe at that time or position, regardless of the wave state and/or wind state at that instant.

The difference between the right and the wrong time reflects the basic point that the ideal is to have the lowest apparent wind speed over the boat during the gybe. Therefore the object is to start the gybe at the moment of highest boat speed possible. So exactly as we sailed low for a few seconds to accelerate a little prior to entering the tack, we sailed high for a few seconds prior to the gybe so as to enter the gybe with higher boat speed. This enables you to execute the gybe with as little interference from the apparent wind as possible. Other outside factors, such as waves or whatever else, become irrelevant because if you have enough boat speed you can steer for balance without difficulty as you turn through any waves.

If you capsize in a gybe, it is the skipper's fault. If the skipper has enough speed he can steer for balance through the gybe. The crew is a factor in the gybe – the skipper is the executor. He steers for balance through the gybe – always.

This is a lesson we learned the hard way – that the most important thing about gybes is that the skipper must always keep his eyes facing forward. I learned this at an Eighteen footer Australian Championships on the Brisbane river where we were the fastest boat (*Banana Republic* at end of first season), but we ended up fourth because I kept on turning backwards in gybes. While this was the most efficient technique ergonomically for the skipper as an individual, we suffered capsizes. Halfway through that event we worked out the what and why of our problem, I forced myself to turn facing forwards, turned steadily and consistently thereafter, the crew were then able to co-ordinate with me, with each other and with the boat, and we never capsized again.

The problem was that any helm who turns aft loses orientation, loses effective control of where he is going, loses steer-for-balance capability, loses his reference point, and so his handling, and particularly loses control of the rate of turn, which becomes inconsistent. The crew had been relying on me to turn the boat at a set rate so that they could do and complete their functions at an equally set rate based on the expected set rate of turn. The problem had been my inconsistency. As soon as I faced forward I was able to retain uninterrupted orientation. This enabled me to turn the boat at a consistent rate of turn, and steer for balance as I turned, and our troubles were over.

This was simply one more example that if you capsize in the gybe it is all the skipper's fault. The skipper should be able to keep the boat upright even if the crew falls over and does a cockroach on the floor.

When to gybe

If you are on a big ocean swell, the worst time to gybe is when you are sailing up the windward face of the wave. If in 20 knots you *must* gybe, find yourself a wave to surf, accelerate and then gybe. This is true of 18s, of yachts, of anything.

The second worst time is right in the middle of a lull because you then have the least boat speed. At these times the boat is sailing its slowest, with rising wind imminent.

This is not quite as bad as gybing at the beginning of the gust when the boat is slow and the sails immediately load up in the gust, but it is almost as bad.

In big ocean swell the best time is when you are sailing/surfing down the leeward face of the wave. The boat is being accelerated down the wave by something other than the wind, so there will be less pressure in the sails which makes it easier.

In gusts, the best time to gybe is just after the peak of the gust has gone past when the wind is abating. The first 20% of the gust is when the wind builds to its strongest and will have accelerated the boat to its highest speed. As soon as you feel the pressure back off, that's the time to gybe. The boat will be at its fastest with least load in the sails through the gybe. It does not look the easiest. It looks as if you are still in the gust, but it is normally the best time to do it.

The mechanics of the gybe

Because the skipper is so important it is proper to expect him to steer accurately through the gybe, and to do little else. We are talking here of three-hander Eighteen footers. The two-hander Eighteens were closer to the 49er – they were much more lively, so were more of a challenge. But they are basically the same.

How you proceed will depend on your level of skill, so let us start with the survival gybe of the typical three-hander Eighteen.

Eighteen footer survival gybe

In the old days, and even now in strong winds, you send the skipper in so he can steer from a secure position, look forward, and identify when and where and what he is going to do. This applies particularly to the situation where you have to gybe, but do not have the speed as in the ideal situation.

In a gybe, crew co-ordination is slaved to sequence rather than rigidly to time as in the tack. For this reason, the crew movements below are described in sequence.

Skipper

- Immediately prior to the gybe, the skipper will take the mainsheet from the sheet hand, move in to sit in the boat on the windward side with his hand on the tiller, scan forward and decide the moment.
- Calls the gybe. This becomes 'Go'. Starts the turn, and steers for balance throughout the turn.

Sheet hand

- At 'Go', the first crew movement is that the sheet hand will stand up and run somewhat forward into the middle of the boat. As he moves he takes the old spinnaker sheet from the forward hand, and trims it in quickly and hard. This to some degree counters the loss of pressure in the spinnaker due to circular airflow, and so either accelerates the boat or at least delays the slowing due to loss of drive force and the added drag of the circular waterflow.
- The sheet hand moving forward early allows the skipper to move across in front of the tiller later, and also allows the sheet hand to concentrate on what is happening with the spinnaker.

Forward hand

- As soon as the sheet hand has moved forward, the forward hand runs between the skipper and the sheet hand and out onto the other wing and normally will hook up and go immediately out onto the wire, and be on the wire by the time the boat is passing through the straight downwind heading.

Sheet hand

- By this time, the sheet hand has picked up the new spinnaker sheet in his other hand.

Straight downwind – Skipper

As the boat passes through the straight downwind heading, the skipper moves across facing forward, grasps the new tiller extension, and moves quickly into the netting of the new windward wing with his foot against the inner rail. He still has the mainsheet. Throughout this process the skipper has been facing forward, controlling the rate of turn and steering for balance through the turn.

Sheet hand

At about this point the new apparent wind will begin to press the spinnaker against the jib. The moment this happens the sheet hand will drop the old spinnaker sheet, and start pulling in the many metres of new sheet to draw the spinnaker clew around the forestay. At the same time, he moves onto the wing and out onto the wire (takes the sheet with him).

Aiming point – acceleration heading – Skipper

As the boat reaches its acceleration heading, the skipper arrests the turn as the spinnaker fills, steers for balance as high as possible for maximum acceleration, curves downwind as the boat accelerates and the apparent wind goes forward, and stabilises on its maximum downwind VMG heading.

Sheet hand

Trims spinnaker for both balance and drive as the boat accelerates. When steady, passes the spinnaker sheet to the forward hand.

Skipper

As soon as the boat is comfortable, the skipper makes his way out, passes the mainsheet to the sheet hand and moves onto the wire – if he needs to be out there.

That is the mechanics of a survival gybe in a three-hander Eighteen footer.

Eighteen footer light air racing gybe

In lighter winds, the normal crew will use the racing gybe. The technique is:

- Just prior to the gybe the sheet hand passes the mainsheet to the skipper, who steers a little high for a few seconds for added speed.
- The skipper calls the gybe, and starts the turn.

- The sheet hand goes in and forward, taking control of the spinnaker sheets.
- The forward hand runs across next.
- The skipper drops the tiller extension and runs through to the other side literally a metre behind the forward hand. He will have accelerated the rate of turn to its maximum, and the dynamics of his running across aft of the centre of gravity will keep the boat turning fast as he runs. If the boat is well balanced (bow not deeply in the water) it will continue to turn fast. Skipper does a funny little movement where he hooks up facing forward and moves out onto the wire at the same time as picking up the new tiller extension. He still has the mainsheet.
- At the appropriate time and heading he will arrest the turn on the optimum heading for acceleration, then do the big bear-away as the boat regains speed.
- As the apparent wind increases and the sails load up, the sheet hand moves onto the wire, passes the spinnaker sheet to the forward hand, and takes the mainsheet from the skipper.

This is a much quicker manoeuvre, with far more room for error – but it works.

49er gybes

In the 49er racing gybe, the skipper goes wing tip to wing tip through the gybe. He starts the turn, then normally goes through just after the forward hand. The dynamics of his accelerating across the boat aft of the centreboard keeps the boat turning fast. The forward hand pauses in the bottom of the boat to pick up the new spinnaker sheet, then moves out and trapezes with one hand with the new sheet in the other hand, and the skipper will get the hook and hook him up, or the skipper does wing tip to wing tip and straight onto the wire.

There are no safety gybes in 49ers because they just don't work. You need all the power you can get for maximum speed for effective steer for balance control. You simply turn with the spinnaker held until there is heeling force in the sails to balance against, then pull the spinnaker clew through deliberately and accelerate carefully.

Eighteen footer – very light air technique

In very light and fickle winds, the fastest way to race Eighteens is to handle them in an unusual way.

In the first Grand Prix year, 1989, we sailed in Canberra (on an inland man-made lake) in mean winds of about 3–4 knots. Particularly when tacking downwind, our 'base' boat speed was 4–5 knots at an apparent wind speed that would just hold the spinnaker up and keep it full. If you were hit by a gust of, say, 2 knots extra wind speed, the boat would rapidly accelerate to 6–8 knots of boat speed. To get this speed you would come up, get the apparent, then do the big bear-away. But what happened then was that at the end of the gust you would have 8 knots of boat speed and the wind would go to nothing, or perhaps 2 knots. At that point it did not matter which way you then pointed the boat, the sails would just blow back along the boat.

This was frustrating. We found it advantageous to change our whole downwind technique so that we did not accelerate, but just got as much depth as we could. We simply changed the way we sailed the boat by not getting speed, but by bearing away to directly downwind. When a gust came we did not move our body weight at all and just pulled away, sometimes quite violently, because with the big rigs any puff would significantly increase the side load on the boat and heel it. So we freed the sheets to bring the apparent wind aft and steered for greatest depth possible at blow-downwind speed rather than steer for optimum tack-downwind VMG at much higher boat speed. This way, at the end of the gust we were still doing only 5–6 knots, but would be aiming much lower down – often at the bottom mark. We then found that at a point early in the lull where our low speed and the lull wind speed were 'right', we could come back up again and use circular airflow to fill the spinnaker and get attached flow again, and in that way keep sailing at respectable speed through the lull instead of waiting at zero speed for a puff to lift the spinnaker off the jib.

It was an interesting exercise. It underlined the property of the Eighteens that it is in the lightest winds that their boat speed to wind speed ratio is the greatest. It is routine to be sailing at 8 knots in 4 knots of breeze.

In fickle winds as in Canberra, the high speeds attainable in the puffs were an embarrassment in the lulls.

Another consequence of this high ratio is that in steady light winds optimum VMG downwind is attained at a heading only about 30° from directly downwind. Above this heading, the apparent wind was so close to the bow that the spinnakers would not stay full, so it was faster to reach two-sail and without spinnaker.

27.11 ■ 29er handling in strong winds

BY SCOTT BABBAGE
IN CONSULTATION WITH DAVID O'CONNOR

USA 29er Championships, Treasure Island, San Francisco; World 29er Championships, Golden Gate, San Francisco

Author's note

Scott (in his early twenties) has sailed Manly Juniors, Flying Elevens, Skiff Moths, foil Moths, Hobies, 29ers, 49ers, Eighteens. His 29er experience is as follows:

Australian 29er Champion	2000	Helm	Helm	SB
Australian 29er Champion	2003	F/hand	David O'Connor
Australian 29er Champion	2004	F/hand	Silja Lehtinen
UK 29er Champion, Weymouth	2004	F/hand	David O'Connor
USA 29er Champion, San Francisco	2005	F/hand	David O'Connor
3rd World Championships, Switzerland	2004	F/hand	David O'Connor
2nd World Championships, SFO	2005	F/hand	David O'Connor
World Champion, Weymouth	2006	F/hand	Silja Lehtinen

Preparation

After our strong results in the moderate wind 2004 European season, David and I split to sail other boats. For San Francisco we both undertook fitness training, and increased our total weight from 125kg to 135kg. We trained both to preserve our light wind speed and primarily to improve handling in stronger winds, otherwise we approached SFO as we approached any other regatta. We had sailed together extensively in the relatively strong winds of Riva (Lake Garda), so were practised and confident of sailing in strong winds. A season on the more powerful Eighteens also provided me with a different perspective on strong winds.

Most of the European entrants seemed neither practised nor confident in strong winds.

Task allocation

When David and I first started sailing 29ers, my role was as much a coach as it was a crew. David was younger (16), smaller, and just moving into 29ers, whereas I had been sailing them for several years. The arrangement was that he would helm, I would sail forward, and because of my experience I would call the strategy and tactics. This worked for us.

San Francisco venues

There were two regattas. The first was the USA Nationals which were sailed in San Francisco Bay close to Treasure Island, east of Alcatraz. Winds were always west, through the Gate. Wind speed was from 15 to 28 knots, averaging about 22 knots. The long fetch from the Gate developed big rolling waves. There was relatively little tidal current. Courses were windward–leeward.

In that regatta our handling and speed both upwind and downwind were quite good. Despite some close calls, our handling got us over the line for the win overall.

The 80 boat World Championships immediately following were sailed in the Gate just off the St Francis Yacht Club. Wind strength was again from 15 to 28 knots, averaging about 18 knots. Tidal current was very strong. Due to the shorter fetch and strong tidal currents, the wind against tide waves were shorter, steeper and irregular.

Strategy

In flood tide, the fastest course to windward was close to the south shore in less adverse current but trickier wind, and in the stronger mid-gate current downwind.

Tactics

Qualifying races reduced the final Gold Fleet to 25, so crowding was never extreme. Because our speed was very good we were prepared, when necessary, to accept small tactical loss in the interests of 'clear lanes' and ability to sail at maximum speed.

Handling

Straight-line speed

We never backed off. We sailed at maximum speed at all times, regardless of conditions. Many crews did not.

Upwind, we moved far enough aft to keep the deck at the bow just above the normal wave crests.

Downwind, we sailed as high as we could to drive the boat as fast as possible, and relied on our speed to swing the apparent wind forward to give us depth. David moved as far aft as he could, I trapezed from the extreme aft ends of the wing gunwales. When faced with abnormally high waves we let the boat heel a little – this presented a component of the area of the lee forward topside as a planing surface to the water, which lifted the bow higher than if we did not heel. In this way, we were able always to overtake the waves without burying into them.

These upwind and downwind straight-line techniques, coupled with reliable tacks and gybes, gave us superior speed and a comfortable win in the USA Nationals in the strong winds and bigger rolling waves without tidal current near Treasure Island. But the Gate proved different and difficult.

Strong-wind tacking

The 29er never really struggles to pull away after a tack. In extreme conditions the safest approach is to ease the jib an inch or two prior to the tack, and to ease and continue to trim the main as necessary, both through the turn and as the crew settle, then sheets are trimmed in as the boat accelerates and is brought up to the desired pointing angle. Simple and slow for safety. We rarely found it necessary to adopt this 'safety' tack technique.

In a 29er, coming out of a racing tack in strong winds calls for critical judgement to stop the tack at the right angle. We did a lot of work on this to get the transfer of balance in synchronism with the steering. If you go too far without the weight yet out, you flip to leeward; if you don't go quite far enough, you go in to windward. So we did a lot of work sailing together until in our judgement we got the steering and transfer of weight both matched to the optimum turning speed for the boat and synchronised between ourselves.

In the 29er I take the mainsheet during the tack; this makes it easier for David to get his tiller movement exactly right. But it makes it trickier when you are coming out of a tack. In strong winds you have to throw a bit of sheet straightaway. I guess if the skipper is tangled up swapping hands on the tiller and has the sheet, he does not have much opportunity to exercise co-ordinated sheet and tiller extension control. Taking this sheeting problem away from the skipper simplified his task, but made mine more difficult.

The (self-tacking) jib sheet we left cleated. The 29er is under-powered and has quite big foils, so it rarely stalled and did not need eased jib sheet. Essentially if the main was ragging before the tack, we were going to need to ease the jib prior to tacking. I eased enough mainsheet to keep the boat flat, then trimmed the mainsail in as I moved out on trapeze. A lot of crews backed off in the stronger breezes and went for safety mode much earlier than we did. We sailed without change in 20, 25, up to 28 knots, primarily because we were used to strong-wind sailing and had confidence. Confidence in strong winds is incredibly important.

Strong-wind gybing

During the USA Championships in the bigger rolling waves (near Treasure Island) and the first three days of qualifying for the Worlds (in the Golden Gate), we were going well but then had a really bad day with trouble on the gybes (see Section 27.11). We lost confidence in our gybing technique and started to capsize. That really rattled us for the rest of the regatta because once a few of the gybes had failed, we lost momentum. That was really, really painful and I think that psychologically we did not handle that too well.

The problem was either misjudging the rate of the turn, or a handling error in which David dropped the mainsheet while changing hands. We coped and we finished second, but … Often we were well placed around the windward mark and fast downwind only to capsize. Our margin was sufficient and our recovery quick enough so that we usually lost only two places, but it was frustrating. We did that quite a lot and it cost us.

Advice re future preparation

Prepare for an 'extreme conditions' regatta by being physically fit, sailing a more powerful boat, and practising in the boat you will sail until you are confident in the expected conditions. As soon as you back off or start to sail conservatively, you don't win and you go over even more frequently.

When difficult strong wind plus irregular short wave conditions are anticipated, consider equipping the boat with twin tiller extensions.

Chapter 28 • Sailing the Foil Moth

by Rohan Veal

Author's note

From the time of the Phoenicians until a century ago, the art of the sailor was to steer to the wind and trim sail. Since the evolution of sliding planks, trapezes and wings, the art of the high performance sailor has been to steer, trim sail and balance. With the development of practical foiling, the art of the foiler is now to steer, trim sail, balance, and control the height at which he flies. This is a new art.

Interest in foil-supported multihull sailboats has been a non-conformist fringe of sailing activity for many decades. Over the past five years, a genre of monohull bifoilers has rapidly gathered strength, proven its practicability, and is quickly establishing itself as one of the fastest of all today's sailboats and with a future potential that is huge. This has been the work of a tiny group: a visionary, a constructor with imagination, and a gifted sailor (see Sections 2.12 to 2.18).

On behalf of readers, I thank Rohan Veal, the sailor, for contributing this chapter.

DEFINITIONS

Wand The tapered glass fibre rod hanging off the bow of the boat that is connected to levers and pushrods along the deck and down the centreboard to the flap on the back edge of the main foil. The wand is held down to the water's surface to 'feel' how high the boat is above the water and to adjust the main foil flap in order to maintain the altitude of the boat at a constant ride height of around 30–60cm.

May stick The forward extension of the wand that 3–4mm elastic is attached to and kept tight in order to pull the wand onto the water's surface.

Ventilate When a lifting foil breaks the surface, the foil is said to 'ventilate'.

Launch 'Launching' is the result of the boat hitting either the back or front slope of a steep wave. The wand is pushed back to induce sudden lift on the main foil, causing the bow to rise up quickly into the air.

Bunny hop After the boat has launched, the usual result is that the main foil will ventilate, but as the rudder foil is still lifting underwater, the bow is pushed down under the water quite hard, as the boat is now pivoting in the air around the centreboard. As a result of this 'bunny hop', the hull may completely submerge underwater, but if the boat is kept flat, the volume of the hull will allow it to come back to the surface.

28.1 ■ Foil Moth experience

In August 2001, Brett Burvill from Perth, Western Australia, experimented with a two-stage T-foil system on his centreboard along with a T-foil rudder with a movable flap on the aft edge that was manually controlled by rotating the tiller extension. The boat flew above the water, but when the stage 1 (upper) foil came out of the water, it ventilated and hence was not smooth enough for stable flight. Around the same time, Ian Ward (Sydney, NSW) and John Ilett (Perth, Western Australia) were also working on slightly different foil arrangements for the Moth. Ward had the idea of using just one hydrofoil on the centreboard and proved successful in flying constantly in moderate conditions. However, it was John Ilett who came up with the arrangement that a majority of the International Moth Class fleet currently use, which is known as a 'bifoiler'.

Ilett devised two simple fully submerged T-foils, one on the bottom of the centreboard and the other on the bottom of the rudder blade. John's brother Garth acted as the test pilot, and quickly learnt to sail fast downwind and on a reach, but could not get the height to sail fast to windward. As a result, he had a lower upwind VMG as compared with the then-current narrow skiff Moths that sailed in displacement mode.

The first time I raced against Garth in his prototype foiler was in my non-foiling Hungry Tiger skiff Moth in the 2002 Australian Championships held in South Australia. At that regatta, water depth issues meant that Garth only used the foils for a few races and so was not able to prove the foiler against the narrow skiff Moths.

Following my win in that championship, I was eager to find out more, so I flew to Perth to sail John's prototype foiler. As soon as I sailed it, I immediately realised its potential and ordered the first production boat. An important point during the testing was that I took my flatter, tighter-leech KA sail to Perth as well and found that it made a big difference when sailing to windward. The tighter leech enabled us to point and sail the foiled boat much higher and faster to windward. We all sailed it and agreed that it was a big improvement.

The biggest gain in VMG upwind came in France during the 2003 World Championships. I had developed some confidence in the boat, and was experimenting with a more efficient windward-going technique by heeling the boat to windward while airborne (now called the 'Veal-Heel') and using a relatively untwisted sail to power it.

Downwind, I had a few altitude control issues in the learning phase because the boat launched out of the water downwind whenever I went through a big wave. Flat water downwind was no problem, but I found the big rolling waves off the French Atlantic coast to be difficult. It was there that I learnt to keep my weight forward (you don't sit back as in normal boats; you keep the weight forward), and the importance of sailing across the wave, not down it. It was also important to sail for the highest water, because if you sail through a trough, it might allow the foil to ventilate and that's not good. So sailing for the highest water was a good rule of thumb to begin with.

I had sailed the boat only a few times before the championships and was constantly changing and exploring ideas. However, I finished a respectable third overall, in what was not only my first overseas regatta, but also my first regatta on foils, so I was still learning a lot. I won a few of the races by a few minutes, so it showed a lot of promise, but I was not consistent enough downwind in waves or in the light airs to secure an overall win.

However, the third placing got a lot of coverage in the media because it proved the potential of a hydro-foiled boat in racing conditions. Six months later I sailed the 2004 Australian National Championships and won eight races straight. But it was not until the World Championships 12 months later, in January 2005 at Black Rock in Melbourne, that the foiler Moth proved itself sufficiently consistent to be universally accepted. At those championships I won all eight races in a wide variety of conditions, and in this way proved consistently superior performance against top international competition. At that regatta, there were about five other foilers and a lot of really good skiff Moth sailors as well.

28.2 ■ Essential prior experience

From my experience, it is not necessary to have mastered a skiff Moth before sailing a foiler. Experience in sailing other skiffs is adequate. Even that is not essential; French sailor Sebastian Josse, who had primarily sailed big boats and windsurfers, was able to handle it in gusty conditions without too much difficulty.

You need to be a good sailor, have a good understanding of apparent wind, good balance, good fitness, reasonable strength. Leg strength and abdominal muscle strength is a benefit for hiking the boat to windward. The mainsheet needs constant trimming, so good shoulder strength is also important. The basic upwind technique is to pull the boat over the top of you and hike comfortably with slightly bent legs. Hiking with straight legs is ideal, as this allows you to get more leverage out over the water. But it is not necessary to be super strong or super fit like other high-performance dinghies.

The tiller extension grip is quite important. Unlike the 470, Laser or any trapezing boat, the tiller should be held across the body, so that your thumb is towards your chest. This allows a slower tiller movement at high speed and allows for the skipper to easily rotate the tiller extension to trim the rudder foil.

28.3 ■ Sailing environment for learning

A relatively steady wind of about 10 knots and no waves is the ideal. Wind that is gusty and shifty makes it more difficult for a beginner.

Avoid significant waves. Waves up to, say, 30cm may be OK because you can clear that chop. Bigger waves are difficult for beginners because they will not have developed quick enough control technique to steer around the troughs as they learn to handle the boat.

To sail the boat, you need 1.5m depth of water as a minimum, ideally with no sand bars, reefs and no weed obstructing you. You can get around weed, but it is better not to have it. Fish and other marine life or other debris in the water can cause problems. If you hit a large jelly fish at high speed, it may catapult you off the boat or, worse still, damage the foil, so that is something to avoid if possible. As the boat is so light, it will just flip over itself if you do hit anything, but it is critical that you let go of the boat and tiller extension, to relieve the boat of the momentum of your weight which may damage it if you hang on. If you are off the boat, the only impact is the boat onto the water and its mass is so small that that does not damage it.

28.4 ■ Handling and preparation onshore

The boats are so light that if the boat is not attached to the trolley the wind can get under the wing and lift the boat out of the trolley. A fully rigged foiler weighs about 30kg and will only take a 10 knot crosswind for the boat to start jumping around. The best trolleys are fairly solid and heavy (stainless steel is best) with a wide wheel base. It is critical that the hull is tied down so it cannot be lifted by the wind. When rigging, it is important to point bow directly into the wind, because the boat when upright will easily blow over if at all crosswind. If it does blow over, the front wing frame corner will hit the ground first, therefore it is recommended to have some protection on these corners such as cutting out and sticking on the corner of an ice-cream container. Ideally it is best to rig in a sheltered area, but if the boat is tied to the trolley correctly and there is no wind protection, it is best to angle the boat away from the wind by 45°, and tip the boat onto the front corner of the wing frame. This is the most stable position for the boat to lie horizontally with the rig up.

Due to safety concerns while sailing and crashing, the practice is growing to wrap padding material like foam around the chainplates on the forward wing beam to protect the sailor in case of an accident. In a few cases, people have been thrown off the boat and have hurt themselves on the stays.

There is not much difference between a skiff Moth and a foiler in the way we rig the boat, except that we use more rig tension because we use a lot of downhaul to flatten the sail and this bends the mast and slackens the stays. It is critical to have sufficient tension (approximately 18 on a Loos Gauge), so the mast never jumps out of the mast step. That has happened.

Because of the stronger apparent wind that the foiler Moth generates, the sails are flatter, but you can flatten more on the water with a lot of downhaul, vang and outhaul tension.

Prior to moving to the water, make sure you have all the retainer pins to secure the centreboard and rudder blade to the boat. It is highly recommended to tie them onto the hull with light shockcord as they can easily get lost when putting the boat in the water. I always carry a spare retainer pin in my lifejacket along with some 1m lengths of 3–4mm Dyneema, just in case. The object is to secure the board with the minimum of time, and get going without delay. All else should be already attached and ready to go before putting the boat in the water.

28.5 ■ Moving to the water – launching

Launching in offshore winds is easiest. There are two options when launching:

1 If a ramp is short, steep and difficult we usually tip the boat over on land, take the trolley off, and fit and secure the foils to the hull so it is ready to sail. Then either one person or two can pick up the hull, carry it to the water, then drop it in, and go. If a third person carries the masthead to stop it dragging, that helps. This is appropriate for Lake Garda where the water becomes deep very quickly and there are queues waiting – also for Woollahra. We simply fully rig the boat ashore, carry it to the water and drop it in, jump in and go.

2 The other option is appropriate for a more shelving bottom. We secure the foils on the trampolines (under the toe straps); and two people lift the boat out of the trolley and carry the boat upright by the wing frame into shallow water. The sailor then pushes the boat out to chest depth – about 1.3–1.5m – tips the boat over, fits the foils from the underside and pins them from the top. You cannot see the deck when inserting the centreboard from the bottom, so we use marks on the centreboard which indicate the depth to which it should be inserted to accept the pin so we can pin it 'blind'. The sailor then connects the wand mechanism to the centreboard and secures the rudder foil in place. When ready, the skipper can right the boat by pulling down on the windward wing frame or standing on the centreboard (close to the hull).

There are different rudder configurations. The Bladerider has a dagger blade and box arrangement; you can lift the rudder higher for shallow water; when you get to deeper water, you can push it down and pin it.

The Fastacraft Prowler has a fixed T-foil rudder so you need to carry the whole assembly of rudder, tiller and extension, until you have enough water to fit it to the gantry and insert the rudder pin. This is a more fiddly assembly, but it is a one-piece unit so there is no relative movement.

It is extremely difficult to launch a foil Moth in onshore winds if there are breaking waves or surf. If the waves exceed 300mm, there is a danger of capsize and a broken mast or foils snapping. I do not recommend this for anyone regardless of experience.

28.6 ■ Moving offshore – also returning

There are two ways to right the boat from the on-its-side foil-fitting position.

If you are standing on the bottom you can jump on the centreboard close to the hull and right it like a normal boat. As it comes up, you throw your leg over the wing bar because you want your weight in the middle at first. Pick up the mainsheet and tiller and quickly bear away to get speed and balance.

The other method is to stand on the centreboard again and pull the windward wing bar down into the water with you. Reach into the boat and grasp the mainsheet and the tiller extension with your lower body still in the water and legs pointing away from the boat. Immediately bear away to sail off on a reach, while swinging your body into the middle of the boat to get balance and the wing frame out of the water.

If there is enough wind, the second method is the easier and faster way to get in and go.

Approaching the shore

Judging depth is always difficult, so the technique is to drop speed to around 1–2 knots when unsure. Sandy beaches are the best. Concrete or rocks are the worst as they can damage the foils if you hit the bottom. When in shallow water, put either leeward or windward wing bar in the water and inch in very slowly until you think the water is shallow enough for you to stand up, but the foils have not yet touched the bottom. Immediately tip it onto its side to remove the foils from the boat.

Alternatively, if the bottom is rough, I will approach slowly as close as I judge safe, tip it onto its side, and swim it ashore by holding onto the forestay. This prevents all foil damage; however, with the Bladerider you can raise your foils and sail into much shallower water if desired.

The optimum technique will depend on the steepness of the bottom, the harshness of the bottom, and your equipment. The same technique applies regardless of the wind direction.

Returning ashore

Once the boat is on its side and you are standing on the bottom holding it, the boat cannot go anywhere so you can disconnect the mechanisms and take the foils out. Usually they float, so if necessary you can leave them in the water (except in an offshore wind).

Normal technique is to right the boat, put the foils into the trampolines, secure them temporarily, and two people carry the boat ashore.

In the case of the Bladerider it is easier to remove only the centreboard. Lift the rudder to its highest in its box and leave it there until the boat is ashore and in its trolley.

If there are two people to carry the boat to the trolley, that is easiest. If not, the boat can be left on its side in 100–200mm of water, you get your own trolley, fit the trolley to the boat while it is on its side in the water, then right it and wheel it ashore by yourself.

28.7 ■ Height control

Height control is a new responsibility in dinghy sailing, and it is shared between sailor and wand.

The wand is attached to the bow and senses the height of the bow above the water. The mechanism between the wand and the flap on the main lifting foil gives fine control of the boat's height. When the boat is too low, the wand will be pressed up and the mechanism will put the flap down and this will bring the boat up. When the boat is too high, the wand comes forward and raises the flap and the boat comes down. This gives very effective fine control of height. But the wand and its mechanism must not be too sensitive, for otherwise the boat would leap up and down as it tried to follow the crest and trough of every wave. The art of the recent equipment development has been to create a sensing mechanism that will give smooth accurate control at the desired average pitch altitude without responding to the crest and trough of every wave.

A second foil attached to the bottom of the rudder blade can also be adjusted by twisting the tiller extension.

The function of this movement is to provide a manual attitude and pitch control.

The practical result is that this type of wand mechanism works very well indeed *provided* the sailor sets the attitude of the foil – that is, his hull – at the approximate angle of attack required for the present and expected speed. At low speed, the wand alone will not lift the boat to start flying unless, and until, the sailor lifts the bow to give the required greater angle of attack to the main foil. The sailor controls the altitude initially by moving his body weight fore-and-aft, and uses the rudder foil for fine adjustment.

Once the boat starts flying it will accelerate quickly. The wand alone cannot stop it climbing too high and launching unless the sailor lowers the bow to about the smaller angle needed at the expected higher speed. Again, the skipper does this primarily by moving body weight forward, and will use the rudder foil adjustment for finer control of altitude.

The end result is that sailing the foil Moth calls for the synchronised co-ordination of steering, sail trimming, and balance needed to sail a fast skiff, plus proactive control of altitude primarily by movement of body weight and supplemented by rudder foil adjustments to enable the wand to do its job of fine control of the flying height.

It's tremendous fun! And it's now the fastest short-course sailing there is.

28.8 ■ Sailing the foil Moth

Displacement sailing

In the displacement mode, the foiler Moth is simply another sailboat, and will sail upwind, crosswind and downwind in the normal manner.

Flying

To start foiling it is necessary to reach at 8–9 knots of boat speed and the boat will simply lift out of the water. It is hard to start foiling if you are sailing either upwind or downwind. The most efficient technique is to reach to start foiling, accelerate crosswind to build apparent wind, then turn upwind or downwind with speed – that is, like an iceboat.

When beginning, the main thing is to get into a reaching position, with body weight positioned in the middle of the wing frame. Newer-model boats do not require much or any effort from the rudder foil control to lift the boat out of the water. The main foil plus the wand configuration should be enough to lift the boat out on a reach.

Take-off speed is about 9 knots boat speed. That will generate enough apparent wind, even in as little as 6 knots of true wind, to get the boat clear of the water and the skipper hiking. The boat must be sailed flat or heeled to windward. If it is heeled to leeward, the foils will push the boat over and the boat will tip over by itself regardless of the skipper's efforts to balance it.

Once it is clear of the water, the boat will go completely silent – no noise at all – and will accelerate immediately to a minimum of 11 knots depending on the wind.

This is new art which differs from normal sailing in two key respects:

1 The first is that to control these boats you need to think control in four dimensions – pitch, altitude, heading and heel. The pitch-speed nexus controls the angle of attack on the foils, and hence the induced drag of the foils. However, it also has an effect on the lee or weather helm on the boat, as the centre of effort can be easily moved fore-and-aft around the centre of lateral resistance on the foils.

2 The second is that the dynamics of these boats – their light weight and high speed – require that height control be proactive rather than reactive. You have to be in charge and the boat has to do what you want it to do. It is important to be proactive and not reactive. If you try to sail by reacting to the boat, you will be too late – it has already happened. The human response is not quick enough. Unless it is firmly controlled, the boat will just do what it wants to do.

An example is if the boat is clear of the water and the bow is up, it will keep lifting. If you do not correct and put the bow down before it is too late it will just launch and turn either way. You have already lost control. The appropriate control is for the skipper to move his weight forward and/or to pitch the bow down to flatten the boat before it lifts too high. You have to anticipate and act first. There is not enough time if you are travelling at 15–18 knots for any corrections to be made once the boat is sailing too high.

As an example, at a recent demonstration day in strong, unsteady wind and small waves, some very good sailors were sailing the foiler for the first time. As a group, they initially sat too far aft. The wand was doing all it could, but the boat's attitude was too nose-high and it just climbed out and launched and they lost control. When they were encouraged to move forward as the boat started to fly, the bow came down, the wand could then look after the altitude, and they were again in control and able to begin to get the feel of this new craft.

Landing

If the beginner wants to progress his skill with a series of short flights, then the technique to bring the boat back down to the water is to stall the sail. This reduces drive force, adds drag, slows the boat without upsetting the balance, and the boat will settle back to the water under control. Whether you are reaching or sailing upwind or downwind, if you sheet in really hard this will stall the main and push the boat down. If you move forward or pitch the bow down with the rudder flap, this will initially reduce drag and accelerate the boat. If you do it to extreme, it will bring the boat down but much more slowly. Another way if you must stop quickly is to heel aggressively and put the wing frame in the water. This will kill the speed very fast, but it may drag the boat around until it is heading in a direction you don't want to go.

Therefore, the efficient, fast and controlled way to land is to stall the sail to reduce drive force and increase drag, and this will stop it flying.

Flying faster

To make the boat sail faster, twist the tiller extension to control the rudder foil to pitch the bow down. This will reduce the angle of attack of the main foil to reduce the drag, and hence speed will increase. Alternatively, the helmsman can move his body weight forward, as this will have the same effect. Flattening the sail by downhaul and/or vang will also reduce drag and increase speed. As the apparent wind increases and goes forward, it will be necessary to sheet in more closely.

The hard-leech fully battened sail acts like a solid wing and always has power. It is important to keep a windward heel 5–10° for maximum speed and lift from the rig and foils. If it is allowed to heel to leeward at all, the foils will push the boat over to leeward, and will result in the leeward wing bar hitting the water, making for a fast capsize.

Because the foil Moth sails so fast with respect to the true wind speed, particularly in lighter winds, the apparent wind is from well ahead of the beam on all points of sailing. As a result there is surprisingly little difference in sail settings between sailing close hauled, reaching and tacking downwind.

Upwind in lighter wind and flat water

Light airs are difficult in that you need 5–6 knots to get it up on foils. Displacement sailing is unstable – not as unstable as the skiff version, but less stable than when foiling. You need good balance to move around the boat to keep it upright, and then a lot of skill to get it up in light airs. Generally this will involve a few quick pumps on the mainsheet, body weight towards the back, mast upright, and lifting the bow with the rudder foil. But if you have around 7 knots of wind you should be able to foil straightaway.

In lighter winds you just give it a go and see how it feels. Reach to start flying and accelerate; only then turn upwind and heel to windward.

Upwind in moderate winds and flat water

To sail upwind needs slightly more windward heel and hard sheeting of the sail.

Upwind in strong winds and flat water

Depending on the skipper's body weight, in +15 knots set a really flat sail, tight leech and exercise firm control. Strong winds are for experienced sailors, not beginners.

Upwind in lighter wind and waves

This requires a tremendous amount of skill, but it may help to try and bounce the boat off the top of a wave to assist with initial flight and acceleration. Once foiling, keep the rig fairly upright in order to stop the wing bars from hitting the water and slowing the boat down.

Upwind in moderate winds and waves

The rig should be fairly upright once again, but with a slight heel to windward if possible, so the wings and skipper can clear the water when hiking.

Upwind in strong winds and waves

These conditions do not present a problem as most beginners fear. The boat should almost float in between the troughs of waves and then just skim the top of the wave's crest. By contouring more along the waves the hull stays clear of the water and the boat can move freely and fast. It really is a lot easier than expected.

Tacking

In order to tack a foiler, it is important to keep it airborne as long as possible. Basically, the skipper should slowly point to windward and move the weight inwards, until the boat hits head-to-wind. At that stage, the boat and the leeward wing will hit the water, killing the majority of the speed. The skipper must quickly jump on the new windward bar to pull the rig over on top of him and keep the leeward wing from going under-water. Bear away past close hauled as quickly as possible to get power in the sail and speed up. The boat should accelerate up to 8–10 knots on a tight reach fairly quickly, and when doing so the boat will lift out of the water. At this point, the skipper should heel the boat over to windward and point up to close hauled at the same time.

When sailing to windward it is possible to keep foiling fast in winds as light as 4 knots, but it is not possible to take off on any point of sailing in winds lighter than 5–6 knots. So when you are foiling through a lull of less than 5 knots and you must tack, it may be safer to gybe and keep up on foils and moving fast, rather than risk tacking, and potentially drop to displacement speed during the tack and not be able to start foiling again.

A few Mothies have done an airborne tack, but it is difficult to keep the hull airborne for the whole way around. The boat needs to spin quite fast and very flat through the tack so you can keep it airborne. The back of the hull might just touch briefly, but it will pop out right away once the boat picks up speed on the new tack. It is important that you select flat water and constant wind to do this, however, otherwise it can throw the boat off balance.

Downwind in lighter winds and flat water

The idea here is to look for pressure and sail as low as possible. Speed is good, but if you are heading in the wrong direction your VMG may be very low. Sail settings are very important here. You need only moderate tension on the vang, outhaul and downhaul. The fuller the sail, the better!

Downwind in moderate winds and flat water

As in lighter winds, but as the apparent wind increases, flatten the sail to reduce drag.

Downwind in strong winds and flat water

As above, but it is possible to sail extremely low, so when gybing you need to sail high after the gybe to get the apparent wind around quickly. A lightweight skipper may not need to let any control lines off downwind as they may be fully powered up already.

Downwind in lighter winds and waves

These are rare but difficult conditions. The decision must be made by the skipper either to sit on the wing bar and sail higher and faster across the waves, otherwise sit in the boat to sail in displacement mode to go low and slow. A VMG GPS will help to determine the best angle to sail on.

Downwind in moderate winds and waves

Depending on the direction of the waves, it is sometimes easier to sit comfortably on the wing covers to sail low, but still foiling at around 10–12 knots of boat speed. This may require the skipper to use aggressive fore-and-aft body movements to stop the bow from pitching too high or digging into the back of a wave. Aggressive rudder angle and trim may also be required to assist the boat in not launching off the back of a steep wave. The alternative to sailing low and slow is to sit on the wing bar and go for speed across the waves.

It is important to look for highest water so that the foils do not ventilate. If the boat looks as though it might launch up into the air off the back of a wave, the skipper can sheet in, heel to leeward, and bear away sharply to reduce lift and power. The boat should slowly come back down to the water across the face of the wave.

Downwind in strong winds and waves

It is important not to try to fly the boat too much. Good technique is to stall the sail and heel the boat to leeward if out of control or over-powered. If there is any sudden acceleration of the boat it will be hard to control and the boat will just launch off a wave and you will lose control. So I always try to sail the boat more slowly than normal downwind to be safe. Sometimes small areas of flat water offer a chance to speed up a bit, but not for too long. I would try and fly across these flat areas, then stall the sail to bring the boat back down on the water before approaching any big waves. Whenever I feel that the boat is trying to come out of the water too high, I bring it down straightaway. This way, you never launch and it is safer to sail downwind than to risk having a good spurt of speed and then crashing and losing 30–60 seconds in righting the boat.

Gybing

A good gybe is critical for a fast downwind leg, and a lot of time can be lost if a gybe is not clean (ie airborne) the whole time. Therefore as I approach a gybe I wait for flat water, regardless of how far past the layline I may have gone, and bear away until the boat slows down to under 15 knots. It is important to keep the boat with no heel, but a slight amount of lift on the bow. This is because when you move to slow down through the gybe, you will need more lift by angle of attack to keep the boat altitude up. If the boat starts to heel to one side or the other, straighten the boat up with small tiller movements (or use slightly more pressure on one side of the hull) until it comes upright. Then continue the turn right through to about 90° to the true wind. Once the apparent wind comes around, then bear away with it. It is important the skipper does not change hands with tiller and mainsheet during the gybe, until the boat is settled down and is sailing fast again on the new gybe. The whole time during the gybe, the boat must not heel over otherwise it will easily lose balance, the wings will hit the water, kill speed instantly, and potentially tip you over.

Mark rounding

The bear-away is pretty simple, but scary to some due to the high speeds. Pull the tiller towards you, the boat bears away, and the wand adjusts the foiling height. The helm needs to be alert to use rudder foil to pitch the bow up or down to keep the boat longitudinally level. The object is to prevent the boat pitching too high or too low and the hull going back into the water, so there may be a little bit of trim needed while bearing away. At the same time, keep it laterally level or heeled to windward. Not much sheet or sail control adjustment is needed (because the apparent wind changes so little at this point).

If after bearing away you want to bear away further and sail fast downwind you can let a little downhaul off and a little vang to get a bit more power from the sail and allow the boat to go lower. With a flat sail, it is hard to go low and fast. The lighter the wind, the more downhaul and vang should be let off. However, it is important to not adjust any control lines until the skipper has complete control of the boat and there is no risk of launching or bunny-hopping the boat.

The opposite applies following a leeward mark rounding. It is important to take a wide rounding and apply the required upwind downhaul, outhaul and vang tension, well before rounding the mark. If you turn too fast, you run the risk of hitting the water and slowing down very quickly.

PART EIGHT

Racing at a High Level

Chapter 29 • *Racing with Speed: 'Connecting the Dots'*

DEFINITIONS

Handling   This is the art of sailing to the next mark as fast as the boat will sail.

Strategy   Strategy is the art of reaching the next mark sooner by taking advantage of observed differences in wind speed, wind direction, sea state and current.

Tactics   This is what you do in addition to handling and strategy because of the presence of an adjacent competing boat or boat(s).

Clock   Small, temporary, always clockwise change in wind direction – that is, as 'veer' in northern hemisphere but not southern hemisphere.

29.1 ■ Strategy   BY FRANK BETHWAITE

The fast handler can sail as fast as any other sailor, but focuses completely on the boat and has not yet learned to look outside the boat. The handler does not see approaching changes and options because he either does not look or does not recognise opportunity in what he sees.

The strategist sails as fast as the handler, but in addition scans continuously. As soon as natural differences occur, the strategist observes them, identifies options, then decides the faster path and sails it.

The tactician sails fast, employs strategy by scanning to identify and then using the natural options, and in addition uses the racing rules to best advantage with respect to adjacent competitor(s).

There are many excellent books about tactics. This chapter will focus on strategy.

The difference between a good boat handler and a successful racing helmsman is that the boat handler gives most or all of his attention to handling the boat. The strategist has developed his skill to the point where he sails as fast as the handler, but with only minimal attention to the boat; he uses most of his time scanning the changing conditions through which he is about to sail. He identifies options as they emerge, and selects and sails the faster path through each option.

This art is perfectly encapsulated by Paul Cayard's analogy of 'connecting the dots'. This chapter will develop his theme.

I have asked a number of the world's successful sailors to describe the way they think about sailboat racing, how they prepare for their regattas, and how they handle 'connecting the dots'. Some sail conventional boats; some sail fast skiffs; some represent youth; some are mature. Their approaches are as different as the people themselves, the boats they sail and the different conditions they race in, but the approaches are all based on the common threads of planning, preparation, scanning while racing, decision, and superb handling skill.

29.2 ■ Connecting the dots   BY PAUL CAYARD

One concept that is important for all racing sailors to understand is that wind velocity changes last much longer and have a much larger effect on speed on downwind legs than upwind legs. How much longer? That depends on the speed of the boat relative to the speed of the wind.

If a boat is travelling at 7 knots upwind in 10 knots of wind, it has nearly 16 knots of apparent wind. If a gust or puff of wind comes along adding 1 knot of wind, this adds approximately 6% more wind. If a boat is travelling downwind at 6–7 knots in 10 knots of wind, it has about 3–4 knots of apparent wind speed. If a 1 knot gust comes along, it increases the apparent wind speed by 30%!

- *Point 1*: Puffs are 3–4 times more powerful downwind than upwind.
  - Next, if a gust or cell of wind comes along, it will last much longer downwind than upwind. How much longer? Let's see.
  - In our example above, the differential between the speed of the boat and the speed of the wind around it was 4 knots downwind and 16 knots upwind. So a gust of wind will 'stay with the boat' and affect the boat about 4 times as long downwind as it would upwind.
  - This effect is greater the faster the boat. Skiffs that go the same speed as the wind downwind may feel the positive effect of a gust for 20 times as long as they would upwind.

- *Point 2*: The positive effect from being in a gust, puff or lull will last 4–5 times longer downwind than upwind.
  - So if gusts are so important, so are holes (areas of less wind). Yes, holes also last longer and have a larger effect downwind than they do upwind.
  - When racing it is important to spot the puffs, and sail a touch higher or a touch lower than optimal to maximise the time you spend in the gust. Sometimes it even pays to gybe or tack for a gust of wind.

In a Sydney address to the 29er Association, I developed this theme by adding:

- Nature never reveals everything about the wind pattern that is approaching.
- No crew ever see everything that Nature reveals.

So the task of the crew becomes:

- Scan continuously to discover what is changing.
- Give shape to what you see. Connect the dots to develop pattern.
- Select and sail the fastest path through the pattern.

I call this 'connecting the dots'.

29.3 ■ Eighteen foot skiff: No 1 course record sail   BY JULIAN BETHWAITE

Author's note

The airline captain, the iceboat sailor (Fig 2.1) and the Eighteen foot skiff sailor (Fig 15.1) have in common that they control wind machines with a performance level such that normal variations from either forecast or carefully considered expectation make little difference to their flight or race.

The airline captain considers the forecast for the part of the world he will fly over, chooses the minimum time route and altitudes, loads appropriate fuel, and follows his flight plan closely. If along the way he can position himself in a favourable 100 knot jet stream for another half hour he will do so, but the difference is likely to be no more than ten minutes at the end of a ten-hour flight.

The skiff crew estimate the most probable wind during the race ahead. They choose their rig and foils, set up their stay tensions, and sail to plan. During the race they scan and respond to kilometre size surges and fades by sailing the surges and avoiding the fades. Shifts they ignore. Gusts are accommodated on a handling, not a strategy, basis.

Buddy Melges makes the point that 'iceboats are for the engineer'. So, I suggest, were the 'no rules' Eighteen foot skiffs.

By the end of that season (see Chapter 15) we had shortened the centreboards to 1700mm and lightened them to 6.5kg. Both the lighter-wind and the stronger-wind boards were near identical in area, but the lighter-wind board used a leading edge radius of about 0.7% of the chord, while the stronger-wind board used about 0.4%. We had shortened the rudder to 850mm (immersed depth), and the centreboard to about 900mm at speed. The sails had been cleaned up and flattened, masts were bending where they should, and the ratios were just about perfect.

The fact that these design and handling refinements had been worthwhile and really worked was affirmed in a very satisfying way. Later in that season in one heat of the World Championships we sailed a race in which, for us, all the factors 'came right'.

The skiffs' No 1 'Round the Islands' course into the prevailing summer afternoon funnelling northeaster has been the same for more than 100 years (Fig 1.22 – three laps from Clark Island to Sow and Pigs Reef and back, with a sail around Shark Island on the first and third laps). We set the all-time record for the No 1 course in 1992 with the Eighteen foot skiff which started the 1991–2 season as *All States* and was re-badged late in the season as *AAMI IV* (Fig 15.1).

The crew was Peter Louden as sheet hand and Peter Warner as forward hand, with me as skipper. This crew had won the Eighteen footer Worlds in 1990–1. The strong funnelling NE sea breeze at 20–22 knots (less than 25) was about as steady as they blow and exactly suited our small rig.

That boat had 17ft-span wings, and at that time we were very actively developing new rig technology. We had identified an important correlation between roach shape and mast bend. We had reduced the area of that particular mainsail by cutting a scallop out of the upper leech to reduce the chord of the upper sail. We had further identified that the mast bend was very sensitive to the height of the forestay attachment point. By altering the attachment point 20–30mm, we were getting significant changes in bend. Also, we were moving the shroud attachment point. Early Eighteen practice was that shrouds attached above the forestay, but we changed progressively to shrouds attaching below the forestay. This geometry generated a lever motion when the masthead bent back that maintained forestay tension. We found the lever dimension to be critical to less than 5mm. That was one of the best and nicest handling rigs we ever developed.

We managed a very good start, and pulled the centreboard way up when we were clear. The boat was moving very fast, the race was one of long tacks, the crew work was impeccable, and we enjoyed a dream run where everything went exactly right.

We were racing both days of the weekends and sailing twice for practice midweek, so our crew teamwork was very good. Eighteen footers are always about the crew, never about the skipper, and Peter Warner and Peter Louden 'bonded' unusually well. The practical result was that Peter Warner anticipated and called the gusts perfectly, that rig responded near-automatically with the upper leech opening and the forestay remaining taut as the mast bent (so we did not lose height), and Peter Louden tightened the mainsheet in the gusts to further flatten the upper main. When handled in this way, the boat pointed higher and sailed faster in the gusts. It was all very polished crew work to optimise the detail development we had put into that rig.

The downwind rides were frightening. The crew work was spot on, so we gybed exactly where we wanted to, and it was a dream sail. I remember one of the runs downwind. Where one normally rounds the Sow and Pigs buoy, sails starboard gybe into and gybes in Chowder Bay (Fig 1.22), on that day we sailed faster and deeper and gybed off Bradleys Head.

We started well, handled the boat without error, made no bad tacks, and managed to ride good surges downwind. The end result was that we finished the No 1 'Round the Islands' course, which has been unchanged for 150 years, in a few seconds less than 50 minutes.

The 'buoy to buoy in a straight line' length of the course is 15.4nm, so the mean 'straight-line' speed around the course was 18.5 knots. Since we necessarily tacked both upwind and downwind, the average boat speed through the water from start to finish substantially exceeded 20 knots.

It is interesting to note that Warwick Rooklyn in the original *AAMI I* also completed a No 1 course race under the time of the old 'best Mammoth' race record, and I think that Michael Spies did too in another B-18. So it was not just us in a freak race. These new, lighter, simpler boats really did sail faster.

The best time posted by a present One-Design Eighteen is a few seconds off 60 minutes. As at 2008, our 50-minute record of 1992 still stands. The boats that year represent the fastest Eighteen foot skiffs ever built.

29.4 ■ Laser: cutting the corners BY MARK BETHWAITE

Author's note

Mark and his distant cousin Warwick have in common that they control wind machines of a performance level such that they look for, and rely on finding and using, the transient but very real variations in wind flow that exist but are not big enough – nor do they last long enough – to be included in the forecast.

Warwick Bethwaite has supported the Canterbury Gliding Club for much of his life, for many years as its president. He and his friends take their pleasure in accepting an aero tow to 3000–4000ft, using local knowledge and skill to thermal soar to 6000–8000ft, at which point they head towards the Southern Alps 20 miles to the west and look for the bottom of likely wave lift. When they sense a wave, they angle back and forth to find the locus of the strongest lift. A few minutes later, they are on oxygen at 20 000–25 000ft, nose down, flaps slightly negative, and flying at 100 knots plus in what must be one of the world's biggest playgrounds.

New Zealand's Southern Alps stretch 1000km from subtropical Golden Bay at the northern extremity to the fjords and glaciers of Doubtful Sound and Puysegur Point to the south. From a noon start on a good day, they can visit either and be back before sundown. This is one of the world's great wave-soaring centres. The whole skill of soaring hinges on locating and using invisible variations in the flow of the invisible high-level wind.

At a smaller scale, Mark has developed to a similar level the art form of scanning, identifying and using useful variations in the flow of the equally invisible surface wind. He looks for key indicators at limit of vision range, and for other indicators at closer range. He fills in the dots and uses the information to such consistent effect that his last six (of eight) world championships have all six been won with a scorecard dominated by firsts with an occasional second. The consistent string of wins repeated six times is compelling evidence that his logic is sound.

The key elements of success in yacht racing are speed through the water, handling skills, strategy and tactics. All have been dealt with extensively in my father's and other books, so I will dwell only on my own approach to strategy.

Before proceeding, I make the unoriginal but vital observation that all four key elements of success are improved by time on the water, particularly training with one or more like-minded competitors. There is no better stimulus for improving boat speed than close-quarter training, and no greater way than training with other boats around close-spaced marks to improve handling skills. There is no greater aid to thinking strategically than being able, through training, to free your mind from the immediate tasks of making the boat go fast and handling it through changes in direction, and there is no better way to sharpen tactical skills than close-quarter training.

Time on the water and training with others should result in needing no more than 5% of your time to be confident of sailing at 95% or better of your optimum speed on any point of sailing. A former coach of mine used to call this 'easy speed'. Total focus on speed – what I call 'grinding' – takes a lot of effort, and does not allow you to think outside the boat.

The 'spare' 95% of your time and mental horsepower can be used to identify, track and resolve strategically important data. Put simply, through training, you can plan better and more quickly, tack or gybe without hesitation, sail to and spend more of your time in stronger wind and/or on the advantaged tack or gybe than your opponent.

A good way of thinking about sailing to windward is to take a helicopter view – say, from an altitude of 1000m above the course and looking upwind. In your mind, overlay a rectilinear grid on that course area, but drawn in the diagonal sense so that the lines represent port and starboard tack headings when the breeze is blowing from the median direction. Think of a chessboard with one corner on the start line or bottom mark, and the opposite corner at the top mark.

The street grid in a city like Sydney, Melbourne or New York (but not London!) is a useful analogy. In the case of Sydney, imagine you are sailing from Darling Harbour to Circular Quay. In New York, it would be Greenwich Village to South East Sea Port and so on.

Now take your thinking back to your boat and establish the bearings of those grid lines by taking port and starboard tack bearings for some time before the start and, critically, continue to update them during the race. Establish clearly the median bearing on port and starboard tack, and thereafter know whether you are on the median bearing, above or below it.

Again, it is very simple, but few people really grasp the imperative of ensuring that you are always sailing at or above the median bearing.

I use the phrase 'cutting the corners' to describe consistently sailing above the median bearings and that this can be achieved in one of two ways – macro and micro.

When sailing to windward in particular, but on all legs of the course, I take first a 'macro' approach to strategy, then a 'micro' one.

The macro approach is to look beyond the immediate to at least 200–500m to windward of where the boat is sailing – to observe what can be observed to allow you to 'cut the corners' when sailing to windward.

Other than when you are the first class to start on an open water course and on a cloudless day, there are usually no lack of indicators in the macro range to windward to predict how the wind will impact you in several minutes' time. These include other boats in your own fleet, boats in other fleets, clouds, land and on Sydney Harbour, flags on the Harbour Bridge, smoke from the funnels of ferries and ships … and the list goes on.

In the macro sense, cutting the corners means sailing consistently above the median bearing through being on the inside of the current phase in the wind pattern. It is likely that you can continue to sail above the median bearing through gusts and lulls. Boat placement on the race course is the way to achieve the macro cutting of the corners and results from continually scanning 200–500m (more if your eyesight is good enough) to windward of where the boat is sailing.

It is relatively simple, having made the observation of a coming clocking or backing phase of the wind, to place yourself on the course to take advantage of it or to minimise the disadvantage. To be more explicit, if you observe a backing phase in the wind from any one or more of the macro indicators, take starboard tack until you meet the backing phase, tack to port, and enjoy the lift. If you observe a clocking phase in the wind, take port tack to place yourself inside the shift, tack to starboard, and again enjoy the ride.

The value of training and hours on the water is that you can spend more time with your head 'out of the boat' rather than focusing on the telltales, sail trim, the bow of the boat as it meets the waves, and all the other issues that come naturally when you are as fully attuned to the boat and water as you are following a period of intensive training. What then makes the difference is the ability to get your head and mind out of the boat and concentrate on placing the boat better on the race course to take advantage of an ever-changing wind pattern.

The micro approach helps you to 'cut the corners' when sailing to windward by identifying and predicting the shorter-term pattern of wind on the water and how it can best be used. Up to and well beyond the design wind, when crews are fully hiked, boats with more wind sail faster. It is as simple as that and applies upwind and downwind.

Returning to the upwind situation, the priority is to place yourself in the vicinity of more wind than your competitors. Sailing faster to windward at its simplest means observing the wind patterns on the water in the 200m to windward of your position, then sailing on alternative tacks to step your way to windward through the areas of greatest wind strength.

This sounds obvious, but it is amazing how few people have the skill to link the gusts with the course of the boat as you make your way to windward. This is another example of connecting the dots.

Taking this to the next level, gusts appear and disappear on the water all the time. The real art of linking these gusts is not just to sail in the observed wind, but to predict where the next gust will form. Wind tends to form and flow in a pattern and it is not unreasonable to expect that pattern to recur and a gust to form where and when a pattern approach suggests it should.

Cutting the corners in the micro sense revolves around placement of the boat on the outside of a gust front and sailing the favoured tack in the gust.

Again taking a helicopter view, but this time at an altitude of only 50m, imagine a gust of wind impacting on the water. A gust is simply a parcel of faster higher-altitude air penetrating the slower-moving lower-altitude air and impacting on the surface of the water. As it impacts, it will not only move downwind, it will also spread across wind in the same way as if a glass of water is thrown onto a table. Most of the water will continue in the direction it is thrown, but a significant element will splay to each side.

It is this splayed wind propagating from the centre of the gust that allows you to cut the corner by sailing the lifted tack on the outside of the gust – on starboard tack if you are on the port side of the gust looking upwind, and on port tack if you are on the starboard side of the gust looking upwind [see Section 3.17].

Linking the gusts (or joining the dots) with your boat's track going to windward has the additional elements, first of predicting where the next gust will be, then being on the favoured tack on the outside of gust fronts rather than having to suffer a header as you sail into the 'wrong' side of it and are forced to sail through it.

When you are really attuned to wind and water it is possible to predict wind direction in an approaching gust. This is to do with how light reflects off the ripples on the water in the approaching gust. It is never the same two days in a row, but in the same way as a world-class tennis or golf player sees the ball 'as big as a football', a world-class sailor develops an intuitive approach to wind on water which simply puts him/her in a class above the rest.

The same strategy of looking for macro and micro elements is relevant when sailing crosswind and downwind. It is difficult on boats without sophisticated instrumentation – as is carried on ocean racing and America's Cup yachts – to track shifts downwind, but the micro wind pattern can certainly be followed, and to the extent that you can track macro elements, your downwind performance will be rewarded.

It is particularly difficult when running in a singlehanded boat to be able to look behind and to windward as often as is required to track the macro pattern, but very good singlehanded sailors seem to manage!

While I now sail a Laser, it really helps if you have good staff. It has been my privilege to sail with Ian MacDiarmid in J24s, Solings, then Etchells, and the following example shows how great observation by your crew and then teamwork can make the difference.

Prior to the 1982 World Soling Championships, Ian MacDiarmid and I plus two others teamed up with a J24 owner and won the Australian then the World J24 Championships. With that training and confidence, in our Soling we won both the Australian and World Soling Championship a few weeks later.

On the run leg of a late race in the J24 World Championships, Dave Curtis, the defending champion, was ahead by a length or so with us second several boat lengths abeam and to leeward. The course was outside Sydney heads in ocean waves and swell. We held position until we saw a particular combination we were awaiting – a forming gust and a set of big waves. At the critical time I luffed to attack Curtis who responded by luffing to keep his distance. With the added speed from the broad reach in the gust, we turned downwind on the first big wave, Ian MacDiarmid made a mighty pump, and we surfed through to the lead which we held to the finish.

In that case, the strategy was to anticipate, wait for, then use the approaching combination of gust and waves, and act at the critical moment so that everything would be in place together 30 seconds later.

Towards the end of the Soling World Championships a month or two later, we were third in a group of leading boats as we approached the finish. The leader was clear ahead. Boat four attacked, and we responded by tacking to maintain cover on four. Boat two responded by tacking to keep touch with three and four. About the fourth tack, Ian MacDiarmid, who was tracking the wind, said, 'Do you realise we are on a 15° lift?'

We re-planned quickly and tightened the cover on four, which tacked to escape. I said 'Dummy' and the crew dummied to the effect that boat two tacked to cover four and the commencing tack by three. But we reversed, did not tack, sailed the lift for 30 seconds, tacked on the next header, crossed the boat that had been two and held second place to the finish.

As I said, it helps to have good staff!

29.5 ■ Tasar: risk management in racing   BY ROB AND NICOLE DOUGLASS

Author's note

'In light air, current is always dominant'. When applied to daily big-fleet light air starts and racing in variable current, this truism grows to become 'The winner of this regatta will be the crew who best understand and manage the risks'. In their pre-regatta work-up, Rob and Nicole Douglass understood the imminent risks and went to unusual lengths to understand these risk factors and to take steps to manage them at three levels:

- By observation they acquired unusually detailed knowledge of the regatta environment.
- Anticipation of personal stress and frustration, together with what to do about it if it occurred.
- A regatta plan to defend their scorecard from crippling penalties.

This approach was successful.

2005 Tasar World Championships, Darwin

We sailed the 2000 Australian Tasar Nationals at Darwin, and finished third. We sailed the 2003 World Tasar Championships in Vancouver Island, Canada, and finished seventh.

When we sailed the 2004 Australian Tasar Championships at Mission Beach (near Cairns), things went horribly wrong both outside the boat and inside at the start of that regatta. While devastating at the time, we later realised that this was really good for us, because, after doing so well in Canada, we knew we could do so much better. So the Darwin 'Worlds' preparation started with ruthless analysis of what went wrong at Mission Beach.

Preparation for the 2005 Worlds – crew co-ordination

Understanding and co-ordination between skipper and crew is critical. As skills of both skipper and crew develop, valuable input can be gained from both parties. But what if there is a difference of opinion that needs to be acted on within the urgent time frame required in a dinghy race? A decision needs to be made, and once it has been made there is no going back, and no point in lamenting an incorrect decision – let alone arguing about it.

As an 11- to 15-year-old Nicole had been happy to work hard and take instructions, and her input up to that point had been almost entirely factual. From 15 through to 17, her knowledge and skills developed rapidly and at an increasing rate. With that knowledge and some confidence came more assertiveness and a greater input, but it also brought the potential for disagreement.

We had not faced this situation together and, from a racing point of view, while there were flashes of brilliance, it was mostly disastrous. If we argued, we sailed slowly. We were both easily distracted from the main game. With a bit more experience, we thought that we had overcome this problem, but after a very poor regatta at Mission Beach we realised that there were still traces of it. At Mission Beach it came home to us just how important teamwork was, so this became the focus of our training – just communicating about everything, rather than arguing about everything.

Further, we realised that I had made some poor decisions because I had allowed myself to become frustrated/preoccupied with either the error or the argument or both. So we revised our joint tasks, and Nicole took on another one – not only to support whatever was decided, but to counter frustration and get me refocused (if necessary) on the next important decision. In retrospect, this decision and conscious reallocation of tasks proved crucial.

All crews will have their own issues to work through and resolve, just as Nicole and I did.

Pre-regatta

We reviewed our research for the 2000 Darwin regatta. We studied and filed the Darwin daily weather data for six weeks prior to travelling to Darwin, and sailed regularly and hard in good competition.

I approached Neville Whittey to coach us. I had never previously approached a coach, but decided to try it because I realised that we were so close to achieving a really good result.

Following the NSW State Championships and with the Worlds ahead, I was worried that there were a number of matters I was not sure of, so I arranged to meet Neville with six pages of questions. His answers reassured me. To most he confirmed that I was thinking the right way. Others were left unresolved, which was fine in that if neither the coach nor I could answer them then nobody could either, so that matter became a matter for decision according to the circumstances of the moment rather than rigid technique.

What Neville brought to us as we worked was confidence. I am an experienced sailor, but am an accountant and not a full-time sailor. I have read the books, and put my experience together with the theory in the books, but there is still the uncertainty that comes with the challenge to my amateur approach by the professional or near-professional sailor. That's where Neville came in – just to talk through a lot of those things: 'Am I right or wrong about that?', 'You are right', 'That's good, I can keep on doing that'. The coach's function was largely to give us confidence that ours would be the best decisions in the conditions, and not to doubt them.

The practical result was that at the Worlds I felt as if I had two minds working. There was my own conviction of 'I've been here and done this, and it worked', and in addition there was a level above, as in: 'I have asked the coach and he agrees'. This gave a more secure base for the next decision up. The effect of this was that when something went wrong, I could 'take it on the chin' but then carry on with the next decision as if nothing had happened rather than agonise over the mistake.

Darwin regatta

The regatta details

This had crystallised into:

- 131 entries who were scheduled to start as one fleet and sail 12 races, three each day.
- To avoid the known wind and tide gradients that affect the normal dinghy course in Fannie Bay, and for adequate room for a 600m start line, the course would be laid 2–3nm offshore to the west of Fannie Bay.

Planning considerations

- Darwin lies on a north–south coast, Arnhem Land to the east, the Timor Sea to the west.
- The normal wind pattern at that season is an offshore easterly 'trade wind' in the morning, light air and a 180° wind change early afternoon as the westerly sea breeze replaces the easterly gradient wind, and the westerly sea breeze later.
- Calm and wind change were to be expected during the midday races.
- The course area chosen was over shallower water just to the south of the deeper shipping channel. This area is characterised by submarine sand ridges and deeper channels that shift position slowly.
- In the course area tidal current is strong.
- During the regatta the midday current would be flood (flowing to the east into Darwin harbour) and increasing day by day.

Work-up and observations

- We arrived a week early, and worked up against the Australian champion.
- The course area to be used for the Worlds was 1–2 miles further offshore than the Darwin Sailing Club's normal dinghy course area. So we consulted local yachtsmen who raced routinely in this further offshore area, and learned
  - The sand ridges had shifted slightly but significantly.
  - Noon wind change was avoided by locals. It could vary from smooth fade then build, to, occasionally, a line of wind at the sea-breeze front as it moved offshore.
- We made a particular point of identifying the positions of shoals and channels in the race area from observations of current differences while we were sailing. When in groups, we watched what was happening to the boat 100m away as well as our speed relative to the boat 20m away. We observed lower current speed over the shoals and faster current through the channels. We referenced the positions of shoals and channels by compass bearings and estimated distances from the No 6 channel navigation buoy.
  We think we did more observing than others around us. Critical to our preparation was that we never stopped observing. We knew what we were looking for and were alert to anything we thought relevant.
- At the end of this process, we were comfortable that we knew the local conditions as well as we could, and better than most competitors.

Final planning

Our view was that in a regatta with 130 starters racing off a 600m start line in dodgy conditions of probable light and variable air and certain strong and variable current, that every boat would probably have one, or more than one, poor race. In these conditions a series of top ten finishes could win.

So we planned to sail, and did sail, a very conservative series. Our objectives were as follows:

- To be consistent.
- To finish each race in the top ten (or better if possible).
- To remain free of punitive penalty points.
- We were not concerned with winning any race.

Re boat speed, we knew that we were in the top five, and that none of the other four was superior in all conditions.

Re starts, our view was that we should be near the favoured position, but did not have to have it. So we started very conservatively. Our object was to be near the favoured end, avoid any potential disaster, look for clear air as soon as possible, and get on with a conservative race.

The regatta

This preparation and planning worked well.

The 'sail conservatively' decision was the key to a progressively more dominant scorecard throughout the regatta. The dodgy second race each day did undo much of the fleet. In the light easterly air at the start, those who crowded the line early were washed over by the inflowing (westerly) tidal current, and had no way of getting back. This behaviour pattern continued despite the introduction of the black flag. A total of 45 boats were black flagged in race two on the first day, and a further 18 in race five on the second. While we risked the starter letting the fleet go (he never did), in these conditions we were prepared to sacrifice a perfect start and a race win for the structure of our scorecard. We stuck to this strategy and by mid-regatta all we had to do was to keep on sailing as we had always sailed. All the pressure was now on those who had to play catch-up but could take no risk because they could not afford even one more bad placing.

The value of some of the detail preparation was shown in the fifth race (the dodgy race on the second day). We had sailed the first race, endured four general recalls, and worked our way through the fleet to 9th when the easterly died as we approached the second leeward, downwind (westerly) mark. The flooding tide was washing us all away from the mark.

The last of the easterly then took the form of a gentle line of wind – the sea-breeze front – that swept up the entire fleet and brought them all up with the leaders. It then fell calm, except for a faint patch of air to the left (south). From 9th we were suddenly 123rd equal. Frustration was extreme. As I boiled and considered sailing towards the dying wind to the left, Nicole said quietly, 'What are you going to do next?' I exploded, 'I can't do anything in this calm.' Nicole said, even more quietly, 'We both know that we cannot do anything now. The question is "What do we do next?"'

She had done her job of sensing and defusing frustration.

With clear thinking restored, I realised that the easterly air to the left was vanishing. We knew we were over a sand ridge in less current, and that the boats to the left were over a channel in a stronger westerly current. So if we stayed where we were we would soon be ahead of 80 boats. Our pre-race observation and preparation was working, and a decision to stay where we were was logical.

I concluded that the line of wind was the sea-breeze front, that it was now to the west of us, that logically the westerly flow of the sea breeze had to start soon, and we knew within 10° where it would blow from. So we stopped trying to run in the vanished easterly, and instead adopted heading and trim for the expected westerly, Nicole hand-held the jib clew, sensed the feeble air, and inch by inch, then metre by metre, we started to move away from the line of boats.

We finished that race 12th, which was our worst regatta placing, but remains the one we value most.

Author's note

Rob and Nicole won that 2005 World Tasar Championship with a series of 'top ten' placings averaging 4.5. They won no race. Their discards were the 12th above and a 9th. In this case, their strength was pre-regatta recognition of unusual risk, and planning to minimise its consequences.

This is a superb example of intelligent regatta planning, preparation and strategy execution at its most complex level.

29.6 ■ 29er: World Championships, Weymouth 2006
BY SCOTT BABBAGE
(IN CONSULTATION WITH SILJA LEHTINEN)

Earlier contacts

Silja Lehtinen and I first thought about sailing a World Championship together at some stage in 2004 when David O'Connor and I were training in Europe prior to the 2004 29er Worlds in Switzerland. We sailed quite a bit against Silja and her brother Lauri, and then went to Finland for more training against them. When we returned to Australia following that trip, I persuaded her to come out and sail with me in the Australian 29er Championships over Christmas 2004.

We won those championships. She helmed; I sailed forward.

We met again a few months later at the 2005 29er Worlds in San Francisco, where I was sailing with David O'Connor. Silja was sailing with a female crew, and in San Francisco's strong winds she did not finish as well as the year before. So we thought, 'Why don't we do another regatta together?', and agreed to sail at Weymouth. David was about to enter the very demanding year 12 at school and had reached the stature where he would in future be sailing 49ers, so our years of sailing together in the 29er were necessarily coming to a close.

Over the following year, Silja no longer owned a 29er so had little opportunity to sail one other than sailing in the Finnish 29er Grand Prix circuit.

I spent the year building a Foil Moth and sailing 49ers and Eighteen foot skiffs, so I too had no opportunity to sail 29ers. As a result, we neither of us had any recent 29er experience prior to the Weymouth Worlds.

Pre-Worlds work-up

We met at Hayling Island to sail together in the UK 29er Nationals which preceded the Weymouth Worlds. At Hayling Island we spent the first week in both boat preparation and in practice sailing to get used to each other again and to rediscover and improve our co-ordination. Silja's technique had matured significantly in the years since we had last sailed together.

Silja's light-air technique is outstanding, and this comes from her background in Finland, which is a light-wind region. Her technique had refined into a 'getting started or restarted' mode; a 'heeled bow-down displacement sailing' mode [see Fig 10.9G] and an 'upright with crew weight far forward' apparent wind mode. Even though we were heavy, by the end of our work-up we could still win races against much lighter people because she knew how to set the boat up in light winds, and how to get it going and keep it going. In light winds a 29er switches between being a displacement boat and an apparent wind boat. Silja would heel the boat bow down and very free in the dead spots. She would start pointing only when she had accelerated and developed good movement, and she would bring it upright to sail it at maximum power and minimum wetted surface as early as possible as soon as it started to move well. The boat would be flat, the weight far forward, sails optimised, minimum movement, very smooth and with very accurate steering.

But the big difference was that in breeze Silja had made an art form of sailing upwind at competitive speed in any mode from pinching to extreme footing, and it required longer than one week for me to learn her new techniques and how best to co-ordinate to support what she was doing in all respects. So during the second week at Hayling Island we sailed the UK 29er Nationals more as a continuation of our training programme than focusing on placing well. It was a light air event in lumpy water, and many boats were sailing with substantially lighter crews. In particular, Paul Brotherton and Marie Shepherd, who won, were sailing at a crew weight 20kg lighter than us, and we could not at that stage match them in light breezes.

From Hayling Island we learned that we were still vulnerable in light winds and vulnerable downwind. We did not have a boat speed advantage, but we were still working on our co-ordination and technique – and still improving. We were fairly confident with the competition after that. We knew who we had to beat and who were the consistent boats.

The performances achieved as our work-up progressed are interesting:

- After one week we had reached the level where we could finish third in the light-air UK Nationals.
- After two weeks we had reached the level where we could finish first equal in the light-air qualifying races that preceded the Worlds at Weymouth.
- By the third week we had reached the level where we could win the Worlds with a few races to spare.

I learned a great deal from sailing with Silja.

29er World Championships at Weymouth, 2006

We could not sail at the Worlds venue at Weymouth until two days prior to the regatta because it was being used for the ISAF Youth Worlds. Silja and I had both sailed regattas at Weymouth previously, so we knew what the conditions there were like. It is a large flat-water harbour that will be the Olympic venue for 2012. It is big enough to fit three courses side by side.

Tide

Tidal currents in the harbour were negligible, and courses were sometimes set outside the harbour. Depending on the course location, in a S/SW breeze the right-hand side sometimes had a beneficial tidal effect. Compared with San Francisco, where tidal current was a huge factor, the current gradients at Weymouth were trivial.

Wind

Winds at Weymouth tend to be steady, with the harbour being enclosed on the western side by a low causeway with Portland Bill, a very big high promontory at its southeastern end. Winds from the south and west and the sea breeze all tend to funnel over the causeway between Weymouth and the promontory as a consistent flow. As in all venues, you end up getting a share of strange winds. There were some days when it was blowing off the sea and funnelling around the Bill and the 49ers would be racing near the (inland) shore in 20 knots, and the 29er course parallel to them would be in 5–8 knots. Somebody sailing offshore would be racing in 3 knots, so it is an area with pronounced gradients caused by local effects plus sea breeze effects at times.

The wind strength changed during the Weymouth event. During the first three days of qualifying it was very light – perhaps 5–8 knots, often lighter. Silja and I were sailing at the same weight, 136kg, as David and I had sailed at San Francisco. At the end of the qualifying races we were tied equal first with Paul Brotherton and Marie Shepherd who were sailing much lighter, so we were very happy to have reached the stage in our work-up where we could now match them in light winds despite the weight difference.

Qualifying

There were 108 entries, and there were three days of qualifying where we raced in four fleets of 27 boats. After each day of qualifying, the fleets were re-seeded by what is now a standard system – they would list the 108 boats according to their accumulated scores then assign them to four separate groups in the order 1, 2, 3, 4 then 4, 3, 2, 1 to generate the next day's fleets. One effect of this system is that often the top few boats never race against one another. At Weymouth, the initial seeded choice of fleets meant that there were no strong light-air teams in our fleet to match us.

After three days of qualifying, the top 25 boats became the Gold Fleet, and the Silver and Bronze fleets each consisted of half the remainder.

Scoring

Each boat carried its *place* into the final races. This practice still varies year by year:

- In Switzerland we carried our *points* right through the regatta. This favoured the top three boats which had generated a large points buffer between 3rd and 4th place, so in the final races the top three could ignore all other boats and race between themselves.
- In San Francisco we carried our *place* of 7th, which was good for us because we were not penalised with a crippling points penalty.
- In Weymouth we again carried our *place* from the qualifying races, this time as a non-droppable score. This was bad for us as we had generated a 15 point buffer between ourselves and the third boat. (In the qualifying races, we finished 1st 6 or 7 times, plus a 2nd and a 5th, which gave us 1st equal on points and 1st on countback.)

Courses and programme

The programme was for up to five races each day, and we raced 15 to 16 races in total. Courses were upwind–downwind, with the start line (which was also the finish line) just to leeward of the leeward gate course marks. Leg length and number of laps (always two or three) were adjusted so the winner's elapsed time was expected to be about 35 minutes. Time limit for the first leg was 15 minutes, and for the whole race was 45 minutes.

Racing

In the World Championship races that followed the qualifiers, our principal opponents were Paul Brotherton and Marie Shepherd. Paul is very experienced, a past European 49er champion, 40+ years old. If they were going to match us boat for boat in very light winds, they would expect to beat us because of their 20kg crew weight advantage.

In the first race in light air, Paul match raced us at the start. He started well – but we did not. He led the fleet, but unfortunately for him the wind had stayed so light that the Race Committee was forced to abandon because nobody finished within the time limit.

By the start of the re-sail, a 12–15 knot sea breeze had set in. Unfortunately for us, our first valid race was an OCS, so thereafter we had to race conservatively. However, through the final series the wind strength progressively increased, so our greater crew weight ceased to be any disadvantage. Our placings that first day were not good – OCS, 3rd, 5th, 7th, but nobody else sailed better so at the end of the first day we were just in the lead.

The second day was quite a long day on the water. The breeze started at 12–15 knots and increased through the day to about 20–22 knots. We scored 3, 1, 4, 1, 2, and finished the day with a 10–12 point buffer between us and the second placed boat, and in addition we now enjoyed a very great psychological advantage.

The last two races that day were quite windy – the wind strength was similar to that at San Francisco. In SFO, the short steep waves and adverse tide in the Gate had slowed the boats to the point where gybes were difficult for the whole fleet. At SFO we, along with the rest of the fleet, had our troubles. At that stage, David was a young and very talented natural sailor who could drive a boat very fast, but could also make costly mistakes. At Weymouth the water was flat and the boats were moving very fast, so the boat handling was quite easy. Silja is a few years older than David, but has much deeper experience. She started in Optimists followed by Bytes and was World Byte champion, and now campaigns in Ynglings for the Olympics. After pioneering the 29er Class in Finland, she has learned to sail the boats the hard way. She is a more mature sailor, a thinking sailor, more analytical. Her boat handling is much more refined, more mechanical in her approach. So in the same winds as at SFO but flatter water, our performance and our manoeuvres were more consistent. Concerning her gybing technique, I could be confident that our turn would be balanced, measured and consistent. In this way, we could approach and exit the gybe in the same way every time.

We used a single tiller extension. However, as between Silja and David, one of the differences in gybing technique is that Silja pre-clears the tiller extension under the mainsheet prior to steering into the turn. That way, she can control the boom through the middle of the gybe without having that moment of danger trying to get the tiller extension through.

At a more general level, with David I tended to scan and advise what was relevant, then called the tactics and he responded. With Silja I scanned and advised in the same way, but Silja's age and experience often led her to question my direction and that made for an interesting departure from the norm. It is often difficult to explain your reasons in the heat of the moment without resorting to unintelligible Australian slang.

The third day of the finals was a stormy day with SW winds 10–12 knots between squalls that blew at up to 18 knots. We sailed on the outside course in waves that were refracted around the Bill to roll south across the course, so we were sailing into the waves on one tack and along them on the other.

David is a keen surfer so has a natural sense in waves. Silja is just a brilliant conscious sailor, and her wave technique was as good as any in the fleet.

We won the first two races, and the regatta was ours barring disaster, so we sailed conservatively for the rest of the third and final day.

Handling technique

Silja is not only a mature sailor with many years of high-level racing experience to draw on. In addition, she has three particular skills at which, once we were fully 'worked up', she was simply better than most of the other competitors.

One is superior light air technique, mentioned above.

The second is that her starting ability is accurate and consistent.

The third is that she could not only change gears fluently in any weight of breeze, she could then sail as fast as any other competitor in whatever mode was appropriate at the moment. She can instantly switch to match any other competitor boat for boat, in any wind at any time, when the tactical situation calls for this. Therefore we could match any boat that was pinching and going high. What we had, and the others *didn't* have, was the ability to switch quickly into a lower, faster maximum VMG mode. Most of the other boats had one upwind mode and nothing else – they had only one gear.

Another strength was that whenever the wind increased from moderate to fresh Silja would always continue working as hard as she could. Most crews started to ease sheet and sail free quite early, often with the skipper sitting in. At that point, Silja would be hiking to extreme to wind the boat up – using all of our crew weight, both of us fully extended, me on trapeze and she hiking at 100% body extension, to keep the main on, to keep the leech up, to keep our height or to give us whatever else we wanted.

The sheet would never begin to go out until she was hiking to the maximum.

Strategy

In terms of strategy, we used a simple formula:

- We relied on her starting skill to start well.
- We relied on her multi-mode flexibility to maintain a clear lane going in the direction we wanted to go on the first work. We probably had a better range of modes upwind than any other competitor. We would change gears adapting to the tactical and strategic situation as appropriate, and did this through accurate trim and steering.
- Our strategy for the whole regatta was to be in the top two or three at the topmark and thereafter hold or improve position. In 29ers, and indeed in all skiffs, that is important because the top few boats will extend their lead and somebody coming from behind will be unable to catch them without a fortunate major shift. So we would start well, choose our lane, use our multi-mode capability to maintain it, then use tactics to put boats away. We did not deal kindly with any of the lead boats near us. All other boats we ignored.

One example of this flexibility and how Silja used it occurred in the first race of the third day. The European champions had been told by their coach to 'gas' us – to put us back into the fleet. At the first tack of the day they tacked very close, directly in front of us, but unfortunately for them they tacked poorly. Like a flash, Silja had borne away and accelerated to take position immediately underneath them. From there we pulled slowly half a length ahead, then we switched gears to climb to windward to lee-bow then cross ahead of them, and from there we adjusted position to increase our lead by 'gassing' them all the way to the layline. They could not deal with this psychologically and raced poorly thereafter.

Our approach enabled us to take the favoured side, to take the first shift. Before long the other competitors got to know how we sailed and avoided us. This had the effect of giving us what we wanted on the start line and up the first work.

Downwind we were never as comfortable or fast as David and I had been downwind. Silja and I rarely passed boats downwind, so we just had to be very quick upwind.

Often at the start we would start not at the favoured end but a little further along the line, with clear air and separation, and we were then able to adopt maximum VMG mode immediately and would roll straight over the top of the boats that were bunched to leeward of us holding each other up. Typically there would be a group of boats at the favoured end, and we would start just above them. Within 200m, we would have rolled them all because of both better air and better VMG. Nobody else could match us in consistent speed across the whole range between pinching and footing.

Tactics

As between San Francisco and Weymouth, at San Francisco David did not have Silja's experience nor multi-mode handling skill nor tactical maturity, and in any case the unusually rough water and strong winds made it counter-productive to adopt a tactical approach.

At Weymouth, the generally lighter winds and flat water invited crews to employ tactics, and Silja's maturity, regatta experience, multi-mode handling capability and tactical skill were decisive.

419

As an example, Silja's technique when we were sailing close to another boat was such that she could always match and usually beat the other vessel. David could lose focus or lose concentration at a critical second and slip back, and it took constant feedback to stay in gear.

Silja and I could adopt whatever mode was best in the tactical and strategic conditions of the moment. Often we would set up the important boats around us to ruin their race. If our competition was tacking below us we would go fast and roll them, and once we were in position they had to tack or take our bad air all the way to the layline. We would not just leave them with separation in a position from which they might gain advantage again. Instead, we would drive them into a situation from which they could not easily recover.

Downwind, Weymouth was not a particularly shifty place so there were neither big gusts nor big shifts to take downwind. In these conditions the technique of sailing to the layline was fastest. Often if we were setting up behind a boat at the windward mark, we would follow them down the run, wait and gybe just inside them on the layline, roll them and beat them to the gate. We picked off boats slowly, one at a time.

Weymouth was such a consistent venue there were no surprises due to unexpected gusts or shifts. Sailing at the front of the fleet we knew that the boats behind were sailing in more disturbed air, so only one or two of the very lightest crews could overtake.

If they were not one of the top three or four, we let them go. If around the topmark there was another boat adjacent that was not one of the top boats, we would talk to them and endeavour to agree to sail as fast as possible without mutual interference. This approach benefited both boats.

So that was it. We concentrated mainly on being quick upwind and manipulating the opposition upwind. Whether in the lead or not, in the lead we sailed to avoid confrontation with all boats other than the top three or four. We quickly established ourselves as unwise to mix with, and as people got to know how we sailed, they avoided confrontations with us.

Author's note

I asked Scott if he would expand on their multi-mode upwind ability – for example, did they mark their sheets? Also, if he would comment on Weymouth in view of the problems when gybing the previous year. Scott again:

I can't think of a way to accurately describe how we replicated our modes unfortunately. We'd go by feel. Our control lines and sheets were unmarked. It did not occur to either of us to consider that we had reached the stage where it was appropriate to mark them. In our work-up we focused on being able to set up quickly and accurately at maximum VMG for the wind and the waves of the moment, then we would practise sailing higher and lower. In this way, we became confident of both the optimum point and also the acceptable range adjacent to that point, and how wide or narrow was that range in differing conditions. This work enabled us to respond to the tactical situation by tuning within an established range to whatever felt good at the time. Luckily, more often than not we got it right.

In terms of set-up we would talk through the options available. If we were feeling bound up, we might raise the board a few inches or go down on the jib clewboard. If we needed power we'd do the opposite, or sail with more sheet tension and less vang to deepen the main.

It was just a balance for what felt good and what matched the conditions. In retrospect, it was all so quick – the preparation of the boat, the UK Nationals, the qualifying races, the Worlds, and it was over. We didn't have either the time or the familiarity with the particular boat to work out an exact formula or set of 'fast numbers'.

Re gybing, I do not know what Silja's exact technique was because I never looked. I didn't look because I didn't need to look. What I know is that her turns were always consistent, with smooth authority uninterrupted by any 'change hands' distraction mid-gybe. The consistency enabled me to synchronise my co-ordination with Silja and with the boat to the point where there was never a problem.

In San Francisco, the thinking during the gybe was on the gybe. In Weymouth, regardless of the wind, as we gybed our thinking was on winning the tactical situation immediately following the gybe. The handling problem had vanished.

Author's note

In this example the regatta environment was one of relatively uniform wind and sea-state conditions. The principal variables would be the behaviour of competitors. A young crew based their work-up, planning and execution on their ability to be good at everything – and particularly good at maintaining competitive windward-going VMG across the wider range of pointing angle (from pinching to footing) in all wind strengths, which is an inherent property of the modern skiff. This enabled them to be slippery in defence and deadly in attack. Focused preparation, deliberate race planning and strategic execution to exploit this particular advantage in sometimes robust weather conditions won them a World Championship.

29.7 ■ 49er: Coaching Gold Medallists

BY EMMETT LAZICH

Author's note

When Moths became narrow skiff Moths, the learning curve to master them was so steep that relatively few sailors made the change successfully. Emmett was one of those who did. A perfectionist, he kept at handling his Moth and applying himself to regatta strategy until he won the Moth World Championship in 1991 and again in 1995.

Emmett's approach is essentially the same as mine and Julian's – measure everything, record it, think about it, analyse it, and in this way learn how to do it better.

He has become a coach at the highest level. Thomas Johanson and Jyrki Jarvi asked him to assist them, and with their skill, assisted by Emmett's coaching, they won the first 49er Olympic Gold Medal at the Sydney 2000 Olympics with a race to spare.

EMMETT LAZICH

Sailed Manly Juniors, Flying Elevens, Lasers, 420s, Moths, Eighteens, 49ers.

Moth World Champion	1991	Japan
Moth World Champion	1995	Australia
3rd Eighteen foot skiff Grand Prix	1997	Australia–New Zealand circuit
6th 49er World Championships	1999	Melbourne, Australia

He then began coaching.

All the early boats and also the Moths were 'wind from behind'-type boats.

I wanted to sail Eighteen foot skiffs, and Bill McCartney (from *Grand Prix Sailing*) loaned us one of the old boats with the flip-flop wings. It was so heavy you couldn't lift it. We would sail it in the winter down at Balmoral. We would sail until dark, then unrig it on the sand beach by the water and bring it up piece by piece because it was too heavy to carry up to the grass. It was so much effort, but we lived for it. I remember it when I see the young guys now in the Eighteens and am a little bit sad that the boats are not as intimidating as they used to be. But when I see their passion, I still remember it.

The Moth without the spinnaker is a total apparent wind vessel on most points of sailing. And with the foil-borne Moths, it is just more accentuated. You live and die by apparent wind strength. But even the skiff Moths are blow-from-behind boats on square runs.

I bought *Nokia*, a modern, light Eighteen, and was abruptly into real apparent wind sailing. The downwind sailing was the major difference. I had always been intrigued by the whole tack-downwind concept. I put a wind indicator on the top of the mast and watched it tacking forward when we gybed sailing faster than the wind in the medium-light breezes where the relative performance of the boat is so high. I thought that was really cool.

A decade later, the general sailing population do not yet begin to understand this concept.

Coaching principles

I coach 49er sailors today with the idea that the better the boat handling and 'flow' and the steadier the speed and the faster you sail, the narrower will be the relevant scan sector on either tack or gybe. The more consistent the speed, the more predictable will be the path along which you are sailing.

If you are looking along those scan lines to see what you will intercept – the true wind you will sail through – there is a win–win situation in that those who sail fastest in straight lines not only benefit from their speed and depth, but also have an easier job with observation, anticipation and strategy because they are reducing the variables.

I was asked to coach the Finnish sailors Thomas Johanson and Jyrki Jarvi:

THOMAS JOHANSON	
Finland, Helm: *Started sailing at age 10 in Optimist*	
4th in Optimist Worlds	1984
4th, 5th and 6th in Europe Dinghy Worlds	
European Laser Champion	1991 also 1992
World Laser Champion, New Zealand	1993
8th in Laser in Atlanta Olympics	1996
3rd in 49er Worlds in Mexico	2000
Gold Medal, 49er class, Sydney Olympics	2000

JYRKI JARVI	
Finland, Forward hand: *Sailed Europe Dinghy, 5o5, 470, 49er*	
5th in 470 Worlds	
3rd in 49er Worlds in Mexico	2000
Gold Medal, 49er class, Sydney Olympics	2000

The Johanson and Jarvi team: early history

TJ and JJ started sailing the 49er when the class was awarded International Status late in 1996. Their early experience is as follows:

TJ is an extremely talented sailor with unusual raw talent in 'feel', and in understanding the wind and water. He is the sort of person who has the potential to pick up very quickly on any new technology.

JJ's function was to keep the boat going, using his logical mind and athletic agility.

Their results as a team were not too good in 1997 and 1998 – or even in 1999. All sorts of things happened, but they slowly improved both the way they worked as a team and the equipment they had to work with. It all started to come together when they finished 3rd in the Mexico 49er Worlds immediately prior to the 2000 Olympics.

I did not start working with them until after the Mexico regatta. Until then, I had been working with another Finnish team. When that team did not qualify, TJ and JJ asked me to work with them, and I accepted with no hesitation. From my own 49er regatta experiences, I understood the problems TJ and JJ were faced with. So my starting point was late, but with a team that had been able to pick up high-level apparent wind racing skills on their own and with minimal coaching due to their own exceptional raw talent. They welcomed me and my assistance, and were an enthusiastic team to work with. We became a close team and, from the start, we aimed high.

Aiming high included the boat and the team support. They detailed the boat to be used at the Games to an exceptionally high level prior to the start of final training. The Finnish team understood that skiff crews when training cannot enjoy rest periods on the water unless appropriately supported, so offered us the use of a coach boat dedicated to the 49er crew.

Task allocation: TJ and JJ

TJ and JJ defined their tasks very clearly, and used what I think is a fairly standard 49er approach.

TJ's tasks

TJ, the helm, was basically the decision-maker. His visual focus was outside the boat; he did the scanning and made the decisions.

TJ and I discussed task allocation right at the beginning, and worked out exactly what would be our approach to getting tasks done and staying happy. This was critical because he and I had to make sure that the coach and the helm were on the same wavelength. We agreed that in terms of strategy and tactics, the boat would run with the helm. As regards keeping the boat going – in terms of issues within the radius of the boat – that was going to be JJ's responsibility.

This approach is very different from what Julian Bethwaite says about how he and his crew handled the Eighteen, but I would say it is more normal in the modern 49er outlook, where the helm has a much larger focal radius, and the forward hand has a much smaller focal radius. There is a good reason for this difference.

If, but only if, you mix and match the controls to set it up correctly, the smaller 49er becomes an amazingly responsive boat. When it is set up properly, its automatic response is such that a helm with a good sense of feel and feedback can rely on the crew and the boat itself to sail at maximum speed. It is this feature of the 49er that enables the helm to focus predominantly way outside the boat. Of course, there is mental multi-tasking and cross-checking – for example, the helm checking waves and power controls.

This does not happen with an Eighteen foot skiff – they are just too manual. Hence the difference of approach between the two classes.

JJ's tasks

While TJ as helm spent his time scanning as above, JJ would predominantly tend the engine room, and cross-check strategy and tactics.

At the beginning of the regatta, JJ was a little unsure of how he would function with TJ under pressure, but he changed very quickly and started to believe that he was the best crew out there. *And*, by the end of the regatta, in my coaching opinion he *was* the best crew out there. It was an amazing transition, which reflects on a lot of factors – their strategy, their speed, their confidence and the way they prepared the boat and everything else that was relevant. As all of these factors built up, their joint confidence soared and they started sailing really well.

Upwind principles

Upwind sailing in apparent wind boats, all of which are light and have big sails, is all about flow and anticipation. If you are going to sail into a lull and you don't know that that lull is going to happen before it happens, you are in big trouble. You have to move the body weight in and sheet in before the rig starts to come over to windward, otherwise you do not sail steadily. So it's all about anticipation and flow and power control, and whether automatic or manual it's about controlling the power smoothly.

I remember that in the Eighteen footer Grand Prix Series era, one of the girls in the hospitality area, who knew nothing about sailing, said to me, 'If you watch the guys that are fast, and you watch the guys that are not going fast, the ones that are fast are upright all the time.' When I thought about it afterwards, I realised that she was more right than she knew. She was thinking 'They just keep it upright', whereas I thought 'If you have a poorly set-up rig, it is difficult for even a skilled dinghy sailor to keep it upright. It is always going to rock around to windward and to leeward.' So whether it is design or preparation or how you sail when you get out on the water, it is only those with good boats and good technique who sail upright and fast. This is exactly what happened to the first Moth sailors who moved to the narrow skiff Moths; in year one our balance was unsteady, but by year two our sailing was smooth, confident, upright and fast.

Upwind, practical: TJ

As helm, TJ predominantly focused outside the boat. His technique when sailing upwind was to scan the quadrant centred on the apparent wind direction at every range from limit of vision to imminent gust. He looked for everything and anything that was relevant, whether distant for strategy or medium-range for tactics or immediate for handling – such as abnormal waves and imminent gust onslaught.

Time allocation mid-leg was to devote most time to scanning at distance for strategy factors, and adequate time was devoted to tactics in the sense that the team object was to avoid tactical issues wherever possible – a 'get out of jail' attitude.

One of the things that TJ and JJ did really well was to avoid getting bogged down in tactics. They were unusual in their ability to sail around the course as if they were the only boat on that course. Many sailors would say 'But you just can't do that', but one of the things that made it possible in their case was that they and their boat did have very good speed in medium to light conditions. They were certainly not slower than anyone else in the generally medium and unsteady conditions of Sydney Harbour in August (late winter). So what happened was that after a few races many of the opposition were reluctant to start alongside them, so right from the start they tended to enjoy clear air. This enabled them to focus more on strategy and boat handling, and less on tactics. They regarded tactics as a distracting side show. They were able to benefit from having the speed to sail clear of the mass for most of the time, and the tactical skill to maximise their clear air.

Upwind, practical: JJ

When sailing upwind, JJ's prime function as forward hand was power control. In response to the minute-by-minute changes in wind and wave, he subtly tweaked sheet, vang, downhaul and camber and adjusted body weight and, when appropriate, co-ordinated with TJ about jib trim. He kept the rig always set up for the middle of the present range of conditions, so that, combined with his fluent body movement, the automatic flexing of the rig to the quicker changes best optimised their speed.

The 49er's hull has a low prismatic coefficient with little volume in the ends, so it is very sensitive to fore-and-aft body weight movement. If the helm is looking 500m up the course, he is not always thinking about fore-and-aft trim, so JJ's function was to sense any error and interrupt TJ if necessary and get him to move a bit to maintain optimum trim and 'flow'.

Lateral body movement is critical, and has a fore-and-aft component as well. When the breeze strengthens it both heels the boat and drives the bow down a little, so the forward hand needs initially to move out and back, then a little forward. When the breeze goes light, there is less power from the rig so the nose pops up initially. So optimum body movement is not just in and out for lateral control, it has an essential initial diagonal fore-and-aft trim component as well which becomes the first movement of a two-stage process. JJ was smooth, accurate and astute with that power control, and it was his skill in handling this that provided the consistent target speed that enabled TJ to do what he was doing so well. Considering their problems in their earlier years together, I found this magnificent to observe as their coach.

This task delegation and execution, plus their level of confidence plus their boat preparation, gave them competitive boat speed. They really were on a roll.

Downwind principles

This is where there is a tremendous difference in approach between blow-downwind boats and tack-downwind boats, which in practice is much harder to grasp. I still remember vividly that when I first started to sail the Grand Prix Eighteens and started thinking through the concept of gybing and imagining the mirror image of being on the other gybe, it was a shock to realise where the new apparent wind would be coming from. But it was true! I learned that the gust you were going to sail through if you gybed the skiff in moderate air was way out ahead of you downwind on the other side. To look far enough downwind I had to walk to the back of the wing and look past the clew and around the back of the mainsail leech. Further, when looking downwind like this I had to learn to estimate the wind strength from reading its effect on backs of the waves.

This concept is something that the sailors of blow-from-behind boats have never experienced and never even imagined. It is still completely foreign to them.

Downwind handling

When I started to work with them, TJ and JJ were sailing the boat in the way that most of the top crews sail mid leg in 2006. The helm scans from the boat to the limit of useful visual range but in two very narrow sectors: one ahead crosswind and slightly downwind for the tack that he is on, and one for the tack that he would be on if he gybed the boat. He would spend about 75% of his time scanning ahead, about 20% scanning the opposite sector, and, say, 5% thinking about the laylines and his opposition and where he is positioning himself relative to them.

That would apply in the middle of the course in 'normal' conditions. Abnormal waves and survival conditions, for example, might call for 25% of the attention, so the other factors would need to be scaled down.

The helm trims the mainsail and the forward hand trims the spinnaker. Co-ordination is essential for smooth power control and boat speed. If you trim the spinnaker alone, you may need a 300mm sheet movement. When the mainsail is also trimmed in co-ordination, the sheet movement to trim the spinnaker will be about halved, and the boat will sail faster. The better you co-ordinate, the less the steering will chase the trim and vice versa, and the more smoothly and faster the boat will 'flow' and the deeper you can steer. So the helm and forward hand always anticipated and trimmed in unison. In a really good gust both body weights would go out a little further, moving together and quickly, the helm would already be pulling away as the gust front reached the boat, and the boat just drove deeper and faster. There was never any hesitation or over-powering in gust fronts. They had already done enough training and hard work together beforehand so the fluency and co-ordination of their downwind handling was near perfect.

Obviously at the top and the bottom of the course other boats are closer and tactical issues will demand more of the helm's scan time. There is so much going on as you approach the bottom gate that you need two sets of eyes to catch everything. At these times the forward hand needs to become the eyes in the back of the helm's head, and in particular to call the approach to either layline. But regardless of tactical preoccupation, spinnaker trim and body movement remains the overriding priority.

You have to get the basics right – consistent, undiminished speed, clean efficient gybes right onto the layline, and planning to remain in clear air. In a 49er in light to medium winds, if you don't approach the bottom gate on the laylines and you are not the lead boat, you invariably get eaten alive.

The three downwind handling techniques

Mode one is light air when you are trying to steer low. In this, the McKee brothers were my role model. The object is to keep the apparent wind forward, but you are easing the spinnaker sheet to get the spinnaker and the main separated. You are trying to get the spinnaker to project out in front of the boat rather than hide behind the mainsail, and you are very carefully using subtle body weight movement – some people think of it as working the windward chine, sailing deep but with the apparent wind still forward. It's easy to stall (for lee-side flow to separate from the spinnaker), and *if* you stall, you nearly stop. When you stall and stop, you have to come up and start again which is very costly.

The McKees were very good at sailing low in wind speeds in which you are not committing too much weight out from the centreline. In Finland there was a great fleet of 49ers that spent much time racing in light air on tight courses, so the Finland crews were already good at this and there was no real need for further coaching.

Mode two is where you are trapezing, but are not yet fully powered up. The Sydney 2000 Olympics were sailed mostly in mode two winds. In mode two, I believe that Chris Nicholson had a head start on everyone for two years because he was so good at mode two sailing.

When you are trapezing but not fully powered, you are trapezing with bodies high, much higher than in mode three – but trapezing nevertheless. You are still trying to sail low, but you are not doing it with eased sheets as in modes one and three. Instead you are oversheeting and doing it with a 'squeeze'. Ease and squeeze instead of ease. So, you oversheet, which momentarily powers and speeds the boat up, and when you have that speed you carefully and subtly steer down and take the extra VMG – but there is such a fine line between doing it correctly and the stall. It should be noted that this will not work with all spinnaker shapes, and possibly will not work with some hull shapes.

As an example, imagine that you are approaching a bottom mark and that you have underlaid so you want to get lower to round the mark.

The typical rookie will bring the body weight in, ease the sheet, and sail slowly down to the mark.

The astute apparent wind sailor will oversheet, power and speed the boat up, and steer down while they have that speed, and time it and do it in such a way that just as the boat stalls the spinnaker comes off as they round the mark. That is something that sailors can relate to. Squeeze it on, sail low while you have the speed, you know that you are going to drop off the plane and stall sometime, but by then you are at the mark. You have done the job and are back sailing upwind again.

The good 49er guys are doing that for the whole downwind leg, but gently, not aggressively, so they never stall. They are 'scalloping' – luffing just before the flow separates. In this way they keep the flow attached and the apparent wind forward and re-establish normal flow and avoid stall and maximise power. The critical factors here are skill in both sail trim and in steering, and in the co-ordination of trim with steering. In this way they can maintain the same speed and sail a mean course lower than the rookie can sail, and they still keep the apparent wind forward. A feature of the 49er is that the spinnaker is cut with twist, so although the lower sail may sometimes stall, the head holds flow and this makes recovery easier. It looks wrong, but it works.

I learned this from observation when competing against Chris Nicholson and Adam Beashel. I had to learn it otherwise we were simply not competitive.

Mode three is easy to understand. This mode starts where you are fully powered, trapezing low, and covers all stronger wind sailing where you are over-powered.

In mode three you sail as high and as fast as you can. Ease as much sheet as you need to keep the boat flat, and trapeze with bodies as far from the centreline as possible. By virtue of the speed you generate, you swing the apparent wind forward and end up sailing low. All sailors can relate to this as soon as they try it.

TJ and JJ and the three modes

At the time I started working with TJ and JJ they were already good at mode one because of the practice in Finland, and also at mode three downwind sailing because of their natural talent. For a while we did not have much mode two wind. As a result, it was only shortly before the Olympics when the weather pattern changed that I realised that they were unaware of the medium to light air mode of sailing a 49er downwind described above.

We discussed it, and I explained to them how to do it. They tried it and were immediately able to feel the results. And that was a big penny that dropped for them just before the Sydney Games. When TJ and JJ picked up on this they were really excited about it and trained hard, and very quickly were able to apply it really well. You could see the excitement. It was two weeks before the Olympics, and they had learned something major.

As it turned out, the Sydney Games were sailed predominantly in mode two downwind sailing conditions. Obviously they had good equipment, but the conditions were such that they could use this technique; it was fresh in their minds and they thrived on it. There were a lot of other factors involved in their victory – for example, the amount of confidence they sailed with and aspects such as that – but they were really on a roll and they were certainly quick during the regatta, and mode two downwind sailing was one of their weapons.

Conclusion

TJ, the helm, was basically the decision-maker – he did the scanning and made the decisions. As regards strategy, as they gained confidence he backed his own judgement to the point of exploiting the gusts and the shifts upwind in a bolder manner than the more conservative Olympic level norm of the other competitors.

JJ kept the boat moving at target speed for more of the time than anyone else. The attitude of both of them was that they were having the regatta of their lives. They were accustomed to and not troubled by the stress of the regatta environment. TJ had won a Laser World Championship and JJ had finished 5th in a 470 Worlds and third in 49ers in Mexico. To them, the Olympics was the best fun they had ever had.

TJ and JJ were brilliant in that despite being bold they were incredibly consistent. My analysis of this is that on the course they were correct about the gusts and the wind shifts about 90% of the time, and my gut feeling is that that is a very good percentage. So they enjoyed the consistency of the conservative sailor while at the same time enjoying the success of the more confident sailor who is 'on a roll' because of good judgement of the gusts and shifts.

They won two races, placed well in all other races, on paper were at least as consistent as any other crew, and this was the approach that won them Gold in Sydney with a race to spare.

Author's note

The 'squeeze and ease' technique described by Emmett is a clever combination of two established dynamic processes: the efficiency of the impulse pump, and the ability of the apparent wind sailboat to sail in more than one mode.

Chapter 23 of *HPS-1* discusses kinetics in depth. To summarise the pump and the impulse-pump:

If in steady flow a wing or sail is trimmed at the maximum angle at which the air will flow still attached to the lee surface (leech ribbons just popping in and out), that wing or sail will develop maximum lift.

If the angle is suddenly increased, the flow will not detach immediately. Momentum will cause it to continue as attached flow. During this brief period the lift will be greater than the steady-state maximum. This situation is unstable and imminent separation is inevitable. But if after a brief pause and prior to separation the trim angle is sufficiently reduced, attached flow can be retained and the situation will shortly return to its steady state. This process, repeated, is 'pumping'.

'Pumping' enables the sailor to apply muscular energy to the system and enjoy a greater momentary lift force and drive force and speed increase.

If the 'pump' is associated with rolling the boat and driving the masthead to windward, so the action of the sail becomes similar to that of a bird that beats its wings, the resulting 'impulse-pump' can absorb much greater muscle force/momentum and deliver a much greater momentary impulse to increase the drive force and speed. This is how birds fly.

The dynamics of the apparent wind sailboat are complex. Section 27.7 describes how an apparent wind boat can be sailed downwind on the same heading in two modes, each of which is stable, and the speed in one mode is near double the speed in the other. What Emmett is saying, and what Johanson and Jarvi demonstrated, is that a third mode is attainable with skill.

The increase of drive force from a skilful impulse-pump will accelerate the boat. This will both increase the speed of the apparent wind and also swing its direction further downwind. The crew can then enjoy three benefits for as long as conditions do not change adversely – the extra apparent wind speed, which sustains the extra boat speed, plus the greater downwind VMG from heading further downwind as they follow the change in apparent wind direction.

This situation is stable, but on the margin of flow stability. If conditions change adversely, separation will occur. But like the pump, if the crew anticipate and luff and ease the spinnaker sheet just prior to flow separation, attached flow can be retained and the process repeated.

In practice what happens is this: every change of boat speed and every change of boat heading, every change of wind speed and of wind direction is sensed by the boat and the crew as a change in the speed and direction of the apparent wind.

Normal apparent wind downwind sailing is to optimise these six factors for maximum downwind VMG.

But if, when conditions are relatively slow and gentle, every puff that heels the boat is responded to, not with body movement adequate to bring the boat upright, but with excess body movement, and the roll to windward is arrested with a synchronised main and spinnaker impulse-pump that increases speed, the whole pattern from then until the next adverse change can be biased with the apparent wind a little stronger, which sustains the added speed and with the boat heading a little further downwind.

Such is the skill of the Gold Medallist.

Index